THE MORTARA CASE AND THOMAS AQUINAS'S DEFENSE OF JEWISH PARENTAL AUTHORITY

JUDAISM AND CATHOLIC THEOLOGY

SERIES EDITORS
Bruce D. Marshall, Southern Methodist University
Matthew Tapie, Saint Leo University

EDITORIAL BOARD
Alan Brill, Seton Hall University
Gavin D'Costa, University of Bristol
Jennifer Hart Weed, University of New Brunswick
David Novak, University of Toronto

To
Rabbi A. James Rudin
whose dedication to Catholic-Jewish relations
opened paths of dialogue and study for future generations.

Copyright © 2025
The Catholic University of America Press
Chapter seven of this book appears in a slightly different form as "The Interpretation
of Romans 11:25–26 in the Architects and Fathers of *Nostra Aetate* and Pope Benedict
XVI," in *The Challenge of Catholic-Jewish Theological Dialogue*, ed. Matthew Tapie,
Alan Brill, and Matthew Levering (Washington, DC: The Catholic University
of America Press, 2025). It is used with permission.

All rights reserved

Copyright claim excludes archival Vatican documents
in Latin or Italian but includes English translations thereof

The paper used in this publication meets the minimum requirements of
American National Standards for Information Science—Permanence of Paper
for Printed Library Materials, ANSI Z39.48-1992.

∞

Cataloging-in-Publication Data on file with the Library of Congress

ISBN (paper): 978-0-8132-3874-6 | ISBN (ebook): 978-0-8132-3875-3

Book design by Burt&Burt
Interior set with Meta Pro and Good Pro News Compressed

THE MORTARA CASE AND THOMAS AQUINAS'S DEFENSE OF JEWISH PARENTAL AUTHORITY

Matthew Tapie

with Original Documents from the Mortara Case

Pro-memoria, Brevi cenni: Italian transcription and English translation by Saretta Marotta

Syllabus: Latin transcription and English translation by Lionel Yaceczko

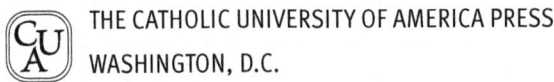

THE CATHOLIC UNIVERSITY OF AMERICA PRESS
WASHINGTON, D.C.

A child naturally belongs to his parents. At first, he is not distinguished from his parent physically so long as he is contained in his mother's womb. Later, after he passes out of the womb and before he has the use of free-will, he is in the care of his parents as in a kind of spiritual womb.

> Thomas Aquinas
> *Questiones Quodlibetales* 2.4.2

❈ ❈ ❈

Evils are not to be done in order that goods may come about, but an evil would be done by taking the little one away from his parents to whom God and nature have made him subject. God also has prohibited such fraud, nor does he want a holocaust to be offered to himself from robbery of possessions or persons.

> John Capreolus
> *Third Book of the Sentences*, Distinction V and VI, q. 4.

❈ ❈ ❈

The Council of Chalcedon, and the councils and controversies that led up to it, were concerned with the mystery of Christ, but they also tell us about the God who became incarnate in Christ. They tell us first that God does not destroy the natural necessities of things he becomes involved with, even in the intimate union of the incarnation. What is according to nature, and what reason can disclose in nature, retains its integrity before the Christian God. And second, they tell us that we must think of God as the one who can let natural necessity be maintained and let reason be left intact: that is, God is not himself a competing part of nature or a part of the world.

> Robert Sokolowski
> *The God of Faith & Reason*

CONTENTS

Preface	ix
Acknowledgments	xv
Abbreviations	xix
Introduction	1

1	Aquinas and the Contemporary Debate on the Mortara Case	23
2	Aquinas in the Mortara Family's Plea: *Pro-memoria* and *Syllabus*	31
3	Aquinas in the Papal Counsel's Reply: *Brevi cenni*	69
4	Papal Teaching and Canon Law on Forced Baptism of Jews	83
5	Aquinas's Defense of Jewish Parental Authority	109
6	Baptism Invitis Parentibus and the Question of the Second Vatican Council's Teaching on Religious Freedom	169
7	The Interpretation of Romans 11:25–26 according to the Architects and Fathers of *Nostra Aetate* and Pope Benedict XVI	195
8	Aquinas and the Incoherence of Baptism Invitis Parentibus	249

APPENDICES: Original Documents from the Mortara Case

Appendix A: *Pro-memoria* (PM)	269
Appendix B: *Syllabus* (SA)	293
Appendix C: *Brevi cenni* (BC)	403
Bibliography	445
Index	463

PREFACE

In March 2018, the Council of Centers on Jewish-Christian Relations (CCJR) invited me to respond to Brown University professor David Kertzer's lecture on the renewed debate in the United States over the Mortara case at the CCJR's annual meeting, which was scheduled to take place in November at Providence College, Rhode Island.[1]

In preparation for the conference, I discovered that my research interests in Thomas Aquinas's thought on Jews and Judaism, and Catholic-Jewish relations, were more intertwined than I realized. The Mortara family, with the help of the Roman Jewish community, had appealed to Aquinas's teaching against forced baptism of Jewish children in their plea for the return of their child, and the Vatican's reply to the family also appealed to Aquinas. As my study of the 1858 case deepened, I learned that there were other nineteenth-century child custody disputes between the Vatican and the Roman Jewish community that cited Aquinas's teaching. This fact seemed to require examination of the question of Aquinas's teaching in its thirteenth-century context as well as its reception history.

I presented my initial findings on this question at the CCJR's annual meeting on November 4, 2018. My presentation consisted of an overview of Aquinas's teaching against forced baptism of Jewish children, and its relation to eighteenth-century papal decrees that legitimized this practice in emergency cases, such as when an infant was near death. A revised and expanded version of the lecture was published as "*Spiritualis Uterus*: The Question of

---

[1] See the introduction for a summary of the facts of the Mortara case. Debate in the United States was rekindled in January 2018, when the Catholic theologian, Romanus Cessario, OP, defended Pope Pius IX's 1858 removal of Edgardo Mortara from his parents. For a discussion of Cessario's article and scholarly reactions, see chapter 1.

Forced Baptism, and Thomas Aquinas's Defense of Jewish Parental Rights," *The Bulletin of Medieval Canon Law* 35 (2018): 289–329.[2]

However, I could not adequately address the question of the interpretation of Aquinas in the Mortara family's plea, and the papal counsel's reply, without access to the original documents from the case.[3] As I discuss below, the family's plea consisted of two parts: *Pro-memoria*, which was mostly in Italian, and the *Syllabus*, which was written in Latin. The other key document was the papal counsel's reply, *Brevi cenni*, which was also written in Italian.[4] The complete documents are housed in the Vatican Apostolic Archives (AAV).

In the spring of 2023, I spent part of my sabbatical in Rome in order to access the AAV and begin the process of transcription and translation of the Mortara family plea and the papal counsel's reply. The translation and publication of the documents into English would make possible not only the study of the relation of Aquinas's teaching to the Mortara case; it would also facilitate study of the theological issues in the case by other scholars. These issues seemed obscured by polemic and controversy. I had the pleasure of working with the Vatican archivist Giovanni Coco, and Saretta Marotta, the Marie Sklodowska-Curie Cofund Fellow at Ca' Foscari at the University of Venice. Dr. Coco and Dr. Marotta assisted me with locating the documents. Dr. Marotta also agreed to transcribe and translate the Italian documents, *Pro-memoria* and *Brevi cenni*. We discovered that the *Syllabus* was a long catalog of theologians and canonists who taught against forced baptism of Jewish children. I invited a classicist familiar with canon law and the translation of hand-written manuscripts, Lionel Yaceczko, Assistant Professor of Classics at Benedictine College, Kansas, to transcribe and translate the *Syllabus*.

Chapters 2 and 3 discuss the interpretation of Aquinas in these documents at the heart of the dispute. As I explain in the introduction,

---

[2] *Spiritualis Uterus* means "spiritual womb," which is a metaphor Aquinas uses to defend Jewish parental authority over their children. Kertzer's lecture was published as "The Kidnapping of Edgardo Mortara: The Continuing Controversy," *SCJR* 14, no. 1 (2019): 1–10.

[3] A 1987 dissertation by Sharon Stahl contains some quotations from incomplete versions of the original documents. Sharon Stahl, "The Mortara Affair, 1858: Reflections of the Struggle to Maintain the Temporal Power of the Papacy," Saint Louis University, 1987. My first attempt to determine the relation of the case to Aquinas's thought was based on this dissertation. See Matthew Tapie, "The Mortara Affair and the Question of Thomas Aquinas's Teaching Against Forced Baptism," *SCJR* 14, no. 1 (2019): 1–18. In chapter 5 of this study, I indicate where my conclusions differ from the *SCJR* article.

[4] David Kertzer mentioned that the *Syllabus* relied on Aquinas but did not indicate which texts, or mention that the papal reply cited Aquinas as well. David Kertzer, *The Kidnapping of Edgardo Mortara* (New York: Vintage, 1998), 145.

transcriptions and English translations of the documents can be found in the appendices of this book. A completely revised and expanded version of my 2018 *Bulletin of Medieval Canon Law* article, which was on Aquinas's thought in its historical context, is the basis of chapter 5.[5]

In my study of the relation of Aquinas's teaching to the difficult history of forced conversion of Jews, I realized that key developments in the history of canon law on baptism of Jewish children *invitis parentibus* (against the will of the parents) were lacking from scholarly presentations of the Mortara case. The contemporary discussion seemed to me to take place in a vacuum unaware of the debates among canonists and theologians that stretched back to the Middle Ages. Providing an overview of this history seemed crucial for understanding the religious issues that surfaced in the Mortara case, which were shaped by arguments *for* baptism of Jewish children invitis parentibus in certain exceptions. My study of the case and its relation to Aquinas's texts therefore required that I become more familiar with developments in papal teaching and canon law on the problem of forced baptism of Jews in general. In chapter 4, I provide a brief survey of this history with attention to key questions in the Mortara case as these relate to Aquinas's teaching.

The study of this history also raised methodological questions. How does one obtain an accurate account of the facts of political, legal, and religious history? How should one approach questions about difficult periods in the history of Christian-Jewish relations, especially as these relate to one's own tradition? Some of these questions were addressed by the Catholic Church in the 1999 International Theological Commission's document, "Memory and Reconciliation: The Church and the Faults of the Past."[6] The rich document was proposed by Joseph Cardinal Ratzinger in view of the Jubilee year 2000, and it provides guidance on the above questions.

On the question of how one obtains an accurate account of the facts of history, "Memory and Reconciliation" says that establishing historical truth by means of historical-critical research is decisive. In a section entitled, "The Interpretation of History," the commission states that "understanding the evidence of the past means reaching it as far as possible in its objectivity through all the sources that are available."[7] The historical-critical utilization of the available sources should aim at the complex task of the reconstruction

---

[5] This chapter renders the previous article mostly obsolete since my reading of the original documents from the case, and expanded study of Aquinas's texts, required that I change some of my conclusions. I discuss these decisions below.

[6] International Theological Commission, "Memory and Reconciliation: The Church and the Faults of the Past" (March 7, 2000), no. 4.1.

[7] "Memory and Reconciliation," no. 4.1.

of a period. This means that obtaining an accurate account of a certain period requires that one consider the work of multiple historians and take documentary evidence seriously. For example, the reconstruction of the facts of the Mortara case requires consideration not only of the scrutinized Mortara memoir but the hundreds of pages of archival sources.

On the question of how one should approach questions about difficult periods in the history of Christian-Jewish relations, the Commission teaches that once facts have been established, it is necessary to evaluate their "spiritual and moral value." This is especially the case when one is evaluating events in the history of Christian-Jewish relations since "the relationship between Christians and Jews is one of the areas requiring a special examination of conscience." The authors state that the history of the relations between Jews and Christians is a tormented one and that the balance of these relations over two thousand years has been negative. "The hostility or diffidence of numerous Christians toward Jews in the course of time is a sad historical fact and is the cause of profound remorse."[8] This introspective approach implies that there is an interdisciplinary and moral theological dimension to the study of the history of Catholic-Jewish relations. Determining the truth in history and in the moral realm requires "the precise correlation of historical and theological judgment." Such study is enhanced by the collaboration of historians and theologians.[9]

From a Catholic perspective, this means that moral evaluation of events in the history of Catholic-Jewish relations requires not only an interdisciplinary approach, but also the cultivation of virtues. Indeed, the authors of "Memory and Reconciliation" teach that the truthful analysis of difficult periods in history can be considered "an act of courage and humility." The virtue of prudence is crucial in this sort of inquiry. Prudence does not mean being cautious or careful.[10] In the Catholic tradition, prudence is the cardinal virtue that allows us to act according to a truthful grasp of the way things are around us, as opposed to the vice of cunning. The cunning person deliberates about action not in accordance with reality but in accord with one's own interests; that is, the way things are is warped to fit what one wants. St. Pope John Paul II modeled the virtue of prudence when he spoke of the "unconditional trust in the power of Truth," and stated that "the Church is certainly

---

[8] "Memory and Reconciliation," no. 5.4; 5.1. The quote regarding the "balance of relations" is from the Commission for Religious Relations with the Jews, *We Remember: A Reflection on the Shoah* (March 16, 1998).

[9] "Memory and Reconciliation," introduction.

[10] William Mattison, *Introducing Moral Theology: True Happiness and the Virtues* (Grand Rapids, MI: Brazos Press, 2008).

PREFACE   xiii

not afraid of the truth that emerges from history and is ready to acknowledge mistakes wherever they have been identified, especially when they involve the respect that is owed to individuals and communities. She is inclined to mistrust generalizations that excuse or condemn various periods."[11]

Near the end of my sabbatical, I met with two librarians at the Biblioteca dell'Archiginnasio in Bologna, Maurizio Avanzolini and Marilena Buscarini. Avanzolini and Buscarini had published a helpful website in 2022 that contains digitized sources from the Mortara case.[12] Both librarians graciously helped me navigate these sources. When I realized that their research also identified some of the locations in Bologna where important events from the case took place, I decided to visit the approximate location where the Mortara home once stood, at Via delle Lame 8, Bologna. After visiting the street, I walked just fifteen minutes through Piazza Maggiore, the city's main square, to the Basilica of San Domenico, which administered the order to have Edgardo Mortara removed from his parents. On the night that the police came to the Mortara home, Edgardo's father made a similar trip from his apartment to San Domenico to request a stay in the order to remove his son. Inside the Basilica of San Domenico is the Arca di San Domenico, which contains the remains of St. Dominic, founder of the Order of Preachers. As I explored the basilica, I entered a side chapel that contained a painting of St. Thomas Aquinas (1225–74) by Giovanni Battista Bertusio (1577–1644), "St. Thomas with the Virgin and Saints Peter and Paul." I was reminded of the towering significance of Aquinas's theology for the Dominicans and the Catholic Church. As I left the basilica, I lit candles for the Mortara parents, Momolo and Marianna, and for Edgardo.

This study attempts to adjudicate the dispute between Pius IX and the Mortara family as it relates to the thought of Aquinas. It attempts to present key elements in the history of canon law on the baptism of Jewish children from the Middle Ages to the present. The study also strives to show that the historical and theological inquiry at the core of the book illuminates contemporary concerns and questions about the Mortara case. These concerns include the question of infant baptism for children of non-Catholic parents, as well as its relation to the Second Vatican Council's teaching on religious freedom and the Jewish people. I offer a discussion and proposals for the

---

[11] "Memory and Reconciliation," introduction; no. 4.2. The quotation of Pope John Paul II is from John Paul II, "General Audience," (September 1, 1999). Pope Francis echoed this aspirational principle when he announced on March 4, 2019, that the Archives of Pope Pius XII would open to historians.

[12] Maurizio Avanzolini and Marilena Buscarini, "Il Caso Mortara," nella Biblioteca dell'Archiginnasio, http://bimu.comune.bologna.it/biblioweb/mostra-caso-mortara/.

various aspects of this challenging issue. In the process, the study demonstrates the relevance of Aquinas's teaching on the natural law for Catholic-Jewish relations today. My hope is that the book can serve as a resource for scholars of Christian-Jewish relations, theologians, pastors, and students who learn of the Mortara case and want to explore the deeper issues.

A comment about Aquinas's texts is necessary. Citations of Aquinas in the Latin are from the critical editions of his texts.[13] My English translations of Aquinas's *Summa theologiae* are based on the Benziger edition unless otherwise noted. I adopt a referencing scheme to Aquinas's *Summa theologiae* to minimize the need for notes. Throughout the body of the text and in the notes, references are given without distinguishing question from article. The abbreviations for the various parts of the article are from the Latin text. Citations will appear in the text and notes as ST I, I.II, II.II, or III, where "I" stands for first part; "I.II" stands for part one of the second part; "II.II" stands for part two of second part; and "III" stands for the third part. The abbreviation "arg." stands for argument (frequently referred to in studies of Aquinas as an "objection"); "s.c." stands for *sed contra*; "co." stands for *respondeo*; and "ad." stands for "reply to argument." So, in ST II.II 10.12 ad. 2, the "10" stands for question 10; "12" for the article; and "ad. 2" stands for reply to the second argument. The various parts of Aquinas's articles are explained in chapter 5. The abbreviations page has a note about this as well. Since Aquinas's texts are easily accessible online, quotations of his texts in Latin have been removed from the notes at the request of the publisher with a few exceptions

---

[13] Critical texts of Aquinas's works are available from Roberto Busa's website, *Corpus Thomisticum*, which presents the entirety of the works of Aquinas in Latin. Busa relies upon the Leonine editions of the *Summa theologiae* and *Quaestiones de quolibet*, which are the texts central to this study. See Roberto Busa, SJ, Enrique Alarcón, and Eduardo Bernot, eds. *Corpus Thomisticum* (Fundación Tomás de Aquino, 2013); See also Sancti Thomae Aquinatis, *Opera omnia: Opera omnia iussu impensaque Leonis XIII. P.M. edita*, t. 4–12 (Ex Typographia Polyglotta S. C. de Propaganda Fide, Romae, 1888–1906); Thomae de Aquino, *Opera omnia jussu Leonis XIII P. M. edita*, t. 25/1–2: *Quaestiones de quolibet* (Roma: Commissio Leonina-Éditions du Cerf, 1996).

ACKNOWLEDGMENTS

Over the last seven years numerous scholars and academic institutions provided different forms of assistance and support throughout various stages of my research. I am grateful first of all to Fr. Kevin Spicer, CSC, who invited me to present my research on the Mortara case as it relates to the teaching of Aquinas at the annual meeting of the CCJR in 2018. If it had not been for this invitation, I do not think I would have engaged the topic.

I am grateful to institutions that provided resources in support of my research. My research trip to Rome in March 2023 was made possible by the Lay Centre at Foyer Unitas, which hosted me as a Visiting Professor. The Lay Centre offers interreligious formation programs and residence for graduate students and faculty conducting research at pontifical universities in Rome. I am grateful to the community of international students and scholars there, as well as the hospitality of staff members Claudia Giampietro, Aline Carbonari Krachevski, and the director of the Lay Centre, Filipe Domingues. Part of my research in Rome was also funded by a grant from the Monsignor Frank Mouch Interreligious Study and Dialogue Endowment, which supports research initiatives at the Saint Leo University Center for Catholic-Jewish Studies (CCJS), where I am fortunate to serve as director. I am grateful to Monsignor Mouch, former president of Saint Leo University, for this support. I am grateful to Fr. Etienne Vetö, former director of the Cardinal Bea Centre for Judaic Studies at the Pontifical Gregorian University, Rome, and now bishop of Reims. At Bishop Vetö's request, the Bea Centre funded my access to the Gregorian University library during my sabbatical. I am grateful to the staff at the Pontifical University of St. Thomas Aquinas, Rome, for their hospitality during my use of their library. I am also grateful for the assistance of the staff at the Daniel A. Cannon Memorial Library at Saint Leo University, including Andrew Venturella.

I am grateful to Giovanni Coco, archivist at the Vatican Apostolic Archives, for assisting me with research at the AAV. I am also grateful to Suzanne Brown-Flemming, director of International Academic Programs at the United States Holocaust Memorial Museum, for sharing with me helpful information on navigating the archives. I am grateful to Tommaso Dell'era for his assistance with locating sources pertaining to the Mortara case. I am grateful to Kenneth Pennington, professor emeritus of canon law at the Catholic University of America, who assisted me with locating some of the sources cited in chapters 4 and 5. I am indebted to Jennifer Hart Weed for her extremely helpful comments on chapter 5. I am also grateful to the following scholars, who read the entire manuscript and provided valuable feedback and suggestions: Peter Ochs, Joseph Sievers, Amy-Jill Levine, Elèna Mortara, Lionel Yaceczko, and Victoria Barnett. Many colleagues shared feedback with me on parts of the manuscript or discussed questions in email correspondence: Kenneth Pennington, Melodie Eichbauer, Kenneth Stow, Bruce Marshall, Matthew Levering, Gavin D'Costa, Thomas Joseph White, Isaac Oliver/de Oliveira, Christian Rutishauser, Reinhard Huetter, Eliot Nidam, Alan Brill, Roger Nutt, Giovanni Coco, James Rudin, Shai Held, Mark Nanos, John Borelli, Karma Ben-Johanan, Eugene Fisher, Pim Valkenberg, Thomas Humphries, Tzvi Novick, Rebecca Carter Chand, and David Maayan. David Maayan is the Maureen and Douglas Cohn Visiting Chair in Jewish Thought at the CCJS, and assistant director of the center. I am privileged to work with him in leading the center, and I am especially grateful for our study sessions in the summer of 2023, where we discussed some of Aquinas's texts. I am also grateful to my students, Grace Cornell and Lili Kozlowski, who serve as undergraduate fellows at the center. They kindly proofread parts of the manuscript. I am also grateful to the former administrator of programs and events at the CCJS, Sasha Bergstrasser, whose administrative assistance made it possible for me to direct the center while on sabbatical. This administrative position was made possible by the generosity of Gail and Paul Whiting, who are longtime friends and supporters of the center.

Several institutions allowed me to present my research to members of the community and to graduate students. I am grateful to Mr. Lawrence Voit, chair of the Christian-Jewish Dialogue at Spring Hill College, who invited me to give a lecture on the topic to a public audience at the Ahavas Chesed Synagogue, Mobile, Alabama, in February 2020. I am also grateful to Gavin D'Costa, visiting professor of interreligious dialogue at the Pontifical University of St. Thomas Aquinas, Rome. D'Costa kindly invited me to share two presentations, "Aquinas's Defense of Jewish Parental Rights" and "Contemporary Questions in the Study of Thomas Aquinas and the Jewish People," with his graduate students in a course entitled "Theologies of

Interreligious Dialogue" at the Angelicum in March 2023. The opportunity to speak with members of the community, as well as teach students, helped me to recognize obstacles to Catholic-Jewish dialogue on the Mortara case. Some were unfamiliar with the history of forced conversions while others were unfamiliar with Catholic teaching on baptism. One attendee of the event in Mobile approached me after my lecture and asked what baptism was. I learned from these experiences that basic explanations of Catholic doctrine, as well as introductions to the difficult history of forced conversions, deepened the understanding of members from both communities. During my lecture at the Angelicum, a Pakistani Catholic graduate student asked me if Aquinas's natural law arguments against the forced conversion of Jewish children could be applied to a similar story that he related about a Catholic girl in Pakistan who was kidnapped while playing outside of her home in Karachi, and then forced to convert to Islam. We discussed how Aquinas's natural law arguments against forced conversion have modern relevance.

I also want to thank John Martino at the Catholic University of America Press. John has been supportive of the project from the beginning, and he was helpful with numerous questions as I worked to bring the manuscript to completion. I am very grateful to my mentor and friend, William Mattison III, for his penetrating questions and his enthusiasm for the project. I am especially grateful to my wife, Carolyn, and daughter, Diana, for their encouragement and patience throughout the process of writing this book.

Feast of St. Thomas Aquinas
Ordinary Jubilee of 2025

ABBREVIATIONS

WORKS OF THOMAS AQUINAS

De mal.	*De malo*
De pot.	*De potentia*
De ver.	*De veritate*
In Isaiam	*Expositio super Isaiam ad litteram*
In Rom.	*Super Epistolam ad Romanos*
Ioan.	*Lectura Super Evangelium S. Ioannis lectura*
QDL	*Questiones Quodlibetales*
Sent.	*Scriptum super libros Sententiarum magistri Petri Lombardi episcopi Parisiensis*
	Citations of *Sent.* appear in the text and notes as follows: Book (I–IV) and followed by "D." for Distinction; "q." stands for question; "a." stands for article; "qa." stands for *quaestiunculae*, which means little questions, referred to here as sub-questions (not all articles contain sub-questions); "arg." is for argument; "co." is for respondeo; and "ad." is for reply to argument. So, *Sent.* IV D. 6, q. 1, a. 2, qa. 3, co. 3, stands for book 4, Distinction 6, question 1, article 2, sub-question 3, respondeo 3.
Sententia Ethic.	*Scriptum super libros Sententiarum*
ST	*Summa Theologiae.* Citations of the ST appear in the text and notes as: ST I, I.II, II.II, or III where "I" stands for first part; "I.II" stands for part one of the second part; "II.II" stands for part two of second part; and

"III" stands for the third part. The abbreviation "arg." stands for argument (frequently referred to in studies of Aquinas as an "objection"); "s.c." stands for sed contra; "co." stands for respondeo; and "ad." stands for "reply to argument." So, in ST II.II 10.12 ad. 2, the "10" stands for question 10; "12" for the article; and "ad. 2" stands for reply to the second argument. The parts of Aquinas's articles are explained in chapter 5.

Super I Cor.   *Super I ad Corinthios*
Super Matt.   *Super Evangelium S. Matthaei lectura*

ARCHIVAL SOURCES

AAV   Archivio Apostolico Vaticano

BC   *Brevi cenni*, Segr. Stato, Rubriche, anno 1864, rubrica 66, fasc. 3, ff. 173r–204v.

PM   *Pro-memoria*, Segr. Stato, Rubriche, anno 1864, rubrica 66, fasc. 1, ff. 167–74.

SA   *Syllabus: Auctoritatum comprobantium Baptisma pueris Iudaeorum invitis parentibus collatum nil prorsus valere*, anno 1864, rubrica 66, fasc. 2, ff 24r–69r.

OTHER WORKS

BMCL   *Bulletin of Medieval Canon Law*, New series

CCC   *Catechism of the Catholic Church*, USCCB, 2nd ed. (Rome: Libreria Editrice Vaticana, 2019).

CIC 1917   *Codex Iuris Canonici Pii X Pontificus Maximi iussu digestus, Benedicti Papae XV auctoritate promulgates* (Rome: Typis Polyglottis Vaticanis, 1917).

CIC 1983   *Codex Juris Canonici auctoritate Ioannis Pauli PP ll promulgatus* (Rome: Libreria Editrice Vaticana, 1983).

CSEL   *Corpus scriptorum ecclesiasticorum latinorum*

Decretum   *Concordia discordantium canonum*

DH   Vatican Council II, *Dignitatis Humanae* (1965).

DS   Heinrich Denzinger, *Enchiridion Symbolorum: A Compendium of Creeds, Definitions and Declarations of the Catholic Church*, ed. Peter Hünermann, 43rd ed. (San Francisco: Ignatius Press, 2012).

GC   "'The Gifts and the Calling of God Are Irrevocable' (Rom 11:29): A Reflection on Theological Questions Pertaining to Catholic-Jewish Relations," Vatican Commission for Religious Relations with the Jews (2015).

Grayzel, vol. 1   Solomon Grayzel, *The Church and the Jews in the XIIIth Century: A Study of Their Relations during the Years 1198–1254*, vol. 1, *Nicaea I to Lateran V* (New York: Jewish Theological Seminary Press, 2011).

Grayzel, vol. 2   Solomon Grayzel, *The Church and the Jews in the XIIIth Century: A Study of Their Relations during the Years 1254–1314*, vol. 2, ed. Kenneth Stow (New York: Jewish Theological Seminary Press, 2012).

Guidelines 1974   "Guidelines and Suggestions for Implementing the Conciliar Declaration Nostra Aetate," Vatican Commission for Religious Relations with the Jews (1974).

JLS   Amnon Linder, *The Jews in the Legal Sources of the Early Middle Ages* (Detroit: Wayne State University Press, 1998).

LG   Vatican Council II, *Lumen Gentium* (1964).

NABRE   New American Bible Revised Edition

NA   Vatican Council II, *Nostra Aetate* (1965).

NCE   *The New Catholic Encyclopedia* 2nd Edition, 15 volumes (Detroit: Gale, 2002).

Notes 1985   "Notes on the Correct Way to Present the Jews and Judaism in Preaching and Catechesis in the Roman Catholic Church," Vatican Commission for Religious Relations with the Jews (1985).

NRSVCE   New Revised Standard Version Catholic Edition

ODCC   *The Oxford Dictionary of the Christian Church*, 3rd ed., ed. F. L. Cross and E. A. Livingstone (New York: Oxford University Press, 2005).

PA *Pastoralis actio: Instruction on Infant Baptism*, Sacred Congregation for the Doctrine of the Faith (1980).

PL Patrologiae Cursus Completus, Series Latina, ed. J.-P. Migne (Paris)

Simonsohn Shlomo Simonsohn, *The Apostolic See and the Jews*, vol. 1–8.

SCJR *Studies in Christian-Jewish Relations*

X Liber extra decretalium, *Corpus iuris canonici*, ed. E. A. Friedberg, vol. 2 (Leipzig: Bernhard Tauchnitz, 1881), 5–928.

INTRODUCTION

Il caso Mortara, or the Mortara case, refers to Pope Pius IX's 1858 removal of a six-year-old Jewish boy, Edgardo Mortara, from his parents, Salomone ("Momolo") Mortara and Marianna Padovani, in Bologna, Italy. Edgardo was born on August 27, 1851. Six years later, rumors that a Jewish boy had been baptized in Bologna, which was part of the territories of the Papal States, reached the Sacred Congregation of the Holy Office in Rome on October 26, 1857.[1] It was reported that the Mortara family's Christian housekeeper, Anna Morisi, claimed to have baptized Edgardo after he had fallen ill as an infant one winter and was allegedly in danger of death.[2]

The precedent in cases of emergency baptism in the Papal States was that only one witness, usually the Christian who baptized the child, was sufficient to prove that the child was close to death. In this region of Italy, the relationship between church and state was very different from our contemporary context.[3] Since the pope had both spiritual and temporal authority in the

---

[1] This title is anachronistic, but "Holy Office" is used frequently by historians. In 1542, Pope Paul III established the commission to oversee matters of faith. It was known as the Sacred Roman and Universal Inquisition, and was initially a tribunal for cases of heresy and schism. In 1588, and up to the period of the Mortara case, its responsibilities extended to everything relating directly or indirectly to faith and morals. It underwent reorganizations in the twentieth century that included changes in title to Sacred Congregation of the Holy Office in 1908, and Sacred Congregation for the Doctrine of the Faith in 1965. Since 2022, it is named the Dicastery for the Doctrine of the Faith.

[2] According to the court testimony of the family doctor, Edgardo was never in danger of dying and had fallen ill in the summer when he was over a year old.

[3] Stefania Tutino, "Ecclesiology/Church-State Relationship in Early Modern Catholicism," in *The Oxford Handbook of Early Modern Theology, 1600–1800*, ed. Ulrich L Lehner et al. (New York: Oxford, 2016), 150–64; Owen Chadwick, *The Popes and European Revolution* (New York: Oxford University Press, 1981), 554. The contemporary Catholic approach to the relationship between the Church and modern society is represented in the Second Vatican Council's 1965 Pastoral Constitution on the Church in the Modern World, *Gaudium et Spes*. Vatican Council II, *Gaudium et*

Papal States, ecclesiastical laws were the basis of civil society. Canon law and civil law stipulated that all baptized children must be raised Catholic.

On June 23, 1858, the Holy Office authorized Father Pier Feletti, the inquisitor of the Church of San Domenico, in Bologna, to send police to the Mortara home to remove Edgardo and transport him to Rome, where he would eventually be raised by Christians. Edgardo would be educated at San Pietro in Vincoli, and enter the Canons Regular of St. Augustine. He would become a priest and professor. The case triggered international controversy. Some scholars argue that it even played a role in the political events leading up to the beginning of Italy's unification.[4]

Although many have a general impression of this painful chapter in Catholic-Jewish relations, few have read the account of the separation of Edgardo from his parents according to the documentary evidence found in the Archivio di Stato di Bologna, and few realize that the case continues to impact contemporary Catholic theology, canon law, and Catholic-Jewish relations.[5]

When Edgardo's father, Momolo, returned home on the evening of June 23, 1858, he discovered the police in his apartment asking his wife, Marianna, to make a list of the names of their seven children. After ensuring that all the children were accounted for, the police Marshal informed the parents that their son, Edgardo, had been baptized, and that they had orders to take the child. Momolo insisted that he and Marianna had no knowledge of the baptism, and that it must be a mistake.

Momolo then gained permission from the Marshall to go see Fr. Feletti, who had ordered the removal of the child, less than a mile away from the Mortara apartment, at the Church of San Domenico. Feletti told Momolo that the boy had been secretly baptized and that he could not deviate from orders he had received: "Far from acting lightly in this matter, I have acted

---

Spes (December 7, 1965). See Joseph Cardinal Ratzinger, "On the Status of Church and Theology Today," in *Principles of Catholic Theology: Building Stones for a Fundamental Theology*, trans. Sister Mary Frances McCarthy, SND (San Francisco: Ignatius Press, 1982), 378–79.

4 Gianfranco Miletto, "Mortara Case," in *Religion Past and Present*, ed. Hans Dieter Betz (Leiden: Brill, 2011).

5 My account of Edgardo's removal is based upon the court testimony about the events of June 23–24, 1858, given by Edgardo's father, mother, the policeman who removed him, and the inquisitor. The transcripts of the 1860 trial of the inquisitor, Father Feletti, are from the Archivio di Stato di Bologna ("Causa di separazione violenta del fanciullo Edgardo Mortara . . . contro Feletti Frate Pier Gaetano, 1860") and summarized in David Kertzer, *The Kidnapping of Edgardo Mortara* (New York: Vintage, 1998), 6. The archives contain several hundred pages of testimony about the events. There are also hundreds of documents on the case in the Vatican Apostolic Archives, and in the historical archives of the Jewish community of Rome. These sources provide the most accurate account of the case.

in good conscience, for everything has been done punctiliously according to the sacred Canons." Momolo asked Feletti to reveal why he thought the child had been baptized since no one in their family was aware of it.[6] Feletti replied that the information about when and how the baptism occurred was confidential. He decided to grant a twenty-four-hour delay of the removal. For this reason, two police officers were stationed in the parents' bedroom overnight to ensure the family did not flee. Marianna stayed on a sofa bed in her bedroom with Edgardo and held him throughout the night. A neighbor recounted that Edgardo's siblings begged the police not to take their brother.

The next day, after a request for a second stay was denied by Feletti, Momolo decided it was best that Marianna and Edgardo's siblings be taken to the home of a friend, Giuseppe Vitta, so they would not witness the police carrying the child away: "Seeing my wife in a deplorable state, indeed driven almost insane, I decided it was best if she were taken from the house so that she wouldn't be made to see the separation, for the sight would have killed her." In the afternoon, neighbors and friends had to carry Marianna out of the apartment. They also transported the other children.

At around 8 p.m., the police marshal took Edgardo from his father's arms and descended the stairs of the Mortara apartment to a carriage waiting in the street. Momolo and his friend Giuseppe Vitta followed the marshal down the stairs, but Momolo apparently fainted. A Catholic neighbor and friend of Vitta, Antonio Fachini, reported what he saw:

> As I was walking down via Lame, I found a carriage standing in front of the house that the Mortaras were then living in, and I saw a policeman stationed at the door. I was stupefied by this, all the more so when I heard shouts coming from the stairs from someone, and then I saw another person rushing out of the door calling to me, "Come! Come see, Fachini! What a pathetic picture!" It was the Jew Vitta, a friend of mine. When I asked him what was going on, he told me to come in. I went into the building with him, and saw at midstairs a policeman who was coming down with a boy in his arms, and just behind him, out cold and lying across the stairs, the Jew Mortara. . . . We rushed to help him, and carried him into

---

6 As discussed in chapters 4 and 6, the baptism of a Jewish child *morti proximus* (close to death) against the will (or without the knowledge) of the parents was lawful and encouraged according to the laws of the Papal States. "Since this may happen, that a child of Hebrew parentage be found by some Christian to be close to death, he will certainly perform a deed which I think is praiseworthy and pleasing to God, if he furnished the child with eternal salvation by purifying water." Pope Benedict XIV, *Prostremo Mense* no. 8, February 28, 1747, in *DS*, 2555. Ambiguity concerning what constituted close to death meant that the decision was made by the one who baptized the child. This opened loopholes for maidservants to baptize Jewish children who were ill but not near death.

his home, where we put him down on a sofa.... If I'd only found a couple of dozen of my friends, I would've tried to follow the carriage, stop it, and take the boy so that he could be given back to his poor parents.[7]

Edgardo was taken to Rome where he would eventually be raised by Catholics, including Pius IX himself. Despite international protests and pleas from the family, the pope said he could not return the child for reasons based in the laws that governed the ghettos of the Papal States.[8]

In October 1858, Edgardo's parents were allowed to visit him at the House of Catechumens in Rome, in the presence of the rector, a priest, and members of a religious order. During the visit the rector appealed to the parents to join their child by converting and stated that Edgardo was destined to work for the conversion of his family. Apart from these monitored visits in the months after the removal, Edgardo was not permitted to see his parents, brothers, or sisters until he was an adult.[9]

Momolo would travel across Europe to plead for assistance in getting his child back. His frequent campaigns and advocacy would ruin his business and force the family to live on donations taken up at synagogues. With the help of the Jewish community of Rome, which had become familiar with canon law on forced baptism, Momolo and Marianna would submit a two-part document, entitled *Pro-memoria* and *Syllabus*, that argued for the return of their child. The document appealed to the teaching of St. Thomas Aquinas (1225–74) against forced baptism of Jewish children. However, Pius IX's counsel, which responded directly to the Mortara plea, also cited Aquinas's teaching to argue that the child's baptism was valid and that according to canon law he belonged to the Church.[10] The request of the parents was denied.

Momolo died in 1872, after years of advocating for the return of his son. One year after Momolo's death, in 1873, Edgardo was ordained a priest at the age of twenty-one, and would take the name of Pius IX, whom he considered his spiritual father. He also added Maria to his name, since he had a devotion to the Virgin Mary. Fr. Pio Maria Mortara would see his mother again in 1878, twenty years after the separation.[11]

---

[7] Kertzer, *The Kidnapping of Edgardo Mortara*, 12.

[8] The legal reasons for the pope's decision will be discussed in chapters 3, 4, and 6. As discussed below, the position of the papal counsel is outlined in their reply to the Mortara family, entitled *Brevi cenni*, which is included in Appendix C.

[9] Elèna Mortara, *Writing for Justice: Victor Séjour, the Kidnapping of Edgardo Mortara, and the Age of Transatlantic Emancipations* (Chicago: Dartmouth College Press, 2015), 174–75.

[10] I discuss these documents in greater detail below.

[11] Mortara, *Writing for Justice*, 174–75.

INTRODUCTION

Some Catholic newspapers and articles reported positive accounts of the removal of Edgardo Mortara from his parents, and asserted that his baptism was miraculous, and that he had even wanted to become a Christian. In the decades that followed, Fr. Pio would travel widely, including to the United States, teaching a similar version of the story. According to Fr. Pio's account of the events, he had expressed a desire to leave his home to become Catholic, and his removal was carried out with gentleness and persuasion. The testimony from his father, mother, and the police who removed him contradicted these claims. In an 1888 memoir, he defended Pope Pius IX's decision and argued that his removal was not an injustice but was guided by divine providence because it was carried out according to the laws of the Papal States.[12] Fr. Pio believed that God had moved his Christian housekeeper to rescue him from his family, who he thought practiced an obsolete religion. He regretted that he was unable to convince them to convert to Christianity. According to Fr. Pio, if it had not been for Pius IX's action and resolve to adhere to his duties in the face of international pressure, he would not have devoted his life to teaching the Catholic faith. Fr. Pio died on March 11, 1940, in Belgium, at the age of eighty-eight, two months before the Nazis invaded the country.

This book is a theological study of the central religious documents in the Mortara case with attention to the teaching of St. Thomas Aquinas. The study attends to the question of how Aquinas was interpreted in the 1858 dispute between the Mortara family and Pope Pius IX, as well as in the contemporary theological debate about the case. The study also examines the question of baptism for infants of non-Catholic parents in emergency situations.

---

[12] There are problems with the memoir, which was published by the Italian journalist Vittorio Messori. Messori claimed he found the original version, written in Spanish, in Rome's Canons Regular archive, and then he translated it into Italian for publication. The Italian version was then translated into English and published as *Kidnapped by the Vatican? The Unpublished Memoirs of Edgardo Mortara* (San Francisco: Ignatius Press, 2017). However, the original document Edgardo wrote in Spanish differs in many passages from what Messori translated into Italian. Messori was asked by *The Atlantic* to explain the discrepancies, and he attributed any errors to the English translation, which he said he did not get to review. Yet the same discrepancies appear in the Italian version he prepared himself. When he was asked to comment on specific passages, he did not respond. David Kertzer compared the Italian version of the Mortara memoir published by Messori with the original Spanish version. Messori's version has numerous changes to the original, including the addition and deletion of entire paragraphs. The changes are common to both published versions of the Mortara memoir in Italian and English. See David Kertzer, "The Kidnapping of Edgardo Mortara: The Continuing Controversy," *Studies in Christian-Jewish Relations* 14, no. 1 (2019): 1–10; and "Edgardo Mortara's Doctored Memoir of a Vatican Kidnapping," *The Atlantic*, April 15, 2018. A more reliable version of the memoir is Marco Cassuto Morselli, *Il Memoriale di Edgardo Mortara* (Rome: Marietti, 2024).

However, it may not be clear why a study of the Mortara case and Aquinas's thought is necessary.

For some, the Mortara case may seem as if it is another difficult chapter in the history of Catholic-Jewish relations that is thankfully behind us. Did not the Catholic Church condemn displays of antisemitism directed against Jews "at any time and by anyone" in *Nostra Aetate* in 1965 (hereafter, *NA*)?[13] Additionally, the Church teaches that children who die without baptism are entrusted to the mercy of God.[14] For those interested in the Mortara case, a thorough history based on archival sources has already been written.[15] Why highlight again this difficult topic that remains an open wound for the Jewish community and helps kindle anti-Catholic sentiment concerning deeds of the distant past?

There are multiple reasons why studying this subject is helpful. The Mortara case raises two important questions that impact Catholic theology and canon law, as well as Catholic-Jewish relations.[16] The first question concerns whether Aquinas is interpreted correctly in the Mortara case and in the contemporary debate. The second question is on the relationship of current canon law on the baptism of infants of non-Catholic parents to the Second Vatican Council's teaching on religious freedom and to Catholic-Jewish relations. Below I detail these questions with attention to the primary focus of this study: the teaching of Aquinas as it relates to the Mortara case.

WHETHER AQUINAS IS INTERPRETED CORRECTLY IN THE MORTARA CASE AND IN THE CONTEMPORARY DEBATE

In January 2018, controversy over the Mortara case reemerged in the United States with the publication of an essay written by the Catholic theologian

---

13 *NA*, 4.

14 "As regards children who have died without Baptism, the Church can only entrust them to the mercy of God, as she does in her funeral rites for them. Indeed, the great mercy of God who desires that all should be saved, and Jesus' tenderness toward children which caused him to say: 'Let the children come to me, do not hinder them' (Mk. 10:14; cf. 1 Tim. 2:4), allow us to hope that there is a way of salvation for children who have died without Baptism." *CCC*, 1261. See also the International Theological Commission's teaching, "The Hope of Salvation for Infants Who Die without Being Baptized" (April 20, 2007), no. 66, 67, 102–3.

15 Until recently, the case attracted little attention from historians. The first book-length historical study is Kertzer's *Kidnapping*, 299.

16 "Canon" (Greek for rule, norm, standard, or measure) is another name for a law in the Code of Canon Law. Canon law is a code of ecclesiastical laws governing the Catholic Church. In the Latin of the Western Church, the governing code is the 1983 Code of Canon Law, which is a revision of the 1917 Code of Canon Law.

INTRODUCTION

Romanus Cessario, OP, in which he defended Pius IX's decision to separate Edgardo from his parents.[17] In order to forestall anti-Catholic sentiment in reaction to an upcoming film about the case, Cessario argued that the removal of Edgardo from his parents is what canon law and Aquinas's theology of baptism required. Scholars criticized Cessario's defense of Pius IX, and cited Aquinas's teaching against forced baptism of Jewish children.[18]

However, this theological debate has overlooked the fact that the question of how Aquinas's teaching against forced baptism of Jewish children applied to the Mortara case was at the center of the dispute between the family and the Vatican in 1858. As mentioned above, the Mortara family and the Vatican's papal counsel both appealed to Aquinas's teaching in support of their arguments for and against the removal of Edgardo. Who had the correct interpretation of Aquinas's thought?

In what follows, I show that the divergent interpretations of Aquinas's teaching, and the disagreement between the Mortara family and the papal counsel, can only be understood in the context of the two-part document produced by the Mortara family and the Roman Jewish community, *Pro-memoria* and *Syllabus*, and the papal counsel's reply, *Brevi cenni*. The Mortara family's two-part document and the Vatican reply are part of the archives of the pontificate of Pius IX, which were released in 1967 and are housed in the Vatican Apostolic Archives (AAV). These Italian and Latin documents from the AAV, which had not previously been transcribed, edited, or translated into English, are published here for the first time.[19]

---

[17] Romanus Cessario, OP, "Non Possumus," *First Things* (February 2018): 55–58. The Order of Preachers, abbreviated OP and also known as the Dominicans, is a Catholic mendicant order founded in France by a Spanish priest, saint, and mystic, St. Dominic, in 1215. The Dominicans are one of the four great mendicant orders of the Catholic Church. Cessario's essay is a review of the English version of Mortara's memoir by Messori, *Kidnapped by the Vatican?*

[18] See chapter 1 for the reactions to Cessario's essay.

[19] The Mortara family was assisted by the scholars of the Roman Rabbinate in the task of collecting previous cases of forced baptism where the outcome was favorable to them, as well as papal bulls and other ecclesiastical decisions on the matter. The first part of the document is entitled *Pro-memoria*, which can be found in AAV, Segr. Stato, Rubriche, anno 1864, rubrica 66, fasc. 1, ff. 167–74. *Pro-memoria* is a fifteen-page manuscript handwritten in Italian. The second part of the document is the *Syllabus*, which is a ninety-two-page manuscript handwritten in Latin. The *Syllabus* is entitled *Auctoritatum comprobantium Baptisma pueris Iudaeorum invitis parentibus collatum nil prorsus valere*, in AAV, Segr. Stato, Rubriche, anno 1864, rubrica 66, fasc. 2, ff 24r–69r. The translation of the title is "Syllabus of authorities proving that baptism for the children of Jews conferred with the parents unwilling has no further validity." The papal counsel's reply is called *Brevi cenni* (the complete title is "Brief notes and reflections on the Pro-memoria and Sillabo: Writings presented to the Holiness of Our Lord Pope Pius IX concerning the baptism conferred in Bologna on the child Edgardo son of the Jews Salomone and Marianna Mortara"). *Brevi cenni e reflessioni* can be found in the files of the secretary of state. See AAV, Segr. Stato, Rubriche, anno 1864, rubrica 66, fasc. 3, ff. 173r–204v. *Pro-memoria* will be cited in footnotes as

The aim of this study is to adjudicate whether Aquinas is interpreted correctly in the 1858 dispute, in the contemporary debate about the case, and in contemporary Church teaching on the baptism of infants invitis parentibus in emergency situations.[20] To determine the answer to these questions the study will consider a set of important sub-questions throughout: What did Aquinas teach about the question of forced baptism of Jewish children in the thirteenth century? How was his teaching interpreted by the parties in the Mortara case?

The question of whether Pius IX's action was justified is related to the inquiry, but it is not the aim of this study. The study of the theology and the legality of Pius IX's actions must be separated. Pius IX's actions were legal at the time according to the law of the Papal States. The alleged baptism and separation of Edgardo from his parents was not a crime when it happened because there was no law that prohibited it. In fact, there was law that expressly encouraged such baptisms, and required separation if these were discovered.

However, this study answers whether Aquinas's teaching supports certain theological assumptions in nineteenth-century canon law that made Pius IX's decision possible: that is, whether it is ever theologically justified to baptize an infant of non-Catholic parents invitis parentibus; whether such baptisms would be valid; and whether, on Aquinas's terms, a child baptized invitis parentibus must be removed from its parents.

These questions might strike the reader as idiosyncratic since some may not be familiar with Catholic teaching on the purpose and necessity of baptism, not to mention the ancient practice of infant baptism in cases of emergency. What is baptism, and what is baptism in cases of urgent necessity? On the other hand, those who are familiar with the Church's teaching on the necessity of baptism might assume that the baptism of children of non-Catholics in danger of death was a commonplace practice in the tradition. Surely the practice of baptizing children of "unbelievers" in danger of death is related to situations that were already well known in the patristic

---

PM, followed by the folio number and then page number in Appendix A. The *Syllabus* will be cited in footnotes as *SA*, followed by the respective author paragraph number, and then page number in Appendix B. *Brevi cenni* will be cited as *BC*, followed by the document page number, and then page number in Appendix C. For more details on the archival sources, see Saretta Marotta's notes to *PM* in Appendix A.

20 Again, *Invitis parentibus* means against the will of parents. It will be used frequently throughout the study to refer to the baptism of children of non-Catholics against the will of their parents. In the context of the nineteenth-century Roman ghetto, "against the will of the parents" also included the meaning "or without their knowledge," because it was understood by all that Jews did not want their children baptized without their permission in either case, i.e., Jews did not want their children baptized secretly or against their express protest.

era (for example, when a Christian attended the bedside of a dying child of non-Catholic parents). It would seem that baptizing children in cases of danger of death is not about the children of non-Catholic parents per se.

To address these concerns, it is important to briefly introduce the purpose and necessity of baptism in Catholic teaching, as well as the practice of baptizing infants in cases of emergency. According to the Catechism, baptism is the basis of the whole Christian life, the door that gives access to the other sacraments.[21] In the Fall of Adam, all have inherited original sin and Christ alone possesses the antidote and treatment whereby the person is cured and made healthy through the medicine of baptism. In the Catholic theological perspective, original sin is like a disease. As Herbert McCabe has observed, "Original sin means sin with which we are infected from our origins. The word 'original' refers not to the origin of mankind in Adam but to my origin, my coming into being. It is the sinfulness I have from my beginnings, as distinct from the evil due to particular individual choices." Original sin refers first of all to the condition in which a person comes into being. It is something like a hereditary defect though sin itself is not a matter of physical structure. Rather, original sin refers to a deprivation of divine life, which manifests itself in the domination of death, and the "malfunctioning of our desires and emotional life."[22]

Christ instituted the sacrament of baptism as the remedy for sin, and the Catholic Church teaches that it is necessary for salvation for those to whom the gospel has been proclaimed.[23] To baptize means to "plunge" or

---

[21] A catechism is a text that contains the fundamental Christian truths formulated in a way that facilitates their understanding. The *Catechism of the Catholic Church* is a summary of the essential elements of the Catholic faith. On June 25, 1992, Pope John Paul II officially approved the *Catechism of the Catholic Church*. Hereafter, it is abbreviated as *CCC*. The sacraments are "efficacious signs of grace, instituted by Christ and entrusted to the Church, by which divine life is dispensed to us." *CCC* 1131.

> The visible reality we see in the Sacraments is their outward expression, the form they take, and the way in which they are administered and received. The invisible reality we cannot "see" is God's grace, his gracious initiative in redeeming us through the death and Resurrection of his Son. The saving words and deeds of Jesus Christ are the foundation of what he would communicate in the Sacraments through the ministers of the Church. Guided by the Holy Spirit, the Church recognizes the existence of Seven Sacraments instituted by the Lord. They are the Sacraments of Initiation (Baptism, Confirmation, the Eucharist), the Sacraments of Healing (Penance and the Anointing of the Sick), and the Sacraments at the Service of Communion (Marriage and Holy Orders).

United States Conference of Catholic Bishops, "Sacraments and Sacramentals," (February 22, 2024).

[22] Herbert McCabe, *God Still Matters*, ed. Brian Davies (New York: Continuum, 2002), 170–71.

[23] "The Church does not know of any means other than baptism that assures entry into eternal beatitude and this is why she takes care not to neglect the mission she received from the Lord to see that all who can be baptized are 'reborn of water and the Spirit.'" *CCC* 1257.

"immerse" and this plunge into water symbolizes the catechumen's burial into Christ's death, from which she rises up by resurrection with him.[24] "The baptised are thus configured to Jesus Christ: 'We were buried therefore with him by baptism into death, so that as Christ was raised from the dead by the glory of the Father, we too might walk in newness of life' (Rom 6:4)."[25] For this reason, baptism is the sacrament of eternal well-being.[26] And baptism is the sacrament by which a person enters the Church.[27]

Since all are born with a fallen human nature and wounded by original sin, children also have need for the new birth in baptism.[28] This is why the practice of infant baptism is an immemorial tradition of the Church, and popes and councils often intervened to remind Christians of their duty to have their children baptized.[29] "Baptism is administered to infants, who are free from personal sins, not only in order to free them from original sin, but also to insert them into the communion of salvation which is the Church, by means of communion in the death and resurrection of Christ."[30] In the sacrament of baptism, the human person is freed from original sin and reborn as a child of God and member of Christ's body; through the grace of Christ received in baptism, the person shares in the divine nature. In normal circumstances, baptism is a moment of joy and celebration for the child's parents, their godparents, and the child's family.

According to the current Code of Canon Law, baptism of adults and infants is administered according to specific liturgical prescriptions.[31] However, in cases of urgent necessity, such as the danger of death, only those

---

[24] "Baptism, confirmation, and the Eucharist lay the foundations of every Christian life." *CCC* 1212. "Baptism is the beginning of new life in Christ; confirmation is its strengthening; and the Eucharist nourishes the disciple with Christ's Body and Blood for the person's transformation." *CCC* 1275.

[25] "The Hope of Salvation for Infants," no. 62.

[26] William Harmless, SJ, "Christ the Pediatrician: Infant Baptism and Christological Imagery in the Pelagian Controversy," *Augustinian Studies* 28, no. 2 (1997): 21.

[27] *CCC* 1277; *LG*, 1, 8.

[28] *CCC* 1250.

[29] *CCC* 1252; *PA*, 6.

[30] "The Hope of Salvation for Infants," no. 7.

[31] *Codex Iuris Canonici* or Code of Canon Law, hereafter, *CIC* 1983. Some examples are as follows: an adult is to be baptized in his or her parish church and an infant in the parish church of the parents unless a just cause suggests otherwise. The parents of an infant to be baptized and those who are to undertake the function of sponsor are to be instructed properly on the meaning of this sacrament and the obligations attached to it. The water to be used in conferring baptism must be blessed. It is recommended that baptism be celebrated on Sunday, if possible, at the Easter Vigil. See *CIC* 1983, 850–60.

INTRODUCTION

things required for the validity of the sacrament must be observed.[32] An adult in danger of death can be baptized if he or she has some knowledge of the truths of the faith, manifests the intention to receive baptism, and promises to observe the commandments of the Christian religion.[33] An infant in danger of death is to be baptized without delay.

The emergency baptism of adults and children is a longstanding practice that reaches back to the patristic era. Indeed, it is likely that emergency baptism was a frequent occurrence, as indicated by Christian inscriptions from the end of the second or beginning of the third century.[34] Augustine mentions baptizing children of pagan parents, but these parents had decided to bring their children to baptism because they thought the sacrament would heal their children from illness or help them to retain good health.[35] Those who brought children to baptism in the early church were often mothers who sought baptism for their infants because of the possibility that the children might die. Like many theologians before him, Aquinas discussed the emergency baptism of infants as well as adults.[36] He held that if an adult was threatened with the danger of death, she should be baptized only if she manifested a desire to receive baptism.[37] In line with this ancient tradition, Aquinas taught that the baptism of infants should not be deferred because the danger of death is always to be feared in children.[38] He even taught that if death is imminent, an infant should be baptized even if the child has not yet entirely come forth from the womb.[39]

---

[32] *CIC* 1983, 850; *CCC* 1256. "In case of necessity, anyone, even a non-baptized person, with the required intention, can baptize, by using the Trinitarian baptismal formula. The intention required is to will to do what the Church does when she baptizes. The Church finds the reason for this possibility in the universal saving will of God and the necessity of Baptism for salvation."

[33] *CIC* 1983, 865 §2.

[34] The emergency baptism of children had begun at the latest by 200 CE. Everett Ferguson, *Baptism in the Early Church: History, Theology, and Liturgy in the First Five Centuries* (Grand Rapids, MI: Eerdmans, 2009), 627, 857, 372–77.

[35] Augustine lived from 354 to 430 CE and was one of the most influential Latin Fathers of the Church. For a discussion of this case in Augustine's *Letter 98* see chapter 5. St. Augustine, *Letter 98*, in *The Works of St. Augustine Part II, Letters Vol 1: 1–99*, trans. Roland Teske, SJ (Hyde Park, NY: New City Press, 2001), 426–32.

[36] See Ferguson's discussion of the practice of emergency baptism in the early church. The theologians who discussed emergency baptisms of infants include Tertullian, Gregory of Nazianzus, and Augustine, among others. Ferguson, *Baptism in the Early Church*, chapter 21, 595, 788.

[37] ST III 68.12 ad. 3.

[38] ST III 68.3 ad. 1.

[39] ST III 68.11 ad. 4. See also *Sent.* IV, D. 4, q. 3, a. 1, qa. 2, co. 2.

However, the emergency baptism of infants was not administered to the children of non-Catholic parents against their will.[40] Arguments for baptizing Jewish children against the will of their parents emerged for the first time in the thirteenth century. This is, in part, why Aquinas refers to the arguments for baptizing Jewish children against the will of their parents as novel. He also argues that such a practice was never the custom of the Church:

> The custom of the Church has maximum authority and must be observed in all matters.... *Now it was never the custom of the Church to baptize the children of the Jews against the will of their parents,* although at times past there have been many very powerful catholic princes like Constantine and Theodosius, with whom most holy bishops have been on most friendly terms, as Sylvester with Constantine, and Ambrose with Theodosius, who would certainly not have failed to obtain this favor from them if it had been at all reasonable. It seems therefore hazardous to repeat this assertion, that the children of Jews should be baptized against their parents' wishes, in contradiction to the Church's custom.[41]

For Aquinas, custom (*consuetudo*) "has the force of law" if it is done repeatedly and proceeds from a deliberate judgment of reason.[42] It was only during Aquinas's lifetime that theologians began to propose that Jewish children be baptized against the will of their parents to provide the children with salvation.

The thirteenth-century proposals to apply the ancient practice of emergency baptism to the infants of Jewish families ran against the law of the Church. Specifically, the proposals ran against the repeated papal condemnations of forced baptism, including those of Pope Gregory the Great (r. 590–604). Aquinas's response to the proposals as well as the response of his Dominican defenders is the major focus of this book.[43]

---

40 The early church did not baptize the unwilling. Harmless, "Christ the Pediatrician," 29. Sometimes Christians in the Roman Empire brought children who were not part of their household to baptism if the children did not have parents or guardians, or if they had been abandoned. For example, in *Letter 98*, Augustine says such children are often taken in by consecrated virgins and brought forward for baptism. Augustine, *Letter 98*, 426–32. See also Tarsicius J. van Bavel, OSA, "Augustine on Baptism: *Letter 98*," *Augustinian Heritage: A Review of Spirituality and Tradition* 39, no. 2 (1993): 191–212.

41 ST II.II 10.12 co. Emphasis added.

42 ST I.II 97.3 co. "Custom has the force of a law, abolishes law, and is the interpreter of law."

43 Aquinas was educated by Benedictine monks at Monte Cassino and joined the Dominican friars in 1244. Many of the Dominicans who came after him adopted and defended aspects of his thought.

INTRODUCTION   13

I argue that Aquinas constructed a multifaceted defense of Jewish parental authority against what he viewed as hazardous arguments for forced baptism of Jewish children offered by his contemporaries.[44] Aquinas defined Jewish parental authority as a natural right (*ius naturale*), which he understood as an aspect of the human person's participation in the natural law or God's wise governance of the created order. For Aquinas, the natural law is "the bridge" between his view of God's providence and human moral and legal norms.[45] He also used the phrase *ius paternae potestatis* or "right of parental authority," which was the term used by his interlocutors when they debated whether Jewish children can be baptized against the will of their parents.[46] Aquinas's view should not be confused with modern theories of rights or the notion of a subjective power of individuals. And he did not formulate a doctrine of natural rights.[47] However, Aquinas did argue that the children of unbelievers are under the authority of their parents by natural right, which he understood in theological terms. As I explain below, this theological notion of a natural right can be considered a fundamental aspect of what Jean Porter has called Aquinas's "dynamic conception of the natural law."[48] For this reason, references to *ordinem iuris naturalis* (order of natural right) throughout Aquinas's defense of Jewish parental authority will sometimes be translated as the "order of the natural law."

Aquinas defended the authority Jewish parents have over their children against a variety of arguments concocted to justify forced baptism of Jewish children. One argument particularly relevant to the Mortara case, is that the theologians proposed that Jewish children should be baptized *invitis parentibus* to provide them with salvation.

---

[44] ST III 68.10. As I explain in detail in chapter 5, Aquinas's teaching can also be found in ST III 10.12 and *QDL* 2.4.2. The rights of European Jewry were rooted in Roman law and papal decrees. See Edward A. Synan, *The Popes and the Jews in the Middle Ages* (New York: Macmillan, 1965), 17–30.

[45] Jean Porter, "Eternal Law, Natural Law, Natural Rights: Freedom and Power in Aquinas," in *The Cambridge Handbook of Natural Law and Human Rights*, ed. Tom P. S. Angier, Iain T. Benson, and Mark Retter (New York, NY: Cambridge University Press, 2022), 191.

[46] The term was borrowed from Roman family law and originally referred to the power that the male head of a family exercised over his children. *QDL* 2.4.2 s.c.; ST II.II 10.12 s.c.

[47] Porter, "Eternal Law," 200. For an excellent discussion of the conceptual origins of the idea of natural rights as these relate to the natural law tradition, see Porter's "Eternal Law." See also Jean Porter, *Natural and Divine Law: Reclaiming the Tradition for Christian Ethics* (Grand Rapids, MI: Eerdmans, 1999), 273; Brian Tierney, *The Idea of Natural Rights* (Grand Rapids, MI: Eerdmans, 1997), 44; and Brian Tierney, *Liberty & Law: The Idea of Permissive Natural Law, 1100–1800* (Washington, DC: The Catholic University of America Press, 2014), 69–91.

[48] Porter, "Eternal Law," 191.

In his response to this argument, Aquinas taught "that no one ought to break the order of the natural right whereby a child is in the custody of its father, in order to rescue it from the danger of eternal death."[49]

Aquinas also insisted that it was the Jewish parents' duty to look after the salvation of their children and that it would be "repugnant to natural justice, if a child . . . were to be taken away from its parents' custody, or anything done to it against its parents' wish."[50] Aquinas used a memorable metaphor to persuade his interlocutors. He taught that the natural right of Jewish parents to care for their children is like a "spiritual womb" that must not violated by Christians: "A child naturally belongs to his parents. At first, he is not distinguished from his parent physically so long as he is contained in his mother's womb. Later, after he passes out of the womb and before he has the use of free-will, he is in the care of his parents as in a kind of spiritual womb."[51]

Aquinas's teaching won the day, and for hundreds of years canonists rejected baptism invitis parentibus, in part because of his arguments. However, the practice of forced baptism of Jewish children in certain exceptions was eventually codified by Pope Benedict XIV (1740–58) for the Roman ghetto in 1747. The policy included the following exception, among others: if a Christian found a Jewish child close to death, it would be meritorious and praiseworthy to provide salvation by baptizing the child even if the parents are opposed.[52] This is the exception that was upheld by Pius IX in 1858.

Aquinas argued strongly against the practice three times, calling it "not at all reasonable." The question of Aquinas's teaching is relevant not only to the Mortara case but other cases as well. Indeed, Aquinas's teaching was not only appealed to by the Mortara family, but by multiple families of the Roman ghetto. As we shall see in chapters 4 and 6, the removal of Edgardo Mortara was one of many cases where a child was separated from his or her Jewish parents after a baptism against their will or without their knowledge. Under the law that required all Christian children to receive a Christian upbringing, the consequence of these baptisms was the removal of the children from

---

[49] ST III 10.12 ad. 2; *QDL* 2.4.2 ad. 2; ST III 68.10 ad. 1. Eternal death refers to the permanent separation of the soul from God. Aquinas concluded that infants who die without baptism do not know what they are deprived of, and hence do not suffer from the privation of the beatific vision. For Aquinas, though unbaptized infants who die were deprived of the beatific vision (or "final end" in which one attains perfect happiness), they enjoyed a natural beatitude and the absence of any suffering since they did not commit any actual fault. "The Hope of Salvation for Infants," no. 23. See also *De mal.* 5.3.

[50] ST II.II 10.12 co.

[51] *QDL* 2.4.2. co.

[52] *DS*, 2555.

their parents. The policies eroded Jewish parental rights in the Papal States in the eighteenth and nineteenth centuries.

CANON 868 §2, THE SECOND VATICAN COUNCIL'S TEACHING ON RELIGIOUS FREEDOM, AND CATHOLIC-JEWISH RELATIONS

In addition to the above historical-theological questions about Aquinas's teaching, the contemporary debate about the Mortara case also raises the question of the relationship of canon 868 §2 to the Second Vatican Council's teaching on religious freedom and to Catholic-Jewish relations today.

As the defenders of Pius IX's decision argue, the Mortara case is a matter of theological principle and canon law. The 1983 Code of Canon Law states that for a baptism to be lawful at least one of the parents of a child (or the person who lawfully holds their place) must give consent. However, canon 868 §2 still has the exception, which states that an infant of non-Catholic parents is lawfully baptized if in danger of death, even if the parents are opposed to it.[53]

A few canon lawyers have expressed hesitation about the application of this canon because of the Second Vatican Council's teaching on religious freedom. One element of this teaching is that in matters religious every manner of coercion should be excluded: "It is one of the major tenets of Catholic doctrine that man's response to God in faith must be free: no one therefore is to be forced to embrace the Christian faith against his own will. This doctrine is contained in the word of God and it was constantly proclaimed by the Fathers of the Church."[54]

Others assert that the current canon was not crafted with the issues of the Mortara case in mind, or that the canon should not be followed since a Jewish child should never be baptized against the will of parents despite the canon. "If the child's parents are not Christian, but belong to some other faith, such as Judaism, no Catholic should baptize that child, even in danger of death.... Baptism should never be done in violation of fundamental church doctrine on religious liberty. That would be a travesty of the law."[55] However,

---

53 *CIC* 1983, canon 868 §2.

54 *DH*, 10.

55 According to Fr. John Huels, a canon lawyer who taught at St. Paul University in Ottawa: The usual situation today for the application of this canon is that one or both parents have abandoned practice of the Catholic faith, but they come from a Catholic family, so one or more grandparents and/or other close relatives are keenly interested in seeing that a child in danger of death gets baptized. In that situation, I have always taught seminarians and other students that the priest, or other minister, should advise the

another commentator on the canon speaks of the child's entitlement to baptism outweighing parental rights: "In danger of death, the will of God that all be baptized and the consequent entitlement of the child to baptism, take precedence over the parents' rights."[56]

The forced removal of a baptized child of non-Catholic parents is no longer possible in our contemporary political context since there are no laws requiring Christian children to receive a Christian education after the dissolution of the Papal States in 1870. Nevertheless, the existence of the current canon that allows for baptism of such infant children of non-Catholic parents *invitis parentibus* raises questions. What is the historical context of canon 868 §2? What are the specific reasons for baptizing a child of non-Catholic parents against the will or without the knowledge of its parents?

In addition to these questions concerning the Second Vatican Council's teaching on religious freedom, the separation of Edgardo Mortara from his parents as well as the existence of the current canon has damaged Catholic-Jewish relations. In response to Cessario's defense of Pius IX, the late archbishop of Philadelphia, Charles Chaput, lamented that Cessario's defense of Pius revived a controversy that has "left a stain on Catholic-Jewish relations for 150 years." "The Church," wrote Archbishop Chaput, "has worked hard for more than 60 years to heal such wounds and repent of past intolerance toward the Jewish community. This did damage to an already difficult effort."[57]

The descendants of the Mortara family have expressed that they continue to suffer the repercussions of Pius IX's decision. In the words of a living member of the Mortara family, Elèna Mortara, the incident remains "an open wound ... something we still discuss at every Passover."[58] Elèna is the great-granddaughter of Edgardo's older sister, Ernesta Mortara. Ernesta

---

grandparent or other relative to baptize the infant secretly. This can only be done if the child truly is in danger of death. The relative should baptize the child himself or herself. The Catholic minister should not, lest there be repercussions if the parents hear about it, for example, a lawsuit against the church. If the child's parents are not Christian, but belong to some other faith, such as Judaism, no Catholic should baptize that child, even in danger of death. . . . Baptism should never be done in violation of fundamental church doctrine on religious liberty. That would be a travesty of the law.

See John Allen Jr., "Relatives of Kidnapped Boy Ask for Rule Change," *National Catholic Reporter* 36, no. 38 (September 1st, 2000): 12.

56 Francis G. Morrisey, ed., *The Canon Law: Letter & Spirit; A Practical Guide to the Code of Canon Law* (Dublin: Veritas Publications, 1995), 478.

57 Archbishop Charles J. Chaput, "The Mortara Affair, Redux," *Jewish Review of Books*, January 29, 2018.

58 Elèna Mortara cited in Anna Momigliano, "Why Some Catholics Still Defend the Kidnapping of Edgardo Mortara," *The Atlantic*, January 24, 2018.

was eleven years old when she witnessed the removal of her younger brother, and she was haunted by the events until the end of her life: "The sinister memory came back to her obsessively as an old woman, even on her death bed, when she desperately implored people around her not to take her children away from her." [59] According to Elèna, "The trauma of the event was deeply engraved in the family's collective consciousness."[60]

The family has also expressed concerns about canon 868 §2. After hearing of Pope John Paul II's September 2000 decision to beatify Pope Pius IX, the family made a public statement requesting that the Vatican revoke the canon: "Normally as Jews we would not make demands of another religion. But because of what our family faced, and because of the unexpected exaltation of Pius IX, we feel we have the moral authority and the duty to address a law that goes against the rights of people to raise their children according to their beliefs."[61]

Another reason for this study is that although there is popular interest in the case in the United States and Italy, there is no in-depth theological discussion of the case available to assist theologians, pastors, laypersons, and students with the above questions. The interest is due, in part, to a 2023 Italian film about the case, *Kidnapped: The Abduction of Edgardo Mortara* (*Rapito* in Italian).[62] The question that will likely be on the minds of those who see the film is whether the teaching of the Catholic Church supports kidnapping Jewish children. The answer is that it absolutely does not. Nonetheless, the above questions remain.

Aquinas is considered one of the most revered teachers in the Christian theological world. Although a few scholars have commented upon his teaching against forced baptism, they have not placed this teaching in the context of medieval canon law debates on whether it is permissible to forcibly baptize Jewish children. Furthermore, there are no studies of the interpretation of Aquinas's teaching on this topic by his Dominican followers, the parties in the 1858 Mortara case, or in contemporary theological discourse on the

---

[59] Mortara, *Writing for Justice*, 173.

[60] Mortara, *Writing for Justice*, 176.

[61] Elèna Mortara made the appeal in an interview on August 17, 2000. The family did not receive a reply. John Allen Jr., "Pope of Infallibility Set for Beatification: Pius IX, a Controversial Choice, Issued 'Syllabus of Errors,'" *National Catholic Reporter* 36, no. 38 (September 1, 2000): 12.

[62] Marco Bellocchio, "Kidnapped: The Abduction of Edgardo Mortara," IMDB, https://www.imdb.com/title/tt14137416/. Another film on the subject was also announced, "The Kidnapping of Edgardo Mortara," to be directed by Steven Spielberg. However, it is believed at the time of this writing that Spielberg will not make the film. IMDB, https://www.imdb.com/title/tt3675680/.

case.[63] *The Mortara Case and Thomas Aquinas's Defense of Jewish Parental Authority* illuminates the scholarly discussion by providing the first book-length study of Aquinas's teaching against forced baptism of Jewish children and aspects of its reception history.

The first chapter introduces readers to contemporary theological debate about the case. I show that both critics and defenders of Pius IX appeal to the teaching of Aquinas to make their arguments, which raises the question of how Aquinas's teaching is rightly understood to apply to this case.

The second chapter analyzes the arguments of the Mortara family's *Pro-memoria* and *Syllabus* with attention to how the authors of the documents interpret Aquinas's teaching against forced baptism of the children of non-Catholics or "unbelievers."[64] I identify the questions at the time of the Mortara case, such as what constitutes an illicit baptism and a valid baptism, and I explain what each party understood as Aquinas's answers to the questions. I show that Aquinas's teaching against baptism of Jewish children *invitis parentibus* was carried forward by his Dominican followers from the late thirteenth century into the middle of the sixteenth century. Two of these Dominicans have become famous for their defense and consolidation of Aquinas's teachings: John Capreolus (c. 1380–1444), known as the "Prince of Thomists," and Sylvester Mazzolini di Prierio (c. 1460–1523).

The third chapter analyzes the papal counsel's reply to the Mortara family, entitled *Brevi cenni*, which appealed to Aquinas to defend Pius IX's decision to remove Edgardo from his parents. The aim of this chapter is to examine how the authors of the papal counsel's reply interpret Aquinas's teaching against forced baptism. The same questions that guided our study of Aquinas's texts in the *Pro-memoria* and *Syllabus* guide the analysis of *Brevi cenni* throughout this chapter. How do the authors of the Vatican document interpret Aquinas's teaching against forced baptism? What were the key questions on forced baptism as these related to Aquinas's teaching?

---

[63] The following scholars have commented upon Aquinas's teaching against forced baptism with attention to historical context in scholarly articles or book chapters: Marcia L. Colish, *Faith, Fiction and Force in Medieval Baptismal Debates* (Washington, DC: The Catholic University of America Press, 2014), 229; Jennifer Hart Weed, "Aquinas on the Forced Conversion of the Jews," in *Jews in Medieval Christendom: "Slay Them Not"*, ed. Kristine T. Utterback and Merrall L. Price (Études sur le Judaïsme Médiéval 60, Leiden: Brill, 2013), 129–46; "Faith, Salvation, and the Sacraments in Aquinas: A Puzzle Concerning Forced Baptisms," in *Philosophy, Culture, and Traditions* 10 (2014), 95–110; John Y. B. Hood, *Aquinas and the Jews* (Philadelphia: University of Pennsylvania Press, 1995), 89; Matthew Tapie, "*Spiritualis Uterus*: The Question of Forced Baptism, and Thomas Aquinas's Defense of Jewish Parental Rights," *BMCL* 35 (2018): 289–329.

[64] The term in the documents of the Mortara case is "infidel," which we translate throughout as "unbeliever." Although the term *non-Catholic* is preferable, it would be anachronistic to apply it to the 1858 documents and to Aquinas's writings.

How are Aquinas's texts understood to apply to the arguments *for* Pius IX's decision to remove the child from his parents? Our concern is to clarify the key questions on Aquinas's teaching in the 1858 debate. The identification of these questions is a necessary first step in evaluating the significance of Aquinas's teaching for the contemporary debate about the case and the question of baptism invitis parentibus in contemporary canon law. I show that three questions were at the heart of the dispute: whether Aquinas holds that forced baptism of Jewish children is lawful or licit (including in certain exceptions); whether forced baptism of a child of unbelievers is nevertheless a valid baptism; and the question of whether Jewish parents lose their rights over their children if they are baptized.

The fourth chapter sets the stage for our study of Aquinas's thought by setting it in its thirteenth-century context. As the late Catholic moral theologian Servais Pinckaers, OP, has observed, a "historical study of the Angelic Doctor's texts and thinking gradually opens to us many perspectives that a purely speculative study cannot grasp. The historical approach facilitates a re-reading that is renewed, more precise, and vastly richer—a great advantage to theological reflection."[65] I try to do this by providing an overview of papal teaching and canon law on forced baptism of Jews. I introduce readers to the policies on forced baptism of Jews produced by various canonists. The chapter shows that the basic distinction between illicit and valid baptism is assumed by theologians and canonists of the Middle Ages, and that the prohibition against forced baptism of Jewish children is altered by the codification of exceptions designed to address specific problems in the Roman ghetto in 1747.

The twofold aim of the fifth chapter is to analyze Aquinas's thought with attention to the key questions that emerged in the 1858 debate, and adjudicate whether Aquinas's teaching is interpreted correctly by the papal counsel and the Mortara family. I show that the context of Aquinas's teaching against baptism invitis parentibus is the fallout from the mid-thirteenth-century Christian discovery of the Talmud and other rabbinic literature. Some Christians responded to the discovery of this literature with a campaign to coerce Jews to convert to Christianity. The campaign included strategies that broke from the Augustinian tradition of toleration, such as proposals for baptizing Jewish children against the will of their parents. I also explain the multifaceted rationale behind Aquinas's rejection of the claim that Jewish children should be baptized invitis parentibus, and his defense of Jewish parental authority. I show that Aquinas defended Jewish parental authority

---

65 Servais Pinckaers, OP, *The Sources of Christian Ethics* (Washington, DC: The Catholic University of America Press, 1995), 237.

by working to overcome a perceived conflict between grace and the parental rights of unbelievers, that is, the Roman legal institution of patria potestas.

For Aquinas, the demands of natural justice are expressions of God's wisdom. Since the care that Jewish parents provide their children is a natural right, their authority over their children cannot be opposed to God's grace. Through this natural law argument, Aquinas reframes the parental rights of unbelievers in theological terms. I also show that Aquinas argued against the claim that one should baptize a child of unbelievers to save the child's soul because the order of the natural right should not be violated for theological reasons. Here, I also address whether Aquinas teaches that Jewish parents lose their rights over their children if they are baptized. I argue that on Aquinas's terms, taking away a Jewish child from his or her parents is considered stealing. For Aquinas, the Church does not have a right over children of unbelievers if they are baptized.

The sixth chapter analyzes the context and purpose of canon 868 §2 with attention to the previous Code of Canon Law (*CIC* 1917), the Second Vatican Council's Declarations, *Dignitatis Humanae* (hereafter, *DH*) and *NA*, and the teaching of Aquinas. Canon 868 §1 of the 1983 Code of Canon Law (*CIC* 1983) states that for a child to be licitly baptized at least one of the parents (or the person who lawfully holds their place) must give consent. In §2, it adds the exception mentioned above: "An infant of Catholic parents, indeed even of non-Catholic parents, is lawfully baptized in danger of death, even if the parents are opposed to it." How is the canon related to previous canon law on baptism invitis parentibus? Moreover, it seems that a baptism of a Jewish child against the will of its parents today is in tension with the Second Vatican Council's teaching on religious freedom. What is the relationship of this canon to the Church's contemporary teaching?

I argue that the rationale for baptizing children of non-Catholics invitis parentibus in danger of death is a problem for two reasons. First, the premise behind the canon, which asserts that the salvation of the child outweighs parental rights, emerged as part of a policy that separated Jewish families of the Roman ghetto in the eighteenth and nineteenth centuries. Second, the canon is incoherent because it sets parental rights, which are in the order of the natural law, against the divine law, that is, the supernatural gift of grace received in the sacrament of baptism. As several of Aquinas's Dominican defenders argue, "Evils are not to be done in order that goods may come about."[66] I also show that the question of the canon's relation to the Second

---

[66] In response to the argument that a child of unbelievers should be baptized invitis parentibus to save it from spiritual death, the Dominican defenders of Aquinas's teaching paraphrase the Apostle Paul's words in Romans 3:8: "Some people slander us by saying that we say, 'Let us do

Vatican Council's teaching on religious freedom surfaced in the 1970s, after the Commission for the Revision of the Code of Canon Law began revising the 1917 *CIC*. The drafting committee charged with formulating the canons on the sacraments modified the canon on baptism invitis parentibus to align it with *DH* and the natural law. The committee rejected baptism invitis parentibus by turning canon 750 §1 of the 1917 *CIC* on its head. The committee changed the norm on infant baptism in danger-of-death situations so that it was the opposite: the baptism of an infant against the wishes of non-Catholic parents was judged illicit. However, this modification was then reversed so that in the final version of the 1983 *CIC*, baptism of an infant in danger of death invitis parentibus was deemed lawful. I argue that in order for the canon to be aligned with the teaching of the Second Vatican Council, as well as Aquinas's teaching, the canon should not be deleted but revised.

The seventh chapter takes a step back and asks a larger question about the Catholic concern for the salvation of the Jews. This concern motivated the theological arguments for forced baptism of Jewish children after the Christian discovery of the Talmud in the thirteenth century, in the eighteenth century, in the nineteenth century, and today. The chapter argues that when the architects and fathers of *NA* decided to drop from the declaration a statement expressing a hope for Jews to enter the Church, they appealed to Romans 11:25–26.[67] I show that the fathers' decision to reject a call for Jews to enter the Church was based on a particular interpretation of Paul's admonishment of gentile followers of Christ in Romans 11:25–26 to recognize the mystery of Israel. The Council fathers and architects understood the Apostle Paul to teach that the salvation of the Jewish people is a mystery beyond human understanding, which must be left to God. In the mystery of God's merciful providence, the salvation of the Jewish people is certain and takes place after the full number of the gentiles have entered the Church. And this mystery does not entail a duty to seek the conversion of Jews. Therefore, there is no Catholic duty to persuade or invite Jews to baptism. Rather, the Church calls Catholics to study and dialogue with their Jewish neighbors.[68]

---

evil so that good may come'?" (NRSVUE). The Dominicans echo Aquinas's uses of the phrase in ST III 68.11 ad. 3: "We should 'not do evil that there may come good' (Romans 3:8)."

67 "For I do not want you to be unperceptive, brothers and sisters, about this mystery, so that you would not be mindful only for yourselves, because for a while a callus has formed for the protection of the injured branches of Israel, until the fullness of the nations shall commence. And then all Israel will be made safe." Mark Nanos, Literal-Oriented Translation of Romans 11:11–32 from Appendix, in *Reading Romans within Judaism: The Collected Essays of Mark D. Nanos*, vol. 2 (Eugene, OR: Cascade, 2018), 287.

68 *NA*, 4: "This sacred synod wants to foster and recommend that mutual understanding and respect which is the fruit, above all, of biblical and theological studies as well as of fraternal dialogues." See also principle 3 of the USCCB, "Statement of Principles for Catholic-Jewish

I also show how ideas from within the "Paul within Judaism" school of biblical scholarship and in Pope Benedict XVI's biblical exegesis reinforce the interpretation of Romans 11:25–26 of the architects and fathers of *NA*.

In the eighth chapter, I summarize the findings of the study with attention to claims of contemporary defenders of Pius IX's decision to remove Edgardo Mortara from his parents. Since contemporary defenders of Pius IX's decision to remove the child from his parents assume a dichotomy between natural law and grace, their position conflicts with Aquinas's teaching. I argue that their claims are opposed to Aquinas's thought because baptism invitis parentibus is incoherent on Aquinas's terms. The argument that the salvation of a child of non-Catholics is more important than the natural law assumes the nominalist premise that God is in a competitive relation with the world and ultimately indifferent to the nature of the human person whom he created in his own image. On the contrary, Aquinas's view of natural law is an objective order of equity established by nature, which is an expression of God's wise governance of creation.

This book constitutes the first theological analysis of the Mortara family's plea and the papal counsel's reply. It is also the first analysis of Aquinas's theology as it is interpreted in the original documents of the Mortara case, and it is the first book-length study of Aquinas's teaching against baptism of Jewish children in its thirteenth-century context, not to mention its reception history among Dominican defenders of Aquinas and in the Church's contemporary teaching on baptism for infants of non-Catholic parents.

Additionally, this study of Aquinas's thought has contemporary relevance. Aquinas's teaching was misinterpreted and distorted by some before and during the Mortara case. His teaching on some of the key questions of the case has been misinterpreted and distorted since that time. Part of my aim is to carry forward the Dominican defense of Aquinas's teaching and to address what are misinterpretations of this teaching in those who support baptism of non-Catholic children invitis parentibus during and after the Mortara case. By setting his thought in its thirteenth-century context, it becomes possible to demonstrate the significance of Aquinas's teaching for contemporary theological debate about the case, as well as the above questions in canon law and Catholic-Jewish relations.[69]

Dialogue," October 2, 2009: "Catholics have a sacred responsibility to bear witness to Christ at every moment of their lives, but lived context shapes the form of that witness to the Lord we love. Jewish-Catholic dialogue, one of the blessed fruits of the Second Vatican Council, has never been and will never be used by the Catholic Church as means of proselytism—nor is it intended as a disguised invitation to baptism."

[69] Marie-Dominique Chenu, OP, *Towards Understanding Saint Thomas*, trans. A. M. Landry and D. Hughes (Chicago: Henry Regnery, 1964).

1

AQUINAS AND THE CONTEMPORARY DEBATE ON THE MORTARA CASE

In January 2018, debate over the Mortara case reemerged in the United States with the publication of Dominican theologian Romanus Cessario's essay defending Pope Pius IX's 1858 decision to remove Edgardo Mortara from his parents in Bologna, Italy.[1]

Some scholars criticized the theological claims of Cessario's essay, citing Aquinas's teaching against forced baptism of Jewish children. Since Cessario and his critics appeal to Aquinas to argue for and against Pius IX's decision to remove Edgardo Mortara, it raises the question of how the scholars in this debate understand Aquinas's teaching to apply to the case.

In this brief chapter, I examine the use of Aquinas in contemporary arguments about the Mortara case. I show how contemporary thinkers employ Aquinas's texts in their arguments, and what questions they understand as central to the discussion. I argue that the contemporary discussion lacks awareness of the complexity of the case because it has ignored the history of forced baptisms of Jews and has overlooked that Aquinas's teaching was claimed by both sides of the 1858 dispute.

I proceed in two steps. In the first section, I outline some contemporary defenders of Pius IX with attention to how they understand Aquinas's teaching to support the removal of Edgardo from his parents. In the second section, I outline some contemporary critics of Pius IX with attention to how *they* understand Aquinas's teaching to apply to the case.

---

[1] Romanus Cessario, "Non Possumus," *First Things* (February 2018): 55–58. The case also caused controversy in the United States in 1858. See Bertram Wallace Korn, *The American Reaction to the Mortara Case: 1858–1859* (American Jewish Archives, 1957). Korn's book has been criticized for inaccuracies.

AQUINAS AND THE CONTEMPORARY DEFENDERS OF PIUS IX'S DECISION TO REMOVE EDGARDO MORTARA

Cessario's argument is that an accurate understanding of the Catholic teaching on baptism allows one to see that Pius IX's decision was not only just but an important act of piety and strength: "In order to forestall wrong and unwarranted interpretations, which may include allusions to child abuse, Catholics and other people of good will must acquire a right understanding of baptism and its effects."[2]

In Cessario's view, one must look beyond the human pathos of the case and recognize deeper realities. The removal of Edgardo Mortara was required by the law of the Church and the Papal States, because of the deeper realities of the power and permanence of baptism and the logical, political consequences of receiving this sacrament. From the Catholic theological perspective on baptism, Cessario argues that one can see that the removal of Mortara was not a kidnapping but "a relocation of an immortal soul into the Christian life, kindly arranged by divine Providence."[3]

Cessario's argument is as follows:

1. An infant in danger of death can be baptized licitly even against the will of non-Catholic parents. Cessario cites the 1983 *CIC* 868 §2, which states that "an infant of Catholic parents or even of non-Catholic parents is baptized licitly in danger of death even against the will of their parents."[4]

2. Baptism seals a person with an indelible spiritual mark that configures a person to Christ.

3. The law of the Church and the civil law of the Papal States required that legitimately baptized children receive a Catholic education.[5]

4. Therefore, Pius IX was right to remove Edgardo from his family and provide him with a Catholic upbringing.

On the point that baptism is indelible, Cessario appeals to Aquinas's theology of baptism.[6] For Cessario, baptism of an infant against the will of the parents is lawful and efficacious, and if civil law mandated Catholic children to be raised by Catholics, then it seems to follow that the relocation

---

2 Cessario, "Non Possumus," 56.
3 Cessario, "Non Possumus," 56.
4 *CIC* 1983; Cessario, "Non Possumus," 56.
5 Cessario, "Non Possumus," 55.
6 ST III 63.1–6.

of Edgardo is not an affront to religious liberty but, especially given the difficulty of the situation, a courageous commitment to the Church's teaching on the efficacy of baptism.

For Cessario, it was faith that bound Pius to give the child a Catholic upbringing that his parents could not. To misunderstand these divine sacramental realities is to leave oneself open to the danger of accommodation to modern liberalism and anti-Catholic sentiment. If one conceives of the Mortara case as a kidnapping, one has fallen victim to modern indifference to theological claims and perhaps anti-Catholic prejudice.[7] In Cessario's view, the Mortara case exacerbated anti-Catholic sentiment in the United States, and prejudiced manipulation of the Mortara case has not disappeared.

Cessario thinks the more important issue is that the case highlights a theological concern that Jewish and Christian communities share: "Jews and Christians alike pledge a higher loyalty that they honor in ways that seem incomprehensible to the world. It is a secularist denial of those higher loyalties that threatens both synagogue and Church."[8]

In the postscript to his *The Unpublished Memoirs of Edgardo Mortara*, the Italian Church historian, Vittorio Messori, examines Mortara's personal archive and also defends the abduction.[9] For Cessario, Messori, and others, the morality of Pius IX's actions are viewed differently based on whether one accepts the truth of the Catholic faith: "In the light of the faith, what the pope did can be seen as not only legally justified but also morally justified; in the darkness of a total rejection of the faith, it appears unconscionable."[10]

AQUINAS AND THE CONTEMPORARY CRITICS OF PIUS IX'S DECISION TO REMOVE EDGARDO MORTARA

Several scholars and writers denounced Cessario's essay and briefly mentioned what they understood as the theological issues raised by the case. Most of the reactions appeared as brief articles in Catholic magazines. The Italian Church historian Massimo Faggioli criticized Cessario's essay as an example of a Catholic traditionalism that ignores the Second Vatican

---

[7] Cessario, "Non Possumus," 56. Cessario's view echoes themes in the American Catholic reaction to the controversy in 1858, which emphasized that those critical of Pius IX were motivated by anti-Catholic prejudice. Korn, *The American Reaction to the Mortara Case*.

[8] Cessario, "Non Possumus," 58.

[9] Vittorio Messori, *Kidnapped by the Vatican? The Unpublished Memoirs of Edgardo Mortara* (San Francisco: Ignatius Press, 2017) 190.

[10] Roy Schoeman, foreword to Messori, *Kidnapped by the Vatican?*, ix.

Council's teaching on the Jewish people, religious liberty, and freedom of conscience.

> Cessario's *First Things* article is an example of the extremism on the side of continuity: it ignores completely the development of Catholic teaching on Jews and Judaism, on religious liberty, and on the freedom of conscience approved by Vatican II, confirmed and repeated by all the popes of the post-Vatican II period. It assumes that the Catholic magisterial tradition that followed and changed nineteenth-century Catholicism is not authentic Catholic teaching.[11]

The American Catholic writer Rod Dreher called Cessario's essay shocking, monstrous, and grotesque. "They stole a child from his mother and father! And here, in the twenty-first century, a priest defends it, saying it was for the child's own good." Dreher asserted that Cessario's position is wrong, but he admitted the Mortara case poses difficult and challenging questions. "Christians really do believe that baptism is a permanent thing. We really do believe that Christianity is objectively true."[12]

Robert Miller, a professor of law at the University of Iowa, argued that Cessario's piece is "statist." Miller gives Cessario the benefit of the doubt that the baptism was lawful and licit. Miller then argued that because the baptism was licit, it does not follow that the state had a right to remove a child from their parents: "Cessario has shown that, assuming the truth of the Catholic faith, Mortara had a supernatural, theological right to a Catholic upbringing and education, with a correlative duty in the Church (particularly the pope), to provide him one. That may well be so, but a moral claim (much less a supernatural moral claim) does not, without more, support a moral right in the state to enforce that claim."[13]

Some scholars cited Aquinas's teachings in their criticism of Cessario's essay. Princeton University professor Robert George called the piece an embarrassment, and cited Aquinas:

> The taking of the child by force from his parents and family was an abomination and defending it is an embarrassment. The gross, unspeakable injustice of such an action (and of its predicate, namely, baptizing a

---

[11] Massimo Faggioli, "Obsessed with Continuity: What an Essay on the Mortara Kidnapping Confirms," *Commonweal*, January 20, 2018.

[12] Rod Dreher, "The Edgardo Mortara Case," *The American Conservative*, January 9, 2018, http://www.theamericanconservative.com/dreher/the-edgardo-mortara-case/.

[13] Robert Miller, "The Mortara Case and the Limits of State Power: *First Things* Should Disavow Fr. Cessario's Defense of Pius IX in the Mortara Case," *Public Discourse*, January 11, 2018.

child against the will of its parents) was well understood by the early and medieval church and was affirmed and explained by Aquinas. Christians, including popes, can commit, and sometimes have committed, profoundly un-Christian acts—and can, and have, committed them in the name of Christianity. This, shamefully, was such a case.[14]

The American journalist Michael Sean Winters claimed that Cessario had made suspect claims based on a "sectarian theological point," which Winters understood as rooted in Aquinas's teachings: "[Cessario's] whole argument is premised on certain Thomistic understandings of how grace *must* work."[15]

For Winters, Cessario was using a theological principle about grace and baptism to overturn other principles such as mercy, the importance of Catholic-Jewish relations, and the teaching of St. Pope John Paul II. He also claimed that Cessario's piece represented a failure to recognize and respect human dignity: "Only a failure to recognize the human dignity of our Jewish brothers and sisters can account for the crime then, or for Cessario's attempts to excuse it now."

A few scholars elaborated upon Aquinas's teaching. Nathaniel Peters, senior fellow of the St. Paul Center for Biblical Theology, argued that although Cessario extensively quotes Aquinas on the indelible character of baptism, he "passes over Aquinas's treatment of who should receive baptism."[16]

Peters cited one of the places in the *Summa* that Aquinas takes up the question and explained that for Aquinas, children who do not yet have free will are under the care of their parents according to the natural law. For Peters, the importance of the sacraments cannot become an excuse for violating natural justice. Additionally, Peters also argued that Aquinas thought that even though Christian kings and princes may have had civil power over Jews it did not follow that they had the power to overthrow the order of natural or divine law.

The medieval historian Kevin Madigan also argued that Cessario failed to mention Aquinas's arguments against forced baptism of Jewish children. For Madigan, Aquinas's views subvert Cessario's attempted vindication of Pius IX: "The unparalleled authority within the Catholic Church of Thomas Aquinas—who in turn relies upon Augustine, canon law, and the natural

---

[14] Robert George, cited in Dreher, "The Edgardo Mortara Case."

[15] Michael Sean Winters, "Fr. Cessario's Edgardo Mortara Essay Is Inexcusable," *National Catholic Reporter*, January 19, 2018, https://www.ncronline.org/news/people/distinctly-catholic/fr-cessarios-edgardo-mortara-essay-inexcusable.

[16] Nathaniel Peters, "Grace Builds upon and Doesn't Destroy Nature: On First Things, Baptism, and the Natural Family," *Public Discourse*, January 15, 2018.

law—argues against Cessario." Madigan concluded that "Thomas certainly would have disapproved. Cessario seems oddly blind to how his most cherished authorities fundamentally undo his entire case."[17]

Holly Taylor Coolman, a Catholic theologian at Providence College, said Cessario's argument was "deeply damaging and misguided."[18] Coolman's response aimed to identify pertinent theological questions raised by the case, with attention to the need for dialogue: "Substantive engagement with the material issues is the very thing we need most." According to Coolman, the first issue the Mortara affair raises is that of nature and grace. Coolman argued that Aquinas's dictum that grace does not destroy but rather perfects nature implies that the natural bond between parent and child must not be destroyed. In Coolman's view, the Mortara case also raises the question of the relationship between church and state and questions related to the Church's teaching on the Jewish people in *NA*.

The Catholic theologian Matthew Levering has also responded to the controversy denouncing the kidnapping and Pius IX's decision. Levering evaluates the decision of Pius IX from a theological perspective informed by the writings of Aquinas. He outlines and repeats Aquinas's critique of forced baptism of Jewish children in ST II.II 10.12 and ST III 68.10. He applies Aquinas's discussion of justice to the Mortara case and argues that love of God does not mean overturning justice toward one's neighbor, including non-Catholic parents. In his critique of contemporary defenders of Pius IX, Levering argues that Pius IX's forcible removal of Edgardo Mortara was a grave abuse of power.[19]

CONCLUSION

This contemporary theological debate has overlooked the fact that the question of Aquinas's teaching on forced baptism was at the center of a rather extensive exchange between the Mortara family and the Vatican's papal counsel in 1858. As explained in the introduction, the Mortara family, with the assistance of the Jewish community in Rome, submitted a formal document that argued that the child must be returned because the Church, according to Aquinas, prohibits baptizing the children of unbelievers without the consent

---

[17] Kevin Madigan, "We Cannot Accept This," *Commonweal*, January 25, 2018.

[18] Holly Taylor Coolman, "The Vatican Kidnapped a Jewish Boy in 1858. Why Are We Still Talking about It?," *America*, January 31, 2018.

[19] Matthew Levering, *Engaging the Doctrine of Israel: A Christian Israelology in Dialogue with Ongoing Judaism* (Eugene, OR: Cascade, 2021). In the seventh chapter of the book, Levering discusses the case and relies, in part, upon my 2018 article in the *Bulletin of Medieval Canon Law*.

of their parents. The Mortara family's document appealed to some of the same teachings in Aquinas cited by the above critics of Cessario.

However, the papal counsel's refutation of the Mortara family's plea also appealed to Aquinas's teaching in order to defend the decision to separate the child from his parents. That Aquinas's teaching is cited as the authority for and against the return of the child to his family in the 1858 exchange raises questions about the interpretation of Aquinas's teaching as it relates to the case.

How do the authors of the Mortara family plea and Vatican documents interpret Aquinas's teaching against forced baptism? What were the key questions on forced baptism of Jewish children as these related to Aquinas's teaching?

The next chapter attempts to clarify the key questions on Aquinas's teaching in the debate between the Mortara family and the Vatican's papal counsel. Without access to the original documents in the 1858 exchange, the contemporary theological discussion lacks an understanding of the questions in the dispute as these relate to Aquinas's theology, as well as the full significance of Aquinas's teaching against forced baptism of Jewish children. I hope to show that the identification of these questions is a helpful first step in evaluating the significance of Aquinas's teaching as it relates to the case.

2

AQUINAS IN THE MORTARA FAMILY'S PLEA: *PRO-MEMORIA* AND *SYLLABUS*

The Mortara family submitted to the Vatican a two-part plea document, *Pro-memoria e Sillabo*, referred to hereafter as *Pro-memoria* and *Syllabus*. *Pro-memoria* and *Syllabus* appealed to Aquinas's teachings to argue the child must be returned because the Church prohibits baptizing children of unbelievers without the consent of their parents.[1] However, the papal counsel's reply to the Mortara family's document, entitled *Brevi cenni e riflessioni sul Pro-memoria e Sillabo* (Brief notes and reflections on the *Pro-memoria e Sillabo*), referred to hereafter as *Brevi cenni*, also appealed to Aquinas to defend Pius's decision to remove Edgardo from his parents.[2]

How do the authors of the Mortara and Vatican documents interpret Aquinas's teaching against forced baptism? What were the questions on forced baptism as these related to Aquinas's teaching? This chapter examines how the authors of the Mortara family's *Pro-memoria* and *Syllabus* interpret Aquinas's teaching. The aim is to clarify questions on Aquinas's teaching in the plea and explain how Aquinas's texts are understood to apply to the arguments *against* Pius IX's decision to remove the child from his parents. The next chapter will focus on the Vatican's reply to the family's plea with attention to the same question: how do the authors of the papal counsel's

---

[1] As explained above, *Pro-memoria* will be cited in footnotes as *PM*, followed by the folio number and then page number in Appendix A. The *Syllabus* will be cited in footnotes as *SA*, followed by the respective author paragraph number, and then page number in Appendix B.

[2] The complete title is, "Brief notes and reflections on the *Pro-memoria* and *Sillabo*: Writings presented to the Holiness of Our Lord Pope Pius IX concerning the baptism conferred in Bologna on the child Edgardo son of the Jews Salomone and Marianna Mortara." As explained above, *Brevi cenni* will be cited as *BC*, followed by the folio number, and then page number in Appendix C.

reply understand Aquinas's texts to apply to the arguments *for* Pius IX's decision to remove Edgardo from his parents?

I proceed in three steps. In the first section, I analyze the arguments of the Mortara family's plea, *Pro-memoria*, with attention to how the authors interpret Aquinas's teaching. In the second section, I analyze the second part of the plea, the *Syllabus*, with attention to how the authorities in the document interpret Aquinas's teaching. In the third section, I summarize the interpretation of Aquinas's teaching according to the authors of the *Pro-memoria* and *Syllabus*.

AQUINAS IN THE MORTARA FAMILY'S *PRO-MEMORIA*

In this section, I discuss the authorship and structure of *Pro-memoria* and *Syllabus*. I also outline the arguments of *Pro-memoria* with attention to how Aquinas's teaching is applied to the issues in the Mortara case.

Pro-memoria and *Syllabus* is a two-part plea document that argues for the return of the Mortara child to his parents. The documents were written with the assistance of the Jewish community in Rome, which had become familiar with canon law. As we shall see in chapters 4 and 6, the removal of Edgardo Mortara was one of many cases where a child was removed from his or her Jewish parents after a clandestine baptism. These baptisms were sometimes administered to Jewish children by Christian maidservants without the knowledge of the parents.

The author of the plea is unknown and is most likely a Catholic theologian or canon lawyer. The papal counsel's reply refers to the author of *Pro-memoria* as "the anonymous Theologian and Canonist."[3] Since the institution of the ghettos in the Papal States by Pope Paul IV in 1555, Jews could not exercise the liberal professions.[4] For this reason, Jews relied upon Christian lawyers.

The first part of the plea, *Pro-memoria*, is a fifteen-page memo handwritten in Italian. The document summarizes the facts of the case, as well as general theological arguments for the return of Edgardo to his parents.[5] The second part of the plea, the *Syllabus*, is a fifty-page document that is handwritten in Latin. The *Syllabus* contains excerpts from the writings of Catholic theologians and popes. It also contains several very brief excerpts from canon lawyers. In addition to the *Pro-memoria* and *Syllabus*, the

---

3 *BC*, 4, 407.
4 See chapter 4.
5 *PM*, f. 167r–167v, 169.

Mortara family's plea included three appendices: Edgardo's birth certificate; a medical report certifying that Edgardo's illness at the time of his baptism was not life-threatening; and the text of a 1639 Church decision in a case of forced baptism.

Both *Pro-memoria* and *Syllabus* rely heavily on the teachings of Aquinas. In the *Pro-memoria*, Aquinas is cited five times and is referred to as "S. Thomas" and "the Angelic Doctor." The theologians and canonists in the *Syllabus* cite Aquinas thirty-eight times and refer to him as "S. Thomas," "Blessed Thomas," and "the Divine Thomas." Let us first examine the main argument of *Pro-memoria* and its interpretation of Aquinas's teachings.

The main argument of *Pro-memoria* is that the Mortaras' child must be returned because the Church does not allow children of unbelievers to be baptized without the consent of their parents, and if they are baptized such baptisms are invalid. After a brief section summarizing the facts of the Mortara case, *Pro-memoria* sets forward an argument for religious freedom of non-Christian parents over their children.

The argument is based on Christian principles. The Christian faith "shines" with a certain "consecration of human reason." This sacred principle of reason is a design of God, for whom it would take "only one act of His Eternal will to overthrow the present order of things." It is in this sacred concept of reason that there is an "absolute inviolability of man in the forum of his conscience."

This sacred principle of human reason is something all humans share, both Catholics and non-Catholics: "Catholicism is the religion for which, in the field of human relationships in this life, the distinction between Christian and unbeliever disappears, leaving only man with . . . his dignity as a human being, as the image of God inscribed on his immortal soul."[6] God permits that several religions exist on earth and "each person believes that the path she or he follows is the only path that God has laid out, and that this path is shaped by the wisdom of ancestors."[7]

Because reason is a design of God, the use of force has no place in religion. Only "persuasion has exclusive dominion." Although Christianity is "the most industrious of all religions in constantly procuring new proselytes for its doctrines, it has no principle which directly or indirectly authorizes the use of violence for this purpose."[8] *Pro-memoria* argues that God is not

---

6 *PM*, f. 170r, 279.

7 *PM*, f. 168r, 273.

8 *PM*, f. 168r, 273.

pleased with "imposed religion" because God has given the human person free will and this is a principle of the natural law:

> An imposed religion would lead to aversion and contempt for that religion itself. The Lord, who has given man free will, is pleased only with voluntary offerings: and if such violence against the law of nature would be a cruel insult to Him . . . it would be no less a grave offense to Him to presume to substitute His will for man's, as if to correct the inscrutable orders of His Providence.[9]

The authors argue that Christianity manifests an open aversion to the use of any means other than persuasion and gentleness. This is because the free will of the person is a sacred feature of the natural order established by God's providence.

These principles are referred to as "powerful reasons of gentleness and universal tolerance," which the document then applies to the issue of forced conversion of adults and children invitis parentibus. The Church "has always felt compelled to condemn the unenlightened zeal of those who believed they would gain merit with God by the forced conversion of unbelievers." And these principles of justice are eternal, invariable, and remain despite the abuses and violence committed in "non-voluntary baptism."[10]

The second argument of *Pro-memoria* is that forced baptisms of adults and children are not only "abominable" but are invalid based on the fact that only parents can answer for their children. "Baptism administered to an adult who has not given his consent is therefore considered null and void."[11] In the same way that a forced baptism of an adult is invalid, the authors ask why baptism of children invitis parentibus should not also be judged invalid. "Are not both acts equally abominable to the Church? Do not both acts equally violate the norms of its government? Or is the authority of a father over his children . . . less certain than man's mastery over himself?" In other words, a father's authority over his child is absolute: "There is nothing that can better belong to us than our children, who are our own flesh and blood."[12] And this authority is the design of Providence. Parents alone must answer for their children. In fact, the primary parental duty is the education of children. It is

---

9 *PM*, f. 168v, 275.
10 *PM*, f. 168v, 275.
11 *PM*, f. 168v, 275.
12 *PM*, f. 169r, 275.

in this duty that "paternal authority assumes its most solemn and powerful character."[13]

Pro-memoria argues that before a son has the rational and moral capacity for his own actions, he is, according to "divine and human laws," bound to his father.[14] The authors then quote Aquinas's teaching on this point in III 68.10 co.:

> If, however, they have not yet the use of free-will, according to the natural right they are under the care of their parents as long as they cannot look after themselves. For which reason we say that even the children of the ancients "were saved through the faith of their parents." Wherefore it would be contrary to natural justice if such children were baptized against their parents' will; just as it would be if one having the use of reason were baptized against his will.[15]

The authors assert that the words of "the Angelic Doctor could not be more precise and perfect." They also comment on the last line of the quote, regarding an adult (one having the use of reason), and argue that since the baptism of an unwilling adult is wrong, so is the baptism of a child *invitis parentibus*.[16]

The authors also cite Aquinas's teaching in ST II.II 10.12 co. to argue that if the children of unbelievers were baptized *invitis parentibus* there is "a real danger that they will abandon the faith once they have grown up."[17]

Pro-memoria also addresses the question of the validity of a forced baptism. Since baptism requires matter, form, and the intention of the recipient, a forced baptism of a child lacks a key element. Before a child has reason, the will of the child is represented by the will of the parents.[18] So, the authors argue that one of the conditions for carrying out the sacrament is missing. It is certain there was no "interpretative will" of the parents, by which the authors mean a positive intention for baptism on behalf of the recipient.

To illustrate the point, the authors once again make a comparison to forced adult baptism:

---

13 *PM*, f. 169r, 275.

14 *PM*, f. 169r, 275.

15 For some quotes of Aquinas in the *PM* and *SA*, I have used the English translation of Aquinas's text from the Benziger edition. See, for example, *PM*, f. 169r–169. However, I have translated *ius naturale* as natural right not natural law, though Aquinas thinks natural right is an aspect of natural law. I discuss this in chapter 5.

16 *PM*, f. 169v, 277.

17 *PM*, f. 169v, 277.

18 Following Aristotle, Aquinas does not think that minor children, the developmentally handicapped, or the mentally ill have the use of reason.

> Here the comparison already established between the baptism of adults and that of children necessarily returns. A man who has never given any sign of inclination to the faith, and who has been baptized while asleep, would not be considered as bound to Christianity, since, in the absence of his consent, one of the necessary conditions for the efficacy of the sacrament would be lacking. But in the present case such a condition was likewise lacking, so why should it be judged differently?[19]

Just as one who is baptized while sleeping would not be considered a Christian, so a child baptized against the will of his parents would not receive the character of the sacrament.

The authors then anticipate a possible objection. Some might reply that the intention of the Church stands in place of the will of the unbelieving parents. On the contrary, they argue that if the interpretive will of the Church is sufficient for baptism *invitis parentibus*, why is the Church's intention insufficient for the baptism of an adult person while sleeping? "Here it will be answered that the authority of the Church compensates for the defect of the paternal will. But if this were so, why does it not also compensate for the lack of the direct will, so that baptism administered in sleep to an adult is also valid?"[20]

The authors of *Pro-memoria* then argue that the intention of the Church prevails only when the parents are Christians. Jewish parents enjoy parental rights over their children, and this is "an unconditional possession which the Church recognizes." Furthermore, Jewish parents are not subject to the spiritual jurisdiction of the Church, and this is true in the case of Edgardo:

> Since Edgardo's parents are not subject to the spiritual dominion of the church, nor did their lack of assent (even if this baptism was certain) be compensated for by the church's intention, in which their will is not to be confused, it would undoubtedly appear from this that one of the three requirements for the sacramental act is lacking, and since this defect would invalidate it in an adult, would it not be sufficient reason to invalidate it in little Edgardo, thus returning him to his parents?[21]

According to the authors, this view finds valid support in "the doctrines of eminent and revered writers." The *Pro-memoria* then lists several cases

---

19 *PM*, f. 171r, 283.

20 *PM*, f. 171r, 283.

21 *PM*, f. 171v, 283. The argument resembles Aquinas's teaching in ST II.II 10.9 ad. 2 on this point: "The Church does not exercise judgment against unbelievers in the point of inflicting spiritual punishment on them."

where secular and ecclesiastical authorities condemned forced baptism invitis parentibus, or declared it invalid, and ordered that the baptized Jewish children be returned to their parents.[22]

The arguments of *Pro-memoria* can be summarized as follows: 1) Free will in things that are of God is a sacred principle established by God in the order of the natural law. 2) According to Aquinas, it is not the custom of the Church to forcibly convert non-Christians or to forcibly baptize children of unbelievers invitis parentibus. 3) Since the Church has no spiritual jurisdiction over the children of unbelievers, the Church's intention cannot represent the intention of Jewish parents as it does Christian parents. 4) If such forced baptisms of children invitis parentibus do occur, these baptisms are invalid, and the children must be returned to their parents.[23]

Pro-memoria concludes by stressing that the parental authority of "the Israelite" is an inviolable gift from God, and that this teaching is proclaimed by the Christian religion:

> The desolation of a father, the monomaniacal anguish of a mother at the loss of one of their children, would already be a serious argument to provoke a compassionate judgment on the part of the high governing authorities of that religion . . . but it is not only the cry of grief that calls for the return of their Edgardo to the Mortara couple. It is also the. . . paternal authority, which they inviolably received from God, and which was inviolably proclaimed by this religion in the Christian as well as in the Israelite.[24]

Pro-memoria is then followed by the *Syllabus*, which reinforces the above claims with extended excerpts from six Dominican theologians who base their arguments against baptism invitis parentibus on Aquinas's writings. We now turn our attention to the arguments of the fifty-page *Syllabus*, and its catalog of excerpts. I analyze how the theologians understand Aquinas's teaching to apply to the question of baptism of Jewish children invitis parentibus.

---

22 *PM*, f. 172r–173r, 285–87.

23 Sharon Stahl also noticed some of these themes, though the basis of her study was a version of the document that was missing pages. Sharon Stahl, "The Mortara Affair, 1858: Reflections of the Struggle to Maintain the Temporal Power of the Papacy," PhD diss., Saint Louis University (1987).

24 *PM*, f. 173v, 289.

AQUINAS IN THE DOMINICAN THEOLOGIANS OF THE *SYLLABUS*

The full title of the *Syllabus* is "Syllabus of authorities proving that baptism for the children of Jews conferred with the parents unwilling has no further validity." Support for the general arguments of the Mortara position in *Pro-memoria*, as outlined above, is reinforced throughout the *Syllabus* with excerpts from the works, among others, of the following French, Italian, and Spanish Dominican theologians: Durandus of Saint-Pourçain (c. 1270–1334); Peter Paludanus (c. 1275–1342); John Capreolus (c. 1380–1444); Cardinal Juan de Torquemada (c. 1388–1468); Archbishop Ambrosius Catharinus (c. 1484–1553); and Sylvester Mazzolini di Prierio (c. 1460–1523).[25] What follows is a brief introduction to each Dominican followed by a summary of their arguments against baptism of Jewish children invitis parentibus with attention to how they interpret Aquinas's teaching.

Most of the excerpts in the *Syllabus* are taken from their commentaries on Peter Lombard's *Book of Sentences*.[26] Lombard's *Book of Sentences* was composed during the 1150s and since 1225 had become the primary text for theology at Paris. Theologians would write commentaries on the *Sentences* by considering both sides of a debate about a particular question. The questions

---

[25] Several shorter excerpts from various canonists and theologians are also included in the *Syllabus*. I lack the space to provide a comprehensive analysis of each thinker's excerpt in the *Syllabus*. The authors of these excerpts all reject the practice of baptism of children of unbelievers invitis parentibus, and those who consider the question of the validity of such baptisms claim that these baptisms are invalid. For example, the *SA* includes an excerpt from Petrus Ancharanus who was born c. 1333 in Tuscany.

> He studied Roman law at Perugia under Baldus and later Canon law at Bologna under Bartholomeus de Saliceto. In 1402 Ancharanus was called to a chair in canon law in Ferrara where he remained until 1405. Ancharanus then returned to Bologna. In 1409 he attended the Council of Pisa as a representative of the University of Bologna. He attended also the opening of the Council of Constance, but remained only a short time before returning to Bologna where he died in 1416.

Kenneth Pennington, *Medieval and Early Modern Jurists* (1993), available online at http://legalhistorysources.com/biobibl.htm. There are also brief excerpts from Paulus Cartesius and Marcus Antonius Natta (or Marco Antonio Natta) in the *SA*. According to Alberto Lupano, Natta was a prolific jurist who lived in the sixteenth century and produced many works. His consilia were especially widely used and printed. He worked primarily in Northeast Italy. Alberto Lupano, "Natta, Marco Antonio," *Dizionario biografico dei giuristi Italiani*, 2 vols., ed. Italo Birocchi et al. (Bologna: Societa Editrice il Mulino, 2013), 2:1414.

[26] Most of the commentaries focus on Distinction IV, chapter 4, "That some receive sacrament and thing, others the sacrament and not the thing, others the thing and not the sacrament." Peter Lombard, *The Sentences*, book 4: *On the Doctrine of Signs*, trans. Giulio Silano (Toronto: Pontifical Institute of Medieval Studies, 2010). See Distinction IV, c4 n1. Baptism is treated in book 4, Distinctions II–VI. See also Marcia L. Colish, *Peter Lombard*, 2 vols. (Leiden: Brill, 1994); Philipp W. Rosemann, *Peter Lombard* (New York: Oxford University Press, 2004).

were related to ancient topics such as Christ, creation, and the sacraments, with the order determined by Lombard's famous work.[27]

This style of theological commentary was used by many Thomists to advance specifically Thomist theses against Scotist and nominalist positions. However, sometimes Dominican theologians would engage other Dominicans who were perceived to depart from Aquinas. The intention to defend Aquinas's thought is most explicit in the work of Capreolus:

> My intention is to introduce nothing of my own, but only to relate opinions that seem to me to have been those of Saint Thomas, and to introduce no proofs for the conclusions other than his own words, except rarely. Furthermore, I plan to introduce, in the proper place, objections [or arguments] of Aureolus, Scotus, Durandus, John of Ripa, Henry, Guido of Carmello, Garo, Adam, and others who attack Saint Thomas, and to solve these objections [or arguments] by means of what Saint Thomas said.[28]

In their commentaries on Lombard's *Sentences*, theologians would also take the opportunity to engage other theologians on questions of current interest. The excerpts from the *Syllabus* demonstrate that Dominican theologians writing well after Aquinas's lifetime were concerned to defend his position against theologians who argued for the forced baptism of Jewish children invitis parentibus.

The theologians in the *Syllabus* appeal mostly to Aquinas's teaching in ST III 68.10, yet their arguments also echo texts from the two other places in Aquinas's corpus in which he treats the topic, ST II.II 10.12 and *Quodlibetales Questiones* 2.4.2.[29] In chapter 5 of this book, I examine the texts of Aquinas cited by these Dominican authors and adjudicate whether their interpretation of Aquinas is correct. In this chapter, I only indicate where themes and arguments in the Dominicans correspond to arguments in Aquinas's texts and present their understanding of the meaning of Aquinas's teachings.

In the style of the Parisian commentary tradition, many of the authors in the *Syllabus* first set out the reasons argued by their contemporaries for baptizing children of unbelievers against the will of their parents. They refer

---

[27] The first book is on God, the second on creation, the third is on Christ, and the fourth is on the sacraments and the last things. On the development of the commentary tradition, see Philipp Rosemann, *The Story of a Great Medieval Book: Peter Lombard's Sentences* (Toronto: University of Toronto Press, 2007).

[28] John Capreolus, *On the Virtues*, trans. Kevin White and Romanus Cessario, OP (Washington, DC: The Catholic University of America Press, 2001), xxviii.

[29] Again, the *Summa theologiae* will be referred to as ST II.II (*Secunda Secundae*) or ST III (*Tertia Pars*); *Quodlibetales Questiones* will be referred to as *QDL*.

to these reasons as objections, which function much like the "arguments" in Aquinas's articles, a term which refers to the reasons of his contemporaries. But *objicere* does not have the meaning that the word denotes today. *Objicere* in the context of the genre of the *disputare* or disputed question means *inducere rationes*, or "to bring in reasons" or arguments in favor of one side.[30] Most of the authors list arguments similar to those listed by Aquinas in ST III 68.10. Some also list arguments from Aquinas's text in ST II.II 10.12. So, the below list reflects all arguments from Aquinas's contemporaries for baptizing children of unbelievers against the will of their parents from ST III 68.10 as well as ST II.II 10.12. The arguments are abbreviated as A1, A2, et cetera for the purpose of labeling the below Dominican's references to Aquinas's lists of arguments.

The objections or arguments are as follows: A1: The first argument can be referred to *as the argument from unbelief in parents*. Unbelief is grounds for severing a marriage. Since unbelief is grounds for severing marriage, it is also grounds for abrogation of parental rights of unbelieving parents. Therefore, children of Jews can be removed from their unbelieving parents and given to others. A2: The second argument can be referred to as *the argument from the danger of spiritual death*. The argument is that it would be a sin to *not* baptize children of unbelievers against the will of their parents and provide salvation for their souls since these children are in danger of spiritual death. A3: The third argument can be referred to as *the argument from the power of kings and princes:* The argument is that since unbelievers are under the power of kings and princes, no injustice would be done to them if they were baptized against the will of their parents. A4: The fourth argument is *the argument from God's ownership of children*. The argument is that since all persons belong more to God than to their natural father, it is not unjust if Jewish children are baptized against their parents' will. A5: The fifth argument is *the argument from the duty to baptize*. Baptism, not preaching, is most effective at achieving salvation. If a preacher fails to preach it is a threat to him because he has been entrusted with the duty of preaching. Likewise, those who could baptize a Jewish child and do not do it are therefore also in danger and even guilty of sin.[31]

---

30 Marie-Dominique Chenu, OP, *Toward Understanding Saint Thomas*, trans. A. M. Landry and D. Hughes (Chicago: Henry Regnery, 1964), 94.

31 A few of the opinions listed by the Dominican theologians in the *Syllabus* are more elaborate than those in Aquinas's texts. Some of the below arguments elaborate upon A3 and add an objection that is not in Aquinas's text: that Christian rulers can earn merit if they offer the children of Jews to baptism because this brings salvation to the children and honors God.

The respective answers to these arguments advanced by the Dominican authors echo many of Aquinas's positions in ST II.II 10.12, ST III 68.10, and QDL 2.4.2. The Dominican authors echo reasons in Aquinas's respondeo or the part of his articles in which he provides his answer to a question. The reasons from Aquinas's answers are abbreviated below as R1, R2, et cetera and are inserted into the Dominican's excerpts for ease of reference.[32] Several of Aquinas's positions were already mentioned above in the *Pro-memoria*. This is because the authors of the *Pro-memoria* attempted to summarize the Thomistic positions of the *Syllabus*.

R1. *The argument from the custom of the Church*: It is against the custom of the Church to forcibly baptize unbelievers, and this is clear because the early leaders of the Church did not request this from Christian emperors.

R2. *The argument from danger of future rejection of the faith*: Children baptized against the will of their parents would later reject the faith by reason of their natural affection for their parents, and this would be detrimental to their souls and the faith.[33]

R3. *The argument from the natural and divine law that the human person comes to know God through reason*: Since the human person comes to know God through reason and will, forced baptism of adults is against the natural law. Likewise, it would be contrary to the natural law if the children of unbelievers were baptized against their parents' will just as it would be if an adult with the use of reason were baptized against his will.[34]

R4. *The argument from natural law that children are contained under the care of parents as a kind of spiritual womb*: Baptism of Jewish children invitis parentibus is against the natural law because the children of the Jews are contained under the care of their parents as under a kind of *spiritualis uterus* (spiritual womb) before they have the use of reason.[35]

---

[32] The location and order of these reasons in Aquinas's texts will be discussed at length in chapter 5.

[33] The assumption here is that rejection of the faith is worse than not believing.

[34] One of Aquinas's texts appeals to the Decretals of Pope Gregory IX, which quoted the Fourth Council of Toledo, on this point. Only the first part of canon 57 of the Council is included in ST III 68.10 s.c.

[35] In ST II.II 10.12 co., Aquinas argues baptizing children of unbelievers invitis parentibus "is against natural justice. For a child is by nature part of its father: thus, at first, it is not distinct from its parents as to its body, so long as it is enfolded within its mother's womb; and later on after birth, and before it has the use of its free-will, it is enfolded in the care of its parents, which is like a spiritual womb." He uses the phrase again in *QDL* 2.4.2.

R5. *The argument from natural law that nothing can be done to children against the will of their parents*: Christians cannot take away the children of unbelievers.

R6. *The argument from the "faith of the parents"*: Under divine law, the parents are the ones responsible for the faith of children and so nothing with regard to divine law is to be done against their will. This is why it is said of old, before circumcision was given, the children of the ancients were "saved through the faith of their parents."

The thinkers in the *Syllabus* also develop arguments that go beyond Aquinas's reasons, as will be explained below.

Durandus of Saint-Pourçain

The first excerpt in the *Syllabus* is from the *Commentary on the Sentences* of Durandus of Saint-Pourçain (c. 1275–1334), a French Dominican theologian and bishop.[36] Durandus entered the Dominican order at Clermont. Some have characterized his thought as nominalist, and others say his teaching is not easy to describe and classify.[37] Nevertheless, he was accused by some of his Dominican colleagues of erroneous teaching, especially on issues where he departed from Aquinas, such as metaphysics and epistemology.[38] Despite censures, Durandus was promoted and completed his doctorate in theology at Paris, and he found favor with popes Clement V and John XXII.

Durandus says there are two points surrounding the question of "whether the children of unbelievers ought to be baptized with their parents unwilling according to Thomas, III.68.10": "The first is whether unbeliever adults could licitly be compelled to the faith and to the things that are of the faith, for example baptism and things of this manner. The second is whether unbeliever little ones who lack the required use of reason could licitly be

---

[36] The *Syllabus* uses his Latin name, Durandus. See his *In Petri Lombardi Sententias theologicas commentarium libri IIII*, in *Sent.* IV. D. 4., 2 vols. (Venice: Ex Typographia Guerraea, 1571; repr., Ridgewood, NJ: Gregg Press, 1964). See also J. A. Weisheipl, "Durandus of Saint-Pourçain," *NCE*, 2nd ed. (Detroit: Gale, 2003), 4:947–49; "Durandus of Saint-Pourçain," in *ODCC*, 520.

[37] See the collection of essays on Durandus's *Sentences* commentary by Andreas Speer et al., *Durand of Saint-Pourçain and His Sentences Commentary: Historical, Philosophical, and Theological issues* (Leuven: Peeters, 2014).

[38] Romanus Cessario, *A Short History of Thomism* (Washington, DC: The Catholic University of America Press, 2003), 56. Durandus was the subject of several censures by a theological commission appointed by the Dominican Master General and was obligated to produce a corrected version of his commentary on the *Sentences*.

baptized with their parents, guardians, or others who have care of them, being unwilling, or without their knowledge."[39]

Durandus's answer to the first question appeals to the example of early "Saints and all the Doctors" who did not request such a practice (R1). For these early leaders of the Church, in fact, the name of "neighbor" applied to every person.[40] Furthermore, adult unbelievers cannot be forced to the act of believing; someone is able to be induced to believe through persuasion and examples as declared by the Fourth Council of Toledo (R3).[41] To "induce or to push or to compel an unbeliever by threats and punishments to profess the faith or to receive baptism is not licit."[42]

Additionally, it is not permitted to take away the things of unbelievers, much less a child (R5), which is "dearer to its father than any possessed thing."[43] Children of unbelievers must not be baptized invitis parentibus because "from natural and divine law it is prohibited for anyone to desire the neighbor's things, and much more to take them away in secret or through violence against his will."[44]

Durandus also lists the arguments *for* baptizing Jewish children invitis parentibus that are listed in ST III 68.10: One should baptize children of unbelievers to "meet the danger of eternal death" and provide salvation for their souls (A2); since man belongs to God from whom he has a soul, more than to his own father, it is not unjust to take away children from their parents to baptize them (A4); Christian princes can earn merit if they offer the children of Jews to baptism for the salvation of the children and honor of God, not to force their parents to believe (A3).[45]

His response to these arguments repeats and develops themes in Aquinas: that man is ordered to God through reason, through which he is able to come to know God; that children before the use of reason are under the care of parents according to natural and divine law; that they may not be "snatched away" to be freed from the danger of eternal death (R3, R5). He also adds a line from St. Paul—"Evils are not to be done in order that goods may come about"—that Aquinas uses in another question on the sacrament of

---

[39] Durandus no. 6 in *SA*, 295.

[40] Durandus no. 8 in *SA*, 299.

[41] Durandus no. 4 in *SA*. The Fourth Council of Toledo will be discussed in chapter 4. See also *JLS*, 486, 295.

[42] Durandus no. 7 in *SA*, 297.

[43] Durandus no. 8 in *SA*, 299.

[44] Durandus no. 8 in *SA*, 299.

[45] Durandus no. 2 in *SA*, 295.

baptism.[46] Durandus also develops Aquinas when he says that if an individual or prince takes away a child from an unbeliever with the latter unwilling, and offers it to baptism, he would offer to God "a sacrifice of robbery" (R4).

Durandus then takes up the question of the validity of forced baptisms of Jewish children: "It is asked . . . if they should in fact be baptized, whether they are truly baptized." He summarizes the argument as follows:

> And it is argued that little ones of unbelievers baptized with the parents unwilling receive the true sacrament, because unbeliever parents do not have greater right over their little children than faithful parents do, but the little ones of faithful parents when baptized with the parents unwilling do receive the true sacrament: therefore similarly the little ones of unbeliever parents, if they should be baptized with the parents unwilling, would receive the true sacrament.[47]

This opinion is not in Aquinas's list of arguments against his position and so developed after his lifetime; it is that the unbelieving parents do not have greater rights than Christian parents.[48] This theme would be taken up at greater length by other Dominicans.

Durandus's answer to this argument is that the reception of any sacrament requires intention of the will. "If in fact someone were to be baptized, confirmed, ordained, or immersed unwilling, one would not receive any sacrament." He then cites St. Jerome's Commentary on Matthew 28:18 ("So teach all nations, baptizing them. . . ."). Jerome says, "Teach all nations, then, when they are taught, bathe them in water; for it is not able to happen that the body should receive the sacrament of baptism unless the soul beforehand shall have taken up the truth of the faith."[49]

Furthermore, in the children of unbelieving parents there is no will or intention "as is plain on its own."[50] A child, before it has the use of reason and will, is ordered to God through the reason and will of those under whose care it is subject, and matters relating to God regarding them must be done according to their disposition (R4).

---

46 Durandus no. 9 in *SA*, 299. An echo of Rom 3:8: "Some people slander us by saying that we say, 'Let us do evil so that good may come'?" (NRSVUE) in ST III 68.11 ad. 3: "We should 'not do evil that there may come good' (Romans 3:8)."

47 Durandus no. 11 in *SA*, 299.

48 Durandus no. 11 in *SA*, 299.

49 Durandus no. 7 in *SA*, 2, 297. *St. Jerome Commentary on Matthew*, trans. Thomas P. Scheck (Washington, DC: The Catholic University of America Press, 2008), 327.

50 Durandus no. 13 in *SA*, 301.

> But the unbeliever father does not abuse his paternal power if he should keep his little son in the rite that he himself observes; and so the care of the son is not able licitly ... to be taken away from him and committed to another from whose will he would be baptized; because of which the son of a faithful parent is able licitly to be baptized with the father unwilling, and receive the true sacrament, but not the son of an unbeliever parent.[51]

Since the will of the parents is the representative will of the little child, if one should in fact be baptized there is no baptism.[52]

Durandus illustrates his teaching that the sacrament requires intention with an analogy to the baptism of a sleeping adult. The analogy was employed above, in the *Pro-memoria*:

> If any adult were to be so raised that he had heard nothing about the faith, and were only in original sin, if such were to be sleeping and in sleeping be baptized, it is settled that there would be no baptism of such a one, not because in his will would baptism find a barrier more than in a little one, but because the will of receiving baptism would be lacking.[53]

Peter Paludanus

The *Syllabus* then presents the teaching of the French Dominican theologian and patriarch of Jerusalem, Peter Paludanus (c. 1275–1342). Paludanus entered the Dominican order at Lyons. After studying theology at Toulouse, he was sent to Paris to lecture on the *Sentences* as successor to Durandus. He would later be appointed to a commission that investigated books 2 and 3 of Durandus's commentary on the *Sentences*. In general, Paludanus responded to the nominalist tendencies in theology caused by Ockham's influence.[54] Paludanus also became patriarch of Jerusalem in 1329, and he wrote a concordance to Aquinas's *Summa theologiae*.

---

51 Durandus no. 24 in *SA*, 309.

52 Durandus no. 13 in *SA*, 301.

53 What of those unbelievers who are near death, and unable to think about or express a possible desire to be baptized? It would seem logical to baptize them to prevent them from going to hell. But Aquinas thinks "a person should not be baptized while asleep, except he be threatened with the danger of death. In which case he should be baptized, if previously he has manifested a desire to receive Baptism." ST III 68.12 ad. 3. For more analysis on Durandus's view of forced baptism of adults as it relates to Aquinas's teaching see Colish, *Peter Lombard*, 307–8.

54 Cessario, *Short History*, 55.

The excerpt in the *Syllabus* is taken from Paludanus's commentary on the *Sentences*.[55] The excerpt begins with the question of "whether the children of unbelievers who lack the use of reason are to be baptized with their parents unwilling." Paludanus lists opinions or arguments in favor of forced baptism of Jewish children. The opinions are similar to those listed by Durandus.

The first opinion is that "earthly princes can licitly, and even meritoriously take away the children of Jews and offer them to baptism" because they do this for the salvation of the children and to honor God (A3). Additionally, this opinion also argues that if these children are baptized, they receive "true"—that is, valid—baptism because "for the reception of baptism it suffices that there be found no barrier of contrary will, as is plain in the little ones of Christians; but in the little ones of Jews there is no barrier of proper will; therefore they receive it."[56] This argument is, once again, not in Aquinas's texts.

Paludanus's answer echoes themes from Aquinas's teaching (R3–5) but also develops the teaching through an analogy to forced marriage. He says that "these reasons are not compelling." First, for the same reason that a prince is not able to force a Jewish father to baptism, he is not able to force the father's son. "For the will of the father is considered the will of the son." Paludanus argues that just as the prince could not contract marriage vows for a son or for a daughter with the father unwilling, he could not make the father marry against his will. In affairs of human law, the prince can dispose with an unwilling father as he wishes but "not in affairs that are regarding natural and divine right."[57]

Paludanus's second point addresses the question of validity of forced baptisms of children. His discussion of the question is extensive and develops Aquinas's themes considerably. He is once again concerned to respond to the claim that the children of unbelievers who receive such baptisms receive the sacrament because there is "no contrary will in a child."

Paludanus argues that if they should be baptized "they do not receive baptism." Why? "The first reason is that all are free in affairs that correspond to natural and divine law" (R3). Receiving baptism pertains to the divine law. And the care of little ones, until they reach the age of reason, is with the

---

55 The *Syllabus* uses his Latin name, Paludanus. For his commentary on the *Sentences* see Petrus de Palude, *Quartus Sententiarum liber*, ed. Vincent Haerlem (Paris, 1514); F. Stegmüller, *Repertorium commentariorum in Sententias Petri Lombardi* (Würzburg: Schöningh, 1947), l: 327–28. See also Jean Dunbabin, *A Hound of God: Pierre de La Palud and the Fourteenth-Century Church* (New York: Oxford University Press, 1991).

56 Paludanus no. 2 in *SA*, 311.

57 Paludanus no. 3 in *SA*, 311.

parents according to natural law (R4).⁵⁸ Therefore, only the will of the parents is the "representative will" of little ones before such time as they should have the use of reason. Repeating Aquinas, he says that is why it is usually said that of old, before circumcision was given, they were "saved in the faith of their parents" (R6).⁵⁹ Paludanus also cites the Fourth Council of Toledo's prohibition of forced baptism (R3).⁶⁰ For these reasons, "no one can licitly take them away from them to be baptized" (R5).⁶¹

Paludanus also considers another rather elaborate argument beyond those listed in Aquinas's texts. The argument sought to overturn the parental rights of unbelievers by saying that the Church's intention can replace the intention of unbelieving parents just as the Church's intention is sufficient for the baptism of children who have Christian parents. Paludanus is the first of several Dominicans in the *Syllabus* to address the question of whether the intention of the faithful can stand in place of the intention of unbelievers with regard to their children.

Paludanus then describes the logic of the argument as follows. If a father were to teach his son or daughter bad morals, for example that his son should commit adultery, or that his daughter should become a prostitute, his guardianship would be taken away and he would be deprived of *patria potestas* (parental rights).⁶² But teaching unbelief to a child is even worse than teaching bad morals. Since "spiritual fornication is worse, and does more harm to Christian civilization, much more should the offspring be taken away from him if he wants to make it an adulteress to the faith."⁶³ Additionally, the representative intention for the child of unbelievers belongs not only the parents but more to the "spiritual adopting parents"—that is, to the Church.⁶⁴ "The will of the Church is more the representative will of the little one than the will of the parent of the flesh."⁶⁵ The claim is that the direct intention and representative will of the community of the faithful is sufficient to count as the will of the recipient. The analogy is that since the son of a faithful Christian can be baptized even if the Christian father is unwilling for some reason,

---

58 In the thirteenth century, the age that children could be baptized without the consent of parents or guardians was seven years old. Grayzel, vol. 2, 14.

59 Paludanus no. 5 in *SA*, 315.

60 Paludanus no. 4 in *SA*, 313. For the text of canon 57 see *JLS*, 486.

61 Paludanus no. 4 in *SA*, 313.

62 Paludanus no. 6 in *SA*, 315. Literally, "power of a father," which was a term understood to refer to the Roman legal tradition of parental rights.

63 Paludanus no. 6 in *SA*, 315.

64 Paludanus no. 10 in *SA*, 319.

65 Paludanus no. 13 in *SA*, 319.

the child receives true baptism. Therefore, if the children of the Jews should be baptized, they receive the true sacrament. "The faith of those who offer them is enough for little ones, with no mention of the faith of the parents."[66]

Paludanus then responds by making an important distinction: the Jewish people are outside the Church. He argues that "it is not so with the little ones of unbelievers, because before baptism they are not of the Church in such a way that the will of the Church could thus be able to be their representative will."[67] The Christian who "offers" the little one has "no right in someone else's son," and nor does the Church. Christian parents or the Church are able to offer the little ones of Christians but not the little ones of Jews or unbelievers of any kind.

For Paludanus, the question of whether a forced baptism of a child of unbelievers is valid is directly impacted by this distinction: "If they should receive baptism being forced and not consenting, nothing is done.... In the things that are of the pure divine law they require a true or representative will: it ought not to be done, nor, if it is done, is it valid."[68] For Paludanus, only the will of the unbelieving parents is the representative will of their children before the children have the use of reason (R3).

Paludanus also teaches that there is divine prohibition of forced baptism of Jews in Scripture. He appeals to Psalm 59:12, which in this context is intended to highlight Augustine's famous teaching that no one should forcibly separate Jews from Judaism.[69] "The Psalm says, 'Do not kill them, lest ever my peoples be forgotten' (Ps. 59.12)." Paludanus adds, "For we have it handed down from the scriptures that it is not the will of God that they should be killed."[70] Aquinas does not use this argument in his defense of Jewish parental authority, but he assumes the doctrine of Jewish witness and toleration of Jewish worship elsewhere.[71]

Paludanus adds a second Augustinian argument based in Scripture for why the Jewish people should not be forcibly converted: "Likewise according to the prophecies, they are to be converted at the preaching of Enoch and Elijah, wherefore until then God wants the heart in its blindness to be

---

[66] Paludanus no. 11 in *SA*, 319.

[67] Paludanus no. 13 in *SA*, 319.

[68] Paludanus no. 20 in *SA*, 329.

[69] Paludanus no. 16 in *SA*, 323. See Paula Fredriksen, *Augustine and the Jews: A Christian Defense of Jews and Judaism* (New York: Double Day, 2008), 304, 364. The psalm functions in Augustine's sermons as a metaphor for his witness doctrine, which includes the claim that God wills the freedom of Jewish practice.

[70] Paludanus no. 16 in *SA*, 323.

[71] ST II.II 10.11 co.

tolerated. But if either they or their children were to be baptized with them unwilling then no time would be found for Enoch and Elijah; nor, consequently, would the prophecies be made to come true."[72] According to "the prophecies" (Mal 4:5–6), the deliverance and restoration of Israel takes place at the Second Coming, when the "two witnesses" mentioned in Revelation 11:3 will return and preach to the Jewish people. This tradition was rooted in Augustine, who understood the two witnesses in Revelation 11:3 to refer to Enoch and Elijah, who were both taken up into heaven. Augustine thought John the Baptist was called Elijah because he was a symbol, or type, of the eschatological figure, Elijah, who would precede the Second Coming of Christ. Augustine taught that Elijah would come back to preach and reveal the Christological meaning of Scripture to Jews.[73] Paludanus therefore draws upon an Augustinian doctrine that prohibits the killing of Jews and pinpoints conversion of Jews beyond the present age.

Paludanus deploys this Augustinian eschatology to defend Jewish parental authority. He argues that if the Jewish people are converted before the Second Coming, then there would be no time for the preaching of Enoch and Elijah, and thus the prophecies of Malachi would not be fulfilled.[74] Paludanus then adds that "God has chosen not armed men, the strong and the powerful, but what is weak and contemptible in the world, to convert men by the sword of the mouth not the material one."[75]

Like Durandus, Paludanus also responds to a version of the argument based on the danger of spiritual death. The children of unbelievers may certainly be baptized against the will of their parents in order to save them from spiritual death (A2):

---

[72] Paludanus no. 16 in *SA*, 323.

[73] St. Augustine, *The City of God*, books 11–22, trans. William Babcock (Hyde Park, NY: New City Press, 2013). See Augustine's discussion of the "return of Elijah" in book XX.27–29. For Augustine, Moses and Elijah had contact with Christ even during their earthly lives. For this reason, they understood the allegorical meaning of historical events that took place before Christ.

[74] Elijah (ninth century BCE) is held to be the greatest Hebrew prophet. Along with Enoch, he did not die but went up into heaven (2 Kgs 2:1–18). In Malachi 4:3–6, Elijah's return was held to be a necessary prelude to the deliverance and restoration of Israel: "See, I will send you the prophet Elijah before the great and terrible day of the LORD comes. He will turn the hearts of parents to their children and the hearts of children to their parents." In the New Testament (e.g., Mark 9:4), Elijah appears as the typical representative of the prophets. In Augustine's view, John the Baptist was called Elijah because he was a symbol of the eschatological figure who would precede the Second Coming of Christ. Augustine's view was endorsed in theological manuals. Enoch was the father of Methuselah. Enoch "walked with God and he was not; for God took him" (Gen 5:24). In the Jewish tradition, many legends became attached to him, and in the New Testament his ascension is referred to in Hebrews 11:5. See the entries on Elijah and Enoch in *ODCC*, 542, 550; "Elijah (Second Coming of)," in *NCE*, 2nd ed., 5:159.

[75] Paludanus no. 16 in *SA*, 323. See also Isa 42:2 and Rev 19:15.

> And if it should be argued against these things which have been said, that there is greater need to meet the danger of eternal than temporal death, but the boy who is in danger of temporal death must be helped against the will of his parents, even if out of malice they were to will the opposite, therefore all the more must the children of unbelievers be helped against the danger of eternal death even with their parents unwilling.[76]

Like Durandus, Paludanus replies to this danger-of-death argument by saying that "evils are not to be done in order that goods may come about."[77] But it would be an evil act to take the son of an unbeliever away from him since the son is in the unbeliever's care and is subject to his decisions as far as natural and divine law are concerned (R5).[78] He then offers an analogy to further illustrate the point that evil must not be done in order that goods may come about: just as water is not to be taken away from someone who was unwilling to give their water to baptize a boy, it would be contrary to justice, should a boy be taken from his parents because of baptism.[79] The child's need for salvation does not give the Christian a right or power over the child. To act as if one had power or care over the child would violate natural and divine law.

Paludanus then echoes Aquinas's teachings. If such forced baptisms were licit, the saints and leaders of the Church would have given this counsel to Christian princes, such as Constantine and Ambrose (R1). He also adds that the practice is "very dangerous," because "a boy that has been baptized, until he comes to adult age, could easily withdraw from what he had done through ignorance against the will of those who have care of him" (R2).[80] He repeats Aquinas's teaching that the human person comes to know God through reason and will (R3): "A man is ordered to God through reason and will, by which he comes to know and love Him."[81] "And therefore, the boy, before he has the use of reason, is ordered to God through the reason of his parents, to whose care he lies subject by nature, because of which the things of God are to be done regarding him according to their disposition."[82]

---

76 Paludanus no. 18 in *SA*, 325.

77 Again, this line is a paraphrase of Rom 3:8: "Some people slander us by saying that we say, 'Let us do evil so that good may come'?" NRSVUE. Aquinas also uses the phrase in ST III 68.11 ad. 3: "We should 'not do evil that there may come good' (Romans 3:8)."

78 Paludanus no. 4 in *SA*, 313; no. 19 in *SA*, 327.

79 Paludanus no. 19 in *SA*, 327.

80 Paludanus no. 4 in *SA*, 313.

81 ST II.II 10.12.

82 Paludanus no. 20 in *SA*, 329.

John Capreolus

The next substantial excerpt in the *Syllabus* is from the commentary on the *Sentences* by the celebrated French Dominican theologian John Capreolus (c. 1380–1444).[83] Capreolus, known as "prince of Thomists," lectured at Paris and Toulouse. He was a native of Languedoc and entered the Dominican order at Rodez. He was the regent of studies at Toulouse. Capreolus became known as a defender of a small anti-revisionist movement that sought to defend Aquinas's thought against the influence of Henry of Ghent, Duns Scotus, Durandus, William of Ockham, and others.[84] The renowned twentieth-century Dominican theologian Marie-Dominique Chenu referred to Capreolus as the "first great commentator on Saint Thomas."[85] In 1407, Capreolus was sent to the University of Paris to comment on Lombard's *Book of Sentences*. "Twentieth-century Thomists have, generally, considered him more faithful to the teachings of Aquinas than later commentators such as Cajetan."[86]

Capreolus takes up the question "whether the children of unbelievers are to be baptized with the parents unwilling." Relying upon ST II.II 10.12, Capreolus says Aquinas answers in the negative. Children either have the use of reason or they do not. If they do not yet have the use of free will, according to the natural law they are under the care of their parents. For this reason, it would be against natural justice if such children were to be baptized (R3).[87] Secondly, the Church has never had this custom because it is not in harmony with reason (R1).[88]

Capreolus then explains Aquinas's twofold rationale for the above teachings. First, if it were possible that the children of unbelievers before the use of reason could receive baptism, then when they come to the fullness of age

---

83 The excerpts in the Mortara *Syllabus* correspond to John Capréolus, *Thomistarum Principis Defensiones Theologiae Divi Thomae Aquinatis*, ed. C. Paban and T. Pègues, 7 vols. (1900–1908; repr., Turonibus, 1967), Article 1, Conclusiones, Questio 1, at 113 or PDF #139, available online at https://babel.hathitrust.org/cgi/pt?id=mdp.39015026314594&view=1up&seq=5&skin=2021. The work is entitled *Arguments in Defense of the Theology of Saint Thomas Aquinas*.

84 See "Translators' Introduction" in John Capreolus, *On the Virtues*, xxviii; J. A. Weisheipl, "Capreolus, John," *NCE*, 2nd ed., 3:92–93. John Duns Scotus (1265–1308) was a Scottish Franciscan theologian who became regent master at Paris.

85 Chenu, *Toward Understanding Saint Thomas*, 273.

86 Michael Tavuzzi, "Johannes Capreolus (c.1380–1444)," *Routledge Encyclopedia of Philosophy*, vol. 1 (New York: Taylor and Francis, 1998).

87 Capreolus no. 1 in *SA*, 335.

88 Capreolus no. 1 in *SA*, 335.

they could easily be led by their parents to abandon what they unknowingly received, and this "borders on a ruination of his faith" (R2).[89]

Second, a child is by nature something of the parent, and when in the womb he is not distinguished from the parents. "Afterwards, though, after he comes out from the womb, before he has the use of free will, he is contained under the care of the parents as if within a kind of spiritual womb [*spirituali utero*]" (R4).[90] Capreolus explains that Aquinas means that when children do not have the use of reason they do not differ from an irrational animal and so it would be against natural justice if a boy were to be taken away from the care of his parents (R5), "or that anything should be ordained concerning him with his parents unwilling."[91]

Capreolus then synthesizes a teaching from ST III 68.10 with *Quodlibetales Questiones* 2.4.2: "[Children] are under the care of their parents as long as they cannot look after themselves. For which reason we say that even the children of the ancients were saved through the faith of their parents" (R6).[92] Capreolus adds Aquinas's explanatory line about this phrase: he thinks Aquinas means to say that "faith of the parents" means that "it pertains to the parents to provide for the children regarding their salvation, especially before they have the use of reason. This is what he says." Capreolus explains that based on this text from Aquinas's *QDL*, one should conclude that "nothing that borders on danger to the faith and the derogation of natural law ought to be introduced in the Church, but the baptizing of the little ones of unbelievers with the parents unwilling is a thing of this type."[93]

Capreolus then responds to the argument that Christian rulers can offer the children of Jews to baptism because this brings salvation to the children, and it honors God (A3). Though Scotus is unnamed, Capreolus seems aware of Scotus's argument that forced baptism and depriving the Jews of their freedom to keep their law and rite is not as damaging to Christian society as allowing them the freedom to keep their law.[94] Capreolus understands the Scotist argument to be that forcibly baptized children would be effective in the long-term because the children "after the third and fourth generation would be truly faithful."[95] In response, Capreolus quotes Aquinas's teaching

---

[89] Capreolus no. 1 in *SA*, 335.

[90] Capreolus no. 1 in *SA*, 335.

[91] Capreolus no. 2 in *SA*, 337.

[92] Capreolus no. 2 in *SA*, 337.

[93] Capreolus no. 2 in *SA*, 337.

[94] Duns Scotus, *Ordinatio*, 4. D. 4. pars 4. q. 3.2.

[95] Capreolus no. 3 in *SA*, 337. Scotus discusses the question "whether the children of Jews and unbelievers are to be baptized when the parents are unwilling" in *Ordinatio*, 4. d. 4. pars 4. q. 3.2.

in ST II.II 10.8 that unbelievers such as Jews are in no way to be compelled to the faith since such matters pertain to the divine law (R3).

Like Paludanus, Capreolus consolidates biblical arguments alongside the Augustinian principle of toleration in Psalm 59:12, "Do not kill them, lest ever my peoples be forgotten." He writes, "The divine foreknowledge and prophetic revelation are at the ready, and this alone ought to suffice for what is proposed, namely that they are not to be forced to the faith, because this would be to strive in vain against the divine foreknowledge and revelation."[96] The mention of prophetic revelation here echoes the Augustinian teaching that the salvation of Jews is the responsibility of Elijah and Enoch, as Paludanus also taught.

Moreover, Capreolus insists baptism invitis parentibus would be more damaging to the Church, and "a sin," because such a practice would be an action against God's prohibition. He adds that "evils are not to be done so that goods may come about, nor ought one incur the ruination of his own salvation because of the ruination of someone else's salvation."[97] "It appears, therefore, that neither an Emperor nor a Pope ought to baptize the sons of unbelievers if they are themselves unwilling as long as the children are under the care of the parents from divine or natural law."[98]

Capreolus also includes an exposition of Pope Gregory IX's *Decretals* D. 45, which is cited by Aquinas in ST III 68.10. As will be discussed at length in the next chapter, *Decretals* D. 45 is based on the Fourth Council of Toledo canon 57 (R3).[99] The canon teaches that unbelievers are to be saved willingly, not unwillingly. Capreolus also adds Aquinas's teaching that the human person is "naturally ordered to God through reason, through which he is naturally able to come to know him." Likewise, children, before they have the use of reason, are ordered to God through the reason of their parents. "Things pertaining to God are to be done according to their disposition." "And from this it is apparent that little ones of the Jews before the use of reason cannot without prejudice and injustice be totally taken away from the care of the parents, especially in the things that are of the natural or divine law."[100]

---

[96] Capreolus no. 5 in *SA*, 337. He repeats this line in no. 8.

[97] Capreolus no. 4 in *SA*, 339.

[98] Capreolus no. 4 in *SA*, 339.

[99] "Regarding the Jews, moreover, the Holy Synod has given instruction that no one therefore should bring force for the purpose of belief. For God has mercy on whom he wills. For such are not to be saved unwillingly, but willingly, so that the form of justice may be intact. For just as man is saved by his own will and faculty of judgement, so they must be persuaded, and not rather compelled to convert." For the text of the canon see *JLS*, 486.

[100] Capreolus no. 6 in *SA*, 341.

For Capreolus, the above natural law arguments determine the question of the will of the parents in baptism as well as the question of whether such baptisms would be valid: "Therefore the will of the father is regarded as the will of the son, whence just as he could not baptize his adult son against his will, so also one cannot baptize the underage son against the will of the father, which is the representative will of the son."[101] Only the will of the unbelieving parents can represent their children, and not the intention of Christians: "And again because the little ones from such a baptism would receive nothing, since neither their own will nor a representative will would be present for them, because there is no representative will of little ones before the use of reason except the will of the parents under whose care they are subject."[102]

Capreolus closes by addressing a position that another Dominican theologian, Ambrosius Catharinus, identifies as the position of Cardinal Cajetan: the position that a valid baptism does not require a representative will but only that there be no contrary will to the baptism. "Nor, moreover, does it suffice for the reception of baptism that there be not found the barrier of a contrary will in the one who ought to be baptized, but it is required that the direct or representative intention of receiving baptism is plain."[103]

Against this position, Capreolus stresses that a representative intention on behalf of the recipient is necessary for a valid sacrament, not simply the lack of a contrary will. He also appeals to the analogy of an invalid adult baptism:[104] Baptism requires the intention of receiving the baptism, directly as in the case of an adult, or representatively through parents. "But only the will of the parents is representative will of the little ones before they have the use of reason. Wherefore if a boy were to be baptized with the parents unwilling, it seems that nothing is being done, since their direct and representative will is lacking."[105]

Capreolus closes with another argument that God does not desire for Christians to act in this way toward Jews: "Evils are not to be done in order that goods may come about, but an evil would be done by taking the little one away from his parents to whom God and nature have made him subject. God also has prohibited such fraud, nor does he want a holocaust to

---

101 Capreolus no. 7 in *SA*, 339.

102 Capreolus no. 4 in *SA*, 339.

103 Capreolus no. 8 in *SA*, 339.

104 "If an adult were so brought up that he had not heard about the faith at all, and he were in his original sin, if such a one were to be baptized while sleeping it is settled that nothing would happen, and nevertheless in his will the baptism would find no barrier." Capreolus says that "more therefore is required." Capreolus no. 8 in *SA*, 339.

105 Capreolus no. 8 in *SA*, 339.

be offered to himself from robbery of possessions or persons, as would be done in the proposed."[106]

Ambrosius Catharinus

Ambrosius Catharinus (c. 1484–1553) was an Italian Dominican theologian, bishop, and doctor of civil and canon law. He entered the Dominican order at Florence. He was also a lawyer under Pope Leo X and one of the first theologians to write against Lutheranism. Catharinus's defense of the feast of the Immaculate Conception as well as other doctrines brought him into conflict with Dominican superiors.[107] He published works on predestination, justification, purgatory, and veneration of saints, among other topics. He attended the Council of Trent as a papal theologian from 1545–47 and was made an archbishop of Conza in 1552. His works are characterized by an emphasis on the teaching authority of the Church and a return to Scripture and the Church Fathers.[108] He wrote a commentary on the *Summa theologiae*.

The excerpt from Catharinus begins with "the question of the children of the Jews."[109] He understands his commentary to present the teaching of "Blessed Thomas, which very many follow with good cause." His summary of Aquinas's teaching on the question is similar to the views of the above Dominicans. He follows Aquinas's position in *QDL* 4.2.2.

Catharinus says it is against the custom of the Church to forcibly baptize unbelievers (R1). If children were baptized against the will of their parents they would later reject the faith by reason of their natural affection for their parents (R2). Since the will of the human person is ordered to God through reason, forced baptism of adults is against the natural law (R3). Baptism of Jewish children *invitis parentibus* is also against the natural law because children are under the care of their parents before they have the use of reason (R4).[110]

Perhaps the most distinctive element of Catharinus's excerpt is his engagement with the influential theologian and commentator on the *Summa*

---

106 Capreolus no. 8 in *SA*, 339.

107 "Ambrosius Catharinus," in *ODCC*, 304.

108 Catharinus was appointed bishop of Minori in 1546. J. R. Cooney, "Ambrosius Catharinus (Lancelot Politi)," *NCE*, 2nd ed., 1:347. J. Schweizer, *Ambrosius Catharinus Politus* (Münster: Aschendorff, 1910).

109 Catharinus no. 1 in *SA*, 343. The excerpt is from *De pueris iudaeorum sua sponte ad baptismum venientibus, etiam invitis parentibus, recipiendis: In appendix to Enarrationes in quinque priora capita libri Geneseos* (Romae: Apud Antonium Bladum, 1552).

110 Catharinus no. 2 in *SA*, 345.

theologiae, Cardinal Cajetan (1469–1534).[111] Catharinus is concerned to address Cajetan's argument that baptism of Jewish children invitis parentibus would "receive the effect of baptism and be said to be truly baptized and bound to the Church in the profession of Christ." In Catharinus's view, "Cajetan makes this claim, and further claims that it is of the teaching of Blessed Thomas. But on both counts he is unquestionably wrong."[112]

According to Catharinus, Cajetan's argument is as follows: "For the receiving of the effect of this Sacrament, the consent or the will of the one who is baptized is not required, but it is enough that no one place a barrier, that is, that no one dissents; and this is plain in the children of the faithful. For they, even though they do not consent, attain to the effect of the sacrament."[113] Catharinus understands Cajetan to argue that the sacrament is conferred upon the infant because the infant is passive, and this allows for the intention to be supplied from elsewhere.[114]

Catharinus's reply begins with an example from an adult baptism. It is false to assert that the sacrament is conferred apart from the will and consent of an adult. He says Aquinas also makes this point.[115] "But that the intention of the one who is being baptized is required of any adult, the Blessed Thomas manifestly holds. Whence he says: 'If in an adult were to be lacking the intention of receiving the sacrament, he would need to be rebaptized.'"[116] Catharinus also offers the analogy of a sleeping adult recipient of baptism and says that on Cajetan's terms the forcibly baptized sleeping adult would be "under the jurisdiction of the Church" and compelled to keep the faith. Catharinus argues that since Cajetan does not hold that the adult baptized while sleeping would be compelled to keep the faith, his position that baptism invitis parentibus is a valid baptism is inconsistent.

---

111 Cajetan or Thomas de Vio (1469–1534) wrote an influential commentary on Aquinas's *Summa theologiae*. At the age of sixteen, he entered the Dominican order at Gaeta, receiving the religious name of Thomas. He was the general master of the Dominicans from 1508–18. Pius V ordered his commentary on the *Summa theologiae* to be published with the complete works of Aquinas in 1570 (minus heterodox opinions in the Third Part). The suppressed passages did not touch on basic principles of Thomism. Leo XIII ordered his commentary to be published with the critical edition of Thomas's *Summa* (1888–1906). According to Weisheipl, many of the views he held are not to be found in Aquinas but are the insights that were a result of his own thinking. For example, he held that the immortality of the soul cannot be demonstrated by reason. Some assert that Cajetan stressed the Aristotelianism of Aquinas "often to the detriment of St. Thomas's originality." J. A. Weisheipl, "Cajetan (Tommaso De Vio)," *NCE*, 2nd ed., 4:853–55.

112 Catharinus no. 3 in *SA*, 345.

113 Catharinus no. 3 in *SA*, 345.

114 Catharinus no. 3 in *SA*, 345.

115 ST I.II 113.3 ad. 1; ST III 68.12 ad. 3.

116 ST III 68.7 ad. 2.

Catharinus then says that Augustine teaches that before children have the use of reason, the children can be offered to baptism because they believe through others. "Blessed Augustine also advances this, when he says, 'Mother Church offers her maternal face to her little ones, so that they may be steeped in the sacred mysteries,' and they are rightly called faithful, because they profess the faith in a certain fashion through the words of those who bear them."[117]

But Catharinus says this is not so for unbelievers who do not belong to Mother Church. Like Paludanus and Capreolus, Catharinus notices the distinction between children of unbelievers and children of Christian parents that is required by the divine and natural law. "And let no one tell me, even if the parents should be unwilling, nevertheless the consent and faith can be supplied to the little ones by the Church and the elders of the Church, as we say so regarding the infants of Christians if by chance the Christian parents were to prohibit their baptism."[118] In regard to Christian parents, he says they are "found to be themselves already obligated to the Church, to offer their consent for their children." Moreover, if they do not do this, the Church can supply what Christian parents "wickedly take away from their sons." This distinction between the parents of unbelievers who are not obligated to the Church, and Christian parents who are indeed obligated to the Church, is "not considered by some." For this reason, "they have erred gravely."[119]

Catharinus understands his teaching to extend the teaching of Aquinas: "It must therefore be concluded that, without the will of the parents, the children of Jews (or those who are in any way unbelievers outside the Church) cannot be baptized, and if they should be baptized the baptism is not valid. And no differently did the Divine Thomas teach, but this is necessarily drawn from his teaching, as Capreolus teaches."[120] He also understands his position to consolidate arguments of Paludanus and Capreolus that if forced baptism of Jewish children occurs, these baptisms are nevertheless invalid, and that the Jews are not under the jurisdiction of the Church in spiritual matters. For

---

117 Catharinus no. 7 in *SA*, 349.

118 Catharinus no. 7 in *SA*, 349. Catharinus's insights about the distinction between Christian parents and Jewish parents will come into play later in the adjudication of Aquinas's teaching in ST III 68.9. Cardinal Giovanni Antonio Sangiorgio attends to the same distinction: "And Augustine says this. But no other person's faith suffices in a little one except the faith of the parents, as much because others have no right over him from the parents as because he himself does not pertain to the church except on account of his origin: therefore the faith of the parents is necessary for this baptism." Sangiorgio no. 4 in *SA*, 34. As I show below, the Dominican theologian Prierio says that they would receive the sacrament "only . . . when the unbelieving parents themselves consent that the children be faithful Christians."

119 Catharinus no. 16 in *SA*, 361.

120 Catharinus no. 9 in *SA*, 353.

Catharinus, Aquinas's teaching and the Dominicans that followed him support the claim that the Church cannot supply the intention or representative will in the place of, or over and against, the will of the parents. "According to the truer teaching of others, which certainly is that of Blessed Thomas and Peter Paludanus and Capreolus . . . the Church is not able to supply the place for those who are not hers in any way, which will very much have to be considered."[121]

Catharinus then directly addresses an important argument concerning the interpretation of Aquinas that will be discussed in chapter 5. The claim is that Aquinas thinks that if such a forced baptism does occur, it is a valid baptism. Based on an interpretation of what is implied in Aquinas's argument from future rejection of the faith (R2), some argue that Aquinas thinks forcibly baptized children receive a valid baptism, since how else would they be able to later reject it?

Catharinus responds:

> But still Blessed Thomas's teaching is diametrically opposed. For he argues expressly against that opinion which wanted such children to receive baptism. And showing that this is absurd and false, he said, "For if they were to receive baptism"—he means this word conditionally, as if to say, "If this were true, as you say, that such children receive baptism, afterwards, when they come to the fullness of reason, they could easily become deserters."[122]

The question of the interpretation of Aquinas on the validity of these forced baptisms is the concern of several Dominican theologians. For example, it will also be addressed below by Sylvester Mazzolini di Prierio.

Catharinus then responds to A3, the claim from Duns Scotus that Christian princes can offer the children of Jews to baptism because this brings salvation to the children. He also addresses A2, that since man belongs to God from whom he has a soul, more than to his own father, it is not unjust to take away children from their parents to baptize them. He summarizes the arguments as follows:

> To prohibit them from being baptized—what else is this than to bring death upon them, and that indeed not temporal but eternal? Additionally, isn't a man more a thing of God, and more under his power than that of his parents? If parents use their power over their children badly, i.e. not

---

[121] Catharinus no. 10 in *SA*, 355.
[122] Catharinus no. 9 in *SA*, 353.

taking them to be baptized themselves, then why cannot Princes do this and return the children to God?[123]

In Catharinus's reply, he asks, "How can the removal of the natural and divine law belong to the power of a prince?" Children cannot be compelled to baptism just as their adult parents cannot. "Wherefore I am not able to stop marveling at this opposite teaching of Cajetan, that anyone can be baptized even if he is unwilling."[124] For if God allows for adult unbelievers to "stop themselves from getting salvation, is it any wonder if consequently they can also not be a boon to their children in this matter." Catharinus then explains the rationale of what he understands as the unbeliever's logic for not baptizing his son:

> When he is unwilling to consent to baptism for his son he does this not to destroy him, but to keep him rather, because he thinks that the religion of Christ is false. The parents therefore do not in this way violate the natural law, but they keep it, if their mind should be considered, when they do not apply to their children what they think is harmful to them, and do not choose it for themselves.[125]

God wills all people to be saved, Catharinus explains, and so God calls and invites all. This is because God wills our salvation. Yet, this also requires our will, explains Catharinus, and so he calls and invites us to respond. "But the will of the children, when they do not have reason, is claimed by the parents, which, if they do not offer it, the children are found to be unable to attain salvation."[126]

Catharinus also makes the point that the Jewish people are not obligated to the Church. Since Jewish parents are not obligated to the Church they do not have "the bond of the Spirit" with her. Therefore, reasons Catharinus, their sons are not sanctified, nor are they able to be sanctified through the help of the Church as long as parents are resisting since they are under the "natural law and order, which the Gospel law does not take away" (R3).[127] And the gospel does not violate the natural law since to do so would be "repugnant

---

123 Catharinus no. 11 in *SA*, 355.
124 Catharinus no. 15 in *SA*, 361.
125 Catharinus no. 15 in *SA*, 361.
126 Catharinus no. 13 in *SA*, 359.
127 Catharinus no. 16 in *SA*, 361.

to natural justice." On this point, Catharinus, like Capreolus, appeals to Aquinas's spiritual womb metaphor.[128]

Cardinal Juan de Torquemada

The *Syllabus* also includes an excerpt from the Spanish Dominican theologian Cardinal Juan de Torquemada's (c. 1388–1468) commentary on Gratian's *Decretum*.[129] Torquemada was the dominant papal apologist of the fifteenth century. He served Pope Eugenius IV, working against conciliarism, and was a pro-papal theorist arguing for the pope's sovereignty. The *Syllabus* has an excerpt from his commentary on Distinction 45, entitled "Chapter on the Jews."

He considers four questions: 1) whether Jews are to be compelled to the faith; 2) whether, if they are baptized while unwilling or forced, they receive the sacrament; 3) whether the little ones of the Jews are to be baptized with the parents unwilling; 4) whether their little ones, baptized with parents unwilling, receive the baptismal character.[130]

On the first question, Torquemada lists three arguments made by contemporaries for why Jews should be forcibly converted.[131] He then presents his respondeo or answer by appealing to Aquinas's teaching in ST II.II 10.8: Jews and gentiles who have never received the faith are in no way to be compelled to the faith.

Torquemada also cites Paludanus's Augustinian argument against forced conversion based on "the divine prohibition" on forced conversions in Psalm 59:12. "We have it handed down from the saints, at least, that it is not the will

---

128 "For the son is naturally something of the father. And at first he is not distinguished from the parents according to the body as long as he is contained in the mother's womb. But afterwards, after he is come out of the womb, before he should have the use of free will, he is contained under the care of the parents as if in a kind of spiritual womb." Catharinus no. 2 in *SA*, 345.

129 *Commentarium super toto Decreto* I (Venice, 1578). The Spanish version of the name is Torquemada. The *Syllabus* refers to him as Giovanni di Turre Cremata. He is also known by the Latin name Johannes de Turrecremata. His main works were *Summa de ecclesia* (c.1440–50). See Joseph Canning, "Torquemada, Juan de," in *The Oxford Dictionary of the Middle Ages*, ed. Robert E. Bork (New York: Oxford University Press, 2010), and T. M. Izbicki, *Protector of the Faith: Cardinal Johannes Turrecremata and the Defense of the Institutional Church* (Washington, DC: The Catholic University of America Press, 1981). See also F. Courtney, "Juan de Torquemada," in *NCE*, 2nd ed., 14:112–13.

130 Torquemada no. 1. *SA*, 367.

131 Torquemada no. 2–4 in *SA*, 367. The arguments are, first, that Jews are to be compelled to the faith since Luke 14 says, "Go out into the roads ... and make them enter"; second, that Paul was forced and converted to the faith in Christ through a punishment of his body, and, therefore, the lost should also be forced to the faith; and third, an argument based in a writing of Pope Gregory to Bishop Maximus.

of God that Jews be killed.... Do not kill them, lest my people should be forgotten." Like Paludanus and Capreolus, Torquemada argues that the Jews will be converted by the preaching of Enoch and Elijah at the Second Coming. If their children were to be baptized, then at no time would the prophecy come true.[132] "Thus, God wills their toleration." Torquemada responds to each of the arguments as well.[133]

Torquemada then addresses the second question, whether Jewish adults receive the sacrament if they are forcibly baptized. As with the first question, he lists the opinions, or arguments, why they would receive the sacrament if forcibly baptized.[134]

Some of the opinions on this question concerning adults are not in other writers in the *Syllabus*. For example, the argument that original sin is contracted with no existing assent of the will, and that therefore it seems that baptism similarly could be conferred on someone apart from any consent of the will of the receiver. In his response, Torquemada appeals to "the master," the Franciscan friar and theologian Alexander of Hales (c. 1185–1245), to argue that even though one could present the unbelieving adult with the benefit of baptism, the person does not receive the sacrament if he opposes baptism.[135] "Entrance into the Church by baptism does not exist in an adult except in one who is in some way affirming it." Baptism is not like original sin since baptism "does not look to nature, but rather to the will of the person ... of those who are offering them."[136]

On the third question, whether children of the Jews should be baptized with the parents unwilling, Torquemada lists the arguments from ST II.II 10.12, including A2, that children should be baptized *invitis parentibus* in order to save them from spiritual death.[137] He also lists A1 (unbelief in parents is grounds for severing parental rights) but develops it by adding biblical support to the argument from St. Paul's first letter to the Corinthians. Torquemada also lists A4: since all persons belong more to God than to their natural fathers, it is not unjust if Jewish children are baptized against their parents' will.

---

132 Torquemada no. 6 in *SA*, 369.

133 Torquemada no. 6 in *SA*, 369.

134 Torquemada no. 11 in *SA*, 373.

135 On Alexander of Hales's defense of the traditional view that Judaism must be tolerated in Christian society, see Robert Chazan, *Church, State, and the Jew in the Middle Ages* (New York: Behrman House, 1980), 43–51.

136 Torquemada no. 11 in *SA*, 373.

137 Torquemada no. 12 in *SA*, 373. For the other arguments see also ST II.II 10.12.

In the respondeo Torquemada says that it would not be licit to baptize them if the parents are unwilling, based on Aquinas's teaching, which is "supported and corroborated with multiple reasons." He then lists the arguments of Aquinas in ST II.II 10.12, such as those from the custom of the Church, and the multiple arguments from the natural law (R1–R5). Like the other authors in the Syllabus, Torquemada argues that before children have the use of reason they are in the care of parents, which is "a kind of spiritual womb."[138] He then responds to each of the arguments he listed above (A1, A2, and A3).[139]

Torquemada then takes up the fourth main question, whether their little ones, baptized with parents unwilling, receive the baptismal character.[140] He lists two possible responses. The first affirms that children of unbelievers, if baptized *invitis parentibus*, receive the character of the sacrament. The second response denies this.

According to the first position, it is said that the unbeliever has no more right over his son than the faithful Christian who offers him. If the son of a Christian parent is baptized with the parent unwilling, then the son of the Christian receives true baptism. Similarly, if the son of the unbeliever receives baptism, then he also receives the true sacrament. Secondly, the faith of those who offer the children of unbelievers to baptism suffices for the intention without concern for the faith of the child's parents. Third, for the reception of baptism it suffices that there be no contrary will, which is plain in the children of the Christians who, before baptism, are "equal to the little ones of the Jews." In the children of Jews there is no barrier of contrary will. Therefore, they receive the true sacrament.[141]

The second position denies that the children of unbelievers receive the character of the sacrament. The arguments in response, according to Torquemada, are as follows. His answers and replies to arguments are extensive and so will be incorporated here together.

First, for baptism it is not sufficient that there is simply "no barrier of contrary will in the receiver." Rather, for the sacrament to be valid for such children there must be a direct or representative will in the recipient. Like the other Dominicans, Torquemada offers the analogy of the sleeping adult baptism.[142] He concludes that "if a little one is baptized with the parents

---

[138] Torquemada no. 13 in *SA*, 375.
[139] Torquemada no. 13 in *SA*, 375.
[140] Torquemada no. 15 in *SA*, 377.
[141] Torquemada no. 15 in *SA*, 377.
[142] Torquemada no. 16 in *SA*, 379.

unwilling... nothing happens, since the will, whether direct or representative, is lacking."[143]

Second, the child is a possession of the father according to human law, as a sheep or a lamb is. But those who violently snatch away a child do not for this reason acquire rights and dominion over the child. Those who offer children for baptism must have some right over the children.[144]

In the third reason, Torquemada makes the same distinction as we have seen above in Paludanus, Capreolus, and Catharinus: Jews are not subject to the Church. In the one receiving baptism there is necessarily required the faith of the Church, his own in the case of an adult, or another's in the case of a child. However, in the case of children of unbelievers, "in no way do they have to do with the Church." For the children of unbelievers to receive baptism, the faith of the parents is necessary.[145] "Others get nothing at all over them."

He reiterates the point by comparing the case of the children of Jews with the case of the children of Christians.

> The Church is the representative will of the parent, indeed to speak more truly, the will of the Church is more the representative will of the little one than the will of the carnal parent, because of the fact that legally the will of the carnal parent who is a faithful Christian is subject to the will of the Church, but it is not so regarding the little ones of unbelievers, because before baptism they are not subject to the Church, neither in the reason which is the son's nor in the reason of the parents.[146]

Torquemada concludes that "from all this it is gathered that just as parents are not able to be forced to things pertaining to divine law, and if forced and consenting they receive baptism, nothing is done, so children in things that are of divine law require true or representative will of parents. And it ought not to be done, nor, if it is done, is it valid." Torquemada also says Peter Paludanus follows this opinion and "declares it more."[147]

For Torquemada, the root of this argument for respect of the parental rights over their children is the natural law argument (R3) that "children

---

[143] Torquemada no. 16 in *SA*, 379.
[144] Torquemada no. 16 in *SA*, 379.
[145] Torquemada no. 16 in *SA*, 379.
[146] Torquemada no. 18 in *SA*, 381.
[147] Torquemada no. 17 in *SA*, 381.

before they have the use of reason are ordered to God through the reason of the parents whose care they naturally lie subject."[148]

Sylvester Mazzolini di Prierio

The last Dominican of the *Syllabus* is Italian theologian Sylvester Mazzolini di Prierio (c. 1460–1523). Prierio entered the order in 1475 and "manifested a brilliant grasp of the disciplines in his course of studies."[149] He taught theology at Bologna and was called by Pope Julius II to Rome. On Cardinal Cajetan's advice, Pope Leo X named him master of the sacred palace in 1515. He wrote against Luther's doctrines. Prierio's writings include treatises on numerous subjects, including the works of Aquinas, and he published a 1497 compendium of Capreolus's Thomist theology, which he strove to implement. He also published a handbook on Capreolus in 1521–22.

The excerpt from Prierio is from his *Summa Sylvestrina* (1519), in which he treats the question of baptism, and whether children of Jews can be baptized with the parents unwilling.[150] Prierio first considers a version of the argument from the power of kings and princes (A3). He responds by rejecting the argument and saying that a prince has not more but less power over the children of Jews than over a Jewish father and nevertheless he is not able to force the father to receive baptism (he adds, "Although Scotus hardly concedes this"). Next, he cites Aquinas: "St. Thomas has said that it is illicit in the *Secunda Secundae* Question 10, Article 12, and his foundation is twofold natural equality, because this is repugnant to natural justice."[151]

Echoing Aquinas's teaching, Prierio then explains that "before the use of free will, the children of the Jews are contained under the care of their parents as under a kind of 'spiritual womb'" (R4). He also argues that baptism invitis parentibus is against the custom of the Church (R1). Prierio then explains what Aquinas means in ST III 68.10 when he says that the children of the Jews are "saved in the faith of their parents" (R6): "Whence it is said of

---

[148] Torquemada no. 17 in *SA*, 381. At the end of the excerpt from Torquemada's commentary on Gratian's *Decretum*, Distinction 45, he argues that God's grace is not a necessity of nature. God acts voluntarily through order in the law of his wisdom. The cause of the taking away of grace is not merely he who puts the obstacle in the way of grace, but also God who in his judgment does not impose grace. Torquemada no. 21 in *SA*, 383.

[149] F. C. Lehner, "Mazzolini, Sylvester," *NCE*, 2nd ed., 9:389–90. See also Michael Tavuzzi's *Prierias: The Life and Works of Silvestro Mazzolini Da Prierio, 1456–1527* (Durham, NC: Duke University Press, 1997). He is also referred to as Mazolinus. See Cessario, *Short History*, 68.

[150] Silvestro Mazzolini di Prierio, *Summa Summarum, quæ Sylvestrina dicitur*, vol. 1–2 (Lugdunum, 1519).

[151] Prierio no. 1 in *SA*, 385.

the children of the ancients that they are saved in the faith of their parents, through which fact it is given to be understood that we look to them to provide their salvation."[152]

As was the case of Catharinus, some of the authorities cited in the *Syllabus* are concerned to address what they understand as misinterpretations of Aquinas's teaching to support baptism invitis parentibus. Prierio adjudicates a difficulty in the interpretation of Aquinas's teaching in ST III 68.9, which discusses whether infants should be baptized.

On the question of whether infants should be baptized, it seems that Aquinas's answer indicates that the children of unbelievers, if baptized invitis parentibus, receive the sacrament.[153] Prierio explains that, however, some think the will of another's parents suffices and then the children must be forced to keep the faith, and that Aquinas teaches this in ST III 68.9 (on the question of whether infants should be baptized). "But I do not remember having read that in St. Thomas myself."[154]

This text in Aquinas is mentioned in the Vatican counsel's reply, which will be discussed in the next chapter. It serves as the basis of the argument that the children of non-Christian parents can be "offered" for baptism. As we shall discuss at length in chapter 5, this article in the *Summa theologiae* is *not* on whether to baptize infants against the will of their non-Catholic parents but whether to baptize infants at all. And so, as Prierio observes, the context of Aquinas's teaching must be carefully considered, with attention to an important question: whether the parents are Christian or if they are not Christian, and whether they desire for their children to be baptized for some reason. Prierio says an example is "if [the children] are possessed or tormented by the devil."[155] If they are not Christian, Prierio explains, they would receive the sacrament "only . . . when the unbelieving parents themselves consent that the children be faithful Christians."[156] In other words, for

---

152 Prierio no. 1 in *SA*, 385.

153 It seems Prierio mistakenly interprets one of Paludanus's objections (arguments against his position) as his respondeo.

154 Prierio no. 3 in *SA*, 387.

155 Prierio in *SA*, 389. It will be discussed at length in chapter 5.

156 Prierio no. 3 in *SA*, 387. Another theologian and prelate included in the *Syllabus*, Cardinal Antonio Sangiorgio (1439/1442–1509), also insists that baptism requires not just a lack of a contrary will but a true and representative will. See Sangiorgio no. 3 in *SA*, 363. Sangiorgio, like Paludanus, Capreolus, Catharinus, Torquemada, and Prierio, rejects the claim that a baptism is valid as long as there is no contrary will, which is, again, the position attributed to Cajetan. See Sangiorgio no. 4 in *SA*, 365. Sangiorgio was a professor of canon law and called the cardinal of Alessandria; he was created cardinal priest in 1493 and promoted to titular patriarch of Jerusalem in 1500. He wrote six volumes of commentaries on canon law. See Salvador Miranda,

Prierio, the context of ST III 68.9 is crucial—it seems there are cases where unbelievers might intend for their children to receive baptism.

CONCLUSION

The content of the *Syllabus* shows that theological questions on the validity of forced baptisms of Jewish children were debated by Thomists and others into the 1500s. This study demonstrates that Aquinas's teaching against baptism of Jewish children invitis parentibus was carried forward and developed by his Dominican followers from the late thirteenth century into the middle of the sixteenth century. This defense of Aquinas includes a diverse and, at times, discordant group of Dominicans. Nevertheless, the Dominicans' determinations on the question of whether Jewish children should be baptized invitis parentibus overlap considerably. Two of these Dominicans have become famous for their defense and consolidation of Aquinas's teachings: John Capreolus, "Prince of Thomists," is among this group, as is Sylvester Mazzolini di Prierio. Contemporary scholars are aware that Aquinas was opposed to forced baptism of Jewish children, but until this study the defense and development of his thought by his Dominican disciples was unknown.

The excerpts from the *Syllabus* demonstrate that the Dominican theologians not only defend but also develop Aquinas's position. They advance the various reasons of Aquinas's respondeo against their contemporaries who argue the opposite position. These are represented by Scotus and Cajetan. For the Dominican theologians, the human person is ordered to God because of reason, through which he is able to come to know God. Capreolus makes this argument: "Man is naturally ordered to God through reason, through which he is naturally able to come to know him." Baptism of a child invitis parentibus is invalid; since the implied will of a small child before the use of reason is the will of his parents, there must be intent on the part of the baptized, not simply the lack of an impediment, which would be the case in the baptism of an infant. If these children are baptized, they do not receive true baptism because the reception of baptism requires not simply that there be "no barrier of contrary will" but that there be a representative will. The Church's intention cannot replace the representative will of the Jewish parents. Even the circumstances of death do not negate the accepted custom of

---

"The Cardinals of the Holy Roman Church," a digital resource published by Florida International University Libraries (1998–2023). The resource contains the biographical entries of the cardinals from 492 to 2015, and of the events and documents concerning the origin of the Roman cardinalate and its historical evolution.

the Church that a child of unbelievers may not be baptized without permission of the parents.

The *Syllabus* functions to support the arguments of the Mortara family's *Pro-memoria* by grounding it in interpretations of Aquinas offered by the Dominican theologians. As explained above, the arguments of *Pro-memoria* can be summarized as follows: 1) Free will in things that are of God is a sacred principle established by God in the natural law. 2) According to Aquinas, it is not the custom of the Church to forcibly convert non-Christians or to forcibly baptize children of unbelievers invitis parentibus. 3) Since the Church has no spiritual jurisdiction over the children of unbelievers, the Church's intention cannot represent the intention of Jewish parents as it does for Christian parents. 4) If such forced baptisms of unbelievers' children invitis parentibus do occur, these baptisms are invalid, and the children must be returned to their parents. The *Pro-memoria* therefore reflects the theological positions of the *Syllabus*.

However, the next chapter demonstrates a difficulty with this interpretation of Aquinas. The difficulty that emerges in the 1858 dispute is that Aquinas is claimed by both sides. For example, does Aquinas teach that baptism of the children of unbelievers invitis parentibus is lawful in certain exceptions? Are there any texts in Aquinas that indicate that an unlawful baptism is nevertheless valid on his terms? Are there arguments in Aquinas that unbelievers lose their rights over their children if forced baptisms take place? These questions will be explored in detail in chapter 3.

3

AQUINAS IN THE PAPAL COUNSEL'S REPLY: *BREVI CENNI*

The papal counsel's reply to the Mortara family, entitled *Brevi cenni*, also appealed to Aquinas to defend Pope Pius IX's decision to remove Edgardo from his parents.[1] The aim of this chapter is to examine how the authors of the papal counsel's reply interpret Aquinas's teaching against forced baptism.

The same questions that guided our study of Aquinas's texts in the *Promemoria* and *Syllabus* will guide the analysis of *Brevi cenni* throughout this chapter. How do the authors of the *Brevi cenni* interpret Aquinas's teaching against forced baptism? What were the key questions on forced baptism as these related to Aquinas's teaching? How are Aquinas's texts understood to apply to the arguments *for* Pius IX's decision to remove the child from his parents? Our concern is to clarify the key questions on Aquinas's teaching in the 1858 debate. The identification of these questions is a necessary step in evaluating the significance of Aquinas's teaching for contemporary reflection on the case.

I show that three questions were at the heart of the dispute: whether Aquinas holds that forced baptism of Jewish children is lawful or licit; whether forced baptism of a child of unbelievers is nevertheless a valid baptism; and the question of whether Jewish parents lose their rights over their children if they are baptized. I also identify important sub-questions.

I proceed in two steps. In the first section, I analyze the papal counsel's reply, *Brevi cenni*, with attention to how the authors of the document interpret Aquinas's teaching and apply it to the arguments *for* Pius IX's decision

---

[1] *Brevi cenni* will be cited as *BC*, followed by the document page number, and then page number in Appendix C.

to remove the child from his parents. In the concluding section, I clarify the questions on Aquinas's teaching in the 1858 dispute and explain the aim of the next chapter, which provides an overview of papal teaching and canon law on the liceity of forced baptism and whether or not such baptisms were considered valid. The next chapter sets the stage for a study of Aquinas's thought in its thirteenth-century context.

AQUINAS IN THE PAPAL COUNSEL'S REPLY, *BREVI CENNI*

The papal counsel's refutation of the Mortara family's plea appealed to Aquinas's teaching to defend the decision to separate Edgardo from his parents. The Vatican's response to the plea consisted of a thirty-three-page document, *Brevi cenni*, that attempts to refute their argument. *Brevi cenni* was sent to bishops and nuncios throughout Europe who had requested the Vatican assist them in explaining Pius IX's actions.[2] The document mentions Aquinas twelve times.

The opening paragraphs read as follows:

> The Parents of a child for whom Divine Grace has provided in a unique way, by liberating him from blind Jewish obstinacy, has made him a fortunate son of the Church, have raised petitions and complaints up to the august papal throne in order to obtain the return of their son, who has already been placed in the bosom of the Church and liberated by the Blood of Jesus Christ. . . .
>
> Having brought the request to such a point, it is only right that the alleged authorities and arguments be examined, as set out in the Memorandum and in the Syllabus attached to the Supplication to the Holy Father.
>
> A venal mind and a hired hand have ransacked not a few eminent authors to collect texts and arguments in order to defend a cause which has already been decided by the same authors to whom reference is made, in the opposite direction to the one intended.[3]

Here, two themes immediately surface that will be reinforced throughout the reply. First, from the counsel's perspective, Edgardo's baptism was valid, and this is why he was understood to have *already* been "placed in the bosom of

---

2 At the time of the case, the Italian Jesuit theologian Luigi Taparelli d'Azeglio defended the position of Pope Pius IX in *Civiltà Cattolica*. He did not reference Aquinas's texts in his defense. Taparelli, Luigi d'Azeglio, SJ, "Il Piccolo Neofito Edgardo Mortara," *Civiltà Cattolica* 12 (1858): 385–416; and "Ciò Che Sa e Ciò Che Non Sa: La Revue Des Deux Mondes Intorno ad Edgardo Mortara," *Civiltà Cattolica* 12 (1858): 529–41.

3 *BC*, 2–3, 405–7.

the Church." Second, the theologians and canonists cited by the Mortaras prove the papal counsel's position.

The papal counsel then lists the Mortara's arguments.[4]

1. That the newborn children of the Jews cannot and must not be baptized against the will of their parents.
2. That if these children of an age before the use of reason were baptized in spite of the contrary will of their parents, such baptism would be completely invalid and of no effect.
3. That even supposing such a baptism to be valid, the child must by natural right be returned to the parental authority which claims him with every reason.
4. That in the present case, there is no proof of the baptism allegedly given by the nurse Morisi to the child Edgardo Mortara.
5. For the above reasons, the applicants therefore request the release and return of the son Edgardo to his parents.

The papal counsel then states that in response to the claims, their reply will show the following:

1. The truth of the main assumption has no effect whatsoever on the case of Edgardo Mortara.
2. That the second assertion is reckless, false, contrary to the judgments of all canonists and theologians, and contrary to the constant practice of the universal Church, and has already been condemned by the Holy See in many decisions.
3. That the right of the Church *acquired over* the baptized child is of a higher order and prevails over the paternal right; and that therefore the baptized child must not be returned, but rather kept in Religion.
4. That in Mortara's case there is full canonical proof of the conferring of baptism, so that there is no longer any reason or right to recall the child under parental authority.
5. That therefore the Church—Mother, Teacher, and Sovereign of mankind—does not infringe any right, nor bring any offence, but fulfils her divine mission by protecting her baptized children and removing them from the danger of apostasy.[5]

---

4 *BC*, 3, 405–7.
5 *BC*, 3–4, 405–7.

In the counsel's view, the main assertion of *Pro-memoria* is that in no way can baptism be conferred on Jewish children invitis parentibus. "It is for this reason that the best part of the authorities and texts quoted in the *Pro-memoria*, and also in the *Syllabus*, are directed by the Author to prove this assertion."[6]

The counsel agrees with part of the first point of *Pro-memoria* when it states that the church has always been against forced conversions. It cites Aquinas's teaching in ST II.II 10.12 co. for the first time.

> The solemn prohibition of baptizing the children of unbelievers against the will of their respective parents has always been the universal *maxim of* the Catholic Church. A *maxim* that dates back from St. Thomas as far as the apostolic age. A *maxim* proclaimed by the Holy Fathers. A *maxim* decreed by the General Councils. A *maxim* unanimously taught by all theologians and canonists. A *maxim* sanctioned by the bulls and decrees of many Supreme Pontiffs. A *maxim* eloquently defined by the Holy Doctor quoted above as "a universal custom, which carries with it an irrefutable authority."[7]

According to the papal counsel, however, the papal authorities cited in the Mortara document "are talking about ADULT Jews and unbelievers and not about children who are naturally incapable of violence and threats."[8]

Nevertheless, baptism, even if illicit (i.e., forced baptism), is still valid. Although the Church teaches against forced baptism, if one is baptized even under "terrors and violent chastisements," the character of the sacrament is still received.[9]

The papal counsel explains that even though baptism of Jews by violent means is reproved by Innocent III (r. 1198–1216), the pope also teaches that if a Jew accepts such baptism in order to escape such threats, the baptism is valid. In a footnote to this point, the counsel cites Aquinas's article on the question "Does fear cause involuntariness" in ST I.II 6.6, and asserts that Aquinas teaches that a baptism received under threat is nonetheless valid: "Whoever wishes to know the reason for which such baptism is declared valid, should recall the sublime doctrine of the Prince of Philosophers, St.

---

6 *BC*, 4, 407.
7 *BC*, 5, 407.
8 *BC*, 6, 409.
9 *BC*, 6, 409.

Thomas, on human acts, when he teaches 'what is done out of fear is essentially voluntary.'"[10]

The counsel then states what it understands as a more important point: there are some exceptional cases contemplated by all theologians and canonists in which the Church allows the children of unbelievers to be baptized:

> Moreover, if the Holy Church has always and constantly forbidden to baptize the children of unbelievers invitis parentibus, there are, however, some cases, contemplated by all theologians and canonists, in which it allows these children to be baptized. And as far as the present case is concerned, *it is permitted* to confer baptism on those children, who are near to death, or who morally have no hope of life. The reason for this indulgence is most serious, and it is all due to a tender mother, which is the Church, since, "in such a case *morally speaking*, neither the child is exposed to the danger of apostasy, nor is the minister, but death itself separates him from his parents. . . ." This would be the case of the child Edgardo, who was baptized in clear danger of death, as will be shown below.[11]

For our purposes, it is important to note the papal counsel claims that all theologians and canonists have contemplated the danger-of-death exception. The counsel does not claim that all theologians, including Aquinas, have taught this.[12] As we shall see in the next chapter, lawful baptism of a Jewish child in danger of death invitis parentibus was codified in 1747.

Nevertheless, according to the papal counsel, failing to distinguish between the validity of the baptism and the issue of liceity is the weakness in the position of the *Pro-memoria*. The fact that the Church teaches against forcibly baptizing a child of unbelievers does not change the fact that the baptism had already happened:

> But it does not in any way concern the ALREADY CONSUMMATED FACT. Therefore, if, even in spite of this law, a child of unbeliever parents were to receive baptism, the Church would recognize it as valid, take power over its new child, and use every means, every solicitude, to separate it from the unfaithfulness of his parents, and to nourish it and educate it in the grace of Jesus Christ.[13]

---

10 *BC*, 6, 409.
11 *BC*, 7, 409–11.
12 We will return to this point in chapter 5.
13 *BC*, 8, 411.

The papal counsel then articulates their conclusion on the first point: "It must therefore be concluded that the truth of the [*Pro-memoria*] . . . thesis, based on the law and the custom of the Church, according to which it is forbidden to baptize the children of unbelievers invitis parentibus, has no influence on an *act already consummated*, which is precisely the baptism given to the child Edgardo, son of Salomone Mortara."[14]

The counsel then turns to the second point of *Pro-memoria*, which argues that if a child (prior to the use of reason) was baptized in spite of the contrary will of their parents, such baptism would be completely invalid and of no effect. The argument is that for a baptism to be valid, the representative will of the unbelieving parents is required. This thesis, argues the counsel, is reckless and false.[15]

The counsel recognizes that Aquinas and Duns Scotus held differing options on this question: "St. Thomas . . . prohibits the baptism of the children of unbelievers invitis parentibus, against the opinion of Scotus and some very few of his followers, who maintain instead that the children of unbelievers can be baptized even against the will of their parents."[16]

However, even a baptism of a Jewish child administered against the will of the parents (illicitly, i.e., administered outside of the danger-of-death situation) is nevertheless a valid baptism: "In fact all the theologians and canonists demonstrate the validity of such Baptism without the consent of the representative will of the relatives; and they agree in asserting baptism thus conferred is valid, because it has all the conditions of the true sacrament, namely matter, form, intention, and finally suitable subject."[17]

The counsel then appeals to the teaching of Cardinal Cajetan to make the argument that Aquinas thought a forced baptism of a child would nevertheless be valid: "The Holy Doctor assumes it wherever he speaks of baptism given to the children of unbelievers." The counsel cites Cajetan's conclusion about Aquinas on this question: "[Aquinas] thinks and finally assumes that the children of unbelievers would really be baptized if they were baptized against the will of their parents. It's because he assumes this that he says it's dangerous to baptize the children of unbelievers in this way: because they would easily return to unbelief because of their natural affection for their parents."[18]

---

14 *BC*, 10, 413.

15 *BC*, 10, 413.

16 *BC*, 10, 413.

17 *BC*, 11, 415.

18 *BC*, 11. Again, Cajetan was a Dominican cardinal, born February 20, 1469, in Gaeta, Italy; he died in 1534 in Rome. The counsel cites to his commentary on ST III 68.10 of Aquinas's *Summa theologiae*, 415.

In addition to Cajetan, the counsel cites the 1747 teaching of Pope Benedict XIV (r. 1740–58), and his interpretation of Aquinas on this question. Benedict XIV claimed that on this point there is no disagreement between Duns Scotus and Aquinas: "There is no disagreement on this subject between St. Thomas (and his disciples) and Scotus, since they do not question that baptism can be validly conferred on Hebrew children without the consent of their parents."[19] The Catholic Church, explains the counsel, has never required the will of the parents for baptism to be valid for children who have not yet reached the use of reason.[20] According to the counsel, that a forced baptism of a child is nonetheless valid is the "constant custom of the Church."[21] To claim that the will of the parents is necessary for baptism or "the representative will" would make the sacrament dependent upon a merely extrinsic condition.[22]

> In truth, the sacrament is always valid when the essential conditions and extremes established by the Divine Author are fulfilled. As far as baptism is concerned, nothing more is required for its validity than that the matter be applied with the appropriate form to a suitable subject, which can be even a newborn child, and the minister can be any man, as long as he intends to do *quod facit Ecclesia* [what the Church does].[23]

Moreover, the representative will must be expressed not by the unbeliever parents "but by the Church, Mother and Sovereign of all men, 'because children are not baptized in the faith of their parents but in the faith of the whole Church.'"[24]

The counsel then cites Aquinas's teaching in ST III 68.9 ad. 2 (whether children should be baptized) to argue that in baptism, the will of the child of unbelievers is not represented by its parents but by the Church.[25] In this

---

[19] The counsel cites Benedict XIV's letter to the Viceregent of Rome, no. 26. *BC*, 13, 417. See *DS*, 2552–62; Kenneth Stow, *Anna and Tranquillo: Catholic Anxiety and Jewish Protest in the Age of Revolutions* (New Haven, CT: Yale University Press, 2016), 76; Marina Caffiero, *Forced Baptisms: Histories of Jews, Christians, and Converts in Papal Rome*, trans. Lydia G. Cochrane (Berkeley: University of California Press, 2012), 44–65. Our study of Aquinas's followers in the previous chapter indicates they do in fact disagree with Scotus on this point.

[20] *BC*, 11, 415.

[21] *BC*, 14, 419.

[22] *BC*, 12, 417.

[23] *BC*, 11, 415.

[24] *BC*, 14, 419.

[25] *BC*, 15, 419. Aquinas argues in ST III 68.9 that it is not a hindrance to a child's salvation if their parents are unbelievers and have no faith but still offer them in baptism. Citing Augustine's *Letter 98* to Boniface, he says that this is because the entire community of saints and faithful present

article, Aquinas cites Augustine's teaching on infant baptism: "Children are offered to receive spiritual grace, not so much by those who carry them in their hands, but by the entire community of saints and faithful; in fact, they are to be offered *by all* whom it pleases to offer them, and by whose charity they are joined to the communion of the Holy Spirit."[26] The Angelic doctor, argues the counsel, reflects the doctrine of Augustine. The counsel writes: "Furthermore, Saint Thomas adds, in the same sense as St. Augustine, that in these cases the will of the Church is expressed and applied to the unbeliever child who is baptized by the one person who administers the sacrament."[27] The counsel concludes that therefore "there is a constant and practical tradition of the validity of baptism given to Jewish children without the knowledge or the consent of parents."[28]

To bolster the argument that the baptism of a Jewish child invitis parentibus is nonetheless a valid baptism, the counsel cites the teaching of Benedict XIV once more. A full proof of the argument may be found in his teaching that is "well known to all!"[29] Thus, "the Jewish children who are baptized even without the consent of their parents, receive the sacrament itself and the substance of the Sacrament."[30]

The counsel then addresses the third claim of *Pro-memoria*: that, supposing this baptism to be valid, the child must in any case be returned by right of nature to the parental authority, which claims it with every reason.[31]

In reply to this argument, the counsel answers that the "Church's *acquired* right over the baptized child prevails over the paternal right of the unbelievers."[32] The counsel states that for canonists and theologians "*God alone* must be regarded as the author of the natural right in the unbeliever parents and the author of the divine right." God is the source of all rights

---

children for baptism. However, as I argue in chapter five, the context of Augustine's letter is crucial: the pagan parents discussed in Augustine's letter to Boniface voluntarily brought their children to the Church to be baptized in order to heal them from illness. Aquinas's teaching in the next article, 68.10, insists only unbelieving parents can decide whether to baptize their children. Augustine's letter can be found in St. Augustine, *The Works of St. Augustine Part II, Letters Vol 1: 1–99*, trans. Roland Teske, SJ (Hyde Park, NY: New City Press, 2001), 426–32.

26 *BC*, 14, 419.

27 *BC*, 15, 419.

28 *BC*, 15, 419.

29 *BC*, 15–16, 419–21. The counsel also references five cases and determinations by the Holy Office on baptisms administered to Jewish children by servants and women that were determined valid.

30 *BC*, 16, 421.

31 *BC*, 16, 421.

32 *BC*, 17, 422.

concerning parents and the Church. "God and the unbeliever parents of the baptized child must not be placed before each other as if they were two authorities with jurisdiction over the natural or divine right to possess the child; but God *alone* must be regarded as the author of the natural right in the unbeliever parents and the author of the divine right."[33] The Church's right is, according to the counsel, a "second right," which the Church enjoys over a baptized child: "This second right, which the Church acquires over the baptized *child*, is of a higher and nobler order than the first: *and therefore the right that the Church has acquired by baptism, prevails over the right of the father, which is relinquished for the benefit of the son, to the honor of God, religion and the sacrament, which would suffer grave outrage from the morally certain future apostasy.*"[34] This higher and nobler divine right is, in the counsel's view, generated by the Fourth Council of Toledo, canon 58: "This was very clearly demanded by the Fourth Council of Toledo, canon 58, in the following words: 'We decree that the baptized sons or daughters of the Jews should be separated from their parents, so that they may not be involved in their errors: instead, they should be entrusted to monasteries or to Christian men and women who fear God, so that they may grow in morals and faith.'"[35] Therefore, the Church acquires divine right over the baptized.[36] For this reason, the baptized child "must not be returned."[37]

The counsel then cites Aquinas to try and make two points. First, if a child is baptized and then returned to his Jewish parents, he or she would apostatize. The counsel cites one of Aquinas's arguments (R2) against the practice of baptizing Jewish children against the will of their parents in ST II.II 10.12: "Having reached maturity, they could easily be induced by their parents to leave what they had unconsciously received.... They would easily return to unbelief because of their natural affection for their parents."[38]

Second, if a child were baptized against the will of their parents, the parents would lose their rights over the child. "St. Thomas himself, in asserting that the Church has never been accustomed to baptize the sons of the unbelievers against their will, says, among other reasons, that in such a case the parents would lose all rights over their children, who have passed into the power of the Church by virtue of Baptism.[39] The counsel cites a text

---

33 *BC*, 17, 422.

34 *BC*, 17, 422.

35 *BC*, 17–18, 422. The authors incorrectly reference canon 58 but the text is from canon 60.

36 *BC*, 19, 425.

37 *BC*, 17, 423.

38 ST II.II 10.12 co. in *BC*, 18, 425.

39 *BC*, 18, 425.

from Aquinas's article in ST II.II 10.12: "It would be an injustice to Jews if their children were to be baptized against their will; since they would lose all rights over their children ALREADY FAITHFUL."[40] The counsel interprets this text as confirming their argument that the baptism was valid, against *Pro-memoria*'s argument to the contrary. In the view of the counsel, the text also confirms the non-return of the child argument against *Pro-memoria*'s third point (that the child must be returned). Here, Aquinas is understood to therefore ground the argument that the forced baptism of a Jewish child is nonetheless valid, and that the child should not be returned. The counsel concludes by saying that this text of Aquinas is "a splendid sentence which decides the validity of baptism and the full right of the Church to take possession of these new children of the grace of Jesus Christ."[41]

The counsel then replies to *Pro-memoria*'s fourth point, that there is no proof of baptism of Edgardo Mortara. The counsel argues that in Mortara's case there is "full canonical proof of the conferring of baptism, so that there is no longer any reason or right to recall the child under parental authority."[42] While under oath, the Christian maidservant, Anna Morisi, testified to the Inquisitor of Bologna that she baptized the child when he was about two years old and had a fever.[43] According to the teaching of Benedict XIV, "a single witness, even a woman, is sufficient to testify to the baptism of the children of the Jews, especially in the case of probable death."[44]

The fifth point of the counsel is their conclusion: "That therefore the Church, Mother, Teacher, and Sovereign of mankind, does not infringe any right, nor bring any offence, but fulfils her divine mission by protecting her baptized children and removing them from the danger of apostasy."[45] In the counsel's view, the Holy See has not "minimally violated the paternal rights of his Jewish parents, but, on the contrary, has acted in this delicate matter in a

---

40 ST II.II 10.12 s.c. in *BC*, 19, 425.

41 *BC*, 19, 425.

42 *BC*, 4, 407.

43 *BC*, 27, 435.

44 *BC*, 26, 435.
   In each and every one of the reported Decisions and Decrees of the Holy See in favour of the validity of Baptism conferred on Jewish children invitis parentibus and in which the perpetual separation from the parents is decreed, there is always only one witness, and mostly a woman, who attests to the conferred baptism, and nevertheless there has never been any doubt about the reality of the facts, as can be seen in the cited positions and in many others preserved in the archives of the Supreme Inquisition.
The counsel also states that the danger of death exception had precedent in a 1678 decision of the Holy Office. See *BC*, 28, 438.

45 *BC*, 30, 439.

civil, persuasive and charitable manner."[46] Moreover, the counsel states that the Church has acted on its Divine mission and supreme authority received from God.[47]

The counsel then summarizes the four main points: 1) The Church has always forbidden the baptism of Jewish children invitis parentibus. 2) But if it happens that a Jewish child is baptized, even against the will of his or her parents, the baptism is valid, and in danger of death, even licit; for Aquinas, the intention of the Church is sufficient for the baptism of a child of unbelievers to be valid. In children who are baptized, no intention is necessary, but the Church makes up for it in the person of the one who confers the Sacrament. "Children who do not yet have the use of reason receive salvation not for themselves, but by the act of the church." "This is stated by St Thomas."[48] 3) That the Church has from God the power and the right to take possession of the baptized children of the unbelievers in order to preserve in them the holiness of their received character and to nourish them to eternal life. Finally, in the case of the baptism of Edgardo Mortara, the Holy See exercised its "full and peaceful right to take possession of the child in an entirely civil and charitable manner, and therefore without violating the paternal right, which must yield and be subordinated to that of the Church."[49]

CONCLUSION

This study of the 1858 Vatican reply indicates that the question of Aquinas's teaching as it relates to the Mortara case is more complex than perhaps has been realized. Without the archival documents, contemporary defenders and critics of Pius IX have not been able to set the case in its historical context, obscuring texts in Aquinas that seem to lend support to Pius IX's decision to remove Edgardo from his parents.

For example, the contemporary theological debate about the case has not addressed the text from ST II.II 10.12, cited by the papal counsel, that seems to indicate Aquinas thinks Jewish children should be removed from their parents if they have been baptized: "Now it would be an injustice to Jews if their children were to be baptized against their will, since they would lose the rights of parental authority over their children as soon as these

---

[46] *BC*, 29, 439.
[47] *BC*, 29, 439.
[48] This language is likely from ST III 68.9 ad. 1. *BC*, 30, 439.
[49] *BC*, 30–31, 439.

were Christians."⁵⁰ The difficulty is summarized in this text from the papal counsel:

> The *Doctor Angelicus*, while demonstrating with reason and authority, that the children of the Jews should not be baptized invitis parentibus, also demonstrates in the places cited by the Memorandum and the Syllabus that if baptism is given to such children, it is confirmed and valid, and therefore these children should not be left in the power of parents who would *certainly*, to the detriment of religion and their eternal health, cause them to apostatize from the faith received in infancy.
>
> St. Thomas himself, in asserting that the Church has never been accustomed to baptize the sons of the unbelievers against their will, says, among other reasons, that in such a case the parents would lose all rights over their children, who have passed into the power of the Church by virtue of Baptism. "It would be an injustice to Jews if their children were baptized against their will; since they would lose the rights of paternal authority over their children AS SOON AS THESE WERE CHRISTIANS."⁵¹

The interpretation of Aquinas in the exchange between the Mortara family and the Vatican concerned three questions. The first question is whether Aquinas holds that forced baptism of Jewish children is lawful or licit. The *Pro-memoria* argued that Aquinas was against baptizing children of unbelievers invitis parentibus. The papal counsel agreed but claimed this point is irrelevant to the case because Edgardo had already received a valid baptism. A related question is whether Aquinas teaches that forced baptism of Jewish children invitis parentibus is lawful in certain exceptions, such as the case of an infant in danger of death. The papal counsel claims that all theologians and canonists have contemplated the danger-of-death exception. Is it the case that that the Church has always allowed the children of unbelievers to be baptized who are close to death?⁵²

The second question is whether forced baptism of a child of unbelievers is nevertheless a valid baptism. "Saint Thomas adds that in these cases the intention of the Church is represented and applied to the child of unbelievers, who is baptized by the one person who confers the sacrament."⁵³ According to the papal counsel, Aquinas thinks such a baptism is valid. Does Aquinas teach in ST III 68.9 ad. 2 that the representative will of the child

---

50 ST II.II 10.12.
51 *BC*, 18–19, 425.
52 *BC*, 7, 409.
53 *BC*, 15, 419.

baptized invitis parentibus must be expressed by the Church and not by unbelieving parents? A related question concerns whether Aquinas thinks a coerced baptism of an adult is nonetheless valid. The papal counsel claims that in ST I.II 6.6 Aquinas teaches that a forced baptism is nonetheless valid because even an act motivated by fear remains a voluntary act.

Finally, a third question emerges concerning the consequences of forced but valid baptisms: whether Aquinas teaches that Jewish parents lose their rights over their children if they are baptized. In other words, does Aquinas think that the Church possesses a divine right over baptized children that outweighs the rights of Jewish parents?

The question of Aquinas's teaching in the contemporary theological debate on the Mortara case can be clarified through an analysis of the concerns in the 1858 dispute. The difficulty that emerges is that Aquinas is claimed by both sides. Adjudicating this difficulty requires answering the above questions through a study of Aquinas's teaching.

However, to adequately treat Aquinas's thought requires not only setting his teachings in the context of thirteenth-century debates on baptism invitis parentibus but in the broader context of papal teaching and canon law on forced baptism of Jews and their children, as well as the developments in canonists and theologians on whether such baptisms were lawful and valid.

Therefore, before turning to the texts in Aquinas to answer the above questions, the next chapter provides an overview of papal teaching and canon law on forced baptism of Jews from antiquity to the nineteenth century. This historical context is necessary for understanding Aquinas's teaching as it relates to the Mortara case. The context will also aid our analysis of contemporary teaching on baptism invitis parentibus in emergency situations. In other words, the historical context outlined in the next chapter sets the stage for our inquiry in chapters 5 and 6.

4

PAPAL TEACHING AND CANON LAW ON FORCED BAPTISM OF JEWS

It is impossible to understand Aquinas's teaching against the baptism of Jewish children invitis parentibus without a consideration of the historical conditions under which he worked. The context of his teaching was the problem of forced baptism of Jews in Christian society, and debates among canonists and theologians about whether such baptisms were lawful or valid. The aim of this chapter is to therefore provide an overview of the difficult topic of papal teaching and canon law on forced baptism of Jews from late antiquity to the eighteenth century, with attention to the issues identified in the previous chapter: whether forced baptisms were considered lawful; whether such baptisms were considered valid; and whether Jewish parents lose their rights over their children if they are baptized.[1]

I proceed in four steps. In the first section, I argue that papal policy in late antiquity and the Middle Ages explicitly and repeatedly condemned forced baptism of Jews. In the second section, I show that the condemnation of forced conversions of Jews at the Fourth Council of Toledo (633) also established the precedent of requiring forcibly converted Jews to remain Christian. This precedent raised legal questions among canonists and theologians about what constituted a forced baptism, and whether forced baptisms were valid. In the third section, I show that by the thirteenth century,

---

1 As Benjamin Ravid points out, there is no comprehensive study of the problem of forced baptism in pre-emancipation Europe. Benjamin Ravid, "The Forced Baptism of Jews in Christian Europe: An Introductory Overview," in *Christianizing Peoples and Converting Individuals*, ed. Guyda Armstrong and Ian N. Wood (Turnhout: Brepols, 2001), 157. For this reason, Ravid's overview is a helpful starting point although the important theological debates about forced baptism are not discussed. It should be consulted along with Marcia L. Colish, *Faith, Fiction and Force in Medieval Baptismal Debates* (Washington, DC: The Catholic University of America Press, 2014).

most canonists were no longer focused on the question of whether forced baptism was valid. After the Christian discovery of the Talmud, the debate shifted to whether Jewish children could lawfully be baptized against the will of their parents. Aquinas engaged in this debate three different times in his work. In the fourth section, I show that this debate would be settled by eighteenth-century papal bulls that legalized forced conversion of Jewish children and adults under certain conditions in the Roman ghetto in 1747. These bulls codified baptism of Jewish children "close to death" as meritorious and set the stage for the Mortara case.

PAPAL TEACHING AGAINST FORCED BAPTISM

The earliest Christian arguments against religious coercion are in defense of Christianity: Tertullian (155 or 160–260) and Lactantius (250–325) argued that Christians should be afforded religious liberty by the Roman Empire because enforcing religious practices on unbelievers invites "fakery and fraud."[2] Tertullian, the first thinker in the West to use the phrase "religious freedom," stated that "it is not part of religion to coerce religious practice, for it is by choice not coercion that we should be led to religion."[3] Lactantius argued that the human will can be moved to act "only by words, not by blows."[4]

After Christianity was declared the official religion of the Roman Empire, its popes and princes did not advocate for forced baptism of Jewish communities. Constantine (r. 306–37) upheld the Roman legal policy of Judaism as a *religio licita*. He urged Roman citizens to acknowledge the one supreme God and confess Christ as Savior. But he also said that those who "delight in error" were free to follow their own religion since they deserve "the same degree of peace and tranquility which they have who do believe."[5]

---

[2] Colish, *Faith, Fiction*, 229. According to David Berger, Tertullian and others wrote *Adversus Iudaeos* literature, which contained harsh anti-Jewish language, but this reflected intra-Christian polemics and not an effort to convert Jews. See David Berger, "Mission to the Jews and Jewish-Christian Contacts in the Polemical Literature of the High Middle Ages," *American Historical Review* 91, no. 3 (1986): 575–91. On Tertullian's *Adversus Iudaeos*, see Geoffrey D. Dunn, *Tertullian's Adversus Judaeos: A Rhetorical Analysis* (Washington, DC: The Catholic University of America Press, 2008).

[3] Tertullian, cited in Robert Wilken, *Liberty in the Things of God: The Christian Origins of Religious Freedom* (New Haven, CT: Yale University Press, 2019), 1. Tertullian's point was that coercion in religious matters violates the freedom of human beings, not that it was a right protected by the law.

[4] Wilken, *Liberty in the Things of God*, 20.

[5] Wilken, 27.

The Theodosian Code effectively made the Jews second class citizens by restricting their participation in the political, legal, military, and economic life of the empire. It also guaranteed that Jews could continue to practice their religion. Though the popes enjoyed close relations with Christian emperors, they did not request that the emperors forcibly convert the Jews.[6]

However, the terminology in official documents of the emperors also referred to Judaism as "superstition," the same derogatory term the Roman authorities had used for Christianity. Judaism was seen as a rival and competitor to Christianity, and so this negative language was then "matched by laws designed to hinder the growth of the Jewish religion."[7] Constantine issued discriminatory laws against Jews. The Theodosian Code continued this policy by prohibiting the building of new synagogues, among other laws:

> Jews were prohibited from converting Christians, and Jews who harassed Jewish converts to Christianity were subject to harsh penalties. . . . On the one hand, "the sect of the Jew [was] prohibited by no law," and official policy recognized their freedom to practice their religion. Imperial rescripts reproved zealous Christians who despoiled and destroyed Jewish synagogues. On the other hand, popular sentiment and imperial legislation were nudging the Jews to the margins of society and compromising their legal standing.[8]

As Robert Wilken has observed, despite restrictive tolerance under Christian rule, the standing of Jews in society eroded.[9] The Christian empire enacted anti-pagan policies: pagan temples and cult statues were seized and destroyed and the performance of pagan rites was eventually prohibited. However, despite their eroding standing, Judaism retained privileges and protections.

Jews also suffered outbreaks of violence instigated by Christian mobs, local clergy, and Christian rulers. Cases of forced baptism occurred in 418 on the Island of Minorca in the Mediterranean Sea. The remains of St. Stephen, the first Christian martyr, were discovered in Jerusalem, and several relics were transported to Minorca by Spanish priests.[10] The arrival of the relics provoked a Christian mob to burn the Jewish synagogue there and threaten

---

6 This observation, which echoes Aquinas's teaching, is made by Colish, *Faith, Fiction*, 230.
7 Wilken, *Liberty in the Things of God*, 29.
8 Wilken, 29.
9 Wilken, 28.
10 In Acts 7:8–60, Stephen is put to death by some Jews.

its Jewish community with conversion or death. The bishop demanded that the Jews convert or leave. The incident was a violation of imperial law.[11]

In the same century, Augustine would articulate his theology of protection of the Jews. For Augustine, the Jews were the original people of God, whose revelation makes the Old Testament a sacred book for Christians. In God's providence, Jews and their witness should be preserved until the Last Day. As Solomon Grayzel observed, "It was . . . necessary if the Jews were to be protected, for the Church to refute the argument that the persistence of Judaism or, as churchmen were likely to express it, 'the stubbornness of the Jews,' was contrary to God's will."[12] Augustine's witness doctrine, and his interpretation of Psalm 59:12 as a warning from Christ to not kill the Jews, would have significant impact on papal attitudes toward the necessity of protecting the Jews of medieval society.[13] Augustine taught that no one should forcibly separate Jews from Judaism. "To do so, he insisted, was to contravene God's will."[14]

The general papal approach to the problem of forced conversion would be solidified by letters written by Pope Gregory the Great (r. 590–604). Gregory's letters would influence popes to protect Jewish populations from numerous threats from the fifth to the eleventh century and beyond. His teaching would later come to be known as *Sicut Iudaeis* (Just as the Jews), a phrase taken from the opening line of a letter he wrote in which he rebuked Victor, the bishop of Palermo, in June of 598 for forcibly baptizing local Jews.[15] Gregory wrote, "Just as the Jews ought not have the freedom to dare

---

[11] Colish says the forced baptisms in Minorca set a precedent for Visigothic rulers. Colish, *Faith, Fiction*, 240.

[12] Solomon Grayzel, "The Papal Bull *Sicut Judeis*," in *Studies and Essays in Honor of Abraham A. Neuman*, ed. Meir Ben-Horin, Bernard D. Weinryb, and Solomon Zeitlin (Leiden: Brill, 1962), 247.

[13] St. Augustine, *The City of God*, books 11–22, trans. William Babcock (New York: New City Press, 2013). See Book XVIII.46. In the King James version, the verse reads, "Slay them not, lest My people forget; scatter them by Thy power and bring them down, O Lord our shield." Paula Fredriksen, *Augustine and the Jews: A Christian Defense of Jews and Judaism* (New York: Double Day, 2008), 276–77. Augustine's well known *compelle intrare* argument was aimed at Donatists, not Jews. See Peter Brown, "St. Augustine's Attitude toward Religious Coercion," *Journal of Roman Studies* 54 (1964): 107–16; Robert E. Lerner, *The Feast of St. Abraham: Medieval Millenarians and the Jews* (Philadelphia: University of Pennsylvania Press, 2001).

[14] Fredriksen, *Augustine and the Jews*, 304, 364.

[15] Simonsohn, vol. 1, 3–24. "Sicut Iudaeis non debet esse licentia quicquam in synagogis suis ultra quam permissum est lege praesumere, ita in his quae eis concessa sunt nullum debent praeiudicium sustinere." See Grayzel, "The Papal Bull *Sicut Judeis*," 243–80; Solomon Katz, "Pope Gregory the Great and the Jews," *Jewish Quarterly Review* 24, no. 2 (1933): 113–36.

do in their synagogues more than the law permits them, so ought they not suffer curtailment of those [privileges] which have been conceded them."[16]

Four months later, Gregory wrote again to rebuke the bishop of Palermo, demanding that the Jewish community be compensated for synagogues that the bishop unlawfully seized and "unadvisedly and rashly consecrated."[17] He wrote, "The Jews may in no way be oppressed or suffer any injustice. Moreover, let the books or ornaments that have been carried off be in like manner sought for. And, if any have been openly taken away, we desire them also to be restored without any question."[18] Gregory instructed that the bishop pay the Jews the price of the synagogues and the property attached to them according to a value decided upon by the abbot Urbicus.

Gregory also condemned forced baptism seven years earlier, in June of 591, in letters to the bishop of Arles and the bishop of Marseilles:

> I will not remain silent on how errant souls should be saved. One after another, travelers in the Marseille region have brought to our attention that there are many men of the Jewish faith now living among you in that province. Many of these Jews are brought to the font by force rather than being led to it by preaching. Now, while I value the laudable goal of handing on the faith we profess out of love for our Lord, I am afraid that this intention is futile when it is inconsistent with Holy Scripture. Nor is the effort meritorious or without loss to any souls we seek to snatch in this way. Anyone brought to the font under constraint and not by the sweetness of preaching will return to his original superstition.[19]

In March of 591, Gregory wrote to the bishop of Terracina, regarding the illegal proscription of Jewish religious services. He asserted that using violence to force Jews to abandon their traditions was not effective.

> As for those who disagree with the Christian religion, they must be encouraged and persuaded to join in unity with the faith through kindness and gentleness. It is only with the sweetness of preaching and warnings of the fearsome judgment to come that belief can be invited. They will be repelled by threats and intimidation. In order to make the word of God audible to

---

16 Grayzel, "The Papal Bull *Sicut Judeis*," 245. See Pope Gregory I, "Letters on the Treatment of Jews" (591, 598), in Jacob R. Marcus, *The Jews in the Medieval World. A Source Book: 315–1791* (New York: Hebrew Union College, 1990), 111–13.

17 Grayzel, "The Papal Bull *Sicut Judeis*," 246; Simonsohn, vol. 1, 16.

18 Simonsohn, vol. 1, 16.

19 Simonsohn, vol. 1, 4; see also Colish, *Faith, Fiction*, 232–33.

them, you need to proceed with due kindness, rather than with an excessive harshness that only terrifies them.[20]

Nevertheless, the problem of forced baptism persisted. In 602, Pope Gregory wrote to the bishop of Naples to rebuke him for violating the rights of the city's Jews.

Gregory's policy had a twofold aim: first, to regulate Christian-Jewish interaction as well as safeguard rights codified in the Theodosian Code, which had guaranteed that Jews might continue to practice their religion. But he also did not want Christians to be influenced by Judaism.[21]

> In his effort to instruct other bishops, Gregory appealed to the ancient truth that religion cannot be coerced. The only tool is persuasion. But he lived in a society whose boundaries were defined by religion. Though he recognized that the Jews had a place, Gregory did not want Christians to be influenced by Jewish practices. Christians should not, he said, be tempted to observe the Jewish custom of not working on the Sabbath. He prohibited Jewish ownership of Christian slaves lest the Christian religion be tainted by association with Jewish customs. And he was displeased that in one city the synagogue was so close to the church that Christians could hear [Jews] singing as they prayed. He advised the bishop to find another place for the Jews to gather. Gregory's magnanimity had its limits.[22]

Nevertheless, Gregory repeatedly called on bishops and Christian rulers to allow Jews to freely practice their religion.

Papal teaching in the Middle Ages followed the lines of Augustine and Gregory in condemning forced baptism. But forced baptism was one issue among others. According to Rebecca Rist, papal correspondence up to the eleventh century indicates that when Jews became a subject of interest, it was in reaction to immediate problems. Sometimes the popes were reacting to Jewish complaints of ill-treatment or Christian queries about Jewish status and practice.[23] These letters were written by clergy or rulers. The letters concerned the need to protect Jews from Christians or prevent Jews from influencing Christians, or to grant them privileges or rescind privileges.[24] According to Rist, the issues included existing synagogues (since

---

20 Simonsohn, vol. 1, 3; see also Colish, *Faith, Fiction*, 233.
21 Rebecca Rist, *Popes and Jews, 1095–1291* (New York: Oxford University Press, 2016), 10–11.
22 Wilken, *Liberty in the Things of God*, 30.
23 Rist, *Popes and Jews*, 10.
24 Grayzel, "The Papal Bull *Sicut Judeis*," 243.

new construction was not allowed), Jews and Christian slaves, commercial dealings between Christians and Jews, and the well-being of Jewish converts to Christianity. In general, Jews were allowed to maintain already-established synagogues but not build new ones; they must not employ Christians; they were to be treated fairly in business transactions; and they were to be aided financially following conversion.[25] Papal attitudes toward Jews consisted of a mixture of protection and restriction, sometimes referred to as "dual patronage." The theme can be detected in papal attitudes throughout Christian history. Such themes can be found in letters about Jews issued by Stephen III (r. 768–72), Adrian I (r. 772–95), Nicholas I (r. 858–67), and Leo VII (r. 936–39), among others.[26]

Pope Gregory's policy of protection of Jewish faith and lives was affirmed and restated in numerous papal letters. For example, Pope Alexander II (r. 1061–73) rebuked Landulf, prince of Benevento, for forcing Jews to Christianity: "Our Lord Jesus Christ, we read, forced no one into his service by violence, but rather by humble exhortation, freedom of choice for each one guarded."[27] Alexander cited Gregory on forbidding Christians to harm Jews: "Thus also the blessed Gregory prohibited certain men who were inflamed to destroy them. He denounced it as impious to want to destroy those who had been preserved by the mercy of God."[28] As Robert Chazan has observed,

> The Church proclaimed the fundamental right of Jews to live safely in a Christian society. Although much of the insecurity of Jewish life in medieval Europe stemmed from the theological claims and evocative imagery of the Church, and although important figures in the Church often played a prominent role in inciting anti-Jewish feeling, nevertheless, ecclesiastical leadership resolutely advanced the notion of toleration. Jews were to live in physical safety; they were to be permitted to organize their own affairs within their communities; and they were to enjoy the freedom of worshiping according to their tradition and of following Jewish law.[29]

---

25 Rist, *Popes and Jews*, 10.

26 Rist, 10.

27 Cited in Edward A. Synan, *The Popes and the Jews in the Middle Ages* (New York: Macmillan, 1965), 68.

28 Alexander II, *Placuit nobis* (1603), Simonsohn, vol. 1, 36.

29 Robert Chazan, *Church, State, and the Jew in the Middle Ages* (New York: Behrman House, 1980), 4.

However, papal decrees on the toleration of Jews were not heeded by some. In December 1095–July 1096, Jews in the Rhineland were massacred by Christian mobs on their way to the First Crusade. Some were forcibly baptized. Some bishops tried to intervene. In response to an appeal from the Jews of Rome, Pope Callistus II (r. 1119–24) issued a papal bull in 1120 for the protection of Jews, which he referred to as *Sicut Iudaeis*, a reference to the famous letter of Gregory the Great. The bull was addressed to "all faithful Christians," in order to oppose "the wickedness and avarice of evil men."[30] On penalty of excommunication, Callistus II forbade forced conversions of Jews:

> No Christian shall use violence to force them into baptism while they are unwilling and refuse, but that [only] if any one of them seeks refuge among the Christians of his own free will and by reason of faith, his willingness having become quite clear, shall he be made a Christian without subjecting himself to any opprobrium. For surely none can be believed to possess the true Christian faith if he is known to have come to Christian baptism, not voluntarily, but unwillingly.[31]

The pope also declared that no Christian could harm, rob, or kill Jews; or "change the good customs they have thus far enjoyed"; or desecrate their synagogues and cemeteries or in any way disturb them while they "celebrate their festivals."

Pope Callistus II's papal bull was a consolidated restatement of the principles in Gregory the Great's letters. Callistus's bull would become known as the *Constitutio pro Iudaeis* or "Constitution on the Jews," and it was repeated by popes from the twelfth to the fifteenth centuries. However, the tolerant *Sicut Iudaeis* tradition was not followed by all Christian rulers, canonists, or popes. As Marcia Colish observed, the tradition of Augustinian toleration and *Sicut Iudaeis* was abandoned in some quarters.[32]

---

30 Grayzel, "The Papal Bull *Sicut Judeis*," 245.

31 Wilken, *Liberty in the Things of God*, 37. According to Simonsohn, the bull has not survived and is known only from the quotation in later editions of the text. Simonsohn, vol. 1, 44. Pope Callistus II cited in Benjamin Ravid, "The Forced Baptism of Jews in Christian Europe: An Introductory Overview," 158.

32 Colish, *Faith, Fiction*, 232. Colish identifies various camps in the historiography of Jewish history, including the "lachrymose chronicle" at one pole and the "revisionists" at the other. The former camp tends to view Christian hostility toward Judaism as an ideological given, while the latter reject that view and argue that documentary evidence tells of support and protection of Jews by Christians. A third group, "the historiographical position," can be located between the two poles and argues that evidence is basically local and circumstantial, and factors in one situation may not be present elsewhere. My survey draws upon the views of scholars from each camp. Colish, *Faith, Fiction*, 234–35.

FORCED BAPTISM AND THE QUESTION OF VALIDITY

In his classic book, *The Anguish of the Jews*, Fr. Edward Flannery observed that the problem of forced baptisms opened a "depressing chapter in the histories of Jewry and Christendom."[33] As mentioned above, a recurring problem was the persecution of Jews by zealous Christian rulers and mobs. "Conversion by compulsion gained momentum from the ninth century onward, fueled by the expansion of Christian Europe on the continent and in the Crusades movement."[34] Despite the Church's teaching, Jewish adults and children were forcibly baptized.[35]

The policies on forced baptism of Jews produced in the seventh century by the Toledo Councils of Visigoth Spain decisively shaped how theologians and canonists viewed the question of forced baptisms for centuries. Although scholars debate the motivations behind the Councils, it is clear that after the conversion of King Reccared in 587 Visigoth rulers were concerned to eradicate what they referred to as the "superstition" and "inflexible perfidy" of the Jews.[36]

---

[33] Edward Flannery, *The Anguish of the Jews: Twenty-Three Centuries of Antisemitism*, 2nd ed. (New York: Paulist Press, 2004), 70; Susan White, "Baptism," *A Dictionary of Jewish-Christian Relations*, ed. Edward Kessler and Neil Wenborn (New York: Cambridge University Press, 2008), 47.

[34] Colish, *Faith, Fiction*, 227.

[35] Aviad M. Kleinberg, "Depriving Parents of the Consolation of Children: Two Legal *Consilia* on the Baptism of Jewish Children," in *De Sion exibit lex et verbum domini de Hierusalem: Essays on Medieval Law, Liturgy and Literature in Honour of Amnon Linder*, ed. Yitzhak Hen (Turnhout: Brepols, 2001), 129. See also Cecil Roth, "Forced Baptism in Italy: A Contribution to the History of Jewish Persecution," in *Gleanings: Essays in Jewish History, Letters, and Art* (New York: Bloch, 1967), 240–63; Benjamin C. I. Ravid, "The Forced Baptism of Jewish Minors in Early Modern Venice," *Italia: Studi e ricerche sulla cultura e sulla letteratura degli ebrei d'Italia* 13–15 (2001): 259–301; Martha Keil, "What Happened to the 'New Christians'? The Viennese Gererah of 1410/11 and the Forced Baptism of the Jews," in *Jews and Christians in Medieval Europe: The Historiographical Legacy of Bernhard Blumenkranz*, ed. Philippe Buc, Martha Keil, and John Tolan (Turnhout: Brepols, 2015), 97–114.

[36] Flannery, *Anguish of the Jews*, 75. See Norman Roth's discussion of the motivation of the policies of Visigoth rulers. The Councils, which were a mix of national assembly and Church synod, articulated policies on forced baptism of Jews in the context of what Amnon Linder has referred to as "statewide and state-controlled conversion" (*JLS*, 488). Norman Roth, "Church and Jews," in *Medieval Jewish Civilization: An Encyclopedia*, ed. Norman Roth (New York: Routledge, 2002). Visigoth kings sought a Catholic kingdom, as stated in Toledo VI canon 3: "No one not a Catholic may remain in the kingdom, and all future kings, under pain of anathema, must enforce this law." Regarding Visigoth kings' concerns with perfidy and superstition, see Roth's list of anti-Jewish policies of the Toledo Councils, including Toledo III canon 14. Norman Roth, *Jews, Visigoths, and Muslims in Medieval Spain: Cooperation and Conflict* (Leiden: Brill, 1994), 32. See also Rachel Stocking, "Forced Converts, 'Crypto-Judaism,' and Children: Religious Identification in Visigothic

In 613, King Sisebut (r. 612–21) issued an ultimatum that Jews of the kingdom either convert or be expelled from the country.[37] The resulting forced baptisms were viewed as a problem. The Fourth Council of Toledo, convoked on December 5, 633, by King Sisenand and presided over by St. Isidore of Seville (c. 570–636), legislated against the practice and decreed that kings who ruled cruelly could be excommunicated.[38]

Isidore taught that a person must come to faith by their own free will. Therefore, under no circumstances is faith to be coerced. "Just as man, created with free will, turns away from God voluntarily, so also he returns to Him, believing because of his own conversion of mind. By his own voluntary choice he manifests his freedom of will. And so, having accepted the truth of the faith, he receives the benefit of grace."[39]

Isidore condemned King Sisebut because "he no doubt had zeal but not knowledge, compelling by force those whom one must urge by reasons for faith."[40] The Council addressed the consequences of Sisebut's campaign of forced baptism. In particular, the first part of canon 57 of the Fourth Council of Toledo, citing Romans 9:18, famously condemned the practice of forced baptism:

> On the Jews, however, thus did the Holy Synod order, that no one should henceforth be forced to believe, *God hath mercy on whom he will and whom he will hardeneth*; such men should not be saved unwillingly but willingly, in order that the procedure of justice should be complete; for just as man perished obedient to the serpent out of his own free will, so will any man be saved—when called by the divine grace—by believing and in converting his own mind. They should be persuaded to convert, therefore, of their own free choice, rather than forced by violence.[41]

Additionally, perceived problems emerged in the aftermath of these forced baptisms. It was alleged that forcibly converted Jews continued to practice Judaism.[42] If baptized persons rejected Christianity, this was thought to undermine Christian faith and society.

Spain," in *Jews in Early Christian Law: Byzantium and the Latin West, 6th–11th Centuries*, ed. John Tolan et al. (Turnhout: Brepols, 2014), 243–65.

37 Flannery, *Anguish of the Jews*, 70–71, 75.
38 Roth, *Jews, Visigoths*, 18.
39 Isidore cited in Colish, *Faith, Fiction*, 244.
40 Cited in Flannery, *Anguish of the Jews*, 75.
41 C.57 cited in *JLS*, 486.
42 C.59 cited in *JLS*, 488:
   Many who were formerly elevated from being Jews to the Christian faith are now blaspheming Christ not only by being known to be practicing Jewish rites but even by

In response to this problem, the second part of the Fourth Council of Toledo canon 57 stated that those who had been baptized by force must remain Christian:

> Those, however, who were formerly forced to come to Christianity (as was done in the days of the most religious prince Sisebut), since it is clear that they have been associated in the divine sacraments, received the grace of baptism, were anointed with chrism, and partook of the body and blood of the Lord, it is proper that they should be forced to keep the faith even though they had taken it under duress, lest the name of the Lord blasphemed and the faith they had undertaken be treated as vile and contemptible.[43]

Colish argues convincingly that some of these lines are attributed to Isidore's views, which were not a coherent theological teaching.[44]

Additionally, canon 60 applies the policy (that those baptized under duress must be forced to keep the faith) to forcibly baptized children on the logic that newly baptized Christians must receive a Christian education: "[Baptized] sons and daughters of the Jews should be separated from the company of their parents in order that they should not become further entangled in their deviation, and entrusted either to monasteries or to Christian, God-fearing men and women."[45] The same Council that rejected forced conversions of Jews also had implied that forced baptisms of either adults or children were nonetheless valid. The Council's attempt to deal with Sisebut's forced conversions therefore established the precedent of requiring forcibly converted Jews to remain Christian and of removing baptized Jewish children from their parents.[46]

The consequence of the indelible character of baptism is that an obligation falls upon the baptized to carry out the duties prescribed by the Church. The rationale of the obligation that falls upon the baptized is explained well by Edward Synan: "Theologians early taught that baptism must be held to leave ineffaceable traces, analogous in the order of the spirit to the ineffaceable

---

daring to operate abominable circumcisions; concerning these men, the Holy Council decreed as follows, with the advice of the most pious and most religious prince our lord Sisenand the King, namely that such transgressors should be reformed and recalled to the veneration of the Christian dogma by the episcopal authority.

43 C.57 cited in *JLS*, 486. Linder explains that the Fourth Council of Toledo had dealt with "the existence of crypto-Jews, formally baptized and recognized Christians, alongside communities of non-baptized and openly practicing Jews. The Council condemned on principle any forced baptism and upheld the indelible nature of baptism once it had been duly performed."

44 Colish, *Faith, Fiction*, 242–45.

45 C.60 cited in *JLS*, 488.

46 Colish, *Faith, Fiction*, 248.

brands and tattoos of slaves and soldiers.... The permanence of its effect is absolute."[47] Before the Fourth Council of Toledo, the accepted understanding was that the indelible character of baptism applied only to those who were baptized willingly. After the Fourth Council of Toledo, Jews who were baptized against their will could be required to remain Christians.[48]

It is important to add a caveat about the impact of these canons: Visigothic kings struggled to enforce their own legislation. Forced baptism was a problem in Spain, but protections for Jews varied depending upon the attitudes of local rulers. As Jonathan Elukin has observed, anti-Jewish laws were often ignored or applied inconsistently.[49] Rist makes a similar point: "In the eleventh, twelfth, and thirteenth centuries, popes seem to have generally ignored the Toledan ruling. Even the great twelfth-century legal mind, Alexander III, who in his re-issue of the 'Constitutio pro Iudaeis' insisted again that Jews should not be forced to accept baptism—thereby deliberately recalling Gregory's teaching—never referred to Canon 57 in any of his correspondence concerned with Jews."[50] Moreover, the policy that those who were baptized under duress must keep the faith was called into question by canon 8 of the Second Council of Nicaea (787), which stated that baptized Jews who were not sincere in their conversion and returned to practicing Judaism ought to be rejected by the Church:

> Since some of those who come from the religion of the Hebrews mistakenly think to make a mockery of Christ who is God, pretending to become Christians, but denying Christ in private by both secretly continuing to observe the sabbath and maintaining other Jewish practices, we decree that they shall not be received to communion or at prayer or into the church, but rather let them openly be Hebrews according to their own religion; they should not baptize their children or buy, or enter into possession of, a slave. But if one of them makes his conversion with a sincere faith and heart, and pronounces his confession wholeheartedly, disclosing their practices and objects in the hope that others may be refuted and corrected, such a person should be welcomed and baptized along with his children, and care should

---

47 Synan, *The Popes and the Jews*, 55.

48 Benjamin Ravid, "The Forced Baptism of Jews in Christian Europe," 159; Edward Flannery, *Anguish of the Jews*, 76. See also Norman Roth, "Church and Jews," 169.

49 Jonathan Elukin, *Living Together, Living Apart: Rethinking Jewish-Christian Relations in the Middle Ages* (Princeton: Princeton University Press, 2013).

50 Rist, *Popes and Jews*, 77.

be taken that they abandon Hebrew practices. However, if they are not of this sort, they should certainly not be welcomed.[51]

Following this line of the thought, some rulers allowed Jewish converts to return to their religion.[52] For example, the Holy Roman Emperor Henry IV (r. 1084–1105) allowed Jews who had been converted by force to return to Judaism.[53]

Nevertheless, some papal statements also affirmed the logic of the second part of the Fourth Council of Toledo canon 57 and held that baptized Jews must live as Christians.[54] Pope Hadrian I (r. 772–95) rejected canon 8 of the Second Council of Nicaea.

Forced conversion of Jews was still condemned repeatedly by numerous popes, as indicated by the well-known letter of Pope Gregory IV (r. 827–44), which cites the prohibition of the practice in canon 57. The fact that the prohibition against forced baptism was repeated by popes in the twelfth century indicates that problems remained.

By the twelfth century, the policy of the Fourth Council of Toledo was solidified as canon law.[55] Around 1140, Gratian included canon 57 in *Distinctio* 45 of his *Decretum prima pars* (hereafter D.45).[56] Gratian rejected forced baptism and taught that Jews should not be treated with hostility. He also taught that faith and salvation can be acquired only through the exercise of one's free will. However, he also affirmed that those who had been baptized, including children, must remain Christians. Gratian added the text of the Fourth Council of Toledo canon 60 to *Decretum secunda pars*, *Causa* 28, question 1, c. 11.[57]

---

51 Second Council of Nicaea (787), canon 8, in *Decrees of the Ecumenical Councils Volume One: Nicaea I to Lateran V*, ed. Norman P. Tanner (London: Sheed and Ward and Georgetown University Press, 1990), 145.

52 Roth, "Church and Jews," 168.

53 Grayzel, vol. 2, 166n3.

54 Synan, *The Popes and the Jews*, 60.

55 "Although originally applied to Jews of the Visigoth period, the inclusion of this text in the later *Decretals* made this a binding rule of canon law. While no Jews should be forced to baptism, once baptized, even by force, he must remain a Christian." Roth, *Jews, Visigoths*, 21.

56 Gratian placed three canons treating Jews in D.45 c.3–5, the most important being canon 57 of the Fourth Council of Toledo, which discussed the coerced conversion of Jews to Christianity. He also placed material from the Fourth Council of Toledo in Causa 28. See Kenneth Pennington, "The Law's Violence against Medieval and Early Modern Jews," *Rivista internazionale di diritto comune* 23 (2012): 33. See also Pennington, "Gratian and the Jews," *BMCL* 31 (2014): 116.

57 Canon 60 appears in the *Decretum* II, C. xxviii, q. 1 c. 11.

According to Kenneth Pennington, a crucial problem the jurists would take up was whether these forced baptisms were nevertheless valid.[58] In other words, baptized persons were expected to fulfill their obligations to observe the Christian faith, but should this obligation apply to forcibly baptized persons?[59] D.45 became the text on which jurists and theologians based their discussions of the legality of Jewish conversions for centuries. According to Colish, "Gratian has been regarded both as a stanch opponent of forced baptism and also as the point of departure for the canonical view that it is sacramentally valid. His *Decretum*, indeed, is a source for both of these positions."[60]

Sicut Iudaeis was also included in decretal collections. The decretal was variously attributed to Pope Alexander III (r. 1159–81) or to Pope Clement III (r. 1187–91). After Johannes Galensis had placed it in *Compilatio secunda* 5.4.3 (c. 1210–15), Raymond de Peñafort would enter it into the *Decretals* of Gregory IX (c. 1234).[61]

Nevertheless, jurists sought a definition of forced baptism that rationalized the practice. In 1164, Rufinus of Bologna, an influential canon lawyer at the University of Bologna, composed a *Summa* on Gratian's D.45 and added a principle not found in Gratian, namely, that baptism under threat is permitted: "Rufinus thus goes well beyond Gratian in validating certain forms of battery and intimidation as exceptions to the ban on forced baptism."[62]

According to Colish, other canonists accepted and promoted Rufinus's reading of D.45. Some canonists introduced a distinction to further rationalize forced baptism.[63] Gratian's successors created a distinction between "conditional" and "absolute" coercion.[64] The Italian canonist Huguccio of Pisa (d. 1210) established the legal basis for determining the validity of a forced baptism in his influential *Summa* on the *Decretum* (c. 1188).[65] In a gloss on the Fourth Council of Toledo, he explained what constituted consent of a Jew to baptism by distinguishing between absolute and conditional coercion.

---

58 Pennington, "Law's Violence," 28–29.
59 Synan, *The Popes and the Jews*, 55.
60 Colish, *Faith, Fiction*, 282.
61 X 5.6.9; Simonsohn, vol. 1, 51–52.
62 Colish, *Faith, Fiction*, 283.
63 Colish, 228.
64 Pennington, "Gratian and the Jews," 116.
65 Kleinberg, "Depriving Parents," 130–31.

"Absolute coercion" is where the victim did not consent to baptism at all.[66] Canonists thought absolutely coerced baptisms were without effect because there was no assent.

However, a second form of coercion, referred to as "conditional coercion," is where the recipient gives nominal assent to avoid harm. Huguccio explains: "If someone is baptized under conditional coercion, for example if I say I will beat, rob, kill, or injure you, unless you are baptized, he can be forced to hold the faith, because from conditional coercion an unwilling person is made into a willing person, and as a willing person is baptized. A coerced choice is a choice, and makes consent."[67] Thirteenth-century jurists found Huguccio's definition of conditional coercion persuasive.

In 1219, Alanus Anglicus argued that unbelievers who resist conversion may be compelled to accept baptism by corporal constraints short of death.[68] As Flannery explains, "canonists were of the opinion that whoever did not openly manifest his opposition to baptism at the very moment of its administration was not truly forced, *vere coacti*—even if death itself awaited such opposition—and was therefore validly baptized, incurring all the rights and duties of Christian life."[69]

The validity of conditionally coerced baptisms would be elevated by Pope Innocent III (r. 1198-1216). Innocent's letter *Maiores* (1201) was a reply to a query from Imbertus d'Aiguières, archbishop of Arles, and discussed baptism of infants, the insane, the comatose, and those under duress.[70] Innocent had insisted in another letter that force must not be employed to achieve conversions: "No Christian shall use violence to compel the Jews to accept baptism ... [A]nyone who has not of his own will sought Christian baptism cannot have the true Christian faith."[71]

---

66 Huguccio, cited in Pennington, "Gratian and the Jews," 118: "I distinguish between absolute and conditional coercion: if anyone is baptized by absolute coercion, for example if one person tied him down and another poured water over him, unless he consents afterwards, he ought not to be forced to embrace the Christian faith."

67 Huguccio, *Summa* to D. 45 c. 5 cited in Pennington, "Gratian and the Jews," 118; Mario Condorelli, *I fondamenti giuridici della tolleranza religiosa nell'elaborazione canonistica dei secoli XII-XIX: Contributo storico-dogmatico* (Milan: Dott. A. Giuffrè, 1960), 152-53.

68 Colish, *Faith, Fiction*, 284.

69 Flannery, *Anguish of the Jews*, 76.

70 Innocent III, *Maiores*, September–October 1201, cited in Simonsohn, vol. 1, 16. See also Kleinberg, "Depriving Parents," 132.

71 See the letter of Innocent III forbidding violence against Jews, in *A Source Book for Medieval History*, ed. Oliver J. Thatcher and Edgard H. McNeal (New York: Scribner, 1905), 212.

But there is no express prohibition in *Maiores*. Once an unbeliever had been baptized, even through use of force, Innocent stated that he must observe the Christian faith:

> It is indeed against the Christian religion to force someone consistently unwilling and deeply opposed into the reception and practice of Christianity. But, without absurdity, some distinguish between unwillingness and unwillingness, compulsion and compulsion. One who is impelled to it violently, by intimidation and threats, and receives baptism to avoid suffering harm, is comparable to one who accedes to baptism fictively. He receives the imprint of the Christian character. Since he wills it, in a sense, conditionally, although he does not will it absolutely, he is bound to the observance of the Christian faith.[72]

Innocent's letter confirmed that a conditionally coerced baptism nevertheless imprints an indelible character on the recipient. Yet an absolutely coerced baptism, in which one wholly objected, does not. Recall that the papal counsel cited Innocent's teaching in its reply to the Mortaras' plea.[73] Colish reports that modern scholars have seen Innocent III as both an opponent and a defender of forced baptism.[74]

Nearly all canonists adopted the distinction between conditional and absolute coercions.[75] Raymond de Peñafort added the rule that conditionally forced baptisms were valid to the *Decretals* of Gregory IX (c. 1234): "If forced conditionally, for instance by threats or by confiscation of their goods or by flogging or by other similar force, they accept the sacrament of baptism and afterward leave our faith, they must be compelled to return.... If they were absolutely forced, for instance if they were violently dragged off and water poured over them, then the essence of baptism is not conferred."[76]

The canonists concluded that a forced conversion or baptism of a Jew was "valid if bestowed under only moderate terror."[77] The category of a con-

---

[72] Innocent III to Imbert d'Agueres, archbishop of Arles, September/October 1201, cited in Gregory IX, *Decretals* 10.3.42.3 in *Corpus iuris canonici*, ed. Aemilius Friedberg, 2 vols. (Leipzig: Tauchnitz, 1879–80; repr., Union, NJ: Lawbook Exchange, 2000), 2:646; Colish, *Faith, Fiction*, 287. Fictive baptism is submitting to baptism without spiritual intentions, for example, to gain economic benefits.

[73] *BC*, 6.

[74] Colish, *Faith, Fiction*, 284.

[75] Kleinberg, "Depriving Parents," 133.

[76] Raymond de Peñafort, "Concerning Jews, Saracens, and their Slaves," no. 2, in Chazan, *Church, State, and the Jew*, 38.

[77] Walter Pakter, *Medieval Canon Law and the Jews* (Ebelsbach, Germany: Gremler, 1988), 317.

ditionally forced baptism or coerced-but-valid baptism provided a legal way around the *Sicut Iudaeis* tradition's condemnation of forced conversions. These coerced-but-valid baptisms also raised legal issues, including questions about the consequences of coerced baptisms of Jewish adults and servants, and whether it was lawful to forcibly baptize children.[78]

WHETHER COERCED BAPTISM IS LAWFUL

Thirteenth-century popes increasingly classified Jews as "internal" rather than "external" to Christian society and so subject to papal authority.[79] On June 6, 1242, the Order of Dominican Preachers publicly burned cartloads of books seized from Parisian Jews.

In 1267, Clement IV's papal bull *Turbato corde* granted inquisitors authority to intervene in the affairs of Jewish communities. Clement was concerned that Jewish converts to Christianity, including those who had been forcibly baptized, had returned to Judaism. This was viewed a subversion of the Christian faith, and so Dominican as well as Franciscan friars were tasked with discovering those who were guilty. Benjamin Ravid views *Turbato corde* as nullifying *Sicut Iudaeis* bulls.[80]

After the Christian discovery of the Talmud, canonists and theologians debated whether to baptize Jewish children against the will of their parents. The debate was motivated by those who hoped that if they could not persuade Jewish families to baptism, they could coerce them.[81] The debate focused not on the validity of a forced baptism, that is, whether one who was forcibly baptized received the indelible mark of the sacrament, but on whether it was lawful to forcibly baptize Jewish children even against the will of their parents.

These proposals were new. In the patristic era, emergency baptism of infants was not administered to the children of non-Catholic parents against their will. And the early church did not baptize the unwilling.[82] This is why Aquinas defended toleration of Jewish religious practice and parental authority against these proposals, which he would refer to as hazardous and repugnant to the natural law. Aquinas also taught that the Jewish people

---

78 Pennington, "Law's Violence," 34.

79 Rist, *Popes and Jews*, 213–14.

80 Ravid, "The Forced Baptism of Jews in Christian Europe: An Introductory Overview," 159.

81 Pakter, *Medieval Canon Law and the Jews*, 329.

82 William Harmless, SJ, "Christ the Pediatrician: Infant Baptism and Christological Imagery in the Pelagian Controversy," *Augustinian Studies* 28, no. 2 (1997): 29.

do not belong to the spiritual authority of the Church.[83] We will examine Aquinas's teaching in detail in the next chapter.

It is important for our purposes now, however, to recognize that by Aquinas's lifetime the debate was *not* on whether a forced baptism was valid. That debate among canonists had been settled by Huguccio's distinction between conditionally and absolutely coerced baptisms, and the elevation of the distinction in Pope Innocent III's *Maiores*.

The debate in the thirteenth century was focused on whether Jewish children could licitly be baptized against the will of their parents or invitis parentibus. For example, the influential theologian and philosopher John Duns Scotus (c. 1265/66–1308) argued that Christian rulers had a moral obligation to baptize the children of unbelievers against the will of their parents because the rights of God over children were superior to those of parents.[84] In northern France, theologians argued for forced conversion of Jewish children, and there was an organized movement to baptize Jewish children.[85]

Forced baptism of Jews remained a threat throughout the late Middle Ages.[86] From the fourteenth century onward, jurists and theologians continued to debate forced conversion.[87] As we saw in chapter 2, a number of Dominican theologians argued against forced baptism of Jewish children into the sixteenth century.

Some of these debates would be settled by eighteenth-century papal bulls that codified forced conversions of children and adults. However, before discussing these policies, it is necessary to first examine a sixteenth-century development in the social condition of Roman Jewry that emboldened expectations among authorities of the Papal States that their Jews would convert to Christianity.

According to Ravid, the most remarkable development in the history of forced conversion of Jews occurred at the end of the Middle Ages. In 1391, forced conversion of Jews became much more frequent and prevalent in Castile and Aragon. Under pressure from restrictive legislation and violent mobs, some permanently left Judaism but were referred to as "New Christians" and resented because they were viewed as new socio-economic competitors. However, those who were forcibly baptized and wanted to revert to Judaism, or crypto-Jews, faced extremely negative Christian attitudes and

---

83 ST II.II 10.9, ad. 2; 10.12.
84 John Duns Scotus, *Ordinatio*, 4. D. 4. pars 4. q. 3.2; Colish, *Faith, Fiction*, 304–5.
85 Pakter, *Medieval Canon Law and the Jews*, 326.
86 Pennington, "Law's Violence," 34.
87 Pennington, 43.

were referred to by Christians as Marranos, or "pig." It is in this context that Pope Sixtus IV (r. 1471–1484) authorized the establishment of the Spanish Inquisition to discover and punish crypto-Jews. The presence of Judaism would become intolerable to rulers in Spain. In March of 1492, Ferdinand and Isabella decreed that all the Jews of Spain must leave in four months.[88]

Early in the sixteenth century, the popes maintained a policy of attracting foreign merchants, and issued a safe-conduct inviting Jews to settle with their families in the Papal States if they were New Christians or of "the Jewish nation." Pope Paul III (r. 1534–49) even declared that no official was to bother them with charges of heresy, apostasy, or blasphemy, or to investigate their practices. The pope assured New Christians that they could assume Judaism with impunity in the Papal States. This was reconfirmed by Pope Julius III (r. 1550–55).[89]

By the mid-sixteenth century, however, a harsh papal attitude emerged. Pope Paul IV (r. 1555–59) reversed the tolerant policies of the Papal States that had been established by his predecessors. Kenneth Stow argues that conversion became the aim of papal policy toward Roman Jews, the largest Jewish community in Western Europe.[90] On July 14th, 1555, Paul IV promulgated the papal bull *Cum nimis absurdum* (Since it is completely senseless) at the Basilica of St. Mark the Evangelist in Rome. The bull shaped papal policy toward Jews of the Papal States.

The ghetto revolutionized Jewish residential life: "For nearly two millennia, Jews had mingled freely with Rome's other inhabitants by day or night, admittedly (but not always consistently) limited by restrictive canons."[91] In *Cum nimis*, Paul IV declared that "all Jews are to live in only one [quarter] to which there is only one entrance and from which there is but one exit."[92] Each ghetto was to have only one synagogue in its customary location and all other synagogues were to be demolished. Jews were not allowed to own any buildings.

---

[88] Ravid, "The Forced Baptism of Jews in Christian Europe: An Introductory Overview," 162–63.

[89] Ravid, "The Forced Baptism of Jews in Christian Europe: An Introductory Overview," 165

[90] Kenneth Stow, *Anna and Tranquillo: Catholic Anxiety and Jewish Protest in the Age of Revolutions* (New Haven, CT: Yale University Press, 2016), 68. See also Serena Di Nepi, *Surviving the Ghetto: Toward a Social History of the Jewish Community in 16th-Century Rome*, trans. Paul M. Rosenberg (Leiden: Brill, 2021); Stow, *Theater of Acculturation: The Roman Ghetto in the Sixteenth Century* (Seattle: University of Washington Press, 2000). The Italian ghetto was not a papal invention but was established by the Venetians in 1516, who allowed Jews to settle on a small island called "the ghetto." See Stow, *Anna and Tranquillo*, 71.

[91] Stow, *Anna and Tranquillo*, 69.

[92] Pope Paul IV, *Cum nimis absurdum*, July 14, 1555, www.ccjr.us/dialogika-resources/primary-texts-from-the-history-of-the-relationship/paul-iv.

Moreover, *Cum nimis* declared that toleration of Jewish existence in the Papal States was conditional on conversion. "The Church of Rome tolerates these very Jews . . . to this end: that they . . . should at long last recognize their erroneous ways, and should lose no time in seeing the true light of the catholic faith."[93]

Before 1555, conversion was not the aim of toleration. Rather, toleration in the Papal States was based in the policy of protection of Pope Gregory the Great. "Popes . . . promised Jews protection without a price. . . . Following the teaching of St. Augustine, they believed that Christian theology demanded a certain toleration of Jews and they therefore encouraged Christians to allow them to live unharmed in their midst."[94] However, "after 1555, conversion became, and remained, prime."[95] For instance, the well-known canon lawyer of the period Marquardus de Susannis published a summary of canon law on the Jews and included a conversionary sermon that he composed.[96] We now turn to the eighteenth-century papal bulls that legalized absolutely coerced baptisms of children and adults.

LAWFUL AND MERITORIOUS FORCED BAPTISM IN CERTAIN EXCEPTIONS

For some historians, the eighteenth century was another turning point in the development of papal attitude on the Jews. Their attitude moved toward "an ever-greater intransigence against the Jews and an all-out policy of conversion."[97]

According to Thomas Brechenmacher, however, there remained a strong sense among those in the government of the Papal States that they had a responsibility toward their Jewish population. The government understood this responsibility in terms of the duty of protection.[98] As protectors of Jews, the popes understood that they had a responsibility to safeguard Jews against

---

[93] Paul IV, *Cum nimis absurdum*.

[94] Rist, *Popes and Jews*, 219.

[95] Stow, *Anna and Tranquillo*, 68.

[96] Stow, 69.

[97] Marina Caffiero, *Forced Baptisms: Histories of Jews, Christians, and Converts in Papal Rome*, trans. Lydia G. Cochrane (Berkeley: University of California Press, 2012), 7. David Kertzer makes a similar argument in *Popes against the Jews: The Vatican's Role in the Rise of Modern Anti-Semitism* (New York: Vintage, 2002). See also Giancarlo Spizzichino, "The Ghetto and the Authorities: A Difficult Coexistence," *Et Ecce Gaudium: The Roman Jews and the Investiture of the Popes*, ed. Daniela Di Castro (Rome: Jewish Museum of Rome, 2010), 17.

[98] Thomas Brechenmacher, *Das Ende der doppelten Schutzherrschaft: Der Heilige Stuhl und die Juden am Übergang zur Moderne (1775–1870)*, Päpste und Papsttum, Band 32 (Stuttgart, Germany: Anton Hiersemann, 2004). See also Owen Chadwick, Review of "Das Ende der

attacks by Christians. But as protectors of Christians, the popes also sought to guard Christians from a perceived negative spiritual influence of Jews.

For this reason, Brechenmacher argues that the policy toward the Jews of the Papal States in this period was shaped by a principle of "dual patronage." From Brechenmacher's perspective, there was a conversionary attitude toward Jews, but it was a symptom of the general structural and political crisis facing the Papal States.[99] There was a sense among the popes of the nineteenth century that they had a responsibility to make the Papal States and Rome in particular a beacon of piety and virtue in a world under siege by liberal revolutions.

Nevertheless, the increasingly defensive position of the Church in the eighteenth century caused the concept of dual patronage to become one-sided, and the task of protecting Christians from Jews became more important. According to Stow, the papacy was uneasy about eighteenth-century secular movements and revolutions in France, the Holy Roman Empire, and the United States.[100] This caused pressure on Roman Jews. Marina Caffiero has argued that the questions concerning Jews that were discussed by the Holy Office in the eighteenth century display an increasing interest in Jewish conversion to Christianity.[101] Caffiero's analysis of the cases in the archives also indicates that there was an interest in the expansion of methods to bring about conversions, especially of children and women.[102] This interest is also evidenced in compulsory attendance at sermons on the Sabbath among numerous other restrictions.[103]

It is in this context that the teaching of Pope Benedict XIV (c. 1740–58) marks a decisive moment in the debate among canon lawyers on whether

---

doppelten Schutzherrschaft: Der Heilige Stuhl und die Juden," by Thomas Brechenmacher, *The Catholic Historical Review* 91, no. 1 (2005): 173–75.

[99] Owen Chadwick, *The Popes and European Revolution* (New York: Oxford University Press, 1981).

[100] Stow, *Anna and Tranquillo*, 75.

[101] The archives of the Congregation for the Doctrine of the Faith (known until the end of the Second Vatican Council as the Holy Office) were opened in 1998. Caffiero, *Forced Baptisms*, 6; Anne Jacobson Schutte, "Palazzo del Sant'Uffizio: The Opening of the Roman Inquisition's Central Archive," *Perspectives on History: The Newsmagazine of the American Historical Association*, May 1999, www.historians.org/research-and-publications/perspectives-on-history/may-1999/palazzo-del-santuffizio-the-opening-of-the-roman-inquisitions-central-archive.

[102] Caffiero, *Forced Baptisms*, 6.

[103] Emily Michelson, *Catholic Spectacle and Rome's Jews: Early Modern Conversion and Resistance* (Princeton, NJ: Princeton University Press, 2024).

it was lawful to baptize Jewish children against the will of their parents.[104] Benedict wrote that "it is unlawful to baptize Hebrew children against the will of their parents."[105] On this point, he cites Aquinas in ST II.II 10.12 and the contrary position, that of Duns Scotus:

> Scotus in book 4 [of his *Commentary on the Sentences of Peter Lombard*], dist. 4, q. 9, no. 2, and in questions related to no. 2, thought that a prince could laudably command that small children of Hebrews and unbelievers be baptized, even against the will of the parents.... Nevertheless, the opinion of St. Thomas prevailed in courts ... and is more widespread among theologians and those skilled in canon law.[106]

Benedict was aware of the stature of Aquinas's teaching. He acknowledged that Aquinas's position against forced baptism of Jewish children was accepted by most theologians and canon lawyers over the contrary opinion of Scotus.

However, in the next section of the letter, he overthrows Aquinas's teaching by articulating a list of exceptions to the prohibition on forced baptisms of non-Christian children. In order to understand his list of exceptions, one must recall that the context of the policy was the Roman ghetto.

In the eighteenth century, most Jews could not spend the night outside of the ghetto or have friendly relations with Christians.[107] However, Christians visited the shops and homes of the ghetto in the daytime in order to have clothing repaired, buy secondhand goods, or to work as maidservants for Jews on the Sabbath. Some visitors were *neofiti* or new converts from Judaism to Christianity. According to papal decrees, there was interest in protecting Jews from New Christians who would baptize their children. And Jews had requested that converts be prevented from entering the ghetto and secretly

---

104 *Lettera a Monsignor Archivescovo di Tarso Vicegerente sopra il Battesimo degli Ebrei o infanti o adulti* (February 28, 1747); and *Lettera della Santità di Nostro Signore Benedetto Papa XIV a Monsignor Pier Girolamo Guglielmi Assessore del Sant'Officio sopra l'Offerta fatta dall'Avia Neofita di alcuni suoi Nipoti infanti Ebrei alla Fede Christiana* (December 15, 1751). The two letters were translations of the bulls *Postremo mense* and *Probe te meminisse*, published in Latin on the same dates. For the decrees see *Bullari Romani continuatio Summorum Pontificum* ... in Benedictus XIV, *Opera Omnia*, tt. XVIII-XXIII, vols. 22–32. (Prati, Italy: Typographia Aldina, 1843–67); *DS*, 2552–62. See also Caffiero, *Forced Baptisms*, 44–65; Pennington, "Law's Violence," 40–43.

105 *Postremo Mense*, 7, *DS*, 2553.

106 *Postremo Mense*, 5, *DS*, 2334.

107 Of over forty ghettos in Italy in 1797, there were eight in the Papal States. Brechenmacher argues that in 1775 the Jews of the Papal States did not live strictly isolated in ghettos. At least a third of the approximately twelve thousand Jews lived in more than one hundred small towns and in the countryside.

baptizing children. Baptisms were also initiated by Christian maidservants of Jewish families.[108] Church leaders considered these interactions as transgressions and imposed fines.[109] The concept of dual patronage can be detected in the Holy Office's efforts to prevent Jewish families from employing Christian girls as maidservants. For example, Benedict XIV forbade Catholic midwives to deliver children in the ghetto.

Despite these policies, the clandestine baptism of Jewish children occurred frequently.[110] Indeed, Pope Benedict XIV pointed out that unlawful baptisms of Jewish children and similar events "happened too often in Rome and outside of Rome."[111] To address the problem, Benedict set forth conditions to regulate the practice and listed two hypothetical cases in which baptism is lawful and fitting even if parents protest against it: if a Christian finds a Jewish child close to death, or if a Christian finds a Jewish child alone.

> It is unlawful to baptize Hebrew children against the will of their parents, now, following the order proposed in the beginning, we must take up ... whether any occasion could ever occur in which that would be lawful and fitting. Since this may happen, that a child of Hebrew parentage be found by some Christian to be close to death, he will certainly perform a deed which I think is praiseworthy and pleasing to God, if he furnished the child with eternal salvation by purifying water. If, likewise, it should happen that any Hebrew child has been cast out and abandoned by its parents, it is the common opinion of all and has also been confirmed by many decisions, that the child ought to be baptized, even if the parents protest against this and demand the child back.[112]

Here, baptism invitis parentibus of Jewish children "close to death" or "abandoned" became not only lawful but was declared praiseworthy and pleasing to God.

Regarding a child found alone, Benedict ruled that although Jews enjoy patria potestas over their children, such rights are lost in cases where there is a "state of abandonment." If a Jewish child has been abandoned by its parents, the child can be baptized even if the parents protest. Other exceptions stated that Jewish children could be baptized if the Jewish parents were absent and their guardians consented.[113]

---

108 Caffiero, *Forced Baptisms*, 156.
109 Stow, *Anna and Tranquillo*, 76.
110 Caffiero, *Forced Baptisms*, 150.
111 Pennington, "Law's Violence," 41.
112 *Postremo mense*, 7–9, *DS*, 2554–56.
113 *Postremo mense*, 14, *DS*, 2557.

The exceptions were open to broad interpretations. Ambiguity concerning what constituted "close to death" or "abandoned" meant that the decision was made by the Christian administering the sacrament.[114] Decades after the decrees were promulgated, a petition to the Holy Office from the heads of Jewish families in 1770 stated that "recently, the license taken by various Christians, both men and women, secretly to baptize the little creatures they find in ghetto homes they frequent has become insupportable."[115]

There were other policies that indicated conversionary aims. One important exception to the prohibition on forced baptism of Jewish children which Benedict XIV codified was referred to as "offering." If a Jew converted to Christianity, he had the authority to offer the children of his relatives for baptism.[116] If the paternal grandfather embraced the Catholic faith, he could bring any grandchild to baptism even if the Jewish mother objected.[117] For this reason, if a Jew converted, he or she became a danger to his or her family.

Benedict's decrees consolidated earlier decisions where "parental rights" were interpreted to apply beyond parents, to extended relatives who had converted. "Beginning in the later sixteenth century... expansive legal interpretations were vouchsafing the power of parental consent in an ever-widening circle of relatives: first, with a small step, in 1583, to the parental grandfather, then, in 1751, with a large jump, to the parental grandmother, and, eventually, by 1783, to parental uncles and aunts."[118] Additionally, Roman Jewish leaders (*Fattori*) of the ghetto were warned that they would be held personally responsible if they tried to persuade Jews not to convert to Christianity.[119] The Jewish leaders were also warned against assisting pregnant women whose unborn children had been "offered" (by a converted relative) in escaping Rome.[120] Benedict also ruled that Jewish converts had the right to offer their adult relatives. If the husband converted, he could offer his wife to the Church.

---

[114] "This means that even in this variety of legal baptism, exactly how a Jewish child was judged to be 'alone' and could thus be considered abandoned or exposed remained ambiguous." Caffiero, *Forced Baptisms*, 51.

[115] Stow, *Anna and Tranquillo*, 77.

[116] *Postremo mense*, 15–16, DS, 2557

[117] *Postremo mense*, 17, DS, 2557.

[118] Stow, *Anna and Tranquillo*, 75. Stow has shown that there was already legal precedent that began extending the parental rights beyond the mother and father. Benedict's innovations drew heavily upon the thought of the judge of Torinese Jews Giuseppe Sessa.

[119] Stow, 73.

[120] Stow, 74.

Benedict based these rulings, including the offerings, on a traditional legal principle referred to as *favor fidei*, or "favor of the faith."[121] According to Stow, *favor fidei* was an umbrella principle that referred to action that advanced the faith.[122] *Favor fidei* became the standard for adjudicating decisions where parental rights were perceived to conflict with that which benefited the Church.[123] The exceptions codified the idea that the good of Christian society outweighed all other concerns, including the parental rights of unbelievers.

As mentioned above, some of these principles were already stated in previous cases by some popes and jurists who preceded Benedict XIV. Pope Gregory XIII had appealed to *favor fidei* to allow an offering by a paternal grandfather who had converted to Christianity. Benedict went beyond him by allowing paternal grandmothers to make offerings as well. Benedict XIV refined, focused, and elevated this line of legal reasoning.[124] What makes *Postremo mense* so powerful was that it consolidated previous rulings and applied the principles to the problem of baptism of Jewish children invitis parentibus. The codification of the principles overthrew the traditional prohibition on forced baptism of Jewish children that was solidified by Aquinas. The rulings elevated the concept of the primacy of the Church's rights over and against the parental rights of Jews.[125]

CONCLUSION

To summarize this chapter on forced baptism of Jews in papal teaching and canon law, an unlawful or illicit baptism is baptizing a recipient under absolute coercion—against the express will and protest of the potential recipient or parents of the recipient. Such baptisms were thought to be invalid. Conditional

---

121 Stow, 79–82.

122 Pakter, *Medieval Canon Law and the Jews*, 319. Aviad M. Kleinberg says this teaching can be traced to Raymond de Peñafort's *De Iudaeis*. Kleinberg, "Depriving Parents," 135; Kenneth Stow, "The Cruel Jewish Father: From Miracle to Murder," *Studies in Medieval Jewish Intellectual and Social History: Festschrift in Honor of Robert Chazan*, ed. David Engel, Lawrence H. Schiffman, and Eliot R. Wolfson (*Journal of Jewish Thought and Philosophy*, Supplement 15; Leiden: Brill, 2012), 245–78. The opposite of *favor fidei* was *odium fidei*, which referred to actions that detract from advancing the faith. Stow, *Anna and Tranquillo*, 257.

123 Stow, *Anna and Tranquillo*, 79.

124 According to Stow, Benedict's decisions were based in the legal theory developed by Stefano Graziani in 1625 and perfected by Giuseppe Sessa in 1716.

125 Maria Pia Donato, "Reorder and Restore: Benedict XIV, the Index, and the Holy Office," in *Benedict XIV and the Enlightenment: Art, Science, and Spirituality*, ed. Rebecca Messbarger, Christopher Johns, and Philip Gavitt (Toronto: University of Toronto Press, 2016), 239.

coercion was legal, and its effects permanent. However, conditional coercion was a broad category that included an array of coercive measures that might move a person to consent to baptism in order to avoid harm. The exceptions codified in 1747 expanded the legal category of lawful coercions to include absolutely coerced conversions of Jewish children and adults.

In these measures, the government of the Papal States began to permit absolutely coerced baptisms as lawful, which had not been allowed before.[126] Walter Pakter observed that until the codification of these exceptions, most Italian canonists thought Jews should not be converted in this manner.[127] Taken together, the definition of conditional coercion accepted by many canonists in the thirteenth century, and the list of exceptions applied to Jewish families of the ghetto by Benedict XIV, removed the teeth from the Church's prohibition against forced baptism of Jews, not to mention its numerous restatements issued by popes in the Middle Ages.

In Caffiero's view, Benedict's XIV's letters "were used to transcend tradition ... in particular the authority of St. Thomas, who forbids baptism *invitis parentibus*."[128] As mentioned above, Aquinas addressed the topic of forced baptism of Jewish children three times in his corpus: in the *Summa theologiae* II.II 10.12 and III 68.10, and in *Quodlibetales Questiones* 2.4.2.

However, Pope Benedict XIV's citation of Aquinas raises the question of whether Aquinas's teaching supports Benedict's exceptions to the prohibition against forced baptism of Jewish children. Stow has said the dualistic worldview epitomized by the legal principle, *favor fidei*, can be traced to Aquinas: "*Favor fidei* appears ... notably in Thomas Aquinas's discussion of forced baptism."[129] According to Stow, Aquinas taught that "one must always prefer *favorem fidei*." "No wonder that in critical papal pronouncements of Benedict XIV, the differentiating of *favor* from *odium* comes to the fore."[130]

Did Aquinas teach that one must prefer *favorem fidei*? We now turn to an analysis of Aquinas's teaching with attention to this question, as well as the three key questions identified in our analysis of the papal counsel's reply to the Mortara family: whether Aquinas holds that forced baptism of Jewish children is lawful or licit in certain exceptions; whether forced baptism of a child of unbelievers is nevertheless a valid baptism; and whether Aquinas teaches that Jewish parents lose their rights over their children if they are baptized.

---

126 Stow, *Anna and Tranquillo*, 75.
127 Pakter, *Medieval Canon Law and the Jews*, 330.
128 Caffiero, *Forced Baptisms*, 46; Kleinberg, "Depriving Parents," 145.
129 Stow, *Anna and Tranquillo*, 79.
130 Stow, 80.

5

AQUINAS'S DEFENSE OF JEWISH PARENTAL AUTHORITY

The twofold aim of this chapter is to analyze Aquinas's thought with attention to the key questions that emerged in the 1858 debate and to adjudicate whether Aquinas's teaching is interpreted correctly by the papal counsel and the Mortara family's plea.

I proceed in four steps. In the first section, I show that the context of Aquinas's teaching against baptism invitis parentibus is the fallout from the mid-thirteenth-century Christian discovery of the Talmud and other rabbinic literature. Some Christians responded to the discovery of this literature with a campaign to coerce Jews to convert to Christianity. The campaign included strategies that broke from the Augustinian tradition of toleration. For example, some theologians argued that Jewish children should be baptized against the will of their parents.

In the second section, I answer the first question that surfaced from our study of the 1858 dispute: whether Aquinas holds that forced baptism of Jewish children is lawful or licit, and the related question of whether forced baptism is lawful in certain exceptions, such as to save the soul of an infant from the danger of spiritual death. Here, I explain the multifaceted rationale behind Aquinas's rejection of various arguments that Jewish children should be baptized invitis parentibus and his theological defense of Jewish parental authority. I show that Aquinas defended Jewish parental authority by working to overcome a perceived conflict between the privileges of the Church and the parental authority of unbelievers, that is, the Roman legal institution of patria potestas. Aquinas argued that it is an injustice to violate parental authority for theological purposes since the custom of the Church is opposed to forced baptism, and parental authority is like a *spiritualis uterus* or spiritual womb in the order of natural right, which is an aspect of the

natural law. Aquinas also rejected the argument that one should baptize a child of unbelievers to save the child from spiritual death.

In the third section, I answer whether Aquinas teaches that the forced baptism of a child of unbelievers is nevertheless a valid baptism. I discuss why Aquinas's interest in defending the authority of parents over their children is rooted in his theology of baptism as the sacrament of faith and his understanding of faith as a theological virtue. Here, I also address the difficult question of whether Aquinas thinks coerced baptisms of adults are nonetheless valid.

In the fourth section, I answer whether Aquinas teaches that Jewish parents lose their authority over their children if the latter are baptized. In other words, does Aquinas think that the Church possesses a "second divine right" that outweighs the authority of Jewish parents and that would allow for their removal? I argue that on Aquinas's terms, taking away a child from his or her parents is considered stealing, as John Capreolus recognized. I also show that in Aquinas the Church does not have a right over children of non-Catholic parents if they are baptized and that such children should remain with their parents.

In the conclusion, I adjudicate whether Aquinas's teaching is interpreted correctly by the papal counsel and by the Mortara family's two-part document. I argue that, for the most part, the interpretation of Aquinas in the *Pro-memoria* and *Syllabus* represents a more accurate picture of Aquinas's teaching on the questions that emerged in the 1858 debate. However, the papal counsel's reply is also correct on two points.

THE THIRTEENTH-CENTURY CONTEXT OF AQUINAS'S TEACHING

In the thirteenth century, Christian attitudes toward Jews and Judaism became "essentially suspicious and aggressive."[1] Christian leaders implemented polices that were aimed at defending Christian society from the perceived threat of the Talmud and other rabbinic literature.[2] Some Franciscans and Dominicans used their expanding knowledge of the rabbinic tradition, often sourced by Jewish converts, to organize campaigns that advocated for

---

[1] Grayzel, vol. 2, 3.

[2] Robert Chazan explains that the Christian discovery of the Jewish sources began with Peter the Venerable in the twelfth century and continued with Nicholas Donin in the middle of the thirteenth century. Robert Chazan, *From Anti-Judaism to Anti-Semitism: Ancient and Medieval Christian Constructions of Jewish History* (New York: Cambridge, 2016), 137. See also John Friedman, Jean Connell Hoff, and Robert Chazan, eds., *The Trial of the Talmud, Paris, 1240* (Toronto: Pontifical Institute of Medieval Studies, 2012).

papal and royal support for forced sermons and the confiscation of Jewish books. "There was renewed sensitivity to the age-old question of how those people most directly conversant with God's initial revelation could fail to read its implications correctly. This made the Jews, for some in the Church, a matter of greater concern than their limited numbers warranted."[3] These defensive and aggressive attitudes would mature into "the first truly serious Christian proselytizing campaign among the Jews."[4] According to Robert Chazan, "What emerges most strikingly, is that this mid-thirteenth-century effort breaks new ground in the seriousness of the commitment to win over Jews to the Christian faith."[5]

The leading figures in these campaigns were Jewish converts to Christianity, including the Dominican Nicholas Donin, a French Jew and former Talmud student. Donin converted to Christianity and denounced the Talmud. In a letter to the papal curia in 1236 he claimed the Talmud was not to be tolerated by Christian society.[6] Pope Gregory IX (r. 1227–41) sent letters to monarchs and ecclesiastical leaders across Christendom that included thirty-five accusations against the Talmud that Chazan thinks were likely composed by Donin. The letters reflect elements of Donin's accusations.[7]

---

[3] Robert Chazan, *From Anti-Judaism*, 136–37; Robert Chazan, *Daggers of Faith: Thirteenth-Century Christian Missionizing and Jewish Response* (Los Angeles: University of California Press, 1989), 1, 30.

[4] Chazan, *Daggers*, 1.

[5] Chazan, 3. Scholars largely agree that the mission strategy was new, although there is dispute over its meaning and significance. Robin Vose argues that the idea of a particular Dominican mission that deliberately prioritized and pioneered the conversion of Jews is false. Vose thinks the Dominicans were mostly focused on teaching and eliminating heresy and dissent within the Church.

> External mission was the exception rather than the norm. For the most part medieval Dominicans were neither able nor particularly willing to work toward the conversion of non-Christians. It would be a distortion of history to take their few theoretical statements on mission, combined with an equally few actual examples of proselytizing behavior, and conclude that "serious missionizing" characterized relations between Dominicans and non-Christians throughout the Middle Ages and into the Modern period.

Robin Vose, *Dominicans, Muslims, and Jews in the Medieval Crown of Aragon* (New York: Cambridge University Press, 2011), 250.

[6] Edward H. Flannery, *The Anguish of the Jews: Twenty-Three Centuries of Antisemitism* (Mahwah, NJ: Paulist Press, 2004), 104.

[7] Jews "are not content with the Old Law, which God gave to Moses in writing"; they "affirm that God gave another law that is called Talmud"; the Talmud "contains matter that is so abusive and so unspeakable that it arouses shame in those who mention it and horror in those who hear it"; and the Talmud "is said to be the chief cause that holds the Jews obstinate in their perfidy." Chazan, *From Anti-Judaism*, 137. Gregory IX's letters are published in Simonsohn, vol. 2, 1.172 (June 9, 1239) letter to the Archbishops of France. See also letters 1.171 no. 162 (June 9, 1239) to

In 1240, Donin organized a papally commissioned public trial of the Talmud in Paris that included a disputation between Donin and a panel of four rabbis.[8] "The Talmud was put on trial before a jury of university scholars and a set of northern French rabbis serving as witnesses for the defense. The Talmud was found guilty of at least some of the charges, and one or two years later large quantities of Talmud manuscripts ... were consigned to the flames in one of the major squares of the French kingdom's capital city."[9] Twenty-four wagonloads of Talmudic texts were burned in Paris. Gregory IX ordered the monarchs of Western Christendom to confiscate the Talmud.[10] Some monarchs did not comply, but the papal order to burn the Talmud was carried out multiple times.

Gregory was motivated, in part, by Donin's idea that the elimination of the Talmud would expedite the conversion of Jews.[11] In Chazan's view, Donin "represents a major milestone in the projection of negative imagery of Jewish present and past in medieval Europe."[12] "A clear message had been sent throughout Christendom: rabbis and their books were everywhere under suspicion and threat of prosecution for disseminating allegedly harmful beliefs."[13]

Aquinas lived and worked in the same period in which this proselytizing campaign was born.[14] The campaign eroded the traditional notion of Augustinian toleration and *Sicut Iudaeis*.[15] Aquinas defended this tradition and argued that Jewish religious life must be tolerated.[16] The Jews should be allowed to observe their rites.

The anti-Talmud campaign included a focus on children. "Within a year [of the burning of the Talmud in 1242] they turned their attention from Jews'

William of Auvergne, bishop of Paris, and 1.173 no. 164 (June 20, 1239) to the king of Portugal, in the same volume.

8 Vose, *Dominicans, Muslims, and Jews*, 140.

9 Friedman, *The Trial of the Talmud*, 1.

10 Walter Pakter, *Medieval Canon Law and the Jews* (Ebelsbach, Germany: Gremler, 1988), 322; Benjamin Z. Kedar, "Canon Law and the Burning of the Talmud," *BMCL* 9 (1979): 79–82. Kedar notes that Gregory's successor, Innocent IV, had a far less expansive view of the pope's right to judge Jews.

11 Grayzel, vol. 2, 8–9.

12 Chazan, *From Anti-Judaism*, 139.

13 Vose, *Dominicans, Muslims, and Jews*, 141.

14 Jeremy Cohen, *The Friars and the Jews: The Evolution of Medieval Anti-Judaism* (New York: Cornell University Press, 1982).

15 Grayzel, vol. 2, 9.

16 ST II.II 10.11 ad. 1–3.

symbolic roots to their real branches, their children."[17] "Toward the end of [Aquinas's] career there was... new pressure for taking Jewish children from their parents so that they might be given a Christian upbringing."[18]

Therefore, the context of Aquinas's defense of Jewish parental authority is a period when European Jews and their families faced suspicious and aggressive Christian attitudes, and increased pressure to convert to Christianity.

Aquinas was aware of several arguments that sought to erode the Church's custom against forced baptisms and reframe such acts as lawful if directed at the children of unbelievers. The pressure to baptize Jewish children also occurred in the context of a tension between civil law and canon law and doubts about binding ruling in cases of conflicting opinions.[19] The issue of Jewish parental rights took on significance after Innocent and Clement's decretals recognizing mixed marriages.[20]

Canonists disagreed over the legitimacy of baptizing Jewish children in these contexts. Kenneth Pennington observes that "a significant issue was the fate of Jewish children in families in which one of the parents became Christian or in which the parents did not convert, but in which a child had been baptized."[21]

Gratian had incorporated two canons from the Fourth Council of Toledo dealing with this problem, first *Iudei qui chrstianas* (C.28 q.1 c.10), concerning a child with one Jewish parent, and a second, *Iudeorum* (C.28 q.1 c.11), dealing with involuntary baptism of children with two Jewish parents.[22] The texts involved conflicts between Christian theology and the Roman legal tradition of patria potestas, which concerned "a core of rights and moral obligations to protect the interests of the minor child."[23]

A classic case decided in 1229 by Gregory IX illustrates the conflict that was debated during Aquinas's lifetime. The case revolved around the status of a Jewish child. A Jewish father in Strasbourg converted to Christianity, leaving his devout Jewish wife and four-year old son. Gregory awarded custody to the newly converted father on the basis of both patria potestas and

---

17 Pakter, *Medieval Canon Law and the Jews*, 322.

18 Edward Synan, review of *Aquinas and the Jews*, by John Hood, *Church History Review* 82, no. 3 (1996): 550–51.

19 Robert Chazan, *Church, State, and the Jew in the Middle Ages* (New York: Behrman House, 1980), 27.

20 X 4.14.4; X 5.6.9; Pakter, *Medieval Canon Law and the Jews*, 319.

21 Kenneth Pennington, "Law's Violence," 30.

22 Pakter, *Medieval Canon Law and the Jews*, 318.

23 Pakter, 315.

favor fidei, understood as "the greatest advantage to the Christian faith."[24] "It became a benchmark for deciding the rights of father, mother, and child for centuries."[25]

When Hostiensis defended Gregory IX's decretal, he argued that although the mother had multiple rights to have custody, the converted father's single right of patria potestas was the deciding factor.[26] The Dominican Raymond de Peñafort included Gregory's appellate decision *Ex literis tuis* in the *Decretals* (X 3.33.2).

The pope's statement about patria potestas and *favor fidei*, however, created a problem that perplexed jurists: could a Jewish mother who converted to Christianity be awarded custody *against* the parental rights of a Jewish father? If so, the father's parental rights would be in conflict with that which advanced the Christian faith.[27]

Aviad M. Kleinberg points out that the main problem that needed to be addressed was not the child's consent or lack thereof, but the infringement upon the rights of the (unwilling) parents.[28] The debate concerning forced baptism in Aquinas's age was therefore focused on the question of whether perceived advantages to the Church could override patria potestas.

Various opinions on this question circulated in the medieval academic world. French Dominican theologian William of Rennes (c. 1259) argued around 1235 in his commentary on Raymond de Peñafort's *Summa de casibus* that Jewish children can be "offered" to baptism even if the parents are unwilling:

> But whether they could take their children away and baptize them? I answer: They cannot take away adults unless they have willingly agreed to be baptized. They cannot take away their children if they are not the lords over them. But if truly Jews are slaves to their lords as I believe . . . princes of Jewish slaves can take their children without any injury, since they are slaves Jewish parents do not have any power over their children. Princes can give their children just as he can give his servants to others, or sell them into slavery, so too they may offer them to baptism even if the

---

[24] Pakter, 319; Aviad M. Kleinberg, "Depriving Parents of the Consolation of Children: Two Legal *Consilia* on the Baptism of Jewish Children," In *De Sion exibit lex et verbum domini de Hierusalem: Essays on Medieval Law, Liturgy and Literature in Honour of Amnon Linder*, ed. Yitzhak Hen (Turnhout: Brepols, 2001), 135.

[25] Pennington, "Gratian and the Jews," 119.

[26] Hostiensis, *Lectura on the Decretals Gregorii noni* (Strassburg, 1512) fol. 131rb to X 3.33.2.

[27] Pakter, *Medieval Canon Law and the Jews*, 320; Kleinberg, "Depriving Parents," 135.

[28] Kleinberg, "Depriving Parents," 135.

parents are unwilling. When princes do so they gain merit for saving the children through the sacrament of the faith, provided that they would not compel the parents to convert to the faith.[29]

Rennes's argument was repeated in the writings of others, such as Duns Scotus (1265–1308), and the French Dominican Vincent of Beauvais (d. 1264). Rennes's commentary was also transmitted alongside Raymond de Peñaforte's work in most of the manuscripts, and he enjoyed an almost equal authority during the later Middle Ages.

Aquinas's arguments against these proposals can be seen as an attempt to defend the Catholic doctrine on the fundamental right of Jews to live safely in Christian society, and to practice their religion.[30] We now turn to the analysis of his thought with attention to the arguments for forced baptism of Jewish children written by some of his contemporaries.

WHETHER AQUINAS HOLDS THAT BAPTISM OF JEWISH CHILDREN INVITIS PARENTIBUS IS LAWFUL

In this section, I answer whether Aquinas holds that forced baptism of Jewish children is lawful and whether forced baptism is lawful in certain exceptions. Aquinas addressed the question of whether Jewish children should be baptized invitis parentibus in ST II.II 10.12, written in 1271 or early 1272. He also addressed the question in his *QDL* 2.4.2, which he debated in Paris sometime in 1268–72.[31] Aquinas addressed the topic a third time in ST III 68.10, which

---

[29] William of Rennes, Apparatus on *Summa de casibus* (Rome, 1603) 33a s.v. *aspertatibus*. I am grateful to Kenneth Pennington for sharing with me Rennes's position. See "Guillelmus Redonensis," in *Bio-Bibliographical Guide to Medieval and Early Modern Jurists*, Report no. a260 (Cambridge: Ames Foundation, Harvard Law School, 2023), https://amesfoundation.law.harvard.edu/BioBibCanonists/Report_Biobib2.php?record_id=a260.

[30] Some scholars think Aquinas departs from the tolerant Augustinian tradition. See Jeremy Cohen, *Living Letters of the Law: Ideas of the Jew in Medieval Christianity* (Berkeley: University of California Press, 1999), 372. Cohen extends this argument in *Christ Killers: The Jews and the Passion from the Bible to the Big Screen* (New York: Oxford University Press, 2007).

[31] Quodlibetal Questions (*Quaestiones de Quolibet*) are a collection of texts from disputations over which Aquinas presided while teaching at the University of Paris from 1256 to 1259 and again from 1268 to 1272. English translations of the QDL are based on Turner Nevitt and Brian Davies, *Thomas Aquinas's Quodlibetal Questions* (New York: Oxford University Press, 2020), cited hereafter as *QDL*. Torrell says that questions I–VI and XII come from the period 1268–72, but beyond this it is difficult to situate them with certainty. Jean-Pierre Torrell, *Saint Thomas Aquinas*, vol. 1, *The Person and His Work* (Washington, DC: The Catholic University of America Press, 2023), 396. Davies and Nevitt explain that these questions were not of Aquinas's own choosing but were raised for him to answer in an open forum where the teacher fielded unexpected questions in a public setting. This makes the questions unique among Aquinas's writings since normally he

he wrote in the months before December 1273, before he stopped work.[32] The question in ST II.II 10.12 is entitled, "Should the children of Jews or other unbelievers be baptized against their parents' wishes?" In ST III 68.10 and QDL 2.4.2, the question is stated similarly.[33]

A close reading of Aquinas's texts requires attention to the teaching style of the disputed question and how this teaching style is reflected in his writings. Disputed questions or disputations (*disputationes*) refers to a scholastic teaching style that became prominent at the University of Oxford and Paris around 1256.[34] In a disputation, the magister would select a question, and students would then be required to make arguments for possible answers. The master would then comment on the question and make a formal *determinatio* or answer. He would also respond to student arguments. Aquinas regularly conducted teaching sessions in this style.

In Aquinas's *Summa theologiae*, the basic unit is a written disputation, which is referred to as the *articulus* or article. Collections of articles on different questions were referred to as *summas*. In other words, Aquinas's *Summa theologiae* is not made up of chapters but articles. The parts of the article include the question, arguments, sed contra, respondeo, and the replies to arguments. In each article, a question is raised, with brief arguments (sometimes referred to as objections) for one way of answering it listed first, at the top of the article.

The arguments are then followed by the sed contra. The sed contra, in itself, is not the author's answer; it is commonly misinterpreted because it is usually in opposition to the list of arguments that came before it.[35] The sed contra is usually an expression of a rationale for the opposite position to the arguments. It displays the thinking behind the alternate position. The sed contra is misinterpreted because it is often similar to the answer of the author, which appears in the next section, the respondeo. But the sed contra is *not* the same as the respondeo. The author's position, or respondeo, begins with *respondeo dicendum* (I respond that it is to be said). Aquinas's answers

---

decided what to discuss. "In his quodlibetals we find his report of what he was forced by others to discuss in 'real time.'" Nevitt and Davies, xxiii.

32 The *Tertia Pars* was probably begun in Paris in 1271–72, and Aquinas wrote it until December 1273 in Naples, which is the date he stopped writing. Torrell, *Person and Work*, 333.

33 In ST III 68.10, the question is, "Whether children of Jews or other unbelievers be baptized against the will of their parents?" In QDL 2.4.2, the question is, "It seems that children of Jews should be baptized against their parents' will."

34 My presentation of how Aquinas's writings reflect the structure of the disputed question draws upon the work of Chenu, Torrell, Davies, and Nevitt.

35 Marie-Dominique Chenu, OP, *Toward Understanding St. Thomas Aquinas* (Chicago: H. Regnery, 1964), 95.

also appear in his replies to the arguments, which come last. It is only in the respondeo, and the replies to arguments, that one can determine Aquinas's answer to a question.

For the purpose of clarity, and to avoid redundancy, I discuss all Aquinas's reasons for rejecting the practice of baptism invitis parentibus across the three relevant texts instead of analyzing each text individually. I label the reasons as R1, R2, R3, et cetera (according to the same list used in chapter 2). I set most of Aquinas's texts in the footnotes. I indicate the location of each reason in the text and differences between texts in the footnotes as well. Not all the reasons will be treated in this section since some pertain more to the questions of subsequent sections. After I discuss Aquinas's reasons against baptism invitis parentibus, I discuss all the arguments (or objections) of Aquinas's contemporaries who argued in support of forced baptism of Jewish children. Again, Aquinas lists these arguments against his position in each of his respective articles on the matter. After I list each argument, I then explain Aquinas's replies.

The Argument from the Custom of the Church (R1)

Aquinas thinks the repeated proposals by some of his contemporaries to baptize the children of unbelievers invitis parentibus are not at all reasonable and are in fact hazardous for the Church.[36] He says it would be dangerous

---

36 ST II.II 10.12 co.:
   The custom [consuetudo] of the Church has maximum authority and must be observed in all matters, since the teaching of Catholic doctors has its authority from the Church. Hence we are more subject to the authority of the Church rather than to that of Augustine or Jerome or any other doctor. Now it was never the custom of the Church to baptize the children of the Jews against the will of their parents, although at times past there have been many very powerful catholic princes like Constantine and Theodosius, with whom most holy bishops have been on most friendly terms, as Sylvester with Constantine, and Ambrose with Theodosius, who would certainly not have failed to obtain this favor from them if it had been at all reasonable. It seems therefore hazardous to repeat this assertion, that the children of Jews should be baptized against their parents' wishes, in contradiction to the Church's custom [consuetudinem].
   There are two reasons for this custom. One is on account of the danger to the faith. Children baptized before they have the use of reason, afterwards when they come to perfect age, might easily be persuaded by their parents to renounce what they had unknowingly embraced; and this would be detrimental to the faith.
   The other reason is that it is repugnant to natural justice [iustitiae naturali]. For a child is by nature part of its father: thus, at first, its body is not distinct from its parents, so long as it is in its mother's womb; and later on after birth, and before it has the use of its free-will, it is in the care of its parents, which is like a spiritual womb, for so long as man has not the use of reason, he differs not from an irrational animal; so that even as an ox or a horse belongs to someone who, according to the civil law, can use them as he wishes, as his own instrument, so, according to the natural law [iure

to invent this new strategy when for centuries it had not been the Church's custom to baptize Jewish children against their parents' wishes: "And so it seems dangerous to concoct this assertion about baptizing the sons of Jews even if their parents are opposed, as it is beyond the custom of the Church observed up to this time."[37]

In Aquinas's view, the custom of the Church is against forced baptism, including children of unbelievers.[38] In his answer, he immediately marshals the "maximum authority" of the Church, which he says is to be followed in all matters and is more authoritative than the teachings of any other doctor: "The custom of the Church has maximum authority and must be observed in all matters, since the teaching of Catholic doctors has its authority from the Church. Hence we are more subject to the authority of the Church rather than to that of Augustine or Jerome or any other doctor."[39]

As mentioned above, for Aquinas, custom (*consuetudo*) "has the force of law" if it is done repeatedly and proceeds from a deliberate judgment of reason.[40] For Aquinas, the proposals to apply the ancient practice of emergency baptism to the infants of Jewish families *invitis parentibus* ran against the repeated judgments of the bishops and popes of the Church.

To illustrate his point, Aquinas suggests that his readers consider Pope Sylvester I (r. 314–35) and Bishop Ambrose (374–97). Given their close friendship with Roman emperors, these men certainly would have called for legislation mandating forced baptism of Jewish children, if it were in accord with reason:

> *naturali*], a son, before coming to the use of reason, is under his father's care. Hence it would be contrary to natural justice [*iustitiae naturali*], if a child, before having the use of reason, were to be taken away from its parents' custody, or anything done to it against its parents' wish. As soon, however, as it begins to have the use of its freewill, it begins to belong to itself, and is able to look after itself, in matters concerning the Divine or the natural law [*iuris divini vel naturalis*], and then it should be induced, not by compulsion but by persuasion, to embrace the faith: it can then consent to the faith, and be baptized, even against its parents' wish; but not before it comes to the use of reason. Hence it is said of the children of the fathers of old that they were saved in the faith of their parents; whereby we are given to understand that it is the parents' duty to look after the salvation of their children, especially before they come to the use of reason.

---

37 I borrow "concoct" from Mark Jordan. See his translation in Saint Thomas Aquinas, *On Faith: Summa Theologiae Part 2–2, Questions 1–16*, trans. Mark Jordan (Notre Dame: University of Notre Dame Press, 1990), 210.

38 Aquinas sees D.45, in ST III 68.10 s.c. as representative of the view that forced baptism is against the custom of the Church.

39 ST II.II 10.12 co.

40 ST I.II 97.3 co. Matthew Levering made this observation in his *Engaging the Doctrine of Israel: A Christian Israelology in Dialogue with Ongoing Judaism* (Eugene, OR: Cascade Books, 2021), 414.

Now it was never the custom of the Church to baptize the children of the Jews against the will of their parents, although at times past there have been many very powerful catholic princes like Constantine and Theodosius, with whom most holy bishops have been on most friendly terms, as Sylvester with Constantine, and Ambrose with Theodosius, who would certainly not have failed to obtain this favor from them if it had been at all reasonable. It seems therefore hazardous to repeat this assertion, that the children of Jews should be baptized against their parents' wishes, in contradiction to the Church's custom.[41]

The Argument from Danger of Future Rejection of the Faith (R2)

Next, Aquinas gives two reasons why the custom of the Church is opposed to such forced baptisms. The first reason is labeled here as R2: it actually poses a danger to the faith. The danger is that the children "would be liable to lapse into unbelief, by reason of their natural affection for their parents." Aquinas seems to assume that even if such children were baptized, they would be brought up by their unbelieving parents, and so "might easily be persuaded to renounce what they had unknowingly embraced."[42] We will return to this argument in section 3, since the argument pertains to the question of whether children baptized *invitis parentibus* receive a valid baptism.

The Argument from the Natural and Divine Law That the Human Person Comes to Know God through Reason (R3)

The second reason why the Church is opposed to such baptisms takes up the majority of the *respondeo* and is identified here as R3: baptizing Jewish children against the will of their parents would be repugnant to natural justice (*repugnat iustitiae naturali*). It is repugnant to natural justice because children, like adults, must come to God through reason. First, we will discuss

---

41 ST II.II 10.12 co. In *QDL* 2.4.2 co., Aquinas's *respondeo* also begins with this argument and the text is almost identical to II.II 10.12 co. However, he refers to the proposal as "novel." In ST III 68.10 co., Aquinas does not include the argument that the popes and emperors did not follow this practice, but he does appeal to the custom of the Church: "Therefore it is not the custom of the Church to baptize the children of unbelievers against their parents' will."

42 In *QDL* 2.42, the text is once again almost identical: "Such baptisms are a danger to the faith. If children without the ability to use reason receive baptism, then once they are old enough, their parents could easily get them to abandon what they received in ignorance, which would be to the detriment of the faith." In ST III 68.10 co., Aquinas shortens the argument: "Moreover under the circumstances it would be dangerous to baptize the children of unbelievers; for they would be liable to lapse into unbelief, by reason of their natural affection for their parents."

natural justice. Second, we will discuss why children and adults must come to God through reason.

For Aquinas, natural justice can be considered an aspect of natural law and is universal. Natural justice is the basis of legal justice since it is not subjective but exists always and everywhere. It does not have force only in a certain province, nor does it arise from human conjecture. Why? Aquinas, following Aristotle, argues that natural justice is the same everywhere, among all people, because it is from nature.[43] In the divinely established natural order of things (*naturali ordine ordinatur*) there are principles naturally known to the human person "such as evil must be avoided, no one is to be unjustly injured, and theft must not be committed and so on."[44]

An important natural inclination that Aquinas is concerned to defend as an object of natural justice is the natural inclination of the rational human person to know the truth about God. As will be discussed in the next section at length, Aquinas teaches that in matters concerning divine law a person should only be persuaded to the faith, not moved by compulsion. Aquinas argues that before a child of unbelievers has the use of its free will, it can be baptized only if the parents will this.

> As soon, however, as it begins to have the use of its free-will, it begins to belong to itself, and is able to look after itself, in matters concerning the Divine or the natural law, and then it should be induced, not by compulsion but by persuasion, to embrace the faith: it can then consent to the faith, and be baptized, even against its parents' wish; but not before it comes to the use of reason.[45]

As Aquinas explains in more detail in the reply to the fourth argument, according to the natural law the human person is directed to God by reason. It is through reason that a person comes to know God. This is why a child,

---

[43] *Sententia Ethic.*, lib. 5 1.12 n. 8. See also Aquinas's comment in *Sententia Ethic.*, lib. 5 1.12 n. 3, where he explains that
> natural justice does not consist in what seems or does not seem to be, i.e., it does not arise from human conjecture but from nature. In speculative matters there are some things naturally known, like indemonstrable principles, and truths closely connected with them; there are other things discovered by human ingenuity, and conclusions flowing from these. Likewise in practical matters there are some principles naturally known as it were, indemonstrable principles and truths related to them, as evil must be avoided, no one is to be unjustly injured, theft must not be committed and so on; others are devised by human diligence which are here called just legal enactments.

[44] *Sententia Ethic.*, lib. 5 1.12 n. 3.

[45] ST II.II 10.12 co. In the thirteenth century, the age at which children could be baptized without the consent of parents or guardians was seven years old. After that age a child could choose for itself. Grayzel, vol. 2, 14.

before it has the use of free will, must be brought to God through the reason of its parents, not by compulsion. For Aquinas, this means the child must be brought to God through the parents' decisions on matters concerning divine law.[46]

Aquinas also appeals to the example that a forced baptism of an adult would also be contrary to natural justice, since if an adult unbeliever has reason and free will, then the person controls their own actions in things that are of divine or natural law: "Wherefore it would be contrary to natural justice if such children were baptized against their parents' will; just as it would be if one having the use of reason were baptized against his will."

The Argument from the Natural Law That Children Are Contained under the Care of Parents as a Kind of Spiritual Womb (R4)

Under natural justice we must consider another important term in Aquinas's defense of Jewish parental authority: natural right (*ius naturale*). Indeed, Aquinas says the children of unbelievers must not be baptized against the will of their parents according to the "order of natural right" (*ordinem iuris naturalis*).

What might this mean? In his commentary on Aristotle's *Ethics*, Aquinas identifies the education of offspring as an inclination of nature common to all people and refers to this inclination as a natural right. He also refers to the education of offspring as a natural inclination and precept of the natural law in his "Treatise on Law" in the *Summa theologiae*.[47] Aquinas says elsewhere in the *Summa* that the object of justice is the right or *ius*. Since the natural right of the education of offspring is included under natural justice, Aquinas

---

46 In *QDL* 2.4.2 co., Aquinas's teaching on this point is closely connected with R4, on the spiritual womb, which I will discuss below with. In ST III 68.10 co., this reason is put first, and it is similar to ST II.II 10.12 co. and *QDL* 2.4.2 co., but Aquinas leaves out the spiritual womb metaphor:
  The children of unbelievers either have the use of reason or they have not. If they have, then they already begin to control their own actions, in things that are of Divine or natural law. And therefore of their own accord, and against the will of their parents, they can receive Baptism, just as they can contract marriage. Consequently, such can lawfully be advised and persuaded to be baptized. If, however, they have not yet the use of free will, according to the natural law they are under the care of their parents as long as they cannot look after themselves.... Wherefore it would be contrary to natural justice if such children were baptized against their parents' will; just as it would be if one having the use of reason were baptized against his will.

47 ST I.II 94.2 co. "There is in man an inclination to things that pertain to him more specially, according to that nature which he has in common with other animals: and in virtue of this inclination, those things are said to belong to the natural law, which nature has taught to all animals, such as sexual intercourse, education of offspring and so forth."

thinks the demands of natural justice require that we do no injustice to the children of our neighbors with regard to the education of their children, and that this is part of the natural law.[48] For Aquinas, Jewish parental authority is rooted in the natural law because natural justice requires that Christians render to unbeliever parents the natural right to the education of their offspring. As Jean Porter has argued, men and women have a moral power to demand forbearance from others in some circumstances in Aquinas, on the basis of a right grounded in nature.[49]

This is why Aquinas explains in detail in his *respondeo* that a son is by natural right (*ius naturale*) under his father's care (*sub cura patris*). One of those circumstances is Jewish parental authority over their children. This notion of a parental right included under natural justice can be considered an aspect of what Porter has called Aquinas's "dynamic conception of the natural law."[50] For this reason, references to *ordinem iuris naturalis* (order of natural right) throughout Aquinas's defense of Jewish parental authority can be translated as the "order of the natural law." The natural law, for Aquinas, is the eternal law imprinted on creatures.[51] As will be explained in detail below, the natural law gives creatures their proper inclinations and acts.[52]

Aquinas then elaborates upon why a child is, before having use of reason, part of its parents by natural right through the use of a metaphor that he refers to as a *spiritualis uterus*, or "spiritual womb."[53] He says that a child is by nature part of its father (*Filius enim naturaliter est aliquid*) in two ways: "Thus, at first, it is not distinct from its parents as to its body, so long as it is in its mother's womb; and later on after birth, and before it has the use of its free-will, it is under the care of its parents, which is like a spiritual womb."[54]

---

[48] ST II.II 57.1 co.

[49] Jean Porter, "Eternal Law, Natural Law, Natural Rights: Freedom and Power in Aquinas," in *The Cambridge Handbook of Natural Law and Human Rights*, ed. Tom P. S. Angier, Iain T. Benson, and Mark Retter (New York: Cambridge University Press, 2022), 200.

[50] Jean Porter, "Eternal Law, Natural Law," 191.

[51] See ST I.II 91–92.

[52] ST I.II 91.2 co.

[53] ST II.II 10.12 co.

[54] ST II.II 10.12 co. However, Aquinas says in ST III 68.11 that the child's soul is distinct from the mother's soul. In 68.11 ad. 2, he explains that "an internal member of the mother is something of hers by continuity and material union of the part with the whole: whereas a child while in its mother's womb is something of hers through being joined with, and yet distinct from her." It seems this sense of "continuity and material union of the part with the whole" is perhaps what Aquinas has in mind when he says, in ST II.II 10.12 co., that the child is described as "not distinct from its parents as to its body, so long as it is in its mother's womb."

The child is by nature part of its parents when the body of the child is enfolded or contained (*continetur*) within its mother's womb. Yet a child is by nature part of its parents in another sense. And Aquinas once again uses *continetur* to specify the relation of the child to its parents according to the natural law. After a child is born, he or she is still a part of its parents according to the natural law in that the child is *continetur* within the care of its parents.

Aquinas's womb analogy is intended to highlight how the authority of the Jewish parents over their young child, after he has been born but before he has use of reason, is an expression of God's wise governance of the created order. The natural right of Jewish parents to care for their children is a design of God's divine providence. Human parents participate in this divine providence through their rational capacity, which is also ordered according to God's wisdom. It is through the rational, spiritual nature of each parent's desire for perfection that they are already directed to God. The rational will of the unbelieving parent is therefore not indifferent to God. God is not indifferent to the unbelieving parents. Natural justice requires that others recognize the natural right of the parents. This is, in part, why Aquinas says that children before they have the use of reason are contained under the parents' care like a spiritual womb in the order of natural right.[55]

Aquinas's usage of this metaphor echoes the way he uses *uterus* or womb to describe how infant baptism is somewhat like carnal birth in that the children are dependent upon the action of the Church for spiritual nourishment. In the baptism of children of Christian parents, children do not have faith but they depend upon the Church and the faith of their sponsors for nourishment as they did in the womb of their mothers.[56] Aquinas writes, "The spiritual regeneration effected by Baptism is somewhat like carnal birth, in this respect, that as the child while in the mother's womb receives nourishment not independently, but through the nourishment of its mother, so also children before the use of reason, being as it were in the womb of their mother the Church, receive salvation not by their own act, but by the act of the Church."[57]

Moreover, Aquinas uses the phrase "spiritual womb" as a metaphor for how a person, no matter how old, can enter the Church through the

---

55 *QDL* 2.4.2 co.

56 Aquinas also uses the metaphor to refer to the virginal womb as the shrine of the Holy Spirit wherein the Spirit had formed the flesh of Christ. ST III 28.3 co.

57 ST III 68.9 ad. 1.

sacrament of baptism. He comments on Nicodemus's famous question to Christ in John 3:4: "How can a person once grown old be born again?"[58]

> Regeneration seemed impossible because of the mode of carnal generation. For in the beginning, when a man is generated, he is small in size, so that his mother's womb can contain him; but later, after he is born, he continues to grow and reaches such a size that he cannot be contained within his mother's womb. And so Nicodemus says, *can he enter a second time into his mother's womb and be born again*? As if to say: he cannot, because the womb cannot contain him. But this does not apply to spiritual generation. For no matter how spiritually old a man might become through sin: *because I kept silent, all my bones grew old* (Ps 31:3), he can, with the help of divine grace, become new: *your youth will be renewed like the eagle's* (Ps 102:5). And no matter how enormous he is, he can enter the spiritual womb [*uterum spiritualem*] of the Church by the sacrament of baptism. And it is clear what that spiritual womb [*uterus spiritualis*] is; otherwise it would never have been said: *from the womb, before the daystar, I begot you* (Ps 109:3).[59]

The metaphor Aquinas uses for how the Church nourishes newly born Christians is applied to how Jewish parents nourish and care for their children after they are born. The idea that the children of Jews should be baptized against their parents' wishes is repugnant to natural justice because a child is in the care of its parents by nature, which is like a spiritual womb. That Aquinas would use "spiritual womb" as a metaphor for the care that Jewish parents provide for their children before they have the use of reason indicates his high view of parental authority as an order of the natural law established by divine providence. In using "spiritual womb" he stresses the conjunction of what might seem to some as two apparently opposite spheres, the spiritual and the physical, the supernatural and the natural.[60]

---

58 John 3:1–5, NIV:
> Now there was a Pharisee named Nicodemus, a ruler of the Jews. He came to Jesus at night and said to him, "Rabbi, we know that you are a teacher who has come from God, for no one can do these signs that you are doing unless God is with him." Jesus answered and said to him, "Amen, amen, I say to you, no one can see the kingdom of God without being born from above." Nicodemus said to him, "How can a person once grown old be born again? Surely he cannot reenter his mother's womb and be born again, can he?" Jesus answered, "Amen, amen, I say to you, no one can enter the kingdom of God without being born of water and Spirit."

59 *Ioan.* 3, lect. 1, 438–39.

60 I am indebted to Professor Elèna Mortara for this insight, which she shared with me after reading a draft of this chapter.

Aquinas also reinforces the metaphor and the natural law argument with an analogy from civil Roman law: in the same way that an irrational animal such as an ox can belong to someone by civil law, likewise, a child before it obtains the use of reason, is under the care of its father according to the natural law.[61] Elsewhere, Aquinas says that not even the pope has power to dispense with matters of divine or natural law since their force comes from being divinely established.[62]

The next argument, R5, is that, based on the natural law, nothing can be done to children against the will of their parents. This argument will be considered in section 4 since it pertains to the question of whether such children can be removed from their parents if they are baptized.

The Argument from "the Faith of the Parents" (R6)

Aquinas also roots his argument in Scripture and says that, under the divine law, Jewish parents have a duty to look after the salvation of their children according to the precedent of the "children of the ancients," by which Aquinas means the observation of circumcision among the patriarchs of Israel and their families.[63] For this reason, nothing with regard to divine law is to be done against their will. Aquinas says this is why it is said, before circumcision was given, the children of the ancients were saved through the faith of their parents.[64]

In *QDL* 2.4.2, Aquinas says:

> Once children begin to use free will . . . and are able to make their own decisions in matters of divine or natural law, they can be brought to the faith—not by coercion, but by persuasion—and can accept the faith and consent to be baptized but not before they are able to use reason. Hence the children of the ancients are said to have been saved by *the faith of their parents*, which means that parents are responsible for the salvation of their children, especially before they are capable of using reason.[65]

In ST III 68.10, he writes: "According to the natural law they are under the care of their parents as long as they cannot look after themselves. For which

---

[61] ST II.II 10.12 co.

[62] *QDL* 4.8.2.

[63] Divine law is given by God to direct the human person in an explicit way to her supernatural end. Divine law consists in the Old and New Laws. For the various kinds of law, see ST I.II 91.1–6.

[64] ST II.II 10.12 co.

[65] *QDL* 2.4.2 co. Emphasis added.

reason we say that even the children of the ancients 'were saved through the faith of their parents.'"⁶⁶ And in ST II.II 10.12, Aquinas is even clearer that this appeal to the Old Testament means that it is the duty of Jewish parents to look after the salvation of their own children: "Hence it is said of the children of the fathers of old that they were saved in the faith of their parents; whereby we are given to understand that it is the parents' duty to look after the salvation of their children."

But what does this phrase mean? The phrase "saved by the faith of their parents" is from Peter Lombard's *Sentences*, book 4, I, 8:

> But regarding the men who lived before circumcision, and the women who lived before and after, it is asked what remedy they had against sin. Some say that sacrifices and oblations were helpful to them for the remission of sin. But it is better to say that the men who issued from Abraham were justified by circumcision, and the women by faith and good work, either their own, if they were adults, or their parents', if they were little. As for those who lived before circumcision, children were justified by the faith of their parents, and parents by the power of sacrifices, namely the power which they perceived spiritually in those sacrifices.⁶⁷

In ST III 70.2 (Whether circumcision was instituted in a fitting manner), Aquinas explains that the fathers of old, such as Abraham, received the promise that Christ was to be born of "the Jewish nation" (Gen 22:18, "In thy seed shall all the nations of the earth be blessed") in the rite of circumcision. Circumcision, which was a part of the divine law, was a sacrament given before the Mosaic Law in preparation for baptism. "Moreover, [Abraham] was the first to cut himself off from the society of unbelievers, in accordance with the commandment of the Lord." He explains in III 70.2 ad. 2 that the giving of circumcision took place before the giving of the Mosaic Law because "the body of the faithful" should be gathered by a sensible sign, "which is necessary in order that men be united together in any religion, as Augustine says."⁶⁸

For Aquinas, gathering the Jewish people into the body of the faithful required the institution of circumcision before the giving of the Mosaic Law; and those circumcised carried the promise of Christ in their flesh. The promise of Christ was therefore safeguarded in the body of the faithful

---

66 ST III 68.10 co.

67 Book 4, distinction I, c8. Peter Lombard, *The Sentences*, book 4: *On the Doctrine of Signs*, trans. Giulio Silano (Toronto: Pontifical Institute of Medieval Studies, 2010), 7.

68 ST III 70.2 ad. 3.

by the fathers of old, in particular the parents who taught their families concerning these divine things: "Those Fathers, however, who lived before the Law, taught their families concerning Divine things by way of paternal admonition. Hence the Lord said of Abraham (Genesis 18:19): 'I know that he will command his children, and his household after him to keep the way of the Lord.'"

Therefore, Aquinas's citation of the text from Lombard demonstrates that he thinks the ancient tradition that the children of the Jews received paternal admonition concerning divine things from their parents represents a divine duty of parental authority. Aquinas thinks that this sacred duty of parental authority remained theologically meaningful in the thirteenth century.[69]

We now turn to the arguments *for* baptism of Jewish children against the will of their parents, which Aquinas listed at the beginning of his articles. In ST II.II 10.12, the arguments that Aquinas listed include positions articulated by theologians of his time, such as Rennes. One of the arguments shares a premise with Benedict XIV's 1747 codification of baptism invitis parentibus: providing salvation for the Jewish child justifies violation of the parental right. Because of this connection between the theological rationale underlining this argument and the theological rationale for the exception to forced baptism of Jewish children issued by Benedict XIV, it is worth citing the arguments at length.

The Argument That Unbelief in Parents Is Grounds for Severing Parental Rights (A1)

The first argument *for* baptism invitis parentibus listed in ST II.II 10.12 seems to have aspects of Gregory IX's 1229 case in mind. It can be referred to as the argument that unbelief in parents is grounds for severing parental rights.[70]

Since unbelief of a parent is grounds for abrogation of the parental rights, the children of Jews can be baptized against the will of their parents. Aquinas cites Gratian's *Decretum* C.28 q.1 c.4 and c.5 as authorities for the

---

69 Aquinas does not think the observation of circumcision brings justification as it did before Christ. For the most part, Aquinas thinks these rites *were* but no longer *are* figures of Christ. Nevertheless, Jewish parental authority retains a divine foundation rooted in God's words to Abraham. See chapter 7 for a more detailed discussion of the ongoing theological significance of circumcision in Aquinas.

70 This argument is listed first in ST II.II 10.12 arg. 1 and *QDL* 2.4.2 co. In *QDL* 2.4.2 arg. 1, the argument contains biblical citations that attempt to prove that unbelief dissolves parental rights. The argument is not listed in ST III 68.10.

position. Since this position is listed as the first argument, it can safely be assumed Aquinas thought it was the strongest argument in 1271 or 1272. Aquinas thinks that the first argument is usually the strongest argument against his position. He summarizes the position thus:

> It would seem that the children of Jews and of other unbelievers ought to be baptized against their parents' will. For the bond of marriage is stronger than the right of parental authority over children, since the right of parental authority can be made to cease, when a son is set at liberty; whereas the marriage bond cannot be severed by man, according to Matthew 19:6: "What . . . God hath joined together let no man put asunder." And yet the marriage bond is broken on account of unbelief: for the Apostle says (1 Corinthians 7:15): "If the unbeliever depart, let him depart. For a brother or sister is not under servitude in such cases": and a canon [C.28 q.1 c.17] says that if the unbelieving partner is unwilling to abide with the other, without insult to their Creator, then the other partner is not bound to cohabitation. Much more, therefore, unbelief abrogates the right of unbelieving parents' authority over their children: and consequently their children may be baptized against their parents' will.[71]

The argument is that since an unbelieving spouse can be grounds for severing the marriage bond, unbelief in parents is grounds for severing parental rights.

Aquinas disagrees, since parental authority is based in the natural law and not like the marriage bond, which is based on consent: "In the marriage bond, both husband and wife have the use of the free-will, and each can assent to the faith without the other's consent. But this does not apply to a child before it comes to the use of reason: yet the comparison holds good after the child has come to the use of reason, if it is willing to be converted."[72] In other words, since parental authority is a natural right based in the order of the natural law and not based on consent to a marriage contract, the authority of parents over children cannot be terminated. Here, Aquinas protects Jewish families against an argument that the rejection of the Christian faith invalidates parental authority over their children.[73]

---

71 ST II.II 10.12 arg. 1; *Decretem*, C. 28 q. 1 c. 17.

72 ST II.II 10.12 ad. 1.

73 In my BMC article on Aquinas's teaching in ST II.II 10.12, I said that Aquinas's reply seemed to undermine the claim that unbelief in one parent is grounds for transferring custody of that parent's children to a converted spouse. Tapie, "*Spiritualis Uterus,*" 319. However, in his commentary on the *Sentences*, Aquinas follows the decision of Gregory IX's appellate decision (*Ex literis tuis* in the *Decretals* X 3.33.2) that a child (before he or she reaches the age of reason) of a Jewish convert to Christianity should be awarded custody over against the unbeliever spouse, but the unbeliever spouse has some say in the education of the child: "Notwithstanding that their

The Argument from the Danger of Spiritual Death (A2)

The second argument can be referred to as the argument from the danger of spiritual death. The argument is that it would be a sin to *not* baptize children of unbelievers since these children are in danger of spiritual death. Since they are in such grave danger, and in need of salvation, they can be taken away from their parents and baptized:

> Further, one is more bound to assist a man who is in danger of everlasting death, than one who is in danger of temporal death. Now it would be a sin, if one saw a man in danger of temporal death and failed to go to his aid. Since, then, the children of Jews and other unbelievers are in danger of everlasting death, should they be left to their parents who would imbue them with their unbelief, it seems they ought to be taken away from them and baptized, and instructed in the faith.[74]

Aquinas replies by arguing that in the same way that one should not violate civil law in order to rescue someone who has been legally condemned, no one ought to break the order of the natural right, in which a child is in the custody of its father, in order to rescue it from spiritual death.[75]

> No one should be snatched from natural death against the order of the civil law: for instance, if a man were condemned by the judge to temporal death, nobody ought to rescue him by violence: hence no one ought to break the order of the natural right [*ordinem iuris naturalis*] whereby a child is in the custody of its father, in order to rescue it from the danger of everlasting death.[76]

As mentioned above, Aquinas encourages baptism of children in cases of urgency or danger of death as did many theologians before him.[77] But not

---

mother's submission is necessary for their education." But Aquinas does not extend this policy to extended family members who convert, a development that would come in the late seventeenth century. See *Sent.* IV, D. 39, q. 1 a. 4, ad. 4: "The children have either arrived at the age of maturity, and then are able to freely follow either their believing father or their unbelieving mother; or else they are considered to be in the age of minority, and then they should be given to the believing parent, notwithstanding that their mother's submission is necessary for their education."

74 ST II.II 10.12 arg. 2.

75 In *QDL* 2.4.2 arg. 2, he lists the objection second as he did in ST II.II 10.12 arg. 2. In ST III 68.10 arg. 1, Aquinas cites this argument first, which indicates that by 1273 he thought that the argument from the danger of spiritual death had become more influential.

76 ST II.II 10.12 ad. 2. In a number of places I have amended the Benziger translation to natural right instead of natural law.

77 ST III 68.3 ad. 1. "This decree of Pope Leo, concerning the celebration of Baptism at two seasons, is to be understood 'with the exception of the danger of death' (which is always to be feared in children) as stated above."

for the children of Jews or other unbelievers without their consent.[78] "If a layman were to baptize even outside a case of urgency; he would sin, yet he would confer the sacrament." Nevertheless, deacons can baptize in "cases of urgency" when a bishop or priest are "a long way off."[79] Aquinas does not see the case of urgency applying to the children of unbelievers invitis parentibus. He rejects the argument that a child of unbelievers may be baptized to save it from spiritual death, which means he would reject the application of baptism in cases of urgency to Jewish children in situations of near temporal death. For Aquinas, consequentialist appeals cannot dispense with the natural law since what is contrary to natural justice, such as theft, murder, and the like, is also contrary to grace.[80]

The Argument from the Power of Kings and Princes (A3)

The third argument can be referred to as the argument of Jewish servitude or the argument from the power of kings and princes.[81] The argument is that since slaves are under their master's power, so are unbelievers under the power of kings and princes. Since children of slaves are also slaves, they are under the full authority of the prince. No injustice would be done to them if they were baptized against the will of their parents. Similar arguments based on servitude of the Jews were made by Rennes.[82] Aquinas rejects this position and argues that although Jews are in a state of civil servitude (not slaves or serfs), this does not exclude them from the divine and natural law.[83] "Jews

---

[78] Aquinas thinks children should be baptized quickly if they are in danger of death but not without the consent of parents. He addresses both issues under the same question, ST III 68, "Those who receive baptism" (III 68.3 ad. 1; and III 68.10 co.).

[79] ST III 67.1 ad. 3.

[80] *De mal.* 5.1 ad. 13.

[81] ST II.II 10.12 arg. 3. In *QDL* 2.4.2, he lists the objection third as he did in ST II.II 10.12. In ST III 68.10, the objection is listed second.

[82] That Rennes wrote during Aquinas's lifetime means John Y. B. Hood was correct when he speculated about precursors to Duns Scotus's position: "We know that twenty years after Aquinas's death Duns Scotus openly advocated forced baptism of Jewish children. It seems reasonable to presume Scotus had precursors." Hood, *Aquinas and the Jews* (Philadelphia: University of Pennsylvania Press, 1995), 89. Duns Scotus, *Ordinatio*, 4. d. 4. pars 4. q. 3.2.

[83] ST II.II 10.12 ad. 3. "Jews were legally citizens, certainly not slaves or serfs; canon lawyers and theologians advocated Jewish servitude, not actual serfdom; Jews were subject to certain restrictions not binding on other groups in medieval society. Usually they were subject to secular, not canon law, and problems arose when the Church sought to claim jurisdiction." Rebecca Rist, *Popes and Jews, 1095–1291* (New York: Oxford University Press, 2016), 207–8.

are servants of their lords by civil law, which does not negate the order of the natural right or divine law [*ordinem iuris naturalis vel divini*]."[84]

The Argument of God's Ownership of Children (A4)

The fourth argument can be referred to as the argument of God's ownership of children. The argument is that since all persons belong more to God than to a carnal father, it is not unjust if Jewish children are baptized against their parents' will: "Human beings belong more to God, who gives them their souls, than to their natural parents, who give them their bodies. Therefore, it does not seem unjust for the children of Jews to be taken from their natural parents and consecrated to God in baptism."[85]

Aquinas rejects this argument as well and states that though a child does belong more to God than to a carnal father, the child must be brought to God through reason and through the care of his parents: "Man is ordained unto God through his reason, by which he can know God. Wherefore a child, before it has the use of reason, is ordained to God, by a natural order, through the reason of its parents, under whose care it naturally lies, and it is according to their ordering that things pertaining to God are to be done in respect of the child."[86]

The Argument That Failing to Baptize Is Sinful (A5)

The fifth argument can be referred to as the argument that failing to baptize is sinful.[87] Baptism, not preaching, is most effective at achieving salvation. If a preacher fails to preach it is a threat to him because he has been entrusted with the duty of preaching. Likewise, those who could baptize a Jewish child and do not do it are therefore also in danger, and even guilty of sin.

Aquinas rejects this position as well. Consistent with his last reply, he argues that the guilt of not baptizing a child falls solely with the parents,

---

[84] ST II.II 10.12 ad. 3. See also *QDL* 2.4.2 ad. 3.

[85] *QDL* 2.42 arg. 4; see also ST II.II 10.12 arg. 4; ST III 68.10 arg. 3.

[86] ST III 68.10; ST II.II 10.12: "Man is directed to God by his reason, whereby he can know Him. Hence a child before coming to the use of reason, in the natural order of things, is directed to God by its parents' reason, under whose care it lies by nature: and it is for them to dispose of the child in all matters relating to God." *QDL* 2.4.2 ad. 4: "Human beings are directed to God through reason, by which God can be known. Hence before children have the ability to use reason, they are naturally directed to God through the reason of their parents, who are naturally in charge of them. Thus, parents determine how their children relate to the things of God."

[87] ST II.II 10.12 arg. 5; *QDL* 2.4.2 arg. 5. Aquinas leaves this objection out of his article in ST III 68.10.

and not on another. "To provide the sacraments of salvation for the children of unbelievers pertains to their parents. Hence it is they whom the danger threatens, if through being deprived of the sacraments their children fail to obtain salvation."[88]

The arguments Aquinas lists for baptizing Jewish children invitis parentibus indicate that there were a number of rather sophisticated positions circulating in the middle of the twelfth century that sought to override Jewish parental rights. Some of the positions appeal to canon law and are expressed by Dominican theologians such as Rennes and de Beauvais.

Aquinas thinks these teachings are dangerous innovations that threaten to overturn the law of the Church against forced baptism of unbelievers: "It seems dangerous to introduce the novel claim that the children of Jews can be baptized against their parents' will, contrary to the custom observed in the Church thus far."[89]

Aquinas goes further, though, and explains why such proposals are not at all reasonable, and contrary to the principles of natural law. In doing so, he articulates the theological reasons behind the Church's teaching that no one should be forced to believe, and that unbelievers ought to be saved willingly.

But what is the natural law? Aquinas's argument that Jewish parental authority is in the order of the natural right, which is an aspect of natural justice, assumes a knowledge of the natural law as it relates to the eternal law. Aquinas's above replies are built on the rich theological anthropology in the preceding articles of the *Summa*, including his teaching on the relation of the eternal law and natural law, and the natural inclinations of the human person. To grasp the profound significance of his defense of the authority of Jewish parents over their children, it will help to provide a brief account of his theology of natural law as it relates to the spiritual nature of the human person.[90]

For Aquinas, the Jewish child must be brought to God through the reason of his unbelieving parents. How is this possible if the parent does not have explicit faith in Christ? For Aquinas, all human persons are created in the image of God. Since human persons are created in God's image they are "ordained" or directed to God through the capacities of their natural reason. Aquinas describes God's governance over the things of creation according to his "eternal law."[91] In the wisdom of God's eternal law, the rational capacity of the person carries a spiritual capacity and potential. Therefore, the spiritual

---

[88] ST II.II 10.12 ad. 5; *QDL* 2.4.2 ad. 5.

[89] *QDL* 2.4.2.

[90] A complete account is beyond the scope of this chapter. See Servais Pinckaers, *The Sources of Christian Ethics* (Washington, DC: The Catholic University of America Press, 2005).

[91] ST I.II 91.1.

AQUINAS'S DEFENSE OF JEWISH PARENTAL AUTHORITY

nature of the person comes from God as gift, and this nature is destined to be elevated to grace and return to God through Christ.

The way in which humans share in God's governance of creation is through natural law, which is a participation in the eternal law.[92]

> Now among all others, the rational creature is subject to Divine providence in the most excellent way, in so far as it partakes of a share of providence, by being provident both for itself and for others. Wherefore it has a share of the Eternal Reason, whereby it has a natural inclination to its proper act and end: and this participation of the eternal law in the rational creature is called the natural law. Hence the Psalmist after saying (Psalm 4:6): "Offer up the sacrifice of justice," as though someone asked what the works of justice are, adds: "Many say, Who showeth us good things?" in answer to which question he says: "The light of Thy countenance, O Lord, is signed upon us": thus implying that the light of natural reason, whereby we discern what is good and what is evil, which is the function of the natural law, is nothing else than an imprint on us of the Divine light. It is therefore evident that the natural law is nothing else than the rational creature's participation of the eternal law.[93]

Nature or the human mind is not the cause of the natural law. For Aquinas, the rational nature of the human person is an imprint of the divine light. The rational person participates in God's eternal law through discerning with the light of reason what is good and evil. In Aquinas, natural law is always defined in theological terms.[94]

However, this directedness to God is not explicit knowledge of God on the part of the subject.[95] Rather, the rational appetite is constituted by natural inclinations to the truth and goodness. This inclination to the good includes the good of the education of offspring, as mentioned above. Aquinas

---

92 ST I.II 91.2.

93 ST I.II 91.2 co.

94 Russell Hittinger, *The First Grace: Rediscovering the Natural Law in a Post-Christian World* (Wilmington, DE: ISI Books, 2003), 10.

95 ST I.II 91.4 co.:
> Besides the natural and the human law it was necessary for the directing of human conduct to have a Divine law. . . . First, because it is by law that man is directed how to perform his proper acts in view of his last end. And indeed if man were ordained to no other end than that which is proportionate to his natural faculty, there would be no need for man to have any further direction of the part of his reason, besides the natural law and human law which is derived from it. But since man is ordained to an end of eternal happiness which is inproportionate to man's natural faculty, as stated above (I.II 5.5), therefore it was necessary that, besides the natural and the human law, man should be directed to his end by a law given by God.

considers this inclination a natural right and lists it as a precept of the natural law. The inclinations are natural in the sense that the human person's desire for what is true and good arises spontaneously and directs the person like hunger or thirst directs the appetite.[96] For Aquinas, the natural inclinations are at the source of voluntary free action. "Therefore, those things that are possessed of reason, move themselves to an end; because they have dominion over their actions through their free-will, which is the 'faculty of will and reason.'"[97] But these faculties are only the seeds of right action, which must be cultivated into virtues through a web of virtuous social relationships, including the guidance of parents and teachers.[98]

For Aquinas, the inclination to truth and goodness is not simply a vague concept of the good but has a specific character, which Aquinas imports from Aristotle. The natural inclinations are not directed toward a concept of partial good. Rather, the person's appetite is naturally directed toward a universal concept of the good. For example, "There can be no will in those things that lack reason and intellect, since they cannot apprehend the universal."[99] Although the human person is directed toward a complexity of goods, these are shaped by the person's natural desire for a universal end, or a perfect good that is all-sufficient: "The object of the will is the end and the good in universal."[100] Aquinas says all things that can be desired by the will belong to one genus, the last end (*finis ultimus*) or beatitude (*beatitudo*).[101] And just as all people desire the last end, so the will of an individual person

---

[96] Pinckaers, *Sources of Christian Ethics*, 402.

[97] ST I.II 1.2 co.

[98] "As for his estimation of the efficacy of natural law in the human mind, Thomas never wavered from the judgement that only the rudiments (or the *seminalia*) are known by the untutored mind." Hittinger, *The First Grace*, 10. Alasdair MacIntyre developed a Thomistic account of why social relations are required to cultivate the virtues in his important book *Dependent Rational Animals: Why Human Beings Need the Virtues* (Chicago: Open Court, 1999). He argues that all human animals are, by nature, always vulnerable, and for this reason a web of social relationships is necessary for vulnerable human communities to acquire the virtues. These relationships include: 1) parents, family members, and teachers who train the person not simply to please themselves or others, but to reflect on and act so as to achieve what is good and best, whether this pleases them or not (see chapter 8); 2) social relationships that support the person beyond childhood, such as friendship, neighborhood, and local community (see chapter 9); 3) and, most importantly, all of these people and groups must possess the "virtues of dependence" or the virtue of *misericordia*, which is defined as affectionate regard for people in need who cannot return favors, especially those who are outsiders to the community. For a treatment of *misericordia* see MacIntyre, chapter 10.

[99] ST I.II 1.2 ad. 3.

[100] ST I.II 1.2 ad. 3.

[101] Beatitude is the term for the state in which a person possesses the good completely or perfectly, where no good due to the person is lacking and no inclination of the will is left unsatisfied. ST I.II 1.6.

must be fixed on one last end.[102] The human person is therefore directed to God by reason in the sense that the person's "rational appetite" desires its own perfection, that is, "he desires as his perfect and crowning good."[103]

This rational directedness to the universal good is therefore the unique capacity of the human person to move oneself toward a perceived perfect good, though humans often mistake created imperfect goods for the truly perfect good, who is God. Though the human person may mistake a variety of created imperfect goods, such as wealth, power, or bodily health, as their final end or perfect good, instead of God, it does not change the fact that the subject desires a perfect good. To know and tend toward the nature of an end is proper to the rational nature of the person.[104] And God is the ultimate or last end of the person. For Aquinas, "Nothing can give rest to the human will except a universal good, which is not found in any creature but only in God."[105] "Hence it was necessary for the salvation of man that certain truths which exceed human reason should be made known to him by divine revelation."[106] "The human person attains their last end by knowing and loving God."[107] Commenting on Aquinas's view of the spiritual nature of the human person, Servais Pinckaers writes, "Our instinct for truth and goodness . . . is at bottom an instinct for God."[108]

This is why, in his defense of Jewish parental authority, Aquinas says that it is through reason that a person comes to know God: "Man is ordained unto God through his reason, by which he can know God." This theological claim about the nature of the person as he relates to the natural law is the

---

[102] ST I.II 1.5 co.

[103] ST I.II 1.5 co. "It is therefore necessary for the last end so to fill man's appetite, that nothing is left besides it for man to desire. Which is not possible, if something else be required for his perfection." ST I.II 1.2. As Frederick Bauerschmidt observes, two distinct acts issue from the one power of intellectual apprehending:
> Understanding (*intellectus*), in which we grasp self-evident principles and the conclusion of arguments, and reasoning (*ratio*), in which we work discursively from premises toward conclusions. The twofold acts of intellectual apprehending mirror the twofold acts of the intellectual appetite, which can be divided into will, which is our act of desiring the good as our end, and choice, which is our act of desiring the means to attend the end that we will. This capacity to choose is free (*liberum arbitrium*) because it can choose different means in relation to the end apprehended and willed.

Frederick Christian Bauerschmidt, *Thomas Aquinas: Faith, Reason, and Following Christ* (New York: Oxford, 2013), 233–34.

[104] ST I.II 2.

[105] ST I.II 2.8 co.

[106] ST I 1.1 co.

[107] ST I.II 1.8 co.

[108] Pinckaers, *Sources of Christian Ethics*, 404.

foundation of Aquinas's teaching that children would, in a sense, come to know God through the reason of the parents. "Parents determine how their children relate to the things of God."[109] "Hence a child before having the use of reason, by the natural order is directed to God by the reason of its parents, whose care it is naturally subjected, and it is according to their direction that directs the child in all matters divine."[110]

AQUINAS AND THE QUESTION OF WHETHER FORCED BAPTISMS OF ADULTS OR CHILDREN ARE VALID

The papal counsel's reply to the Mortara family claimed that in ST I.II 6.6 Aquinas teaches that a) although forced baptism of an adult unbeliever is illicit (i.e., unlawful), it is nonetheless a valid baptism because even an act motivated by fear remains a voluntary act; b) the Church's intention stands in place of the unbelieving parents; and c) a clandestine baptism of a Jewish child without the knowledge or against the will of the parents is nonetheless a valid baptism.

Aquinas did not directly address the question of whether a forced baptism of a Jewish child is nevertheless valid as his Dominican defenders did. However, he did address the question of the forced baptism of adults. He is also clear on the requirements for a valid baptism, which he calls the "sacrament of faith."

In this section, I first discuss the forced baptism of adults, and then I discuss what is required for a valid baptism of an infant. I respond to each of the papal counsel's arguments. I argue that although Aquinas teaches that the adult recipient of baptism must intend to receive baptism for the sacrament to be fully efficacious unto salvation, he is aware of the problem of forced conversions, and thinks that a certain type of coerced baptism of adults, although sinful and unjust on the part of the minister, nevertheless imprints what is called a baptismal character if the recipient consents to the baptism. In this section, I also distinguish the imprinting of baptismal character from sanctifying grace, and discuss how the assent to the faith in adults, for Aquinas, must be a voluntary act of the will that cooperates with God's movement of grace. Lastly, I show that Aquinas's teaching on the necessity of the intention in the recipient does not necessarily mean that an unlawful baptism of a child against the will of the parents would be invalid.

---

109 *QDL* 2.4.2 ad. 4.

110 ST II.II 10.12 ad. 4; *QDL* 2.4.2 ad. 4; ST III 68.10 ad. 3.

Throughout the section it will be very important to keep in mind that "more" is required for the valid baptism of an adult than an infant.

Whether Aquinas Teaches That a Forced Baptism of an Adult Is Nonetheless Valid because Even an Act Motivated by Fear Remains a Voluntary Act

Recall that the papal counsel claimed that Aquinas teaches in ST I.II 6.6 (on voluntary and involuntary acts) that a forced baptism is nonetheless valid because Aquinas teaches that even an act motivated by fear is a voluntary act. Below, I examine Aquinas's teaching on the indelible character of baptism and the necessity of the intention of the recipient in adult baptism alongside his teaching on fear and voluntary action. In the second part of the subsection, I discuss why Aquinas thinks the assent to the faith must be a voluntary act that cooperates with God's movement of grace and is free from fear and coercion.

BAPTISMAL CHARACTER AND THE QUESTION OF THE INTENTION IN THE RECIPIENT

For Aquinas, baptism is the "sacrament of faith."[111] It is through the sacrament of faith that the human person is gathered into the congregation of the faithful and incorporated with Christ.[112] The person is made a member of Christ through grace, and the sacraments not only signify but cause grace.[113] In order to address the question of the effects of the sacrament in the case of a coerced baptism of an adult, it will first help to define Aquinas's view of the sacrament of baptism and its effects, which include an indelible character in the soul and sanctifying grace.

Aquinas asks whether a baptism is a mere washing, that is, whether it is reducible to the visible, material only. Some theologians had said baptism is the material of the water, not the act of washing; others said baptism is not mere washing but spiritual regeneration. Aquinas acknowledges that baptism is the act of washing, but it is much more.[114] The sacrament of baptism is not simply symbolic water: "Some have thought that the water itself is the sacrament . . . but this is not true."[115] He explains that baptism "is some-

---

[111] ST III 66.1 ad. 1.

[112] ST III 66.1 ad. 1; ST III 66.3 co.; ST III 66.10 ad. 2.

[113] ST III 62.1 co. Aquinas cites Galatians 3:27: "As many of you as have been baptized in Christ have put on Christ."

[114] Roger Nutt, *General Principles of Sacramental Theology* (Washington, DC: The Catholic University of America Press, 2017), 168.

[115] ST III 66.1 co.

thing real signified by the outward washing." The application of water to the recipient with the prescribed form of the words really does effect interior realities: "The sanctification is not completed in water but a certain sanctifying instrumental virtue, not permanent but transient, passes from the water, in which it is, into man who is the subject of true sanctification."[116] This reality, or effects of grace, is both the baptismal character and inward justification.

It is crucial to grasp that Aquinas follows an already established tripartite formula that had aimed to safeguard the idea that a sacrament was not empty of meaning or ineffective simply because a recipient might lack a proper understanding of the sacrament or had mixed intentions in receiving it. For instance, one might intend to receive the sacrament of baptism or matrimony but have mixed intentions.

For this reason, Aquinas makes a threefold distinction when it comes to a sacrament (or sign) and its effects (or the realities signified).[117] Aquinas says three things may be considered in the sacrament of baptism: 1) "mere sacrament [*sacramentum tantum*]"; 2) "reality and sacrament [*res et sacramentum*]"; and 3) "reality only [*res tantum*]".[118]

The first aspect, mere sacrament, is that which is visible and outward. It is the external, visible, and outward sign that points to something else; this is why Aquinas says, "a sacrament is a kind of sign."[119] This is the water itself and its use in washing.

The second aspect is the interior reality caused by the visible action of washing: this interior reality is the *res et sacramentum*. This interior reality is signified by the visible action. It is this interior reality that Aquinas understands as the baptismal character imparted by divine action: "The baptismal character is both reality and sacrament [*res et sacramentum*]: because it is something real signified by the outward washing."[120] The sacramental character is real: it is a capacity or power in the soul to participate in divine worship of Christ. It is this capacity that disposes the subject to the reception of other sacraments. It is the capacity for participation in Christ's priesthood, which is the foundation of the sacramental liturgy.[121]

---

116 ST III 66.1 co.

117 This threefold distinction is based on the teaching in Lombard's *Sentences* on how some receive the sacrament and not the thing, i.e., the reality, etc.

118 ST III 66.1.

119 ST III 60.1 co.

120 ST III 66.1 co.

121 Nutt, *General Principles*, 156–57.

The interior reality, the character, however, is *also a sign* of something deeper or a superior reality. It is a sign of a further interior reality, the *res tantum* (reality only). This further reality, the *res tantum*, is the sanctifying grace of inward justification in Christ. The *res tantum* is the effect at which the institution of the sacrament of baptism ultimately aims. As Roger Nutt has helpfully explained, "Another way of thinking about the distinction between the *sacramentum tantum*, *res et sacramentum*, and the *res tantum*, is to trace the movement of the sacramental celebration to its ultimate perfection: exterior (rite) to interior (character or the immediate sacramental reality) to superior reality (the ultimate grace or purpose of the sacrament)."[122]

Receiving a valid sacrament of baptism does not mean that the deeper reality of baptism, *res tantum*, is automatically brought to fruition.[123] For an adult who chooses to receive a sacrament but does not really believe or has mixed intentions, there is a defect in their intention and so they really do receive the sacrament, but they do not receive the superior reality of sanctification. Aquinas says that sometimes people intend to receive baptism (or other sacraments) without right faith. Some come to baptism with a defective understanding of what baptism is. Aquinas thinks some do not have right faith when they approach the sacrament since they might even be unwilling to renounce unbelief in Christ or renounce their sins. Therefore, the sacrament of faith does not always cause sanctifying grace, nor does it require faith. In ST III 68.8, Aquinas asks whether faith is required on the part of the recipient. His answer is that the Church's intention in baptizing is that the human person be cleansed from sin, and so for this reason "she does not intend to give baptism save to those who have right faith."[124] This is why the Church asks those who come to baptism whether they believe. A validly celebrated sacrament is not fruitful if there is some obstacle on the part of the adult recipient.

An important distinction emerges here that pertains to our question. The adult person with mixed intentions or without right faith can still receive the sacrament: "Each receives the sacrament if it be conferred on him, though not unto salvation."[125] If anyone comes to baptism without right faith, they receive baptism "outside the Church" and the person "does not receive baptism unto salvation."[126]

---

122 Nutt, 169.

123 Nutt, 171–72.

124 ST III 68.8. ad. 2.

125 ST III 68.8. See ad. 1–4.

126 Aquinas cites Augustine on this point: "Hence Augustine says (De Baptism. Contr. Donat. IV): 'From the Church being compared to Paradise we learn that men can receive her Baptism even

Nevertheless, they do receive the sacramental character, which is a real participation in the priesthood of Christ. The adult who seeks baptism but does not have right faith receives the character of baptism "but not unto salvation" in the sense that they do not receive the ultimate effect of the sacrament, which is sanctifying grace. In other words, it is possible to receive a valid sacrament in that one receives the character of the sacrament, but it may not be fruitful in that it does not provide sanctifying grace, the ultimate purpose of the sacrament. "This clarifies why the sacraments do not work as 'vending machines' of grace, despite the fact that their causality works *ex opere operato*. Simply receiving validly celebrated sacraments is not the same as receiving them spiritually and fruitfully."[127]

The character of baptism, which is a "spiritual seal," is still set upon the recipient in that it is imprinted on the soul as a kind of sign.[128] For Aquinas, the character functions similarly to how a coin is marked for a particular end, such as the exchange of goods. In baptism, the mark is "the character of Christ" for service to God and to worship of God.[129] Again, the effect of the character of baptism is a sealing of the soul for divine worship, which deputizes the person for service in the same way someone might be marked for service in the military.[130] Ideally, the person would receive both character and sanctifying grace through the sacrament of baptism when they are moved by God's grace to assent with intellect and will to the faith voluntarily.[131] In the case of a defect in intention, that is, seeking baptism without a correct understanding of the sacrament, Aquinas says a general intention is sufficient. "Yet even if he think not aright concerning this sacrament, it is enough, for the receiving of the sacrament, that he should have a general intention of receiving Baptism, according as Christ instituted, and as the Church bestows it."[132] In a valid sacrament, the baptismal character remains even if sanctify-

---

outside her fold, but that elsewhere none can receive or keep the salvation of the blessed.'" ST III 68.8. ad. 2.

[127] Nutt, *General Principles*, 172–73.
[128] ST III 63.1 co.; ad. 1, 2.
[129] ST III 63.3 co.
[130] ST III 63.6 co. Baptism confers the power to receive the other sacraments of the Church. Not all sacraments imprint a character in the soul. The three sacraments that imprint a character are baptism, confirmation, and holy orders.
[131] "Hence the human mind whilst it is being justified, must, by a movement of its free-will withdraw from sin and draw near to justice. Now to withdraw from sin and to draw near to justice, in an act of free-will, means detestation and desire." ST I.II 113.5 co.
[132] ST III 68.8 ad. 3.

ing grace is lost through sin. It is through the sacramental character that one has the capacity to return to the Church through penance, if grace is lost.[133]

However, Aquinas also says the baptismal character can only be imprinted upon the soul "provided the other conditions are fulfilled which are essential to the sacrament."[134] What conditions are essential to the sacrament?[135] Aquinas is clear that to receive the indelible character requires matter, form, and intention on behalf of the minister and recipient. The matter is any plain water (ST III 66.3–4); the form is "I baptize thee in the name of the Father, and of the Son, and of the Holy Spirit" (ST III 63.5); and the intention is in the minister (ST III 67.1–8), as well as the general intention of the recipient (68.7). These elements are essential for a valid sacrament. Aquinas says, "Consequently, however much the matter of the sacrament is applied to man, if the due form of the words and the other requisites are missing, the effect of the sacrament does not follow."[136] In another place, Aquinas writes: "As stated above (Question 64, article 3), the sacraments derive their efficacy from Christ's institution of the sacrament when he was baptized."[137] "Consequently, if any of those things be omitted which Christ instituted in regard to a sacrament, it is invalid."[138] The sacrament is invalid if there is a change of form, for example conferring baptism using any other names but the Father, Son, and Holy Spirit.[139] And a baptism without the intention of the recipient requires rebaptism: "When a man is justified by baptism . . . it is necessary for him to intend to receive that which is given

---

[133] "The reason why a baptized child is able to receive Holy Communion and other sacraments but an unbaptized adult who has well-formed faith cannot receive Holy Communion or participate in the sacramental life of the Church can be given in one word—character. By Baptism the child has been consecrated or deputed to join in the sacramental worship of the Church. To accomplish this deputation to participate in these supernatural realities, Baptism (and Confirmation) causes a spiritual power in the soul that gives it a participation in Christ's own priesthood. The unbaptized adult, by contrast, while perhaps enjoying a very mature faith, lacks the capacity to join in the sacramental liturgy because his soul has not been elevated spiritually by the character of Baptism to share in Christ's priestly activity." Nutt, *General Principles*, 157–58, 165.

[134] ST III 68.8 co.

[135] ST III 64.5 ad. 3: "A thing is required in a sacrament in two ways. First, as being essential to it: and if this be wanting, the sacrament is invalid; for instance, if the due form or matter be wanting. Secondly, a thing is required for a sacrament, by reason of a certain fitness. And in this way good ministers are required for a sacrament."

[136] *De ver.* 27.4 ad. 10.

[137] ST III 66.2 co.

[138] ST III 66.6 co.

[139] ST III 66.5 ad. 7.

him."¹⁴⁰ "If an adult lack the intention of receiving the sacrament, he must be rebaptized."¹⁴¹

Aquinas also says an adult unbeliever should in no way be compelled to embrace the faith but persuaded.¹⁴² In ST III 68.7 he is explicit that an essential requirement of the sacrament is the intention of the recipient. It seems the circumstances of a coerced baptism would mean that "consent" to baptism under threat constitutes an involuntary act. A key part of Aquinas's definition of a voluntary action is that it is according to the inclination of the will, and he contrasts this inclination of the will with acts that involve violence, fear, or coercion.

> On the part of the agent, a thing must be, when someone is forced by some agent, so that he is not able to do the contrary. This is called "necessity of coercion." Now this necessity of coercion is altogether repugnant to the will. For we call that violent which is against the inclination of a thing. But the very movement of the will is an inclination to something. Therefore, as a thing is called natural because it is according to the inclination of nature, so a thing is called voluntary because it is according to the inclination of the will. Therefore, just as it is impossible for a thing to be at the same time violent and natural, so it is impossible for a thing to be absolutely coerced or violent, and voluntary.¹⁴³

A valid baptism requires a general intention of the recipient in accord with the inclination of their will. Since an essential part of a voluntary action is that it is in accordance with the inclination of the will of the agent, it seems that forcing someone to accept baptism under threat would constitute necessity of coercion. In other words, the baptism would be involuntary.

Additionally, Aquinas teaches that, in a qualified sense, violence makes an act involuntary.¹⁴⁴ The act of the will is twofold. The first act of the will is "the immediate proper act" proceeding from an interior principle of knowledge, that is, "to wish" to perform some act such as "to walk" and "to speak." Or perhaps we can use the example "to request baptism." The second act of the will is its execution of the wish to perform an action, that is, to put the wish to

---

140 ST III 68.7 ad. 1.

141 ST III 68.7 ad. 2. Catharinus also mentioned this teaching.

142 ST II.II 10.8 ad. 2: "Those Jews who have in no way received the faith, ought not by no means to be compelled to the faith." In ST II.II 10.12 co., Aquinas uses the formula "not by compulsion but by persuasion."

143 ST I 82.1 co.

144 ST I.II 6.4 co.

walk, speak, or to request baptism into action. Aquinas says violence *cannot* be done to the first act of the interior will, that is, the wish to perform acts or the wish not to perform acts. The interior act of the will is only moved by its own inclination, not by an external principle. Violence can only be done to the second act of the will, that is, "to walk" or "to speak" insofar as "violence can prevent the exterior members from executing the will's command." A compelled act, then, is a) from outside the person, that is, "an exterior principle" and b) something against the interior will. "Consequently it is contrary to the nature of the will's own act, that it should be subject to compulsion and violence."[145] This violence causes involuntariness: "Now that which is against nature is said to be 'unnatural'; and in like manner that which is against the will is said to be 'involuntary'. Therefore, violence causes involuntariness."[146] It seems a character would *not* be imprinted on the soul in a coerced baptism since the baptism would be involuntary.

Aquinas also says that acts done through fear are voluntary in a certain respect, and that circumstances must be considered. Aquinas says that according to Aristotle and Gregory of Nyssa, things done through fear are of a "mixed character," being partly voluntary and partly involuntary. "For that which is done through fear, considered in itself, is not voluntary; but it becomes voluntary in this particular case, in order, namely, to avoid the evil feared." Aquinas explains, "But if the matter be considered aright, such things are voluntary rather than involuntary; for they are voluntary simply, but involuntary in a certain respect." Aquinas explains that a singular act done through fear is still an act insofar as it is a singular action performed "here and now," and under other individuating circumstances. Aquinas gives the example of throwing cargo overboard during a storm through fear of the danger. He says such a singular act is "voluntary simply" because it is a principle of action from within. Aquinas also qualifies this by saying that circumstances of a particular case must be considered. Outside this case what is done through fear is involuntary "inasmuch as it is repugnant to the will."[147]

What if a passive subject was baptized against their interior will? The violent movement is done "against the interior inclination."[148] Since the interior will is set against baptism, it seems the circumstances of being baptized by an exterior principle (the violent will of another agent) against the interior inclination of the will would mean the sacrament would be invalid.

---

[145] ST I.II 6.4 co.

[146] ST I.II 6.5 co.

[147] ST I.II 6.6 co. Aquinas also says that a human act is deemed to be voluntary or involuntary according to knowledge or ignorance of circumstances. ST I.II 7.2 co.

[148] ST I.II 6.5 ad. 2.

Recall Cajetan's position was that a valid baptism does not require a representative will *but only that there is no contrary will to the baptism*. Against a similar position, John Capreolus stressed that a representative intention on behalf of the recipient is necessary for a valid sacrament, not simply the lack of a contrary will. Capreolus appealed to the analogy of an invalid adult baptism: "If an adult were so brought up that he had not heard about the faith at all, and he were in his original sin, if such a one were to be baptized while sleeping it is settled that nothing would happen, and nevertheless in his will the baptism would find no barrier." Capreolus concludes that "more therefore is required." Capreolus's statement that "more is required" for the validity of the sacrament points our attention to Aquinas's positive role of the recipient's free will. Capreolus likely has in mind Aquinas's teaching that a person "should not be baptized while asleep" except in cases where he is "threatened with the danger of death." However, one who is asleep and near death can only be baptized if he previously manifested a desire to receive baptism.[149]

However, commentators on Aquinas's teaching on forced baptism have overlooked that in his early thought in the *Commentary on the Sentences* he indirectly addresses the question of whether a coerced baptism of an adult would be valid when he discusses "whether both will and intention are required for baptism." He seems to think the baptismal character is imprinted if there is a general intention to receive the sacrament in order to avoid violence. In other words, he accepts that a conditionally coerced act of the will is nonetheless an act of the will. Aquinas says that for the baptized person to receive the character of the sacrament nothing is required except for "the removal of the impediment, which is nothing other than a will contrary to [the sacrament and the reality behind the sacrament]."[150] Aquinas explains, "Among adults and those having the use of reason, in whom a contrary will can exist either actually or habitually, baptism requires contrition or devotion, to receive the reality behind the sacrament; as well as intention or will, to receive the sacrament."[151] On behalf of the recipient, all that is required for the imprint of the character of the sacrament is the lack of a contrary will.

Aquinas then defines the nature of the contrary will in a way that reflects Pope Innocent III's distinction in *Maiores* between a conditional will and

---

[149] ST III 68.12 ad. 3; ST I.II 113.3 ad. 1.

[150] *Sent.* IV D. 6, q. 1, a. 2, qa. 3, co. 3. The commentary on the four books of Lombard's *Sentences* is the first major work by Aquinas. Torrell, *Person and Work*, 36–53, 332.

[151] Some think that Aquinas does not cite Aristotle's *Nichomachean Ethics* 3.1 in any of his discussions of baptism. Marcia L. Colish, *Faith, Fiction, & Force in Medieval Baptismal Debates* (Washington, DC: The Catholic University of America Press, 2014), 299. However, he does so in *Sent.* IV D. 6 q. 1, a. 2, qa. 3, co. 3.

an absolutely contrary will. He says one who is baptized under threat nevertheless still chooses to receive baptism and so he does receive the sacrament "but not the reality behind it."[152]

> Nevertheless, it should be known that an absolute will [*voluntas absoluta*] to receive what the Church confers is not required in an adult, but it is enough to will it conditionally [*voluntas conditionata*], as happens in matters of mixed willing, which is discussed in [Aristotle's] *Ethics* 3; and thus if it is completely forced, such that its principle is completely external, with the one undergoing it contributing nothing, as when someone is violently dunked while crying out in protest, that person receives neither the sacrament nor the reality behind it. But if it is compelling inducement, as with threats or beating, such that the baptized chooses to receive baptism rather than suffer such things, then he does receive the sacrament, but not the reality behind it.[153]

Therefore, in the *Sentences*, written during 1252–56, Aquinas held that one who receives the sacrament in order to avoid violence receives the character of the sacrament but not sanctifying grace.

In 1273, while writing the third part of the *Summa theologiae*, Aquinas once again addressed the question of whether the intention of receiving the sacrament is required on the part of the one baptized.[154] He did not use the terms absolute will and conditional will, which he used decades earlier in the *Sentences*.[155] In the *Summa theologiae*, Aquinas states that "it is necessary for him to have the will or intention of receiving the sacrament."[156] However, Aquinas also considers an objection against this teaching that an intention is required for a valid sacrament. The objection is that an intention is not necessary in a recipient of baptism because, when some persons are baptized, they are passive. The argument is as follows: "It seems that the intention of receiving the sacrament of Baptism is not required on the part of the one baptized. For the one baptized is, as it were, 'patient' in the sacrament. But an intention is required not on the part of the patient but on the part of

---

152 Innocent III to Imbert d'Agueres, archbishop of Arles, September/October 1201, as cited in Gregory IX, *Decretals* 10.3.42.3 in *Corpus iuris canonici*, ed. Aemilius Friedberg, 2 vols. (Leipzig, Germany: Tauchnitz, 1879–80; repr., Union, NJ: Lawbook Exchange, 2000), 2:646. See also Colish, *Faith, Fiction*, 287.

153 *Sent.* IV D. 6 q. 1, a. 2, qa. 3, co. 3.

154 ST III 68.7.

155 *Sent.* IV D. 6 q. 1, a. 2, qa. 3, ad. 3: "The will or intention is not required for baptism as a cause or disposition to the character but only as removing what prevents it."

156 ST III 68.7 co.

the agent. Therefore, it seems that the intention of receiving Baptism is not required on the part of the one baptized."

Aquinas's reply is that although it is indeed the case that the recipient have the will or intention of receiving the sacrament, he also explains that a passive state is nonetheless a voluntary state: "When a man is justified by Baptism, his passiveness is not violent but voluntary [*non est passio coacta, sed voluntaria*]: wherefore it is necessary for him to intend to receive that which is given him."[157] Aquinas also states that the sacrament is invalid if *a contrary will be expressed* on behalf of the recipient: "The minister of a sacrament acts in the person of the whole Church, whose minister he is; while in the words uttered by him, the intention of the Church is expressed; and this suffices for the validity of the sacrament, except the contrary be expressed on the part either of the minister or of the recipient of the sacrament."[158] This seems to imply that a lack of a contrary will to baptism, that is, not voicing opposition, is considered voluntary passiveness on Aquinas's terms, and could thus be considered a general intention.

Aquinas's view of the role of the will in receiving the sacrament of baptism seems to align with the accepted view among canonists of his day, that "conditional coercion" of an unbeliever to embrace the faith under threat would result in a valid baptism if there was a lack of a contrary will, that is, a passive state where there was no express protest. Aquinas's view develops from the *Sentences* only in that his view that all that is required for the validity of the sacrament is that "no contrary will" be present is clarified: the lack of a contrary will is defined positively as a voluntary, passive state.

It is important to note that Aquinas teaches that an unbelieving adult should not be compelled but persuaded to baptism; and that to compel an unbeliever to baptism is contrary to natural justice.[159] However, for Aquinas, if one chose to receive the sacrament to avoid harm, one would receive the character of the sacrament but not the reality of sanctifying grace. The one who compelled the person to baptism would also sin.

GRACE AND VOLUNTARY ASSENT TO THE THINGS OF THE FAITH

The above technical discussion of how a general intention to be baptized to avoid harm suffices for the imprint of baptismal character provides an incomplete picture of Aquinas's view of the divine purpose and the fruitfulness of

---

157 ST III 68.7 ad. 1.
158 ST III 64.8 ad. 2.
159 ST II.II 10.12 co.

the sacrament of baptism. For Aquinas, forced baptism was considered an act contrary to natural justice and thus sinful.

The sacrament of baptism was instituted by Christ as an instrument to heal the wound of original sin in a person and restore relationship with God. As instruments instituted by Christ, the sacraments not only signify but cause grace. The aim and full fruit of baptism is the unfolding of sanctifying grace and friendship with God. It is through the gift of grace received in baptism that one enters communion with the Passion and resurrection of Christ. For Aquinas, the sacraments of the New Law cause grace not in a mechanistic way but through the intentional and relational action of God in Christ. This is why Aquinas insists that in the sacraments of the New Law a person is incorporated with Christ.[160]

For an adult, this relation with God can only come through a voluntary and trusting assent to the "things of the faith" that is free from fear.[161] For Aquinas, faith is one of the three theological virtues, along with hope and charity. Faith is defined by Aquinas as "a disposition of the mind, by which eternal life is begun in us, making the intellect assent to what is not apparent."[162] In Aquinas, "true faith is a virtue, meaning it is a disposition that inclines us to act well, specifically to know the truth revealed by God."[163] There are two things required for faith:

> First, that the things which are of faith should be proposed to man: this is necessary in order that man believe anything explicitly. The second thing requisite for faith is the assent of the believer to the things which are proposed to him.... Man, by assenting to matters of faith, is raised above his nature, this must needs accrue to him from some supernatural principle moving him inwardly; and this is God. Therefore faith, as regards the assent which is the chief act of faith, is from God moving man inwardly by grace.[164]

---

[160] ST III 62.1 co.

[161] Jennifer Hart Weed, "Aquinas on the Forced Conversion of the Jews," *Jews in Medieval Christendom: "Slay Them Not"*, ed. Kristine T. Utterback and Merrall L. Price (Études sur le Judaïsme Médiéval 60, Leiden: Brill, 2013), 129–46; "Faith, Salvation, and the Sacraments in Aquinas: A Puzzle Concerning Forced Baptisms," *Philosophy, Culture, and Traditions* 10 (2014), 95–110. Weed does not focus on the question of whether a conditionally willed baptism, i.e., under threat, imprints a character on the soul.

[162] Bauerschmidt, *Thomas Aquinas*, 144.

[163] Bauerschmidt, 144.

[164] ST II.II 6.1 co.

Here, the "things proposed" refers to the object of faith, which is first and foremost the "First Truth," God. It is trusting God and believing the articles of faith: "Rather than a blind impulse of trust, faith is, as Augustine said, 'to think with assent.' Faith involves not only saying to God, 'I believe that you are trustworthy,' but also, 'I assent to the truth of what you say.' In this way, faith is a kind of knowledge, with an identifiable cognitive content: the articles of faith."[165]

However, for the sacrament of baptism to be fruitful unto sanctifying grace, the believer must assent voluntarily to the things of the faith. Aquinas says, "Now the act of believing is an act of the intellect assenting to the divine truth at the command of the will moved by the grace of God, so that it is subject to the free-will in relation to God."[166] Since the things of the faith surpass human reason, these do not come to the knowledge of the human person unless God reveals this knowledge. God can reveal this knowledge immediately, as he did with the apostles and prophets. For others, the things of the faith are proposed by God in sending preachers of the faith. Therefore, faith involves the intellect's assent to what is not apparent but revealed by God. The will of the one who approaches the sacrament participates in Christ's gift of grace through their intellectual assent and will.

Aquinas is careful to explain that although some believe at the sight of a miracle or because of hearing a sermon, others might see and hear the same things and not believe. "Hence we must assert another internal cause, which moves man inwardly to assent to matters of faith.... Since man, by assenting to matters of faith, is raised above his nature, this must needs accrue to him from some supernatural principle moving him inwardly, and this is God."[167] This is why Aquinas teaches that faith, "as regards the assent which is the chief act of faith," is a gift from God who moves the person inwardly by grace. "The act of faith, like all other meritorious human actions, is accomplished by the will being moved from within by God's grace."[168] So, faith comes from God who moves the person by grace.

This supernatural and inward movement cooperates with the intellect of the human person. "God does not justify us without ourselves, because while we are being justified we consent to God's justification by a movement

---

165 Bauerschmidt, *Thomas Aquinas*, 145.
166 ST II.II 2.9.
167 ST II.II 6.1 co.
168 Bauerschmidt, *Thomas Aquinas*, 147.

of our free-will. Nevertheless, this movement is not the cause of grace, but the effect; hence the whole operation pertains to grace."[169]

In the context of his teaching on the virtue of faith, Aquinas defines intellectual assent as a voluntary act of choice: "The intellect assents to something, not through being sufficiently moved to this assent by its proper object, but through an act of choice, whereby it turns voluntarily to one side rather than to the other: and if this be accompanied by doubt or fear of the opposite side, there will be opinion, while, if there be certainty and no fear of the other side, there will be faith."[170] If doubt or fear accompany the intellectual assent to the things of the faith, the result is opinion.

For Aquinas, faith is present in the person when the intellect voluntarily assents to the proposed content without fear or doubt. But this movement of the free-will is also "God's motion to justice."

> God moves everything in its own manner. . . . Hence he moves man to justice according to the condition of his human nature. But it is man's proper nature to have free-will. Hence in him who has the use of reason God's motion to justice does not take place without a movement of the free-will. But He so infuses the gift of justifying grace that at the same time He moves the free-will to accept the gift of grace, in such as are capable of being moved thus.[171]

In other words, the person cooperates with grace in the movement of the free-will. The infused virtue of faith is a "total gift from God that can only be caused by God."[172]

This is why, if baptism were applied to an unwilling adult recipient (whether absolutely unwilling or conditionally willing), the sacrament would not cause sanctifying grace "automatically."[173] Sacraments are an instrumental cause of God's power.[174] The sacrament of faith confers grace, yet it is "incomplete" apart from God's power as the principal agent of the instrument.

---

169 ST I.II 111.2 ad. 2.

170 ST II.II 1.4 co.

171 ST I.II 113.3 co. In ad. 1, Aquinas says, "Infants are not capable of the movement of their free-will; hence it is by the mere infusion of their souls that God moves them to justice. Now this cannot be brought about without a sacrament; because as original sin, from which they are justified, does not come to them from their own will, but by carnal generation, so also is grace given them by Christ through spiritual regeneration."

172 William C. Mattison III, *Growing in Virtue: Aquinas on Habit* (Washington, DC: Georgetown University Press, 2023), 172.

173 Weed, "Faith, Salvation," 102.

174 ST III 62.1.

Sacramental grace comes from God and is only efficacious insofar as God moves them according to their institution.[175]

> The sacraments do not work for the production of grace by the power of their own form, for in that case they would work as principal agents; but they work by the power of the principal agent, God, existing in them.... The sacraments have an effect upon grace inasmuch as they are, as it were, moved by God to this effect. And that motion can be considered on the basis of their institution, their sanctification, and their application to the one who goes to the sacraments. They consequently do not have their efficacy after the manner of a complete being, but in a sense incompletely.[176]

The sacraments of the New Law cause grace because these are instituted by God to be employed for the purpose of conferring grace. But without God's power, the efficacy of a sacrament is incomplete. And the power of the sacrament of baptism is from faith in Christ's Passion: "Christ dwells in us 'by faith' (Ephesians 3:17). Consequently, by faith, Christ's power is united to us. Now the power of blotting out sin belongs in a special way to His Passion. And therefore men are delivered from sin especially by faith in His Passion. ... Therefore the power of the sacrament which is ordained until the remission of sins is derived principally from faith in Christ's Passion."[177] Aquinas says that "none but God can cause grace: since grace is nothing else than a participated likeness of the Divine nature."[178] In no case can a person cause the infused virtue of faith. A fruitful reception of the sacrament of baptism is caused by the power of Christ's Passion being united to the person by faith. And only God moves the person's free will to accept the gift of grace, in persons capable of being moved.[179]

Aquinas's theology of the virtue of faith along with his view that God's sanctifying grace is not coercive is the rationale behind his argument that Jews are not to be compelled to the faith because "to believe depends upon the will": "Jews ... are by no means to be compelled to the faith, in order that

---

175 See Weed, "Faith, Salvation," 102.

176 *De ver.* 27.5.

177 ST III 62.5 ad. 2.

178 ST III 62.1 co.

179 "Thomas's discussion of the virtue of faith is something of a balancing act, attempting to do justice to the roles played by the intellect and the will, God's grace and human freedom, as well as the knowing and unknowing—the satisfaction and ongoing desire—that faith involves." Bauerschmidt, *Thomas Aquinas*, 147.

they may believe, because to believe depends on the will."; "Jews . . . ought by no means to be compelled to the faith."[180]

Nevertheless, Aquinas also reiterated the teaching from the Fourth Council of Toledo canon 57, which states that Jews who have received the faith on their own ought to be compelled to keep it.[181] Based on the texts discussed above, this means that if one were coerced to baptism and chose to "receive" the sacrament in order to avoid harm they would not receive sanctifying grace because of the lack of voluntary assent to the things of the faith based in trust in God (rather than fear). But the person would receive the character of the sacrament since a general intention even if willed "conditionally" suffices for a valid sacrament. For this reason, it seems that on Aquinas's terms the person could be compelled to keep the faith despite having received the sacrament under threat of harm.

The historian and rabbi Solomon Grayzel praised Aquinas for his defense of Jewish parental authority, saying, "Nothing of the kind had ever been done by important Christians, either emperors or theologians."[182] However, Grayzel was disappointed by the idea implied in Aquinas's restatement of the Fourth Council of Toledo canon 57, that those who received baptism under threat did so voluntarily.[183]

In the light of our study of the distinction between conditional and absolute coercion in chapter 4, we can see that Aquinas's position reflects the common view of most canonists of his day. The question of the validity of "conditionally" coerced baptisms of unbelievers was settled by Innocent III's *Maiores* roughly a decade before Aquinas was even born.[184]

---

180 ST II.II 10.8 ad. 2.
181 ST II.II 10.8 ad. 2.
182 Grayzel, vol. 2, 8. Grayzel cites ST II.II 10.8 ad. 3.
183 Grayzel, vol. 2, 29. Grayzel comments on ST II.II 10.8 ad. 3, which Aquinas had written concerning those who had an obligation to keep the faith once it had been received:
It may be considered subjective on the part of a Jew to feel that Aquinas's argument on this point is unconvincing, but it does appear unworthy for a man of his intellectual stature to offer the following comparison: "*sicut vovere est voluntatis, reddere autem est necessitates, ita accipere fidem est voluntatis, sed tenere iam acceptam est necessitates*" [Just as taking a vow belongs to the will, and keeping a vow, a matter of obligation, so acceptance of the faith belongs to the will, whereas keeping the faith, once one has received it, is a matter of obligation]. Making a voluntary promise and choosing between life and death are not comparable situations.
184 "Considering that, at that time, almost all conversions from Judaism were the result of riots, with the knife literally at the Jew's throat, it is difficult to see how Innocent's view, and its ultimate inclusion in the *Corpus Juris Canonici*, can be anything but a negation of *Sicut [Judaeis]*." Grayzel, vol. 2, 7.

Whether Aquinas teaches in ST III 68.9 That the Will of a Child of Unbelievers is Represented in Baptism by the Church not its Parents

Recall that the papal counsel claimed that Aquinas teaches in ST III 68.9 that the will of a child of unbelievers is represented in baptism by the Church not its parents. The counsel claimed that "the intention of the Church is represented and applied to the unfaithful child, who is baptized by the one person who confers the sacrament."[185]

Does Aquinas teach in ST III 68.9 ad. 2 that the *representative* will of the child baptized is expressed by the Church and not by unbelieving parents? Again, the context of Aquinas's teaching is crucial. Considering the context requires analysis of the nature of the dispute represented in the question of the article, as well as the concerns and directions of the arguments.

The question of the article is, "Whether children should be baptized." The arguments reject the practice of infant baptism, and answer in the negative: "Children have not the use of free-will ... [and so] they cannot receive baptism; it seems that children cannot be baptized," etc. The concern of the second argument is relevant since it is Aquinas's reply to this argument that is cited by the papal counsel: "Baptism is the sacrament of faith ... but children have not faith, which demands an act of the will on the part of the believer. Nor can it be said that their salvation is implied in the faith of their parents; since the latter are sometimes unbelievers, and their unbelief would conduce rather to the damnation of their children. Therefore it seems that children cannot be baptized."[186] The relevant concern in the argument is that the sin of the unbelieving parents would harm the child after she received the sacrament.

Aquinas's reply is that Christ taught that unless a person is born again of water and the Holy Spirit, he cannot enter the kingdom of God. He also says children should be brought up in things pertaining to the Christian way of life. It became necessary to baptize children, that, in a second birth they might obtain salvation through Christ. In reply to the concern that the lack of faith in unbelieving parents would prohibit the child from receiving the sacrament, Aquinas cites Augustine's words written in *Letter 98* to Boniface, in the fifth century: "Little children are offered that they may receive grace in their souls, not so much from the hands of those that carry them (yet from these too, if they be good and faithful) as from the whole company of the

---

185 *BC*, 15.
186 ST III 68.9 arg. 2.

saints and the faithful. For they are rightly considered to be offered by those who are pleased at their being offered."[187] Aquinas concludes that it is not a hindrance to a child's salvation if their parents are unbelievers and have no faith. In this case, the unbelief of the parents is not a hinderance because the entire community of saints and faithful present the children for baptism.

How can this claim be reconciled with Aquinas's teaching in the very next article, ST III 68.10: "Whether children of Jews or other unbelievers should be baptized against the will of their parents." As explained above, Aquinas teaches there that "if children have not the use of free-will, according to the natural law they are under the care of their parents.... It would be contrary to natural justice if such children were baptized against their parents' will."[188]

However, the context of Augustine's *Letter 98* is crucial for making sense of Aquinas's teaching in ST III 68.9 ad. 2.[189] The context of Boniface's letter concerns parents who participate in pagan worship in Rome *and* desire to have their children baptized. Around 408, Boniface, the bishop of Cataqua in Numidia asked Augustine various questions about baptism, including whether parents who "subject their baptized infants to sacrilegious rites sin

---

[187] Augustine, cited in ST III 68.9 ad. 2. The full text of Aquinas's reply in ad. 2 is as follows: As Augustine says, writing to Boniface (*Cont. duas Ep. Pelag. i*), "in the Church of our Saviour little children believe through others, just as they contracted from others those sins which are remitted in Baptism." Nor is it a hindrance to their salvation if their parents be unbelievers, because, as Augustine says, writing to the same Boniface (Ep. xcviii), "little children are offered that they may receive grace in their souls, not so much from the hands of those that carry them (yet from these too, if they be good and faithful) as from the whole company of the saints and the faithful. For they are rightly considered to be offered by those who are pleased at their being offered, and by whose charity they are united in communion with the Holy Ghost." And the unbelief of their own parents, even if after Baptism these strive to infect them with the worship of demons, hurts not the children. For as Augustine says (Cont. duas Ep. Pelag. i) "once the child has been begotten by the will of others, he cannot subsequently be held by the bonds of another's sin so long as he consent not with his will, according to Ezekiel 18:4: 'As the soul of the Father, so also the soul of the son is mine; the soul that sinneth, the same shall die.' Yet he contracted from Adam that which was loosed by the grace of this sacrament, because as yet he was not endowed with a separate existence. But the faith of one, indeed of the whole Church, profits the child through the operation of the Holy Ghost, Who unites the Church together, and communicates the goods of one member to another."

[188] ST III 68.10.

[189] St. Augustine, *The Works of St. Augustine Part II, Letters Vol 1: 1–99*, trans. Roland Teske, SJ (Hyde Park, NY: New City Press, 2001), 426–32. See also Everett Ferguson, *Baptism in the Early Church: History, Theology, and Liturgy in the First Five Centuries* (Grand Rapids, MI: Eerdmans, 2009), 805.

against them."[190] Boniface reported to Augustine that a child spat out the eucharist "with unusual gestures" after having been offered to demons. The parents' participation in "demon worship" and sacrilegious rites raised the question of whether their request for their children to be baptized should be denied.

The concern could be summarized as "What good would it do to allow a child to be baptized and then raised in such an environment?" Moreover, why would pagan parents want their children baptized anyway? Augustine's reply to Boniface indicates the parents intended that their children receive baptism.

> Do not let it disturb you that some do not bring their little ones to receive baptism with that faith for the purpose of being reborn for eternal life by spiritual grace, but *because they think that they retain or recover their bodily health by this remedy. For they do not fail to be reborn because they are presented by these people with this intention.* After all, through them the necessary actions of the minister and the words of the mysteries are celebrated without which the little one cannot be consecrated. . . . Little ones are, of course, presented to receive spiritual grace, not so much from those in whose hands they are carried, though they do also receive it from them if they are good believing people, as form the universal society of the saints and believers. For they are correctly understood to be presented by all who are pleased that they are presented and by whose holy and undivided love they are helped to come into the communion of the Holy Spirit.[191]

The context of Augustine's letter is that the unbelieving parents bring their children to the Church on their own accord in order to baptize them. The pagan parents thought baptism would heal their children from sickness or retain good health. Augustine explains that, even if parents present their children for baptism for the wrong motives, the Holy Spirit still works through the Church to bring forth children of God. What is important to note here, is that though the pagan parents' intention for baptism of their children was misguided, their intention was for their children to be baptized. Augustine's point is that the intention of the Church suffices despite the misguided intentions of the unbelieving parents. He also says unbelieving parents' sacrilegious rituals will not harm the newly baptized child, and so he approves of their raising the children.

---

[190] Numidia was in North Africa, near modern Algeria. See the commentary of Roland Teske on *Letter 98*, in *Works of Augustine Part II, Letters Vol. 1*, 426.

[191] Emphasis mine.

The historical context of this case from 408 is different from the thirteenth-century case addressed by Aquinas since there were no legal consequences in the fifth century that required removal of baptized children from their unbelieving parents for Christian education. That law would be legislated in 633, with canon 60 of the Fourth Council of Toledo, and even then, it was mostly ignored or inconsistently applied until after Gratian.

The context of the thirteenth century is the fall out of the Christian discovery of the Talmud and the campaign that sought to justify the baptism of Jewish children invitis parentibus using numerous arguments. The pagan children in Boniface's case are not baptized without the knowledge or against the will of their parents. Rather, the voluntary intention of the non-Christian parents is for their children to be baptized despite their mistaken understanding of the purpose of baptism. This is why the Dominican theologian Prierio, who was aware of the context of Augustine's *Letter 98*, argued that the children of unbelievers mentioned by Boniface would receive the sacrament but "only . . . when the unbelieving parents themselves consent that the children be faithful Christians."[192]

Aquinas would have likely understood the context of Augustine's letter to Boniface, and this is perhaps why he sets the question on whether to baptize infants (ST III 68.9) next to the question on whether to baptize the infant children of nonbelievers (ST III 68.10). Perhaps he was aware that Augustine's mention of "offering" children in the teaching of article 9 could be misinterpreted to justify the novel and hazardous proposals for baptizing Jewish children invitis parentibus.

In article 10, Aquinas argues against those who push for baptizing Jewish children invitis parentibus. He insists that only Jewish parents can decide whether to baptize their children. The implication is that the Church's intention *should not* stand in the place of the Jewish parents' will without the parents' knowledge and consent. In the fifth-century case that is the context of ST III 68.9, the general intention of the unbelieving pagan parents is to baptize their children based on the misguided view that baptism is a remedy for bodily health. In the thirteenth-century case faced by Aquinas in ST III 68.10, the question is forced baptism of children of Jews or other unbelievers against their parents' will.

As mentioned above, Aquinas does teach in the *Summa theologiae* that baptism of infants of Christian parents must not be deferred because of the danger of death, as many other theologians held. He says no other spiritual

---

[192] Prierio no. 3 in *SA*, 387.

remedy is available for them besides the sacrament of baptism.[193] If an adult is in danger of death, then baptism should not be deferred. The celebration of baptism can be delayed for adults with the exception of the danger of death (*excepto tamen periculo mortis*).[194] Aquinas adds that the danger of death is "always to be feared in children." The context, however, is the question of deferring baptism in "those who approach baptism," that is, those who willingly approach baptism as adults or the parents of ill children.

Moreover, Aquinas was well aware of Augustine's teaching that unbelievers must not be forced to the faith, and cites Augustine's words on this point:

> He who has the use of free-will, must, in order to die to the old life, "will to repent of his former life"; so must he, of his own will, intend to lead a new life, the beginning of which is precisely the receiving of the sacrament. Therefore on the part of the one baptized, it is necessary for him to have the will or intention of receiving the sacrament.[195]

Therefore, in the context of reading ST III 68.9 and ST III 68.10 together, Aquinas teaches that the Church's intention can of course stand in for the infant children of unbelievers, as it does for Christians generally, but *only if the unbelieving parents will their children to receive baptism*. And Aquinas

---

[193] ST III 68.3. Aquinas teaches that adults have a remedy against original sin: the mere desire for baptism (68.2), which can save them if they happen to die before being baptized. This was a concern because adults might need to defer baptism to Easter and Pentecost to be fully instructed in the faith. Aquinas even mentions the issue of some who come to the Church for baptism with insincere intentions; their baptism should be deferred to give time to instruct them to "safeguard the Church, lest she be deceived through baptism of those who come to her under false pretenses." However, if they are threatened with danger of sickness, these adults should be baptized. In his reply to the first objection, which cites Pope St. Leo the Great's Letter 16.6 to argue that baptism should be delayed until the proper liturgical season, Aquinas writes: "This decree of Pope Leo, concerning the celebration of Baptism at Easter and Pentecost, is to be understood with the exception of the danger of death (which is always to be feared in children) as stated above." Pope St. Leo wrote, in Letter 16.6, "For while we put off the vows of those who are not pressed by ill health and live in peaceful security to those two closely connected and cognate festivals, we do not at any time refuse this which is the only safeguard of true salvation to any one in peril of death, in the crisis of a siege, in the distress of persecution, in the terror of shipwreck." Charles Lett Feltoe, "The Letters and Sermons of Leo the Great," in *Nicene and Post-Nicene Fathers*, Second Series, vol. 12 (repr., Peabody, MA: Hendrickson, 1994), 28. Aquinas explains, "The second objection cites the Council of Agde, (held in 506 CE) canon 34 to argue that Jews who desire baptism should be made to wait eight months to see if they come in good faith: 'This decree concerning the Jews was for a safeguard to the Church, lest they corrupt the faith of simple people, if they be not fully converted. Nevertheless, as the same passage reads further on, *if within the appointed time they are threatened with danger of sickness, they should be baptized.*'" ST III 68.3 ad. 3.

[194] ST III 68.7 ad. 1.

[195] ST III 68.7 co.

argues that the children of unbelievers should not be baptized invitis parentibus even to save them from spiritual death.

Whether a Forced Baptism of a Jewish Child against the Will of the Parents Is Nonetheless a Valid Baptism

A final difficulty regarding the question of validity is raised by Cajetan's interpretation of ST II.II 10.12. As explained in chapter 2, Cajetan's claim is that Aquinas thinks that if such a forced baptism of a Jewish child does occur, it is a valid baptism. Specifically, the argument is that Aquinas's teaching that the baptized children would later reject the faith (R2) implies that Aquinas thinks children baptized without the consent of their parents receive the effects of the sacrament of baptism, since how else would they able to later renounce the faith?[196] Therefore, it seems Aquinas teaches that an unlawful (invitis parentibus) baptism of infant of unbelievers is nonetheless valid.

A possible objection is that perhaps Aquinas intended for the statement in R2 to be a hypothetical example, that is, "If it were possible for the children of unbelievers to receive such baptisms then they would not keep the faith because of the influence of their parents." Something like this seems to be what Catharinus had in mind. He argued that Aquinas was stating a hypothetical case in order to demonstrate how, in practice, such "baptisms" would ultimately harm the Church because the children would be persuaded by their parents to renounce what they had unknowingly received.

> But still Blessed Thomas's teaching is diametrically opposed. For he argues expressly against that opinion which wanted such children to receive baptism. And showing that this is absurd and false, he said, "For if they were to receive baptism"—he means this word conditionally, as if to say, if this were true, as you say, that such children receive baptism, afterwards, when they come to the fullness of reason, they could easily become deserters.[197]

---

[196] The Fathers of the English Dominican Province (Benziger Brothers edition) translate the text of ST II.II 10.12 as: "For children baptized before coming to the use of reason, afterwards when they come to perfect age, might easily be persuaded by their parents to renounce what they had unknowingly embraced; and this would be detrimental to the faith." ST III 68:10 reads: "Moreover under the circumstances it would be dangerous to baptize the children of unbelievers; for they would be liable to lapse into unbelief, by reason of their natural affection for their parents."

[197] Catharinus in *SA* 31. Mark Jordan also translates *Si enem pueri* in Aquinas's statement conditionally: "If children" were to receive baptism they could easily be induced by their parents to set aside what they unknowingly received. Jordan, *On Faith*, 210. Aquinas uses the term in the *Sent* IV, D. 6 q. 1 a. 1 co.: "First, he shows that those who are not yet born, existing in their mothers' wombs, have not received [*non susceperunt*] baptism by their mothers' baptism; hence they must be baptized." In IV, D. 6 q. 1 a. 4, Aquinas lists an argument that in cases of urgency a mother can

Another possible reply to this difficulty is that not all baptisms that are "received" result in sanctification since some receive the material element (the outward sign of visible washing with water) but not the reality of the character or inward justification of sanctifying grace.[198] As explained above, on Aquinas's terms, the application of the sacrament to the recipient and the inward justification are not one and the same. If a child of unbelievers received a clandestine baptism against their will, perhaps it is the "mere sacrament [*sacramentum tantum*]" or washing that the child receives and not the interior reality of the indelible character of baptism.

But Aquinas teaches that, unlike adults who approach the sacrament of baptism with different levels of devotion or various intentions, infants are equally disposed to grace.[199] Children receive the character and the grace of the sacrament because they depend not upon their own will but the faith of those who bring them to baptism. Children receive an influx of grace and virtues from Christ in baptism.[200] Aquinas considers this when he replies to the argument that since infants do not have free will and cannot assent to the things of the faith with a voluntary act, it seems infants cannot cooperate with God's grace. With regard to baptism, Aquinas says, "Infants are not capable of the movement of their free-will; hence it is by the mere infusion of their souls that God moves them to justice. Now this cannot be brought about without a sacrament; because as original sin, from which they are justified, does not come to them from their own will, but by carnal generation, so also is grace given them by Christ through spiritual regeneration."[201] If we return to our discussion of Aquinas's teaching on the virtue of faith, we can see that his theology of the act of faith is present when he discusses "virtual cooperating grace" in infants as this relates to parents and sponsors. Parents substitute their intention for their child at baptism. "According to the Church's ritual, those who are to be baptized ask of the Church that they may receive Baptism: and thus they express their intention of receiving the

---

be killed in order to remove the child for baptism: "Furthermore, eternal death is infinitely worse than bodily death. But the lesser of two evils is always to be chosen. Therefore, the mother should be cut open and the child taken out, so that, baptized, he may be freed from eternal death, and his birth from the womb should not be waited for." He rejects this and replies: "Bad things should not be done so that good things will come, as is said in Romans 3:8. And thus someone should rather allow the infant to perish than perish himself by committing murder against the mother. Similarly, one should rather allow the infant to perish than to perish himself by committing the injustice of baptizing a child against the will of its mother."

198 ST III 66.1.
199 ST III 69.8 co.
200 ST III 69.6 co.
201 ST I.II 113.3 ad. 3.

sacrament."[202] "Just as a child, when he is being baptized, believes not by himself but by others, so is he examined not by himself but through others, and these in answer confess the Church's faith in the child's stead." Although children do not have cooperating grace actually, they possess it virtually through their parents: "Even though there is no cooperating grace in infants actually, there is nonetheless virtually; for the cooperating grace which they have received will be sufficient to cooperate with free choice when they have its use."[203]

In the *Commentary on the Sentences*, Aquinas also says that infants receive the grace of the sacrament unto justification. He cites Peter Lombard: "*All children who in baptism are cleansed from original sin, receive both the sacrament and thing.* However, not only little ones, but also sometimes adults. Nevertheless, with infants there is no doubt that they receive it; there is, however, with adults, for they can impede it by insincerity."[204] "The soul of a child gets grace by the very fact that it is united to Christ through the sacrament of baptism without the exercise of free will. In adults, however, the exercise of free choice is required."[205] From these texts, it seems that Aquinas would hold that infants even if baptized against the will of their parents receive both the sacrament and character.

WHETHER JEWISH PARENTS LOSE THEIR RIGHTS OVER THEIR CHILDREN IF THEY ARE BAPTIZED

As is clear in Aquinas's answers in ST II.II 10.12, ST III 68.10, and *QDL* 2.4.2, he is aware of theological challenges to Jewish parental authority. His defense of Jewish parental authority takes place in the section of the *Summa theologiae* where he discusses the virtue of faith and the vice of unbelief. For Aquinas, the Jewish people are not under the authority of the Church in theological matters: "The Church ... has not the right to exercise spiritual judgment over [pagans and Jews]."[206] "The Church does not exercise judgment against unbelievers in the point of inflicting spiritual punishment on them."[207] Aquinas roots this teaching in Paul: "Now it is not within the competency of the Church to punish unbelief in those who have never received the

---

202 ST III 68.7.
203 *De ver.* 27.5 ad. 16.
204 *Sent.* IV D. 4, *expositio textus*; Peter Lombard, *Sentences*, IV 4.1, (26), 2.
205 *De ver.* 28.3 ad. 14.
206 ST II.II 10.9 co.
207 ST II.II 10.9 ad. 2.

faith, according to the saying of the Apostle (1 Corinthians 5:12)."[208] Augustine held to this ancient principle as well, and stated that the Church does not have spiritual dominion over outsiders. Augustine and Aquinas take Paul's teaching to mean abstention from judging those who are not under Christian law, whom the Church could not discipline.[209] When Aquinas comments on Paul's teaching in 1 Corinthians 5:12, he writes that Paul taught it was not his business to judge unbelievers, but that God will judge those who are outside the Church. "Those who are outside, that is the infidels, will be judged by God." For Aquinas, the Church "has spiritual power over those alone who have submitted to the faith."[210] Since Jews reside outside the Church, they are not subject to the jurisdiction of the Church in spiritual matters.[211]

It is in this context that Aquinas argues against the practice of forcibly baptizing Jewish children. Several of the Dominican theologians recognize this and incorporate the ancient Pauline principle into their arguments against the practice of baptism invitis parentibus. This is, in part, why Aquinas and his Dominican defenders argue that nothing can be done to Jewish children against the will of their parents. We now consider this argument, which we referred to as R5 (the argument from natural law that nothing can be done to children against the will of their parents), which includes the claim that Christians cannot take away the children of unbelievers.[212]

Aquinas assumes that if a child of unbelievers is baptized invitis parentibus, they would nevertheless remain with their parents. This is implied by the fact that Aquinas thinks the children baptized invitis parentibus would later be persuaded by their parents to lapse into unbelief: "Afterwards when they come to perfect age, might easily be persuaded by their parents." And ST III 68:10: "They would be liable to lapse into unbelief, by reason of their natural affection for their parents." If Aquinas thought that parents would lose their rights over such children and that the children would be taken away, why does he seem to assume children remain under the influence of their unbelieving parents?

Aquinas speaks elsewhere of situations where unbelievers raise Christian children. In another place in the *Summa theologiae* he remarks on the need for godparents to concern themselves with the spiritual welfare of their godchildren, especially if the children are brought up by unbelievers: "Consequently

---

208 ST II.II 12.2 co.

209 Grayzel, vol. 2, 12–13.

210 *Super I Cor.*, c. 5, lectio 3. See Vose, *Dominicans, Muslims, and Jews*, 52–53.

211 Aquinas adds that the Church has power over unbelievers only in the sense that it can forbid believers to deal with them.

212 The most extensive argumentation on this point is in ST II.II 10.12 and *QDL* 2.4.2.

[godparents] are bound to watch over their godchildren when there is need for them to do so: for instance when and where children are brought up among unbelievers. But if they are brought up among Catholic Christians, the godparents may well be excused from this responsibility, since it may be presumed that the children will be carefully instructed by their parents."[213] Aquinas refers to the situation of being raised among unbelievers as a danger to the faith of the newly baptized: "Where the danger is imminent, the godparent, as Dionysius says ... should be someone 'versed in holy things.' But where the danger is not imminent, by reason of the children being brought up among Catholics, anyone is admitted to this position, because the things pertaining to the Christian rule of life and faith are known openly by all."[214]

However, the papal counsel cited a text of the sed contra in Aquinas's article in ST II.II 10.12 that seems to indicate that Aquinas thinks parents of children baptized invitis parentibus lose their rights over their children. The sed contra of this article reads as follows: "Now it would be an injustice to Jews if their children were to be baptized against their will, since they would lose the rights of parental authority over their children as soon as these were Christians."[215] From a cursory reading of this part of the article, it seems Aquinas adopts the precedent of the Fourth Council of Toledo canon 60, which teaches that an unlawful baptism of a child results in the removal of the child from the parents.[216]

---

213 ST III 67.8 co.

214 ST III 67.8 ad. 1.

215 ST II.II 10.12 s.c. In ST III 68.10 co., Aquinas sets D.45, the well-known prohibition of forced conversions, in the sed contra: "There is a contrary argument in the Decretum Dist. Xlv, a canon from the Council of Toledo which states: the holy synod commands concerning Jews that henceforward none of them be compelled to believe through violent force (vis): for such are not to be saved against their will, but willingly, that their righteousness may be without flaw." Aquinas puts only the first part of canon 57 of the Fourth Council of Toledo, cited in D. 45, in the sed contra. ST III 68.10 co. is written after ST II.II 10.12 co. It is not clear why Aquinas chose a different sed contra near the end of his life. It is possible that he was aware of potential misinterpretations and abuses of the previous sed contra from ST II.II 10.12; this part of a scholastic article was often misinterpreted as the author's view.

216 As explained in chapter 4, the text of the Fourth Council of Toledo canon 60 was added by Gratian to *Decretum* secunda pars, Causa 28, question 1, c. 11, which states:
> We decree that the sons and daughters of the Jews should be separated from the company of their parents in order that they should not become further entangled in their deviation, and entrusted either to monasteries or to Christian, God-fearing men and women, in order that they should learn from their way of life to venerate the faith and, educated on better things, progress in their morals as well as their faith.

See Chazan, *Church, State, and the Jew*, 24. In ST III 68.10, he does not cite 60, which mentions separation of children from parents. For the text of the Fourth Council of Toledo canon 60, see *JLS*, 488.

Based on the sed contra of Aquinas's article in ST II.II 10.12, the papal counsel argued that Aquinas taught that parents lose their rights over their children if they are baptized. The papal counsel wrote as follows: "St. Thomas himself, in asserting that the Church has never been accustomed to baptize the sons of the unbelievers against their will, says, among other reasons, that in such a case the parents would lose all rights over their children, who have passed into the power of the Church by virtue of Baptism."[217] However, such a misinterpretation of Aquinas's position is due to inattention to the style of the disputed question embedded in the structure of his articles.

As explained above, the sed contra can easily be mistaken for Aquinas's own position because the sed contra typically represents something close to Aquinas's position. However, it is inadequate on its own since he may only agree with part of it.[218] The argument Aquinas places in the sed contra is the preferred argument *against* forced baptism of Jewish children in his time. The preferred argument was based in the Fourth Council of Toledo canons 57 and 60, but the argument also assumed the legal consequences of coerced but valid baptisms in the thirteenth century, since it states that parents would "lose their rights" over the children once the children are baptized. The inviolability of patria potestas was the preferred legal argument against baptism of Jewish children as late as Innocent IV (r. 1243–54). In other words, even if many canonists were opposed to the dangerous practice of forced baptism of Jewish children, they also assumed that a conditionally coerced baptism of an adult or a child of unbelievers was nevertheless valid *and* that children should be removed from the parents.[219] The argument in the sed contra seems to reflect this view.

But this is not Aquinas's position. The sed contra expresses only the preferred position against forced baptism of Jewish children. Aquinas's position is similar to the text in the sed contra but it is also different. Aquinas's position is similar in that he is also against baptizing a child of unbelievers against the will of their parents and seems to think that if such a baptism takes place it is valid. However, his answer is different in that he establishes

---

217 *BC*, 18.

218 "Sometimes [the sed contra] is a simple quotation of an authority, while at other times it offers the sketch of an argument, but rarely more than a sketch. In a few cases, it offers an argument that is no closer to Aquinas's final view than the objections [i.e., arguments]." Frederick Christian Bauerschmidt, "Reading the *Summa Theologiae*," in *The Cambridge Companion to the Summa Theologiae*, ed. Philip McCosker and Denys Turner (New York: Cambridge University Press, 2016), 11–12.

219 "In the case of minors, coercion and assent were irrelevant; all minors were considered Christians after baptism." Pakter, *Medieval Canon Law and the Jews*, 318; Kleinberg "Depriving Parents," 133.

the inviolability of parental authority for unbelievers over their children in the order of the natural law. Aquinas's discussion then spells out the consequences of this teaching. Not only is forced baptism of children of unbelievers contrary to the natural law, but so is taking children away from their parents: "Hence it would be contrary to natural justice, if a child, before having the use of reason, were to be taken away from its parents' care, or to have anything done to it if the parents are unwilling."[220]

When Aquinas refers to a child being "taken away," he uses *subtraho* (to take away, steal). This is the same term he uses in his discussion of vices against the virtue of justice in the second part of the *Summa theologiae*. There, he explains that injury of a neighbor against his will can be done by deeds or words. Deeds that unjustly injure a neighbor include murder, bodily injury, and theft and robbery. Under theft and robbery, Aquinas explains that these acts of injustice against neighbors derive their sinful nature through the taking being involuntary on the part of the person from whom something is taken.[221]

Therefore, not only is Aquinas against the sin of forced baptism of Jewish children against the will of their parents (which is an act he describes as repugnant to the natural law), he is also against the sin of stealing children from their parents. On Aquinas's terms, kidnapping is an odious and grievous sin that inflicts irreparable harm. Kidnapping is a mortal sin for which the pain of death should be inflicted.[222] Therefore, the act of forced baptism of Jewish children invitis parentibus and the thirteenth-century legal consequence of separation constitute a twofold sin against the parents. John Capreolus thought these violent acts constituted robbery: "God also has prohibited such fraud, nor does he want a holocaust to be offered to himself from robbery of possessions or persons, as would be done in the proposed."[223]

CONCLUSION

It will be helpful to summarize the issues according to the key questions that surfaced in the 1858 debate, as well as my answers to each question.

1. *Whether Aquinas holds that forced baptism of Jewish children is lawful or licit, and the closely related question of whether forced baptism is lawful in*

---

220 ST II.II 10.12 co.
221 ST II.II 66.4 co.
222 ST II.II 66.6 ad. 2.
223 Capreolus no. 8 in *SA*, 341.

certain exceptions, such as to save the soul of an infant from the danger of spiritual death.

Aquinas holds that forced baptism of Jewish children is not lawful or licit, nor did he make exceptions for cases of danger of death. For Aquinas, the care of parents for the young child who lacks reason is like a spiritual womb. Through the metaphor of a spiritual womb, he reframes and roots the Roman institution of patria potestas as it had been applied to Jewish parents in theological terms, as an order of natural right, which is an aspect of natural law.

However, the papal counsel leaves out Aquinas's arguments against the idea of baptism of Jewish children *invitis parentibus* in order to provide them with salvation. As Catharinus commented, Aquinas is diametrically opposed to the theological proposals seeking to justify the practice since these violate the natural law. For Aquinas, the baptism of an infant against the will of parents, even to save it from spiritual death, is considered a dangerous innovation that is against the custom of the Church, and that it is an attack on the natural law. The practice is opposed to Aquinas's account of the relationship between the natural law, grace, and God's relation to creation. More will be said about this point in the conclusion of the study.

2. *Whether Aquinas teaches that a forced baptism of a child of unbelievers is nevertheless a valid baptism, and the related question of whether a forced baptism of an adult would be valid.*

Recall that the papal counsel argued that a) the forced baptism of an adult unbeliever is nonetheless valid because even an act motivated by fear remains a voluntary act. This is true since Aquinas's theology of the baptismal character requires at least a general intention, even under duress. In my previous work, I was incorrect when I judged that Aquinas's view of the role of the human will in salvation undermines the accepted view among canonists that a "conditional coercion" is a valid baptism.[224] For Aquinas, the reality of the character is imprinted in the soul so long as there is no contrary will. In a "conditionally" coerced baptism of an adult, the recipient would receive the character of the sacrament but not sanctifying grace.

The papal counsel also claimed that b) based in Aquinas's teaching in ST III 68.9, the Church's intention stands in place of the unbelieving parents. This is a misleading prooftext for the argument that the Church's intention can stand in place of the intention of *unwilling* Jewish parents. The argument lifts Aquinas's interpretation of Augustine's letter to Boniface out of its fifth-century context and ignores the fact that the pagan Roman parents

---

224 Tapie, *"Spiritualis Uterus,"* 314.

intended for their children to receive baptism to restore or retain temporal bodily health. It also sets Aquinas's explicit teaching in ST III 68.10 that only Jewish parents can decide to baptize their children against ST III 68.9.

Finally, the papal counsel argued that c) a forced baptism of a Jewish child without the knowledge or against the will of the parents is nonetheless a valid baptism on Aquinas's terms. Aquinas insists that in baptism infants have intention and faith virtually through the sponsors and parents that present them, and that only the unbelieving parents can decide to offer their children in baptism. Yet R2 seems to imply that if children received a forced baptism, they receive the baptismal character.[225] *Susceperunt* in Aquinas is used mostly in ST III 68.6 and 68.8 to discuss the obligations of those who have received the faith or not. In 68.10, although Aquinas condemns the practice of forced baptism of children of unbelievers, he says that if such children were baptized the children might later return to unbelief (*infidelitatem*), which implies that they receive the sacrament and the reality of the sacrament. I had previously argued that on Aquinas's terms, a forced baptism without the intention of the parents is an invalid baptism.[226] However, Aquinas teaches in the *Summa theologiae* and the *Sentences* that infants receive both the sacrament and the reality of the sacrament. Although Aquinas strongly rejects the proposals for baptism of Jewish children invitis parentibus, he seems to assume that if such an unlawful baptism does occur the child would receive a valid sacrament.

3. *Whether Aquinas teaches that Jewish parents lose their rights over their children if they are baptized.*

Aquinas does not teach that Jewish parents lose their rights over their children if they are baptized. Rather, he teaches that it is against the natural law to have anything done to a child if the parents are unwilling. As explained above, Aquinas places a text in the sed contra of ST II.II 10.12 that states that Jewish parents would lose the rights of parental authority over their children as soon as these were Christians. The papal counsel appealed to Aquinas's sed contra in its argument against the *Pro-memoria* and *Syllabus* that the Mortara child could not be returned to his parents.

However, after reading Aquinas's teachings in the context of the scholastic genre of the disputed question, it is clear that the citation of the sed contra functions (perhaps unintentionally) as a proof text for the papal counsel's position and is not Aquinas's view. The counsel misinterprets the sed contra

---

[225] R2 occurs in in ST II.II 10.12, ST III 68.10, and *QDL* 2.4.2.
[226] Tapie, "*Spiritualis Uterus*," 314. The Dominican theologians of the *Syllabus* held the same position.

for Aquinas's answer to the question in ST II.II 10.12 and reads the statement out of the context of the rest of his robust teaching in the respondeo. Again, it is against the natural law to have anything done to a child if the parents are unwilling. This would, of course, include stealing the child. On this logic, even if a child was forcibly baptized against the will of its parents, it would be contrary to natural justice to remove the child. For Aquinas, the Church does not have a right over children because they were baptized, and if they are baptized, he assumes they remain with the parents. On Aquinas's terms, the "removal" of Edgardo Mortara was a kidnapping.

As mentioned at the close of the last chapter, Kenneth Stow attributes to Aquinas the legal principle *favor fidei*, which was then used by others to justify "offerings" of Jewish children and adults in the Roman ghetto.[227] Stow's claim is that *favor fidei* appears in Aquinas's discussion of forced baptism, and that Aquinas teaches that one must always prefer the principle.

However, the phrase does not occur in Aquinas's corpus. Benedict XIV did not think Jewish parental rights were grounded in the natural law as Aquinas did. Rather, Benedict thought the source of Jewish parental rights was *not* natural or divine law, but human law codified by the Romans.[228] Therefore, the root of the dualistic worldview that set Jewish parental rights against the Christian faith cannot be attributed to Aquinas.

On the question of whether a Jewish parent who converted could gain custody over their child from an unbelieving spouse, Aquinas follows the decision of Gregory IX and awards custody to the father who converts to Christianity with what seems like a caveat that the Jewish mother's permission is required for the Christian education of the child. But there is absolutely no justification in Aquinas for arguing that the rights of parents can be transferred to extended members of the family who convert to Christianity.

Benedict XIV's *Postremo mense* cited Aquinas despite the fact that Aquinas condemned as hazardous the arguments for baptizing Jewish children invitis parentibus in order to provide them with salvation. As we shall see in the next chapter, the citation of Aquinas in *Postremo mense* had the effect of awkwardly linking Aquinas to the 1747 teaching, a distortion of Aquinas's views that would be repeated by others.

Insofar as Aquinas's teaching is concerned, the Mortara family's plea is correct that Aquinas is opposed to coerced baptisms of adults and children of unbelievers. The argument of the Mortara family's plea (and the Dominican theologians they cited), that in Aquinas, the intention of the

---

[227] Kenneth Stow, *Anna and Tranquillo: Catholic Anxiety and Jewish Protest in the Age of Revolutions* (New Haven, CT: Yale University Press, 2016), 80 and fn125.

[228] Stow, 81.

Church *cannot* replace the intention of the parents of unbelievers, is also correct. The Dominican theologians insist that the representative will is a requisite for the sacrament of baptism to be valid, and when they argue that forced baptism of Jewish children is invalid baptism precisely because it lacks the intent of the parents, this view is in agreement with Aquinas's thought, in that it should not be done.

Nevertheless, the papal counsel's claim that a clandestine baptism of a Jewish child without the knowledge or against the will of the parents is nonetheless a valid baptism on Aquinas's terms finds support in his teaching that infants receive the sacrament and the reality of the sacrament.

Our analysis of Aquinas's texts, demonstrates that both canon law justifications for abrogating parental rights of Jews and the argument based on spiritual death were the most prominent arguments set forward for overriding Jewish parental authority of their children at the end of the thirteenth century. Twenty years after Aquinas's death, Scotus advocated for the forced baptism of Jewish children using similar arguments.

Through the metaphor of the spiritual womb, Aquinas provided a robust Christian theological defense of Jewish parental authority over their children. Aquinas's view of natural right is an objective order of equity established by nature, as an expression of God's wisdom.[229] Since the demands of natural justice, for Aquinas, are expressions of God's wisdom, Jewish parental authority is from God.

Despite Aquinas's efforts, some of the arguments for baptizing Jewish children invitis parentibus slowly gained acceptance among some jurists and were then codified in the eighteenth century. As discussed in the last chapter, the argument from the danger of death is a premise in the 1747 policy that asserts it is lawful and meritorious if a Christian were to baptize a Jewish child close to death against the will of its parents. Pius IX's decision regarding Edgardo Mortara was based on this policy.

One implication of this study of Aquinas's defense of Jewish parental authority as an order of the natural law is that his argument denies a premise in the 1747 policy. Aquinas argued that the natural law must not be violated to save a child of unbelievers from spiritual death, and that it is against the natural law to have anything done to a child if the parents are unwilling. This raises the question of the implications of Aquinas's teaching for the contemporary canon on baptism of non-Catholic children in danger of death.

---

[229] Again, for a discussion of the conceptual origins of the idea of natural rights as these relate to the natural law tradition from 1150 to 1250, see Brian Tierney, *The Idea of Natural Rights* (Grand Rapids, MI: Eerdmans, 1997), 44; and Jean Porter, *Natural and Divine Law: Reclaiming the Tradition for Christian Ethics* (Grand Rapids, MI: Eerdmans, 1999), 273.

In the next chapter, we turn to the question of the significance of Aquinas's teaching as it relates to contemporary canon law and the Church's teaching on religious freedom. What is the relationship of the 1747 policy and the 1983 Code of Canon Law, which states that an infant of Catholic parents, indeed even of non-Catholic parents, is lawfully baptized in danger of death, even if the parents are opposed to it?[230]

---

[230] Canon 868 §2, *CIC* 1983.

6

BAPTISM INVITIS PARENTIBUS AND THE QUESTION OF THE SECOND VATICAN COUNCIL'S TEACHING ON RELIGIOUS FREEDOM

Canon 868 §1 of the 1983 Code of Canon Law (*CIC* 1983) states that for a child to be licitly baptized at least one of the parents (or the person who lawfully holds their place) must give consent. It then adds this exception in §2: "An infant of Catholic parents, indeed even of non-Catholic parents, is lawfully baptized in danger of death, even if the parents are opposed to it."[1]

The purpose of this chapter is to examine the historical context and purpose of this canon. How is the canon related to previous canon law on baptism of infants of non-Catholic parents invitis parentibus? Moreover, it seems that a baptism of a Jewish child against the will of its parents would contradict the Second Vatican Council's teaching on religious freedom. What is the relationship of this canon to the Church's contemporary teaching?

This chapter analyzes the historical context and purpose of canon 868 §2 with attention to the previous Code of Canon Law (*CIC* 1917), the Second Vatican Council's Declarations, *DH* and *NA*, and the teaching of Thomas Aquinas.[2] I argue that the theological rationale behind canon 868 §2 is a problem for a few reasons. First, the premise behind the canon, which asserts that the salvation of the child outweighs parental rights, emerged as part

---

[1] *CIC* 1983.

[2] *CIC* 1917. The work is called the 1917 Code of Canon Law, named for the year it was promulgated. English translations are from Edward N. Peters, *The 1917 or Pio-Benedictine Code of Canon Law in English Translation with Extensive Scholarly Apparatus* (San Francisco: Ignatius Press, 2001). Again, *DH* refers to *Dignitatis Humanae* and *NA* refers to *Nostra Aetate*.

of a policy that separated numerous Jewish families in the eighteenth and nineteenth centuries. Second, the canon is theologically incoherent because it sets parental rights, which is a natural right in the order of the natural law, against the divine law. Lastly, I argue the canon runs against the grain of both the teaching of the Second Vatican Council and the thought of Aquinas.

I proceed in four steps. In the first section, I show that the claim that the salvation of the child outweighs parental rights was part of a policy that separated Jewish families in the Papal States. In the second section, I show that the origin of previous canon law on baptism invitis parentibus (750 §§1–2 CIC 1917) is the 1747 papal policy of the Papal States. I examine whether the *CIC* 1917 carried forward the theological rationale behind the 1747 policy. In the third section, I trace the development of canon law on baptism invitis parentibus in the *CIC* 1917 to the *CIC* 1983, with attention to whether the reforms adopted any aspects of the 1747 policy. In this section, I show that a major aim of the Church's intention behind the reform of the *CIC* 1983 was, in part, to bring the law of the Church into accordance with the teaching of the Second Vatican Council. In the fourth section, I show that the premise behind canon 868 §2, that the salvation of the child outweighs parental rights, is in tension with *DH*, the thought of Aquinas, and St. Pope John Paul II's 2000 Jubilee teaching against "violence in service to the truth."[3]

BAPTISM INVITIS PARENTIBUS AND THE SEPARATION OF JEWISH FAMILIES IN THE PAPAL STATES

This section is organized in two parts. The first section begins with a brief analysis of the Sacred Congregation for the Doctrine of the Faith's 1980 Instruction on Infant Baptism, *Pastoralis actio* (*PA*). The second section examines the consequences of the 1747 policy on baptism invitis parentibus in the Roman ghetto with attention to the separation of Jewish families. St. Pope John Paul II referred to this era of history in general as a "troubled period."[4]

PA states that the Catholic Church has always taught that "the practice of baptizing infants is considered a rule of immemorial tradition."[5] Since the sacrament of baptism joins people to the Body of Christ, the Church, it

---

[3] Pope John Paul II, "Apostolic Letter *Tertio millennio adveniente* for the Jubilee of the Year 2000" (November 10, 1994), no. 35.

[4] Pope John Paul II, "Address of the Holy Father John Paul II to an International Symposium on the Inquisition," (October 31, 1998), no. 4.

[5] *PA*, Sacred Congregation for the Doctrine of the Faith, October 20, 1980, 4.

is "an invitation of universal and limitless love."[6] Baptism shares in the Son's paschal mystery, and it is a communication of new life in the Spirit.

Parents present their child for baptism as a part of the entire community of the faithful. *PA* also recognizes limits to the practice of baptism: to admit a child to baptism requires parental consent and a serious assurance that the child will be given a Catholic upbringing. However, *PA* also adds an exception. There are some extreme cases in which parental rights are outweighed by a more important principle:

> Although the Church is truly aware of the efficacy of her faith operating in the Baptism of children, and aware of the validity of the sacrament that she confers on them, she recognizes limits to her practice, since, apart from cases of danger of death, she does not admit a child to Baptism without its parents' consent and a serious assurance that after Baptism it will be given a Catholic upbringing. This is because she is concerned both for the natural rights of the parents and for the requirements of the development of faith in the child.[7]

PA, like the current canon law, *CIC* 1983, allows for baptism of a child of non-Catholic parents invitis parentibus in cases of danger of death. What is the historical context of this canon?

As discussed in chapter 4, a line of thinking concerned with the baptism of Jewish children invitis parentibus in order to provide children with salvation began to develop in the thirteenth century. Canonists and theologians debated the question until the eighteenth century when the question was settled by Pope Benedict XIV's *Postremo mense*.

The 1747 policies had hazardous consequences for Jewish families. As mentioned in chapter 4, Benedict's decrees codified and encouraged the use of the danger-of-death exception. Recall that baptisms of Jewish children by Christian maidservants were a particular problem. Jewish children were entrusted to Christian maidservants due to the lack of Jewish nurses.[8] In Benedict's teaching, no definition was offered for what "close to death" meant, and the judgment of the Christian administering the sacrament was sufficient.[9] Under the law that required baptized children to receive a Christian upbringing, the consequence of such baptisms was the forced removal of

---

6 *PA*, 9–10.

7 *PA*, 15.

8 *BC*, 29.

9 As mentioned earlier, the position of Benedict XIV as well as the papal counsel in the Mortara case was that a single witness was sufficient to attest to the baptism of the children of the Jews, and especially in the case of probable death. *BC*, 26.

Jewish children from their parents. The policies opened loopholes for lawful forced conversions, which set the stage for the Mortara case and other cases.[10]

In November 1814, the governor of Reggio ordered that a seven-year-old child, Saporina De'Angeli, be removed from her Jewish parents because she had been baptized years earlier as a baby by their Catholic maidservant. According to the plea, the local Jewish community requested the return of the child, but the governor denied the request and Saporina was separated from her mother and father.[11]

In July 1844, police removed the nineteen-month-old daughter, Pamela Maroni, from her parents, Abraham and Venturina, in Reggio, Italy. Pamela had been secretly baptized by a Catholic woman who had worked in their home for a few days. The family's request to have the child returned was denied by the archbishop of Modena and the Holy Office in Rome. She was taken to the House of the Catechumens (hereafter Catecumeni) and her parents were not allowed to see her until she became an adult.[12]

Benedict XIV's rulings on the topic remained the law on the matter throughout the nineteenth century. This meant that if authorities in the Papal States were informed about a baptism of a Jewish child, the police removed the child from the parents' home and sent it to the Catecumeni. However, throughout the decades of the nineteenth century, the largest number of forced baptisms came not from Christian maidservants baptizing Jewish children but from offerings of adults and children made by male Jewish family members who had converted.

In 1818, Ezekiel Piatelli, a thirty-three-year-old man from the Roman ghetto, came to the House of the Catechumens.[13] When asked by the rector if he was married and had children, Ezekiel reported that he had a wife and two small children: a three-year-old and an infant. The wife and her children were then taken to the Catecumeni. The children were baptized three days after they arrived; the mother was baptized four months later.

---

[10] Marina Caffiero, *Forced Baptisms: Histories of Jews, Christians, and Converts in Papal Rome*, trans. Lydia G Cochrane (Berkeley: University of California Press, 2012), 15. Caffiero's work confirms Kenneth Pennington's view that Benedict's exceptions were the loophole that led to the Mortara case. Pennington, "The Law's Violence against Medieval and Early Modern Jews," *Rivista internazionale di diritto comune* 23 (2012): 43.

[11] David Kertzer, *The Kidnapping of Edgardo Mortara* (New York: Vintage Books, 2008), 34.

[12] Kertzer, *Kidnapping*, 33. The Catecumeni is where potential converts were instructed and baptized. For the relationship between the ghetto and the House of the Catechumens see Caffiero, *Forced Baptisms*, 11.

[13] David Kertzer, *The Popes against the Jews: The Vatican's Role in the Rise of Modern Anti-Semitism* (New York: Vintage Books, 2002), 56.

In 1816, sixty-three-year-old Sabato Rosselli entered the Catecumeni and was asked to offer his wife and three children. The police were then ordered to take the family from the Roman ghetto. The fifty-year-old wife, Preziosa, told the rector she had no intention of converting, and was locked in *stanze degl'Ostinati* (rooms of the obstinate), where she was pressured to convert.[14] After refusing to convert over a period of twenty days, she was sent back to the ghetto. Her eighteen-year-old son was also held against his will. He also refused to convert, as did his sixteen-year-old brother. The nine-year-old son converted about a month after his arrival.

Recall also that a Jewish convert could offer family members who were not direct dependents. In one case, a Jewish grandfather that converted offered his granddaughter against the will of her father. The girl was seized and baptized against the will of her parents.[15] In 1755, two girls under the age of seven were kidnapped from their widowed mother by their uncle and offered for baptism. Pope Benedict XIV ruled that the rights of the mother were overturned because the salvation provided by baptism was superior to anything a parent could naturally offer.[16]

The neophytes (including recently converted Jews) who lived in the Catecumeni could also obtain merit and recompense through the denunciation of their relatives.[17] A denunciation meant that the Christian submitted testimony that the person had expressed a desire to convert to Christianity.[18] In some of these cases, the police interviewed the accused to see if, in fact, the person had expressed such a desire. In other cases, the person was simply taken to the Catecumeni and subjected to sermons or threats of violence.[19]

The decrees legitimizing baptism invitis parentibus in danger-of-death situations were therefore part of a broader policy that caused the separation of numerous Jewish families in the Papal States. What is the relationship between this historical context and contemporary canon law, which still allows for baptism invitis parentibus in cases of danger of death? We now turn to an examination of the canon on baptism of non-Catholic children

---

14 Kertzer, *Popes*, 58. The limit was forty days.

15 Caffiero, *Forced Baptisms*, 15. See also the 1703 case of Ercole and Ester in Caffiero, *Forced Baptisms*, 14.

16 Caffiero, 41.

17 Caffiero, 13.

18 Caffiero, 147.

19 See the diary of Anna del Monte, who remained a Jew and left a diary recounting her thirteen days in the Catecumeni. Kenneth Stow, *Anna and Tranquillo: Catholic Anxiety and Jewish Protest in the Age of Revolutions* (New Haven, CT: Yale University Press, 2016), chapter 1; Caffiero, *Forced Baptisms*, 157.

in emergency situations in the *CIC* 1917, and whether it carries forward the principle that the Church's concern for the salvation of a child close to death overrides the natural rights of non-Catholic parents.

BAPTISM INVITIS PARENTIBUS IN THE 1917 CODE OF CANON LAW

The *CIC* 1917 or Pio-Benedictine Code of Canon Law is of monumental significance for the Catholic Church.[20] The *CIC* 1917 replaced the *Quinque Libri Decretalium* (1234) of Pope Gregory IX, which had governed the Church for centuries. The chief architect, Pietro Cardinal Gasparri (1852–1934), achieved the distillation of over fifteen hundred years of a vast collection of canonical materials into a single authoritative reference.

Canon 750 §§1–2 stated that in danger of death, the infant child of infidels is licitly baptized even against the will of the parents:

> §1. The infant of infidels, even over the objections of the parents, is licitly baptized when life is so threatened that it is prudently foreseen that death will result before the infant attains the use of reason.
>
> §2. Outside of danger of death, provided provision is made for Catholic education, [an infant] is licitly baptized:
> 1. If the parents or guardians, or at least one of them, consents;
> 2. If the parents, that is, father, mother, grandfather, grandmother, or guardians are no more, or have lost their rights over [the infant] or cannot in any way exercise it.[21]

The footnotes to §1 of the canon cite Benedict XIV's *Postremo mense*.[22] According to Dom Augustine, a Benedictine monk known for his explanations of the 1917 code, the canon was "taken in the main from Benedict XIV."[23] With regard to the danger-of-death exception, he wrote: "Our canon repeats what Benedict XIV pointed out so clearly, that the children of infidels may

---

20 Peters, *The 1917 or Pio-Benedictine Code of Canon Law*, xxiii.

21 Can. 750:
> §1 Infans infidelium, etiam ivitis parentibus, licite baptizatur, cum in eo versatur vitae discrimine, ut prudenter praevideatur moriturus, antequam usum rationis attingat.
> §2 Extra mortis periculum, dummodo catholicae eius educationi cautum sit, licite baptizatur:
> 1. Si parentes vel tutores, aut saltem unus eorum, consentient;
> 2. Si parentes, idest pater, mater, avus, avia, vel tutores desint, aut ius in eum amiserint, vel illud exercere nullo pacto queant.

22 For the text of the footnotes see *CIC* 1917.

23 Dom Augustine, OSB, *A Commentary on the New Code of Canon Law*, vol. 4 (London: Herder, 1920), 54.

be lawfully baptized against the will of their parents only when they are in danger of death."[24]

Recall that Benedict had taught that such baptism of children would be "praiseworthy and pleasing to God."[25] The 1917 *CIC* leaves out this language. And the text of the canon also adds a condition to Benedict's *morti proximus* (close to death) exception. The non-Catholic infant is baptized licitly invitis parentibus only "when life is so threatened that it is prudently foreseen that death will result." The necessity of a prudential assessment of death is an addition. As mentioned above, the lack of definition of what "close to death" meant opened loopholes for Catholic maidservants to baptize Jewish children who were ill. Perhaps the addition of the necessity of a prudential assessment of death was provoked by the Mortara case.

Nevertheless, it is not clear what prudential assessment of death might mean, or who is responsible for such a judgment. Dom Augustine's comment on the canon added a clarification of "prudently foreseen." He asserted that the child must be understood to have no chance of surviving to the age of reason. He also implied that this judgement can be made by a nurse. In a comment that confirms the above analysis of the historical context of this canon, Dom Augustine mentions a hypothetical emergency dealing with "Hebrew parents": "This danger must be such that there is little or no hope of their surviving to the age of discretion. Thus a nurse may baptize the dying child of Hebrew parents."[26]

Dom Augustine also cited one of the legal principles used by Benedict to declare baptism invitis parentibus in certain cases lawful. He explained that Benedict's judgement was "based upon the *favor fidei*, which dictates that the supernatural right should prevail over the natural."[27]

Another commentator, Stanislaus Woywood, OFM, asserted that the principle behind the canon is the infant's right to divine grace: "It is evident that, when the infant is in danger of death, his right to baptism which he gets through the Redemption of Christ is superior to the right of the parents over the child, for he is then in extreme spiritual need in which all inferior rights must give way."[28]

Therefore, the source of the *CIC* 1917 canon on invitis parentibus is the 1747 policy, and the idea that the supernatural right prevails over the merely

---

24 Dom Augustine, 53.

25 *Postremo mense*, 8; *DS*, 2553.

26 Dom Augustine, *Commentary*, 53–54.

27 Dom Augustine, 54.

28 Stanislaus Woywood, *A Practical Commentary on the Code of Canon Law*, revised by Callistus Smith, 2 vols. (New York: Joseph F. Wagner, 1948), 1:378.

natural. The purpose of the canon is to secure the spiritual life of the infant of non-Catholic parents if it is foreseen by a nurse that the death of the child is imminent. That which advances the Christian faith, and the child's spiritual life, are considered superior to the rights of Jewish parents.

Baptism invitis parentibus in canon 750 of the 1917 *CIC* was affirmed by Pius XI in 1929:

> The Church... never tires of defending her right, and of reminding parents of their duty to have all Catholic-born children baptized and brought up as Christians. On the other hand, so jealous is she of the family's inviolable natural right to educate the children, that she never consents, save under peculiar circumstances and with special cautions, to baptize the children of infidels, or provide for their education against the will of the parents, till such time as the children can choose for themselves and freely embrace the Faith.[29]

The footnote for this sentence cites two authorities: the *CIC* 1917, canon 750 §1, and Aquinas's teaching in ST II.II 10.12. The citation of Aquinas is significant because it demonstrates the first papal teaching in the twentieth century to affirm the practice of baptism invitis parentibus alongside Aquinas's teaching.

This continues the attempt, initiated by Benedict XIV, at the integration of Aquinas and exceptions to forced baptism of Jewish children. As I explain in section 4, the 1980 teaching on infant baptism, *PA*, would repeat this mistake. It is a problem because it implies that Aquinas is the source of the teaching on the inviolable natural rights of the parents *and* the exception to baptize invitis parentibus in cases where the infant is near death. But as our analysis of Aquinas's teaching revealed, there is no such exception in Aquinas. Indeed, Aquinas taught that the idea of such a practice was hazardous and against the custom of the Church. We now turn to an analysis of the relevant canon in the *CIC* 1983. Our aim is to trace the development of the canon on baptism invitis parentibus from *CIC* 1917 to *CIC* 1983 with attention to whether the 1983 reforms adopted aspects of the 1747 policy.

BAPTISM INVITIS PARENTIBUS AND THE 1983 CODE OF CANON LAW

In the first part of this section, I trace the development of the canon on baptism invitis parentibus in the *CIC* 1917 to the *CIC* 1983 with attention to whether the reforms carried forward the rationale behind the 1747 papal

---

[29] Pius XI, *Divini Illius Magistri* (December 31, 1929), no. 39.

policy. I argue that that the drafting committee charged with the reform of the canons on the sacraments determined to modify the *CIC* 1917 on baptism invitis parentibus based on their reading of the Second Vatican Council's *DH* as well as the ancient principle that the parental authority of unbelievers is based in the natural law.

Pope John Paul II's introduction to the *CIC* 1983, and the preface to the Latin edition, make the aim of the reform of the 1917 *CIC* clear: "The reform was to be carried out according to the decisions and principles to be determined by [the] Council."[30]

John Paul II promulgated the revised Code of Canon Law on January 25, 1983. On that same day, in the year 1959, his predecessor St. Pope John XXIII had announced both his decision to convoke Second Vatican Council *and* his decision to reform the *CIC* 1917. The reform of the code was subsequently requested by the Council. And the initiative began immediately after the Council closed on December 8, 1965. According to John Paul II, the aim of the reform of the *CIC* 1917 was the renewal of Christian life and bringing the legislation of the church into agreement with the Council's emphasis on this theme.

During the session that inaugurated the reform of the *CIC* 1917, Pope John XXIII gave the Commission for the Code of Canon Law principles to guide their work:

> [The Pope] indicated to the Commission two elements which should underly the whole revision effort. First of all it was not simply a matter of a new organization of the laws as had occurred at the time of the Pio-Benedictine Code; but rather it was also and especially a matter of reforming the norms to accommodate them to a new mentality and new needs even if the old law was to supply the foundation for the work of revision. Careful attention was to be paid to all the decrees and acts of the Second Vatican Council since they contain the main lines of legislative renewal either because norms were issued which directly affected new institutes and ecclesiastical discipline, or because it was necessary that the doctrinal riches of the Council, which contributed so much to pastoral life, have their consequences and necessary impact on canonical legislation. Repeatedly in allocutions, precepts and decisions during the following years, the two above mentioned elements were recalled to the minds of the Commission [for the Code

---

[30] Pope John Paul II, Apostolic Constitution *Sacrae Disciplinae Leges* of the Supreme Pontiff Pope John Paul II for the Promulgation of the New Code of Canon Law, January 25, 1983.

of Canon Law] . . . by the Supreme Pontiff, who continued to oversee the whole enterprise from on high and assiduously pursue it.[31]

After nearly two decades of an extensive revision process that included study, deliberation, and multiple drafts, the 1917 *CIC* was abrogated on November 27, 1983, by the Johanno-Pauline Code of 1983.

The 1983 *CIC* ultimately retained the practice of baptizing infants invitis parentibus. Canon 868 §§1–2 reads as follows:

§1. For an infant to be baptized licitly:
  1. The parents or at least one of them or the person who legitimately takes their place must consent;
  2. There must be a founded hope that the infant will be brought up in the Catholic religion; if such hope is altogether lacking, the baptism is to be delayed according to the prescripts of particular law after the parents have been advised about the reason.[32]

§2. An infant of Catholic parents or even of non-Catholic parents is baptized licitly in danger of death even against the will of the parents.[33]

The new *CIC*, like the *CIC* 1917, once again distinguishes between prerequisites for parents in ordinary situations and in an emergency situation.

868 §1 addresses the ordinary situation. It must be the will of the parents (or at least one of them or the guardian) to have the infant baptized, and parents must accept the responsibility to raise the child Catholic. Drawing upon principles from the 1980 *Pastoralis actio* that suggest postponing baptisms in certain conditions, the canon states that if this responsibility is altogether lacking the baptism should be delayed.[34]

868 §2 addresses the emergency situation. The canon repeats the 1917 Code of Canon Law's adoption of *Prostremo mense*'s codification of baptism invitis parentibus but it applies it to both Catholics and non-Catholics. One

---

[31] Pope John Paul II, Apostolic Constitution *Sacrae Disciplinae Leges*.

[32] Pope Francis's *Motu Proprio*, "De concordia inter Codices" modified no. 2 of 868 §1. Canon 868 §2 was not modified. See Apostolic Letter issued 'Motu Proprio' "De concordia inter Codices" modifying some norms of the Code of Canon Law (May 31, 2016).

[33] Can. 868:
  §1. Ut infans licite baptizetur, oportet:
    1. parentes, saltem eorum unus aut qui legitime eorundem locum tenet, consentiant;
    2. spes habeatur fundata eum in religione catholica educatum iri, firma §3; quae si prorsus deficiat, baptismus secundum praescripta iuris particularis differatur, monitis de ratione parentum.
  §2. Infans parentum catholicorum, immo et non catholicorum, in periculo mortis licite baptizatur, etiam invitis parentibus.

[34] See *PA*, n. 28.

commentator on the 1983 code speaks of the child's "entitlement" to baptism outweighing parental rights: "In danger of death, the will of God that all be baptized and the consequent entitlement of the child to baptism, take precedence over the parents' rights."[35]

However, other canon law scholars have expressed hesitation about the canon's application of the danger-of-death situation to non-Catholic parents because of the teachings of the Second Vatican Council. For example, the canon lawyer John Huels taught that 868 §2 (an infant of Catholic parents or even of non-Catholic parents is baptized licitly in danger of death even against the will of the parents) can only be applied to Catholic parents who have abandoned the practice of the faith but come from a Catholic family:

> The usual situation today for the application of this canon is that one or both parents have abandoned practice of the Catholic faith, but they come from a Catholic family, so one or more grandparents and/or other close relatives are keenly interested in seeing that a child in danger of death gets baptized. In that situation, I have always taught seminarians and other students that the priest, or other minister, should advise the grandparent or other relative to baptize the infant secretly. This can only be done if the child truly is in danger of death. The relative should baptize the child himself or herself. The Catholic minister should not, lest there be repercussions if the parents hear about it, for example, a lawsuit against the church.

When Huels addresses specifically whether 868 §2 applies directly to an infant of parents who are non-Catholic, such as Jewish parents, he says its application in such a case would be an injustice and violate the teaching of the Second Vatican Council: "If the child's parents are not Christian, but belong to some other faith, such as Judaism, no Catholic should baptize that child, even in danger of death.... Baptism should never be done in violation of fundamental church doctrine on religious liberty. That would be a travesty of the law."[36]

Another canon law scholar, John W. Robertson, argued that it is difficult to justify application of 868 §2 to an infant of non-Catholic parents given the Second Vatican Council's teaching on religious freedom: "In view of the

---

[35] Francis G. Morrisey, ed., *The Canon Law: Letter & Spirit; A Practical Guide to the Code of Canon Law* (Dublin: Veritas Publications, 1995), 478.

[36] Fr. John Huels, a canon lawyer who taught at St. Paul University in Ottawa, cited in John Allen Jr., "Relatives of Kidnapped Boy Ask for Rule Change," *National Catholic Reporter* 36, no. 38 (September 1, 2000):12. Althaus Rüdiger also thinks the canon is in tension with Vatican II's affirmation of religious freedom and should not be applied to Jews. Althaus Rüdiger, ". . . etiam invitis parentibus" oder: Heilsgewissheit contra Elternwille Anmerkungen zu einer problematischen Klausel im Taufrecht, in *Theologie und Glaube* 113. Jahrgang, 4. Heft 4, Vierteljahr (2023): 335–46.

teaching of the Declaration on Religious Freedom that no one may be forced to embrace the Christian faith against his or her own will, it is more difficult to justify baptizing an infant, even in danger of death, when the parents (or those who take their place) are opposed."[37]

Additionally, canon law scholars advise that on the question of parental permission, consideration must be given to particular teachings of *DH*, including no. 5: "Each family, as a society that enjoys a proper and fundamental right, has the right to freely order its domestic religious life under the direction of the parents. To these corresponds the right to determine the form of religious education that must be given to their children according to their own religious conviction."[38]

Indeed, the question of the canon's relation to the teaching of the Second Vatican Council surfaced just after the Commission for the Revision of the Code of Canon Law began its work. In the late 1960s and continuing through the mid-1970s, early versions of proposed canons for what would become the *CIC* 1983 were developed by ten drafting committees charged with the formulation of the new law.

In a 1985 article in *The Jurist*, Robertson showed that the drafting committee charged with formulating the canons on the sacraments was determined to modify the 1917 *CIC* on baptism invitis parentibus and bring it into line with *DH* and the natural law.[39]

If we trace the path of the revision process from 1971–80 it will become clear that the process of reform of the *CIC* 1917 surfaced differing opinions on the question of baptizing children of non-Catholics invitis parentibus. Writing about this path, one scholar of canon law observed: "The formulation of canon 868 §2 followed a tortuous path during the code revision process due to differing opinions among the consultors regarding the liceity of baptizing infants in danger of death situations against the explicit wishes of their parents or those who take the parent's place."[40]

The developments during the revision process were as follows. A significant modification was proposed in the drafting committee's first report. The members of the committee modified baptism invitis parentibus in 750 §1 of the 1917 *CIC*. In the first schema of the canons on baptism, the norm

---

37 John W. Robertson, "Canons 867 and 868 and Baptizing Infants against the Will of Parents," *The Jurist* 45 (1985): 631–38.

38 Ángel Marzoa et al., eds., *Exegetical Commentary on the Code of Canon Law*, vol. 3 (Montreal: Wilson & Lafleur, 2004), 468; *DH*, 5.

39 Robertson, "Canons 867 and 868," 631–38.

40 See Kevin T. Hart's commentary on this canon in John P. Beal, James A. Coriden, and Thomas J. Green, eds., *New Commentary on the Code of Canon Law* (New York: Paulist Press, 2000), 1056.

on infant baptism in danger-of-death situations was turned on its head: the baptism of an infant against the wishes of the parents was judged *illicit*.[41]

This judgment was made by the drafting committee based on a survey of papal teaching on religious freedom as well as *DH*. The committee considered a text from Pope Pius XII's 1943 encyclical letter *Mystici Corporis*, which reads as follows:

> Though We desire this unceasing prayer to rise to God from the whole Mystical Body in common, that all the straying sheep may hasten to enter the one fold of Jesus Christ, yet We recognize that this must be done of their own free will; for no one believes unless he wills to believe. Hence they are most certainly not genuine Christians who against their belief are forced to go into a church, to approach the altar and to receive the Sacraments; for the "faith without which it is impossible to please God" is an entirely free "submission of intellect and will." Therefore, whenever it happens, despite the constant teaching of this Apostolic See, that anyone is compelled to embrace the Catholic faith against his will, Our sense of duty demands that We condemn the act.[42]

The encyclical cites Augustine, Vatican I, and the *CIC* 1917 to teach that the decision to become part of the mystical body must be freely made since no one believes unless one wills to believe.

Among other papal statements the drafting committee considered is the 1885 encyclical letter *Immortale Dei* of Pope Leo XIII: "The Church is wont to take earnest heed that no one shall be forced to embrace the Catholic faith against his will, for, as St. Augustine wisely reminds us, 'Man cannot believe otherwise than of his own will.'"[43]

The study group also looked at *DH* 10, which reads as follows:

> It is one of the major tenets of Catholic doctrine that man's response to God in faith must be free: no one therefore is to be forced to embrace the Christian faith against his own will. This doctrine is contained in the word of God and it was constantly proclaimed by the Fathers of the Church. The act of faith is of its very nature a free act. Man, redeemed by Christ the Savior and through Christ Jesus called to be God's adopted son, cannot give his adherence to God revealing Himself unless, under the drawing of the Father, he offers to God the reasonable and free submission of faith. It

---

41 Beal, Coriden, and Green, *New Commentary*, 1056.
42 Pope Pius XII, Encyclical Letter *Mystici Corporis* (June 29, 1943), no. 104.
43 Pope Leo XIII, Encyclical Letter *Immortale Dei* (November 1, 1885), no. 36.

is therefore completely in accord with the nature of faith that in matters religious every manner of coercion on the part of men should be excluded. In consequence, the principle of religious freedom makes no small contribution to the creation of an environment in which men can without hindrance be invited to the Christian faith, embrace it of their own free will, and profess it effectively in their whole manner of life."[44]

The footnote to the line in *DH* 10 that states that the doctrine against forced conversion was constantly proclaimed by the Fathers of the Church appeals to Lactantius, Augustine, and numerous letters of St. Gregory the Great, as well as other sources of Catholic doctrine condemning forced conversion. Some of these sources were discussed in chapter 4 of this book.[45]

The December 1971 journal of the Dicastery for Legislative Texts, *Communicationes*, indicates that the committee modified the canon to state that if the parents are opposed to the baptism the child *cannot* lawfully be baptized even in cases when a child is in danger of death if the parents express opposition: "Thus, if parents express opposition to the baptism of their child, the child may not licitly be baptized even when in danger of death."[46]

The February 1975 schema of the canons produced by the drafting committee then used slightly different and more permissive wording but still prohibited the baptism of a child of either Catholic or non-Catholic parents even in danger of death if parents were opposed to this. The draft of the canon read as follows: "In danger of death the child of either Catholic or non-Catholic parents may be baptized provided the parents or those who take the place of parents are not expressly opposed."[47]

---

44 *DH*, 10.

45 For a helpful bibliography on the original sources in this important footnote to *DH* 10 see David L. Schindler and Nicolas Healy, eds., *Freedom, Truth, and Human Dignity: The Second Vatican Council's Declaration on Religious Freedom; A New Translation, Redaction History, and Interpretation of Dignitatis Humanae* (Grand Rapids, MI: Eerdmans, 2015), 31.

46 *Communicationes*, Pontificia Commissio Codici Iuris Canonici Recognoscendo, vol. 3, no. 2 (Rome: Typis Polyglottis Vaticanis, 1971), 200: "Etiam infantes qui in discrimine vitae versantur et morituri praevidentur, licite non baptizantur, si ambo parentes aut ei qui eorum locum tenent sint expresse contrarii."

47 Schema Documenti Pontificii Quo Disciplina Canonica De Sacramentis Recognoscitur, Pontificia Commissio Codici Iuris Canonici Recognoscendo (Rome: Typis Polyglottis Vaticanis, Februarii, 1975), 23:

§1. Ut infans licite baptizetur, oportet: I) spes habeatur fundata eum in religione catholica educatum iri; 2) parentes, saltem eorum unus, aut qui legitime eorundem locum tenent, consentiant.

§2. Infans, sive parentum catholicorum sive etiam non catholicorum, qui in eo versetur vitae discrimine ut prudenter praevideatur moriturus antequam usum rationis attingat,

The June 1975 journal indicates the drafting committee referenced the Second Vatican Council's teaching on religious freedom to explain its changes to the *CIC* 1917. In particular, the committee appealed to *DH* 10 to argue that the act of faith is of its very nature a voluntary act. In the case of an infant, this free act of the will is made by the parents or those who take the place of parents. Moreover, this free act of the will is made by the parents by virtue of the natural law [*lege naturali*].[48]

The drafting committee's reference to non-Catholic parental authority over their children as part of the natural law is highly significant. It means the committee's initial reform of the canon realigned the Church's law on the subject of baptism of non-Catholic children invitis parentibus with the natural law and what Aquinas understood as the custom of the Church.

The Commission for the Code of Canon Law then reviewed the schema proposals of the drafting committee for the sacraments and made substantial changes to their proposals. The commission altered the draft so that it reflected the previous *CIC* 1917 canon: an infant with non-Catholic parents in danger of death is baptized licitly even if the parents are opposed. They also added a condition concerning the danger of aversion to religion. Robertson observes, "Without explaining the change in the canon, the report indicated that the commission approved a text indicating that an infant in danger of death is licitly baptized even against the will of the parents, unless there is danger of aversion to religion."[49]

In 1980, the Commission for the Code of Canon Law modified the schema again by striking the condition concerning the aversion to religion: "Cardinal Florit wished to omit the phrase ... which would prohibit baptism of an infant in danger of death when there would be danger of aversion to religion, because this aversion to religion would be a lesser evil than not

---

licite baptizatur, dummodo non sint expresse contrarii ambo parentes aut qui legitime eorundem locum tenent.

[48] *Communicationes*, Pontificia Commissio Codici Iuris Canonici Recognoscendo, vol. 7, no. 1 (Rome: Typis Polyglottis Vaticanis, Iunio, 1975), 30:

Ratio huius mutatae normae propositae est quia actus fidei ipsa sua natura voluntarius est et requirit ut homo rationabile liberumque Deo praestet fidei ipsa sua natura voluntarius est et requirit ut homo rationabile liberumque Deo praestet fidei obsequium (cf. Conc. Vat. II, Decl. Dignitatis humanae, n. 10), et quia talem actum voluntarium ponere potest aut ipse baptizandus, si est adultus, aut eiusdem loco eius parentes, qui nempe *lege naturali* eundem, si ipse non iam agere valeat, repraesentant, eiusdem officia atque iura exercentes.

[49] *Communicationes*, Pontificia Commissio Codici Iuris Canonici Recognoscendo, vol. 13, no. 1 (Rome: Typis Polyglottis Vaticanis, 1981), 223–24.

baptizing the infant." The clause "unless there is danger of aversion to religion" was omitted.[50]

The canon lawyer Kevin T. Hart explained that the rationale behind striking the condition was as follows: "That such hatred may result was not as important as the salvation of the infant through baptism."[51] The final version that would be promulgated in the *CIC* 1983 reads: "An infant of Catholic parents, indeed even of non-Catholic parents, is lawfully baptized in danger of death, even if the parents are opposed to it."

BAPTISM INVITIS PARENTIBUS AND THE TEACHING OF THE SECOND VATICAN COUNCIL

The Second Vatican Council teaches that the human person's response to God must be free, and that the act of faith is of its very nature a free act. And because of this it follows that families have the right to order freely their own domestic religious life, under the guidance of the parents.[52] In this section, I argue that the practice of baptism invitis parentibus is in tension with the teaching of *DH* on the voluntary nature of the act of faith, and the religious freedom of parents to order freely their own domestic religious life. For similar reasons, the canon runs against the grain of Aquinas's teaching, as well as John Paul II's teaching against violence in service to the truth.

According to Nicholas Healy, the Second Vatican Council's teaching on religious freedom is rooted in what divine revelation teaches about the dignity of the human person.[53] *DH* 9 states:

---

50 Robertson, "Canons 867 and 868," 637.

51 Beal, Coriden, and Green, *New Commentary*, 1057.

52 *DH*, 5.

53 According to Healy, some understand *DH* as a departure from the true Catholic view that the duty of political authority to care for the common good entails acknowledgment of the truth of the Catholic religion and allows suppression of public manifestations of false religions. Others think *DH* is a break with earlier papal teaching. Still others understand *DH* as a genuine development of doctrine, especially the ancient view that free intelligent human acts and the transcendentality of truth imply a relation to the creator. The end of political authority is the care of the common good with attention to the dignity of human persons. The latter view guides my interpretation of the Council's teaching. See David L. Schindler, "Freedom, Truth, and Human Dignity: An Interpretation of *Dignitatis Humanae* on the Right to Religious Freedom," in *Freedom, Truth, and Human Dignity: The Second Vatican Council's Declaration on Religious Freedom. A New Translation, Redaction History, and Interpretation of Dignitatis Humanae*, ed. David L. Schindler and Nicholas J. Healy Jr. (Grand Rapids, MI: Eerdmans, 2015), 39–210; and Nicholas Healy, "Dignitatis Humanae," in *The Reception of Vatican II*, ed. Matthew Lamb and Matthew Levering (New York: Oxford University Press, 2017), 373.

> The declaration of this Vatican Council on the right of man to religious freedom has its foundation in the dignity of the person.... What is more, this doctrine of freedom has roots in divine revelation, and for this reason Christians are bound to respect it all the more conscientiously. Revelation does not indeed affirm in so many words the right of man to immunity from external coercion in matters religious. It does, however, disclose the dignity of the human person in its full dimensions. It gives evidence of the respect which Christ showed toward the freedom with which man is to fulfill his duty of belief in the word of God and it gives us lessons in the spirit which disciples of such a Master ought to adopt and continually follow. Thus further light is cast upon the general principles upon which the doctrine of this declaration on religious freedom is based. In particular, religious freedom in society is entirely consonant with the freedom of the act of Christian faith.[54]

That the Catholic view of religious freedom is rooted in divine truths about the dignity of human persons becomes especially clear when one considers the interpretation of *DH* in Pope Paul VI, John Paul II, and Pope Benedict XVI.

According to Pope Paul VI, *DH* taught that the human person's relation to God is the enabling ground of freedom.[55] John Paul II's interpretation of *DH* also indicates that the foundation of human freedom is the person's relation to God. In his encyclical letter *Redemptor hominis*, John Paul II explained that *DH*'s concept of religious freedom is grounded in what divine revelation teaches about the human person: "The Declaration on Religious Freedom shows us convincingly that, when Christ, and, after him, his apostles proclaimed the truth that comes not from men but from God, they preserved, while acting with their full force of spirit, a deep esteem for man, for his intellect, his will, his conscience and his freedom. Thus the human person's dignity itself becomes part of the content of that proclamation."[56] The idea that religious freedom is the first and most basic freedom is repeated throughout John Paul II's works.[57] Therefore, the right to religious freedom, for John Paul, is "not merely one human right among others," but "rather [it] is the most fundamental, since the dignity of every person has its first source

---

54 *DH*, 9.
55 Healy, "Dignitatis Humanae," 377.
56 John Paul II, *Redemptor hominis* (March 1979), no. 12.
57 Healy, "Dignitatis Humanae," 376.

in his essential relationship with God the Creator and Father, in whose image and likeness he was created."[58]

Pope Benedict XVI emphasized that religious freedom is rooted in the dignity of the human person, who is created in love and called to live in communion with the truth.[59] For Benedict, the right to religious freedom is rooted in the very dignity of the human person, "whose transcendent nature must not be ignored or overlooked.... This dignity, understood as a capacity to transcend one's own materiality and to seek truth, must be acknowledged as a universal good."[60]

It is important to point out the medieval roots of the theological anthropology behind *DH*'s teaching as well as the popes' interpretation of this teaching. *DH* teaches that the "act of faith is of its very nature a voluntary act."[61] According to David Schindler's important study, "Freedom, Truth, and Human Dignity: An Interpretation of *DH* on the Right to Religious Freedom," the Second Vatican Council's teaching on the right to religious freedom presupposes an ancient-medieval understanding of the spiritual nature of the human being and human act, and the transcendental nature of truth.[62] Indeed, the theological anthropology behind *DH* aligns with Aquinas's argument for why baptizing Jewish children against the will of their parents is repugnant to the natural law.

To articulate the ancient-medieval understanding of the person at the core of *DH*, Schindler draws upon Dominican scholar Servais Pinckaers's interpretation of Aquinas's teaching on the spiritual nature of the human act as it relates to natural and divine law.[63] Through this Thomistic lens, Schindler argues that *DH* affirms the subjectivity of the human person while simultaneously securing a link between this subjectivity and the order of truth, especially religious truth. For instance, *DH* 3 teaches the following:

> Further light is shed on the subject if one considers that the highest norm of human life is the divine law—eternal, objective and universal—whereby God orders, directs and governs the entire universe and all the ways of the human community by a plan conceived in wisdom and love. Man has been made by God to participate in this law, with the result that, under the gentle

---

[58] John Paul II cited in Healy, "Dignitatis Humanae," 376.

[59] Healy, "Dignitatis Humanae," 379.

[60] Benedict XVI, "Message for the Celebration of the World Day of Peace" (January 2011), no. 2; Healy, "Dignitatis Humanae," 379.

[61] *DH*, 10.

[62] Schindler, "Freedom, Truth, and Human Dignity," 39–210.

[63] Schindler, 60.

disposition of divine Providence, he can come to perceive ever more fully the truth that is unchanging. Wherefore every man has the duty, and therefore the right, to seek the truth in matters religious in order that he may with prudence form for himself right and true judgments of conscience, under use of all suitable means.

Truth, however, is to be sought after in a manner proper to the dignity of the human person and his social nature. The inquiry is to be free, carried on with the aid of teaching or instruction, communication and dialogue, in the course of which men explain to one another the truth they have discovered, or think they have discovered, in order thus to assist one another in the quest for truth.[64]

Schindler argues that in this text from *DH*, freedom or interiority of the person's social nature is first positively—not negatively or indifferently—related to the world and to God.[65] "The human being, as a creature, stands in an original relationship of truth with the world and with God, a naturally given relationship that he is called to freely and intelligently realize over a lifetime."[66]

As I argued in the last chapter, this positive directedness of human reason and will toward God is recognized by Aquinas: "Man is ordered to God because of reason, through which he is able to come to know God."[67] For Aquinas, since all human persons are created in the image of God, they are directed to God through their rational appetite for the universal good. God's grace elevates the person's natural desire for the perfect good by revealing that God in Christ is the perfect good, the First Truth. However, God's grace does not move the person's rational appetite to assent to the faith in a coercive way but in accordance with the rational nature of the human person. Aquinas calls baptism the sacrament of faith. The act of faith is defined by Aquinas as a voluntary intellectual assent to the articles of faith proposed to the intellect. God desires to know and love the human person according to the intrinsic nature of the person, that is, through their reason and will.

Recall that Aquinas applied this same understanding of the directedness (or natural inclination) of human intellect and will to the natural law precept of the education of offspring and the desire for God in his defense of Jewish parental authority over their children. Jewish parents enjoy the God-given

---

[64] *DH*, 3.

[65] Schindler, "Freedom, Truth, and Human Dignity," 103–5.

[66] Schindler, 102.

[67] ST II.II 10.12 ad. 4.

natural right of authority over their children and the duty to look after the salvation of their children, especially before they come to the use of reason:

> As soon, however, as [the child] begins to have the use of its free-will, it begins to belong to itself, and is able to look after itself, in matters concerning the Divine or the natural law, and then it should be induced, not by compulsion but by persuasion, to embrace the faith: it can then consent to the faith, and be baptized, even against its parents' wish; but not before it comes to the use of reason.[68]

Aquinas's defense of Jewish parental authority as a natural right in the order of the natural law therefore aligns with the ancient-medieval understanding of the spiritual nature of the human being and human act that is at the heart of *DH*'s teaching.

The right to religious freedom in *DH* must be understood not primarily as a negative freedom from coercion, although this is indeed essential. Religious freedom in *DH* is defined positively as the person's natural inclination to seek the truth and the good in relation to God and to other human creatures. For Aquinas, the natural law was also positively expressed in the form of precepts and natural inclinations that guide the person to truth and goodness.[69]

In Schindler's view, this interpretation of *DH* is confirmed in the teaching of John Paul II and Benedict XVI. Their teachings develop further the relationship of God and truth implied in the medieval conception of the spiritual, interior-subjective nature of the human act, and of this act's original-transcendental ordering toward the world.[70] It is on the basis of this positive definition of freedom as essential to human action that *DH* teaches that the voluntary nature of the act of faith precludes coercion. This is why *DH* 1 teaches that "in no other way does truth impose itself than by the strength of truth itself, entering the mind at once gently and with power."[71] Schindler explains,

> All persons have the right to seek the truth, ultimately about God, *in freedom, because all persons share in the spiritual nature of the human act ordered to the transcendental nature of truth, and are (thereby) obliged to*

---

[68] ST II.II 10.12 co.

[69] Schindler, "Freedom, Truth, and Human Dignity," 174n51; see also Servais Pinckaers, *The Sources of Christian Ethics*, trans. Mary Thomas (Washington DC: The Catholic University of America Press, 1995), 405.

[70] Schindler, "Freedom, Truth, and Human Dignity," 105.

[71] *DH*, 1.

seek the truth about God. This means that there can be no entry into truth, rightly understood, no legitimate promotion of the person's movement toward truth, that does not presuppose and demand respect for the interior self-determining, hence free, activity proper to the spiritual nature of the person.[72]

The spiritual nature of the person then, requires respect and excludes coercion. *DH* 10 teaches, "It is therefore completely in accord with the nature of faith that in matters religious *every manner of coercion* on the part of men should be excluded."[73] "In religious matters the person is to be kept immune within civil society from any kind of human coercion."[74]

DH's teaching excludes the coerced adult baptisms discussed in chapter 4, whether conditional or absolute.

Additionally, *DH* teaches that the same freedom that belongs to individual persons must also be recognized for the family, and when persons act together in community.[75]

> Each family, as a society in its own original right, has the right to order freely its own domestic religious life, under the guidance of the parents. Parents also have the right to determine the way in which religious instruction will be handed on to their children, in accord with their own religious beliefs. The civil power must therefore acknowledge the right of parents to choose with true freedom among schools or other means of education, and must not unjustly burden them on account of this freedom of choice, whether directly or indirectly. Furthermore, the rights of parents are violated if their children are forced to attend lessons that are at odds with the religious beliefs of their parents, or if a single system of education is imposed that excludes all religious formation.[76]

It seems difficult to reconcile this robust articulation of parents' rights over the education of their children with baptism of a non-Catholic child against the will of its parents. Contrary to canon 868 §2, *DH* teaches that the parents of non-Catholics, not the Church, have the right to determine the way in which religious instruction will be handed on to their children. Therefore, *DH*'s teaching excludes baptizing an infant child in danger of

---

72 Schindler, "Freedom, Truth, and Human Dignity," 83.
73 *DH*, 10; Healy, "Dignitatis Humanae," 371. Emphasis added.
74 *DH*, 12.
75 *DH*, 4.
76 *DH*, 5.

death against the will of its non-Catholic parents since this clearly constitutes an act of human coercion.

Canon 868 §2 can also be examined in the light of John Paul II's Jubilee teaching that rejected "violence in service of the truth." This teaching is best understood in light of *DH* 12, which declares that the Church has carefully protected and handed on the teaching on religious freedom she has received from Christ and the apostles.[77] "In faithfulness therefore to the truth of the Gospel, the Church is following the way of Christ and the apostles when she recognizes and gives support to the principle of religious freedom as befitting the dignity of man and as being in accord with divine revelation."[78] *DH* then makes an important acknowledgment that raises the question of departures from the Church's doctrine on religious freedom that she received from Christ and the apostles. *DH* states, "In the life of the People of God, as it has made its pilgrim way through the vicissitudes of human history, there has at times appeared a way of acting that was hardly in accord with the spirit of the Gospel or even opposed to it."[79]

DH 12 therefore laid a foundation that John Paul II would build upon in the decades after the Council. Healy points out that John Paul II's teaching on religious freedom includes his repentance for past actions by members of the Church. John Paul II can be seen to implement *DH* 12 by examining the historical record and calling attention to those times in history when members of the Church departed from the spirit of Christ and the gospel.[80]

In his *Tertio millennio adveniente*, John Paul II specifically addressed violence "in certain centuries" and said that the Church has an obligation to express profound regret for these actions:

> Another painful chapter of history to which the sons and daughters of the Church must return with a spirit of repentance is that of the acquiescence given, especially in certain centuries, to intolerance and even the use of violence in the service of truth. It is true that an accurate historical judgment cannot prescind from careful study of the cultural conditioning of the times, as a result of which many people may have held in good faith that an authentic witness to the truth could include suppressing the opinions of others or at least paying no attention to them. Many factors frequently

---

77 *DH*, 12.

78 *DH*, 12.

79 According to *DH*, 12, despite human failures and departures, the "teaching of the Church has nonetheless always stood firm, that no one is to be forced to embrace the faith."

80 Healy, "Dignitatis Humanae," 377; Pope John Paul II, "Apostolic Letter *Tertio millennio adveniente* for the Jubilee of the Year 2000" (November 10, 1994), no. 33.

converged to create assumptions which justified intolerance and fostered an emotional climate from which only great spirits, truly free and filled with God, were in some way able to break free. Yet the consideration of mitigating factors does not exonerate the Church from the obligation to express profound regret for the weaknesses of so many of her sons and daughters who sullied her face, preventing her from fully mirroring the image of her crucified Lord, the supreme witness of patient love and of humble meekness. From these painful moments of the past a lesson can be drawn for the future, leading all Christians to adhere fully to the sublime principle stated by the Council: "The truth cannot impose itself except by virtue of its own truth, as it wins over the mind with both gentleness and power."[81]

Pope John Paul II's 1998 address to an international symposium on the Inquisition applied his Jubilee teaching against violence in service to the truth to the period in which the Mortara case took place:

Ladies and Gentlemen! The problem of the Inquisition belongs to a troubled period of the Church's history, which I have invited Christians to revisit with an open mind. As I wrote in the Apostolic Letter *Tertio millennio adveniente*: "Another painful chapter of history to which the sons and daughters of the Church must return with a spirit of repentance is that of the acquiescence given, especially in certain centuries, to intolerance and even the use of violence in the service of the truth" (n. 35).[82]

CONCLUSION

It is not clear how the practice of baptizing infant children of non-Catholic parents invitis parentibus can be reconciled with the Church's teaching on religious freedom. According to the Second Vatican Council, "It is one of the major tenets of Catholic doctrine that man's response to God in faith must be free: no one therefore is to be forced to embrace the Christian faith against his own will."[83] As Pope Benedict XVI has said, "Parents must be always

---

[81] Pope John Paul II, *Tertio millennio*, no. 35.
[82] Pope John Paul II, "Address of the Holy Father John Paul II to an International Symposium on the Inquisition" (October 31, 1998), no. 4.
[83] *DH*, 10.

free to transmit to their children, responsibly and without constraints, their heritage of faith, values and culture."[84]

In 1747, Pope Benedict XIV attempted to synthesize Aquinas's teaching with a policy that sought to limit indiscriminate baptisms of Jewish children, but the policy also defined types of forced baptism as lawful. Citing Aquinas's thirteenth-century teaching against forced baptism of Jewish children alongside the exceptions to the practice had the effect of blending Aquinas's teaching with the line of reasoning from Duns Scotus that forced baptism of Jewish children is meritorious. This caused a distortion of Aquinas's teaching that has lasted for hundreds of years. The blending of Aquinas's teaching with the danger-of-death exceptions is evident in the papal counsel's reply to the Mortara family, *Brevi cenni*. This blending is also evident in some contemporary teaching documents on infant baptism.

For example, *PA* states that the Church has a concern for the natural rights of parents, but the document's restatement of the danger-of-death exception links Aquinas with baptism invitis parentibus in danger-of-death situations. This is evident in footnote 27 of section 15 of *PA*. The authors understand baptism invitis parentibus as a longstanding tradition rooted in *Prostremo mense* as well as Aquinas: "There is a longstanding tradition, appealed to by St. Thomas Aquinas (Summa Theologica, IIa-IIIae [sic] q. 10, a. 12, in c.) and Pope Benedict XIV (Instruction Postremo Mense of February 28, 1747, 4–5: DS 2552–2553), against baptizing a child of unbelieving or Jewish parents, except in danger of death (CIC, can. 750, par. 2) against the parents' wishes."[85] This footnote mistakenly presents baptism invitis parentibus in cases of danger of death as a tradition rooted in the *Summa theologiae* II.II 10.12. The 1747 policies have been mistakenly attributed to Aquinas at least three times since the eighteenth century: in the papal counsel's reply to the Mortara family; in Pope Pius XI; and in *PA*. As discussed at the end of chapter 5, this mistake has also been repeated by some contemporary scholars.

As explained in the previous chapter, Aquinas argued against the position that parental rights should be overturned to provide salvation for Jewish children. For Aquinas, parental authority over a non-Catholic child before the use of reason is like a spiritual womb established by God in the order of the natural law. The child's need for salvation does not justify breaking the natural law.

Since the premise of the current canon on invitis parentibus is that a child's salvation outweighs the rights of non-Catholic parents in a case of urgency, the canon is in tension with the teaching of Aquinas. In order for

---

[84] Benedict XVI, "Message for the Celebration of the World Day of Peace," no. 4.
[85] *PA*, section 15, footnote 27.

the current canon to be aligned with the teaching of the Second Vatican Council and Aquinas's teaching, the canon should be modified so that it directly states that for an infant of non-Catholic parents to be baptized licitly, one or both parents or the person who legitimately takes their place must consent. If only one parent consents, the child may be baptized only if the other parent does not object.

The concern for the salvation of the Jewish people motivated arguments for forced baptism of Jewish children in the thirteenth century, the eighteenth century, and the nineteenth century. These arguments were driven, in part, by the assumption that Catholics have a duty in the present age to seek the conversion of the Jewish people. The next chapter, therefore, takes a step back and asks a larger question about Christ and the salvation of the Jewish people according to the architects and fathers of the Second Vatican Council Declaration *Nostra Aetate*. The chapter examines the theological reasons behind the decision of the architects and fathers to drop from *NA* a statement expressing a hope for Jews to enter the Church in the present age.

7

THE INTERPRETATION OF ROMANS 11:25-26 ACCORDING TO THE ARCHITECTS AND FATHERS OF *NOSTRA AETATE* AND POPE BENEDICT XVI

According to the Pontifical Commission for Religious Relations with the Jews (CRRJ), there cannot be two ways of salvation since Christ is the redeemer of the Jews and the gentiles.[1] Yet the CRRJ insists that this Christological redemption is a mystery that excludes missionary efforts to convert the Jewish people. The authors of the document then cite a line from *Nostra Aetate* (hereafter *NA*) and say that it is the Church's expectation that the Lord will bring about the hour of the salvation of the Jewish people, "when all peoples will call on God with one voice and 'serve him shoulder to shoulder.'"[2] The architects of *NA* drafted this line under the guidance of the Secretariat for Promoting Christian Unity, which had been commissioned by St. Pope John XXIII to study the Church's relationship to the Jewish people. The line was inspired, in part, by the eschatological vision of St. Paul concerning the mystery of Israel in Romans 11:25–26: "I do not want you to be unaware of this mystery, brothers [and sisters], so that you will not become wise [in] your own estimation: a hardening has come upon Israel in part, until the full number of the Gentiles comes in, and thus all Israel will be saved."[3]

---

[1] GC, 37.

[2] The line from *NA*, 4 reads, "In company with the Prophets and the same Apostle, the Church awaits that day, known to God alone, on which all peoples will address the Lord in a single voice and 'serve him shoulder to shoulder.'"

[3] Rom 11:25–26, NABRE.

However, in 1964, members of the Central Coordinating Commission and the Commission on Faith and Morals appealed to this same text in Romans to argue that *NA* should express a hope for Jews to enter the Church. Some interpreted the proposal as a call to conversion.[4] The proposed language was ultimately dropped by the Council fathers after considerable deliberation.

What did the Council fathers say in their deliberations about the question of conversion and the universal saving significance of Jesus Christ for the Jewish people? Scholars have overlooked that the architects and Council fathers of *NA* appealed to a theological interpretation of Romans 11:25–26 in their response to the proposal. In this chapter, I argue that the rejection of the proposal for *NA* to express a hope for Jews to enter the Church was not based in pragmatic concerns but in Scripture, and, therefore, in the deposit of faith. The fathers' rejection of the text calling for Jews to enter the Church was based in a particular interpretation of Paul's admonishment of gentile followers of Christ in Romans 11:25–26 to recognize the mystery of the salvation of Israel. The fathers interpreted this mystery to mean that the salvation of the Jewish people takes place on a day known to God alone, and that it therefore does not entail a Catholic duty to seek the conversion of Jews.[5] In the light of the Council's deliberations on the question of conversion and the salvation of the Jewish people, we can say that *NA*'s language, which states, "In company with the Prophets and the Apostle the Church awaits that Day known to God alone," implies this teaching. I also show that ideas in the "Paul within Judaism" school of biblical scholarship, and in Pope Benedict XVI, reinforce the interpretation of Romans 11:25–26 in the architects of *NA*. Indeed, Benedict XVI's biblical exegesis confirms their interpretation of Romans 11:25–26 as excluding a Christian duty to seek the conversion of Jews. The Council fathers' interpretation of these texts is illuminated and

---

4 The proposed language read as follows: "It is also worth remembering that the union of the Jewish people with the Church is part of the Christian hope. Therefore, following the teaching of the Apostle (Romans 11:25) the Church waits with unshaken faith and deep longing for the entry of that people into the fullness of the people of God established by Christ." The text of the drafts is accessible at the website of the Council of Centers for Christian-Jewish Relations: https://ccjr.us/dialogika-resources/documents-and-statements/roman-catholic/second-vatican-council/na-drafts.

5 In Catholic theology, a mystery is "a hidden reality or secret. More specifically, in the theology of revelation, a truth that human beings cannot discover except from revelation and that, even after revelation, exceeds their comprehension. In addition to this primary meaning . . . the term has other connected meanings that should be kept in mind: (1) in soteriology, the great redemptive acts of God in history, especially in Jesus Christ; (2) in the theology of worship, the sacramental reenactment of the redemptive deeds of Christ." Avery Dulles, "Mystery (in Theology)," in *NCE*, 2nd ed. (Washington, DC: The Catholic University of America Press, 2003), 10:82–85.

deepened in the teaching of Benedict XVI because he makes explicit the biblical reasons why there is no duty for Catholics to seek the conversion of Jews in the age of the gentiles. This rejection of a duty to seek the conversion of the Jewish people is highly significant because it is based in the deposit of the faith, not pragmatic concerns.

This chapter is organized in four sections. In the first section, I discuss what the CRRJ has referred to as a "highly complex theological question": how can Christian belief in the universal salvific significance of Jesus Christ be combined in a coherent way with belief in the never-revoked covenant of God with Israel? I show that the CRRJ's 2015 document "The Gifts and the Calling of God" (GC) not only asks Catholics to focus on this question but also suggests that the Second Vatican Council's interpretation of Romans 11:25-26 is an important guide for Catholic reflection. However, it does not articulate why. In the second section, I remedy this problem by examining the biblical rationale for why the architects and Council fathers' interpretation of Romans 11:25-26 led them to reject the proposal for a call for Jewish people to enter the Church. In the third section of the chapter, I discuss a recent Catholic proposal that the "hardening" of Israel mentioned in Romans 11:25 should be correlated with the moral theological concept of "invincible ignorance." I then draw upon Aquinas to suggest a more positive Catholic interpretation of Jewish religious life after Christ. In the fourth section, I argue that ideas from within the "Paul within Judaism" school of biblical scholarship and in Benedict XVI's biblical exegesis confirms the interpretation of Romans 11:25-26 in the architects of *NA*. On the question of how belief in the universal salvific significance of Jesus Christ can combined in a coherent way with belief in the irrevocable covenant of God with Israel, Benedict's teaching is clearer and more coherent than GC.

CHRIST AND THE SALVATION OF THE JEWISH PEOPLE

The claim that God's covenant with the Jewish people is irrevocable has become commonplace in Catholic teaching. The teaching is established in the thought of St. Pope John Paul II, and it is included in the Catechism of the Catholic Church.[6] In the 2015 Vatican document "The Gifts and the Calling of God Are Irrevocable," the Pontifical Commission for Religious Relations

---

6 Pope John Paul II, "Address to Representatives of the West German Jewish Community," Mainz, 1980, https://www.ccjr.us/dialogika-resources/documents-and-statements/roman-catholic/pope-john-paul-ii/jp2-80nov17.

The teaching is based in Rom 11:29, which reads, "For the gifts and the call of God are irrevocable." NABRE. See *CCC* 121: "The Old Covenant has never been revoked."

with the Jews reiterated this teaching.[7] The document aimed to advance Catholic theological reflection on questions in Catholic-Jewish dialogue on the fiftieth anniversary of *NA*. Among the many suggestions for topics of reflection, the authors state that Catholics must reflect on the relationship between God's irrevocable covenant with the Jewish people and another statement of Catholic faith: the universality of salvation in Jesus Christ.

An entire section of the seven-part document is entitled "The universality of salvation in Jesus Christ and God's unrevoked covenant with Israel." The section opens by explaining that the universal and exclusive mediation of salvation through Jesus Christ belongs to the core of Christian faith: "The Christian faith confesses that God wants to lead all people to salvation, that Jesus Christ is the universal mediator of salvation, and that there is no 'other name under heaven given to the human race by which we are to be saved' (Acts 4:12)."[8]

However, the next paragraph adds an explanation to prevent misinterpretation. Though there is one path to salvation according to the Church, this does not mean that the salvation of the Jewish people is undermined: "From the Christian confession that there can be only one path to salvation, however, it does not in any way follow that the Jews are excluded from God's salvation because they do not believe in Jesus Christ as the Messiah of Israel and the Son of God."[9] And the next paragraph sets forth a "highly complex theological question" that, according to the authors, Catholics must continue to study: "Another focus for Catholics must continue to be the highly complex theological question of how Christian belief in the universal salvific significance of Jesus Christ can be combined in a coherent way with the equally clear statement of faith in the never-revoked covenant of God with Israel."[10] This complex question concerning the relationship of Christ and Israel is not new. In *NA* section 2, the Council affirmed that Christ is "the fullness of religious life."[11]

Some scholars understand this Christological fulfillment language to undermine the positive affirmation of the election of the Jewish people in section 4.[12] A related approach proposes two paths of salvation, one for

---

[7] Hereafter GC. See GC, preface.

[8] GC, 35.

[9] GC, 36.

[10] GC, 37.

[11] *NA*, 2: "Indeed, [the Church] proclaims, and ever must proclaim Christ 'the way, the truth, and the life' (John 14:6), in whom men may find the fullness of religious life, in whom God has reconciled all things to Himself."

[12] *NA*, 4: "God holds the Jews most dear for the sake of their Fathers; He does not repent of the gifts He makes or of the calls He issues—such is the witness of the Apostle." See Paul Knitter,

Christians and another for Jews. These approaches attempt to alleviate the tension between Christ and God's election of the Jewish people by revising the Church's Christology. Both are ruled out by the CRRJ.[13]

The CRRJ also rules out what it refers to as a "replacement theory" approach to the question of the saving significance of Jesus Christ and the Jewish people.[14] Although it is not addressed in GC, one version of this replacement theory is the claim that Judaism is a fulfilled and obsolete religion. It is important to say that this claim is not merely contentious in the context of Catholic-Jewish dialogue.[15] Such a view is contradicted by numerous affirmations of postbiblical Judaism in the teaching of the CRRJ, and especially in papal utterances made to Jewish communities.

Additionally, Catholics must also be sensitive to the fact that Christian anti-Judaism was deployed by antisemitic thinkers and politicians in the years leading up to and during the Second World War. Antisemitic Christian language about Judaism helped fuel resentment of the place of Jews in modern German society during what Saul Friedländer has called the years of persecution.[16] German liberals and nationalists demanded the replacement of Jewish identity "for the sake of what that they saw as a higher particularist identity, that of the modern nation-state."[17] The concept of outsider applied to the Jew by antisemitic thinkers "owed its tenacity not only to Jewish difference as such but also to the depth of its religious roots. Whatever else could be said about the Jew, he was first and foremost the 'other,' who had rejected Christ and revelation."[18]

"Nostra Aetate: A Milestone in the History of Religions? From Competition to Cooperation," in *The Future of Interreligious Dialogue: A Multireligious Conversation on Nostra Aetate*, ed. L. Charles Cohen, Paul Knitter, and Ulrich Rosenhagen (Maryknoll, NY: Orbis, 2017), 45–60.

13 "It is the belief of the Church that Christ is the Savior for all. There cannot be two ways of salvation." GC, 37.

14 "Replacement" is defined by the authors of GC as the claim that "the promises and commitments of God would no longer apply to Israel because it had not recognized Jesus as the Messiah and the Son of God, but had been transferred to the Church of Jesus Christ which was now the true 'new Israel', the new chosen people of God." GC, 17.

15 The document does not address this view, which is represented by the medieval concept of the cessation of the law. The cessation of the law is where Jewish religious life is fulfilled by Christ and rendered obsolete for Jews after the Passion. See my discussion of this view on the cessation of the law in my book *Aquinas on Israel and the Church: The Question of Supersessionism in the Theology of Thomas Aquinas* (Eugene, OR: Wipf & Stock/Pickwick, 2014).

16 Saul Friedlander, *Nazi Germany and the Jews*, vol. 1: *The Years of Persecution, 1933–1939* (New York: HarperCollins, 1997).

17 Friedländer, 82.

18 Friedländer, 84. As Peter Ochs has observed, "while Nazism was itself anti-Christian, it inherited the anti-Semitism that was a de facto consequence of Christian supersessionism. Thus, whatever its formal, theological justification or non-justification, supersessionism shows itself

For Catholics after the Shoah to affirm or imply the medieval view of Jewish religious practices as "dead" represents a failure to cultivate what St. John Paul II referred to as a "moral and religious memory."[19] Before and during the Second World War, German intellectuals called for the disappearance of the Jewish people by way of assimilation, legal exclusion, or expulsion. In this contemporary context, Christian usage of language that Judaism is obsolete for Jews (especially Jews who reject Christianity) become a counter-witness to the gospel.[20]

According to GC's teaching, these approaches can be said to err in the lack of attention to how the question of the saving significance of Christ and the election of the Jewish people must be viewed in light of the mystery Paul mentions in Romans 11:25–26. GC uses the term *mystery* in the context of the question of the saving significance of Christ and the Jewish people multiple times.

The fifth part of GC highlights the importance of Paul's use of the concept of mystery in Romans 11. The first and second occurrences appear

---

to be lethal as a public teaching." Peter Ochs, *Another Reformation: Postliberal Christianity and the Jews* (Grand Rapids, MI: Baker Academic, 2011), 1–2.

19 See Pope John Paul II's teaching on this topic:
   While bearing their unique witness to the Holy One of Israel and to the Torah, the Jewish people have suffered much at different times and in many places. But the Shoah was certainly the worst suffering of all. The inhumanity with which the Jews were persecuted and massacred during this century is beyond the capacity of words to convey. All this was done to them for the sole reason that they were Jews. The very magnitude of the crime raises many questions. Historians, sociologists, political philosophers, psychologists and theologians are all trying to learn more about the reality of the Shoah and its causes. Much scholarly study . . . remains to be done. But such an event cannot be fully measured by the ordinary criteria of historical research alone. It calls for a "moral and religious memory" and, particularly among Christians, a very serious reflection on what gave rise to it. The fact that the Shoah took place in Europe, that is, in countries of long-standing Christian civilization, raises the question of the relation between the Nazi persecution and the attitudes down the centuries of Christians towards Jews.
"We Remember: A Reflection on the Shoah," Commission for Religious Relations with the Jews, 1998, http://www.christianunity.va/content/unitacristiani/en/commissione-per-i-rapporti-religiosi-con-l-ebraismo/commissione-per-i-rapporti-religiosi-con-l-ebraismo-crre/documenti-della-commissione/en1.html.

20 "It is appropriate that, as the Second Millennium of Christianity draws to a close, the Church should become more fully conscious of the sinfulness of her children, recalling all those times in history when they departed from the spirit of Christ and his Gospel and, instead of offering to the world the witness of a life inspired by the values of faith, indulged in ways of thinking and acting which were truly forms of counter-witness and scandal." Pope John Paul II, *Tertio Millennio*, no. 33. See also the use and extension of this term in the important document from the International Theological Commission, "Memory and Reconciliation," no. 1.3, 5.3, 5.4.

immediately after the document highlights that St. Paul negates the question he himself posed, whether God repudiated his own people:

> That the Jews are participants in God's salvation is theologically unquestionable, but how that can be possible without confessing Christ explicitly, is and remains an unfathomable divine *mystery*. It is therefore no accident that Paul's soteriological reflection in Romans 9–11 on the irrevocable redemption of Israel against the background of the Christ-*mystery* culminate in a magnificent doxology: "Oh, the depth of the riches and wisdom and knowledge of God! How inscrutable are his judgments and how unsearchable his ways" (Rom 11:33).[21]

The third usage of *mystery* occurs immediately after the introduction of the "highly complex theological question" (how Christian belief in the universal salvific significance of Jesus Christ can be combined in a coherent way with the never-revoked covenant of God with Israel). The authors cite *NA* to explain that "Christ is also the Redeemer of the Jews in addition to the Gentiles. Here we confront the *mystery* of God's work, which is not a matter of missionary efforts to convert Jews, but rather the expectation that the Lord will bring about the hour when we will all be united, 'when all peoples will call on God with one voice and "serve him shoulder to shoulder"' (*Nostra Aetate*, no. 4)."[22]

Therefore, GC clearly emphasizes that the concept of mystery is key for Catholic reflection upon the question of the Jewish people and the saving significance of Christ. The direct reference to *NA*'s mention of the hour when all people will be united indicates that the authors of GC understand the Council's teaching as significant for reflection on why missionary efforts to convert Jews are excluded. But the authors do not articulate how the Council fathers interpreted the mystery of Israel's salvation.

I now turn to an analysis of the interpretation of Romans 11:25–26 in the architects and fathers of *NA*. I argue that the rejection of the proposal for the declaration to express a hope for Jews to enter the Church was based, in part, on an eschatological interpretation of Paul's admonishment of gentile followers of Christ in Romans 11:25–26 to recognize the mystery of Israel's salvation.

---

[21] GC, 36. Emphasis added.
[22] GC, 37. Emphasis added.

THE INTERPRETATION OF ROMANS 11:25-26 IN THE ARCHITECTS AND FATHERS OF *NOSTRA AETATE*

In the first part of this section, I discuss the architects of *NA* and their positive affirmation of Jewish election and peoplehood. In the second part, I show that their rejection of the proposal to include a call for the Jewish people to enter the Church in *NA* was based on an interpretation of Romans 11:25–26, not merely pragmatic concerns.[23]

The architects of *NA* wrestled with the complex question of the Jewish people and the saving significance of Christ before and during the Second Vatican Council. In the years leading up to the drafting of *NA*, the Council fathers elevated a teaching from Paul's letter to the Romans that had been buried by negative Christian language about the Jewish people.

Certain elements of the premodern Catholic view of Jews and Judaism reflect a strong connection between the election of Israel and the Jewish Christ. Church fathers and medieval theologians taught that Jesus was Jewish; that he was circumcised on the eighth day and lived "under the law."[24] As argued in chapters 2 and 5, Aquinas also taught that the Jewish people do not belong to the spiritual authority of the Church, and he defended toleration of Jewish worship and parental authority.[25] Augustine and Aquinas taught that the presence of Jews was beneficial to Christian society and argued that the Jewish people should therefore be tolerated.[26] The theological claims provided a foundation for policies of restricted tolerance, though the policies were not followed by all princes and popes.

Moreover, the positive views were intertwined with claims that the Jews were scattered throughout the diaspora as a punishment by God for rejecting Christ. And some would argue against the principles of the more tolerant Augustinian tradition. As discussed in chapters 4 and 5, Aquinas's contemporaries, including the Franciscan theologian Duns Scotus and others, claimed that force should be used to convert Jews, including their children. The positive statements concerning the Jewish people in the tradition were often

---

[23] Some understand the Council's rejection of a call for conversion as a pragmatic response to public controversy over leaked drafts of the statement. For one example of this common view see Karma Ben-Johanan, *Jacob's Younger Brother: Christian-Jewish Relations after Vatican II* (Cambridge, MA: Harvard University Press, 2022), 35, 71.

[24] Aquinas engaged in extended reflections on the nature and purpose of Christ's circumcision, for example in ST III 37.

[25] ST II.II 10.9, ad. 2; 10.12.

[26] St. Augustine, *The City of God, Books 11–22*, trans. William Babcock (Hyde Park, NY: New City Press, 2013), XVIII.46; Paula Fredriksen, *Augustine and the Jews: A Christian Defense of Jews and Judaism* (New York: Doubleday Religion, 2008), 276–77.

buried by negative theological attitudes, severely discriminatory policies, and outbreaks of violence. Contrary to Paul's warning in Romans 11:20 ("Do not become proud, but stand in awe"), a boasting against the Jewish people was cemented in theological writings and some papal utterances.[27] As Pope Benedict XVI has said, relations between Jews and Christians in this period can be described as "a long and difficult history."[28]

The positive Pauline ideas about the Jews in *NA* would be recovered in the Christian theological struggle against Nazi racial antisemitism in central Europe in the years just before the Holocaust.[29] The Catholic theologians and architects of ideas in *NA*, John M. Oesterreicher and Karl Thieme, among others, fought to prevent the synthesis of Catholicism with Nazism during the rise of the Third Reich.[30] In their confrontation with racial antisemitism these theologians were forced to question negative Christian arguments invoked by the Nazis, such as that Jews were under a divine curse for deicide and that Judaism was an obsolete religion.

For example, through an exchange with Martin Buber in 1948, Thieme came to recognize that what was needed to overcome Christian antisemitism was the rejection of its theological source, namely, the Christian teaching that Israel "according to the flesh" was a people God willed only in the past but no longer.[31] Thieme challenged this teaching by drawing upon Paul's words in the letter to the Romans that Jews remain dear to God despite unbelief in Christ.[32] The breakthrough idea, for Thieme, was that a Jewish person, not

---

[27] This attitude of superiority assumed the erroneous deicide charge based in interpretations of Matt 27:25. The false charge was rejected at the Second Vatican Council, in NA no. 4. See also 1 Thess 2:14–16, NABRE. Pope Gregory IX's call for the confiscation of the Talmud is an example of this attitude. By the mid-sixteenth century, Catholic-Jewish relations deteriorated under Pope Paul IV.

[28] "Before the recent crimes of the Nazi regime and, in general with a retrospective look at a long and difficult history, it was necessary to evaluate and define in a new way the relationship between the Church and the faith of Israel." Pope Benedict XVI, "Christmas Address to the Roman Curia," December 22, 2005, https://ccjr.us/dialogika-resources/documents-and-statements/roman-catholic/pope-benedict-xvi/b16-05dec22.

[29] John Connelly, *From Enemy to Brother: The Revolution in Catholic Teaching on the Jews, 1933–1965* (Cambridge, MA: Harvard University Press, 2012).

[30] John Marin Oesterreicher was an Austrian Jew who converted to Catholicism and was ordained a Catholic priest. Karl Thieme was a German theologian and Protestant convert to Catholicism.

[31] The classic phrase from Paul should not be interpreted pejoratively. As Oesterreicher explained, the phrase "does not stigmatize the Jews for any supposed carnality, sensuality, or worldliness. It refers simply to the Israel that has come forth by natural generation." Oesterreicher, *The New Encounter: Between Christians and Jews* (New York: Philosophical Library, 1986), 289n23.

[32] Rom 11:28–29, NRSVCE.

only as an individual but precisely as a Jew, can be pleasing to God.[33] Thieme was able to assemble these ideas about the Jews and make the argument that even after the Passion of Christ, the Jewish people remained dear to God unto the end of time.

Some of these ideas would be incorporated into *NA* and approved by the Council fathers. They exalted the Pauline teaching recovered by the Catholic anti-Nazi thinkers that the Jewish people remain dear to God: "As Holy Scripture testifies, Jerusalem did not recognize the time of her visitation, nor did the Jews in large number, accept the Gospel; indeed not a few opposed its spreading. Nevertheless, God holds the Jews most dear for the sake of their Fathers; He does not repent of the gifts He makes or of the calls He issues—such is the witness of the Apostle."[34] The Council fathers were aware of texts indicating that some Jews in first-century Jerusalem did not accept the gospel. However, the line they adopted to address the opposition of some Jews to the gospel is immediately followed by "nevertheless," or in the Latin of the declaration, *nihilominus*. Nevertheless, "God holds the Jews most dear."[35]

Which Jews did the Council fathers have in mind? Was it only the biblical Jews of Paul's time? *Lumen Gentium*, Vatican II's Dogmatic Constitution on the Church, affirmed the election of the Jews as a people with its distinction between the Israelite fathers and "this people": "On account of their fathers *this people* remains most dear to God, for God does not repent of the gifts He makes nor of the calls He issues."[36] In *NA*, the Council also rejected the idea that the Jewish people were a people like any other in its deliberate use of the phrase "Abraham's stock" or "offspring" to refer to the Jews *as a people* instead of only a religion.[37] *NA* is therefore about the Jewish people, and it affirms that God holds these particular people, the offspring of Abraham,

---

33 Thieme wrote, "Precisely for the Jews according to the entirety of divine revelation certain promises continue to be in force, so that one can assume that even in distance from Christ the Jewish people enjoys special guidance and special grace." Cited in Connelly, *From Enemy to Brother*, 205.

34 *NA*, 4.

35 *LG*, 16. Emphasis added.

36 "Mysterium Ecclesiae perscrutans, Sacra haec Synodus meminit vinculi, quo populus Novi Testamenti cum stirpe Abrahae spiritualiter coniunctus est." Connelly, *From Enemy to Brother*, 191. See Isa 41:8 and Jer 33:26, NABRE. Thomas Stransky translates *stirpe* as "offspring." See his translation of the text of *NA* in *Nostra Aetate: Celebrating Fifty Years of the Catholic Church's Dialogue with Jews and Muslims*, ed. Pim Valkenberg and Anthony Cirelli (Washington, DC: The Catholic University of America Press, 2016), xxi.

37 The recognition of the permanence of Judaism as a religion would come later, in the documents issued by the CRRJ in 1974, 1985, and 2015.

most dear.³⁸ Though the declaration did not mention an "irrevocable covenant" with the Jewish people as John Paul II would speak of decades later, *NA* affirms that God holds the Jews as a people most dear. The declaration also historically rejected the deicide charge, collective guilt, and antisemitism.

This positive view of the special status of the Jewish people based in Romans was advanced amidst critical questions.³⁹ For example, Jean Daniélou made his doubts about the positive teaching known in private to the Dominican exegete Jacque Dupont: "They want to say that the Jewish people is not a people like the others.... This reflects Jewish ideology but not Christian theology. As we see it, the fleshly Israel lost all its privileges, and we have inherited them. Israel is now a people like all the others, exactly like all the others."⁴⁰ The French Dominican and archeologist Pierre Benoit, who joined the subcommittee drafting the statement on the Jews in the fall of 1964, argued a similar point in a memorandum he submitted before the final vote on *NA*.

However, Oesterreicher anticipated Benoit's objections and insisted that if Paul had wanted to say Jews were like all other peoples he would have, but instead he argued that Christians must not make themselves superior to the branches. This language was a reference to Romans 11:18: "Do not boast against the branches. If you do boast, consider that you do not support the root; the root supports you."⁴¹

As evidenced by these citations of Scripture, the solution to the "two-thousand-year-old problem of the relation of the Church with the Jewish

---

[38] Some have interpreted a recent statement from the CRRJ (GC 39) to teach that *NA* is not about the Jews. But the overinterpretation of the Council that concerned the CRRJ is the claim that *NA* taught that there exists an irrevocable covenant: "Because it was such a theological breakthrough, the Conciliar text is not infrequently over-interpreted, and things are read into it which it does not in fact contain. An important example of over-interpretation would be the following: that the covenant that God made with his people Israel perdures and is never invalidated. Although this statement is true, it cannot be explicitly read into 'Nostra aetate' (no. 4)." See GC, 39. The context of the declaration as well as the text of the declaration concerns the whole people, not their ancient Israelite fathers only.

[39] Giovanni Miccoli thinks the real reason for the opposition from those in the Curia and the conciliar minority to the positive language on the Jews in *NA*, 4, was a deeper antisemitism evidenced in "books, short works, and leaflets circulated far and wide among the fathers" that claimed the right of the Church to defend itself against "Jewish aggression." After learning of the leaflets, Fr. Congar wrote in his journal of September 28, "Anti-Semitism is not dead!" Giovanni Miccoli, "Two Sensitive Issues: Religious Freedom and the Jews," In *History of Vatican II*, vol. 4: *Church as Communion: Third Period and Intersession, September 1964–September 1965*, ed. Giuseppe Alberigo and Joseph Komonchak (Maryknoll, NY: Orbis, 2003), 156–57. However, for some, questions of biblical interpretation were at stake.

[40] Connelly, *From Enemy to Brother*, 261.

[41] Connelly, 263; Rom 11:18, NABRE.

people was sought by the drafters of *NA* at a profoundly biblical level."[42] Bea and the drafters of *NA* oriented the Church's understanding of its relation to the Jews to Romans. In a plea to the Council fathers to make the statement on the Jews part of the Council proceedings, Bea argued that "the aim of this very brief decree is to call to the attention of Christ's faithful these truths concerning the Jews which are affirmed by the apostle and contained in the deposit of faith, and to do this so clearly that in dealing with the children of that people the faithful will act in no other way than did Christ the Lord and his apostles Peter and Paul."[43] Likewise, Oesterreicher said the Council's intention was "to restore the Pauline view of the Jewish people and to put an end to certain interpretations of Scripture which contracted its true meaning."[44]

Some responded with appeals to Galatians and Hebrews and claimed that the Jews' role in history as the chosen people was made obsolete and that the New Covenant had replaced the Old Covenant.[45] Why should Romans 9–11 guide the Church's reflection on Judaism rather than other parts of the New Testament? The architects rightly pointed out that Romans was Paul's final epistle, and it represented his mature views of the Jewish people after the Passion of Christ and the preaching of the gospel. Chapters 9–11 of Romans also represented Paul's *only* pastoral letter directly instructing gentile believers about the Jewish people.[46]

In the summer of 1964, Luigi Ciappi, the personal theologian of Pope Paul VI and member of the Commission on Faith and Morals, sent a memorandum to the pope requesting that language be added to the statement on the Jews that urged the Jewish people to accept Christ. Ciappi argued that the unbelief of Jews in Christ cannot be defined as invincible ignorance, and requires a Catholic duty to work for the conversion of the Jewish people:

> The infidelity of the Jews is not simple, inculpable ignorance of Christ, but is a positive infidelity, even if judgment on individuals is reserved to God alone. Therefore the Church cannot be uninterested in their conversion or

---

[42] Augustin Cardinal Bea, *The Church and the Jewish People: A Commentary on the Second Vatican Council's Declaration on the Relation of the Church to Non-Christian Religions* (New York: Harper and Row, 1966), 7.

[43] John M. Oesterreicher, "Declaration on the Relationship of the Church to Non-Christian Religions," in *Commentary on the Documents of Vatican II*, vol. 3: *Declaration on the Relationship of the Church to the Non-Christian Religions: Dogmatic Constitution on Divine Revelation; Decree on the Apostolate of the Laity*, ed. Herbert Vorgrimler (New York: Herder and Herder, 1969), 54.

[44] Oesterreicher, "Declaration," 45.

[45] Connelly, *From Enemy to Brother*, 225.

[46] Connelly, 256.

leave them "in good faith," and simply pray for them. In the text of the declaration the drafters have not had the courage to mention explicitly either the duty of Catholics to work for the "conversion" of the Jews or the serious duty of the Jews to acquire a better knowledge of the Christian religion.[47]

Members of the Central Coordinating Commission and the Commission on Faith and Morals then altered the draft of the statement on the Jewish people that had been prepared by Cardinal Bea's Secretariat for Promoting Christian Unity.[48]

They reinserted text expressing a hope for the union of the Jewish people with the Church that had been dropped from an earlier version.[49] The reinserted text appealed to Paul's teaching in Romans 11:25: "It is also worth remembering that the union of the Jewish people with the Church is part of the Christian hope. Therefore, following the teaching of the Apostle (Romans 11:25) the Church waits with unshaken faith and deep longing for the entry of that people into the fullness of the people of God established by Christ."[50]

---

[47] Miccoli, "Two Sensitive Issues," 150; Connelly, *From Enemy to Brother*, 257–58. As I discuss below, Ciappi's argument highlights one of the problems with applications by Catholics of the category of invincible ignorance to Jews.

[48] Correspondence with John Borelli.

[49] Oesterreicher, "Declaration," 67–86.

[50] The first draft of the "Decree on the Jews" (*Decretum de Iudaeis*) that was prepared by Cardinal Bea contained a statement on the "union of the Jewish people with the Church." It was completed in early December 1961 but was never submitted to the Council. It reads as follows:
> Furthermore, the Church believes in the union of the Jewish people with herself as an integral part of Christian hope. With unshaken faith and deep longing the Church awaits union with this people. At the time of Christ's coming, "a remnant chosen by grace" (Rom 11:5), the very first fruits of the Church, accepted the Eternal Word. The Church believes, however, with the Apostle that at the appointed time, the fullness of the children of Abraham according to the flesh will embrace him who is salvation (Rom 11:12, 26). Their acceptance will be life from the dead (Rom 11:15).

The statement was dropped from subsequent drafts until it was reinserted by the Coordinating Commission in the September 1964 draft entitled "The Jews and Non-Christians." Additionally, the preparatory study on the Declaration included dogmatic principles such as "the final reconciliation of the Church and the people of Israel," and it stated that "a view of the Church that did not include this imperishable hope seemed to the Subcommittee's members incomplete." Oesterreicher, *The New Encounter*, 139. Additionally, the preliminary study written by Oesterreicher also requested that the Council teach that "the Church is the Church of Jews and Gentiles. The reconciliation of both in Christ prefigures and announces the reconciliation for all human beings in the Church, which, therefore, makes her the core of humankind." Oesterreicher, *The New Encounter*, 145. Connelly does not include these details, which gives the impression that the idea of expressing the Christian desire for union with the Jewish people originated only with members of the Coordinating Commission. Connelly, *From Enemy to Brother*, 253. Oesterreicher did not propose the change in 1964, but he rejected the idea that the controversial text itself represented a call to conversion. Moreover, he would also come to the conclusion that Romans 11:25–26 did *not* support the proposed language. The drafts are accessible at the website of

The addition of these lines raised the question of whether *NA* should call for the Jewish people to enter the Church.

Cardinal Bea's reaction to this revision by the Central Coordinating Commission was negative. He indicated to the Council fathers that his secretariat was not responsible for this revision.[51] Oesterreicher would also come to the conclusion that Romans 11:25–26 did *not* support the proposed language. Over two dozen bishops and cardinals made interventions during debates at the Council on September 28 and 29, 1964.

Several Council fathers argued that Paul's teaching in Romans 11:25–26 indicates *not* that the Jews should enter the Church in the present age, but that the salvation of the Jewish people is a mystery that exceeds the grasp of human reason, and that it does not concern methods of human persuasion. Their interventions indicate that the fathers understood Romans 11:25–26 to mean that the salvation of the Jewish people is hidden in the wisdom and knowledge of God.

Oesterreicher thought the interventions were so important that they should "always be printed alongside the Declaration itself, as they support, explain and sometimes also develop it."[52] Some of the interventions that touch on Romans 11:25–26 are as follows:

Achilles Cardinal Liénart (Lille, France):

> In the Epistle to the Romans (11: 26–29) [Paul] declares that God is faithful and that "the gifts and the call of God are irrevocable" even after sin; there he explains how marvelously and mysteriously in the full working out of providence the salvation of the Jews will again be included in the history of Redemption after the full number of the gentiles have entered, and thus all will be saved.... And so, that our catechesis and preaching may be faithful, it is necessary for our Sacred Synod to explicitly declare . . . that the Jews,

---

the Council of Centers for Christian-Jewish Relations: https://ccjr.us/dialogika-resources/documents-and-statements/roman-catholic/second-vatican-council/na-drafts.

51 Cardinal Bea also wrote to the members of the secretariat on July 17, 1964, explaining what happened:

> After we had submitted the text of De Iudaeis, as approved in the March plenary session, to the Coordination Commission [*sic*], this Commission to a certain extent assumed responsibility for the content and wording of the draft. The question may now arise as to whether the Secretariat wishes to assume full responsibility for the printed text on the Jews, since this new draft neither reproduces completely our revision nor has it been voted upon in a subsequent session of the Secretariat.

"Augustine Cardinal Bea to members of the Secretariat," AAV, *Conc. Vat. II*, Box 1454 Secretariatus ad Christianorum Unitatem Fovendam Busta #8.

52 Oesterreicher, "Declaration," 67.

in accordance with divine Providence's hidden disposition of mercy, have a place reserved for them in the present economy of salvation.[53]

Archbishop O'Boyle (Washington, DC):

The destiny of the Jewish people depends completely on the dispositions of divine Providence and the grace of God. Therefore, if we express our hope in words that lead the Jews to interpret them as a definite and conscious intention to work for their conversion, we will build another high wall that separates us from a holy and fruitful dialogue with the Jewish people. . . . I can add: In expressing the hope for conversion of the Jews and of all the other peoples, the declaration in lines 23–27 goes beyond the limits of precise Catholic teaching. For, in the declaration the text of St. Paul's epistle to the Romans 11:15 is cited where the apostle uses words that are so indefinite and mysterious that even Catholic exegetes propose very different interpretations. Therefore, it would be better if we would admit the limitations of our knowledge, and the hidden ways of divine Providence. It would be better if we were to express our hope for the conversion of the Jews in such a way that the Jews themselves would understand our respect for their sincerity and our humble knowledge of the truth that the mystery of salvation does not depend on us, but on the sublime action of God. I, therefore, propose that the following words be substituted for the paragraph in question: "It is worth remembering that the uniting of the Jews and ourselves is part of Christian hope. The Church with unshaken faith and with an earnest desire looks forward to this union from God in his time, in a way that is hidden in His wisdom (cf. Rom 11:25–26)."[54]

Cardinal Lercaro (Bologna, Italy):

The "union of the Jewish people with the Church," of which our Declaration speaks, could easily give rise to suspicion, that is, be understood in a crude and superficial sense. Our desire is, however, simply to profess the faith and hope of Paul, namely that God "has not rejected his people whom he foreknew" (Rom 11:29), that [the Jews] are "beloved" of God (Rom 11:28), and that "their full inclusion" is not yet revealed (Rom 11:12). But in what way will their full inclusion be revealed? Certainly in ways that are religious and mysterious, whose mystery we must respect. Those ways are hidden

---

[53] The text is available from the website of the Council of Centers for Christian-Jewish Relations: https://ccjr.us/dialogika-resources/documents-and-statements/roman-catholic/second-vatican-council/na-drafts.

[54] Oesterreicher, "Declaration," 71. O'Boyle incorrectly cited Rom 11:15 instead of 11:25.

in the wisdom and knowledge of God. Therefore they should not be confused with the ways of men, that is with the methods of propaganda and the human arts of persuasion. Jews and Christians will be guided to the common, eternal, messianic paschal meal, not by changes in this world but by the eschatological destiny of souls.[55]

Bishop Daem (Antwerp, Netherlands):

The Christian must bear in mind that in accordance with the divine decree the Jews and we Christians are moving towards the same fulfilment—the revelation of God's mercy in a common Covenant. We must follow this divine decree, not by means of an unseemly proselytism, but in plain dealing and complete humility.... Let us therefore, reverend Fathers, choose this twofold standpoint of humility and of sharing in a common hope, in order... the better to walk in the light of Pauline teaching.[56]

Archbishop Elchinger (Strasbourg, France):

Our Declaration must, however, avoid any kind of call for the conversion of the whole Jewish people, as has indeed in a certain sense already been done. At the present time it is simply impossible for the Jews to conceive that for them to pass over to the Gospel of Christ is no defection, but their true fulfillment. We do not and cannot yet know that hour appointed by God of which St. Paul speaks in his letter to the Romans, that is, the hour of the final union of the chosen people in its entirety.[57]

Twelve speakers wanted the lines revised.[58] As indicated by records of the deliberations, several of the Council fathers suggested that the proposed lines be revised based on the idea that respect for the mystery of Israel was incompatible with proselytism: "Many fathers asked that in the expression of this hope, since it concerns the mystery of Israel, any appearance of proselytism be avoided."[59]

However, a crucial point for our purposes is that the architects and the fathers of NA recognized that Romans 11:25–26 indicated that the question

---

55 Oesterreicher, 75.

56 Oesterreicher, 80.

57 Oesterreicher, 77.

58 Oesterreicher, *The New Encounter*, 229.

59 Acta Syn. III.8, 648. The Synodal Acts of the deliberations are available at Council of Centers for Christian-Jewish Relations: https://ccjr.us/dialogika-resources/documents-and-statements/roman-catholic/second-vatican-council/na-debate.

of Jewish salvation is a mystery that takes place on a day known to God alone, and so it exceeds the grasp of human reason. Rather than reading 11:25–26 as biblical justification to call for Jews to enter the Church in the present age, they realized these verses should be read eschatologically, with a recognition of the mysterious ways of God's providence and the limitations of human reason.

This is clear from their insistence that the question of Christ and the salvation of the Jews "should not be confused with the ways of men"; is hidden in Divine Providence; and is "hidden in the wisdom and knowledge of God." And this divine wisdom with regard to the question of the salvation of the Jewish people is contrasted with the "conscious intention to work for their conversion" and "human persuasion."

From the Council fathers' perspective, 11:25–26 cannot be used to justify a Christian duty to encourage the Jews to enter the Church. Such a reading would distort Paul's letter. This argument was also made by the Swiss Jewish historian Ernst Ludwig Ehrlich of B'nai B'rith in an exchange with Oesterreicher. Ehrlich pointed out to Oesterreicher in a letter that the reading of Romans 11:25–26 suggested by some members of the Curia was wrong. "Please do yourself and me a favor . . . [and] hurry to the Secretariat and show the people there that the text is simply wrong, and that a well-grounded New Testament reading must be found. . . . Any notion of conversion is excluded entirely. . . . I really cannot understand how they could claim to be making reference to Paul."[60] The point that surfaced in this exchange was that Romans 11:25–26 does not mention the entry of the Jewish people into the Church. Rather, Paul says that in the present time a "hardening" has come upon Israel, and that this hardening takes place as the gentiles enter the Church.[61] Paul expected the full number of the gentiles to "come in" during the present age. Israel's salvation is an eschatological hope directed at the end of time.[62]

Oesterreicher agreed that Paul's vision was an eschatological hope and that the text of Paul's teaching did *not* justify the idea that the Jews should enter the Church now.[63] He therefore suggested a line be inserted that he

---

[60] Ehrlich cited in Connelly, *From Enemy to Brother*, 255. See "Ehrlich to Oesterreicher," 10 September 1964, SHU-SCC, JMO Collection, RG 26.4.1, box 2.

[61] As I explain in the next section, "hardening" is a problematic translation.

[62] Again, Rom 11:25–26, NABRE, reads: "I do not want you to be unaware of this mystery, brothers [and sisters], so that you will not become wise [in] your own estimation: a hardening has come upon Israel in part, until the full number of the Gentiles comes in, and thus all Israel will be saved."

[63] He also thought the lines of the proposed draft had been "greatly misunderstood." "An unprejudiced reader . . . who examines the statement carefully is bound to conclude that it does not

borrowed from Thieme's reading of Romans 11:25–26.[64] Thieme's line references the eschatological vision of Zephaniah 3:9: "For then I will make pure the speech of the peoples, that they all may call upon the name of the LORD, to serve him with one accord." The Zephaniah text, therefore, was selected with the theological intention of interpreting Paul's eschatological vision correctly. The Zephaniah text would then be synthesized with the fathers' eschatological interpretation of Paul's vision of Jewish salvation in 11:25–26.[65]

The final text of *NA*, which was promulgated by Pope Paul VI on October 28, 1965, after the final vote ("yes": 2221; "no": 88), reads as follows: "In company with the Prophets and the Apostle, *the Church awaits that day*, known to God alone, on which all people will address the Lord in a single voice and 'serve Him shoulder to shoulder.'" As Cardinal Bea remarked: "The Declaration . . . seeks to show that despite all this the Jewish people is still most dear to God and that at *a future time*, known to God alone, all men, including the Jews, will serve him with one heart and mind."[66]

Therefore, the architects and fathers of *NA* decided to reject the call for the Jewish people to enter the Church based on the interpretation of Romans 11:25–26 that understands the Church to await the salvation of the Jewish people as an eschatological reality, not an expectation for the present time. The line mentioning "the Prophets and the Apostle" that was inserted into *NA* was inspired by this interpretation. Although the quotation of Romans 11:25–26 was dropped from the body of the text, the line retained the reference to Paul's eschatological vision since it referenced not only Zephaniah but "the Apostle" and "the Church awaits that day," and it cited Romans 11 in the footnote. The drafters selected this reading of the Apostle's vision over the edits made in the previous version, which were advanced by Ciappi's proposal that it was the *duty* of Catholics to work for the "conversion" of the Jews in the present age. The fathers' eschatological reading of "that day" motivated their rejection of the text that was understood as a call for Jews to enter the Church now. Therefore, the lines calling for entry of Jews into

---

recommend a 'mission to the Jews,' but expresses simply and solely the belief that at the end of time God will gather into union with Himself all who profess His name." Oesterreicher, *The New Encounter*, 193. See also Connelly, *From Enemy to Brother*, 255–56.

64 Connelly, *From Enemy to Brother*, 254–55. Thieme had already come to this view earlier. Oesterreicher was only beginning to accept Thieme's position. Thieme passed away in July 1963, one year prior to the Central Coordinating Commission's revisions to Bea's draft.

65 Zeph 3:9, NABRE.

66 Bea, *The Church and the Jewish People*, 51. Emphasis added.

the Church were rejected by the fathers and architects of *NA* on theological and not merely pragmatic grounds.[67]

Cardinal Bea understood this well, which is why he taught that the foundation of *NA*'s teaching on these points was deeply biblical. There is a future day, known to God alone, when all Israel will be united with the fullness of the gentiles.[68] Bea said that Paul's teaching on the "hardening of Israel" revealed a "mysterious fact": "In God's plan, the 'lack of faith' of this people is only provisional (though it may last for thousands of years)."[69]

As I argue below, the Council's vision of the certainty of the salvation of the Jewish people shares aspects of the teachings of the Dominican theologians who defended Aquinas's teaching against baptism of Jewish children *invitis parentibus*. They insisted that when it comes to the conversion of the Jews, the Church must await the return of the Prophet Elijah. In a similar spirit, although seemingly unaware of this medieval teaching, the Council fathers taught that when it comes to the Church and the question of the salvation of the Jews, now is a time of waiting. According to the Council, the prophets (which would include, of course, Elijah) wait for this day, as does the Apostle Paul. In the present time, the Church must also wait for this day. Bea referred to this view as "Israel in the sight of God." I will discuss this highly important view below.

The thinking of most of the architects of *NA* evolved considerably on these issues. Both Oesterreicher and Thieme had originally thought the conversion of the Jewish people was a necessity. Thieme would eventually conclude that there was no duty to convert Jews but that there was instead a vocation of the Jews, which Christians must learn to respect. He realized that God willed the existence of the Jewish people today for a particular mission.[70]

---

[67] As is well-known, knowledge of the proposed revision compelled Abraham Joshua Heschel to declare that he was "ready to go to Auschwitz any time, if faced with the alternative of conversion or death." "Ecumenism: What Catholics Think about Jews," *Time*, September 11, 1964. Connelly says there is little doubt that Bea and his theological advisors had the sentiments of Heschel and other Jewish observers in mind in the fall of 1964. In Oesterreicher's view, however, the final draft was as a result of multiple influences, in the context of a fresh appreciation of Scripture and the actions of the Council Fathers. Connelly, *From Enemy to Brother*, 257.

[68] "The new version points to a day-to-come, when concord and harmony will reign." Oesterreicher, *The New Encounter*, 231.

[69] Bea, *The Church and the Jewish People*, 98–99.

[70] "The Jew who fulfills the purpose of his existence in the economy of salvation makes a contribution to fulfilling the will of God. Has not Israel been made an escort to the nations (like Socrates to the Athenians... breaking them constantly, never letting them sleep, warning us any time our belief threatens to become superstition)? Does not Israel always wake us up when we think we

Likewise, Oesterreicher eventually abandoned the idea that there was a Christian duty to seek conversion of the Jews and adopted Thieme's line of thought.[71] Oesterreicher observed:

> The "totality" of humanity according to God's plan is made up of Israel and the nations, who are to be finally united in the one and only Covenant. If you put things that way, it is clear that the last days have not yet been fulfilled.... Christians tend to forget sometimes that they are still waiting for the coming in glory of their Messiah ... Israel on the other hand must remain faithful as long as the times are not accomplished; it is still loved by God because of his election and because of the Patriarchs. God's gifts and his call cannot be abolished.[72]

Additionally, Bea understood *NA* to teach that Israel's salvation is in God's hands. Israel's "lack of faith [in Christ] is only for a time, until the day—known to God alone, as the Declaration says—when the full number of the gentiles has come into the kingdom of God and so all Israel will be saved."[73]

As we shall see below, Pope Benedict XVI interpreted Paul along similar lines. Benedict also taught that, according to Scripture, the salvation of the Jewish people is in God's hands, and now is the time for the gentiles to enter the Church. There is also an affirmation of a special election and vocation of the Jews in Benedict's teaching, and he rejects the idea that there is a Catholic duty to seek the conversion of the Jews.

THE "HUMAN VIEW OF ISRAEL" AND "ISRAEL IN THE SIGHT OF GOD"

Oesterreicher acknowledged the possibility of different interpretations of Romans 11:25–26 and said that it could not be the task of the Council to choose a particular interpretation of these famous verses.[74] However, the exchange between Oesterreicher and Ehrlich and the debates and final text of the declaration indicate that Oesterreicher and the Council did indeed

---

have found the perfect societal order but it is not the Kingdom of God?" Thieme, cited in Connelly, *From Enemy to Brother*, 274.

71 Oesterreicher, *The New Encounter*, 139.

72 Oesterreicher, cited in Connelly, *From Enemy to Brother*, 284.

73 Bea, *The Church and the Jewish People*, 100–101.

74 Oesterreicher, *The New Encounter*, 139. He states that there were "two ways of understanding future 'conversion' of Israel" among the fathers of the Church. "The majority of exegetes, past and present, agreed that the Apostle was speaking of the salvation of Israel according to the flesh." Oesterreicher, 139. As I explain below, Aquinas understands Paul's words that all Israel shall be saved to apply to Israel of the flesh.

make decisions about these verses. The architects and fathers interpreted the meaning of Paul's words as follows: 1) "All Israel will be saved" in verse 26 refers to Israel according to the flesh, that is, ethnic Israel.[75] 2) In the mystery of God's merciful providence, the salvation of the Jewish people is certain and will take place on that day known to God alone but only after the full number of the gentiles have entered the Church. 3) This mystery does not entail a duty to seek the conversion of the Jews.

As is well known, standard translations of Romans 11:25–26 render the verses as follows: "I do not want you to be unaware of this mystery, brothers, so that you will not become wise [in] your own estimation: a hardening [pōrōsis; πώρωσις] has come upon Israel in part, until the full number of the gentiles comes in, and thus all Israel will be saved."[76]

In the first part of this section, I discuss a Catholic proposal that the "hardening" of Israel mentioned in verse 25 should be correlated with the moral theological concept of invincible ignorance (nonculpable wrongdoing). I then draw upon aspects of Aquinas's view of the meaning of post-biblical Jewish worship to suggest a more positive interpretation of Jewish religious practice after the Passion of Christ. I argue that the primary way the Jewish people are related to Christ is through their ongoing election and divine worship, which remains a figure of the Christian faith in general and of the Second Coming of the circumcised and glorified body of Christ in particular.

The "Human View of Israel"

In a thoughtful and constructive proposal, Gavin D'Costa attempted to articulate a Catholic doctrinal ground for the religious life of Judaism after the Passion of Christ. Drawing upon Romans 11:25–26, D'Costa argues that Paul's use of πώρωσις (pōrōsis) should be correlated with invincible ignorance or non-culpability. As mentioned above, the term is frequently translated in English as "hardening," and this is, in part, why D'Costa suggests the term could be understood to refer to the subjective, non-culpable state of Jews toward Christ: "Rabbinic Judaism, as a group, cannot be blamed and are

---

75 In other words, verse 26 refers to ethnic Israel instead of only Jews who had decided to follow Christ, or the remnant of Israel, according to other interpreters in history.

76 Rom 11:25–26, NABRE. The Greek text reads as follows: Οὐ γὰρ θέλω ὑμᾶς ἀγνοεῖν, ἀδελφοί, τὸ μυστήριον τοῦτο, ἵνα μὴ ἦτε ἑαυτοῖς φρόνιμοι, ὅτι πώρωσις ἀπὸ μέρους τῷ Ἰσραὴλ γέγονεν ἄχρι οὗ τὸ πλήρωμα τῶν ἐθνῶν εἰσέλθῃ, καὶ οὕτως πᾶς Ἰσραὴλ σωθήσεται.

not culpable, in remaining Rabbinic Jews. Could we interpret Paul in this manner?"[77]

In Catholic theology, the language of invincible ignorance provides a way of evaluating wrongdoing and blame in situations where people act in good faith but have an erroneous conscience, that is, they are wrong about what they think they should do, so they *act* wrongly as well. D'Costa's aim in using this term in his theological reflection on Judaism is, in part, to explain why Catholics can affirm the religious life of rabbinic Judaism after the Passion of Christ, in contrast to what is understood as the standard Christian condemnatory view of rabbinic Judaism. Why should Christians affirm Jewish religious practice today, despite Christ's fulfillment of the law? D'Costa argues that Christian violence against the Jewish people has obscured the gospel from view. A person may be invincibly ignorant after hearing the gospel because of the scandalous behavior of Christians. Since the identity of Jesus has been obscured by Christian injustice against Jews, the negative view of Christ among most Jews is understandable. The mistaken view of Christ is due to ignorance, and so there is no culpability for the misunderstanding.[78]

Although invincible ignorance may apply in cases where there is a misunderstanding of the Church's teaching about Christ, the use of the category begs the ancient question of the theological status of Jews and Judaism outside the Church. I want to suggest that the use of the category of invincible ignorance might be helpful but only if it can adequately address four issues. First, if we are not careful, a correlation of "hardening" with invincible ignorance can obscure the context and point of Paul's teaching in Romans 11:25–26 by losing sight of the distinction between what Cardinal Bea referred to as the "human view" of Israel and "Israel in the sight of God." Second, the correlation does not address the problem of "vincible ignorance" or the idea of a "culpable rejection." In other words, if Jews can only observe Judaism if they do not know of, or misunderstand, the Church's teachings about Christ, this seems to imply that Jews who do know of these teachings and reject Christianity are in mortal sin. Third, the correlation can encourage a focus upon the subjective states of conscience in Jews and distract from the

---

[77] Gavin D'Costa, *Catholic Doctrines on the Jewish People after Vatican II* (New York: Oxford University, 2019), 58–59. D'Costa provides a systematic theological treatment of some of the most difficult doctrinal questions on the Jewish people that have emerged since the Second Vatican Council. Although I disagree with some of the conclusions of the book, it represents one of the most serious and thoughtful attempts at a constructive Catholic theology of Jews and Judaism since the Council.

[78] D'Costa, *Catholic Doctrines*, 41–43. "This allows for probably the majority of Jews' rejection of the gospel as an act that might well be in good faith." D'Costa, 38–39.

objective reality of God's divine activity as it relates to the mystery of Israel. Lastly, applying invincible ignorance to the Jewish people today can obscure an important question faced by the architects and fathers of *NA*. I address each of these issues below.

Concerning the first issue, the correlation of invincible ignorance with the common English translation "hardening" can make it seem as if Paul is mostly concerned with the subjective wrongdoing of Jews in his day. This implies that Paul thought the existence of Jews and Judaism after the Passion of Christ was an unintended state of affairs that God otherwise prefers not to exist. But this assumption seems incompatible with Paul's positive affirmation of the election of Israel (Rom 11:28) and his teaching on the "mystery" or role of Israel (11:25–26) in bringing about the salvation of the fullness of the gentiles. In other words, a focus on the subjective response of Israel to Paul's preaching of the gospel leaves one with an incomplete picture of Paul's teaching about Jews and Judaism after Christ. Cardinal Bea referred to this incomplete picture as the "the human point of view" of why some Jews had rejected Paul's preaching of the gospel. Bea asked, "How can we explain the refusal of the majority of the Jewish people to accept the Gospel?"[79] For Bea, Paul answers this question in two ways. First, Paul provides the immediate subjective cause of refusal or the "the human point of view."[80] On this subjective level, some of the Jews to whom he preached rejected the claim that righteousness came through Christ, the cornerstone of the divine plan of salvation. However, Bea says this human view is incomplete because it is only empirical: "St. Paul, however, does not stop at the immediate and so to say empirical reason. He looks deeper into the merciful plan of God.... In God's plan, the lack of faith [in Christ] of his people is only provisional."

This deeper view is what Bea referred to as "the position of Israel in the sight of God."[81] From the human and empirical point of view, the Christian may see Israel only in terms of unbelief in Christ. But from the view of Israel in the sight of God, one sees Israel against the backdrop of a positive and divine objective plan. Bea says Israel's "lack of faith is only for a time, until the day—known to God alone, as the Declaration says—when the full number of the gentiles has come into the kingdom of God and so all Israel will be saved." To interpret the Jewish people through the human point of view of Israel's response to Christ is to neglect Paul's teaching that gentiles must be

---

[79] It seems problematic to use the language of "the majority of the Jewish people" since most Jewish people at that time lived in the diaspora, outside of Jerusalem, and so they were unaware of the teaching of the apostles.

[80] Bea, *The Church and the Jewish People*, 97.

[81] Bea, 98.

aware of the objective reality of God's providential care for the Jewish people and their future restoration.[82] God holds the Jews most dear, and God wills their existence throughout the present age so that the full number of the gentiles have time to enter the Church. The ongoing existence of Israel plays a positive role in God's divine plan despite the rejection of the gospel.[83]

The second issue with the correlation of invincible ignorance with the common English translation "hardening" is that it does not attend to the problem of vincible ignorance. A hypothetical example may help to illustrate how the terms invincible and vincible ignorance are used to evaluate wrongdoing and blame in the Catholic moral tradition.[84]

Vincible ignorance: Let us say that a person is driving down a road and is pulled over by the police. The officer informs the person that he was speeding through a school zone, going 45 in a 25-mph zone. The person could respond that he was acting in good faith and did not know it was a school zone, and so he should not get a ticket. But the person would get a ticket. As a driver, it is his responsibility to know the speed limit and to keep an eye out for school zone signs. The person really thought that the limit was 45 mph and acted accordingly. Here is a simple example of following one's conscience when it is wrong, or an "erroneous conscience." The ignorance about the speed limit is *vincible*, meaning the person could have overcome his ignorance. In fact, the person was obligated to pay attention to speed limit signs, and so the person is morally responsible for not knowing better. The person acted wrongly, but should have known better, and so is blameworthy. Vincible ignorance means one is blameworthy because one could have gained access to the necessary information for acting rightly.

Invincible ignorance: But perhaps the person was paying attention, and the last speed limit sign stated that the limit was 45 mph. Since no new sign appeared, the person assumed that 45 mph was the limit. However, it turns out that there was a school zone sign marking the change to 25 mph, but when the person drives back, out of frustration, in order to discover whether he truly was inattentive, the person finds that the school zone sign

---

[82] This interpretation corresponds to modern interpretations as well. "Paul insists that Israel's lack of conviction in the good news is an anomaly. They have heard the message (Rom 10.14–18)—it was witnessed in their own scriptures, after all (3.2, 20–21)—yet they remain 'disobedient and contrary,' while the gentiles have found the god they did not seek (10.18, 20–21). The only explanation is that God, once again, is controlling events." Paula Fredriksen, *Paul: The Pagans' Apostle* (New Haven, CT: Yale University Press, 2017), 160.

[83] Fredriksen, 160–62.

[84] I borrow this example from the discussion of prudence and conscience in chapter 5 of William Mattison, *Introducing Moral Theology: True Happiness and the Virtues* (Grand Rapids, MI: Brazos Press, 2008).

was knocked over for some reason. The person was still speeding and violating the law. The question is not whether the person violated the law, because speeding in a school zone is a violation. The question is whether the person is blameworthy for that violation. In this case, the person truly had no way of knowing the law. So, the person acted wrongly but the person is *not* blameworthy since there was no access to the necessary knowledge. Invincible ignorance means one is not blameworthy because one did not have access to the necessary information *and* there was no way to acquire access to the information.

On this logic, to be in a state of nonculpable, invincible ignorance with regard to unbelief in Christ (i.e., to be wrong about Christ and not blameworthy), a non-Christian must have no access to the Church's teaching about Christ, or the understanding of the teaching about Christ could be distorted by the history of Christian violence. Of course, some do lack understanding of the Church's teaching about Christ, or their understanding of Christ is distorted by the history of Christian violence toward Jews. From this perspective, although some are mistaken to practice Judaism after Christ comes (the assumption here, which I return to below, is that God no longer wills that it be practiced) they are certainly not blameworthy for this.

However, in Romans 9–11, Paul is *not* in anguish over Jews who lack information or misunderstand the gospel. In other words, invincible ignorance based in misunderstanding of the gospel is not the issue. Rather, Paul is in anguish about Jews who have rejected the gospel and so he is trying to discern God's divine plan. As Pope Benedict XVI observed, "[Paul] was met with rejection which he thought was foretold in Isaiah 6:9–10."[85]

Moreover, in the context of the historic dialogue between Christians and Jews that was advanced by the Second Vatican Council, both communities can distinguish the Church's teaching about Christ from the history of Christian violence. Many Jewish thinkers reject the Church's teaching about Christ not because of the history of Christian violence but because they have a different interpretation of Scripture and of the character of the messianic era. For many educated lay persons, rabbis, and scholars, the disagreement between Judaism and Christianity is not based in misperceptions but in complex philosophical and theological reasons. Therefore, invincible

---

[85] Pope Benedict XVI, "Grace and Vocation without Remorse: Comments on the Treatise De Iudaeis," *Communio: International Catholic Review* 45, no. 1 (Spring 2018): 164. "The entirety of Romans 9–11 functions to explain why so few Jews have become convinced that Jesus is the Messiah." Matthew Thiessen, *A Jewish Paul: The Messiah's Herald to the Gentiles* (Grand Rapids, MI: Baker Academic, 2023), 153. "They have heard the message (Rom 10:14–18)—it was witnessed in their own scriptures, after all (Rom 3:2, 20–22)—yet they remain 'disobedient and contrary,' while the gentiles have found the god they did not seek (10.18, 20–21)." Fredriksen, *Paul*, 160.

ignorance is not at issue in the context of Catholic-Jewish dialogue. The participants in a dialogue would not seem to meet the criteria for invincible ignorance to the degree that they understand and reject Christological claims. The more difficult question in the context of the dialogue called for by the Second Vatican Council is not the question of invincible ignorance but vincible ignorance. This is where one acts wrongly (according to traditional medieval interpretations of rabbinic Judaism), but should have known better, and so is blameworthy. The challenge is evident in Luigi Ciappi's above mentioned memorandum to Pope Paul VI. Ciappi argued that "infidelity" or resistance of Jews to Christ cannot be defined as nonculpable and therefore required a Catholic duty to work for the conversion of the Jewish people.[86] The application of invincible ignorance does not address the question of a "culpable rejection."[87]

Third, the correlation of invincible ignorance with "hardening" can also distort the reading of the Catechism:

> When one considers the future, God's People of the Old Covenant and the new People of God tend towards similar goals: expectation of the coming (or the return) of the Messiah. But one awaits the return of the Messiah who died and rose from the dead and is recognized as Lord and Son of God; the other awaits the coming of a Messiah, whose features remain hidden till the end of time; and the latter waiting is accompanied by the drama of not knowing or of misunderstanding Christ Jesus.[88]

It might seem at first glance that the Catechism's mention of not knowing and misunderstanding implies the category of invincible ignorance.[89] But the Catechism also says that the features of the Messiah awaited by the Jewish people "remain hidden till the end of time." The idea of the Messiah's hidden features seems important since the objective truth is not only that the Messiah has come; it also includes the truth that he will come again in glory

---

[86] Ciappi wrote, "The infidelity of the Jews is not simple, inculpable ignorance of Christ, but is a positive infidelity, even if judgment on individuals is reserved to God alone." The application of invincible ignorance does not address the question of a "culpable rejection." In this perspective, it seems a Jewish thinker would sin if they refused to embrace the Catholic faith after having come to understand it. "Some Jews may sin in refusing to embrace the truth as they freely and fully come to understand it viz. Jesus is the Jewish messiah." D'Costa, *Catholic Doctrines*, 43.

[87] In this perspective, it seems a Jewish thinker would sin if they refused to embrace the Catholic faith after having come to understand it. "Some Jews may sin in refusing to embrace the truth as they freely and fully come to understand it viz. Jesus is the Jewish messiah." D'Costa, *Catholic Doctrines*, 43.

[88] *CCC* 343.

[89] D'Costa, *Catholic Doctrines*, 61.

to judge the living and the dead. Insofar as the Jewish people are concerned, the Messiah's features are hidden for reasons related to the mystery that the fullness of the gentiles must enter the Church before all Israel is saved.

Therefore, the drama of salvation history is not simply a straightforward case of a misunderstanding about accessible knowledge. If we focus only upon subjective states in this eschatological context, we can miss the fact that the "drama of not knowing" involves God's mysterious divine activity in willing a state of affairs that mercifully benefits the gentiles and all Israel. This is why Paul declares, "O the depth of the riches and wisdom and knowledge of God! How unsearchable are his judgments and how inscrutable his ways!"[90]

Lastly, the fourth issue with applying invincible ignorance to Jews and Judaism is that it obscures a fundamental question faced by the Council fathers who drafted *NA*: In what way, exactly, are the Jewish people dear to God apart from any subjective responses to the Church's teaching concerning the universal saving significance of Jesus Christ? What is the theological value of Jews and rabbinic Judaism outside of the Church?[91]

---

[90] Rom 11:33, NRSVCE.

[91] To affirm only that God wills that Judaism continue in the Jews who follow Christ implies that God is indifferent to whether Jews and Judaism exist outside the Church. The argument that God desires for Judaism to continue in Jews who follow Christ seems to beg these ancient questions. I do not intend to imply that Jewish identity is cancelled in conversion to Christianity, or that Jews who follow Jesus have no place in God's plan. The question of whether Jews who follow Christ should observe "Jewish practices" within the Church today is important. The Church cannot forget she is a Church of Jews and gentiles in her initial apostolic and prophetic foundational architecture. As I showed in my study of Aquinas's Ephesians commentary, Aquinas refers to the apostles and prophets as the "two walls" of the temple of Christ's body, since the Church is constituted in its foundation by the Jewish prophets and the Jewish apostles. Michael Wyschogrod's question of whether Jews who follow Christ today must continue to observe what they understand as Jewish practices is not the same question as whether ongoing Judaism has positive theological value outside of the Church. I discuss the importance of this distinction in chapter 1 of my book *Aquinas on Israel and the Church: A Study of the Question of Supersessionism in the Theology of Thomas Aquinas* (Eugene, OR: Pickwick/Wipf & Stock, 2014). I do not think Jews who follow Christ should be disallowed from observing practices they understand to be Jewish, but such practices cannot be required by Church law. This is because, as Augustine and Aquinas taught, Judaism is not within the spiritual jurisdiction of the Church, i.e., the Church has no spiritual authority over Judaism. ST II.II 10.9 ad. 2; see also 12.2. "The Church has no jurisdiction over unbelievers." Here, Aquinas follows an ancient principle, based on 1 Cor 5:12–13, that the Church does not have spiritual dominion over outsiders. See Grayzel, vol. 2, 12–13. Matthew Levering's view of these complex questions is relevant here:

> It seems to me that Christians would thereby be proclaiming that living Judaism has no say over what counts as Judaism. Rabbinic Judaism would simply be ruled out of court. In other words, ignoring the rabbinic authorities' decision over what counts as Judaism would be even more accurately described as supersessionism than the action that generated the problem of supersessionism in the first place, namely Paul's and others' disagreement with other Jews over what constituted the Messianic fulfillment.

Yet if God intends the cessation of Torah in its original mode, how can God also will that Jews and Judaism continue until the full number of the gentiles enter the Church and Israel is saved? How can God will that Judaism no longer be practiced *and* that Judaism continue unto the end of time? A difficulty based in Romans 11:25–26 emerges, but it can be resolved by heeding Pope Benedict XVI's teachings on these themes, which we will discuss below. The difficulty can also be addressed through a study of Paul's warning to recognize the mystery of God's positive purposes in his election of the Jewish people unto the end of time. Paul's warning in 11:25 encourages gentile followers of Christ to engage in precisely this sort of reflection: "I do not want you to be unaware of this mystery . . . so that you will not become wise in your own estimation."[92]

What is the mystery that Paul speaks of? As I explain below, the mystery is the Apostle's teaching that the universal saving mission of the Church is bound up with and depends upon the existence of ethnic Israel, the root of the Church, unto the end of time. In the present age, a certain time known to God alone is required for gentiles to enter the Church. And Israel according to the flesh will also be saved; this will occur at the end of time, on that day awaited by the prophets, the Apostle, and the Church. The ingathering of the nations into the Church in the present age is therefore dependent upon the existence of ethnic Jews today. If there are no Jews in the world, the biblical prophecy of the prophets and the Apostle collapses.

The last several popes' positive language about the Jewish people and their religious life can be seen as an attempt to explore the positive purposes of God's election of the Jews in the time of the gentiles. Their teachings emphasize that rabbinic Judaism is spiritually alive, and that this spiritual life of Judaism and Jewish interpretation of the Bible enrich the Church. For example, in his Apostolic Exhortation *Evangelii Gaudium*, Pope Francis says that Judaism is a living religion and that it is life-giving for the Church: "God continues to work among the people of the Old Covenant and to bring forth treasures of wisdom which flow from their encounter with his word.

Matthew Levering, *Jewish-Christian Dialogue and the Life of Wisdom: Engagements with the Theology of David Novak* (New York: Continuum, 2010), 25. The problem of ignoring the rabbinic authorities' decision over what counts as Judaism surfaces in D'Costa's proposal: "Who then owns the term Jew in the modern context?" Gavin D'Costa, "Response from the Author to Reviews of *Catholic Doctrines on the Jewish People after Vatican II*," *Studies in Christian-Jewish Relations* 15, no. 1 (2020): 18. The challenge is whether the religious life of rabbinic Judaism can be interpreted more benevolently, which I understand to be D'Costa's intention. For one of the most helpful descriptions of the challenge, see Michael Wyschogrod, "A Jewish Reading of St. Thomas Aquinas," in *Understanding Scripture: Explorations of Jewish and Christian Traditions of Interpretation*, ed. Clemens Thoma and Michael Wyschogrod (Mahwah, NJ: Paulist, 1987), 125–38.

92 Rom 11:25, NABRE.

For this reason, the Church also is enriched when she receives the values of Judaism."[93] As D'Costa argues, in the thought of St. Pope John Paul II, Pope Benedict XVI, and Pope Francis there is a "growing sense of the spiritual vitality and significance of present-day Judaism and its traditions."[94]

"Israel in the Sight of God"

The above discussion of the question of whether Jews who observe the law after Christ are in mortal sin brings the difficulty with a human reading of the cessation of the ceremonial law into focus. The problem is that in some traditional formulations of the issue, observance of the ceremonial law in its original mode is no longer understood to connect Israel to Christ but to deny Christ. The rationale is as follows: All ceremonies are professions of faith. Professions of faith are made in word and deed. If such professions in word or deed are false professions, then the one making such a profession sins mortally. Since Christ has already come, it is false to declare that he will come, which was the primary purpose of worship in the original mode. Therefore, the one observing a sacrament for declaring Christ will come makes a false profession of unbelief and sins mortally. The old sacraments are evaluated here based on the subjective dimension of the intention of the one who participates in the sacrament with an eye toward whether the sacraments are efficacious or effect grace. Since the old sacraments no longer prefigure the Passion, the old sacraments do not cause grace because the sacraments are understood to no longer unite one to Christ.[95]

However, there was also an objective dimension to the way Jewish religious life or the old sacraments witnessed to Christianity after the coming of Christ, despite the issue of whether the sacraments were efficacious, and despite subjective dispositions of unbelief. The popes of Aquinas's day developed this objective dimension in response to Christian mob violence against Jews.

In numerous papal bulls, Pope Gregory IX and Innocent IV defended Jewish existence in Christian society with more theologically elaborate

---

[93] Pope Francis, "Apostolic Exhortation *Evangelii Gaudium* of the Holy Father Pope Francis to the Bishops, Clergy, Consecrated Persons and the Lay Faithful on the Proclamation of the Gospel in Today's World" (November 24, 2013), no. 249.

[94] D'Costa, *Catholic Doctrines*, 19. "The cultic religious rituals of Rabbinic Judaism are alive and lifegiving, not dead and deadening." D'Costa, *Catholic Doctrines*, 188. In D'Costa's proposal, this affirmation of Jewish religious practice holds only for those who are invincibly ignorant of Christ. D'Costa, *Catholic Doctrines*, 43.

[95] On Aquinas's terms, the old sacraments did not cause grace in and of themselves but only insofar as the sacraments pointed to the reality of Christ's Passion.

arguments than those found in Pope Gregory the Great's letters.[96] To repel violent attacks upon Jews, the popes of Aquinas's day made theological arguments that God had preserved Jewish existence outside the Church. The arguments could be summarized under the following general principle: despite the subjective state of unbelief in Christ in the Jews living in the Middle Ages, God intends for his elect people to exist unto the end of time because this benefits the Christian faith. These popes argued that the Jewish people are related to Christ and the Christian faith even as they remain outside the Church: "Their relation with Christians is useful and, in a way, necessary; for they bear the image of our Savior, and were created by the Creator of all mankind," and "their fathers were made friends of God." [97] The popes argued that the existence of the Jews is of itself proof of the truth of the story of Christ: "The proof of the Christian faith comes . . . from their archives" and the prophets testify that they shall be saved in the end of days.[98] "They have been preserved specifically to testify to the orthodox Faith."[99] Though Jews reject or do not understand the Christian interpretation of Scripture, these people bear the image of the Savior and are the guardians of Scripture. The popes also understood the Bible, specifically in the teaching of the Prophets and in Christ, to demand that the conversion of Jews be awaited patiently: "The Lord mercifully expects their conversion in accordance with prophetic testimony."[100] Some of these theological arguments that the Jewish people continue to witness to the Christian faith on an objective level are reflected in Aquinas, since he teaches that the rites of the Jews figured the Passion but *also the Christian mode of life in general* and the Second Coming in particular. I will return to Aquinas's views momentarily since aspects of his teaching reflect some of these views.

As Pope Benedict XVI observed, Judaism always maintained a special position and was not simply submerged in the world of other religions: "It was clear to the Church that Judaism is not one religion among others but stands in a unique situation and therefore must be recognized as such by the Church. On this basis the idea developed in the Middle Ages of the pope's

---

[96] See Grayzel's helpful summary of these teachings in Grayzel, vol. 2, 9–12. The defense of the Jews in Pope Gregory IX and Innocent IV also contains language that accuses Jews of blasphemy and deicide and thus reveals how the teaching of contempt was tethered to positive ideas.

[97] Pope Gregory IX, "To the Archbishops and Bishops of the Kingdom of France," April 6, 1233, cited in Grayzel, vol. 2, 201.

[98] Pope Gregory IX, "To the Archbishop of Bordeaux and to the Bishops of Saintes," September 5, 1236, cited in Grayzel, vol. 2, 227.

[99] Pope Innocent IV, "To the King of Navarre," October 7, 1246, cited in Grayzel, vol. 2, 261.

[100] Pope Innocent IV, "To the King of Navarre."

THE INTERPRETATION OF ROMANS 11:25–26

twofold obligation of protection: on the one hand, the Christians must be defended against the Jews, but also the Jews had to be protected. They alone in the medieval world could exist alongside Christians as a *religio licita*."[101]

The teaching of the Second Vatican Council affirmed this special status of the Jewish people: "The Jews in large number, [did not] accept the Gospel; indeed not a few opposed its spreading. Nevertheless, God holds the Jews most dear for the sake of their Fathers."[102] How is this special status of Jews outside the Church related to Christ and the Church?

Lumen Gentium defines the relation of Jews and Judaism to the Church positively, through the promise of Christ given to the Jewish people, and the flesh of that people from whom Christ was born: "In the first place we must recall the people to whom the testament and the promise were given and from whom Christ was born according to the flesh."[103]

In the CRRJ's 1985 document "Notes on the Correct Way to Present Jews and Judaism in Preaching and Catechesis in the Roman Catholic Church," the authors affirm the permanence of Israel according to the flesh as a sign "to be interpreted": "The permanence of Israel (while so many ancient peoples have disappeared without trace) is a historic fact and a sign to be interpreted within God's design."[104] The authors then turn to the olive tree metaphor of Romans 11, and quote a statement of St. John Paul II that the special status of the Jewish people is expressed well by St. Paul's olive tree metaphor: "It remains a chosen people, 'the pure olive on which were grafted the branches of the wild olive which are the gentiles.'"[105] Judaism could be

---

[101] Pope Benedict XVI, "Grace and Vocation," 169.

[102] *NA*, 4.

[103] *LG*, 16.

[104] In the Catechism, the ancient practice of typological reading is encouraged, as it holds together the unity of the Old and New Testaments. *CCC* 128: "The Church, as early as apostolic times, and then constantly in her Tradition, has illuminated the unity of the divine plan in the two Testaments through typology, which discerns in God's works of the Old Covenant prefigurations of what he accomplished in the fullness of time in the person of his incarnate Son." *CCC* 129: "Christians therefore read the Old Testament in the light of Christ crucified and risen. Such typological reading discloses the inexhaustible content of the Old Testament; but it must not make us forget that the Old Testament retains its own intrinsic value as Revelation reaffirmed by our Lord himself." The CRRJ also discusses typological reading and says it must be used with care, and that the Old Testament "retains its own value as Revelation." "We should be careful to avoid any transition from the Old to the New Testament which might seem merely a rupture." "Notes on the Correct Way to Present the Jews and Judaism in Preaching and Catechesis in the Roman Catholic Church," Vatican Commission for Religious Relations with the Jews (1985), 3–8 (hereafter Notes 1985).

[105] John Paul II, "To the Delegates of the Episcopal Conferences for Relations with Judaism," March 6, 1982. Section 6 not only implies that God wills the existence of the Jewish people as a sign; the section can also be seen to reject the anti-Jewish elements of Augustine's typological

said to continue to function as an ongoing sign in God's design through a reflection on the "root" in St. Paul's statement in Romans 11:18: "Remember that it is not you that support the root; but the root that supports you." This root could be interpreted to refer to the distinctiveness of the flesh of that particular people, or, as *Lumen Gentium* states, the flesh of that people from whom Christ was born. The Pauline idea that the Church draws present sustenance from this elect people implies that their ongoing physical existence is vital for the life of the Church.

Perhaps the support that the root that is Israel continues to provide the Church can be clarified through the Thomistic view of the figuring function of the old sacraments. As I have argued elsewhere, the Thomistic conception of the old sacraments as figures of Christ deserves to be explored for positive meaning especially after the Second Vatican Council's recovery of the teaching that the promise of Christ was given to the Jewish people, and Christ came from the flesh of this people; that God continues to hold this people most dear; and that the Church, along with the prophets and the Apostle Paul, awaits the day of the salvation of this people.[106]

In Aquinas, observance of the ceremonial law after the Passion of Christ was understood as a subjective declaration of unbelief on behalf of those who resisted faith in Christ and participated in these sacraments. However,

---

reading of the story of Cain and Abel. St. Augustine, *Answer to Faustus, A Manichean: The Works of St. Augustine Part I*, vol. 20, trans. Roland Teske, SJ, ed. Boniface Ramsey (Hyde Park, NY: New City Press, 2007). See also Aquinas's approving description of this reading of Gen 4 in his commentary on Matt 27:25. *Super Matt.*, 27.1.2343. I have shown elsewhere that alongside positive statements on the Jews there are also punitive supersessionist and economically supersessionist views in Aquinas. See Tapie, *Aquinas on Israel and the Church*.

[106] Perhaps it is appropriate to address a possible objection to this sort of constructive Christian theological account of Judaism. Some might say Christian systematic theological reflection in this area is misguided at best and is a violation of the other's self-identity. Jews do not recognize the intrinsic relationship between Israel and the Church that Catholics see. However, it is impossible to establish a non-theological conception of the other, especially from within a tradition-based inquiry. Additionally, the importance of theology in Jewish-Catholic dialogue is a theme that runs through Catholic teaching on Jews and Judaism, from *NA* all the way to Pope Francis. And the writing of *NA* would not have been possible without "internal" theological reflection on the Church's relationship to Judaism and the Jewish people. A cursory reading of the deliberations of the Council indicates that it was precisely theological reflection and debate that helped move *NA* to promulgation. And, yet, there also existed "external" theological exchanges between Catholic theologians and Jewish scholars during and after the war that shaped conversations about the themes of the declaration. Thieme's exchange with Buber is an example; Ehrlich's exchange with Oesterreicher is another. In other words, it is a both/and: internal theological reflection *and* external dialogues enabled the development of doctrine that is *NA*. I think a Christian theological account of Judaism is a necessity for Christians because of the person of Christ and the nature of Catholic theology, but this task should include striving to understand how Jews define themselves; dialogue with Jewish thought; and utmost respect for the special status of Judaism as external to the Church.

in some places in Aquinas's thought the old sacraments also pointed to an objective Christian reality apart from the subjective intention of the recipient of the sacrament. The figuring function of the old sacraments was connected to the Augustinian legacy of a special status for Jews and Judaism outside the Church.

This special status of the Jews as the people who received the promise of Christ is the ground of the ongoing positive function of the old sacraments. Aquinas, writing at the end of his life in the late thirteenth century, stressed that the Old Testament was good and authored by God; and that the Jewish people were the elect people from whom Christ came. Aquinas absorbed the "witness of the Apostle" (his title for St. Paul) concerning the ongoing election of the Jewish people.[107] Aquinas, citing Augustine, taught that questioning the election of the Jewish people was an error: "And if again it is asked why [God] chose this people, and not another, that Christ might be born thereof; a fitting answer is given by Augustine: 'Why He draws one and draws not another, seek not to judge, if you wish not to err.'"[108]

For Aquinas, the literal meaning of the ceremonies of the old law before the Passion of Christ is that these laws consecrated the Jewish people to the worship of God in a special way. Aquinas divides the ceremonies of the old law into four categories: 1) *sacrificia* or sacrifices; 2) *sacra* or sacred things; 3) *sacramenta* or sacraments; and 4) *observantiae* or observances. All of these categories are referred to together as *caeremoniae veteris legis*. The 1) *sacrificia* include sacrificial animals offered by the Levite priesthood. 2) *Sacra* include instruments such as the temple, tabernacle, and the vessels. 3) *Sacramenta* include circumcision, "without which no one was admitted to the legal observances" and the eating of the paschal banquet.[109] Aquinas refers to the paschal banquet as an observance, but it is treated in the same article on sacraments, indicating that Passover, for him, may fit into both *sacramenta* and *observantiae* categories. 4) *Observantiae* mostly refers to dietary regulations. All of these precepts are ceremonial in character in the sense that they give public expression to divine worship.

---

[107] Aquinas wrote in his commentary on St. Paul's letter to the Romans, "For if the Jews' prerogative were abrogated on account of the unbelief of some, it would follow that man's unbelief would nullify God's faithfulness—which is an unacceptable conclusion." *In Rom.*, 3.1.249. See also Tapie, *Aquinas on Israel and the Church*; and Joseph Sievers, "'God's Gifts and Call Are Irrevocable': The Reception of Romans 11:29 through the Centuries and Christian-Jewish Relations," in *Reading Israel in Romans: Legitimacy and Plausibility of Divergent Interpretations*, ed. Cristina Grenholm and Daniel Patte (Harrisburg, PA: Trinity Press International, 2000), 144.

[108] ST I.II 98.4.

[109] ST I.II 102.5.

According to Aquinas, the latter two, that is, the 3) sacrament of circumcision and 4) observance of dietary regulations, along with Passover, function together to consecrate the Jewish people in a special way to the worship of God. Aquinas says the literal, rational cause for the *observantiae* of the law is the "special prerogative of that people."[110] He therefore recognizes the importance of ceremonial law categories 3 and 4 for the distinctiveness of the Jewish people. The temple sacrifice (or *sacrificia*) and sacred things (or *sacra*), such as the tabernacle, are not tied to the "special prerogative of that people." Again, the special prerogative of the people is tied to circumcision, Passover, and dietary laws. The special status or prerogative of this divine worship reflects God's choice of this particular people because the worship "consecrated" the people to God.[111] Therefore, the literal meaning of the old sacraments, for Aquinas, was that it enclosed this particular people, and not another people, in the worship of the God of Israel.

It is well known among Thomists that the figurative meaning of these old sacraments pointed to Christ's Passion. Yet, the signification of the old sacraments pointed not only to the biblical promises and prophecies concerning the Passion of Christ.[112] In Aquinas, the objective dimension of the signification of the old sacraments also pointed forward to aspects of the Christian faith in general, and in a way that seems to echo the thought of Gregory IX and Innocent IV on Jews as a sign of Christ. In what way might elect Israel continue to "figure" the Christian faith, even after the Passion of Christ? The ongoing figuring function of the old sacraments could be described as twofold: Jewish worship points to the Christian faith in general, and it points to the distinctive human nature of Christ in his incarnation, resurrection, and Second Coming in particular.

First, the general way in which the ceremonial law continues to figure Christ can be explained by way of the claim Aquinas makes concerning the rites continuing to figure the Christian faith, not only the Passion. In ST

---

110 ST I.II 102.6.

111 ST I.II 102.5–6.

112 For the most part, Aquinas thinks these rites *were* but no longer *are* figures of Christ. For instance, Jeremy Cohen is correct that the language about the ceremonies of the old law as "figures of present benefit" that belong to Israel according to the flesh are eventually applied to Christians in Aquinas's comments on Rom 9:4–5. I am grateful for his helpful correction on this point, although there are other positive ideas in the Romans commentary. Jeremy Cohen, "Supersessionism, the Epistle to the Romans, Thomas Aquinas, and the Jews of the Eschaton," *Journal of Ecumenical Studies* 52, no. 4 (Fall 2017): 527–53. I depart from those elements of Aquinas's doctrine where there is an insistence that the ceremonial law was *only* a figure of the Passion of Christ. In my view, the old sacraments continue to figure the Christian faith and the Second Coming. For this reason, the sacraments cannot be said to be superfluous in the time before the Second Coming.

II.II 10.11, the old sacraments are described as present tense *figura* after the Passion, and in his discussion of unbelief (*infidelitas*) as a vice against faith, and whether such unbelief should be tolerated in Christendom, Aquinas states that Jewish rites should be tolerated because of a particular good: "Thus from the fact that the Jews observe their rites, which, of old, foreshadowed the truth of the faith which we hold, there follows this good—that our very enemies bear witness to our faith, and that our faith is represented in a figure, so to speak."[113] The standard view is confirmed when Aquinas says the rites prefigured the truth of the Christian faith in the past. However, Aquinas then says that in the worship of the Jews of his day there remains a continuing figuring function in relation to the Christian faith. The rites continued to bear witness to Christianity in the thirteenth century despite subjective unbelief in Christ.[114] This text is noteworthy because Aquinas does not refer to Jewish worship only as rites that *were figures* of the Christian faith, which was the function of Jewish worship before Christ. Rather, Jewish worship is said to continue to figure the Christian faith. In another place in the *Summa theologiae*, he says the rites figure "the Christian mode of life" in general, and not only the Passion: "All these things happened to them in figures. Consequently, the reasons for these observances may be taken in two ways, first according to their fittingness to the worship of God; secondly according as they foreshadow something touching the Christian mode of life."[115] As mentioned above, Aquinas's thought seems to echo Gregory IX's and Innocent IV's defense of Jews and Judaism as an ongoing sign of Christ in the face of Christian violence.

---

113 ST II.II 10.11: "Ex hoc autem quod Iudaei ritus suos observant, in quibus olim praefigurabatur veritas fidei quam tenemus, hoc bonum provenit quod testimonium fidei nostrae habemus ab hostibus, et quasi in figura nobis repraesentatur quod credimus."

114 Bruce Marshall made this point in a 2009 essay, "Quasi in Figura":
   Given the tremendous weight Thomas ascribes to the figurative meaning of Jewish worship *before* Christ, to say that this worship retains a figurative significance after Christ is not a trivial claim. If Jewish worship even now attests Christian truth in a figurative way, it must somehow still do what it *did* from the beginning: point to Jesus Christ in its own distinctive fashion, join the faithful worshipper to his incarnation and passion, and so confer the grace of justification.

Bruce Marshall, "Quasi in Figura: A Brief Reflection on Jewish Election, after Thomas Aquinas," *Nova et Vetera*, English edition, 7, no. 2 (2009): 483. Aquinas's teaching differs from Augustine's classical apologetic function of the doctrine of Jewish witness. Augustine's teaching on the apologetic function of Judaism does not teach that Jewish worship is a figure of Christ. Rather, Augustine's witness doctrine teaches that when the Jews embrace their Scriptures, they unknowingly prove that Christians do not make up the prophecies about Christ. My aim here is to develop this insight. As I argued above, Aquinas's thought echoes Gregory IX's and Innocent IV's defense of Jews and Judaism as ongoing sign of Christ.

115 ST I.II 102.6.

Based on this text in Aquinas, one can say that the Jewish people who received the promise of Christ are therefore related to the Church in that they continue to bear the promise of Christ unto the end of time. As I have argued elsewhere, it is my view that this relation can be expressed in what Aquinas understood as the three "appearances of the Son of God": incarnation, resurrection, and Second Coming.[116]

First, consider that Christ was circumcised on the eighth day. In this event in the early life of Christ, a direct link between the permanent election of Israel, the Torah, and the Church's faith in the incarnation becomes manifest. The circumcised body of Christ is a permanent reminder that he was conceived by the power of the Holy Spirit in the womb of his Jewish mother and circumcised on the eighth day. According to Aquinas, the first reason that Christ was circumcised was "in order to prove the reality of his human nature, in contradiction to the Manicheans, who said that he had an imaginary body."[117] The ongoing physical existence of ethnic Israel therefore is sustenance for the Church in that Israel witnesses, in the time of the gentiles, to the reality of Christ's human nature: that Jesus Christ was really born.

A second sense in which the people is a sign corresponds to the second appearance of the Son of God, the resurrection. Since Christ's resurrected body retains its wounds, Jewish circumcision could also be said to figure the circumcised Jewish flesh of Christ's resurrected and glorified body. Far from fulfilling and destroying the law, Christ fulfills and upholds the Torah in his circumcised and glorified body. This is because even as he is seated at the right hand of God his body retains its circumcision. Therefore, the ongoing distinctiveness of Jewish flesh maintained in the Jewish practice of circumcision remains a figure or sign not only of the incarnation, but of Christ's resurrection: that Jesus Christ's body died and that Jesus Christ's body was raised and glorified.

The third way in which the people is a sign corresponds to the third appearance of the Son of God, the Second Coming. The permanent distinctiveness of the Jewish people, as well as their prayer for the throne of David and Zion, is a sign that figures the perfect state of peace at the Second

---

116 According to Aquinas there is a threefold appearing of the Son of God. Aquinas, *In Isaiam*, Prologue. See also Pope Benedict's discussion of the threefold scheme of salvation history of *umbra* (shadow)—*imago* (image)— and *veritas* (truth). The Church fathers described the movement of history in this threefold scheme and understood the present age as *imago*, that is, a transitory state of time. This is the time of the gentiles who have not yet arrived at the plain truth of seeing Christ face to face. Perhaps Aquinas's "threefold appearing" of the Son of God can be considered a helpful set of distinctions for understanding the relation Christ to the Jewish people in the time of *umbra*, *imago*, and *veritas*. Pope Benedict XVI, "Grace and Vocation," 176.

117 ST III 37.1.

Coming. The faith of the Church includes belief in the Second Coming of Christ, when he will appear in what Aquinas calls the land of the living, when the dead will rise. Circumcision today could be said to figure the reality of the resurrected body of Christ at the Second Coming in a twofold sense that corresponds to 1) Christ's circumcised and glorified body at the Second Coming and 2) the bodies of those resurrected from the dead. First, the rite of circumcision today figures the circumcised and glorified body of Christ the deliverer who will come from Zion to judge the living and the dead, when all Israel will be saved. Second, circumcision could be said to continue to figure what the Church Fathers and Aquinas called the "eighth era." In their reflections on why circumcision took place on the eighth day, the fathers said the eighth day was a symbol that referred to the eighth era, which they understood as the resurrection of the dead.[118] In line with this patristic tradition, Aquinas states that circumcision was a figure of the resurrection of the dead in the eighth age and of the removal of corruption from the bodies of the elect: "The figurative reason for circumcision was that it foreshadowed the removal of corruption, which was to be brought about by Christ, and will be perfectly fulfilled in the eighth age, which is the age of those who rise from the dead."[119] In his commentary on Romans, Aquinas says this again. Circumcision prefigures the resurrection of the dead, "when all possibility of suffering and death is removed from the bodies of the elect."[120] Circumcision can therefore be said to signify both the circumcised and glorified body of Christ as well as his removal of corruption from human bodies and the earth in the land of the living.

The removal of corruption and death will apply to the Jewish people, since on Aquinas's terms the elect includes the ethnic Jewish people who will be saved at the end of time. When Aquinas comments upon Romans 11:28 that "as regards election [the Jews] are beloved," he says that one can expect that the redemption of the Israel of the flesh is reasonable because this people is the elect people of God: "As regards those elected from that people, salvation was obtained. For if they are dear to God, it is reasonable that they be saved by God: the eye has not seen, O God, besides you, what things you have prepared for them that wait for you (Isa 64:4)."[121] Since the old sacraments figure not only the Passion of Christ, but all three appearances

---

[118] Jean Daniélou, *The Bible and the Liturgy* (Notre Dame, IN: University of Notre Dame Press, 1966), 262–86.

[119] ST I.II 102.5 ad. 1.

[120] *In Rom.*, 4.2.348.

[121] *In Rom.*, 11.4.923. See also Jeremy Cohen, *The Salvation of Israel: Jews in Christian Eschatology from Paul to the Puritans* (New York: Cornell University Press, 2022).

of Christ, it seems that any anagogical interpretations of circumcision would continue to figure the perfect fulfillment of God's promises to the Jewish people on that day known to God alone, and this is despite subjective dispositions to Christ.[122]

Therefore, we can add a third figuring function to the ongoing practice of circumcision. Jewish worship points to 1) the Christian faith in general; 2) the distinctive human nature of Christ in his incarnation, resurrection, and Second Coming; and 3) to that day known to God alone when elect Israel will be saved by Christ in his circumcised and glorified body at the Second Coming, after the full number of the gentiles enter the Church.[123]

In line with the above emphasis on "that day" in the architects and fathers of *NA*, Jewish religious practice after the Passion figures that day which Christians confess in the Creed: "He will come again in glory to judge the living and the dead and his kingdom will have no end." *Lumen Gentium*, no. 16, teaches that the people to whom the promise of Christ was given and from whom Christ came remains dear to God.[124] In what sense was the promise of Christ given to that people? As explained in chapter 5, Aquinas taught that the fathers of old, such as Abraham, received the promise that Christ was to be born of "the Jewish nation" (Gen 22:18: "In thy seed shall all the nations of the earth be blessed") *in the rite of circumcision*. The rite of circumcision is the sign of this promise. The giving of circumcision took place before the giving of the Mosaic Law because "the body of the faithful" should be

---

[122] See the statement of the CRRJ, in Guidelines 1974, section 2, on Christ's perfect fulfillment: When commenting on biblical texts, emphasis will be laid on the continuity of our faith with that of the earlier Covenant, in the perspective of the promises, without minimizing those elements of Christianity which are original. We believe that those promises were fulfilled with the first coming of Christ. But it is none the less true that we still await their perfect fulfillment in his glorious return at the end of time.
The Pontifical Biblical Commission also stated that the Jewish messianic hope reflects a possible reading of the Bible that deserves respect but that is not held by Christians: "Christians can and ought to admit that the Jewish reading of the Bible is a possible one, in continuity with the Jewish Sacred Scriptures from the Second Temple period, a reading analogous to the Christian reading which developed in parallel fashion. Both readings are bound up with the vision of their respective faiths, of which the readings are the result and expression. Consequently, both are irreducible." Pontifical Biblical Commission, "The Jewish People and Their Sacred Scriptures in the Christian Bible" (2001), no. 22.

[123] Since Jewish worship points to the Christian faith and the body of Christ after the Passion, it would seem to join the faithful worshipper to Christ. Perhaps this is one way to coherently explain how Jews remain objective participants in salvation despite subjective dispositions to Christ. GC, 36.

[124] *LG*, 16: "In the first place we must recall the people to whom the testament and the promises were given and from whom Christ was born according to the flesh. On account of their fathers this people remains most dear to God."

gathered by a sensible sign.¹²⁵ The promise of Christ given to that special people in the rite of circumcision is also the promise of Christ's perfect fulfillment of God's promises when "out of Zion the Deliverer shall come." Therefore, this particular people, the body of the faithful, bear the imprint of God's promise of Christ irrevocably despite the fact that, as NA 4 makes clear, "the Jews in large number [did not] accept the Gospel." As Kendall Soulen observes, "God's election of Israel comes with no expiration date. *It does so precisely because of its orientation to Jesus Christ.*"¹²⁶

ROMANS 11:25-26 AND THE EXEGESIS OF POPE BENEDICT XVI

In this final section, I argue that ideas from within the "Paul within Judaism" school of biblical scholarship, and in Pope Benedict XVI's biblical exegesis, reinforce the interpretation of Romans 11:25–26 in the architects and fathers of NA. The Council fathers' interpretation of these texts is affirmed and deepened in the teaching of Benedict XVI because he makes explicit the teaching from the Council debates that there is no duty for Catholics to seek the conversion of Jews in the age of the gentiles.

The Mystery of the Protective Callus over Israel

Let us first turn to the question of the interpretation of Romans 11:25–26. A more coherent and helpful argument for Christian affirmation of Jewish religious practice after the Passion is possible if we not only jettison the idea of invincible ignorance but also reject the problematic use of the term "hardening" of Israel.

This requires adjusting the lens on our reading of Romans 11:25–26 to detect the eschatological vision of the Apostle Paul that was elevated by the fathers of NA. Again, the problem with the standard translation of "hardening" is that it shifts the theological spotlight to a perceived epistemological disposition in Jews. When this negative disposition is read into the text it distracts from the overarching point of chapter 11. Paul's aim in his famous olive tree analogy at the center of chapter 11 is to admonish gentile followers of Christ to adopt an attitude of awe (v. 20: "Do not become proud but stand in awe"), and to not be ignorant of a particular mystery: the Jewish people

---

125 ST III 70.2 ad. 3.

126 R. Kendall Soulen, *Irrevocable: The Name of God and the Unity of the Christian Bible* (Minneapolis, MN: Fortress Press, 2022), 95.

remain dear to God and deeply important to the Church's universal saving mission even in distance to Christ.[127]

Another way of interpreting Romans 11:25 shifts the focus from subjective dispositions to a focus on God's positive purposes in electing Israel of the flesh until the Second Coming. Mark Nanos translates v. 25–26 as follows: "For I do not want you to be unperceptive, brothers [and sisters], [about] this mystery [mustérion; μυστήριον], so that you would not be mindful [only] for yourselves, because for a while a callus [porosis; πώρωσις] has formed for [the protection of the injured branches of] Israel, until the fullness of the nations shall commence. And then all Israel will be made safe [or saved]."[128] Nanos argues that πώρωσις (from πωρόω), traditionally translated as "hardening," evokes the idea of Pharaoh's hardened heart. But Paul does not use the Greek word for Pharaoh's hardened heart (sklayros; σκληρός) in Romans 11:25 to refer to Israelites. Rather, the word he uses, πωρόω, is a medical term referring to the formation of a "callus" to protect a wounded limb.[129]

A callus involves a type of hardening that is not a negative attribute but a protective and healing attribute. Unlike the negative case of a hardened heart, a callus on a damaged limb "promotes healing, *protecting* the injured area so that life can be conducted in and through it, thus serving the interests of the

---

[127] Romans is written to gentile Christ followers and to them alone, though Paul does think that Jews must become obedient to the good news. But proclaiming the gospel to the Jewish people was Peter's task, and it was ultimately not received by the Jewish people. Thiessen, *A Jewish Paul*, 151, 154.

[128] Mark Nanos, Literal-Oriented Translation of Romans 11:11–32 from appendix, in *Reading Romans within Judaism: The Collected Essays of Mark D. Nanos*, vol. 2 (Eugene, OR: Cascade, 2018), 287. Since a mystery cannot fully be grasped by human reason, the NABRE translation of the phrase "I do not want you to be unaware of this mystery" seems preferable to the NRSVCE's "I want you to understand this mystery." Daniel Patte makes a similar point in his essay "A Post-Holocaust Biblical Critic Responds," in *Reading Israel in Romans: Legitimacy and Plausibility of Divergent Interpretations*, ed. Cristina Grenholm and Daniel Patte (Harrisburg, PA: Trinity Press International, 2000), 231.

[129] Mark Nanos, "'Callused,' Not 'Hardened': Paul's Revelation of Temporary Protection until All Israel Can Be Healed," in *Reading Romans within Judaism*, 153–78. According to Nanos, πωρόω is not a word common to the Tanakh. It is used once in the Septuagint (Job 17:7) to refer to eyes growing dim from grief, but Nanos argues that this is not the best term to express such an idea. Πώρωσις is not used in the Pseudepigrapha, Josephus, or Philo. The term is common in medical discussions in antiquity. According to Hippocrates, *De alimento* 54, it has to do with a process of healing following an injury: "Marrow nutriment of bone, and through this a callus forms." Nanos reports that the term is also used in Celsus's *De Medicina* and *Aretaeus*, which "explains how to bind a broken bone tightly because in this position a callus grows." There is no evidence that πώρωσις was used to refer to the heart during Paul's time, but it is used later, in Mark 3:5, John 12:40, and in the Pauline tradition responsible for Eph 4:18. Nanos, "'Callused,' Not 'Hardened,'" 155. See also Nanos's introductory essay on Romans in Amy-Jill Levine and Marc Zvi Brettler, eds., *Jewish Annotated New Testament*, 2nd ed. (New York: Oxford University Press, 2017), 285–86, 308–12.

overall body (or plan), so that it can be restored (saved, healed, rescued)."[130] This interpretation is fitting given Paul's olive tree analogy, which immediately precedes verses 25–26.

The positive purpose of this protective callus that has formed upon Israel is the mystery Paul speaks of in 11:25. Paul says, "I do not want you to be unperceptive ... about this mystery ... because for a while a callus has formed until the fullness of the nations shall commence." As Soulen has observed, the mystery is *not* that all Israel will be saved. The mystery is *how* all Israel will be saved. The idea that Israel will be saved by God is unsurprising as the theme is pervasive in Scripture. The mystery that Paul refers to in Romans 11:25 is *the manner* in which the salvation of Israel will take place:

> Paul announces ... God's immediate intervention on Israel's behalf at the end of the age: "Out of Zion will come the Deliverer." [But for] Paul ... there is nothing mysterious about this aspect of his announcement. Few themes are more prevalent throughout the Scriptures than God's eschatological intervention on Israel's behalf. Rather, the mystery that Paul announces touches on a different point entirely, namely, the *manner* in which God will intervene on Israel's behalf. This will happen, Paul affirms, after "the full number of the Gentiles has come in." "And so," that is, in this way, "all Israel will be saved."[131]

To be aware of the mystery of the callus is to recognize that in God's wisdom, the Jewish people not only remain beloved of God (v. 28) unto the end of time, but their ongoing existence supports the full number of the nations entering the Church.

A callus has formed on part of Israel because God is protecting and preserving them. Protecting them from what? The painful division among Jews, Christ-following Jews, and Christ-following gentiles in the first century over the announcement that salvation has come from the Jews in Jesus Christ; and its secondary cause of the nations' boasting against Israel. Why does God preserve this particular people unto the end of time? This people is dearly beloved of God because he chose them; and the mission to the gentiles depends on ethnic Israel's ongoing distinct existence. "For God the salvation of the Gentiles is bound up with the salvation of Israel, just as Israel's salvation is of importance to all the Gentiles."[132] The Church's mis-

---

130 See Nanos's comments on Rom 11:26 in the *Jewish Annotated New Testament*.

131 R. Kendall Soulen, *The God of Israel and Christian Theology* (Minneapolis, MN: Fortress Press, 1996), 174.

132 Johannes Munck, *Paul and the Salvation of Mankind*, trans. Frank Clarke (Richmond, VA: John Knox Press, 1959), 259.

sion to the gentiles "draws sustenance from the root of that well-cultivated olive tree on to which have been grafted the wild shoots, the gentiles."[133] In the present time, a protective callus has formed over the Jewish people so they can flourish until the fullness of the nations commences, and then all Israel will be restored. Here, a permanent distinction between the Church and Judaism after the Passion of Christ is defined positively yet with a view of their eschatological interdependence.

The mystery of the callus is a symbol of God's positive will that Jews and Judaism maintain a distinctive existence now and unto the end of time. The mystery of this divinely willed callus shifts our focus to the necessity of Christian awareness of three fundamental beliefs: 1) ethnic Israel remains dear to God in the time before the Second Coming (11:29), or as *NA* stated, God holds the Jews most dear; 2) that Israel's ongoing existence supports the full number of the gentiles entering the Church (11:25); 3) and that after the gentiles enter the Church all Israel shall be saved (11:26). Judaism's presence in the world is a part of God's mysterious plan of salvation. It is in this sense that divine protection and restoration of Israel are objective realities despite subjective Jewish dispositions to Christ.

As the drafters of *NA* perceived, this situation is a mystery in which the divine will is inscrutably involved. The idea of a protective callus also strongly resonates with themes in the Church's traditional teaching, expressed by Augustine, Pope Gregory the Great, and the numerous papal decrees that set out the official position of the papacy regarding the freedom of the Jews. In this sense, *NA*'s affirmation of the special status of the Jewish people echoes the premise of the tradition that God wills that the Jewish people exist in safety outside of the Church and unto the end of time.

Pope Benedict XVI on Romans 11:25-26

The above interpretation of Romans 11:25–26 also aligns with Pope Benedict XVI's endorsement of what we might call "the argument from exception" view that there is no duty to convert the Jewish people in the present time.

This argument from exception is based not in pragmatic reasons but in Scripture and tradition. It is based in the eschatological discourse of Jesus in the Synoptic Gospels, the Apostle Paul, the Book of Revelation, and in Augustine (as well as Aquinas).

---

[133] GC, 34, affirms this interpretation of the Council when it says, "This image represents for Paul the decisive key to thinking of the relationship between Israel and the Church in the light of faith. With this image Paul gives expression to the duality of the unity and divergence of Israel and the Church."

THE INTERPRETATION OF ROMANS 11:25-26

Pope Benedict argued that according to the Synoptic Gospels, the end of time can only come when the gospel has been brought to the gentiles.[134] "In my analysis of the eschatological discourse of Jesus...I have shown that according to Jesus' understanding of history, a 'time of the Gentiles' comes between the destruction of the temple and the end of the world."[135]

For Benedict XVI, the "time of the Gentiles" concept is also in the Apostle Paul. Like the fathers and architects of NA, Paul only described Israel's conversion in prophetic terms. This Pauline fact "inevitably rules out any attempt at an empirical explanation which would denature prophecy by turning into empty speculation."[136]

In Benedict's discussion of Romans 11:25-26, he says that Paul taught that the present time is the time of the gentiles and that a proper understanding of this time impacts the question of salvation of the Jews:

> Here I should like to recall the advice given by Bernard of Clairvaux to his pupil Pope Eugene III on this matter. He reminds the Pope that his duty of care extends not only to Christians, but: "You also have obligations toward unbelievers, whether Jew, Greek, or Gentile" (*De Consideratione* III/i, 2). Then he immediately corrects himself and observes more accurately: "Granted, with regard to the Jews, time excuses you; for them a determined point in time has been fixed, which cannot be anticipated. The full number of the Gentiles must come in first" (*De Consideratione* III/i, 3).[137]

To further explicate the meaning of Romans 11:25-26, Pope Benedict cites the interpretation of the theologian Hildegard Brem: "In the light of Romans 11:25, the Church must not concern herself with the conversion of the Jews, since she must wait for the time fixed for this by God, 'until the full number of the Gentiles come in' (Rom 11:25).... On the contrary, the Jews themselves are a living homily to which the Church must draw attention."[138] Commenting on the timing of the salvation of the Jewish people, Benedict said, "It is in fact still our belief as Christians that Christ is the Messiah of Israel. It is in God's

---

[134] Pope Benedict XVI, *Jesus of Nazareth*, vol. 2: *Holy Week: From the Entrance into Jerusalem to the Resurrection* (San Francisco: Ignatius, 2011), 42.

[135] Pope Benedict XVI, "Grace and Vocation," 175.

[136] Joseph Ratzinger, *Eschatology: Death and Eternal Life*, 2nd ed., trans. Michael Waldstein (Washington, DC: The Catholic University of America Press, 1988), 200.

[137] Pope Benedict XVI, *Jesus of Nazareth*, 44.

[138] Pope Benedict XVI, *Jesus of Nazareth*, 45.

hands, of course, just in what way, when, and how the reuniting of Jews and Gentiles, the reunification of God's people, will be achieved."[139]

Additionally, Benedict argues that the Book of Revelation supports this eschatological vision when it speaks of two groups of the redeemed, Israel and a great multitude.

> Not only does St. Paul speak of "all Israel being saved," but also the Book of Revelation of St. John sees two groups of the redeemed: 144,000 from the twelve tribes of Israel (which expresses in another language the same thing that Paul meant by the phrase "all Israel"); and next to them, "a great multitude that no man can number" (Rv 7:9) as the representation of the saved pagan world.[140]

In Benedict's teaching, the Church must not concern herself with the conversion of the Jews because this is the time of the gentiles.[141] Rather, the integrity of the mission of Israel in the era of grace must be acknowledged. These themes can be detected in several of Benedict's statements:

> In the meantime, Israel retains its own mission. Israel is in the hands of God, who will save it "as a whole" at the proper time, when the number of the Gentiles is complete. The fact that the historical duration of this period cannot be calculated is self-evident and should not surprise us. But it was becoming increasingly clear that the evangelization of the Gentiles was now the disciples' particular task.[142]

In what way was the disciples' task of evangelization of the gentiles becoming "increasingly clear"? In one of Paul's speeches at the end of Acts, he references a second vision of the resurrected Jesus that occurred while Paul was praying in the temple (Acts 22:17–21), and Jesus directs his mission away from Jerusalem to the gentiles. The vision is often overlooked because of the more frequent references to his first vision of Christ (Acts 9:3–5; 22:6) on the road to Damascus. Concerning this second vision during his prayer in the temple, Paul says, "After I had returned to Jerusalem and while I was praying in the temple, I fell into a trance and saw Jesus saying to me, 'Hurry and get out of Jerusalem quickly, because they will not accept your testimony

---

[139] Pope Benedict XVI, *God and the World: A Conversation with Peter Seewald* (San Francisco: Ignatius Press, 2002), 150.
[140] Pope Benedict XVI, "Grace and Vocation," 169.
[141] Pope Benedict XVI, "Grace and Vocation," 169.
[142] Pope Benedict XVI, *Jesus of Nazareth*, 46.

about me. . . . Go, I shall send you far away to the Gentiles.'"[143] For Paul, the knowledge that some Jews would not accept the gospel is revealed to him directly by Christ, and it is confirmed in his experience. "It was necessary that the word of God be spoken to you first, but since you reject it . . . we now turn to the Gentiles. For so the Lord has commanded us."[144] "From now on I will go to the Gentiles."[145] In his mature ministry, Paul's discussions with Jews are aimed at clarifying that he had not made any accusations against his own nation, Israel (Acts 28:19), but that his teaching was misinterpreted by Jews. Some Jews mistakenly thought Paul was instructing Jews to abandon Moses and to not observe the law.[146] According to Acts, Paul's last attempt in Rome to convince Jews about Jesus ends in a dramatic citation of Isaiah 6:9-10 ("You will indeed listen, but never understand"), and a declaration of the turn to the gentiles: "Let it be known to you then that this salvation of God has been sent to the Gentiles; they will listen."[147] The citation of Isaiah at the end of Acts indicates that any Jewish mission is over given this situation of the emergence of a callus on part of Israel.[148]

The turn to the gentiles is a biblical idea that leads Benedict to affirm that although Christians await, with the Apostle and the prophets, the salvation of the Jewish people, there is no mission to Israel today. Rather, Israel has its own mission: "Israel still has a mission to accomplish today. We are in fact waiting for the moment when Israel, too, will say Yes to Christ, but we also know that while history still runs its course even this standing at the door fulfills a mission, one that is important for the world. In that way this people still has a special place in God's plans."[149] "Even if Christians look for the day when Israel will recognize Christ as the Son of God and the rift that separates them will be healed, they should also acknowledge God's providence, which has obviously given Israel a particular mission in this 'time of the Gentiles.'"[150]

According to Benedict, this reading of the New Testament is the "correct understanding" but one that has been obscured: "The beginnings of the correct understanding have always been there, waiting to be rediscovered,

---

143 Acts 22:17-18, NABRE.

144 Acts 13:46, NABRE.

145 Acts 18:6, NABRE.

146 Whereas, in Paul's view, this teaching was for the gentile followers of Jesus. See Acts 21:21-24, NABRE.

147 Acts 28:26-28.

148 See also Rom 11:7-12.

149 Pope Benedict XVI, *God and the World*, 149.

150 Pope Benedict XVI, *Many Religions–One Covenant*, 109.

however deep the shadows [obscuring it]."¹⁵¹ "Israel's mission has always been present in the background."¹⁵²

The CRRJ seems to adopt a similar view in GC 40 when it rejects institutional mission to the Jews: "The Church is therefore obligated to view evangelization to Jews... in a different manner from that to people of other religions and world views. In concrete terms this means that the Catholic Church neither conducts nor supports any specific institutional mission work directed toward Jews."¹⁵³

However, GC then introduces an idiosyncratic distinction between "institutional Jewish mission" and Christian mission in personal life, which appears nowhere else in Vatican documents and seems to undermine the special requirements of Catholic-Jewish dialogue: "While there is a principled rejection of an institutional Jewish mission, Christians are nonetheless called to bear witness to their faith in Jesus Christ also to Jews, although they should do so in a humble and sensitive manner, acknowledging that Jews are bearers of God's Word, and particularly in view of the great tragedy of the Shoah."¹⁵⁴ GC 42 then states that "Christian mission means that all Christians,

---

151 Pope Benedict XVI, *Jesus of Nazareth*, 44. Some might view Benedict's 2008 change to the Good Friday prayer in the Tridentine Liturgy to indicate ambiguity in his views or endorse a duty to convert Jews. However, he said his intention in drafting the new prayer was the exact opposite. He intended to shift the prayer in the old liturgy, which was still in use by some, away from conversion of the Jews in a missionary sense to language that reflects the eschatological emphasis of the Second Vatican Council:

> The old formulation really was offensive to Jews and failed to express positively the overall intrinsic unity between the Old and New Testament. For this reason, I believed that a modification of this passage in the old liturgy was necessary, especially, as I have already said, out of consideration for our relation with our Jewish friends. I altered the text in such a way as to express our faith that Christ is the Savior for all, that there are not two channels for salvation, so that Christ is *also* the redeemer of the Jews, and not just of the Gentiles. But the new formulation also shifts the focus from a direct petition for the conversion of the Jews in a missionary sense to *a plea that the Lord might bring about the hour of history when we may all be united.*

Pope Benedict XVI, *Light of the World. The Pope, the Church, and the Signs of the Times; A Conversation with Peter Seewald* (San Francisco: Ignatius Press, 2010), 107 (emphasis mine). Benedict also explained that he was not aware that the current heading mentioning conversion was added to the prayer until after the change. He said the heading does not belong there, and that it should be eliminated. Pope Benedict XVI, *Last Testament: In His Own Words*, ed. Peter Seewald, trans. Jacob Phillips (London: Bloomsbury, 2017), chapter 12, 248–49, note ii.

152 Pope Benedict XVI, *Jesus of Nazareth*, 44.

153 GC, 40.

154 GC, 40. The term *institutional mission* is from Cardinal Kurt Koch. See Philip Cunningham, "The Sources Behind 'The Gifts and the Calling of God Are Irrevocable' (Rom 11:29): A Reflection on Theological Questions Pertaining to Catholic-Jewish Relations on the Occasion of the 50th Anniversary of Nostra Aetate (no. 4)," *SCJR* 12, no. 1 (2017): 27. The term is based on the thesis that there was never a specific and exclusive mission to the Jews in the Church's history. However, the

in community with the Church, confess and proclaim the historical realization of God's universal will for salvation in Christ Jesus (cf. 'Ad Gentes' 7)."[155] The citation is to Vatican II's *Ad Gentes* 7, which could be interpreted to imply that there is a duty to preach the gospel to Jews: "Therefore . . . a necessity lies upon the Church (1 Cor. 9:16), and at the same time a sacred duty, to preach the Gospel."[156]

Is there a duty for Catholics to proclaim the gospel to Jews? The term *proclamation* was defined in 1991 by the Pontifical Council for Interreligious Dialogue in *Dialogue and Proclamation*: "It is an invitation to a commitment of faith in Jesus Christ and to entry through baptism into the community of believers which is the Church. This proclamation can be solemn and public, as for instance on the day of Pentecost (cf. *Ac* 2:5–41), or a simple private conversation (cf. *Ac* 8:30–38)."[157] However, on whether there is a duty for Catholics to proclaim the gospel to Jews, *ABialogue and Proclamation* cites NA, and states that Jewish-Christian dialogue has its own "special requirements": "Because the spiritual patrimony common to Christians and Jews is so great (NA 4), dialogue between Christians and Jews has its own special requirements. These are not dealt with in this document."[158] The authors then

---

organized response to the Christian discovery of the Talmud and forced sermons in the thirteenth century problematize this claim. Emily Michelson has also shown that forced conversionary sermons to Jews in early modern Rome were mandated by a papal bull and took place weekly in public for 250 years. Emily Michelson, *Catholic Spectacle and Rome's Jews: Early Modern Conversion and Resistance* (Princeton, NJ: Princeton University Press, 2024), 1.

155 GC, 42.

156 The necessity of universal mission was expressed in Vatican II's *Ad Gentes*, Pope Paul VI's Apostolic Exhortation *Evangelii Nuntiandi*, and St. Pope John Paul II in *Redemptoris Missio*. In *Evangelii Nuntiandi* 22, proclamation is only one aspect of a broader definition of evangelization: "This proclamation—*kerygma*, preaching or catechesis—occupies such an important place in evangelization that it has often become synonymous with it; and yet it is only one aspect of evangelization." Vatican Council II, *Ad Gentes* (December 7, 1965); Pope Paul VI, Apostolic Exhortation *Evangelii Nuntiandi* (December 8, 1975); John Paul II, Encyclical Letter *Redemptoris Missio*: On the permanent validity of the Church's missionary mandate (December 7, 1990).

157 In *Dialogue and Proclamation* sections 8–10, the term *evangelizing mission* is used for evangelization in its broad sense, while the more specific understanding is expressed by the term *proclamation*. No. 10 defines proclamation as invitation to a commitment of faith in Jesus that can be private or public:
> Proclamation is the communication of the Gospel message, the mystery of salvation realized by God for all in Jesus Christ by the power of the Spirit. It is an invitation to a commitment of faith in Jesus Christ and to entry through baptism into the community of believers which is the Church. This proclamation can be solemn and public, as for instance on the day of Pentecost (cf. *Ac* 2:5–41), or a simple private conversation (cf. *Ac* 8:30–38). It leads naturally to catechesis which aims at deepening this faith. Proclamation is the foundation, centre, and summit of evangelization (cf. EN 27).

158 *Dialogue and Proclamation*, fn18.

point the reader to other CRRJ documents for a "full treatment" of these requirements.[159] In these rich CRRJ documents, the emphasis on the aim of dialogue is the task of understanding Judaism and Jewish self-definition in joint study, and how to correctly present Jews and Judaism in Catholic teaching. Nevertheless, both documents affirm that in virtue of the Church's divine mission, she must proclaim Jesus Christ to the world.[160]

Moreover, in GC 42, which was published in 2015, the proclamation of the faith is included under the document's section 6 heading, "The Church's mandate to evangelize in relation to Judaism."[161] In section 7, "The goals of dialogue with Judaism," there is no mention of the special requirements of dialogue or a clarification of the relationship of dialogue to proclamation.

Based on the confusing use of terms such as evangelization, witness, mission, dialogue, and proclamation, one could conclude that the CRRJ teaches that there is a duty to invite Jews to convert to Christianity. Since the definition of *proclamation* includes a persuasive intent to invite others to enter the Church, some understand the CRRJ's GC document to teach that there is an evangelizing mission to the Jews that includes efforts to persuade Jews to Christianity.[162] Moreover, some also understand Jews who follow Christ to have a special role in the Christian mission to the Jews.[163] *Dialogue and Proclamation*, section 10, defines proclamation as invitation to a commitment of faith in Jesus that can be private or public. Since teaching is the sacred duty of bishops and priests, should Catholic pastors assist this special mission to the Jews and invite Jews who follow Christ to speak at diocesan outreach events, with the hope that Jews attend and embrace the Catholic faith? The special status of Jewish-Catholic dialogue disappears in this question.

---

[159] See Guidelines 1974; Notes 1985.

[160] Guidelines 1974, section 1, cites *Ad Gentes* 2, which states, "The pilgrim Church is missionary by her very nature, since it is from the mission of the Son and the mission of the Holy Spirit that she draws her origin, in accordance with the decree of God the Father." Notes 1985, section 7, cites to section 1 of Guidelines 1974.

[161] GC 40–43.

[162] D'Costa, *Catholic Doctrines*, 150–51. Philip Cunningham acknowledges that some may understand the CRRJ to teach here that Catholics should dialogue with Jews in hopes that their Jewish partners will be moved to embrace Christian faith. However, he says GC 42 should be considered in light of other statements on the special status of Catholic-Jewish dialogue and the aim of such dialogue in other Vatican documents. See Philip Cunningham, "Gifts and Calling: Coming to Terms with Jews as Covenantal Partners," *Studies in Christian-Jewish Relations* 12, no. 1 (2017): 10.

[163] D'Costa, *Catholic Doctrines*, 186. As indicated in chapters 5 and 6, the belief that Jewish converts to Christianity have a special role in preaching to other Jews is not a new idea.

As scholars have pointed out, Vatican documents, including GC, use a confusing array of terms—such as evangelization, witness, mission, dialogue, and proclamation—inconsistently. This inconsistency creates confusion since the terms can be read in contradictory ways.[164] It also presents difficulties on the ground where Catholics seek to implement the study and dialogue with Jews called for by *NA* and the last five popes.[165] That the USCCB had to clarify its own approach to dialogue with Jews in 2009 is evidence of the confusion at the practical level: "Catholics have a sacred responsibility to bear witness to Christ at every moment of their lives, but lived context shapes the form of that witness to the Lord we love. Jewish-Catholic dialogue, one of the blessed fruits of the Second Vatican Council, has never been and will never be used by the Catholic Church as means of proselytism—nor is it intended as a disguised invitation to baptism."[166] GC 42 sits in tension with this USCCB dialogue principle and the teaching in other Vatican documents and papal utterances that there are special requirements in Catholic-Jewish dialogue.

On the question of whether there is a Catholic duty to invite Jews to embrace the Catholic faith, Pope Benedict's teaching is much clearer and more coherent than GC. According to Benedict, the Church's "missionary mandate is universal—with one exception: a mission to the Jews was not foreseen and not necessary because they alone, among all peoples, knew the 'unknown God.'"[167] Benedict taught that Christians can learn a great

---

[164] Both D'Costa and Cunningham have said the use of the terms in these documents is confusing. D'Costa, "Response from the Author," 10; D'Costa, *Catholic Doctrines*, 147.
   This cluster of terms can be understood in nearly contradictory ways. To sketch the alternatives in binary fashion: Does "evangelize" mean that Christians should: (A) encourage Jews to be baptized or (B) work with Jews in service to the Reign of God? Does "mission" to Jews after *Nostra aetate* mean: (A) to seek to bring them to faith in Christ or (B) to engage in mutually enriching religious dialogue with them? Does "witness" mean that Christians explain their faith to Jews: (A) to bring them to faith in Christ or (B) to share reciprocally the experience of covenantal relationship with God? Do Catholics "dialogue" with Jews (A) in the hope that they will turn to Christ or (B) to deepen a relationship of mutuality?
Cunningham, "Gifts and Calling," 6–7.

[165] "This sacred synod wants to foster and recommend that mutual understanding and respect which is the fruit, above all, of biblical and theological studies as well as of fraternal dialogues." *NA*, 4.

[166] USCCB, "Statement of Principles for Catholic-Jewish Dialogue," October 2, 2009, https://www.usccb.org/beliefs-and-teachings/ecumenical-and-interreligious/jewish/upload/Statement-of-Catholic-Principles-for-Catholic-Jewish-Dialogue-2009.pdf.

[167] Christian M. Rutishauser, "Not Mission, but Dialogue," in *Neue Zürcher Zeitung*, December 1, 2018, 45. That the Jewish people possess the knowledge of God is also something Aquinas assumed. Aquinas applies Christ's words to the disciples from John 15:15 ("I have called you friends") directly to the Jews on account of their receiving "the knowledge of God" (i.e., the old

deal from Jewish exegesis and that the Catholic-Jewish dialogue should be about Scripture, not proclamation.[168] The dialogue aims at mutual respect and understanding, which includes explanation of the coherence of Catholic doctrine and biblical interpretation. But the aim of dialogue is not proclamation; it does not include any invitation to the Jewish dialogue partner to convert to Catholicism.

Moreover, since Pope Benedict's teaching that there is no Christian duty to seek the conversion of Jews is rooted in the New Testament, it means he not only affirms the interpretation of Romans 11:25–26 in the architects and fathers of *NA*, he also develops this teaching.[169] Perhaps one of Benedict's most significant theological contributions to the new encounter between the Church and the Jewish people is how his exegesis deepens the biblical basis for the Council's rejection of a call for Jews to enter the Church in the time of the gentiles.[170] If one adjusts the lens of inquiry to detect both the Council and Pope Benedict's interpretation of Romans 11:25–26, a significant biblical convergence comes into view.

The architects and fathers of *NA* decided to reject the call for the Jewish people to enter the Church based on the biblical argument that the salvation of the Jewish people is an eschatological reality foretold by the Prophets and the Apostle Paul. Therefore, for Benedict, the conversion of Jews is *not* a duty of Catholics or an expectation for the present, and this view is rooted in Scripture. For Benedict, the New Testament teaches that the Jewish people "are not excluded from salvation, but they serve salvation in a particular way, and thereby they stand within the patience of God, in which we, too, place our trust."[171] This helps to clarify that the Council fathers' rejection of a call for the Jewish people to enter the Church is based not in a preference for ambiguity or public pressure but what the deposit of faith testified concerning the mystery of Israel.

---

law): "The words of God were committed to them, as to his friends: I have called you friends." *In Rom.*, 3.1.250.

168 Pontifical Biblical Commission, "The Jewish People and Their Sacred Scriptures in the Christian Bible," preface.

169 The connections between the Council and Benedict on these biblical mysteries of the faith, however, are missed if Benedict's contributions to Catholic-Jewish relations are interpreted through a rationalist lens, or how he is perceived by the public, or if the Council is interpreted to have political rather than dogmatic intentions.

170 Benedict's contribution as biblical theologian also meant that he could not only reject antisemitism and the deicide charge along with *NA* and other popes; his study *Jesus of Nazareth* also explained exactly why these hideous falsehoods had no biblical basis.

171 Pope Benedict XVI, *God and the World*, 150.

Although GC clearly emphasizes that the concept of mystery is key for Catholic theological reflection upon the question of the Jewish people and the saving significance of Christ, the document fails to recognize the significance of the interpretation of Romans 11:25–26 in the Council fathers and architects and how their interpretation impacts the question of whether there is a duty to convert Jews to the Catholic faith.[172]

In the light of Benedict's teaching, the wisdom of the Council becomes clearer, and we can see that the question of whether a Christian mission to the Jews is appropriate is the wrong question. The question is whether Christians will heed Paul's warning to recognize God's positive purposes in the election of Israel and the mystery of Israel's salvation in the age of the gentiles.

It is also important to recognize that Pope Benedict's exegesis is significant not on its own but as an expression of the tradition regarding the special position of the Jews in the Augustinian witness doctrine: "The Fathers say that the Jews, to whom Holy Scripture was first entrusted, must remain alongside us as a witness to the world."[173] Benedict's approach to recognizing that the differences between Jews and Christians will not be resolved in the time of the gentiles expresses this Augustinian tradition in an implicit and positive way: "As far as is humanly foreseeable, this dialogue will never lead to the unity of the two interpretations within ongoing history. This unity is reserved to God at the end of history."[174]

Augustine held that the differences between the Christian and Jewish readings of Scripture would be addressed only at the Second Coming with the return of Elijah, whom he said was "still alive because he was caught up from this human world in a fiery chariot." Augustine understood Malachi 4:5–6 as a prophecy that Elijah will teach the Jewish people on that day that NA says the Church awaits along with the prophets and the Apostle. In Malachi, Elijah's return was held to be a necessary prelude to the deliverance and restoration of Israel: "I will send you the prophet Elijah before the great and terrible day of the LORD comes. He will turn the hearts of parents to their children and the hearts of children to their parents."[175] Augustine thought that upon Elijah's return at the Second Coming, Elijah would proclaim to the Jewish people the Christological interpretation of the law of Moses: "It

---

[172] Pope Benedict XVI's teachings on the special status of the Jewish people, including his view that Israel retains its own mission in the time of the gentiles, were not incorporated into GC.

[173] Pope Benedict XVI, *Many Religions–One Covenant*, 104–5.

[174] Pope Benedict XVI, "Letter from Benedict XVI to Rabbi Arie Folger," in Pope Benedict XVI, *What is Christianity? The Last Writings* (San Francisco: Ignatius Press, 2023), 99.

[175] Mal 4:5–6, NRSVCE.

is very often on the lips and in the hearts of the faithful that in the last time, before the judgement, this great and wonderful prophet Elijah will expound the law to the Jews."[176] Augustine says that when Elijah returns on that day, Elijah will teach that the Father loves the Son "so that the Jews . . . will come to love this same Son, who is our Christ. For, to the Jews, God now has his heart turned away from our Christ, since this is what they think."[177]

Benedict's thought on this important question can therefore be seen as an expression of the longstanding tradition in the Church fathers and numerous papal decrees that Judaism stands in a special position and its autonomy must therefore be respected and protected. When these protections functioned to provide religious freedom for the Jewish people, the Church's tradition can be said to have honored the mystery of the divinely willed protective callus over Israel. The view of the architects and fathers of NA significantly elevates the authority of this biblical prophecy in the tradition concerning the fact that the salvation of the Jewish people is an eschatological reality, and not an expectation for the present. The Council's teaching that the Church awaits that day foretold by the prophets and the Apostle therefore implies a eschatological principle that was assumed by Aquinas and his Dominican defenders: the witness of biblical prophecy is that God wills the Jews to exist unto the end of time despite the question of subjective Jewish responses to Christ.

CONCLUSION

The Christian notion of a duty to convert Jews is prominent in Christian history, and, at times, has motivated grave injustices against the Jewish people and their families. These injustices have caused great pain for Jews and scandals for the Church, as is the case in the kidnapping of Edgardo Mortara and in the removal of other Jewish children from their families. If all Jews converted would there be a theological loss? How would this effect the Church's mission to the gentiles, and its claims about the biblical prophecies concerning the advent of Christ and the human nature of Christ? According to Pope Benedict XVI, "Israel is undeniably still the possessor of Sacred Scripture. . . . The fact remains that it preserves in its hand the Sacred Scriptures of divine

---

176 Augustine, *The City of God*, book 20, 29.

177 Augustine, *The City of God*, book 20, 30. Readers should note the deicide charge in this text. The Second Vatican Council rejected the deicide charge in *NA*, 4. "What happened in His passion cannot be charged against all the Jews, without distinction, then alive, nor against the Jews of today. . . . The Jews should not be presented as rejected or accursed by God, as if this followed from the Holy Scriptures."

revelation. The Fathers of the Church, such as Saint Augustine, emphasized that there must be an Israel that does not belong to the Church in order to bear witness to the authenticity of the Sacred Scriptures."[178] To use Paul's metaphor in Romans 11, what would happen to the olive tree if there were no root? How could "all Israel be saved" if there were no Jews left on that day for which the Church is supposed to wait?

Duns Scotus was aware of how the Christian claim that there is a duty to convert the Jews in the era of grace undermined biblical prophecy.[179] He recognized that the claim contradicted the Apostle Paul's eschatological vision that all Israel will be saved by God at the end of time. If all Jews converted in the present age, then the biblical prophecies about the salvation of Israel could not come true. As a solution to this problem, he proposed that a group of Jews be stationed on a remote island so there would be a small number that could be saved and thus the prophecy would be fulfilled.[180] As the Dominican defenders of Aquinas's teaching asked: if Christians convert the Jews in the present age, what role would be left for Elijah upon his return at the Second Coming?

In the corridors of the Council, the drafters of NA were faced with the complex theological question which the fifth part of GC asks Catholics to study today: the question of Christ and the salvation of the Jewish people. The architects and fathers of NA, along with Pope Benedict XVI, set this question against the background of Romans 11:25-26. They interpreted Paul's words as follows: 1) "All Israel will be saved" in verse 26 refers to Israel according to the flesh, that is, ethnic Israel. 2) In the mystery of God's merciful providence, the salvation of the Jewish people is certain and takes place after the full number of the gentiles have entered the Church. 3) This mystery does not entail a duty to seek conversion of the Jews. NA does not teach explicitly that there is no duty to seek the conversion of the Jews. But in the light of

---

[178] Pope Benedict, "Grace and Vocation," 169.

[179] Simonsohn, vol. 7, 29, 255.

[180] Colish says that Scotus concedes that the witness of the Jews should be preserved until they are gathered in and converted on the Last Day. Colish, *Faith, Fiction*, 305. See Duns Scotus, *Ordinatio*, 4. d. 4. pars 4. q. 3.2.:
>I say that for those who are so few and so tardily to be converted (because the fruit for the Church will be slight and there will be no propagation from them of sons in the Christian Law), there is no need for so many Jews, in so many parts of the world, to persist in retaining their Law for so great a length of time; but it would be sufficient for some few, sequestered in some island, to be permitted to keep their law, and about them the prophecy of Isaiah would at length be fulfilled.

See also Nancy L. Turner, "Jewish Witness, Forced Conversion, and Island Living: John Duns Scotus on Jews and Judaism," in *Christian Attitudes toward the Jews in the Middle Ages*, ed. Michael Frassetto (New York: Routledge, 2007), 183-209.

the Council fathers' answer to the question of conversion of Jews, based in Romans 11:25–26, we can say that the Declaration's language that "the Church awaits that Day known to God alone" implies this teaching. And it is an important line of interpretation that is elevated by Pope Benedict XVI's exegesis and his insistence upon dialogue, not mission. Indeed, Benedict XVI helps illuminate the Council's efforts to restore the truths taught by the Apostle, and, therefore, contained in the deposit of faith.

8

AQUINAS AND THE INCOHERENCE OF BAPTISM INVITIS PARENTIBUS

The aim of this chapter is to summarize the findings of the study with attention to the claims of contemporary defenders of Pius IX's decision to remove Edgardo Mortara from his parents. I argue that their claims are opposed to Aquinas's thought because baptism invitis parentibus is not only repugnant to the natural law and a sin, but it is also incoherent since it assumes that God is in a competitive relation with creation, and indifferent to the spiritual nature of the non-Catholic parents whom he created in his image.

I proceed in two steps. First, I summarize the conclusions of the study with attention to the claims of the contemporary defenders of Pius IX. I show that their claims assume a dichotomy between natural law and grace that is in conflict with Aquinas's teaching. I then explain why the premise behind canon 868 §2, that the divine will that all children receive salvation outweighs the natural bonds between parents and their child, is incoherent on Aquinas's terms.

SUMMARY OF FINDINGS

This study of Aquinas and the Mortara case has shown that soon after Edgardo was removed from his parents, the Mortara family submitted a formal document that argued that, based on the teachings of Aquinas, the child must be returned. However, the papal counsel's refutation of the Mortara family plea also appealed to Aquinas's teaching in order to defend the decision to separate Edgardo from his parents. That Aquinas's teaching was cited as the authority for and against the return of Edgardo to his family

raised questions about the interpretation of Aquinas's teaching on forced baptism as it relates to the Mortara case.

The following question guided the study of the original documents from the 1858 case: how do the authors of the Mortara family's *Pro-memoria* and *Syllabus* and the Vatican document *Brevi cenni* interpret Aquinas's teaching against forced baptism? This study demonstrated that Aquinas's teaching against baptism of Jewish children invitis parentibus was carried forward by his Dominican followers from the late thirteenth century into the middle of the sixteenth century. *Pro-memoria* and *Syllabus* argued that Aquinas was not only against baptizing children without the consent of parents for multiple reasons; the Dominicans also held that Aquinas's teaching supports their arguments that if baptisms invitis parentibus occurred then nothing happens, since the interpretive will for the children of the Jews can only be expressed by their Jewish parents, who are not under the spiritual jurisdiction of the Church.

However, the papal counsel argued that based on Aquinas's teachings: 1) The Church has always forbidden the baptism of Jewish children invitis parentibus. 2) But if it happens that such a baptism occurs, the baptism is valid, and in danger of death it is even licit; the counsel also argued that the intention of the Church and not the parents, is all that is needed for the baptism of a child of unbelievers to be valid. In children who are baptized no intention is necessary, but the Church makes up for it in the person of the one who confers the sacrament. 3) That the Church has from God the power and the right to take possession of the baptized children of the unbelievers.

My study of the documents from the case revealed that the key questions on Aquinas's teaching in the debate between the Mortara family and the papal counsel were as follows: 1) whether Aquinas holds that forced baptism of Jewish children is lawful or licit in order to provide salvation for the child; 2) whether forced baptism of a child of unbelievers is nevertheless a valid baptism; and 3) whether Aquinas teaches that Jewish parents lose their rights over their children if they are baptized. I showed that the identification of these questions is a helpful first step in evaluating the significance of Aquinas's teaching.

However, before examining Aquinas's texts on baptism invitis parentibus, it was necessary to study the context of his teaching: the problem of forced baptism of Jews in Christian history, and debates among canonists and theologians about whether such baptisms were lawful or valid. For this reason, I presented an overview of papal teaching and canon law on forced baptism of Jews from antiquity to the eighteenth century, with attention to the issues identified in the 1858 debate. I showed that thirteenth-century proposals to apply the ancient practice of emergency baptism to the infants

of Jewish families ran against the law of the Church. Specifically, it ran against the repeated papal condemnations on baptism of unbelievers against their will. It was only during Aquinas's lifetime, in the thirteenth century, that theologians began to propose that Jewish children be baptized against the will of their parents in order to provide the children with salvation. I also argued that 1747 papal decrees codified forced baptism of Jewish children in certain exceptions, and that these decrees overturned Aquinas's teaching.

Next, I analyzed Aquinas's teaching and adjudicated whether the parties in the 1858 debate interpreted Aquinas correctly. To the first question, 1) whether Aquinas holds that forced baptism of Jewish children is lawful or licit: I argued that for Aquinas, the care of parents for the young child who lacks reason is like a spiritual womb. Through the metaphor of a spiritual womb, Aquinas reframed the Roman institution of patria potestas in theological terms, as a natural right in the order of the natural law. This move provided a robust theological defense of Jewish parental authority. I also demonstrated that there are problems with the papal counsel's interpretation and application of Aquinas to the Mortara case. The papal counsel ignored the theological argument against the practice of baptism of Jewish children invitis parentibus, which called Benedict XIV's policy of baptizing Jewish children in danger of death into question. Aquinas is diametrically opposed to the proposals seeking to justify the practice, including the argument that providing salvation to the child justifies violating the natural law. I argued that the assertion that the authority of Jewish parents can be violated to provide salvation to a child sets the order of the natural law against the eternal law and the divine law.

For Aquinas, since unbelieving parents are created in the image of God, they are directed to God through their rational appetite for the universal good. God's grace elevates the person's natural desire for the perfect good by revealing that God is the perfect good, the First Truth. However, God's grace does not move the person's rational appetite to assent to the faith in a coercive way but in accord with the rational nature of the human person. God desires to know and love the human person according to the intrinsic nature of the person, that is, through their reason and will.

To the second question, 2) whether forced baptism of a child of unbelievers is nevertheless a valid baptism: Recall that the papal counsel's reply to the Mortara family claimed that in ST I.II 6.6 Aquinas taught that a) the forced baptism of an adult unbeliever is nonetheless valid because even an act motivated by fear remains a voluntary act; b) the Church's intention stands in place of the unbelieving parents; and c) a forced baptism of a Jewish child without the knowledge or against the will of the parents is nonetheless a valid baptism.

Concerning the first claim, I showed that the counsel ignored Aquinas's teaching that a valid baptism requires the intention of the recipient. Nevertheless, if a person chose to accept baptism under fear of a threat, the baptism would imprint a character on the soul and be valid according to Aquinas. Reception of the sacrament on these terms would not provide sanctifying grace, which only comes through intellectual assent and voluntary belief in the faith. Concerning the second claim, the argument reads Augustine's letter to Boniface out of its fifth-century context and ignores that the pagan parents intended for their children to receive baptism to restore or retain temporal bodily health. Concerning the third claim, although Aquinas condemns the practice of forced baptism of children of unbelievers, he implies that their baptisms would be valid.

To the third question, 3) whether Aquinas teaches that Jewish parents lose their rights over their children if they are baptized: recall that the papal counsel argued that Aquinas teaches that Jewish parents lose their rights over their children if they are baptized. The papal counsel appealed to Aquinas's sed contra in its argument against the *Pro-memoria* and *Syllabus* that the child cannot be returned to his parents. I argued that the counsel misinterprets the sed contra for Aquinas's answer to the question in ST II.II 10.12 and reads the statement out of the context of the rest of his teaching in the respondeo. This teaching holds that it would be contrary to natural justice, if a child, before having the use of reason, were to have anything done to it if the parents are unwilling. On this logic, stealing a child would still be contrary to natural justice even if a child was forcibly baptized against the will of the parents. For Aquinas, the Church does not have a right over children because they were baptized, and if they are baptized, he thinks they remain with their parents.

I concluded that insofar as Aquinas's teaching is concerned, the Mortara family's plea is correct that Aquinas is opposed to forced baptisms of adults and children of unbelievers. The papal counsel left out that Aquinas is also opposed to baptisms of Jewish children invitis parentibus to provide them with salvation. The argument of the Mortara family and Dominican theologians that, in Aquinas, the intention of the Church should not replace the intention of the parents of unbelievers is also correct. The Dominican theologians insist that the representative will is a requisite for the sacrament of baptism to be valid and that forced baptism of Jewish children is invalid precisely because it lacks intent of the parents. Nevertheless, the papal counsel's claim that a clandestine baptism of a Jewish child without the knowledge or against the will of the parents is nonetheless a valid baptism finds support in Aquinas. Such a baptism would be illicit but valid.

My analysis of Aquinas's texts also demonstrates that both canon law justifications for abrogating parental rights of Jews and the argument based on saving a child from spiritual death are the most prominent arguments set forward for overriding Jewish parental rights at the end of the thirteenth century. As discussed in chapter 4, the argument from the danger of death is a premise in Benedict XIV's 1747 policy that asserts it is lawful and meritorious if a Christian were to baptize a Jewish child close to death against the will of their parents.

One implication of this study of Aquinas's teachings is that his argument denies a key premise for the exception to forced baptism of Jewish children articulated in Benedict XIV's letters and adopted by Pius IX. Aquinas argued that the natural law must not be violated to save a child of unbelievers and that nothing can be done to a child if the parents are unwilling. Since Aquinas's teaching calls the rational of this policy into question, it also raises the question of the theological coherence of the current canon.

In chapter 6, I analyzed the historical context and purpose of canon 868 §2 with attention to the previous Code of Canon Law (*CIC* 1917), the Second Vatican Council's Declarations, *DH* and *NA*, and the teaching of Aquinas. I argued that the theological rationale behind canon 868 §2 is a problem for a few reasons. First, the premise behind the canon, which asserts that the salvation of the child outweighs parental rights, emerged as part of a policy that caused the separation of numerous families in the Roman ghetto in the eighteenth and nineteenth centuries. Second, I argued that the canon is theologically incoherent because it sets the parental authority of non-Catholics, which is in the order of the natural law, against the divine law. I also argued that the canon runs against the grain of the teaching of the Second Vatican Council, the thought of Aquinas, and the teaching of St. Pope John Paul II.

I also showed that Benedict XIV attempted to synthesize Aquinas's teaching with Scotus's nominalist view of God's power over parental rights. Citing Aquinas's teaching against forced baptism of Jewish children alongside the 1747 exceptions to the practice had the effect of blending Aquinas with the practice of forced baptism of Jewish children in danger-of-death situations. This caused a distortion of Aquinas's teaching that has lasted for over two hundred years. As discussed in chapter 3, the blending of Aquinas's teaching with the danger-of-death exceptions is evident in the papal counsel reply to the Mortara family. This blending of Aquinas and Scotus is also evident in contemporary teachings on emergency baptism invitis parentibus.

The last chapter took a step back and asked a larger question about the longstanding Christian concern for the salvation of the Jews. In particular, the chapter examined the decision of the architects and fathers of *NA* to drop from the declaration a statement expressing a hope for Jews to enter

the Church. I argued that the rejection of the text calling for Jews to enter the Church was based in a particular interpretation of Paul's admonishment of gentile followers of Christ in Romans 11:25–26 to recognize the mystery of Israel. The architects and fathers of *NA* confronted the centrality of the mystery of Israel and interpreted Paul's words as follows: 1) "All Israel will be saved" refers to Israel according to the flesh; 2) the salvation of the Jewish people is certain but the how and when is a mystery that exceeds the grasp of human reason; 3) and that this mystery does not entail a duty to seek conversion of the Jews. In the light of the Council's deliberations, the language of *NA* that the Church awaits the day implies this teaching. I showed that the rejection of the proposal for *NA* to express a hope for Jews to enter the Church was not based in pragmatic concerns but in Scripture, and, therefore, the deposit of faith. I also argued that Pope Benedict XVI's biblical exegesis confirms the fathers' interpretation of Romans 11:25–26 as excluding a Christian duty to seek the conversion of Jews.

THE CONTEMPORARY DEFENDERS OF PIUS IX'S DECISION TO REMOVE EDGARDO MORTARA

Aquinas's thought provides profound reasons to reject arguments defending Pius IX's decision to remove Mortara from his parents. It is deeply misleading to cite Aquinas as theological support for the clandestine baptism of Mortara since Aquinas stands on the side of a tolerant Augustinian tradition that defends Jewish worship and Jewish authority to determine the religious life of their families. As I argued in chapter 5, the papal counsel's argument stands in line not with Aquinas but with a tradition represented by Rufinus of Bologna, William of Rennes, Vincent de Beauvais, and Duns Scotus.

The same can be said for the positions of some contemporary defenders of Pius IX. For example, Romanus Cessario implies that the baptism and removal of a child against the will of its parents is what Aquinas's theology of baptism requires. When Aquinas is read in historical context, it is clear that he argued against theological and legal arguments quite similar to some contemporary defenders of Pius IX's decision to remove Mortara from his parents. The contemporary defenders of Pius IX assume a nominalist theology where "higher loyalties" to the Christian faith override the parental rights of unbelievers: "The Catholic perspective is based on a hierarchy that cannot possibly be ignored without unhinging the doctrine of the faith itself: when

a right in the natural order conflicts with another in the supernatural order, the latter necessarily prevails."[1]

The historian Aviad M. Kleinberg describes this view: "Since there can be no higher goal than defending and promoting Christian faith, other considerations must give way to this basic policy."[2] In a similar spirit, Cessario asks: "Should putative civil liberties trump the requirements of faith? ... The honor we give to mother and father will be imperfect if we do not render a higher honor to God above."[3] Cessario thinks the more important and deeper lesson that the Mortara case highlights is Jews and Christians alike pledge a higher loyalty that they honor in ways that seem incomprehensible to the world.[4]

Insofar as Aquinas's teaching is concerned, the baptism of Edgardo Mortara, or any child, against the will of non-Catholic parents is a dangerous practice that is contrary to the custom of the Church and the natural law. Aquinas consistently rejected the legal and theological proposals that attempted to justify these acts. When Aquinas's teaching is considered in the context of thirteenth-century arguments for forcibly converting Jewish children, it is clear that he defended Jewish parental authority in a culture that took the conversion of Jews seriously. He did so by working to overcome what seemed to some jurists as a perceived conflict between the Christian faith and rights. For Aquinas, the care that Jewish parents provide to their children is a natural right and precept of the natural law that cannot be opposed to God's grace.

---

[1] Vittorio Messori, *Kidnapped by the Vatican? The Unpublished Memoirs of Edgardo Mortara* (San Francisco: Ignatius Press, 2017), 35.

[2] Aviad M. Kleinberg, "Depriving Parents of the Consolation of Children: Two Legal *Consilia* on the Baptism of Jewish Children," in *De Sion exibit lex et verbum domini de Hierusalem: Essays on Medieval Law, Liturgy and Literature in Honour of Amnon Linder*, ed. Yitzhak Hen (Turnhout: Brepols, 2001), 135.

[3] Romanus Cessario, "Non Possumus," *First Things* (February 2018): 58.

[4] Cessario, "Non Possumus," 58. Other Catholic thinkers also emphasize this human versus supernatural theme, insisting that a materialistic view prevents one from seeing the deeper reality of the abduction. The Italian Church historian Vittorio Messori also defends the abduction. See Messori, *Kidnapped by the Vatican?*

GOD, CREATION AS RELATION, AND THE INCOHERENCE OF BAPTISM INVITIS PARENTIBUS

According to one contemporary commentator on the 1983 *CIC*, the divine will of God and the child's right to salvation take precedence over parental rights: "In danger of death, the will of God that all be baptized and the consequent entitlement of the child to baptism, take precedence over the parents' rights."[5] Since it is the divine will that all children receive eternal salvation, it seems this outweighs the natural bonds between parents and their child. And since children are vulnerable to sickness and accidental death at all times it would seem reasonable to baptize them as soon as possible. As Duns Scotus argued, God has a greater right over the children than parents do.[6] Moreover, one might argue that the political context of the Mortara case is different than our contemporary context. Today, there are no consequences for such emergency baptisms against the will or without the knowledge of non-Catholic parents, such as removal of baptized children for Christian education. Perhaps a Christian should baptize an infant of unbelievers clandestinely since it would be good to provide the child with salvation and restore its relationship to God.

However, on Aquinas's terms, the problem with the practice of baptism invitis parentibus runs deeper than the potential negative consequences or aversion to religion that such an act may provoke. Aquinas held that the practice was an injustice that went against the law of the Church, the natural law, and was "not at all reasonable."[7]

The practice is opposed to the teachings of numerous popes from the time of Augustine to the thirteenth century and beyond. Some contemporary Catholic defenders of the practice stress the concern is to avoid the damnation of the child. But such a concern reflects, in part, Augustine's teaching on the condemnation of the unbaptized, including infants who die without baptism.[8] However, Augustine had access to political power in the Roman emperor Honorius (r. 393–423), as is evident in the Church's response to the Donatists. Yet he did not request the emperor use force to baptize Jewish children and save them from damnation. Pope Gregory the Great adopted Augustine's view of the destiny of unbaptized infants. Yet he also condemned

---

5 Francis G. Morrisey, ed., *The Canon Law: Letter & Spirit; A Practical Guide to the Code of Canon Law* (Dublin: Veritas Publications, 1995), 478.

6 Duns Scotus, *Ordinatio*, 4. d. 4. pars 4. q. 3.2.

7 ST II.II 10.12 co.

8 *PA* 16–19; *De pecc. mer.* 1.16.21 (CSEL 60, 20f.); *Sermo* 294.3, *Patrologia cursus completa, series latina* (PL), J. P. Migne, ed., 38, 1337; *Contra Iulianum* 5.11.44 (PL 44, 809).

forced baptism of Jews and insisted that Christians protect and defend the Jewish people from injustice: "The Jews may in no way be oppressed or suffer any injustice."[9]

Second, on Aquinas's terms, the act of baptism invitis parentibus is a mortal sin. The problem is the baptism itself, apart from consequences, since it is a baptism of a child of non-Catholic parents without their permission. This act is a sin against natural justice because the child of non-Catholics is under its parents' care by the order of the natural law, which means nothing can be done to it against its parents' intentions.[10] For this reason, the parent's authority over the child cannot be violated by a well-intentioned Christian. For Aquinas, the parents' authority over the child is a natural right, and the care that they provide it is a divinely ordained part of the natural order. As the prince of Thomists, John Capreolus, has said, "Evils are not to be done in order that goods may come about."

Third, the claim that God's grace must overcome the nature by which the person is subject to God's providence is incoherent. The argument for baptizing a child against the will of its non-Catholic parents in cases of near death assumes the divine will must overcome the will of non-Catholic parents. As mentioned above, this hierarchy is described by defenders of Pius IX's decision to remove Edgardo Mortara from his parents. Fr. Pio Mortara himself described the hierarchy of divine over human will in baptism invitis parentibus in cases of danger of death:

> What the parents are neither able nor willing to give the helpless child—in other words, truth, virtue, holiness in germinal form, Christ, God, and Paradise as an inheritance—all this God gives him, and he gives it to him because He wants to.... The divine will prevails over petty human reason. Here parental authority is in a state of incapacity.... Parental authority ... in the case that concerns us, harmful to the child's eternal salvation, is replaced by the authority of the heavenly Father.... God chooses this soul, takes it for Himself, justifies it, and claims it. Who would dare to ask God why?[11]

---

[9] Simonsohn, vol. 1, 16.

[10] ST II.II 59.4. "Now every injury inflicted on another person is of itself contrary to charity, which moves us to will the good of another. And so since injustice always consists in an injury inflicted on another person, it is evident that to do an injustice is a mortal sin according to its genus."

[11] Pio Maria Mortara, "The Mortara Child and Pius IX. The Autobiographical Account of the 'Mortara Case' Written by the Protagonist, Reverend Father Pio Maria Mortara, CRL," in Messori, "Kidnapped by the Vatican?," 160–61. Marco Cassuto Morselli, *Il Memoriale di Edgardo Mortara* (Rome: Marietti, 2024), 156–57.

The will of God that all receive salvation is understood to conflict with the human will of the parents, which is a lower authority. And the lower human authority must be overturned in order to restore the child's relationship with God.

The idea that God's will is in conflict with human freedom is rooted in a nominalist view of God and God's relation to creation. According to Servais Pinckaers, a nominalist concept of God emerged in Christian theological writings in the years after Aquinas died. This concept ran against Aquinas's thought in its emphasis that God's will was identified as over against the natural inclinations of the human person:

> Reflection on [God] would focus henceforth on his free and sovereign will far more than on his wisdom, truth, and goodness. God's freedom was sovereign, absolute, and identified, so to speak, with his being. . . . Nothing could limit this freedom . . . especially not any nature. God being creator through the sheer power of his will, there could not exist in creation, or even within man, any nature or natural inclination that might impose on God or restrain or orient his action. Furthermore, one could not speak of a nature or natural qualities in God which would call for our respect, since freedom was his supreme quality.[12]

Such a vision of God's power as indifferent to creation redefined the relation between the human person and God as a relation of opposition. "The divine and human freedom were conceived as two absolutes, but with this difference: God was omnipotent in regard to his creatures and could, consequently, impose his will upon us."[13]

As Russell Hittinger has argued, such an understanding of the relation of God's will and human will sets grace against nature since it requires that God's grace must eventually unseat the natural law:

> This would destroy the metaphysical continuity between the various dispensations of divine providence. For if God is to govern, he will have to supersede, if not destroy, the jurisdiction constituted (allegedly) by human causality. Insofar as the natural law is regarded as the foundation of the moral order, and insofar as that is thought to be cause (and not merely discovered) in some proper and primary way by human cognition, God will have to unseat the natural law.[14]

---

[12] Servais Pinckaers, *The Sources of Christian Ethics*, trans. Mary Thomas (Washington DC: The Catholic University of America Press, 1995), 342.

[13] Pinckaers, *Sources of Christian Ethics*, 247.

[14] Russell Hittinger, *The First Grace: Rediscovering the Natural Law in a Post-Christian World* (Wilmington, DE: ISI Books, 2003), 10.

The conflictual relationship between divine will and human will therefore breaks apart the Thomistic conception of God's providence.

As the Catholic theologian David Burrell has shown, God is not in a competitive relationship with the world.[15] Burrell argues that Aquinas's philosophical use of the formula "God is the beginning and end of all things" is crucial for distinguishing God from the universe and obtaining a proper understanding of creation as a relation to God.

Aquinas said that "we cannot know what God is, but only what he is not.... So to study Him, we study what he has not."[16] Burrell explains that this is not just pious talk. "Aquinas works to show under one rubric after another how it is that our discourse fails to present God."[17] Whatever is the beginning and end of everything else cannot itself be one of those things.[18] God cannot be qualified, defined, categorized, specified, or compared with anything else. God does not possess composition of matter and form, or potency and act. Indeed, the language of the "simpleness" of God is shorthand for saying God lacks composition; it is intended to point to God as beginning and end of all things, and is not a characteristic of God.[19] This is, in part, why Aquinas says "God is not a species, nor an individual, nor does he have a difference or definition, for a definition is made from genus and species."[20]

Why is this important? Aquinas's philosophical grammar rules out the possibility of identifying God as a special object or being.[21] Since God is the beginning and end of all things, we cannot say that God's existence is externally caused. Aquinas says, "The very fact that God's existence itself subsists without being acquired by anything, and as such is limitless, distinguishes it from everything else."[22] What are we saying if we say God is subsistent existence itself? "We would be saying all that we can about God. Yet we have no way of fitting that statement into the rest of our discourses."[23] "God escapes our grasp on every count."[24] God does not contain potentialities, so in him nature must not differ from existence.[25] The best way to articulate this is to

---

15 David Burrell, CSC, *Aquinas: God and Action*, 3rd ed. (Eugene, OR: Wipf & Stock, 2016).
16 ST I, intro.
17 Burrell, *Aquinas*, 15.
18 Burrell, 14.
19 Burrell, 18, 20.
20 *De pot.* q. 7, a. 3.
21 Burrell, *Aquinas*, 16–18.
22 ST I 7.1 ad. 3.
23 Burrell, *Aquinas*, 61.
24 Burrell, 21.
25 ST I 3.4 co.

say that God's nature is itself existence, or God is his own existence, *ipsum esse subsistens* (existence or act of existence itself).[26] God's essence is to exist, or as Burrell puts it, "To be God is to be to-be." This phrase gestures toward the fact that God's lacking limits does not mean God lacks identity.[27] "If God were one type of being, he could be caught in the net of conceptual knowledge and the prohibition of such a 'catching' is the practical purpose of the claim that he is to-be itself."[28] For Aquinas, then, God's nature transcends anything that we can apprehend in our present state.[29] If God were anything other than the act of to-be, he would be one type of being among many.[30]

This understanding of God as pure act is crucial for a proper understanding of the relation of God to creation. Since God is the beginning and end of all things, he is incommensurate with any single thing he causes. Aquinas reminds us that when we speak of God making and producing things, we speak by analogy of the way we understand things, since no human experiences the universal production of things.[31] To acknowledge God to be creator is an article of faith and a turning point, since it is the recognition of the "emanation" of all being and time from God.[32] Anything that has being must receive it from the one whose nature is to-be itself. Since it is God's nature to exist, Aquinas says that it follows that created existence is his proper effect, just as fire itself sets other things on fire. Created existence itself "participates" in God in the sense that it has a relation of dependence from the one whose nature is simply to-be.[33] All creatures exist only by participation in the inexhaustive act of existing which is the Creator. No creature can be without this participation.[34] Created existence is thus causally related to God's creative activity so that the creature itself is a relation. This means that creation should not be mistaken as mere fact or a given. To illustrate

---

26 ST I 3.4 co.

27 Burrell explains that "to-be" expresses the nature of God: that which we cannot know. Aquinas clarifies this usage in I 3.4 ad. 2: "The verb 'to be' is used in two ways: to signify the act of existing, and to signify the mental uniting of predicate to subject which constitutes a proposition. Now we cannot clearly know the being of God in the first sense any more than we can clearly know his essence." Burrell, *Aquinas*, 48, 55.

28 Robert Barron, *The Priority of Christ: Toward a Postliberal Catholicism* (Grand Rapids, MI: Brazos Press, 2007), 219.

29 Burrell, *Aquinas*, 61.

30 Barron, *The Priority of Christ*, 219.

31 Burrell, *Aquinas*, 153.

32 Burrell, 153.

33 Burrell, 154.

34 David B. Burrell, *Towards a Jewish-Christian-Muslim Theology* (Oxford: Wiley-Blackwell, 2011), 21–22.

this point, Burrell says, "I cannot exercise my existence. If something exists it simply is, and we speak on analogy here, an act that does not originate with us." As Burrell points out, the intellectual turning point in Augustine's journey was his attunement to how all creatures relate to God, hearing them say, "We did not make ourselves."[35] To speak of "creation," then, means that we are not speaking of any ordinary production. For this reason, Aquinas says, "Creation is nothing other really than a kind of relation to God."[36] Creation is "a relation" to God, and it is a relation of radical dependence.[37]

If creation is relation to God, then God cannot be in a competitive relationship with creatures.[38] In a helpful discussion of Aquinas's view of creation as relation to God, Bishop Robert Barron explains that God does not enter into the nexus of conditioned relations, interacting with other similar things. "On the contrary, the web of interdependent realities as a whole is brought into being by that which remains necessarily other." Barron explains that this is the case even as God exerts primary causality that gives rise to the being of the world through an infinite variety of secondary causes, which retain their own integrity and uniqueness as causes. "Even as he enters most intimately into creation, grounding it and sustaining it, he must allow it to be itself, for to do otherwise would be to compromise his own otherness."[39] God's involvement with the creature is not competitive but intimate, because God sustains the deepest center of a creature's existence.[40] "God is the ground of any and all creaturely activities, emotions, reactions, and passions and hence is more, not less, connected to the creature."[41]

Creation as relation has what Barron refers to as an "other-enhancing quality."[42] God does not create out of need but out of a desire to share his goodness with what is other. And God "lets the other be in the very act of constituting that other as other."[43] This includes sustaining the being and the power to act for all of his creatures, since to withhold causal integrity to natural creation would mean withholding goodness from what he has

---

35 St. Augustine, *The Confessions*, trans. Maria Boulding, OSB, ed. John E. Rotelle, OSA, vol. 1 of *The Works of Saint Augustine* (Hyde Park, NY: New City Press, 1997), 228.
36 *De pot.* q. 3, a. 3.
37 Burrell, *Aquinas*, 154–56.
38 Barron, *The Priority of Christ*, 224.
39 Barron, 220.
40 Barron, 223–24.
41 Barron, 224.
42 Barron, 221.
43 Barron, 221.

made.⁴⁴ For Aquinas, the otherness of God is what permits God to operate so thoroughly among creatures without compromising their causality. Aquinas says that "the higher a cause is, the more universal and efficacious it is, and the more efficacious it is, the deeper it penetrates into its effect."⁴⁵ In other words, divine freedom can come intimately close to human freedom and not compromise it. Though the human person is other than God, the person participates in God's eternal law through existing and longing for the universal true and good. As explained above, the human person's rational participation in the eternal law is nothing other than the natural law.⁴⁶

Since God is not a highest being among beings but is wholly other, he "can operate in the realm of beings nonviolently, or as the book of Wisdom has it, 'sweetly.'"⁴⁷ The above explanations from Burrell and Barron on the proper understanding of the relation between God, creation, and human freedom can help us see that God does not act coercively against that which is other than God. "[If] God were a finite thing, his relation to others would be interruptive and invasive." Indeed, the divine relation to creation is peaceful rather than coercive: "In him there is a love utterly untainted by violence."⁴⁸

Behind this metaphysics is the distinctive relationship that obtains between the divine and human nature in Christ.⁴⁹ In Jesus Christ, God becomes human not by overwhelming the integrity of human nature. Rather, two natures, divine and human, come together without mixing, mingling, or confusion. Jesus is fully human and fully divine. The two exist in mutual perfection. In Christ, God and creature, divine will and human will, come together in such a way that neither is compromised. As Robert Sokolowski has argued, God does not destroy the natural necessities of things he becomes involved with since nature retains its integrity before the Christian God:

> The Council of Chalcedon, and the councils and controversies that led up to it, were concerned with the mystery of Christ, but they also tell us about the God who became incarnate in Christ. They tell us first that God does

---

44 Barron, 227.

45 *De pot.* q. 3, a. 7.

46 "Now among all others, the rational creature is subject to Divine providence in the most excellent way, in so far as it partakes of a share of providence, by being provident both for itself and for others. Wherefore it has a share of the Eternal Reason, whereby it has a natural inclination to its proper act and end: and this participation of the eternal law in the rational creature is called the natural law." ST I.II 91.2.

47 Barron, *The Priority of Christ*, 228. Wisdom 8:1: "She reacheth therefore from end to end mightily, and ordereth all things sweetly." Douay-Rheims 1899 American Edition.

48 Barron, *The Priority of Christ*, 225.

49 Barron, 221.

not destroy the natural necessities of things he becomes involved with, even in the intimate union of the incarnation. What is according to nature, and what reason can disclose in nature, retains its integrity before the Christian God. And second, they tell us that we must think of God as the one who can let natural necessity be maintained and let reason be left intact: that is, God is not himself a competing part of nature or a part of the world.[50]

God is not a competitive being among many or a mind who struggles over and against other minds for authority.

God governs and redeems creation by cooperating with the spiritual nature of the human person, not by destroying that nature. For Aquinas, since all human persons, including non-Catholic parents, are created in the image of God, they are directed to God through their rational appetite for a complete and all-sufficient happiness. This is, in part, why God does not justify us without ourselves; rather, faith requires the voluntary intellectual assent to God's movement of grace. In this way, grace does not destroy or overturn the participation of non-Catholic parents in God's eternal law in situations where children are in danger of death. In such a tragic situation, the charitable act would be to do all one could to save the natural life of the child and assist the child's parents. According to God's providence, it is through the spiritual nature of the parents that a child comes to know and love God. God guides humanity to return to him through knowledge and by love.[51] To hold that a Christian should baptize a child of non-Catholics in danger of death without their knowledge or against their will assumes that God is in a competitive relation with creation and indifferent to the spiritual nature of the parents.

❀ ❀ ❀

The Mortaras were not the first Jewish family to appeal to Aquinas's teaching to defend against kidnappings of their children. Italy's Jewish communities had become familiar with canon law on matters affecting them. On the question of forced baptism, the major communities regularly exchanged documents.[52] This study of the Mortara Syllabus indicates that the Jews appealed not only to Aquinas's teachings but to a Dominican tradition that rigorously

---

50 Robert Sokolowski, *The God of Faith & Reason: Foundations of Christian Theology* (Washington, DC: The Catholic University of America Press, 1995), 35–36.
51 Michael S. Sherwin, *By Knowledge & By Love: Charity and Knowledge in the Moral Theology of St. Thomas Aquinas* (Washington, DC: The Catholic University of America Press, 2005).
52 David Kertzer, *The Kidnapping of Edgardo Mortara* (New York: Vintage, 2008), 144.

defended Jewish parental authority as a spiritual womb in the order of the natural law, which must not be violated.

The Jews of the Roman ghetto appealed to Aquinas's teaching in at least two other cases. As discussed in chapters 4 and 6, before the Mortara affair Roman Jewish children and adults were abducted from the Roman ghetto and coerced into baptism. Roman Jewish responses to these forced baptisms sometimes included formal legal pleas submitted to the Vatican.

In 1713, Mazaldo Cohen, the three-and-a-half-year-old daughter of Sara Cohen, was taken to the House of Catechumens for conversion by Sara's brother-in-law, Israel Jona, who had himself converted. Sara appealed to the congregation with the support of a Christian lawyer, Francesco Maria Spannocchi.[53]

Spannocchi argued to the congregation that Aquinas prohibited the baptism of small children invitis parentibus, which they claimed covered both father and mother. The petition argued for the mother's guardianship and claimed that her brother-in-law had kidnapped her daughter. The rector of the House of Catechumens, Don Crisante Cozzi, argued that the child was not kidnapped but came to convert by divine will, since the child had made the sign of the cross.[54] The final decision was against the mother. After two months of separation from her daughter, Mazaldo, Sara Cohen asked to be baptized at the House of Catechumens.

In another case, in 1762, Stella, who was three, and Ester, who was six, were taken from their Jewish parents because they had been offered by their Jewish grandmother, who had converted. The grandmother also offered the unborn child of the pregnant daughter-in-law, Allegrezza, who publicly opposed the offering. The children were taken by force from their parents.

Their defense was handled by a Roman lawyer, Carlo Luti, who represented Jews in defense of parental rights cases. Luti also appealed to Aquinas: "As could be expected, the petition cited the authority of St. Thomas and the canonists who prohibited the baptism of children without the consent of the parents."[55]

The plea was denied, however, on the basis of concern for the soul of the infant, and what the counsel regarded as the failure of the parents to guide him: "When those who by nature should guide him are in disagreement among

---

[53] Marina Caffiero, *Forced Baptisms: Histories of Jews, Christians, and Converts in Papal Rome*, trans. Lydia G Cochrane (Berkeley: University of California Press, 2012), 83.

[54] Caffiero, *Forced Baptisms*, 84–85.

[55] Caffiero, 117.

them, [the infant] should have the Church come to his aid by always preferring the sentiment of the person who will assure his salvation with Baptism."[56]

As is clear from these cases and the Mortara family's *Pro-memoria* and *Syllabus*, Aquinas's teaching was viewed by advocates of Jewish parental rights as an important defense against forced baptism of children. The Roman lawyer Luti's plea is representative of the challenge since it highlights that Aquinas's teaching was known in the eighteenth century but it was ineffective in the face of appeals to higher loyalties or the favor of the faith.[57] Luti wrote, "But if things continue in this manner, we shall soon see the offering of any relative approved, not to mention any Jew in the Ghetto, and the opinion of St. Thomas, which is said to be followed, will have only the honor of being commonly printed in the books, but will be trampled on the more and more when it comes to putting it into practice."[58] Luti's comments that Aquinas's teaching will be printed but not followed remains relevant. As discussed in chapter 6, Aquinas's texts have been cited three times alongside of the baptism invitis parentibus in danger of death teaching.

Part of the aim of this study has been to highlight the Dominican defense of Aquinas's teaching on these matters and to address what are misinterpretations of his teaching in those who support baptism of non-Catholic children invitis parentibus. Moreover, the study carries forward the Dominican tradition of defending Jewish children from Christian violence in Ambrosius Catharinus, Peter Paludanus, John Capreolus, Juan de Torquemada, and Sylvester Mazzolini di Prierio.

Today, there is a need to recover and apply Aquinas's teaching on these difficult matters. Since Aquinas's thought denies the rationale behind the danger-of-death exception, it also denies the premise of canon 868 §2, that the will of God that all receive salvation takes precedence over non-Catholic parents' rights, which are rooted in the natural law. As mentioned above, the drafting committee charged with formulating the revision of the 1917 canons on the sacraments modified the canon on baptism invitis parentibus in an attempt to align it with the Second Vatican Council. The committee argued for the modification based on *DH* 10 and the principle that non-Catholic parental authority is an order of the natural law. But this modification was later rejected and, therefore, not included in the 1983 *CIC*. In order for 868 §2 to be aligned with the natural law, the Second Vatican Council, and Aquinas, the canon should be modified so that it directly states that for an infant of non-Catholic parents to be baptized licitly, one or both parents or the person

---

56 Caffiero, 121.
57 Caffiero, 19.
58 Caffiero, 120.

who legitimately takes their place must consent. If only one parent consents, the child may be baptized only if the other parent does not object. In addition to the above theological issues, the current canon strains Jewish-Catholic relations. As a living member of the Mortara family has said, "Making the forced baptism of children licit against the will of the parents, for fear of the eternal damnation of their soul, is a dangerous and now unacceptable practice."[59]

Aquinas argued that the practice was dangerous in the thirteenth century. Through the metaphor of the spiritual womb, he reframed the Roman institution of patria potestas in theological terms, by defining it as a natural right. Aquinas's view of natural right is an objective order of equity established by nature, as an expression of God's wisdom.[60] Since the demands of natural justice, for Aquinas, are expressions of God's wisdom, Jewish parental authority is from God.

According to Aquinas, not even the pope has power to dispense with matters of divine or natural law. "The pope cannot dispense with matters of divine law or natural law since their force comes from being divinely established."[61] The spiritual womb of non-Catholic parents is not destroyed in the context of God's supernatural gift of grace since "grace does not destroy nature but perfects it."[62]

---

[59] Elèna Mortara, "Ancora sulla breccia: battesimi forzati e codice canonico," in *150 Anni sulla breccia: Roma, una capitale in trasformazione*, ed. Marisa Patulli Trythall (Roma: Nova Delphi Libri, 2021), 290–91.

[60] Jean Porter, *Natural and Divine Law: Reclaiming the Tradition for Christian Ethics* (Grand Rapids, MI: Eerdmans, 1999), 273.

[61] *QDL* 4.8.2. "The pope cannot dispense with matters of divine law or natural law since their force comes from being divinely established. . . . Hence the pope can dispense with all such determinations of human law; it is only those of natural law and the articles of faith and the sacraments of the New Law that he cannot dispense with, since he could not possibly do so for the truth, but only against the truth."

[62] *ST* I 1.8 ad. 2.

APPENDICES
ORIGINAL DOCUMENTS FROM THE MORTARA CASE

Appendix A: *Pro-memoria* (*PM*)   **269**
Italian transcription with English translation

Appendix B: *Syllabus* (*SA*)   **293**
Latin transcription with English translation

Appendix C: *Brevi cenni* (*BC*)   **403**
Italian transcription with English translation

APPENDIX A

PRO-MEMORIA (PM)
Source: AAV, Segr. Stato, Rubriche, anno 1864, rubrica 66, fasc. 1, ff. 167-74.

[f. 167r]

PRO-MEMORIA

Il 24 giugno del corrente anno 1858 in Bologna venne strappato ai suoi genitori Israeliti il fanciullo Edgardo Mortara di non ancora anni sette (allegato N. 1), adducendosi che il medesimo fosse stato battezzato clandestinamente. Il desolato padre domandò più volte, ma sempre invano, le minute circostanze del fatto, per cui lo si privava del figlio. Solo dopo varie settimane conobbe per indiretta via che all'Anna Morisi già serva di casa uscì detto molti mesi addietro con altra fantesca di avere, ad istigazione di certo

ENGLISH TRANSLATION
Translated by Saretta Marotta

[f. 167r]

PRO-MEMORIA

On 24th June 1858 in Bologna, the child Edgardo Mortara, not yet seven years old (see the attachment no. 1), was taken from his Jewish parents, on the grounds that he had been baptized clandestinely.[1] The distraught father asked several times, but always in vain, for exactly what reason his son had been taken from him. It was only after several weeks that he learned indirectly that Anna Morisi, who was a servant in the house, had told another maid many months ago that she had baptized the child Edgardo. She said

---

1 Here, *Pro-memoria* refers to the first exhibit, the birth certificate of Edgardo Mortara.

Sig. Lepori, droghiere, battezzato, niuno presente, il bambino Edgardo, caduto sull'età di un anno gravemente malato, e che un tale discorso ebbe luogo in occasione che, essendo per morire altro figlio dei Mortara, veniva la Morisi interessata da quell'altra serva a conferirgli il battesimo, il che essa non volle fare altrimenti.

Il Mortara dinnanzi a cotale esposizione del fatto trova da osservare:

1. Che veramente l'Edgardo nell'età poco più di un anno ammalò, ma di semplice febbre verminosa, tanto comune ai bambini; onde lo stato di lui non era per isvegliare serii timori in chicchessia (allegato n 2). Non esisteva dunque la condizione, in cui si permette di battezzare i bambini degl'infedeli *invitis parentibus,* cioè la fondata certezza di morte inevitabile. Infatti sarebbe in contraddizione colle massime della Chiesa sull'autorità paterna (di cui più innanzi) il credere ciò autorizzato prima che la vicina morte non vada sottraendo i figli all'autorità dei genitori. Supposto [f. 167v] un momento che la evidenza della poca entità di quella malattia, bastevole ad impedire ogni inquietudine nei parenti dell'Edgardo, non rifulgesse al pensiero della troppo amorevole fantesca, non è già egualmente supponibile che dinnanzi all'altrui falsa estimazione, possa una legge declinare dalla verace essenza dei rapporti stabiliti alla sua applicazione.

2. L'avvenimento tal quale narrasi non diè luogo ad esame, non a confronto di testimoni. Mentre è assioma giuridico che *"quanto crimen est gravius, tanto praesumptiones debent esse vehementiores, quia ubi maius periculum ibi cautius est agendum"* (abbas Panormitan) e mentre non si torrebbe mai alcuno giudizialmente dal più lieve possesso, senza il corredo d'irrefragabili prove, si vorrà ora sulla semplice e nuda assertiva di una fantesca stabilire un fatto, cui si darebbe per conseguenza di orbare un padre ed una madre della loro prole? E per vero non mancano gravi autori in materia canonica, i quali nella sola circostanza della deficienza di testimonii, scorgono sufficiente ragione per dichiarare la nullità di simili battesimi.

that she had baptized him at the age of one year, without any witnesses, at the instigation of a certain Mr. Lepori, a grocer, because the child was then seriously ill. Such a conversation had taken place on the occasion that, as another Mortara child was about to die, Morisi had been asked by the other maid to baptize him, but Morisi refused to do such a thing again.

Given this presentation of the facts, Mortara has some observations to make:

1. It is true that Edgardo fell ill at the age of a little more than a year, but with a simple vermin fever, so common among children that his condition was not likely to arouse serious fear in anyone (see the attachment no. 2).[2] Therefore, the condition under which the Church allows the baptism of the children of unbelievers *invitis parentibus*, that is, the well-founded certainty of inevitable death, did not exist.[3] In fact, it would be contrary to the Church's maxims on paternal authority (mentioned here below) to believe that this is permitted before near death takes the children away from the authority of their parents. But let us suppose for a moment that the clear signs of the non-seriousness of that illness—signs which were sufficient to dispel all anxiety in Edgardo's relatives—did not shine in the eyes of the too affectionate maid. Even if this were the case it would still be inconceivable that the validity of a law could be undermined by an error of judgment committed by others.

2. The event [of baptism] as reported [by Morisi] did not give rise to any verification or comparison with witnesses. However, there is a juridical axiom which dictates that *"the more serious the crime, the more rigorous must be the presumptions, because where the danger is greater, one must be more cautious"* (Abbas Panormitanus).[4] Besides, no one would ever be judicially deprived of the weakest possession, without irrefutable evidences. And would one now wish to establish as certain a fact, on the basis of the simple and bare assertion of a nursemaid, which would lead to depriving a father and a mother of their child? And indeed, there is no shortage of authoritative canonists, who consider the mere circumstance of lack of witnesses to be sufficient reason to declare such baptisms null and void.

2 In this case, the *Pro-memoria* attaches the testimony of the physician Pasquale Saragoni, who certified that the illness suffered by Edgardo Mortara, at the age of about one year, was minor and certainly nothing that could be interpreted by anyone as life-threatening. The text of this attachment was published, among others, by André Vincent Delacouture, *Roma e la opinione pubblica d'Europa nel fatto Mortara. Atti, documenti, confutazioni* (Torino: Unione tipografico-editrice, 1859), 73.

3 *Invitis parentibus*: against the will of the parents.

4 Niccolò Tedeschi (1386–1445) was a Benedictine canonist, also known as "Abbas Panormitanus" or simply "Panormitanus." Panormitanus wrote numerous commentaries on various decretals, arguing for the superiority of general councils over the pope. He was one of the authors mentioned in the *Syllabus auctoritatum comprobantium* attached to the Mortaras' appeal to the pope.

Felin Super Decret. Lib. V Rit. 6 Cap. IX - ibi (in notis): Si puer (iudaeus) debite fuerit per saecularem baptizatus, aliis non existentibus, talis puer non dicitur baptizatus.

Ita Petrus de Ancharano, in cons. 195 incipit secundum ea est, Marquardus in tractatu de iudaeis pars 3 cap 2 n. 6 ubi late discutit hanc difficultatem.

3. La Morisi ha parlato dopo cinque anni di assoluto silenzio sull'accaduto. Perciò non è infondato il sospetto che essa abbia potuto non ricordare perfettamente di avere in allora adempiuto a tutte le esigenze del rito battesimale, colla gelosa precisione richiesta alla validità di questo sacramento, tanto più che in detta epoca essa, non ancor giunta al sedicesimo di età, trovavasi rozza ed inesperta quant'altri mai.

[f. 168r] Premesse queste brevi considerazioni sul merito del fatto, avuto riguardo alla sua legale autenticità ed al reale aspetto delle cose, si passerà agli argomenti generali dai quali traggono altresì conforto i coniugi Mortara che le benigne autorità, cui è devoluto il sentenziare, siano per restituire ad essi il figlio.

É cosa oramai da veruno ignorata che lo spirito del Cristianesimo è spirito di mansuetudine e di carità. Quantunque la più operosa fra tutte le religioni in procacciare sempre nuovi proseliti alle sue dottrine, non havvi in essa principio che direttamente o indirettamente autorizzi d'impiegare all'uopo la violenza, o che piuttosto non manifesti un'aperta avversione all'uso di tutti altri mezzi, che non siano la persuasione e la dolcezza (vedi i testi in fine).

Felinus (Commentary on Gregory's Decretals, book V, rit. 6, chapter 9, in the notes): "If a (Jewish) child has been baptized, even correctly, by a lay person without witnesses, he should not be considered be baptized." *The same said Peter of Ancarano (Consilium 195, incipit II) and Marquardus de Susannis (De judaeis, part III, chapter 2, n. 6, where he deals extensively with this problem).*[5]

3. Morisi spoke after five years of absolute silence on the matter. It is therefore not unreasonable to suspect that she might not have been able to remember perfectly whether she had fulfilled all the requirements of the baptismal rite, with the jealous precision required for the validity of this sacrament, all the more so since at that time she, not yet sixteen years old, was as rough and inexperienced as ever.

[f. 168r] After these brief remarks on the facts, their legal authenticity and their reality, we will turn to the general arguments from which the Mortara couple also derive the hope that the benevolent authorities, to whom the judgment is entrusted, will want to return their son to them.[6]

It is a fact now ignored by no one that the spirit of Christianity is a spirit of meekness and charity. Although it is the most industrious of all religions in constantly procuring new proselytes for its doctrines, it has no principle that directly or indirectly authorizes the use of violence for this purpose. Rather, it manifests an open aversion to the use of any means other than persuasion and gentleness (see the texts at the end).[7]

---

[5] Felino Maria Sandeo (1444–1503), Peter of Ancarano (Pietro d'Ancarano, 1333–1416), and Marquardus de Susannis (Marquardo Susanna, 1508–78) were all Italian canonists quoted in the *Syllabus auctoritatum comprobantium*.

[6] There is another version (we will call it the "versio altera") of the *Pro-memoria*, which can be found in the AAV, Segreteria di Stato, rubrica 66, fasc. 2, ff. 7–15, and which at this point adds numerous pages of Latin quotations from various authors that differ from those found in the *Syllabus* as well as from those (much fewer in number) found in the version of the *Pro-memoria* transcribed and translated here (the "versio primaria"). For this translation, we have chosen to transcribe and translate the *versio primaria* because: 1) it is the one to which the *Brevi cenni*, the reply of the Holy See, responds; 2) the *versio primaria* is also found in the (Archivio di Stato) in Bologna; 3). Finally, it is the versio primaria that was sent by the circular letter of the Secretariat of State to the Apostolic Nuncios together with the *Brevi cenni*. It is not known why the Vatican Archives also kept the *altera* version or what its provenance is. To see the content of this *versio altera*, see Sharon Stahl, "The Mortara Affair, 1858: Reflections of the Struggle to Maintain the Temporal Power of the Papacy" (PhD diss., Saint Louis University, 1987), which bases her reflections only on this version of the *Pro-memoria*.

[7] The reference is to the *Syllabus auctoritatum comprobantium*, which gathers in fifty pages dozens of Latin quotations from jurists and theologians (with the notable omission of St. Thomas Aquinas) who support the thesis of the invalidity of baptisms *invitis parentibus*.

Certo che fra i sensi di giustizia e di umanità, onde rifulge il Cristianesimo, non poteva mancare la consacrazione religiosa di quel principio di ragione che prescrive l'assoluta inviolabilità dell'uomo nel foro della sua coscienza. Iddio cui basterebbe un solo atto dell'eterno volere per isconvolgere l'attuale ordinamento delle cose, permette che più religioni esistano sopra la terra, mentre una sola deve essere secondo la quale egli gradisce il culto degli uomini. Le convinzioni in noi trasfuse sulle ginocchia della madre, fan credere a ciascuno, che la sola strada da lui seguita è quella tracciata da Dio a servire Iddio, cui perciò si temerebbe tradire col distaccarsene. É dunque sempre un nobile motivo quello che ci tiene attaccati alle avite credenze, perché l'uomo non si arrende mai all'errore che gli sembri tale. E male opererebbe la forza dove ha esclusivo dominio la persuasione: una religione imposta equivarrebbe all'avversione ed al disprezzo della religione stessa. Il Signore, [f. 168v] che dava all'uomo il libero arbitrio, solo gradisce le offerte volontarie, e se atroce ingiuria sarebbe cotale violenza contro il diritto di natura, non meno grave offesa recherebbe anche d'altro lato alla Divinità, presumendo sostituirsi al di lei volere, quasi a correggere gli ordini imperscrutabili della sua Provvidenza.

Basandosi in queste potenti ragioni di mitezza e di tolleranza universale, la Chiesa fu del continuo in sull'avviso per condannare il poco illuminato zelo di coloro che avessero creduto guadagnare merito appo Dio colla forzata conversione degl'infedeli. E per vero, dal momento che i principi teologici del Cristianesimo davano come propria conseguenza quel solenne principio di morale *"Ama il prossimo come te stesso"*, stabilivasi, qualunque ne fosse la credenza sul destino riserbato agl'infedeli dal Giudice Supremo, che il fatto della religiosa loro esistenza, poteva bensì apparire una sventura agli occhi della Chiesa, non mai un delitto, da punirsi col misurare per essi ad una stregua di giustizia diversa da quella usata pei Cristiani, i rapporti, quanto meno, di ragione naturale. Ora è indubitato che i potenti motivi onde vengono impediti con tanta severità i battesimi non volontarii, rimangono nel pieno loro vigore anche di fronte all'azione consumata, poiché il vincolo risultante dalla esecuzione di un fatto non obbliga, a senso di qualunque legge chi non prestò il suo volere all'atto di cotale esecuzione, né può l'abuso seguito delle cose più sacre alterare i rapporti della giustizia, eterni ed invariabili, per determinare che la violenza pesata alle sue bilance non sia sempre violenza.

Surely, among the sentiments of justice and humanity with which the Christian faith shines, the religious consecration of that principle of reason, which prescribes the absolute inviolability of man in the forum of his conscience, could not be absent. God, to whom it would take only one act of His Eternal will to overthrow the present order of things, allows several religions to exist on earth, although there is only one according to which He pleases men to worship Him. The beliefs that have been instilled in us since we were on our mother's knees, make each of us believe that the path we follow is the only path that God has laid out for us to follow Him, so each of us is afraid of betraying God Himself if we deviate from that path. Therefore, it is always a noble motivation that keeps us attached to the beliefs of our ancestors, so that man never gives in to what he believes to be an error. And force would operate wrongly where persuasion has exclusive dominion: an imposed religion would lead to aversion and contempt for that religion itself. The Lord, [f. 168v] who has given man free will, is pleased only with voluntary offerings: and if such violence against the law of nature would be a cruel insult to Him, on the other hand, it would be no less a grave offense to Him to presume to substitute His will for man's, as if to correct the inscrutable orders of His Providence.

Relying on these powerful reasons of gentleness and universal tolerance, the Church has always felt compelled to condemn the unenlightened zeal of those who believed they could gain merit with God by procuring the forced conversion of unbelievers. And indeed, since the theological principles of the Christian faith have as their consequence the solemn principle of morality, *"Love your neighbor as yourself,"* the Church, whatever the belief about the destiny reserved for the unbelievers by the Supreme Judge, established that the fact of their religious existence could appear as a misfortune in the eyes of the Church, but never as a crime to be punished. Much less to be punished by applying to them a measure of justice different from that applied to Christians, at least in the relations governed by natural law. Now it is undeniable that the compelling reasons for which non-consensual baptisms are so strongly discouraged remain in full force even in the face of the accomplished fact. Indeed, under any law, the lien resulting from the execution of an act does not bind the one who has not consented by his will to the execution itself. Nor can the abuse committed in the most sacred things change the rules of justice, eternal and unchangeable, to determine that violence weighed on its scales is not always violence.

Il battesimo conferito all'adulto, il quale non vi abbia prestato il proprio consenso, è pertanto ritenuto nullo; e perché non si giudicherebbe egualmente di quello amministrato ad un bambino *invitis parentibus*? L'atto cui diedesi luogo [f. 169r] verso l'uno e verso l'altro non è abbominato in pari grado dalla Chiesa? Non viola in egual modo le norme del suo governo? O forse è meno inconcussa, meno certa ed assoluta della padronanza che l'uomo ha di se stesso, l'autorità di un padre verso i proprii figli? Ma non v'ha nulla che possa appartenerci meglio dei figli, sangue del sangue nostro, parte migliore di noi, destinata a continuare la nostra esistenza per la catena delle generazioni, sacro deposito a noi affidato dalla Provvidenza per doverne soli rispondere ad Essa. Nello integro sviluppo delle facoltà che costituiscono l'uomo, dando la capacità morale delle proprie azioni, il figlio rimane vincolato al padre solamente pei legami del rispetto, della gratitudine e dell'amore, ma prima che egli abbia raggiunto questo periodo della vita, né le divine né le umane leggi riconoscono in lui personalità distinta da quella del padre.

La educazione della prole, primo degli obblighi inerenti al nome di padre, è l'oggetto in cui assume più di solennità e di vigore la potestà paterna, onde il figlio nato per decreto provvidenziale da un israelita deve essere per tutti Israelita, fino a tanto che non voglia altrimenti il padre od egli stesso fatto adulto, e perciò non vi ha potere che valga nei termini del giusto e dell'onesto ad imporgli altre credenze di quelle ricevute dall'insegnamento paterno, quando la volontà del genitore è sua volontà, allo stesso modo che non varrebbe quando egli fosse emancipato a se stesso.

S. Thom 3 Quaest. 67:

> *(Infidelium filiis). Si vero nondum habent usum liberi arbitrii, secundum ius naturale sunt sub cura parentum, quandiu ipsi sibi providere non possunt. Unde etiam et de pueris antiquorum dicitur quod salvabantur in fide parentum. Et Ideo contra iustitiam naturalem esset, si tales pueri invitis* [f. 169v] *parentibus baptizarentur, sicut etiam si aliquis habens usum rationis baptizarentur invitis.*

Baptism administered to an adult who has not given his consent is therefore considered null and void; and why should it not be judged equally if administered to a child *invitis parentibus*? [f. 169r] Are not both acts equally abominable to the Church? Do not both acts equally violate the norms of its government? Or is the authority of a father over his children less incontestable, less certain and less absolute, than man's mastery over himself? But nothing can belong to us more than our children, who are our own flesh and blood, the best part of us, destined to continue our existence through the chain of generations, the sacred deposit entrusted to us by Providence, so that we alone must answer for them. In the integral development of the faculties that constitute man, including the acquired moral capacity for his own actions, the son remains bound to the father only by the bonds of respect, gratitude, and love. But before he has reached this point, neither divine nor human laws recognize a personality distinct from that of the father.

The education of progeny, first of all of the duties inherent in the name *father*, is the object in which paternal authority assumes its most solemn and powerful character. Hence, the son born to an Israelite by the decision of Providence must be an Israelite for everyone, until either the father or he himself, having come of age, shall will otherwise. Therefore, no power within the bounds of justice and honesty can impose upon the Israelite son other beliefs than those he has received from his father's teaching, both when he is of the age when the will of the parent is for all his will, and when he becomes an adult.

S. Thom, III, Quest. 68

> (Sons of unbelievers) If, however, they have not yet the use of free-will, according to the natural law they are under the care of their parents as long as they cannot look after themselves. For which reason we say that even the children of the ancients "were saved through the faith of their parents." Wherefore it would be contrary to natural justice if such children were baptized against their parents' will; just as it would be if one having the use of reason were baptized against his will.[8]

---

[8] English translations of Thomas Aquinas are based on the Benziger edition of the *Summa Theologica: Summa Theologica*, trans. Fathers of the English Dominican Province (New York: Benziger Brothers, 1947).

Non potrebb'essere più preciso e perfetto, secondo che qui afferma l'Angelico Dottore, il parallelo dell'uno e dell'altro attentato dinnanzi agli ordini immutabili della giustizia, e quindi come non si saprebbe avvisare cagione di differenza nella colpabilità di chi amministra il battesimo all'adulto non volente, e di colui che l'adopera in un fanciullo ad onta del paterno volere, così non è dato conoscere per qual titolo non abbia a giudicarsene eguale l'effetto in ambo i casi.

Forse dirà taluno che il diverso giudizio avrà in ciò fondamento, che il bambino incapace ancora di ferme convinzioni, non subisce azione coattiva nella sua coscienza, ed è ben facile rivolgerne i pensieri ad una novella fede, la qualcosa non potrebbe egualmente avvenire in un adulto. Si oppone in primo luogo che non motto vi sarebbe a calcolare pei voluti effetti sull'accennata diversità di condizione, conforme sentenziò S. Tommaso con altri autorevoli scrittori:

S. Thom. 3 Quaest. 67: *"Est periculosum filios infidelium baptizare quia de facili ad infidelitatem redirent propter naturalem affectum ad parentes."*

Ugolin de officio et potestate Episcopi part. 1, *Cap. 23*: *"Filii hebraeorum qui usum rationis non habent, invitis parentibus baptizandi non sunt, ut dixit Gloss. in cap. Iudaeorum 28 Quaest 1 et sequitur eum Abb. in cap. Sicut Iudaeis et Rubric. in Clement. 1 § 8. quaest. 5 de Iudaeis, et S. Thom. 2.2. quaest. 10, artic. 12, ubi contrariam opinionem iuri naturali repugnare asserit et consuetudini Ecclesiae quandoquidem periculum est ne grandiores facti fidem deserant. Hanc opinionem magis communem receptam etiam testatur. Felinus in cap. Sicut Iudaeis n. 1 et per bullam* [f. 170r] *Martini V."*

The parallelism between these two abuses of the immutable rules of justice could not be more precise and perfect than what the Angelic Doctor affirms here. Therefore, just as there is no difference between the guilt of one who administers baptism to an unwilling adult and that of one who administers it to a child against the father's will, why should not the effect of such abuses be the same in both cases?

Perhaps someone will say that the difference in judgment is based on the fact that the child, not yet capable of firm convictions, is not subject to coercion in his conscience since it is quite easy for his thoughts to turn to a new faith, and this is something that could not be the same for an adult. It is objected, first of all, that there are no quotations [from jurists in support of this thesis] with regard to the aforementioned diversity of situations and their effects, where St. Thomas and other authoritative writers stated [that they are] identical:[9]

S. Thom, III, Quest. 67: "*It would be dangerous to baptize the children of unbelievers, for they would be liable to lapse into unbelief, by reason of their natural affection for their parents.*"

Bartolomeo Ugolini, *De officio et potestate Episcopi*, part 1, chapter 23:[10] "*The children of the Jews who have no use of reason must not be baptized against the will of their parents, as it says in* [omitted] *and S. Thomas, Part II.II, question 10, art. 12, where he assert that a contrary opinion is incompatible with natural law and the custom of the Church when there is a real danger that they will abandon the faith once they have grown up. Felinus (chapter "as the Jews," n. 1) and the Bull of Martin V also testify that this view was the most widely accepted interpretation.*"[11]

---

[9] Here the Italian text is very cryptic. We translated as "there are no quotations" the phrase "non MOTTO vi sarebbe a calcolare." *Motto* is an archaic term (from the French *mot*) for "word, sentence." So—translating very freely—we can assume that the text means to say that there are no legal sources to support the thesis of a different situation between the forced baptism of an adult and that of a child, while Thomas and other jurists maintain that they are equal conditions with equal effects.

[10] Bartolomeo Ugolini (c. 1540–1610) was a canon lawyer from the diocese of Rimini.

[11] Here Ugolini succinctly lists several authors in support of his thesis, giving references to their works in abbreviated form; only his quotations of St. Thomas and Felinus, which are given with their statements in full, have been left in this translation.

In secondo luogo non si discorre qui di esaminare quello che potrà accadere sull'animo del fanciullo, non definibile d'altronde con precisione, vertendo la tesi indistintamente sull'età minorile. É invece proposito di riconoscere quanto avviene del padre, la cui volontà è per ogni ordine di legge volontà del figlio. Finalmente qui non si tratta di stabilire la estrinseca opportunità di un dato sistema di condotta, onde pigliare le mosse dal prudente esame del plausibile e dell'effettuabile. É bensì quistione di un fatto da bilanciarsi cogli eterni principi del giusto e dell'onesto, superiori a qualunque umana contingenza. É quistione di due diritti, riconosciuti in pari grado d'inviolabilità, dei quali verrebbe negato all'uno, la giustizia resa all'altro.

Quella religione adunque innanzi al cui mite discernimento sparisce nei rapporti di questa vita il Cristiano e l'infedele, per rimanere l'uomo coi sentimenti, colla dignità dell'uomo, colla immagine di Dio nell'anima sua immortale, potrebbe non avere conformato uno de' suoi decreti, qualunque sia l'evento e l'individuo cui si riferisca, ai principi assoluti dell'ordine morale? E dove proclamando la carità universale faceva guerra a tutti gli abusi della forza, vorrebbe mai convalidare un atto eseguito in spreto a' suoi comandi per strappare un figlio dal cuore de' genitori israeliti, a costo fors'anco della loro esistenza? E convalidarlo nel tempo stesso che, solo cangiata una circostanza meramente estrinseca lo giudicherebbe irrito e nullo? E mentre di fronte a tante eresi ed alle orgie del filosofismo, anatemizzava le micidiali dottrine che attaccano la società nelle sue basi, la famiglia e la proprietà, avverrebbe mai per essa che il gemito della desolazione sorgesse fra i vincoli spezzati della famiglia [f. 170v] per accusare una somma ingiustizia?

Altro argomento onde i coniugi Mortara ripetono la restituzione del figlio, è nelle volute condizioni perchèil battesimo imprima indelebilmente il suo carattere, il quale argomento è d'altronde quello stesso dell'autorità paterna, guardato sotto diverso punto di vista.

Queste condizioni sono adunque stabilite nel concorso della materia, della formula e della volontà. Quando fra vari requisiti stabiliti indispensabilmente all'efficacia di un dato atto, fosse permesso bilanciare il grado comparativo della loro importanza, è senza dubbio che l'ultimo accennato avrebbe a giudicarsi come il più necessario. E per vero la Chiesa riconosceva eziando oltre il battesimo di sangue, quello consistente nel semplice desiderio (Tertull. Baptism XII, Origen in Joh. 1, 6, n. 26, S. Agost. De Bapt. Cap. 4). Fu nell'idea di questo battesimo che S. Ambrogio riconfortava i pensieri di coloro che avessero dubitato intorno alla salvezza dell'Imperatore Valentiniano, ucciso prima di essere battezzato.

[f. 170r] Secondly, it is not a question here of examining what may happen to the child's soul, which, moreover, cannot be precisely defined, since the thesis refers indiscriminately to the age of minority. Rather, the purpose here is to recognize what happens to the father, whose will is, by every system of law, the son's will. Finally, here it is not a question of establishing the extrinsic appropriateness of a given method of conduct, starting from a prudent consideration of what is plausible and feasible. It is rather a question of a fact to be weighed against the eternal principles of right and honesty, superior to any human contingency. It is a question of two rights, recognized as having an equal degree of inviolability, one of which would be denied the justice done to the other.

Catholicism is the religion for which, in the field of human relationships in this life, the distinction between Christian and unbeliever disappears, leaving only man with his feelings, with his dignity as a human being, as the image of God inscribed on his immortal soul. Could such a religion make a decree, regardless of the event and the individual to which the decree refers, not in conformity with the absolute principles of the moral order? Would this religion, which proclaims universal charity by waging war against all abuses of force, ever want to validate an act performed in defiance of its precepts, which snatches a son from his Israelite parents, perhaps even at the cost of seeing them die of grief? Would it like to validate an act that it would consider null and void if only a mere extrinsic circumstance were to change? Finally, if Catholicism, in the face of the many heresies and the orgies of philosophism [of our time], anathematizes the deadly doctrines that attack society at its very foundations, which are the family and property, would it ever find itself accused of a supreme injustice by the groaning desolation that arises from the family bonds it has broken?

[f. 170v] Another argument from which the Mortara couple insist on the restitution of their son is the conditions required for baptism to indelibly imprint its character, which is the same argument as that of paternal authority, viewed from a different angle.

These conditions are therefore established in the combination of matter, formulation, and will. If, among the various requirements indispensable to the efficacy of a given act, it were possible to measure the degree of their importance in relation to each other, the last, the will, would undoubtedly be judged to be the most necessary. And indeed the Church also recognized, in addition to the baptism of the blood, that which consists in the simple desire (Tertullian, *On Baptism*, XII; Origen in John 1:6, 26; S. Augustine *De Baptismo*, chapter 4). It was with this form of baptism in mind that St. Ambrose comforted those who had doubts about the salvation of the Emperor Valentinian, who was killed before being baptized.

Orat funebr. in obitu Valentiniani N. 51 Audio vos dolere quod non acceperit sacramenta baptismatis. Dicite mihi quid aliud in nobis est, nisi voluntas, nisi petitio? Atqui etiam dudum hoc votum habuit, ut antequam in Italiam venisset initiaretur et proxime baptizari se a me velle significavit.

Il costume della Chiesa, fino dai primi secoli, di non conferire il battesimo agl'infedeli se non dopo una fondata istruzione ed un catecumenato sostenuto a lungo, dimostra all'evidenza che si vuole fede ben salda ed illuminato volere a potere conseguire il sacramento del battesimo. In ordine all'infante senza ragione per credere e senza volere, [f. 171r] per determinarsi all'uopo, supplisce la fede e la volontà dei parenti, ritenuta a ragione interpretativa della sua, in assoluta dipendenza ch'egli è dai medesimi.

Nel caso di cui si tratta non sarebbe intervenuto alla consumazione del presunto battesimo la volontà espressa del battezzando, trattandosi di un bambino in età poco più d'un anno. Certo egualmente che non vi avrebbe avuto luogo volontà interpretativa, dacché i genitori dell'Edgardo, costituiti esclusivamente nella facoltà di assentirlo, erano e sono alieni da ciò, come seguaci del Mosaismo. È dunque evidente la mancanza di una delle condizioni *sine qua non* ad effettuare il sacramento e così la ragione di restituire l'Edgardo ai suoi parenti.

Qui ritorna di necessità il paragone già stabilito fra il battesimo dell'adulto e quello del fanciullo. L'uomo che non diede mai indizio di essere inclinato alla fede, battezzato che egli fosse dormendo, non lo si considererebbe tenuto al Cristianesimo, essendo mancata col di lui assenso, una delle prerogative necessarie ad imprimere il carattere al sacramento. Ma nel fatto in questione mancò parimenti siffatto requisito, e perché se ne giudicherebbe altrimenti?

Qui ci si risponderà che l'autorità della chiesa supplisce al difetto della volontà paterna. Ma ciò essendo, e perché non supplirà alla deficienza della volontà diretta, e quindi non sarà valido anche il battesimo amministrato nel sonno all'adulto? Perfettamente eguale in ambi i casi lo stato passivo del battezzando, onninamente eguale la deficienza della richiesta intenzione, e si negherà in ordine al primo ciò che si ammette per il secondo? Esisterebbe mai un principio che in faccia alle medesime circostanze dovesse spiegare diverse ed opposte conseguenze? Inoltre non si saprebbe spiegare il [f. 171v] concorso di questa volontà là dove si tratti di avvalorare ciò che avviene in opposizione colla medesima. Ed infatti alla stregua di una tale opinione non sorgerebbe più ostacolo per conferire il battesimo a tutti gl'infedeli, volenti o non volenti, giacché non avendosi altra mira, se non il conferimento del battesimo, questo troverebbesi adempiuto in qualunque ipotesi colla sola intenzione della imperante.

Funeral oration for Valentinan, 51: But I hear you lamenting the fact that he did not receive the sacraments of baptism. Tell me what else is there in us except the will, except the request? Yet he already had the specific desire to receive the sacraments of initiation before he came into Italy, and he recently noted that he wanted to be baptized by me.

The practice of the Church, from the earliest centuries, of not conferring baptism on unbelievers except after well-founded instruction and a long catechumenate, clearly shows that firm faith and enlightened will are required to be able to receive the sacrament of baptism. In the case of an infant who has no rational capacity to believe and no will, [f. 171r] this is compensated for by the faith and the will of his relatives, who are rightly considered to be his interpreters since he is absolutely dependent on them.

In the case in question, the express will of the person to be baptized did not intervene to confirm the alleged baptism, since the child was little more than one year old. It is equally certain that there was no interpretative will, since Edgardo's parents, who were the only ones who could consent to the act on his behalf, were and are outside the Catholic faith, as followers of Mosaism. It is therefore clear that one of the *sine qua non* conditions for carrying out the sacrament is missing, and thus the reason for returning Edgardo to his relatives.

Here the comparison already established between the baptism of adults and that of children necessarily returns. A man who has never given any sign of inclination to the faith, and who has been baptized while asleep, would not be considered as bound to Christianity, since, in the absence of his consent, one of the necessary conditions for the efficacy of the sacrament would be lacking. But in the present case such a condition was likewise lacking, so why should it be judged differently?

Here it will be answered that the authority of the church compensates for the defect of the paternal will. But if this were so, why does it not also compensate for the lack of the direct will, so that baptism administered in sleep to an adult is also valid? In both cases, the passive state of the person being baptized is perfectly equal, as is the lack of the required intention; why, then, is the former denied what is admitted for the latter? Would there ever be a principle which in the face of the same circumstances would have to explain different and opposite consequences? [f. 171v] Moreover, it would not be possible to explain the concurrence of this will where it is a question of corroborating what happens in opposition to it. In fact, on the basis of such a view, there would be no more obstacle to the conferring of baptism on all unbelievers, whether willingly or unwillingly, since, having nothing else in view but the conferring of baptism, this would be fulfilled in any case by the sole intention of the prevailing will.

É evidente d'altronde in termini di ragione e di fatto, che i moti di una volontà sono operativi unicamente sul campo abbracciato dalla potenza che le corrisponde. Ora la volontà efficiente della Chiesa in ciò che riguarda le rispettive sanzioni religiose è solo presumibile dove le coscienze recano nelle proprie convinzioni il suggello del suo spirituale dominio. Onde circa il battesimo dell'infante *invitis parentibus* potrà ben dirsi aver supplito la intenzione della Chiesa, quando i genitori sono nel grembo della Chiesa stessa, e perciò obbligati dal vincolo di sudditanza a seguire ciecamente quello che essa prescrive, non già dove i medesimi non subordinati, come è del caso in proposito, alla sua spirituale giurisdizione, trovansi in faccia a lei nell'intero possesso dell'autorità paterna sulla coscienza dei figli, possesso incondizionato, da lei riconosciuto e segnato al rispetto universale.

Non essendo i genitori dell'Edgardo soggetti all'imperio spirituale della Chiesa, né avendo perciò supplito (quando pur certo l'allegato battesimo) al mancato loro assenso l'intenzione della medesima, in cui non va confusa la loro volontà, apparendo da ciò indubitatamente la deficienza di uno dei tre requisiti, onde si compie l'atto sacramentale, ed essendo tale difetto per invalidarlo in un adulto, non sarebbe egli motivo sufficiente per invalidarlo nel piccolo Edgardo, restituendolo così alle preghiere dei genitori?

[f. 172r] Chi scrive non avrebbe rivolto i pensieri a siffatti ragionamenti, qualora non gli fosse occorso un valevole appoggio nelle dottrine di egregi e venerati scrittori i quali finirono per conchiudere la nullità dei battesimi *invitis parentibus* ovveramente quando non avesse rinvenuta l'applicazione di simili dottrine in epoche vicine e lontane per parte delle varie autorità secolari ed ecclesiastiche.

It is, moreover, evident from reason and fact that the desires of a will are effective only in the sphere over which a power is exercised which is in accordance with that will. Now the efficient will of the Church in what concerns the respective religious sanctions is only presumable where consciences bear in their convictions the seal of its spiritual dominion. Therefore, with regard to the baptism of the infant *invitis parentibus*, it can well be said that the intention of the Church prevails when the parents are in the womb of the Church itself, and therefore obliged by the bond of subjection to it to follow blindly what the Church prescribes. But this cannot be the case if they are not subject to its spiritual jurisdiction, as is the case here, where these parents stand before the Church in the full possession of the father's authority over the conscience of the children, an unconditional possession that the Church recognizes and to which it owes universal respect.

Since Edgardo's parents are not subject to the spiritual dominion of the church, nor was their lack of assent (even if this baptism was certain) compensated for by the church's intention, in which their will is not to be confused, it would undoubtedly appear from this that one of the three requirements for the sacramental act is lacking, and since this defect would invalidate it in an adult, would it not be sufficient reason to invalidate it in little Edgardo, thus returning him to his parents' prayers?

[f. 172r] The writer would not have turned his thoughts to such reasoning if he had not found valid support in the doctrines of eminent and revered writers, who ended up concluding the nullity of baptisms *invitis parentibus*, or really if he had not found the application of similar doctrines in times near and far on the part of the various secular and ecclesiastical authorities.[12]

---

12 The Mortara family was assisted by the Roman Jewish community and the scholars of the Roman Rabbinate in the task of collecting previous cases of forced baptism where the outcome was favorable to them, as well as papal bulls and other ecclesiastical decisions on the matter.

Il Bursatto nel Consil. 231 n. 6 narra il fatto che qui si riporta colle stesse sue parole:

> "Hoc primum probatur altero decreto Martini V haebreis anno 1429 concesso quo inter caetera disposuit: neminem ex iudaeis vel eorum filiis, qui duodecimum annum suae aetatis nondum peregerunt, aut aliter doli mali vel discretionis capaces non fuerint sine expresso parentum aut altero eorum consensu non baptizari. Secundo ex quadam sententia lata in una causa Ianuensi confirmata, in iudicatam transita ac exequita, tum a Rege tum a Pontefice Paolo III seu ab eo delegato anno 1539, dum puer haebreus filius aetatis annorum septem baptizantus invitis parentibus fuit per sententiam restitutus in contradictorio iudicio donec aetatem duodecim annorum compleret praestita per eos fideiussione de illo tum Episcopo praesentando, et de non subornando, vel retrahendo eum a Christiana religione".

Per altra sentenza del Card. Francesco Sfondrati eseguita in Roma il 27 giugno 1547 e registrata negli atti di Pietro Reverio, pubblico notaio, fu decretata la restituzione dell'Angelo e del Samuele, fanciulli israeliti, quantunque battezzati, ad un certo Vitale, loro legittimo *tutore*, depositati prima da esso dugento scudi d'oro quale garanzia dell'obbligo assuntosi di presentare a chi di ragione, i due pupilli per farne interrogare la volontà sulla religione da seguire, tosto che avessero [f. 172v] compiuto il dodicesimo anno della loro età.

Il 10 Febbraio 1639 il Vicario di Mons. Scipione Agnello Maffei, Vescovo di Casale, emanò per ordine della S. Congregazione de' Vescovi, una Notificazione, ove fra le pene comminate a quelli che ardissero battezzare i fanciulli ebrei *invitis parentibus*, si dichiara eziando che non verrebbe riconosciuto valido l'abusato atto sacramentale (Allegato n.3).

L'anno 1728 l'Inquisizione di Torino ordinò che fosse restituita ai genitori una lattante battezzata dalla balia cristiana (questo fatto rilevasi da una supplica degl'Israeliti del Littorale e Friuli Austriaco a S. E. R. Mons. Paolucci Nunzio e Legato a latere del Sommo Pontefice l'anno 1739).

APPENDIX A

Bursatti, in his *Consilia* 231, n. 6, narrates a fact, which is reported here in his own words:[13]

> "The first evidence of this comes from another decree of Martin V, granted to the Hebrews in the year 1429. Among other things, it decreed: 'None of the Jews, or their children, who have not attained the age of twelve years, or who are otherwise incapable of malice or discernment, shall be baptized without the express consent of their parents. Secondly, from a certain judicial sentence given in a case decided in court and executed in January 1539 by both the King and Pope Paul III or his delegate, when a child, the son of Jews, aged seven years, and baptized against the will of his parents, was returned to his parents, who gave a guarantee that, when he was twelve years old, they would present him to the bishop, and would not corrupt him or take him away from the Christian religion."

By another decree of Card. Francesco Sfondrati, executed in Rome on June 27, 1547, and recorded in the acts of Pietro Reverio, public notary, it was decreed that Angelo and Samuele, Israelite children, although baptized, were to be returned to a certain Vitale, their legitimate legal guardian, who first deposited two hundred gold scudi as a guarantee of the obligation he assumed to present the two pupils, as soon as they had completed the twelfth year of their age, to the competent authority in order to have their will questioned as to the religion to be followed.

[f. 172v] On February 10, 1639, the Vicar of Archbishop Scipione Agnello Maffei, Bishop of Casale, by order of the Holy Congregation of Bishops, issued a Notification in which, among the penalties imposed on those who dared to baptize Jewish children *invitis parentibus*, it was stated that the abused sacramental act would not be recognized as valid (see attachment no. 3).[14]

In 1728, the Inquisition of Turin ordered the return of an infant baptized by a Christian wet nurse to her parents (this fact is mentioned in a petition of 1739 from the Israelites of the Austrian Litoral and Friuli to H. E. R. Msgr. Paolucci Nuncio and Legate *a latere* of the Supreme Pontiff).

In Rome, in 1840, the armed forces appeared at the door of Mr. and Mrs. Cremieux, French Israelites, and asked for a newborn baby girl of theirs, as she had been baptized in Fiumicino. They did not want to surrender the

---

13 Francesco Odoardo Bursatti (seventeenth to eighteenth centuries), a jurist of Mantuan origin, was the author of the work "Francisci Bursatti consilia seu Responsa."

14 Attachment no. 3 was the copy of this notification from 1639. For the text see Delacouture, *Roma e la opinione*, 74–75.

A Roma nel 1840 si presentò la forza armata presso i coniugi Cremieux israeliti francesi, richiedendo una loro neonata perché battezzata a Fiumicino. La bambina non fu voluta consegnare, e la Superiore Autorità dopo matura discussione non ne fece altra domanda ai genitori.

Carlo VI imperatore concedeva l'anno 1740 agli Ebrei di Gorizia il seguente rescritto:

> "Tutti gli Ebbrei assieme uniti nel nostro Friuli e Littorale Austriaco domiciliati, hanno umilmente supplicato a inibbire tali attentati con successivamente ordinare che tali creature in simile maniera battezzate debbano senza dimora ai loro genitori restituirsi per fino che arrivati loro all'età di anni 14 siano in stato di poter da se soli eleggere una religione. Disapprovando noi ora gli attentati predimostrati tendenti contro la legge della natura e religione ed in conseguenza volendo che gli ebbrei sopranominati restino in tutto e per tutto mantenuti nei privileggi Cesarei a' medesimi concessi, perciò si ha clementissimamente ordinati che per primo si debba insistere debbitamente affine vengano subbito [f.173r] restituiti alli sopradivisati ebbrei, e nella potestà de' loro genitori, le creature nella maniera predescritta rapite, e che di presente forse vengano ancora trattenute, nell'avvenire poi sotto pene sensibili ecc."

La stessa premura dimostrò S. M. Amedeo re di Sardegna. Difatti nel suo Codice Regio dato alle stampe il 1728 fece inserire il seguente articolo: *"Che i fanciulli Ebrei contro il paterno volere battezzati debbano riconsegnarsi ai genitori, inflitta la pena di tre tratti di corda e di scudi trecento d'oro al Cristiano che battezzasse e detenesse la Creatura."*

Il 16° fra i capitoli onde gli Israeliti furono ricevuti in Rovigo ha le seguenti parole: *"che niuno possa deviare alcuno dei suoi figli senza il volere del padre e madre sotto niun pretesto, anco di battesimo, nemmeno niuno di casa sua di meno età di anni dodici, e disviandolo tutto quello che si facesse nella persona di quelle creature non sia di alcun valore."*

APPENDIX A

child, and the Superior Authority, after careful consideration, made no further request to the parents.[15]

In 1740, Emperor Charles VI granted the Jews of Gorizia the following royal decree:

> "All the Jews residing in our Friuli and Litoral Austria have humbly requested that such abuses be prevented and that such creatures baptized in this way be ordered to return immediately to their parents until, after reaching the age of fourteen years, they are in a state to be able to choose a religion for themselves. We now disapprove of the aforesaid abuses, which are contrary to the law of nature and religion, and consequently we desire that the above-mentioned Jews maintain in all respects the imperial privileges granted to them. Therefore it is ordered, with supreme clemency, that, in the first place, the creatures abducted in the manner before described, and which at the present time are still retained, if any, [f.173r] be immediately and duly returned to the aforesaid Jews, and to the authority of their parents. In the second place, for the future, punishments are hereby ordered [against those who], etc."

The same concern was shown by His Majesty Amadeo, King of Sardinia. In fact, he had the following article inserted in his Royal Code, which was printed in 1728: "That Jewish children who have been baptized against their father's will must return to their parents, and that the penalty of three lengths of rope and three hundred gold scudi is imposed on the Christian who baptizes and detains the child."

The sixteenth chapter of the conditions with which the Israelites were received in Rovigo has the following words: "No one shall, under any pretext, even of baptism, convert any of the children [of Judaism] without the will of their father and mother, nor take out of their house any who are less than twelve years old; Whatever has been done in the person of those creatures to convert them shall be of no value."

In 1852, the Israelite Pincherli family of Verona was ordered to surrender to the ecclesiastical authorities a girl who had been baptized five years earlier by her nurse or maid.[16] After being able to take the girl far away, the

---

15 In *Brevi cenni*, the Holy See devoted much space to the refutation of this precedent, providing ample details about it. In particular, the intervention of the French authorities to defend the rights of their fellow citizens: the Montel-Cremieux couple were in fact French citizens who sought the help of the French ambassador to the Holy See. The question of the responsibility of the state with regard to its citizens was used by the Holy See in *Brevi cenni* to say that the Holy See had jurisdiction and responsibility for the child not only as the Church, but also as the state, since the Mortara family lived in Bologna.

16 The Pincherli case was argued on behalf of the Mortara family, since it occurred during the pontificate of Pius IX. *Brevi cenni* did not respond to this case, nor did it mention it. Stahl, in

Nell'anno 1852 alla famiglia Israelita Pincherli di Verona fu comandato di consegnare all'Autorità Ecclesiastica una fanciulla battezzata da cinque anni dalla nutrice o dalla cameriera. Dopo di aver potuto allontanare la ragazza, il padre umiliò riverente istanza, perché si desistesse da ogni richiesta. Gli fu accordato, a patto che giunta questa sua figlia all'età di 14 anni, l'avrebbe presentata a chi di diritto, per sentire da lei se voglia seguitare nella religione del padre, o abbracciare la cattolica.

Potrebbero forse aggiungersi ulteriori esempi analoghi ai precedenti, qualora non fosse mancato il tempo alle ricerche, o vi fosse meno di difficoltà per eseguirle con utile risultato. Ma non è poco il narrato fin qui a manifestare [f. 173v] che anche in epoche meno propizie alle sorti degli Israeliti, né certo così illuminate come la nostra dal benefico sole della civiltà, lo zelo fortemente sentito della religione condannava di nullità quegli atti sacrileghi, con che il falso zelo, ovveramente l'odio e la vendetta ascose in mentite sembianze, cercavano gettare l'afflizione senza conforto tra le famiglie Israelitiche, spogliandole irreparabilmente contro le umane e le divine istituzioni dei cari oggetti della paterna tenerezza. Ed oggi avrebbero meno a sperarvi i genitori dell'Edgardo, mentre lo stesso verace zelo dispensato a più alti ed esquisiti sensi di ragione e di umanità, parla nel cuore e nella mente della Suprema Autorità giudice della loro causa? Non era forse dopo avere interrogato l'oracolo della Chiesa che Principi tanto divoti della cattolica religione emanavano le accennate disposizioni ad invalidare i battesimi abusati negl'infanti israeliti? E non era la voce della Chiesa quelli di Vescovi e Sommi Pontefici, quando colpivano della stessa sentenza i medesimi atti?

La desolazione di un padre, l'angoscia monomaniaca di una madre sulla perdita di un loro figlio, sarebbero già un grave argomento di mite consiglio nell'alto governo di quella religione, che ha viscere di umanità per ogni sventura. Ma non è solamente il grido del dolore che invoca pei coniugi Mortara la restituzione del loro Edgardo, è ancora il sentimento della paterna autorità che ebbero inviolabilmente da Dio, e che inviolabile fu proclamata così nel Cristiano, come nell'Israelita da questa religione: è l'elocubrata argomentazione di eletti ingegni, onore e decoro delle ecclesiastiche dottrine; è l'esempio autorevole di un passato, ove ben altra che non al presente [era] la pubblica ragione dei socievoli rapporti; è la giustizia, la mansuetudine, [f. 174r] la carità che han sede nella mente e nel cuore del Magnanimo Pontefice e de' suoi degni Ministri, cui spetta il decretare sull'invocata restituzione.

father made a reverent plea to desist from all demands. This was granted on the condition that when his daughter reached the age of fourteen, he would present her to the proper authorities to hear whether she wished to follow her father's religion or embrace Catholicism.

Further similar examples might perhaps be added to the above mentioned, if there had not been lack of time for research, or if it had been less difficult to perform them with useful results. [f. 173v] But what has been said so far is not so small as to show how, even in ages less favorable to the destiny of the Israelites, and certainly not so enlightened as ours by the beneficial sun of civilization, the strongly felt true zeal of religion condemned those sacrilegious acts as null and void, by which the false zeal, or indeed hate and revenge concealed under false guises, have sought to cast uncomfortable affliction among the Israelites families, depriving them irreparably, against human and divine laws, of the dear objects of paternal tenderness. And should Edgardo's parents have less reason to hope today, when the same true zeal of religion, expressed with the highest and most exquisite sense of reason and humanity, is evidently in the heart and mind of the Pope, Supreme Authority, Judge of their cause? Was it not after having consulted the opinion of the Church that Princes so devoted to the Catholic religion issued the aforesaid decrees invalidating abusive baptisms of Israelite infants? And was it not the voice of the same Church, that of those bishops and Supreme Pontiffs who [previously] pronounced the same sentence of nullity on the same acts?

The desolation of a father and the monomaniacal anguish of a mother at the loss of one of their children would already be a serious argument to provoke a compassionate judgment on the part of the high governing authorities of that religion that has human viscera of emotion for every misfortune. But it is not only the cry of grief that calls for the return of their Edgardo to the Mortara couple. It is also the feeling of the paternal authority, which they inviolably received from God, and which was inviolably proclaimed by this religion in the Christian as well as in the Israelite. It is the elucidated argumentation of eminent minds, authoritative jurists, honor and decorum of ecclesiastical doctrines. It is the authoritative example of a past, in which the conditions of social relations were very different from those of today. It is the justice, it is the meekness, [f. 174r] it is the charity that reside in the mind and in the heart of the magnanimous Pontiff and of his worthy Ministers, to whom the decision of the requested restitution is incumbent.

"The Mortara Affair, 1858," hypothesized that the most likely explanation for the decision in the Pincherli case was that it remained a local affair. Perhaps the publicity of the Mortara case, with the involvement of the Roman authorities up to Pius IX himself, made a different outcome impossible, since a renunciation of the rights of the Church would have been linked to the attitude of the Holy See in the face of the birth of the unified Italian state and the struggle to maintain temporal power in the face of an increasingly secular Europe.

APPENDIX B

SYLLABUS (SA)
Source: AAV, Segr. Stato, Rubriche, anno 1864, rubrica 66, fasc. 2, ff 24r-69r.
Transcription

Syllabus auctoritatum comprobantium baptisma pueris Iudaeorum invitis parentibus collatum nil prosus valere.

I.PRAEF. **(F27R)** DURANDUS DE SANCTO PORTIANO IN SENTENTIAS LIB. IV DISTINCT. IV. QUEST. VI. UTRUM FILII INFIDELIUM DEBENT BAPTIZARI INVITIS PARENTIBUS EORUM THOM. 3. Q. 68 ART. 10.

1. Deinde quaeritur in speciali de filiis infidelium, utrum debeant baptizari invitis parentibus, et si de facto baptizentur utrum sint vere baptizati. Quantum ad primum videtur quod parvuli Iudaeorum vel aliorum infidelium debeant baptizari invitis parentibus, quia magis est occurrendum

ENGLISH TRANSLATION
Translated by Lionel Yaceczko

Syllabus of authorities proving that baptism for the children of Jews conferred with the parents unwilling has no further validity

I.PREF. DURANDUS OF SAINT-POURÇAIN ON THE *FOUR BOOKS OF SENTENCES*, DISTINCTION 4, QUESTION 6. WHETHER THE CHILDREN OF UNBELIEVERS OUGHT TO BE BAPTIZED WITH THEIR PARENTS UNWILLING ACCORDING TO THOMAS, ST III, Q. 68, A. 10.

1. The next question asks specifically about the children of unbelievers, whether they ought to be baptized with their parents unwilling, and, if they should in fact be baptized, whether they are truly baptized. As much as pertains to the first, it seems that the little ones of the Jews or other unbelievers

periculo mortis aeternae, quam mortis temporalis, sed parvulo existenti in periculo mortis temporalis subveniendum est contra voluntatem parentum, etiam si ex malitia vellent oppositum. Ergo multo magis subveniendum est pueris infidelium in periculo mortis aeternae etiam invitis parentibus, quod fit dum baptizantur eorum parvuli quare, etc.

2. Item quilibet homo magis est Dei, a quo habet animam, quam patris a quo habet corpus: non ergo videtur injustum si pueri infidelium parentibus auferrentur et Deo per baptismum consecrarentur.

3. Item principes Christiani possunt offerre pueros Iudaeorum baptismo: imo videntur in hoc mereri si hoc faciunt propter salutem puerorum et honorem Dei, et non ut parentes cogantur ad credendum, quia illud non est licitum.

4. In contrarium arguitur quia non minorem potestatem habet dominus temporalis super parentem Iudaeum quam super ejus filium. Sed constat quod princeps non potest licite compellere Iudaeum adultum ad baptismum suscipiendum in se, ut habetur distinct. 43 ex Concilio Toletano (f27v), ubi dicitur sic: Iudaeis praecepit Sancta Synodus nemini ad credendum vim inferre, ergo non debet eis vim inferre auferendo filium ut baptizetur, cum voluntas parvuli sit voluntas patris quousque filius habeat usum rationis.

5. Item quia si hoc esset licitum, probabile esset quod primitivi Sancti et Rectores Ecclesiae hoc consuluissent terrenis principibus quos habuerunt valde favorabiles: ut Sylvester Constantinum, et Ambrosius Theodosium. Hoc autem nusquam leguntur fuisse, ergo non est probabile quod hoc possit fieri licite.

6. Responsio. Circa questionem sunt duo. Primum est an infideles adulti possint licite compelli ad fidem et ad ea quae sunt fidei puta baptismum et huijusmodi. Secundum est an infideles parvuli carentes debito usu rationis possint licite baptizari invitis vel ignorantibus parentibus eorum seu tutoribus, vel aliis habentibus curam eorum. De his enim duobus aliquid tactum est arguendo.

ought to be baptized even if their parents should be unwilling, because we must rather meet the danger of eternal death than of temporal death, but the little one being in danger of temporal death must be helped against the will of the parents, even if out of malice they were to will the opposite. Therefore much more should the children of unbelievers be helped in danger of eternal death, even though the parents should be unwilling, which happens when their little ones are baptized, wherefore, etc.

2. Likewise a man is more God's, from whom he has his soul, than his father's, from whom he has his body: it does not therefore seem unjust if the children of unbelievers were to be taken away from their parents and consecrated to God through baptism.

3. Likewise Christian princes can offer the children of Jews to baptism: indeed they seem in this to earn merit if they do this because of the salvation of the children and the honor of God, and not in order that the parents be forced to believe, because that is not licit.

4. On the contrary it is argued that the temporal lord has no lesser power over the Jewish parent than over his son. But it is settled that a prince is not able licitly to compel a Jewish adult to receive baptism in himself, as is held in the 43rd distinction of the Council of Toledo, where it is said thus: The Holy Synod instructs that no one should bring force upon Jews to believe. Therefore one should not bring force by taking away a child from them so that it should be baptized, since the will of the little one is the will of the father until the child has the use of reason.

5. Likewise because if this were licit, it would be probable that the early Saints and Leaders of the Church would have given this counsel to the earthly princes whom they held in strong favor, as Sylvester did Constantine, and Ambrose did Theodosius.[1] But nowhere do we read that they did this, therefore it is not probable that this could be done licitly.

6. Response: There are two points surrounding the question. The first is whether unbeliever adults could licitly be compelled to the faith and to the

---

[1] All footnotes in the translation of the *Syllabus* are from the translator. During Silvester I's papacy (r. 314–35), under the patronage of Emperor Constantine I (c. 274–337), several important churches were built in Rome, including the Lateran Basilica and St. Peter's. Ambrose was bishop of Milan (374–97) when that city was sometimes the location of the western imperial court and therefore the de facto capital of the western half of the empire. Theodosius reigned 379–95 and was on such good relations with Ambrose that the latter even dared a famous public rebuke of him (on which see Paulinus, *Vita Ambrosii*, in Roy J. Deferrari, ed., *Early Christian Biographies* [Washington, DC: The Catholic University of America Press, 1952], 25–66; and Ambrose, *Letter 41*, in Ambrose, *The Letters of St. Ambrose, Biship of Milan*, trans. H. Walford [London: James Parker, 1881]).

7. Quantum ad primum sciendum est quod cum credere sit actus intellectus, et ea quae sunt merae fidei non possunt demonstrari vel sic evidenter probari, ut eis necessario assentiat intellectus, ideo nullus potest necessitari vel cogi simpliciter ad actum credendi; potest adhuc induci aliquis persuasionibus et exemplis, et hoc semper fuit licitum. Inducere autem seu impellere vel compellere infidelem minis et poenis ad profitendam fidem vel ad suscipiendum baptismum non est licitum. Cujus ratio est quia quum homo sit homo per rationem, nullus homo potest rationabiliter (f28r) et licite compelli ad ea quae sunt supra rationem et utentibus sola ratione naturali, videretur esse contra rationem. Sed actus credendi et ritus exterior fidei sunt supra rationem humanam, et infidelibus utentibus sola ratione naturali videntur esse contra rationem, ergo infideles adulti non possunt rationabiliter et licite ad talia compelli vel impelli minis et poenis temporalibus. Et si de facto aliquis invitus baptizaretur, confirmaretur, ordinaretur, vel immergeretur, talis non reciperet aliquod sacramentum nec rem sacramenti. Unde beatus Hieronymus exponens in quadam homilia illud Matthei ultimi: Ita *docete omnes gentes baptizantes eos*, et dicit sic, docete *omnes gentes deinde doctos intingite aqua; non enim potest fieri ut corpus baptismi recipiat sacramentum, nisi anima ante fidei veritatem susceperit.*[a] Postquam autem aliquis voluntarie credidit, et Sacramentum fidei suscepit, ex tunc compellendus est ad servandum ritus fidei, quia licet fides sit supra rationem, et ob hoc nullus sit ad eam suscipiendam cogendus, tamen ex quo aliquis voluntarie eam susceperit, et eam servare promisit, rationabile est quod ad hoc compellatur. Studiose enim agendum est ut ea quae promittuntur, opere compleantur, ob quam causam haeretici compelluntur ad servandam veram fidem, quia vere baptizati et profitentur se esse vero Christianos.

---

[a] Hier. *Comm. in Matt.* (PL 26, Col. 218B): *docete omnes gentes baptizantes eos in nomine Patris, et Filii, et Spiritus sancti*. Primum docent omnes gentes, deinde doctos intingite aqua. Non enim potest fieri ut corpus baptismi recipiat sacramentum, nisi anima ante fidei susceperit veritatem.

things that are of the faith, for example baptism and things of this manner. The second is whether unbeliever little ones who lack the required use of reason could licitly be baptized with their parents, guardians, or others who have care of them, being unwilling, or without their knowledge. For it has been touched upon somewhat in the arguing of these two points.

7. As pertains to the first, it must be known that, since believing is an act of the intellect, and those things that are of pure faith are not able to be demonstrated or in this way able to be proved through evidence, so that the intellect should assent to them by necessity, therefore no one is able to be made or simply forced to the act of believing; a person can still be induced by persuasion and examples, and this has always been licit. But to induce or to push or to compel an unbeliever by threats and punishments to profess the faith or to receive baptism is not licit. The reason for this is that since a man is man through reason, no man can rationally and licitly be compelled to those things which are concerned with reason: even for those who use only natural reason, it seems to be contrary to reason. But the act of believing and the exterior rite of faith are concerned with human reason, and to unbelievers using only natural reason they seem contrary to reason, therefore adult unbelievers are not able rationally and licitly to be compelled or forced to such through threats and temporal punishments. And if in fact someone were to be baptized, confirmed, ordained, or immersed unwillingly, such a one would not receive any sacrament, nor the matter of the sacrament. Whence the blessed Jerome, explaining in a certain homily the last chapter of Matthew, says, "So teach all nations, baptizing them," and he says as follows: "Teach all nations, then, when they are taught, bathe them in the water; for it is not able to happen that the body should receive the sacrament of baptism unless the soul beforehand shall have taken up the truth of the faith."[2] But after someone has voluntarily believed, and taken up the sacrament of the faith, from that time he can be compelled to keep the rite of the faith, because although the faith is concerned with reason, and because of this no one should be forced to take it up, nevertheless from the time when someone shall have taken it up voluntarily, and promised to keep it, it is reasonable that he be compelled to it. For it should be zealously seen to that effort be made to fulfill promises that are made, for which reason heretics are compelled to keep the true faith, because they have been truly baptized and profess themselves to be Christians in truth.

---

2 Jerome, *Commentary on Matthew*, 28:19: *Teach all nations, baptizing them in the name of the Father, and of the Son, and of the Holy Spirit.* "First they teach all nations, then when they have been taught they bathe them in the water. For it is not able to happen that the body receive the sacrament of baptism, unless the soul has beforehand received the truth of the faith."

8. Quantum ad secundum, scilicet, an parvuli filii infidelium sint baptizandi invitis parentibus vel tutoribus, seu aliis habentibus curam eorum, respondetur: de jure naturali et divino prohibetur cuilibet concupiscere res proximi sui, et multo magis tollere clam vel per violentiam contra (f28v) ejus voluntatem, sed secundum Sanctos et omnes Doctores nomine proximi intelligitur omnis homo, ergo in isto casu non licet Christianis auferre per violentiam res et bona infidelium, multo minus filios, et offerre eos baptismo. Quia si hoc liceret, aut liceret personae privatae aut publicae potestati: non personae privatae, quia pares sunt, et par in parem non habet imperium; nec potestati publicae, quia sicut prius potestas publica non potest licite bona istius infidelis auferre pro voluntate sua, sicut nec alicujus fidelis, multo minus filium, qui est patri charior quacumque re possessa, imo sicut princeps auferrens res talis infidelis, et offerens eos Deo, offerret sacrificium de rapina sic princeps fidelis auferrens infideli filium eo invito, et offerens eum baptismo, offert Deo sacrificium de rapina.

9. Ad primum argumentum dicendum quod nulli est subveniedum in periculo corporali contra ordinem juris civilis, unde si quis a suo judice rite condemnetur ad mortem, non est per violentiam eripiendus; similiter contra ordinem juris naturalis vel divini, quod filius <est> sub cura parentum non est eripiendus ut liberetur a periculo mortis aeternae. Non enim sunt facienda mala ut veniant bona. Hoc autem esset, si filius infidelis baptizaretur invitis parentibus, quorum curae subest de jure naturali et divino.

10. Ad secundum dicendum quod homo ordinatur in Deum per rationem, per quam potest Deum cognoscere, et ideo puer antequam habeat usum rationis ordinatur in Deum per rationem eorum quorum curae subjacet; propter quod secundum eorum dispositionem sunt circa eum [*emendavi*, cum *cod.*] agenda divina (f29r), et quia pueri [*emendavi*, pauperi *cod.*] parentum infidelium non possunt licite ab eorum cura subtrahi, ideo non licet pueros eorum ipsis invitis auferre.

11. In quaestione autem utrum parvuli infidelium baptizati invitis parentibus suscipiant verum sacramentum sic proceditur. Et arguitur quod parvuli infidelium baptizati invitis parentibus suscipiant verum Sacramentum quia parentes infideles non habent majus jus in filiis suis parvulis, quam fideles parentes, sed parvuli parentum fidelium baptizati invitis parentibus suscipiunt verum sacramentum: ergo similiter parvuli parentum infidelium si baptizentur invitis parentibus susciperent verum Sacramentum.

12. Item sicut est baptismus fluminis, sic est baptismus sanguinis, sed pueri occisi pro Christo invitis parentibus receperunt et modo reciperent

8. As much as pertains to the second, that is to say, whether the little children of unbelievers should be baptized with their parents, guardians, or others who have care of them unwilling, the response is: from natural and divine law it is prohibited for anyone to desire the neighbor's things, and much more to take them away in secret or through violence against his will, but according to the Saints and all the Doctors, in the name *neighbor* is understood every person, therefore in that case it is not permitted for Christians to take away through violence the things and goods of unbelievers, much less the children, and offer them to baptism. Because if this were permitted, it would be permitted either to a private person or to a public power: not to a private person, because they are equals, and an equal does not have command over an equal; nor to public power, because, just as before, public power is not able licitly to take away the goods of the unbeliever without his own will, just as neither can it do so to any faithful person, much less his child, which is dearer to its father than any possessed thing—nay, even as a prince, taking away the things of such an unbeliever and offering them to God, would offer a sacrifice of robbery, so a faithful prince taking away the child from an unbeliever with the latter unwilling, and offering it to baptism, offers to God a sacrifice of robbery.

9. To the first argument it must be said that no one must be helped in bodily danger contrary to the order of civil law, whence if anyone should be rightly condemned to death by his judge, he is not to be snatched away by violence; similarly, it is against the order of natural or divine law because the son under the care of his parents is not to be snatched away to be freed from danger of eternal death. For evils are not to be done in order that goods may come about. This however is what it would be, if the son of an unbeliever were baptized with the parents unwilling, under whose care he is from natural and divine law.

10. To the second it must be said that man is ordered to God through reason, through which he is able to come to know God, and so the child before he has the use of reason is ordered to God through the reason of those under whose care he is subject; because of which the things relating to God are to be done regarding him according to *their* disposition, also because the children of unbeliever parents are not able licitly to be taken away from their care, therefore it is not permitted to take their children away from them if they are unwilling.

11. So now we proceed in the question whether the little ones of unbelievers baptized with the parents unwilling receive the true sacrament. And it is argued that little ones of unbelievers baptized with the parents unwilling receive the true sacrament, because unbeliever parents do not have greater

remissionem originalis peccati, ergo similiter pueri baptizati invitis parentibus reciperent verum sacramentum et effectum Sacramenti.

13. In contrarium arguitur quia ad receptionem cujuslibet sacramenti requiritur intentio seu voluntas recipiendi ipsum propria vel interpetrativa, sed in parvulo filio parentum infidelium, si baptizaretur invitis parentibus, non est voluntas vel intentio propria suscipiendi baptismum, ut de se patet. Nec interpetrativa cum baptizaretur invitis parentibus quorum voluntas est interpetrativa voluntatis filii parvuli: ergo si talis de facto baptizetur nullus est baptismus. Minor de se manifesta est, sed major probatur, quia si aliquis adultus sic nutritus esset quod nihil audisset de fide, et esset solum in originali, si talis dormiret et dormiendo baptizaretur, constat quod nullus esset talis baptismus, non quia in voluntate (f29v) ejus inveniret baptismus obicem plus quam in parvulo, quia deficeret voluntas suscipiendi baptismum, erga ad susceptionem baptismi requiritur voluntas suscipientis propria, si sit adultus, vel interpetrativa si sit [*emendavi*, sint *cod.*] parvulus, et haec fuit major: sequitur ergo conclusio.

14. De quaestione ista dicunt quidam quod parvuli infidelium quorumcumque, si baptizarentur invitis parentibus, recipiunt verum sacramentum et rem sacramenti: quorum ratio est quia ad susceptionem veri baptismi sufficit quod non inveniatur in suscipiente obex contrarie voluntatis, ut patet in parvulis Christianorum, qui ante susceptionem baptismi sunt pares parvulis infidelium, sed in parvulis Iudaeorum vel quorumcumque infidelium non est obex contrariae voluntatis respectu suscipientis baptismum, ergo tales, si de facto baptizarentur etiam invitis parentibus, suscipiunt verum sacramentum et rem sacramenti. Pro hac opinione videtur esse illud quod scribitur de consecr. di. 4 Cap. parvuli fideles vocantur, ubi videtur insinuari quod parvulis sufficit fides offerentium nulla facta mentione de fide parentum, et respondent isti ad rationem in oppositum negando majorem propositionem, quia, ut dicunt, ad veram receptionem baptismi non requiritur voluntas recipientis propria, nec interpetrativa, et ad probationem ejus dicunt quod postquam puer venit ad annos discretionis pie creditur quod Deus movet ipsum ad salutem per instinctum interiorem, vel aliquam motionem exteriorem in generali, vel in speciali revelando ea quae sunt fidei, sine qua non est salus, vel saltem quod cogitet de sua salute, et de mediis (f30r) perducentibus ad salutem: et si tali motui generali vel speciali non acquiescant tunc ponit obicem, vel contrariae voluntatis, si renuat procurare media suae salutis, vel cujusdam indignitatis, si post talem instinctum negligeret, quia qui in nullo se juvat quando potest indignus est quod ab alio juvetur, et si talis dormiens baptizaretur de facto nihil proficeret quia non reciperet verum sacramentum, nec aliquem effectum sacramenti, si vero tali instinctu acquiescat, jam

right over their little children than faithful parents do, but the little ones of faithful parents when baptized with the parents unwilling do receive the true sacrament: therefore similarly the little ones of unbeliever parents, if they should be baptized with the parents unwilling, would receive the true sacrament.

12. Likewise just as there is the baptism of the stream, so there is the baptism of the blood, but children killed for Christ with their parents unwilling have received and just then would receive the remission of original sin: therefore similarly children baptized with the parents unwilling would receive the true sacrament and the effect of the sacrament.

13. On the contrary it is argued that the reception of any sacrament requires the intention or the will—one's own or a representative's—of receiving it, but in the little child of unbeliever parents, if it be baptized with the parents unwilling, there is no will or proper intention of receiving baptism, as is plain on its own. Nor is there representative will, since it was baptized with the parents unwilling, and their will is the representative of the will of the little child: therefore if such a one should in fact be baptized there is no baptism. The minor point is manifest on its own, but the major point is proven on the grounds that if any adult were to be so raised that he had heard nothing about the faith, and were only in original sin, if such were to be sleeping and in sleeping be baptized, it is settled that there would be no baptism of such a one, not because baptism would find a barrier in his will more than in a little one, but because the will of receiving baptism would be lacking, since for the receiving of baptism is required the proper will of the one receiving it, if he should be an adult, or the representative will, if he should be a little one, and this was the major: therefore the conclusion follows.

14. On that question some say that the little ones of whatsoever unbelievers, if they were to be baptized with the parents unwilling, receive the true sacrament and the matter of the sacrament: and their reason is that for the receiving of true baptism it is enough that there be not found in the one who receives it the barrier of a contrary will, as is plain in the little ones of Christians who before the reception of baptism are the equals of the little ones of unbelievers. In the little ones of the Jews or whatsoever unbelievers, there is no barrier of contrary will in respect of the one receiving baptism, therefore such, if they were in fact baptized even with the parents unwilling, receive the true sacrament and the matter of the sacrament. In favor of this opinion seems to be that which is written in the *De Consecr. Di.* chapter 4: they are called faithful little ones, where it seems to be insinuated that the faith of those who offer them is is enough for the littles ones, with no mention made about the faith of the parents, and they respond to the reasoning on

habet baptismum in voto generali vel speciali implicite vel explicite. Et si baptizaretur dormiens recipit verum baptismum et ejus effectum. Non quia ad susceptionem baptismi requiratur voluntas propria vel interpretativa per se, sed solum ad removendum obicem voluntatis contrariae vel negligentis. Et istud habet locum in adulto, in parvulo autem nullus talis obex inveniri potest, quum non possit habere usum voluntatis. Propter quod nec voluntas propria nec interpretativa requiritur ad hoc ut suscipiat verum baptismum.

15. Quidquid sit de conclusione. Responsio tamen ad rationem non valet. Primo quia licet pium sit credere quod venienti ad annos discretionis Deus inspiret per se ipsum vel alterum hominem vel angelum, interius vel exterius, in generali vel in speciali, quod quaerat ea quae sunt suae salutis, nullus tamen dicit quod inspiratio fiat semper homini statim quando venit ad annos discretionis, sed sufficit quod fiat ei post moram temporis, si vivat secundum dictamen rectae rationis naturalis, et illud est magis rationabile quam primum, quia congruum est quod bene utenti ratione naturali Deus inspiret ea quae sunt fidei (f30v) et super rationem et non prius. In illo ergo medio tempore ante inspirationem factam si talis dormiat et baptizetur, non potest dici quod in eo sit obex contrariae voluntatis ad baptismum nec negligentiae, et tamen non reciperet verum baptismum, ergo non sufficit in adulto quod baptismus non inveniat obicem, sed requiritur aliqua voluntas suscipiendi baptismum.

APPENDIX B

the other side by denying the major proposition, because, as they say, for the true reception of baptism there is not required the proper will of the one who receives it, nor even that of a representative, and for the proving of this they say that after the child comes to the age of discretion there is pious belief that God moves him to salvation through an interior impulse or some exterior movement in general, or specifically by revealing those things that are of the faith, without which there is no salvation, or at least something for him to think about concerning his own salvation, and about the means that bring him to salvation: and if to such a movement, general or specific, they should not acquiesce, then he puts a barrier, either of a contrary will, if he should refuse to foster the means of his salvation, or of a sort of unworthiness, if afterwards he were to neglect such an impulse, because he who helps himself in no way when he can is unworthy to be helped by another, and if such a one sleeping were to be baptized in fact it would do him no good because he would not receive the true sacrament, nor any effect of the sacrament; but if he should acquiesce to such an impulse, he already has baptism in general or specific prayer, implicitly or explicitly. And if he were to be baptized sleeping he receives true baptism and its effect. Not on the grounds that for the reception of baptism there be required the proper or representative will by itself, but only for the removing of the barrier of the contrary will or of the one who is neglecting. And it has that place in an adult, but in a little one no such barrier is able to be found, since he could not have the use of the will. For which reason neither the proper will nor the representative is required for him to receive true baptism.

15. What should be said in conclusion: Nevertheless the response does not prevail in relation to the reasoning. In the first place because although it be pious to believe that for the one coming to the age of discretion God inspires by himself or through another person or an angel interiorly or exteriorly, in general or specifically, that he should seek the things that are for his own salvation, nevertheless no one says that inspiration should always happen to a man immediately when he comes to the age of discretion, but it is enough that it happen to him after a period of time if he should live according to the dictates of right natural reason, and that is more reasonable than the first, because it is logical that if one use natural reason well, God would inspire him with the things that pertain to the faith, and that He should do so after reason and not before. Therefore in that middle time before the inspiration has happened, if such a one should sleep and be baptized, it cannot be said that in him there is the barrier to baptism of contrary will, nor of negligence, and nevertheless he would not be receiving true baptism; therefore it is not enough in an adult that baptism not find a barrier, but some will of receiving baptism is required.

16. Secundo quod posito quod talis inspiratio fieret homini statim quando venit ad annos discretionis, non oportet tamen quod statim acquiescat, vel contradicat, sed potest sine culpa quacumque tenere consensum in suspenso et deliberare si talis inspiratio est a Deo an non, et deliberando dormire, et tunc in eo non est obex contrariae voluntatis ad baptismum nec negligentiae, et tamen si de facto baptizetur non est verus baptismus, ergo ut prius in adulto non sufficit non invenire obicem, sed requiritur aliqua voluntas suscipiendi baptismum.

17. Tertio quia isti videntur sibi contradicere, dicunt enim (et est verum) quod necessarium est ad salutem tali adulto post inspirationem sibi factam velle quaerere media per quae pervenitur ad salutem; sed medium maxime necessarium est baptismus. Ergo necessarium est ad salutem quod voluntas istius in generali vel in speciali implicite vel explicite sit de baptismo suscipiendo secundum se tamquam de medio necessario ad salutem, et non ad removendum obicem contrariae voluntatis vel negligentiae, cujus contrarium ipsi dicunt et male; quia tamen obex numquam fuit in voluntate istius, qui post inspirationem vel admonitionem sibi factam (**f31r**) vult quaerere media suae saluti necessaria. Ridiculum est autem dicere quod aliquid sit necessarium ad removendum impedimentum quod nec est, nec fuit.

18. Quarto quia renuere vel negligere quaerere baptismum non potest esse impedimentum suscipiendi ipsum, nisi quia velle suscipere est ad hoc dispositio necessaria in adulto, quia renuere vel negligere non impediunt potentiam voluntatis secundum se sed solum impediunt eam ab actu volendi, si ergo velle suscipere baptismum non sit in adulto dispositio necessaria ad baptismum secundum se, sequitur quod nolle seu renuere vel negligere ipsum non erunt impedimenta. Non enim impediant nisi velle oppositum quod secundum te non est per se necessarium ad suscipiendum baptismum etiam in adulto; quae omnia sunt inconvenientia et sibi invicem repugnantia, et sic patet quod praecedens ratio non est in aliquo soluta.

19. Dicendum est ergo aliter ad quaestionem praedictam circa quam declarabantur tria. Primum est quod in adultis requiritur voluntas propria suscipiendi baptismum, et in parvulis requiritur voluntas interpretativa. Secundum est cujus vel quorumsit illa voluntas quae dicitur esse voluntas interpretativa parvulorum. Et tertio apparebit illud quod principaliter quaeritur videlicet an parvuli infidelium baptizati de facto invitis parentibus suscipiant verum baptismum.

16. Second, because, as it is posited that such inspiration happened to a man immediately when he came to the age of discretion, nevertheless it is not necessary that he acquiesce or reject it immediately, but he is able without any fault whatsoever to hold consent in suspense and to deliberate if such inspiration is from God or not, and in deliberating to sleep, and then in him there is not the barrier to baptism of contrary will nor of negligence, and nevertheless if in fact he should be baptized it is not true baptism, therefore, as before, in an adult it is not enough not to find a barrier, but some will of receiving baptism is required.

17. Third, because they seem to contradict themselves, for they say (and it is true) that it is necessary for salvation for such an adult after the inspiration has been made unto him to want to seek the means through which one arrives at salvation; but the means that is preeminently necessary is baptism. Therefore it is necessary for salvation that the will of that one be in general or specifically, implicitly or explicitly, about the receiving of baptism as the necessary means to salvation in its own right, and not for the removing of the barrier of contrary will or negligence, of which they say the contrary, and they say wrongly; because nevertheless there was never a barrier in the will of that one who, after the inspiration or admonition was made to him, wants to seek the means necessary for his own salvation. But it is ridiculous to say that something should be necessary for removing an impediment that neither does exist nor has existed.

18. Fourth, because rejecting or neglecting to seek baptism cannot be an impediment to receiving it except for the fact that wanting to receive it is the necessary disposition for this in an adult, because rejecting or neglecting do not impede the power of the will according to itself, but only impede it from the act of willing. If therefore wanting to receive baptism should not be the necessary disposition in the adult for baptism according to itself, it follows that not wanting or rejecting or neglecting it will not be impediments. For they would not impede anything except wanting the opposite, which according to you is not by itself necessary for receiving baptism even in an adult; all which statements are inconsistent and in conflict with themselves, and thus it is plain that the preceding reasoning is not in any way undone.

19. It must therefore be said otherwise to the aforesaid question regarding which there were three declarations. The first is that in adults there is required the proper will of receiving baptism, and in the little ones there is required the representative will. The second is whose or whosesoever is the will that is said to be the "representative will" of little ones. And third will appear to be that which principally is being asked: namely, whether the

20. Quod in adultis requiratur voluntas recipiendi baptismum patet faciliter ex his quae dicta sunt in praecedenti quaestione. Nam Christus mittens post resurrectionem discipulos ad praedicandum dixit: Docete omnes gentes, baptizantes eos etc. Ubi dicit Hieron: quod non potest fieri quod corpus baptizati recipiat Sacramentum, nisi ante anima fidei (f31v) veritatem susceperit. Ex quo sic arguitur, infidelis adultus qui jam voluntatis suae arbiter constitutus est simili modo se debet habere ad fidem et ad fidei Sacramenta et maxime ad baptismum, qui est primum fidei Sacramentum et per quae sit transgressus in consortum fidelium, sed talis adultus non potest credere si volens ergo nec baptizari, et si de facto immergatur vel aspergatur aqua et dicantur verba, "Ego te baptizo," nullum est sacramentum; requiritur ergo in adultis baptizandis voluntas propria.

21. In parvulis autem sufficit voluntas aliena quae sit interpretativa voluntatis [*emendavi*, voluntates *cod.*] parvulorum, quia in in [*sic*] ipsis est solum originale peccatum, quod contractum est ex voluntate primi parentis quae fuit aliquo modo voluntas omnium qui descensuri erant ab eo per viam naturalis generationis proxime vel remotae, et ideo ad deletionem ejus per baptismum sufficit in parvulis voluntas aliena quae sit [*emendavi*, sint *cod.*] interpretativa voluntatis eorum. Et confirmatur quia quidquid est necessitate [*emendavi*, necessitates *cod.*] in uno est de necessitate sacramenti in omnibus; in similibus quidem similiter, et in proportionalibus proportionaliter, sed voluntas recipiendi baptismum est de necessitate sacramenti in adultis habentibus usum rationis et discretionis, ergo voluntas suscipiendi baptismum est in parvulis de necessitate sacramenti, non quidem similiter, quia non possint consimiliter habere usum propriae rationis et voluntatis sicut adulti, sed proportionabiliter in quantum convenit pro eis voluntas aliena, quae tamen est voluntas eorum interpretativa. Et sic patet primum.

22. Quantum ad secundum, scilicet, cujus vel quorum sit illa voluntas interpretativa parvulorum dicendum est, quod est (f32r) voluntas habentium curam parvuli et isti in primo gradu regulariter sunt parentes parvulorum, quamdiu vivunt: voluntas enim patris reputetur voluntas filii quamdiu caret usu rationis. Unde pater testatur pro filia et eligit ei sepolturam. Decedentibus autem parentibus curam parvulorum habent tutores eorum si sint, et si non sint, sicut esset de parvulo exposito coram hospitali, de quo nescitur quorum est filius curam ejus habebit, qui eum in cura sua recipiet; quia quod in nullius jure est occupanti conceditur. Et si talis non sit qui eum in cura sua recipiat, remanet saltem in cura Ecclesiae, si sit filius alicujus fidelis vel si reperitur inter fideles quia idem praesumitur. Quod autem

little ones of unbelievers who have in fact been baptized *invitus parentibus* receive true baptism.

20. The fact that in adults the will of receiving baptism is required is easily plain from the things that have been said in the preceding question. For Christ sending his disciples to preach after the resurrection said: "Teach all nations, baptizing them, etc." And Jerome says there: "It is not able to happen that the body of the baptized receive the sacrament, unless the soul should have beforehand received the truth of the faith." And so from this it is argued that the unbeliever adult who already has been made the arbiter of his own will in a similar way must dispose himself in relation to the faith and to the sacraments of the faith (and especially to baptism, which is the first sacrament of the faith), and such things as he has entered through into the fellowship of the faithful. But such an adult is therefore not able to believe unless he be baptized willingly, and even if in fact he be immersed or sprinkled with water and the words "I baptize you" be said, there is no sacrament; one's own will, therefore, is required, in baptizing adults.

21. In little ones, however, another's will that is representative of the will of the little ones is enough, because in them there is only original sin, which was contracted from the will of the first parent, which was in some way the will of all who were to descend from him through the way of proximate or remote natural generation, and so for the removal of it through baptism another's will is enough in little ones, since it is representative of their will. And it is confirmed that whatever is of necessity in one is of necessity of the sacrament in all; in similar cases similarly, and in proportional ones proportionately. The will of receiving baptism is of necessity of the sacrament in adults who have the use of reason and discretion, and therefore the will of receiving baptism is in little ones of the necessity of the sacrament, not indeed similarly, on the grounds that they cannot in like manner have the use of their own reason and will as adults can, but proportionately, inasmuch as another's will is fitting for them, which nevertheless is representative of their will. And thus the first is plain.

22. As much as pertains to the second, that is to say, whose or of what persons is the representative will of little ones, it must be said that it is the will of those who have the care of the little one and those in the first respect are regularly the parents of little ones, as long as they are alive: for the will of the father should be considered the will of the son as long as he lacks the use of reason. Whence the father testifies for the daughter and makes the choice of burial for her. But when the parents decease, their guardians have care of the little ones, if there should be any, and if there be none, as it would be in the case of a little one exposed before a hospital, regarding which it is not known whose

voluntas habentium curam parvulorum sit voluntas interpretativa eorum, patet ex dictis in praecedenti quaestione, videlicet quod homo ordinatur in Deum per rationem et voluntatem, quibus potest eum cognoscere et amare. Et ideo puer antequam habeat usum rationis et voluntatis ordinatur in Deum per rationem et voluntatem illorum quorum curae subjacet, et secundum eorum dispositionem sunt circa eum agenda divina.

23. Quantum ad tertium, videlicet an parvuli infidelium baptizati de facto invitis parentibus recipiant verum baptismum, respondetur: Cum parvuli parentum infidelium non possint eis licite auferri et alterius curae subjici viventibus parentibus et invitis, tunc non apparet [quod *delevi*] si tales pueri de facto baptizentur invitis [*emendavi*, invitos *cod.*] parentibus quo modo suscipiant verum sacramentum, quia non concurrit voluntas suscipiendi nec directa nec interpretativa, quarum tamen altera necessaria requiritur, ut probatum est.

24. Ad argumenta in oppositum respondendum est: ad primum, (f32v) quod non est simile de parvulis parentum fidelium et parentum infidelium, quia potestas patris fidelis super filium subjacet potestati publicae seculari et Ecclesiastici, et ideo si pater abutatur potestate sua quam habet circa curam pueri, potest juste privari paterna potestate et cura filii committi alii, quia non exhiberet se tamquam patrem sed tamquam hostem; et sic est de patre fideli qui nollet filium suum baptizari, propter quod cura pueri potest juste sibi auferri et alteri committi de cujus voluntate puer baptizetur; sicut de jure civili auferenda esset patri filia quam vellet prostituere, et filius quem [*emendavi*, quam *cod.*] vellet docere malos mores, puta quod esset adulterandum vel furandum. Pater autem infidelis non abutitur patria potestate si teneat filium parvulum in ritu quem ipsemet servat; et ideo non potest licite propter hoc sibi auferri cura filii et alii committi de cujus voluntate baptizetur; propter quod filius parentis fidelis potest licite invito patre baptizari, et suscipit verum sacramentum, non autem filius parentis infidelis. Ad secundum dicendum quod parvuli occisi pro Christo etiam invitis parentibus sicut fuerunt innocentes fuerunt salvati, et nunc etiam salvaretur parvulus si occideretur in odium Christi—et illud cum esset ex proprio merito, quia nullum est in parvula, nec ex natura facti nec ex opere operato, cum martyrium non sit sacramentum, sed ex abundanti pietate Dei; ideo ibi non requiritur voluntas propria vel aliena sicut te requiritur in baptismo fluminis, quo est sacramentum.

child it is, he will have care of it who receives it in his care; because what lies in the right of no one is granted to the possessor. And if there should not be such a one as to receive it in his care, it remains at least in the care of the Church, if it should be the child of one of the faithful or if it is found among the faithful, because it is presumed to be the same. Now, the fact that the will of those having care of the little ones is their representative will is plain from what was said in the preceding question, namely that a man is ordered to God through reason and will, by which he comes to know and love Him. And so a child, before it have the use of reason and will, is ordered to God through the reason and will of those under whose care it is subject, and matters relating to God regarding them must be done according to their disposition.

23. As much as pertains to the third, namely whether the little ones of unbelievers who have in fact been baptized with their parents unwilling receive true baptism, the response is: since the little ones of unbeliever parents are not able licitly to be taken away from them and subjected to the care of another as long as their parents are living and unwilling, it does not then appear, if such children should in fact be baptized with their parents unwilling, how they should receive the true sacrament, because there is no concurrence of the will of the one receiving, whether the direct or the representative will, of one or the other of which there is still a necessary requirement, as has been proven.

24. To the opposing arguments it must be said in response: to the first, that regarding the little ones of faithful parents and of unbeliever parents it is not alike, because the paternal power of a faithful person over the son lies subject to the secular and the ecclesiastical public power, and so if the father abuses his power that he has regarding the care of the boy, he is able to be deprived justly of his paternal power and the care of the son to be committed to another, on the grounds that he would not be showing himself to be a father but as if an enemy; and so it is regarding a faithful father who is unwilling that his son be baptized, because of which the care of the boy is able to be justly taken away from him and committed to another from whose will the boy would be baptized; just as in civil law it would be that a daughter should be taken away from a father if he wanted to prostitute her, and a son if he wanted to teach him bad morals, for example that he ought to commit adultery or theft. But the unbeliever father does not abuse his paternal power if he should keep his little son in the rite that he himself observes; and so the care of the son is not able licitly because of this to be taken away from him and committed to another from whose will he would be baptized; because of which the son of a faithful parent is able licitly to be baptized with the father unwilling, and receive the true sacrament, but not the son of an unbeliever

II.PRAEF. **(F33R)** PETRUS DE PALUDE IN 4 *SENTENTIARUM QUAESTIO* 4. DISTINCTIO 4. DE BAPTISMO. QUAERITUR UTRUM INVITIS PARENTIBUS SINT BAPTIZANDI PUERI INFIDELIUM RATIONIS USU CARENTES.

1. Circa pueros infidelium est distinguendum: aut habent usum rationis, tunc possunt baptizari etiam invitis parentibus, sicut matrimonium contrahere; aut non habent, tunc circa hoc triplex opinio, utrum si sint invitis parentibus baptizandi.

2. Prima opinio duplex. Nempe principes terrenos posse licite imo meritorie auferre pueros Iudaeorum, et eos baptismo offerre; imo videtur in hoc mereri quia hoc faciunt propter salutem puerorum et honorem Dei, non ut parentes cogantur ad credendum; quod illud non est licitum. Et hoc est primum dictum. Secundo dicitur quod pueri si baptizati suscipiunt verum baptismum. Et probatur sic: ad susceptionem baptismi sufficit quod non inveniatur obex contrariae voluntatis, ut patet in parvulis Christianorum; sed in parvulis Iudaeorum non est obex propriae voluntatis; ergo suscipiunt. Et dico propriae voluntatis in percipiente non in parente, alias peccata primorum parentum nocerent et transirent ad filios; quod non est verum.

3. Sed hae rationes parum cogunt. Prima non quia princeps non potest cogere patrem ad baptismum ita non potest cogere patrem in filium. Voluntas enim patris voluntas filii reputatur, et sic pater testatur filio sicut et sibi: et eligit ei sepulturam sicut et sibi. Unde sicut filium adultum contra ejus voluntatem baptizare non potest, nec debet contra voluntatem ipsius filii; sic nec filium **(f33v)** impuberem contra voluntatem patris, quae est dispositiva de filio: quia illo jure valet testamentum pupillare factum a patre quantum testamentum adulti sui juris factum ab eo. In his autem quae sunt juris humani potest disponere princeps patre invito (sicut et de ipso patre), sed non in his quae sunt de jure naturali vel divino: nam non posset contrahere sponsalia pro filio vel pro filia patre invito (sicut nec ipsum patrem invitum posset uxorare).

parent. To the second it must be said that little ones killed for Christ even with the parents unwilling, as they were innocent, have been saved, and now also a little one would be saved if he were to be killed for hatred of Christ—even though that would be outside of proper merit, because there is none in a little girl, nor from the nature of the deed nor by the work done, since martyrdom is not a sacrament, but from the abundant love of God; therefore there is no requirement there of one's own will or that of another, as is required in the baptism of the stream from which is the sacrament.[3]

II.PREF. PETER PALUDANUS (C. 1275–1342), OP; THE LATIN PATRIARCH OF JERUSALEM (1329).[4] ON THE *FOUR BOOKS OF SENTENCES*, QUESTION 4, DISTINCTION 4, ON BAPTISM. IT IS ASKED WHETHER THE CHILDREN OF UNBELIEVERS WHO LACK THE USE OF REASON ARE TO BE BAPTIZED WITH THEIR PARENTS UNWILLING.

1. Regarding children of unbelievers a distinction must be made: either they have the use of reason, and then they can be baptized even with their parents unwilling, just as they can contract matrimony; or they do not have it, and then regarding this there is a threefold opinion regarding the question of whether they are to be baptized with their parents unwilling.

2. The first opinion is twofold. Of course earthly princes can licitly, even meritoriously, take away the children of Jews and offer them to baptism; in fact there seems to be merit in this because they do this for the salvation of the children and the honor of God, not so that their parents should be forced to belief; because that is not licit. And this is the first word on it. The second word is that children, if baptized, receive true baptism. And it is proven thus: for the reception of baptism it suffices that there be found no barrier of contrary will, as is plain in the little ones of Christians; but in the little ones of Jews there is no barrier of proper will; therefore they receive it. And I say of the proper will that it is in the one that receives it, not in the parent, otherwise the sins of the parents would cause harm and transfer to the children; which is not true.

3. But these reasons are not compelling. The first one is not, because a prince is not able to compel the father to baptism, so he is not able to compel the father in regard to his son. For the will of the father is considered the will of the son, and thus the father bears witness for his son even as he does for himself: and he chooses burial for him even as he does for himself. Whence just

---

[3] There may be a mistake in the Latin here, as *parvula* (feminine, "little girl") makes less sense in the context than *parvulus*, the masculine equivalent, which is is found in many places in this paragraph. We note, however, that *filia* (daughter) does also occur in this paragraph.

[4] Referred to in Latin as Paludanus or Paludensis, but also in French as de la Palu.

4. Ad secundum dicendum est quod est obex voluntas parentum, et ideo non baptizatur. Et cum dicitur quod peccata parentum non transeunt ad filios, verum est directe quasi quia nascendo ab eis contrahant peccata eorum, sicut contrahunt peccatum Adae; sed indirecte et per accidens bene potest pater impedire bonum filii etiam spirituale. Et ideo est secunda opinio huic contraria quae ponit quod non est licitum parvulos Iudaeorum parentibus auferre et eos baptismo offerre, et si de facto baptizentur non suscipiunt baptismum. Ratio prima est: in his quae competunt jure naturali et divino omnes sunt liberi. Similiter baptizari pertinet ad jus divinum, ergo cum cura parvulorum de jure naturali et divino competant quantum ad hoc parentibus manifestum est quod nemo possunt eis licite auferri ut baptizentur. Secundo quia constat quod princeps non potest licite Iudaeum [*cod.*pc, Iudaeorumac] compellere ad actum baptismi percipiendum in se, ut habetur in di. XIV ex Concilio Tolletano [*sic*] ubi dicitur sic, De Iudaeis [*emendavi*, jadaeis *cod.*] praecipit sancta Synodus nemini ad credendum vim inferre; et non potest eis inferri vim auferendo filium ut baptizetur; cum voluntas filii parvuli sit voluntas patris quousque habeat usum rationis. (**f34r**) Tertio quia si hoc esset licitum credendum est, quod primitivi Sancti et Rectores Ecclesiae hoc consuluissent terrenis principibus quos habuerunt valde favorabiles, ut Silvester Constantinum et Ambrosius [*emendavi*, Ambrosium *cod.*] Theodosium, quod nunquam legitur hoc fecisse. Ergo non est probabile quod hoc possit licite fieri. Quarto quia hoc non esse securum, sed valde periculosum: nam puer baptizatus dum veniret ad aetatem adultam posset de facili resilire ab eo quod fecisset ignorans contra voluntatem habentium curam ejus. Ex quibus probatur quod non est licitum principibus terrarum auferre filios Iudaeorum et offerre eos baptismo.

as he is not able to baptize the adult son against his will, nor ought he against the will of the son himself; so also one ought not to compel a juvenile son against the will of the father, which is dispositive regarding the son: because by that right the orphan testament made by a father has force as much as the testament of his own right made by him as an adult. In affairs, however, that are of human right, a prince can dispose with the father unwilling (just as he can also regarding the father himself), but not in affairs that are regarding natural or divine right: for he could not contract marriage vows for a son or for a daughter with the father unwilling (just as he could not make the father himself marry against his will).

4. To the second it must be said that the will of the parents is a barrier, and therefore he is not baptized. And when it is said that the sins of the parents do not transfer to the children, it is true directly, as if on the grounds that in being born they contract their sins from them, just as they do in fact contract the sin of Adam; but indirectly and by accident the father is quite able to impede even the spiritual good of the son. And so the second opinion is contrary to this, which posits that it is not licit to take away the little ones of Jews from their parents and offer them to baptism, and if in fact they should be baptized they do not receive baptism. The first reason is that all are free in affairs that correspond to natural and divine law. Similarly being baptized pertains to divine law; therefore since the care of little ones corresponds to natural and divine law, as far as this is concerned it is manifest with respect to parents that no one can licitly take them away from them to be baptized. Secondly, because it is settled that a prince cannot licitly compel a Jew to the act of receiving baptism in itself, as is held in distinction 14 of the Council of Toledo, where it is said as follows: "Regarding Jews the holy Synod instructs no one to bring force to make them believe," and force cannot be brought upon them in the taking away of the son for him to be baptized; since the will of the father is the will of the little son until such time as he should have the use of reason. Third, because if this were licit, it must be believed that the early Saints and Leaders of the Church would have given this counsel to those earthly princes whom they held in strong favor, as Silvester did Constantine and Ambrose did Theodosius, but we do not read that they ever did. Therefore it is not probable that this could be done licitly. Fourth, because of the fact that this is not secure, but very dangerous: for a boy that has been baptized, until he comes to adult age, could easily withdraw from what he had done through ignorance against the will of those who have care of him. From which arguments it is proven that it is not licit for princes of nations to take away the children of Jews and offer them to baptism.

5. Secundo opinio probatur sic, scilicet, quia si baptizentur non suscipiunt baptismum: quia ad susceptionem baptismi non sufficit quod non inveniatur obex contrariae voluntatis in eo qui debet baptizari, sed requiritur intentio percipiendi baptismum directa vel interpetrativa. Et probatur quia si adultus aliquis sic nutritur esset quod nihil omnino audisset de fide et esset in solo originali, si talis dormiret, et dormiendo baptizaretur, constet quod nihil fieret, ut probatur ex praecedentibus, et tamen in voluntate ejus baptismus nullum obicem inveniret. Plus ergo requiritur: scilicet, intentio suscipiendi baptismum directa vel interpetrativa in parvulo. Sola autem voluntas parentum est voluntas interpetrativa parvulorum antequam habeant usum rationis; propterea quod consuevit dici quod antiquitus ante datam circumcisionem salvabantur in fide parentum, non aliorum, nisi quatenus gerebant vicem parentum. Ergo si invitis parentibus baptizaretur parvulus, nihil videretur fieri, cum desit voluntas eorum directa et **(f34v)** interpetrativa.

6. Cavillantur rationes: sed licet hae rationes (saltem duae primae) sint tactae superius contra aliam opinionem, tamen ad eas posset sic instari, et primo cum prima, unde posset sic dici ad minorem quod aeducatio [sic] liberorum est de jure naturali quod omnia animalia docet, sicut doctrina in moribus de jure gentium. Si tamen pater vellet docere filium malos mores, non esset permittendum: puta quod esset moechandum, quod esset furandum et hujusmodi. Imo juste haec sibi prohiberentur, et sibi tutela filii auferretur, et merito privaretur jure patriae potestatis. Sic patri auferenda esset filia quam vellet prostituere. Cum ergo fornicatio spiritualis sit pejor, et magis noceat civilitati Christianae, multo magis auferenda est sibi proles quam vult facere a fide adulteram.

7. Ad Secundam rationem potest sic respondere: quod contra voluntatem suam directam vel interpetrativam nullus est baptizandus, scilicet, voluntas patris non est voluntas filii, nisi in bonis filiis et in quibus tantum se exhibet pium patrem, non autem hostem; sicut tutores et curati dantur quando bene administrant, non autem quando pupillum spoliant. Praeterea si voluntas parentum non requiritur ad baptismum, ergo contraria voluntas non impedit baptismum, quum sit oppositum in opposito, et propositum in proposito. Sed si puer non habeat patrem nec matrem, sed ambo sint mortui, cum

5. Secondly, the opinion, that if they should be baptized they do not receive baptism, is proven thus: for the reception of baptism it is not enough that there should be found no barrier of contrary will in him who must be baptized, but there is a requirement for the direct or representative intention of the reception of baptism. And it is proven that if any adult were so brought up that he should have heard nothing at all about the faith and were only in original sin, if such a one were to sleep, and in sleeping be baptized, it is settled that nothing would happen, as is proven from the preceding arguments, and nevertheless in his will the baptism would find no barrier. Therefore, more is required: that is to say, the direct or representative intention of receiving baptism in the little one. Moreover, only the will of the parents is the representative will of little ones before such time as they should have the use of reason; and that is why it is usually said that of old, before circumcision was given, they were saved in the faith of their parents, not of others except insofar as they played the role of parents.[5] Therefore, if a little one were to be baptized with the parents unwilling, it would seem to be the case that nothing happens since their direct and representative will is lacking.

6. The reasons quibble; but although these reasons (at least the two first ones) are touched upon above against the other opinion, nevertheless in relation to them it could be insisted as follows: firstly with the first, whence it could so be said in regard to the minor, that the education of children is of natural right that teaches all animals, just as teaching in morals is of the law of nations. If nevertheless the father were to want to teach his son bad morals, it would not be a thing to be permitted; for example, that he should commit adultery, that he should commit theft, and things of this manner. Nay, rather, these things would justly be prohibited him and the guardianship of the son taken away from him, and with good reason would he be deprived of the right of patria potestas.[6] In this way the daughter would be taken away from the father if he wanted to make her a prostitute. Since therefore spiritual fornication is worse, and does more harm to Christian civilization, much more should the offspring be taken away from him if he wants to make it an adulteress to the faith.

7. To the second reason one can respond as follows: that no one is to be baptized against his own direct or representative will; that is to say, the will of the father is not the will of the son, except in good children and in those to whom

---

5 See Rom 4:11–17.

6 *Patria potestas* (the power of the father): in ancient Roman law, this accorded to the *paterfamilias* (father of the household) absolute authority over members of his household. The term is not found in the current Code of Canon Law (*CIC* 1983).

non desit remedium salutis sive sit fidelium, sive infidelium filius, potest et debet baptizari, et parentis gerens officium qui ejus curam gerit hoc facere potest, sicut nutritur ex pietate puer (**f35r**) expositus cujus parentes ignorantur. Si igitur sine voluntate parentum potest esse verus baptismus, et contra voluntatem eorum similiter. In habenti enim usum rationis eorum voluntas non requiritur ad effectum, et per consequens nec contraria voluntas impedit effectum, licet ad hoc potest dici quod voluntas non requiritur nec per oppositum impeditur quando non habet parentes, vel quando finita est tutela parentum.

8. Ad tertiam dicendum quod propter scandalum in principio Ecclesiae multa omittebantur et dissimulabantur quae modo non dissimulantur. Tunc enim haeretici ad fidem non cogebantur (quod tamen juste poterant), ne videatur [*emendavi*, videntur *cod.*] fides viribus, non virtutibus prosperare. Tunc enim Ecclesia pugnabat solum gladio oris, nunc autem etiam gladio materiali pugnat contra hostes fidei.

9. Ad quartam potest dici quod magis est verisimile quod non reddeat ad fidem in qua non est nutritus, quam si esset in ea nutritus. Unde magis probabiliter timetur quod manens in Iudaeismo in perpetuum non convertatur vel quod conversus pervertatur (sicut saepe accidit) quam si a puero esset conversus et inter Christianos solos conversatur; quia tunc raro ad Iudaeismum redit. Si dicatur quod hoc videtur contra naturam, sicut mulier habens filium suum mortuum quae alterius filium surripuit cui [*emendavi*, eui *cod.*] justo judicio redditus fuit, et in perdicibus una alterius ova surripuit et quae non peperit fovet. Dicendum est quod non est similiter in proposita quia pia fraus est hic et nutrix est mater; mater autem noverca.

he shows himself a loving father only and not an enemy, just as guardians and caretakers are given when they discharge their function well, but not when they deprive the orphan. Furthermore, if the will of the parents is not required for baptism, then the contrary will does not impede baptism, since it is opposed in the opposed, and proposed in the proposed. But if the boy should have neither father nor mother, but both be dead, since there is not lacking the remedy of salvation, whether it be the son of faithful Christians or of unbelievers, he can and ought to be baptized, and the one who carries out the duty of the parent, who takes care of him, is able to do this, just as an exposed boy whose parents are not known is brought up out of love. If therefore without the will of the parents there can be a true baptism, it is also able to happen similarly against their will. For in one who has the use of reason their will is not required for the effect, and consequently nor does a contrary will impede the effect, even though it can be said to this that the will is not required or impeded by the opposite when he does not have parents, or when the guardianship of parents is ended.

8. To the third it must be said that in the beginning because of scandal many things of the Church were omitted and dissembled that are now not dissembled. For then heretics were not forced to the faith (which nevertheless they could have done justly), lest the faith should seem to flourish because of violence, not virtue. For then the Church was fighting only with the sword of the mouth, but now it even fights against the enemies of the faith with the material sword.

9. To the fourth it can be said that it is more likely that he would not respond to the faith in which he was not raised than if he were raised in it. Whence it is feared as more probable that he should remain in Judaism forever and not convert, or that he would convert and relapse (as often happens), than if he were converted from boyhood and lives among Christians only, because then he rarely returns to Judaism. If it should be said that this seems to be against nature, as if a mother with a dead son has stolen another woman's son, and restitution has been made to her after a just judgment; or in partridges, as if one has stolen the eggs of another and fosters those that she has not borne; it must be said that it is not similarly so in the proposed, because there is a pious fraud: here the "mother" is a nurse, there a stepmother is the mother.[7]

---

7 For the partridge, see Jer 17:11: "*Perdix fovit quae non peperit,*" or "The partridge has fostered a brood that she has not borne."

10. Quinta ratio in hoc verum dicit in majore quod requiritur intentio vera vel interpetrativa, nec sufficit non haberi obicem, sicut in illo qui haberet legem naturalem et fidem. Sicut in minori, posset dici quod intentio in (f35v) terpetrativa non est solum parentum carnalium, sed magis spiritualium, sicut olim salvebantur in fide parentum, id est, Ecclesiae; quae tunc erat non solum parentum carnalium, sed magis parentum legalium, sive spiritualium vel adoptantium. Unde cum iste qui agit curam salutis animae exhibeat se patrem, alias vero hostem ex quo iste qui quasi adoptat eum exhibet se parentem et ille tamquam patrinus pro eo respondit qui gerit vicem Ecclesiae, intentio et voluntas interpetrativa parentum spiritualium intervenit, et hoc sufficit. Si enim tutor personae et curator rerum succedit loco parentum, multo magis isti qui quasi parentibus furiosis existentibus tutelam et curam filiorum suscipiunt.

11. Tertia opinio est quae tenet viam mediam, scilicet, quod non est licitum baptizari filios Iudaeorum invitis parentibus, si tamen fiet vere baptizati sunt. Primum probatur ut supra in secunda opinione. Secundum probatur sic: quia non potius jus habet infidelis supra filium quam fidelis, sed si filius fidelis Christiani baptizetur invito patre, recipit verum baptismum. Ergo similiter si baptizetur filius Iudaei recipit verum Sacramentum. Pro hac opinione videtur verum esse quod dicitur de consec. d. IIII e. parvuli fideles vocantur, ubi videtur insinuari quod parvulis sufficit fides offerentium nulla facta mentione de fide parentum.

12. Primus articulus comuniter conceditur, scilicet, quod non licet principibus Christianis parvulos Iudaeorum auferre parentibus et eos baptismo offerre, sed quidam hoc concesso secundum articulum reputant dubium: nempe quod si baptizentur, sint vere baptizati.

13. (f36r) Unde solvuntur rationes ad hoc inductas sic. Cum enim dicitur quod filius parentis Christiani possit baptizari invitis parentibus et suscipiet verum baptismum, ergo similiter de filio infideli dicendum quod non valet, quia Ecclesia prodest fidelibus non solum in actibus civilibus, sed in iis etiam quae ad cultum Dei pertinet. Ideo si Christianus utatur re sua contra divinum cultum [*emendavi*, cultura *cod.*], non injuriatur ei Ecclesia si privet eum re sua et deputet eam ad divinum cultum. Et in hoc casu voluntas Ecclesiae est voluntas parvuli interpretativa, quia hoc in casu Ecclesia habet interpretari voluntatem parentum, imo, ut verius dicatur, voluntas Ecclesiae est

10. The fifth reason speaks truth in this respect: in the major, because the true or representative intention is required, and it is enough that there is held to be no barrier, as in the one who had the natural law and faith. Just as in the minor, it would be said that representative intention is not only of the parents of the flesh, but more of the spiritual ones, as once they were saved in the faith of the parents, that is, of the Church, which at that time was not only the parents of the flesh, but more so the parents of the law, or the spiritual or adopting parents. Whence when he who takes care of the salvation of a soul shows himself to be a father, but otherwise an enemy from the time when he who adopts him shows himself a parent, and he responds for him as a godfather who plays the role of the Church, the intention and representative will of spiritual parents intervenes, and this is enough. For if the guardian of a person and the caretaker of his affairs succeeds to the place of the parents, much more do they who take up guardianship and care of children for parents who are still alive but insane.

11. The third opinion is the one that holds the middle way, that is to say, that it is not licit that the children of Jews be baptized with the parents unwilling, but if it does happen then they really are baptized. The first is as above in the second opinion. The second is proven thus: because the unbeliever has no more right over his son than the faithful Christian does, but if the son of a faithful Christian should be baptized with the father unwilling, he receives true baptism. Therefore, similarly if the son of a Jew should be baptized, he receives the true sacrament. In favor of this opinion that which is said seems to be true in *On Consecration*, distinction 4: little ones are called "faithful," where it seems to be implied that the faith of those who offer them is enough for little ones, with no mention made of the faith of the parents.

12. The first article is commonly conceded, that is to say, that it is not permitted for Christian princes to take away the little ones of the Jews from their parents and offer them to baptism, but some concede this and still consider the second article to be in doubt: whether if they should be baptized they would truly be baptized.

13. Whence the reasons that have been brought in support of this are resolved as follows. For when it is said that the son of the Christian parent could be baptized with the parents unwilling, and will receive true baptism, therefore similarly regarding the son of the unbeliever it must be said that it does not have validity, because the Church profits the faithful not only in civil acts, but also in those which pertain to the worship of God. Therefore, if a Christian should use his means against the worship of God, the Church does not injure him if it should deprive him of his means and designate it for the worship of God. And in this case the will of the Church is the representative will of

magis voluntas parvuli interpretativa quam voluntas parentis carnalis, eo quod de jure voluntas parentis fidelis subest voluntati Ecclesiae. Non sic autem est de parvulis infidelium, quia ante baptismum non sunt Ecclesiae, nec ratione sui, nec ratione parentelae, ut sic voluntas Ecclesiae possit esse voluntas eorum interpretativa.

14. Decretum etiam allegatum non cogit: quia offerentes parvulum, non offerunt eum vice sua, cum nihil juris habeant in filio alieno; nisi hoc procedat de voluntate parentum, cum supponamus ea titulo quaestionis quod quis offerat eum invitis parentibus, nec vice Ecclesiae, cum ante baptismum non habeat jus in parvulo parentis infidelis. Canon igitur alligatus loquitur in casu in quo offerentes gerunt vicem parentum aut Ecclesiae, quod potest esse in parvulis Christianorum, non autem in parvulis Iudaeorum vel quorumcumque infidelium. Et confirmo quod non est simile de fideli et infideli, quia (f36v) non solum illud est possibile, imo est licitum et debitum, nec esset acquiescendum fidelibus parentibus. Similiter nec haereticis, si nollent filium baptizari, sed de filio infidelis quidquid sit de facto, saltem de jure certum est quod baptizari non debet, ergo non est simile.

15. Praeterea rogante fideli matre ut aubaptizaretur [sic] sed renuente gentili patre, baptisma dilatum est, quasi Ecclesia noluerit eum baptizare invito parente, quamvis hoc mater vellet; ergo multo minus utroque parente invito. Sed quidquid sit de paganis, videtur quod Ecclesia possit compellere Iudaeos et filios eorum ad baptismum, sicut filios Christianorum, quia parentes eorum fuerunt Christiani, et ad legem Moysi et ad susceptionem legis Christianae per se et per tota posteritate sua se obligabant, cum sit eadem fides modernorum et antiquorum, et eadem Ecclesia, quae est una columba. Ergo sicut haeretici ab Ecclesia gentium exeuntes ad eam cogi possunt, et ipsis invitis forte filii Graecorum, ad ritum nostrum licite attrahuntur, sic et Iudaei filii Sanctorum patrum maxime quia et ipsi ad legem Moysi sese obligaverunt. Exequutio autem pertinet ad judicium Ecclesiae legis veteris sicut et legis novae. Sicut ergo haereticos legis novae professores Ecclesia cogit ad ipsius observantiam secundum verum ipsius intellectum et sensum, quia obligando se ad eam obligant se ad verum intellectum, quamvis ipsi non obligent se ad eam secundum verum intellectum et sensum suum; similiter Iudaei professores legis Moysi, quamvis non obligaverint se ad legem Moysi secun(f37r)dum verum intellectum, sed secundum suum, cogendi tamen sunt, ut videtur ad hoc ipsum, et etiam liberi eorum ideo etc. Videtur etiam quod omnis paganus possit cogi. Sicut enim omnis paganus posset puniri a principe Catholico propter crimen, unde Saracenus si homicidium committeret, Parisius juste suspenderetur, ita, cum infidelitas sit majus peccatum, cum ipse teneatur ad suscipiendam legem Christi et fidem, non suscipiendo

the little one, because in this case the Church has to translate the will of the parents, nay, rather, to say it more truly, the will of the Church is more the representative will of the little one than the will of the parent of the flesh, because of the fact that the will of the faithful parent is by right subject to the will of the Church. But it is not so with the little ones of unbelievers, because before baptism they are not of the Church in such a way that the will of the Church could thus be able to be their representative will, neither on their own account nor on account of their parentage.

14. The alleged decree also is not compelling, because those who offer the little one do not offer him in their own stead, since they have no right in someone else's son, unless this should proceed from the will of the parents, although we hypothesize these things under the title of the question, that "someone offers him with the parents unwilling"; nor in the Church's, since before baptism She has no right over the little one of an unbeliever parent. The alleged Canon therefore speaks in the case in which those who offer play the role of the parents or of the Church, which can be the case in the little ones of Christians, but not in the little ones of Jews or whatever kind of unbelievers. And I confirm that the cases are not alike for the faithful Christian and the unbeliever, because not only is that possible, it is even licit and ought to happen, nor would faithful Christian parents even have to acquiesce to it. Similarly, neither would heretics, if they were unwilling for their son to be baptized, but regarding the son of an unbeliever, whatever may be the case in fact, at least by right it is certain that he ought not to be baptized, therefore it is not alike.

15. Furthermore, when a faithful Christian mother asks for him to be baptized, but a gentile father refuses, baptism is delayed, as if the Church will have been unwilling to baptize him with the parent unwilling, although the mother would want this; therefore much less if both parents are unwilling. But whatever be the case regarding pagans, it seems that the Church could compel Jews and their children to baptism, just as She can the children of Christians because their parents were Christians, and they obligate themselves to the law of Moses and to the reception of the Christian law for themselves and for their whole posterity, since the faith of the moderns and of the ancients is the same, and the same Church, which is one dove. Therefore, just as heretics coming out from the church of the gentiles can be forced to it, and perhaps the children of the Greeks, even if they themselves be unwilling, are licitly brought to our rite, so also the Jewish children of the Holy fathers, especially because they also obligate themselves to the law of Moses. But the execution pertains to the judgment of the Church of the old law as it does also to that of the new law. Therefore, just as the Church forces professors of

eam peccat. Cum igitur peccatum omissionis sit peccatum poena dignum, sicut peccatum commissionis, sicut posset ab Ecclesia puniri de blasphemia et contumelia Creatoris, sic possunt omnes infideles puniri, quia non recipiunt nec fidem nec Sacramenta Ecclesiae ut sic indirecte eam suscipiant.

16. Sed licet ita videtur esse secundum rationem, aliter tamen est secundum divinam prohibitionem. A scripturis enim traditum habemus quod non est voluntas Dei ut occidantur. Ps, "Ne occidas eos ne unquam obliviscantur populi mei." (Ps. 58.12) Item secundum prophetias, predicatione Enoch et Heliae sunt convertendi, unde usque tunc vult Deus cor in sua caecitate tollerari. Si autem vel ipsi, vel eorum filii ipsis invitis baptizarentur tunc nulli tempore. Enoch et Heliae invenirentur; nec per consequens prophetiae verificarentur.

17. Similiter idem videtur de aliis infidelibus, quia ab Apostolis traditum habemus, ut ad fidem nemo invitus trahatur vel cogatur, sicut patet per ea quae Beatus Iacobus dixit Hermogeni et Fileto. Et Apostolus ait, "Quid ad nos de his qui foris sunt judi(f37v)care?" Unde non homines armatos, fortes et potentes, sed infirma et contemptibilia mundi elegit Deus, ut gladio oris non materiali homines convertat. Unde de aliis criminibus possunt juste infideles a fidelibus puniri, quia Deus non prohibuit et ratio naturalis dictat, de crimine autem infidelitatis non. Unde sicut mulier si ordinetur, non solum peccat, sed etiam nihil recipit, quia Deus ordinavit quod vir et non mulier ordinetur; sic Deus ordinavit quod adultus volens voluntate propria et parvulus voluntate parentum baptizetur, unde aliter nihil agitur. Item sicut non est capax baptismi, sic nec puer sine voluntate parentum. Sed istud exemplum nihil valet, quia ex quo homo est, susceptivus baptismi est, sed praeter

the new law who are heretics to the observance of it according to the true understanding and sense, because in obligating themselves to it they obligate themselves to the true understanding, even though they do not obligate themselves to it according to their own understanding and sense, similarly the Jews, who are professors of the law of Moses, even though they have not obligated themselves to the law of Moses according to the true understanding, but according to their own, nevertheless are to be forced, as it seems in relation to the very matter at hand, and their children, too, therefore etc. It also seems that every pagan could be forced. For just as every pagan would be able to be punished by a Catholic prince because of a crime—whence a Saracen, if he were to commit homicide, if he were a Parisian he would justly be hanged—so, since unbelief is a greater sin, since he would be held to the reception of the law and faith of Christ, he sins by not receiving it. Since therefore the sin of omission is a sin worthy of punishment, just as the sin of commission is, as he could be punished by the Church for blasphemy and contumely of the Creator, so can all unbelievers be punished, because they do not receive either the faith or the sacraments of the Church in such a way as to receive it indirectly.

16. But although it seems to be so according to reason, nevertheless it is otherwise according to the divine prohibition. For we have it handed down from the scriptures that it is not the will of God that they should be killed. The Psalm says, "Do not kill them, lest ever my peoples be forgotten" (Ps 58:12). Likewise according to the prophecies, they are to be converted at the preaching of Enoch and Elijah, wherefore until then God wants the heart in its blindness to be tolerated. But if either they or their children were to be baptized with them unwilling then no time would be found for Enoch and Elijah; nor, consequently, would the prophecies be made to come true.

17. Similarly it seems to be the same with other unbelievers, because we have it handed down from the Apostles that no one should be drawn or forced to the faith unwilling, as is plain through what the Blessed James said to Hermogenes and Philetus.[8] And the Apostle says, "How is judgment of

---

[8] In the "Life of James the Greater" (chapter 99) in the thirteenth-century hagiographical anthology the *Golden Legend* (*Legenda Aurea*), by Jacopo da Voragine, the apostle is said to have come to Judea after preaching in Spain. There he provoked the opposition of Hermogenes, an enchanter (*magus*), who sent his follower Philetus to refute James in public. When Philetus instead converted at James's preaching, Hermogenes then tried magic, then sending demons; both of these efforts were turned back on the aggressor, until Hermogenes was at James's mercy and James freed him, saying, "It does not belong to our teaching that anyone should be converted unwilling [*non enim disciplinae nostrae est ut invitus aliquis convertatur*]." Finally, Hermogenes brought his magical books and offered to burn them, whereupon James directed him to cast them into the sea.

hoc requiritur ad essentiam baptismi intentio sua vel alterius deo non est proprium exemplum.

18. Sed quod aliqui dicunt, quod decretum Ecclesiae nihil juris habet in parvulis non baptizatis, sed in parvulis baptizatorum, non videtur valere, quia eo ipso quo homo committit crimen haeresis cujus cognitio pertinet ad Ecclesiam, Ecclesia habet aliquid juris in eo, et fit de foro Ecclesiae. Cum igitur peccatum originale solo judicio Ecclesiae possit purgari, scilicet, sacramento baptismi quod est Eccleesiae solius, ergo eo ipso quia habet originale, habet in eo aliquid Ecclesia, imo cum nihil possit solvi aut ligari nisi a superiore nisi esset Ecclesiae subditus, non posset Ecclesia per aliquod Sacramentum ei exhibitum ipsum solvere a culpa nec a poena. Sed ad hoc dicitur quod adultus se subijicit voluntate propria, parvulus autem se subjicere non **(f38r)** potest. Unde oportet quod parens eum subdat; cui natura eum subjicit subijcit et procuratorem fecit. Si dicatur quod illud crimen non contraxit in terra Ecclesiae quando non est natus de ventre fideli nec de patre fideli, non videtur valere, quia dictum est Petro: Quodcumque solveris super terram, etc. (Mt. 16.19) Unde mundus totus est per navicula. Ita enim habuit sedem in Anthiochia sicut in Roma, et ubicumque vult potest esse sedes sua, etiam in Babylonia. Unde cum habeat plenitudinem potestatis in omni terra et in omni homine eam habet et sic nec parentes nec ipsi se subjiciant: Deus tamen subiecit sibi omnem hominem unde hoc non facit defectus juris: sed prohibitio superioris, unde et de aliis criminibus punit infideles, sed de isto non, quia Deus prohibet; cui coacta servitia non placent. Et sic Ecclesia potest de his qui foris sunt judicae, sicut potest arcere infideles a comunione fidelium propter peccatum in moribus, non propter peccatum in fide, quod est in eorum vita. Et si arguatur contra ea quae dictae sunt, quod magis est occurendum periculo mortis eternae quam temporalis, sed puero existenti

those who are outside concern us?" (1 Cor 5:12).[9] Whence God has chosen not armed men, the strong and the powerful, but what is weak and contemptible in the world, to convert men by the sword of the mouth, not the material one.[10] Whence unbelievers can justly be punished by the faithful for other crimes, because God has not prohibited it and natural reason dictates it, but not for the crime of unbelief. Whence just as if a woman should be ordained, not only does she sin, but she also receives nothing, because God has ordained that man and not woman should be ordained, so God has ordained that the adult willing with his own proper will, and the little one with the will of the parents, should be baptized, whence otherwise nothing actually happens. Likewise, just as he is not capable of baptism, so neither is a boy without the will of his parents. But that example has no validity, because the example is not proper to God, from whom he is man and is susceptible of baptism, but beyond this there is required for the essence of baptism his own intention or that of another.

18. But what some say, that the decree of the Church has no force of law in little ones who are not baptized, but in little ones of the baptized, does not seem valid, because on account of the very fact that man commits the crime of heresy whose thinking pertains to the Church, the Church has some force of law in him, and it happens in the public eye of the Church. Since therefore original sin can only be purged by the judgment of the Church, that is to say, by the sacrament of baptism that belongs only to the Church, therefore for this very reason, because it has the original, the Church has some force of law in him; as a matter of fact, since nothing can be loosed or bound except by a superior unless he should be subordinate to the Church, the Church could not by any sacrament that itself has been offered to him free him from fault or punishment. But to this it is said that an adult subjects himself by his own proper will, but a little one is not able to subject himself. Whence it is necessary that the parent, to whom nature has made him subject, and whom nature has made caretaker, should make him subject. If it should be said that he has not contracted that guilt in the land of the Church since he was not born of the womb of a faithful Christian or from a faithful Christian father, it does not seem valid, because it was said thus to Peter: "Whatsoever you loose on earth, etc."[11] Whence the whole world is in the barque. For he had his seat in Antioch just as he had it in Rome, and his seat can be wherever he

---

9 The New Testament authors (except for the evangelists), as well as the Fathers generally, used the terms "within" or "inside" and "without" or "outside," both in Latin and in Greek, to refer to Christians and non-Christians respectively.

10 See Isa 42:2 and Rev 19:15.

11 Matt 16:19.

in periculo mortis temporalis subveniendum est contra voluntatem parentum, etiam si ex malitia vellent oppositum, ergo et multo magis subveniendum est pueris infidelium contra periculum mortis aeternae etiam invitis parentibus. Respondetur et bene, quod nulli subveniendum est in periculo corporali contra ordinem juris civilis. Unde si quis a judice rite condemnetur ad mortem non est per violentiam deripiendus.

19. Et similiter contra ordinem (f38v) juris naturalis et divini; quia filius qui est sub cura parentum non est eripiendus ut liberetur a periculo mortis eternae. Non enim sunt facienda mala ut veniant bona. Hoc autem fieret si filius infidelis parentibus auferretur quorum curae subest quantum est de jure naturali et divina, quia, sicut non est auferenda aqua propria alicui eo invito ad puerum baptizandum, si nollet eam dare gratis nec pro pecunia, quia esset contra justitiam, sic nec puer auferendus est parentibus propter baptismum. Nec obstat si licet auferre panem propter necessitatem proximi relevandam extremam, vel aquam propter sitim, quia aqua et panis sunt ad hoc ex sua natura ut succuratur corpori, sed ad subveniendum animae non nisi ex positiva institutione sicut propter mortem licet recipere elemosynam ab excomunicato, non tamen ei loqui vel ad missam eum recipere [*emendavi*, cum rceipere *cod.*] si aliter mortem intentet extra de his quae vi metusve causa fiant c. sacris. Quia cibus est de se remedium contra mortem, et similiter potus, non sic autem loquela vel missa, sicut non licuit Susannae adulterari ut mortem evaderet, imo, si medici dicerent, et verum esset, nisi infirmus fornicationem fecerit morietur, nullo modo fornicari liceret. Sed nec contrahere liceret religioso vel voto obligato propter tale periculum, sicut propter tale periculum contrahere liceret non obligato ad continentiam. Sed de aqua videretur quod posset auferri propter puerum baptizandum quia etsi usus ejus non sit per se ad lavandam animam, est (f39r) tamen ad lavandum corpus et lotione etiam corporis indiget propter corporis salutem in

wants it to be, even in Babylon. Whence since he has the fullness of power in all the earth and he has it in every person, and thus neither do the parents nor they themselves subject themselves to him: nevertheless God has subjected every person to himself, whence it is not lack of legal force that does this, but the prohibition of the superior, whence he even punishes unbelievers for other crimes, but for this one he does not, because God, to whom forced servitude is not pleasing, prohibits it. And thus the Church is able to judge regarding those who are outside, just as it is able to keep unbelievers from the communion of the faithful because of sin in morals, not because of sin in faith, which is in their life. And if it should be argued against these things which have been said, that there is greater need to meet the the danger of eternal than temporal death, but the boy who is in danger of temporal death must be helped against the will of his parents, even if out of malice they were to will the opposite, therefore all the more must the children of unbelievers be helped against the danger of eternal death even with their parents unwilling. The response is also well made that no one in bodily danger must be helped against the order of civil law. Whence if anyone should be duly condemned to death by a judge he is not to be snatched away by violence.

19. And similarly against the order of natural and divine law, because the son who is under the care of the parents must not be snatched away to be freed from danger of eternal death. For evils are not to be done in order that goods may come about. But this would happen if the son of an unbeliever were to be taken away from the parents to whose care he is subject as far as natural and divine law are concerned, because, just as someone's own water should not to be taken away from him against his will for baptizing a boy, if he were to be unwilling to give it for free or even for money, because it would be contrary to justice, so neither should a boy be taken from his parents because of baptism. Nor is there an obstacle if it is permitted to take bread away on the grounds of relieving the extreme necessity of one's neighbor, or water because of health, because water and bread are for this by their nature, that is, for the body to be helped, but for the helping of the soul not so, except from positive institution, just as it is permitted because of death to receive alms from an excommunicated person, yet not for him to speak or to welcome him to Mass, if otherwise he should be at the point of death, apart from the sort of reasons that are made from force or for the sake of fear with the sacred rites. Because food is of itself a remedy against death, and similarly drink, but speech or the Mass are not so, just as it was not permitted for Susanna to commit adultery to escape death, on the contrary, if the physicians were to say, and it were true, that unless a sick man commits fornication he will die, he would still in no way have license to commit fornication. But it would not

resurrectione. Unde sicut si vita pueri sine balneo non posset servari, propter hoc posset aqua auferri, ita videtur et hic.

20. Sed non est similiter quia lotio corporis de natura Sua est materia balnei non sic autem est causa resurectionis nisi ex divina institutione. Si vero secundo contra dicta arguitur quia quilibet homo magis est Dei a quo habet animam quam parentis a quo habet corpus, non igitur videtur injustum si pueri infidelibus auferantur et Deo per baptismum consecrentur. Respondetur et bene quia homo ordinatur in Deum propter rationem, per quam potest Deum cognoscere. Et ideo puer, antequam habeat usum rationis, ordinatur in Deum per rationem parentum, quorum curae naturaliter subjacet, propter quod secundum eorum dispositionem sunt circa eum agenda divina. Unde si puer parentes non habet, vel non comparent, quicumque vult loco parentum ei sit et sicut in nutriendo sic in baptizando, et sufficit quod non appareat voluntas parentum contraria. Et siquidem pater et mater Iudaei mortui essent sicut aliquando pater moritur relicta uxore pregnante quae etiam moritur in partu; vel moriuntur antequam puer habeat usum rationis, tunc propinqui [*cod.pc*, propingue *cod.ac*] de genere suo erunt tutores legitimi loco parentum. Unde non deberet nec posset baptizari ipsis invitis, sicut nec parentibus invitis. Sed si non apparent nec parentes nec propinqui, loco parentum succedit quicumque vult. Et ideo quicumque vellet posset eum tunc baptismo offerre quia naturalis ratio dictat quod cui **(f39v)** parens deficit alius parens sit, sicut una avis alias pullos nutrit quando mater deficit. Ex quibus omnibus colligitur quod sicut parentes non possunt cogi ad ea quae sunt purae fidei supra legem naturae, et si coacti non consentientes baptismum recipiant, nihil est factum, sic filii contra eorum voluntatem; in his quae sunt puri juris divini voluntatem veram requirunt vel interpretativam: non debet fieri nec factum valet.

be permitted, either, for a religious or one under a vow to have intercourse because of such a danger, just as because of such a danger it would not be permitted for someone who is not bound to continence to have intercourse. But regarding water it would seem that it could be taken away because of the baptizing of a boy, because even if the use of it should not be by itself for the cleansing of the soul, it is still for the cleansing of the body and he needs the washing of the body, too, because of the salvation of the body in the resurrection. Whence just as it is the case that, if the life of a boy could not be saved without the bathing, then water could be taken away for this reason, so also it seems to be the case here.

20. But it is not alike, because the washing of the body of its nature is the matter of the bath, but it is not thus the cause of resurrection except by the institution of God. But if in the second place it is being argued against what has been said that any person is more of God from whom he has his soul than of his parent from whom he has his body, it does not therefore seem unjust if children be taken away from unbelievers and consecrated to God through baptism. The response is well made, too, that man is ordered to God because of reason, through which he is able to come to know God. And therefore the boy, before he has the use of reason, is ordered to God through the reason of his parents, to whose care he lies subject by nature, because of which the things of God are to be done regarding him according to their disposition. Whence if a boy does not have parents or they are not in evidence, whoever is willing may serve in the place of parents for him, as in his upbringing so in baptizing, and it is enough that there should not appear a contrary will of the parents. And as a matter of fact if the father and the mother, being Jewish, were dead, as sometimes the father dies leaving a pregnant wife behind, who also dies in childbirth; or they die before the boy has the use of reason, then the next of kin for him will be his lawful guardians in the place of the parents. Whence he ought not, nor could he be baptized with them unwilling, just as he could not with his parents unwilling. But if neither the parents nor the next of kin are in evidence, whoever is willing succeeds to the place of the parents. And so whoever might be willing would be able to offer him then to baptism, because natural reason dictates that one who is without a parent should have another parent, just as one bird brings up chicks from another when the mother is lacking. And from all this we gather that just as the parents cannot be forced to the things that are of the pure faith beyond the law of nature, and if they should receive baptism being forced and not consenting, nothing is done, so their sons against their will; in the things that are of the pure divine law they require a true or representative will: it ought not to be done, nor, if it is done, is it valid.

III.PRAEF. **(F40R)** PAULUS CARTESIUS PROTONOT. APOST. IN 4. *SENTENTIARUM* DE BAPTISM. DIST. 1.

1. Contra opinionem, nempe quod filios Iudaeorum invitis etiam parentibus geniali aqua madefieri posse fervidius concaluit Petrus Paludensis. Divus autem Thomas orthodoxeo senatui tantum auctoritatis impertit ut magis ritibus ejus parendum esse arbitretur quam edictis decretisque eorum qui Divorum fastis adscribuntur. Itaque eam rem ad Senatum refert a quo sciat numquam repugnantium parentum filios hoc latica lotos. At mihi quidem hujus rei ratio duplex videri solet quarum una ob impendentis periculi magnitudine, altera quae juri naturae repugnat. Nam si liberi simul ac nati sunt, nec dum mentis praestantiam nacti hoc roris perfusu madefierent facile, progrediente aetate, parentum admonitu impelli possent ut id defererent quod essent improvida aetati irretiti. Alteram vero naturae contrariam censemus propterea quod natura quidpiam parentum filius putatur. Nam primo a parentibus corporis natura non secernitur quamdiu parentis alvo confinetur, sed cum maturus partus exit antequam liberam animi optionem nanciscatur parentum disciplina tamquam rationis quodam alvo continetur; at quamdiu rationis est impos paulum admodum a pecudum natura discrepat. Ex quo quidem quemadmodum quispiam civium jure in equos aut canes jus et dominatum habet, quibus ut est collibitum utatur, ita natura jure parentes in liberos rationis expertes imperium et dominatum nanciscuntur. Ex quo concedi fas est contra naturam videri liberos in erepundiis **(f40v)** a parentum complexu evellere ac eos nondum rationis compotes ad aliquod certum vitae genus applicare.

III.PREF. PAULUS CARTESIUS, APOSTOLIC PROTONOTARY, ON THE *FOUR BOOKS OF SENTENCES*, DISTINCTION 1, ON BAPTISM.

1. Against the opinion, namely that the the sons of Jews can be steeped in the water of generation even if the parents are unwilling, Peter Paludensis has argued too hotly. The divine Thomas, on the other hand, has imparted such authority to the orthodox curia as to think that its rites should be obeyed more than the edicts and decrees of those who are enrolled in the register of the divines. And so he refers this matter to the curia by whom he may know that children of parents who are opposing it are never washed in the water thereby. But to me at least there usually seems to be a twofold reason for this matter, and of these the one is because of the magnitude of the impending danger, the other that it opposes the law of nature. For if children, as soon as they are born, and while they have not yet gotten presence of mind, were easily steeped in this abundance of dew, when their age advances at the admonition of the parents they could be compelled to defer it on the grounds that they would be enmeshed in imprudent age. But the other we think contrary to nature because of the fact that the son is thought to be by nature something of the parents. For in the first place, the nature of the body is not distinguished from the parents as long as it is confined in the womb of the parent, but when the mature fetus comes out, before it acquires the mental freedom of choice it is contained in the discipline of the parents as if in a kind of womb of reason; but as long as it is incapable of reason, it differs rather little from the nature of cattle.[12] From which indeed, just as any citizen rightly has right and mastery over horses or dogs to use them according to his pleasure, so by nature parents rightly acquire command and mastery over their children who are not partaking of reason. And from this it is right to concede that it seems to be against nature to tear children away from the

---

12 In this sentence Cartesius twice uses the term *alvus*, which we have translated as *womb*. The authors quoted in the *Syllabus* regularly use the term *uterus*, which we have also translated as *womb*. We thus lose a distinction that is present in the Latin here. Cartesius, however, indulges in a turgid style, often preferring rarer words and more modifiers where other authors in the *Syllabus* express the same ideas with more economy and limited vocabulary. For example, Cartesius uses the phrase "not partaking of reason" (*rationis expertes*) where other authors in the *Syllabus* generally say "not yet having [or before] the use of reason." The authors in the *Syllabus* use the phrase "use of reason" (*usus rationis*) in this way fifty-three times, whereas Cartesius alone uses the adjective *expers*. The current *Code of Canon Law* uses the phrase eighteen times, including wherever it addresses the applicability of law to children (e.g., Cann. 1322–24 on those affected by drunkenness or mental disturbance and Can. 1478 on children). Similarly, Cartesius alone uses the noun *ros* (dew), which is used far more by poets than prose authors, rather than the more pedestrian and common noun *aqua* (water), which appears fifteen times in the *Syllabus* to refer to the water of baptism. We need infer little theological significance, therefore, from Cartesius' use of *alvus* instead of *uterus*. His tendency to prefer the rarer word is sufficient explanation.

IV.PRAEF. (F41R) MARSILIUS *SUPER QUATUOR LIBROS SENTENTIARUM* IN 4. QUAEST. 4A. QUAERITUR UTRUM PARVULI INFANTULI CITRA USUM RATIONIS SICUT BAPTIZANDI.

1. Primo dicitur quod parvuli fidelium etiamsi parentes nolent sunt baptizandi, habens enim [est] Ecclesia jus super illos majus quam parentes, eo quod parentes abrenunciaverunt omnibus pompis Sathanae et consequentia infidelitati per se et per pueris suis. Secundo quod non sint pueri infidelium invitis parentibus baptizandi patet quod sicut parentes non compelluntur fidem recipere et possunt alia sua bona libere possidere, ita nec pueri eorum eis invitis cum plus diligant pueros quam [*emendavi*, quod *cod.*] coetera bona. Et cum sint sub dominio parentum et de jure naturali curae parentum commituntur nemo potest tollere jus naturale auctoritate [*emendavi*, aucthoritate *cod.*] filii subsunt parentibus et eorum dispositioni usque ad rationis.

2. Si autem de facto baptizarentur utrum essent vere baptizati et acciperent rem Sacramenti? Dicunt quidam quod sic, quia ibi est intentio debila, forma, et materia, quamvis secundum cor non debeat fieri, quia non sunt facienda mala ut eveniant bona. At quod est probabilius quum hujusmodi foveris desit voluntas propria, et voluntate interpretativa subsunt parentibus; ideo ibi totaliter deest voluntas, quia non subsunt Ecclesiae. Et cum nullus accipiat sacramentum nisi secundum voluntate propria vel aliena; quod ibi omnino nihil fieret quoad Sacramenti caractherem vel rem. Materia enim non est apta circa quam sacramentum exhibetur plusquam canis. Et ideo si tales ad usum rationis venientes affectaverint se esse christianos, ipsi fovent (**f41v**) reabaptizandi.

3. Utrum adulti facti impotentes uti ratione sint baptizandi. Distinguitur secundum Thomam. Vel sunt a nativitate vel ex accidenti. Si a nativitate vel sunt filii [*emendavi*, filio *cod.*] fidelium, tunc baptizandi sunt etiam parentibus invitis, eo quod Ecclesia habet jus super eos, et quaerit filiorum salutem. De talibus enim est sicut de his qui ratione uti non possunt infantibus, ex quo ex infantia semper manent sine usu rationis. Si vero fuerint infidelium filii, videtur quod sicut pueri eorum eis invitis non sunt baptizandi et ita nec isti, quia semper manent sub dominio [*cod.pc*, dommio *cod.ac*] parentum vel eorum cura et ideo nisi illi vellent baptizari non debent quia deest voluntas propria vel interpretativa.

embrace of their parents in their infancy and to apply them, when they are not yet in possession of reason, to any certain kind of life.

IV. PREF. MARSILIUS ON THE *FOUR BOOKS OF SENTENCES*, ON BOOK 4, QUESTION 4. THE QUESTION IS WHETHER THE LITTLE BABIES WITHOUT THE USE OF REASON ARE TO BE BAPTIZED (SO TO SPEAK).

1. First it is said that the little ones of the faithful, even if their parents do not will it, are to be baptized. For the Church is holding a right over them more than the parents, because of the fact that the parents have renounced all the show of Satan and the consequences of unbelief for themselves and for their children. Second, the fact that the children of unbelievers are not to be baptized with the parents unwilling is plain because just as the parents are not compelled to receive the faith and can possess their other goods freely, so neither are their children, if they are unwilling, since they love their children more than the rest of their goods. And since they are under the dominion of their parents and are from natural law committed to the care of the parents—no one can take away the natural law—the children are under the parents' authority and their disposition until the age of reason.

2. But if in fact they should be baptized, the question is whether they were truly baptized and would receive the reality of the sacrament. Some say yes, that there is weak intention, form, and matter, although according to the heart it should not happen, because evils must not be done for good outcomes. But when the proper will of a supporter of this kind is lacking, and they are under the representative will of the parents, and so there the will is totally lacking, because they are not under the Church, and since no one receives a sacrament except according to his own or another's will, what is more probable is that in that case nothing at all would happen, as far as the character or reality of a sacrament is concerned. For the matter is not apt regarding which the sacrament is offered any more than in the case of a dog. And so if such, on coming to the use of reason, have shown that they feel that they are Christians, they themselves support being re-baptized.

3. Whether those who have become adults, yet are incapable of reason, are to be baptized: We distinguish according to Thomas. They are so either from birth or from accident. If from birth they are, for instance, children of faithful Christians, then they are to be baptized even with the parents unwilling, because of the fact that the Church has a right over them, and it seeks the salvation of the children. For regarding such it is as it is regarding infants who are not able to use reason, from the fact that from infancy they always remain without the use of reason. But if they are children of unbelievers, it seems that just as their children are not to be baptized with them unwilling,

4. Siquis haberet parvulum judei commissum et in periculo mortis positum, baptizaret sub hac conditione, "Si pater tuus voluerit cras consentire, ego te baptizo in nomine Patris etc." Quaeritur an puer sit baptizatus vel non: et quamvis videtur quod sic, quia illa conditio non tollit formam nec diminuit. Respondetur hic quod ille puer non sit baptizatus, quia non est baptizatus ante positam conditionem, cum non sit baptizatus non consentiente patre ut prius dictum fuit. Quia in baptismo cum parochus [*emendavi*, pariochus *cod.*] infidelium nequeat dirigi ad salutem nisi per parentes quorum est de jure naturali pro illa aetate ei providere non potest dari baptismum, nisi de facto eorum consensus adsit sint de facto baptismus suum effectum non [*addidi* non] exprimit.

V. PRAEF. **(F42R)** F. JOANNES CAPREOLUS *IN TERTIO LIB. SENTENT.* DISTINCT. V ET VI. QUAEST. 4A. UTRUM PARVULI INFIDELIUM SINT INVITIS PARENTIBUS BAPTIZANDI.

1. Pueri infidelium filii nondum habentes usum rationis non sunt baptizandi invitis parentibus. Hanc conclusionem ponit Sanctus Thomas [*emendavi*, Thoma *cod.*] ubi sic dicit, "Pueri infidelium filii aut habent usum rationis aut non. . . . Si nondum habent usum liberi arbitrii, secundum jus naturale sunt sub cura parentum, et ideo esset contra justitiam naturalem si tales [*emendavi*, talis *cod.*] pueri invitis parentibus baptizarentur. . . . Ecclesia autem nunquam hanc consuetudinem tenuit." Maximam auctoritatem [*emendavi*, authoritatem *cod.*] habet Ecclesiae consuetudo quae semper est in omnibus aemulanda, quia et ipsa doctrina Catholicorum dictorum ab Ecclesia auctoritatem [*emendavi*, authoritatem *cod.*] habet. Unde magis standum est auctoritati Ecclesiae quam auctoritati [*emendavi*, aucthoritati *cod.*] Augustini vel Hieronymi vel cujuscumque Doctoris. Hoc autem usus Ecclesiae numquam habuit, nempe quod Iudaeorum filii invitis parentibus baptizarentur, quamvis fuerint vel tractis temporibus multi Catholici et potentissimi principes, ut Constantinus et Theodosius et alii plures, quibus familiares fuerunt Sanctissimi Episcopi, ut Sylvester Constantino et Ambrosius Theodosio, qui nullo modo praetermisissent hoc ab eis impetrare, si hoc esset consonum rationi.

APPENDIX B

and so neither are they, because they always remain under the dominion of the parents or their care, and so unless they were willing to be baptized they ought not to, because the proper or representative will is lacking.

4. If anyone had a little one of a Jew entrusted to him and that had been put in danger of death, he would baptize it under this condition, "If your father willingly consents tomorrow, I baptize you in the name of the Father, etc." There is a question whether the boy is baptized or not: and although it seems the answer is yes, because that condition does not take away the form, nor diminishes it, the response here is that that boy would not be baptized, because he is not baptized before the condition has been settled, since he is not baptized if his father is not consenting, as was said before. Because in baptism since the priest is not able to be directed to the salvation of the unbelievers, except through the parents to whom it belongs from natural law to provide for him for that time of life, baptism is not able to be given, unless in fact their consent should be present, the baptism in fact does not express its effect.[13]

V. PREF. BR. JEAN CAPRÉOLUS IN *THIRD BOOK ON THE SENTENCES*, DISTINCTIONS 5 AND 6, QUESTION 4. WHETHER THE LITTLE ONES OF THE UNBELIEVERS ARE TO BE BAPTIZED WITH THE PARENTS UNWILLING.

1. Male sons of unbelievers that do not yet have the use of reason are not to be baptized with the parents unwilling. Saint Thomas posits this conclusion when he says as follows: "Male sons of unbelievers either have the use of reason or they do not. . . . If they do not yet have the use of free will, according to natural law they are under the care of their parents, and therefore it would be against natural justice if such boys were to be baptized with the parents unwilling. . . . The Church, moreover, has never had this custom."[14] The custom of the Church has the greatest authority, which is always to be emulated in all things, because the very teaching of the said Catholics also has authority from the Church. Whence we must stand more by the authority of the Church than the authority of Augustine or Jerome or whatsoever Doctor. The use, however, of the Church never did hold this, namely that the children of Jews be baptized with the parents unwilling, although there have been even for extended periods of time many Catholic and most powerful princes, as Constantine and Theodosius and quite a lot of others, with whom most holy bishops have been close, as Sylvester was

---

[13] The original manuscript does not contain the "not," which is incoherent.
[14] See ST III 68.10 co., which is here partially quoted but much adapted to the present purpose.

2. Et hujus ratio duplex est, una quidem propter periculum fidei. Si enim pueri nondum usum rationis habentes baptismum susciperent, postmodum cum ad perfectam aetatem venirent de facili possent a parentibus induci ut relinquerent [*emendavi*, relinquerentur *cod.*] quod ignorantes susceperunt, quod vergeret in fidei detrimentum. Alia vero ratio est quia repugnat justitiae naturali. Filius enim naturaliter est **(f42v)** aliquid patris, et primo quidem a parentibus non distinguitur secundum corpus quamdiu in matris utero continetur. Postmodum vero postquam ab utero egreditur, antequam usum liberi arbitrii habeat, continetur sub cura parentum sicut sub quodam spirituali utero. Quamdiu nempe usum rationis non habet, puer non differt ab animali irrationali. Unde contra justitiam naturalem esset si puer antequam habeat usum rationis a cura parentum subtrahatur, vel de eo aliquid ordinetur invitis parentibus. Unde de pueris antiquorum patrum dicitur quod salvati sunt in fide parentum, per quod datur intelligi quod ad parentes pertinet providere filiis de salute sua, praecipue antequam habeat usum rationis. Haec ille. Similia verba ponit in 2. *Quolibet* q. 7, ex quibus potest formari talis ratio pro conclusione: nihil vergens in periculum fidei et derogationem juris naturalis induci debet in Ecclesia, sed baptizare parvulos infidelium invitis parentibus est hujusmodi. Ergo.

3. Quoad potestatem principum Christianorum super Iudaeos dicimus quod illa non se extendit ad hoc quod cogat subditos obedire Deo de novo, scilicet illos qui numquam fidem susceperunt, ad hoc quod eam suscipiant. Unde S. Thomas scripsit: "Infidelium quidam sunt qui numquam susceperunt fidem, sicut et Iudaei, et tales [*emendavi*, talis *cod.*] nullo modo compellendi sunt ad fidem, ut ipsi credant, quia credere est voluntatis. Alii vero infideles sunt qui fidem Christi susceperunt et eam prophitentur, sicut haeretici, et tales compellendi sunt ut impleant quod promiserant, et teneant quod semel susceperunt."[b] Haec ille, ad hoc igitur facit illud quod ipse dicit prima secundae q. 91. art. **(f43r)** 4. nempe quod de his potest homo legem ferre de quibus potest judicare. Iudicium autem hominis non potest esse de interioribus motibus qui latent sed solum de exterioribus qui apparent. (Refert hic quae dixit Petrus de Palude).

---

[b] ST II.II 10.8 co.: Respondeo dicendum quod infidelium quidam sunt qui nunquam susceperunt fidem, sicut gentiles et Iudaei. Et tales nullo modo sunt ad fidem compellendi, ut ipsi credant, quia credere voluntatis est. . . . Alii vero sunt infideles qui quandoque fidem susceperunt et eam profitentur, sicut haeretici vel quicumque apostatae. Et tales sunt etiam corporaliter compellendi ut impleant quod promiserunt et teneant quod semel susceperunt.

to Constantine, and Ambrose to Theodosius, who in no way would have omitted to get their permission for this, if this were in harmony with reason.

2. And the reason for this is twofold, but single in danger to faith. For if children not yet having the use of reason were to receive baptism, afterwards when they were come to the fullness of age they could easily be led by their parents to abandon what they unknowingly received, and this borders on a ruination of his faith. But the other reason is that it is repugnant to natural justice. For the son is by nature something of the father, and at first he is not distinguished from the parents according to the body as long as he is contained in the mother's womb. Afterwards, though, after he comes out from the womb, before he has the use of free will, he is contained under the care of the parents as if within a kind of spiritual womb. That is, as long as he does not have the use of reason, a boy does not differ from an irrational animal. Whence it would be against natural justice if a boy, before he should have the use of reason, should be taken away from the care of his parents, or that anything should be ordained concerning him with his parents unwilling. Whence it is said of the children of the fathers in ancient times that they are saved in the faith of their parents, through which it is given to be understood that it pertains to the parents to provide for the children regarding their salvation, especially before they have the use of reason. This is what he says. In the second *Quodlibet* q. 7 he posits similar words, from which such an account can be formed for a conclusion: nothing that borders on danger to the faith and the derogation of natural law ought to be introduced in the Church, but the baptizing of the little ones of unbelievers with the parents unwilling is a thing of this type.[15] Therefore.

3. As far as relates to the power of Christian princes over Jews, we say that it does not go so far that it compels subjects in original obedience to God, that is to say, those subjects who never have received the faith, to the point that they should receive it. Whence St. Thomas has written: "There are certain of the unbelievers who never have received the faith, even as the Jews, and such should in no way be compelled to the faith in such a way that they themselves should believe, because believing is characteristic of the will. Other unbelievers there are, however, who have received the faith of Christ, and profess it, such as heretics, and such are to be compelled to fulfill what they had promised, and keep to what they had once taken up." That is what he says, which is why he says to this effect what he says in the *Prima Secundae* q. 1, a. 4., namely that man can bear the law regarding the things about which he

---

[15] See *QDL* II, q. 4 a. 2 co. If we look at q. 7, however, we find no mention of children and *usus rationis*.

4. Apparet igitur quod nec Imperator nec Papa debet filios infidelium ipsis invitis baptizare, quamdiu pueri ex jure divino vel naturali subsunt curae parentum. Et principalis ratio est quia Deus prohibet ne infideles aut eorum filii ante usum rationis cogantur ad suscipiendam fidem vel baptismum, sed specialis ratio est de parvulis, quia hoc faciendo fieret injuria parentibus, et contra jus naturale. Et iterum quia parvuli ex tali baptismo nihil susciperent cum nec adesset eis voluntas propria nec interpretativa, quia voluntas interpretativa parvulorum ante usum rationis non est nisi voluntas parentum, quorum curae subsunt. Posito autem, sed non concesso, quod minus malum esset Iudaeis, aut aliis infidelibus privari libertate servandi legem suam et ritus, quam habere libertatem servandi tamen privanti eos tali libertate et cogenti ad servandam legem Christi esset deterius et peccatum quia ageret contra prohibitionem Dei. Ipsis etiam Iudaeis et infidelibus poneretur scandalum, quia gravius peccarent agendo contra legem et sacramenta Christi suscepta quam ante susceptionem. Et dato quod talium filii post tertiam et quartam generationem bene educati essent vere fideles, tamen non sunt facienda mala ut eveniant bona nec propter detrimentum alienae salutis debet quis propriae salutis incurrere detrimentum.

5. In promptu est divina praescientia et revelatio prophetica et hoc solum debet sufficere ad propositum (f43v) quod scilicet non sunt cogendi ad fidem quia hoc esset frustra niti contra divinam praescientiam et revelationem. Exemplum vero Sisebuti prohibetur imitandum in sacro canone, nec laudatur de tali coactione, sed de pia intentione, sicut patet dist. 45. ubi sic dicitur, "De Iudaeis autem praecepit Sancta Synodus nemini deinceps ad credendum vim inferre. Cui enim Deus vult miseretur. Non enim tales salvandi sunt inviti sed volentes, ut integra sit forma justitiae. Sicut enim homo propria arbitrii voluntate atque facultate ut convertantur suadendi sunt non potius compellendi." Hoc concilium Toletanum.

is able to judge. Now man's judgment cannot be about interior movements that lie hidden, but only about exterior ones that are apparent. (Here what Peter Paludanus has said is relevant.)

4. It appears, therefore, that neither an Emperor nor a Pope ought to baptize the sons of unbelievers if they are themselves unwilling, as long as the children are under the care of the parents from divine or natural law. And the principal reason is that God forbids that unbelievers or their children before the use of reason should be forced to receive the faith or baptism, but there is a specific reason regarding little ones, that by doing this an injustice would be done to the parents, and it would be against natural law. And again because the little ones from such a baptism would receive nothing, since neither their own will nor a representative will would be present for them, because there is no representative will of little ones before the use of reason except the will of the parents under whose care they are subject. Now as it was posited, but not granted, that it would be less bad for Jews or other unbelievers to be deprived of the freedom of keeping their law and rite than to have the freedom of keeping it, nevertheless for the one depriving them of such freedom and forcing them to keep the law of Christ it would be more damaging, and a sin, because it would be an action against God's prohibition. For the Jews themselves, and for unbelievers, it would mean setting a scandal, because they would sin more gravely by acting against the law and sacraments of Christ after they had been received than before their reception. And though it be granted that the sons of such, having been well educated, after the third and fourth generation would be truly faithful, nevertheless evils are not to be done so that goods may come about, nor ought one incur the ruination of his own salvation because of the ruination of someone else's salvation.

5. The divine foreknowledge and prophetic revelation are at the ready, and this alone ought to suffice for what is proposed, namely that they are not to be forced to the faith, because this would be to strive in vain against the divine foreknowledge and revelation. Now, the commendable example of Sisebut is prohibited in the sacred canon, and he is not praised for this sort of compulsion but for his pious intention, as is plain in Distinction 45, where it says as follows: "Regarding the Jews, moreover, the Holy Synod has given instruction that no one therefore should bring force for the purpose of belief. For God has mercy on whom he wills. For such are not to be saved unwillingly, but willingly, so that the form of justice may be intact. For just as man is saved by his own will and faculty of judgment, so they must be persuaded, and not rather compelled, to convert." This the Council of Toledo.[16]

---

[16] Sisebut (d. 621) was a Visigothic king and friend of Isidore of Seville. The latter was the leading light of the Fourth Council of Toledo (633). The quoted text is a partial paraphrase of canon 57,

6. His omnibus addi potest quod homo naturaliter ordinatur ad Deum (S. Thom.) per rationem per quam naturaliter eum cognoscere potest. Unde puer antequam habeat usum rationis naturali ordine ordinatur ad Deum per rationem parentum quorum curae naturaliter subjacet, et secundum eorum dispositionem sunt agenda divina. Ex quibus apparet quod parvuli Iudaeorum ante usum rationis non possunt sine praejudicio et injustitia totaliter subtrahi curae parentum, potissime in his quae sunt juris naturalis vel divini.

7. Voluntas igitur patris voluntas vilii reputatur, unde sicut filium adultum contra ejus voluntatem baptizare non posset, sic nec filium impuberem [*emendavi*, impuberam *cod.*] contra patris voluntatem quae est dispositiva de filio.

8. Nec ad susceptionem autem baptismi sufficit quod non inveniatur obex contrariae voluntatis in eo qui debet baptizari, sed requiritur intentio suscipiendi baptismum directa vel interpretativa quod patet, quia si adultus (f44r) aliquis sic esset nutritus quod nihil omnino audisset de fide, et esset in suo originali, si talis dormiendo baptizaretur constat quod nihil fieret, et tamen in voluntate ejus baptismus nullum obicem inveniret. Plus ergo requiritur, scilicet, intentio percipiendi baptismum (directe vel interpretativa), directa in adulto, interpretativa in parvulo, sola autem voluntas parentum est voluntas interpretativa parvulorum antequam habeant usum rationis. Quare si invitis parentibus puer baptizaretur nihil videtur fieri, cum desit eorum voluntas directa et interpretativa. Ad ea vero quae fiunt circa parvulum ante usum rationis, nullum habitum moralem aut intellectualem causant in eo, et ideo non inclinatur ad talia, potissime cum fiunt ipso ignorante et contra voluntatem parentum suorum, ad quos naturaliter afficitur. Et quidquid sit de [*emendavi*, se *cod.*] hoc tamen non sunt fienda mala ut eveniant bona, fieret autem malum subtrahendo parvulum parentibus quibus eum Deus et natura subjecit. Deus etiam prohibuit talem fraudem nec vult holocaustum offerri sibi de rapina rerum aut personarum sicut fieret in proposito.

6. To all these things it can be added that man is naturally ordered to God (St. Thomas) through reason, through which he is naturally able to come to know him. Whence a boy, before he should have the use of reason, is in the natural order ordered to God through the reason of the parents to whose care he lies naturally subject, and things pertaining to God are to be done according to their disposition. And from this it is apparent that little ones of the Jews before the use of reason cannot without prejudice and injustice be totally taken away from the care of the parents, especially in the things that are of the natural or divine law.

7. Therefore the will of the father is regarded as the will of the son, whence just as he could not baptize his adult son against his will, so also one cannot baptize the underage son against the will of the father, which is the representative will of the son.

8. Nor, moreover, does it suffice for the reception of baptism that there be not found the barrier of a contrary will in the one who ought to be baptized, but it is required that the direct or representative intention of receiving baptism is plain, because if an adult were so brought up that he had not heard about the faith at all, and he were in his original sin, if such a one were to be baptized while sleeping, it is settled that nothing would happen, and nevertheless in

---

which refers to Sisebut and to compulsion and reads thus:
> De Iudeis autem praecepit sancta synodus, nemini deinceps ad credendum vim inferre. Cui enim vult deus misereri, et quem vult indurat. Non enim tales inviti salvandi sunt, sed volentes ut integra sit forma iustitiae. Sicut enim homo propria arbitrii voluntate serpenti oboediens periit, sic vocante se gratia dei propriae mentis conversione homo quisque credendo salvatur. Ergo non vi sed libera arbitrii facultate ut convertantur suadendi sunt non potius impellendi. Qui autem iam pridem ad christianitatem coacti sunt, sicut factum est temporibus religiosissimi principis Sisebuti quia iam constat eos sacramentis divinis adsociatos, et baptismi gratiam suscepisse, et chrismate unctos esse, et corporis domini et sanguinis extitisse participes, oportet ut fidem etiam quam vi vel necessitate susceperunt tenere cogantur, ne nomen domini blasphemetur, et fides quam susceperunt, vilis ac contemptibilis habeatur.

(Regarding the Jews, moreover, the holy synod has given instruction that no one therefore should bring force for the purpose of belief. For God has mercy on whom he wills, and hardens whom he wills. For such are not to be saved unwillingly, but willingly, so that the form of justice may be intact. For just as man perished by his own will of judgment in obeying the serpent, so with the grace of God calling him is each man saved in the conversion of his own heart by believing. Therefore not by force but by the free faculty of judgment they must be persuaded, and not rather compelled, to convert. But those who already long ago have been forced to Christianity, as was done in the times of the most religious prince Sisebut, because it is already settled that they have been associated with the sacraments of God, and received the grace of baptism, and been anointed with the chrism, and been sharers in the body and blood of the Lord, must be forced to keep the faith—even that which they received by force or necessity—lest the name of the Lord be blasphemed, and the faith that they have received be held cheap and contemptible.)

(f44v)
VI. (F45R) NOTANDUM

1. Teste Sylvestro De Prierio nec non Ambrosio Catharino, ut infra videbimus, e doctrina Divi Thomae necessario elicitur, quemadmodum scripsit Capreolus, baptismum collatum sine voluntate parentum non valere, nec aliter Sanctum Ecclesiae Doctorem unquam docuisse confirmant.

(f45v)
VII.PRAEF. (F46R) AMBROSIUS CATHARINUS DE PUERIS IUDAEORUM ETC.

1. Est ergo Sententia B. Thomae quam merito plurimi sequuntur, qui distinguit de pueris Iudaeis. Aut enim inquid habent usum rationis, aut non. Si habent possunt baptizari invitis parentibus. si non habent non possunt. Idque his rationibus probat. Prima est quia hoc consuevit numquam Ecclesia, cijus auctoritatem ipse merito magnificat, et praeponendam censet etiam sanctorum doctrinis, in hunc modum concludens. "Et ideo periculosum videtur hanc assertionem de novo inducere, ut praeter consuetudinem in Ecclesiam hactenus observatam Iudaeorum filii invitis parentibus baptizentur.

his will the baptism would find no barrier. More therefore is required, that is to say, the intention of receiving the baptism (directly or representatively: direct in the adult, representative in the little one, but only the will of the parents is the representative will of the little ones before they have the use of reason). Wherefore if a boy were to be baptized with the parents unwilling, it seems that nothing is being done, since their direct and representative will is lacking. But as far as it relates to the things that are done concerning a little one before the use of reason, they cause no moral or intellectual state in him, and so he is not inclined to such, especially when they are done with himself being ignorant and against the will of his parents, with whom his affections naturally lie. And whatever comes of this, nevertheless evils are not to be done in order that goods may come about, but an evil would be being done by taking the little one away from his parents, to whom God and nature have made him subject. God also has prohibited such a cheat, nor does he want a holocaust to be offered to himself from the robbery of possessions or persons, as would be being done in the proposed.

VI. NOTE

1. With Sylvester de Prierio as witness, as well as Ambrose Catharinus, as we shall see below, from the teaching of the Divine Thomas the necessary conclusion is drawn, as Capreolus has written, that the baptism that is conferred without the will of the parents is not valid, and they confirm that no Holy Doctor of the Church has ever taught otherwise.

VII. PREF. AMBROSIUS CATHARINUS (C. 1484–1553) ON THE CHILDREN OF JEWS, ETC.[17]

1. Here then is the opinion of Blessed Thomas, which very many follow with good cause, when he rules on the question of the children of Jews. For they either have the use of reason, or they do not. If they do, they can be baptized with the parents unwilling. If they do not, they cannot. And he proves this with the following arguments. The first is that the Church has never had this custom, and he with good reason makes much of her authority, and he is of the opinion that it is to be put even before the teachings of the saints, drawing his conclusion in the following manner. "And therefore it seems dangerous to introduce this claim again, that the children of Jews should be baptized with the parents unwilling, contrary to the custom observed in the Church up to this point.

---

[17] Ambrosius Catharinus, born Lancelot Politi, became a Dominican in 1517.

2. "Hujus ratio est duplex. Una quidem propter periculum fidei. Si enim pueri nondum usum rationis habentes baptismum susceperint, postmodum quum ad perfectam aetatem pervenirent facile possent a parentibus induci ut relinquerent quod ignorantes susceperant, quod vergeret in fidei detrimentum. Alia vero ratio est quia repugnat iustitiae naturali. Filius enim naturaliter est aliquid patris. Et primo quidem a parentibus non distinguitur secundum corpus, quamdiu in matris utero continetur. Postmodum vero, postquam ab utero egreditur, antequam usum liberi arbitrii habeat, continetur sub parentum cura sicut sub quodam spirituali utero. Quamdiu etiam usum rationis non habet puer, non differt ab animali irrationali. Unde sicut bos et equus est alicujus ut utatur eo quum voluerit secundum jus civile sicut proprio instrumento [*emendavi secundum Thomam*, strumento *cod.*]. Ita de jure naturali est, quod filius antequam habeat usum rationis sit sub cura patris. Unde contra justitiam naturalem esset quod filius antequam (f46v) habeat usum rationis a parentum cura subtrahatur, vel de eo aliquid ordinetur invitis parentibus."[c]

3. Sed nunc illud vertunt in dubium an, si contra jus invitis parentibus baptizentur, recipiant effectum baptismi et vere baptizati dicantur, et obligati Ecclesiae in professione Christiana. Cajetanus hoc asserit, et illud amplius hoc esse ex doctrina B. Thomae. Sed in utroque absque dubio fallitur. Producendae ergo sunt rationes ejus primum et post confutandae. Prima et maxima ejus ratio haec est. Quia ad recipiendum Sacramenti hujus effectum non exigitur consensus aut voluntas ejus qui baptizatur, sed satis est non ponere obicem, hoc est, non dissentire; quod in pueris fidelium patet. Ipsi enim non consentientes consequuntur sacramenti effectum. Nec putandum est secus esse in adulto aut necessitate sacramenti in uno non potest dici esse de essentia aut necessitate in alio.

4. Et adiuvans hanc opinionem, ne quis diceret (quod tamen D. Thomas constanter dicit et B. Augustinus) in pueris voluntatem et consensum patris esse interpetrative voluntatem et consensum pueri, ac propterea necessario voluntatem requiri ejus qui baptizatur saltem interpetrative: ut huic obstaret responsioni ait, "Voluntas parentum non est dispositio aliqua, sed sola appropinquatio patientes adagens puta ministrum conferentem sacramentum. Constat enim approximantem passivum activo non esse necessarium ex parte patientis. Tum quoniam aliunde potest suppleri; puta ex approximatione agentis ad patiens vel ex removente obstaculum. Tum quoniam extrinsecum hoc est. Patet vero voluntatem (f47r) parentis solummodo approximare passivum activo offerendo infantem baptismo ex eo quod si

[c] *QDL* II, q. 4 a. 2 co.

2. "The reason for this is twofold. One is because of the danger to the faith. For if children that do not yet have the use of reason should have received baptism, afterwards when they come to the fullness of age they would easily be induced by their parents to abandon that which they had received in ignorance, and this would border on a ruination of their faith. But another reason is that it is repugnant to natural justice. For the son is naturally something of the father. And at first at least he is not distinguished from the parents according to the body as long as he is contained in the mother's womb. But afterwards, after he is come out of the womb, before he should have the use of free will, he is contained under the care of the parents as if in a kind of spiritual womb. Also, as long as the boy does not have the use of reason, he does not differ from an irrational animal. And from this he is as someone's ox or horse, so that he uses him whenever he wants according to civil law as his own chattel. So it is of natural law that the son should, before he have the use of reason, be under the care of the father. Whence it would be against natural justice that the son, before he should have the use of reason, should be taken away from the care of the parents, or that anything concerning him should be ordained with the parents unwilling."[18]

3. But now they are calling it into question whether, if they should be baptized with the parents unwilling, contrary to right, they would receive the effect of baptism and be said to be truly baptized and bound to the Church in the profession of Christ. Cajetan makes this claim, and further claims that it is of the teaching of Blessed Thomas.[19] But on both counts he is unquestionably wrong. His arguments therefore must first be produced and afterwards refuted. His first and most important argument is as follows. For the receiving of the effect of this sacrament, the consent or the will of the one who is baptized is not required, but it is enough that no one place a barrier, that is, that no one dissent; and this is plain in the children of the faithful. For they, even though they do not consent, attain to the effect of the sacrament. And we must not think that relation to the being or necessity of a sacrament in an adult in one case is not able to be said to be of essence or necessity in another.

4. And in support of this opinion, lest anyone should say (yet which the Divine Thomas and Blessed Augustine definitely say) that in children the will and consent of the father is the representative will and consent of the boy, and therefore necessarily the will of him who is being baptized is required, at least representatively: in opposition to this response he says, "The will of

---

[18] The quotation is almost exact, with a single scribal error.

[19] Cardinal Thomas de Vio Cajetan (1469–1534), who became a Dominican in 1484 and wrote a commentary on Thomas Aquinas's *Summa Theologica*.

Iudaeus faceret filium baptizare non ut nutriretur Christianus, sed totaliter nutriendum Iudaeum, ob solamque corporis sanitatem vellet infantem baptizare, et hoc ipsum diceret et compelleret ministrum ad baptizandum vel ipsemet baptizaret, in veritate infans esset baptizatus; et tamen tunc paterna voluntas nec ex charitate nec ex spe nec ex fide nec ex Ecclesiae voluntate ibi compararetur, quoniam Ecclesia si sciret resisteret tali oblationi. Nihil ergo facit oblatio pueri nisi quod approximat passivum agenti, injuriamque paternae tollit auctoritatis quae illi irrogaretur si infans patre invito baptizaretur. Sufficit ergo in baptizando non inveniri obicem voluntatis contrariae ad hoc, ut caracterem suscipiat ex baptismo."

5. Haec ille, in quibus certe tot sunt errores quot verba; quae id circa libuit recitare ut qui huic auctori plus nimio tribuunt, cogitantes absurda quae hoc in loco protulit, discant caetera etiam cum judicio expendere.[d] Manifesto itaque ipsos errores. Primum quod ait absque voluntate et consensu adulti conferri [*emendavi*, conferiri *cod.*] sacramentum, omnino falsum est, et contra rationem, et contra omnium sapientium doctrinam. Porro enim adultum dormientem baptizatum ac propterea absque ejus consensu et voluntate, profecto hic recepit Sacramentum juxta hanc Cajetanum doctrinam. Et quum recipit Sacramentum invenitur sub jurisdictione Ecclesiae, et ideo obligatur servare Christianitatem quam vere non est professus, et hoc concedit Cajetanus. Ergo potest ab Ecclesia compelli (f47v) ad servandam Christianitatem. Istud autem est quod ipse negat, et cum hoc concedit praemisso unde hoc necessario sequitur. Si ex vi sacramenti tenetur servare Christianitatem cur ad hoc nequeat compelli? Ait quia absurdum est eum qui non consensit posse compelli. Imo non absurdum si ad hoc tenetur. Compelli aliquem ad id quod tenetur non est absurdum. Sed illud vere absurdum quod Cajetanus concessit, nempe talem absque suo consensu obligari Ecclesiae ad Christianitatem servandam. Quo concesso, sicut necesse est confiteri quod obligatur Ecclesiae, ita etiam confiteri necesse est quod possit compelli.

[d] cf. Terence, *Phormio* 2.4.14: quot homines tot sententiae: suus cuique mos.

the parents is not a disposition, but only an approach that compels passive subjects, for example the minister conferring the sacrament. For it is settled that the the passive that approaches the active is not necessary on the part of the passive. Also since it can be supplied from elsewhere; for example from the approach of the agent to the passive or from the one removing the obstacle. Also since this is extrinsic. But it is plain that the will of the parent only approaches the active by offering the passive infant to baptism, from the fact that if a Jew were to cause the baptizing of his son, not so that he might be raised a Christian, but entirely to be raised as a Jew, and only wanted to baptize the infant for the healthiness of the body, and he were to say this very thing, and compel the minister to baptize or even baptize him on his own, the infant would in truth be baptized, and nevertheless then the father's will would then be produced not from charity, nor from hope, nor from faith, nor from the will of the Church, since the Church, if she knew it, would resist such an offering. Therefore the offering of a boy does nothing except that it approaches the passive to the agent and takes away the injury to the father's authority that would be inflicted on him if the infant were to be baptized with the father unwilling. Therefore it suffices in baptizing that there be not found a barrier of contrary will for him to receive the character from baptism."

5. This is what he says, in which there are surely as many errors as words; and one would like therefore to recount them, so that those who give too much credit to this authority may think on the absurdities that he has produced in this passage and learn also to judge the rest with discretion. And so I am making plain the errors themselves. First, when he says that the sacrament is conferred apart from the will and consent of the adult, it is entirely false, and contrary to reason, and contrary to the teaching of all the wise. For furthermore if a sleeping adult is baptized and therefore it is done without his consent and will, of course he receives the sacrament according to this teaching of Cajetan. And when he receives the sacrament he is found to be under the jurisdiction of the Church, and therefore he is obligated to keep the Christianity that he did not really profess, and Cajetan concedes this. Therefore, he is able to be compelled by the Church to keep Christianity. But that is the thing that he himself denies, and with this he yields to the premise from which this necessarily follows. If he is held by the force of the sacrament to keep Christianity, why would he not be able to be compelled to this? He says because it is absurd that he who has not consented be able to be compelled. On the contrary, it is not absurd if he is held to this. That someone be compelled to that which is held is not absurd. But that is truly absurd which Cajetan has granted, namely that such a one be obligated to the Church for

6. Considera, acute lector, monstra quae in hac doctrina inveniuntur. Primum: sine suo consensu quis obligatur Ecclesiae ad servandum quod non promisit servare. Secundum: obligatus ad servandum non potest compelli. Et ut tertium monstrum agnoscas, quaere ab illo. Numquid non erit absurdum ut non consentiens obligatur [*emendavi*, obligetur *cod.*] ad servandam Christianitatem? Fatetur enim hoc ipse sed respondit his verbis. Uno inconvenienti dato, multa inconvenientia sequi possunt. Et ideo dato hoc inconvenienti quod minister temere baptizaret adultum neutrum non est mirum sequi aliud inconveniens, scilicet quod talis esset de jurisdictione Ecclesiae ratione Sacramenti, ut non esset compellendus ad Christianitatem servandam, quia nunquam consensit sed dormiens baptizatus est. Haec ille. Sed tu insta, et dic: Si uno dato inconvenienti multa sequuntur, cur non concedis esse compellendum eum qui non promisit? Hoc est nempe inconveniens videlicet: ut ille qui non promisit compellatur, non autem quod non compellatur. Propterea si est inconveniens absurdum quod quis obligetur (f48r) non consentiens, cur tu hoc absurdum admittes? Ais: hoc absurdum ex alio sequitur, videlicet quod quidem temere baptizavit. Ergo aliena temeritas me obligat absque ullo meo consensu? Quis adeo immania monstra poterit admittere, vel non protervus defendere? Illud vero mirum, quod afferat pro sua opinione Innocentium, qui dixit tunc imprimi characterem quum [*emendavi*, quem *cod.*] obex contrariae voluntatis non invenitur. Innocentius manifeste praesupponebat requiri voluntatem in adulto ad hoc, ut baptismi sacramentum perciperet, et non erat ibi sermo de adulto qui nec dissensum nec consensum ostendit. Nam ut imprimitur character in dormienti vel amenti palam exigit ipse priorem voluntatem eorum, nec aliter Ecclesiam consuevisse docet.

7. Quod vero a quolibet adulto qui baptizatur requiratur ejus intentio manifeste B. Thomas tenet. Unde ait: Si in adulto deesset intentio suscipiendi Sacramentum, esset rebaptizandus. Idem probat Scotus, Durandus, Petrus de Palude, Archiepiscopus Antoninus et cuncti concordes. Recte ergo argumentatus est Durandus, ut probaret in pueris voluntatem et consensum recipiendi Sacramentum esse de essentia Sacramenti. Si hoc in adultis ergo in pueris. Accepit pro re manifesta quia in adultis eorum consensus requireretur. Unde B. Thomas cum circa rem propositam disputaret, et de more argumentaretur, primum pro parte falsa ad probandum invitis parentibus pueros Iudaeos posse baptizari, ajebat: "Quilibet homo magis est Dei quam Patris carnalis; non ergo est injustum auferri pueros a patribus carnalibus

keeping Christianity apart from his own consent. And when this is granted, just as it is necessary to confess that he be obligated to the Church, so also it is necessary to confess that he could be compelled.

6. Consider, careful reader, the monstrosities that are found in this teaching. First: without his own consent someone may be obligated to the Church for keeping what he did not promise to keep. Second: after being obligated for keeping it, he is not able to be compelled. And to acknowledge a third monstrosity, ask him yourself. Will it not be absurd that one who is not consenting should be obligated to keep Christianity? For he affirms this himself, but responds with these words. Once the one inconsistency is given, many inconsistencies can follow. And therefore with this inconsistency given, that the minister would rashly baptize an adult, neither is it any wonder that another inconsistency follows, that is to say, that such a one would be of the jurisdiction of the Church in regard to the sacrament, so that he should not be compelled to keep Christianity, because he never consented but was baptized while sleeping. This is what he says. But insist, and say: if with the one inconsistency given many follow, why do you not grant that he is to be compelled who has not promised? Of course, the following is inconsistent, namely, that he who has not promised should be compelled, but not that he should not be compelled. Therefore, if there is an absurd inconsistency that someone should be obligated when he does not consent, why will you admit this absurdity? You say: this absurdity follows from another, that is, that he baptized him rashly. Therefore would someone else's rashness obligate me apart from any consent of mine? Who will be able to admit monstrosities so huge, or not shamelessly defend them? But it is amazing that he proposes Innocent on the side of his opinion, who said that a character is imposed at that time when the barrier of a contrary will is not found. Innocent obviously presupposed that the will is required in the adult for him to receive the sacrament of baptism, and there was not there a word about an adult who shows neither dissent nor consent. For when the character is imposed on one sleeping or mad he himself openly requires their prior will, and he teaches that the Church has not been accustomed to do otherwise.

7. But that the intention of the one who is being baptized is required of any adult, the Blessed Thomas manifestly holds. Whence he says: "If in an adult there were to be lacking the intention of receiving the sacrament, he would need to be rebaptized."[20] Scotus, Durand, Peter Paludanus, Archbishop Antoninus, and many who agree approve of the same. Rightly then did Durand argue to prove that in children the will and consent of receiving

20 ST III 68.7 ad. 2.

et conservari Deo." Respondit hoc pacto: "Homo ordi(f48v)natur ad Deum per rationem. Unde puer antequam usum rationis habeat a naturali ordine ordinatur in Deum per rationem parentum, quorum curae naturaliter subjacet, et secundum eorum dispositionem sunt divina agenda." Haec ille. Et iterum quaerens utrum pueri sint baptizandi et de more arguens pro parte falsa, quia in baptismo requiritur intentio et professio fidei et bonae conscientiae [*emendavi*, conscentiae *cod.*] interrogatio in Deum, et concludens pro veritate, quod possint ac debent baptizari respondit argumentis. Primum quod pueri antequam usum rationis habeant [*emendavi*, abeant *cod.*] quasi in matris Ecclesiae utero existentes per illam spiritualem recipiunt vitam. Adducit et B. Augustinus, qui ait, "Mater Ecclesia os maternum parvulis praebet, ut sacris mysteriis imbuantur," et recte fideles vocantur, quia fidem per verba gestantium quodam modo profitentur et promittentes habentur, cum per eorumdem verba gestantium Diabolo [*emendavi*, Diabulo *cod.*] et huic seculo abrenunciare monstrentur.[e] Et ad Bonifacium ait. "In Ecclesia Salvatoris pueri per alios credunt."[f] . . . Certe in baptismo initur pactum cum Deo, ut ritus ipse solemnis docet; ergo mutuus consensus requiritur. B. Chrysostomus [*emendavi*, Crysostomus *cod.*] dixit: "Sicut homo non potest facere bonum nisi habuerit auxilium Dei, ita Deus non operetur bonum in homine nisi ipse voluerit." Quamobrem nequeo desinere admirari hanc adversam Cajetani doctrinam: posse aliquem baptizari etiam invitum. Inviti enim illi pueri censendi sunt quum sunt inviti parentes, quorum voluntas puerorum esse voluntas censetur. Sicut enim si parentes consentirent intelligeretur puer consensisse, ita dissensus parvulorum. Nec dicat mihi quisque, etiam (f49r) si sint inviti parentes [*emendavi*, parentis *cod.*] tamen potest suppleri consensus et fides parvulis ab Ecclesia et majoribus Ecclesiae, sicut dicimus de infantibus Christianorum si forte Christiani parentes prohiberent baptismum ipsorum.

[e] See Augustine, *De Peccatorum meritis et remissione*, ed. C. F. Urba and J. Zycha (Vienna: CSEL, 1913).

[f] ST III 68.9 ad. 2.

the sacrament is of the essence of the sacrament. If this is true in adults then it is in children. He accepts it as an obvious reality that in adults their consent is required. Whence Blessed Thomas, when he was disputing about the proposed matter, and was arguing in his usual way, first spoke on the false side to approve the idea that Jewish children could be baptized with the parents unwilling: "Any person is more of God than of his carnal Father; it is not therefore unjust that children be taken away from their carnal parents and saved for God."[21] He responds in this way: "Man is ordered to God through reason. Whence a boy, before he has the use of reason, is ordered toward God by the natural order through the reason of the parents, under whose care he naturally lies subject, and according to their disposition are the things relating to God to be done."[22] This is what he says. And again asking whether children should be baptized and arguing in his usual way for the false side, that in baptism the intention is required, and the profession of faith and the interrogation of good conscience toward God, and concluding in favor of the truth, that they could and ought to be baptized, he responds to the arguments. First, that children before they have the use of reason, being as if in the womb of mother Church, receive through her the spiritual life. Blessed Augustine also advances this, when he says, "Mother Church offers her maternal face to her little ones, so that they may be steeped in the sacred mysteries,"[23] and they are rightly called the faithful, because they profess the faith in a certain fashion through the words of those who bear them, and are held to be making the promises when they are shown to renounce the Devil and this world through the words of the same who bear them. And he says this to Boniface. "In the Church of the Savior the children believe though others." ... Certainly in baptism there is initiation into the relationship with God, as the solemn rite itself teaches; therefore mutual consent is required. Blessed Chrysostom has said: "Just as man is not able to do good unless he has God's help, so God would not do good in man unless he wills it himself." Wherefore I am not able to stop marveling at this opposite teaching of Cajetan, that anyone can be baptized even if he is unwilling. For the children are to be judged unwilling when the parents, whose will is judged to be the will of the children, are unwilling. For just as if the parents were to consent the boy would be understood to have consented, so it is with the dissent of the little ones. And let no one tell me that even if the parents should be unwilling, nevertheless the consent and faith can be supplied to the little

---

21 See *QDL* II, q. 4 a. 2 arg. 4.

22 *QDL* II, q. 4 a. 2 ad. 4.

23 See Augustine, *De Peccatorum*.

8. Nunc superest illa expedire quae adjecit Cajetanus ex propriis et illud primum, quod voluntas parentum non est dispositio aliqua, sed sola appropinquatio patientis ad agens. Nam hoc unde probat? Similiter aut dicetur in illum quod consensus adulti non sit dispositio, ac propterea ipse etiam invitus posset baptizari, quod est absque ulla dubitatione falsissimum. Si ejus voluntas non requiritur, ejus (ut ita dicam) voluntas non deberet obstare, sicut nec obstat parvulis qui invitis parentibus baptizantur, quorum parentum voluntas et noluntas puerorum voluntas et noluntas interpretative censetur. Praeterea si consensus parentum est solummodo appropinquatio passivi ad agens, certe agens non agit in passivum sine appropinquatione passivi ad se. Nec valet quod ait posse appropinquationem alio modo fieri, nimium si ipsum agens appropinquet sibi passivo, quoniam tale agens, qui est Deus, ut agat in passivum exigit appropinquationem passivi ad se, sicut scriptum est: Appropinquate Deo, et appropinquabit [*emendavi*, approbinquabit *cod.*] vobis.[g] Cum omnes simus naturae alienati a Deo inimici illi, et hoc sit obstaculum quo minus non illi appropinquare valeamus, et illi [*emendavi*, ille *cod.*] nobis nisi hoc obstaculum tollatur nulla fiet appropinquatio. Sed sicut ab initio voluntate saltem parentum quae interpetrative fuit nostra ab ea recessimus ita ut postmodo necesse est ut voluntate saltem parentum, (f49v) quae nostra sit interpetrative, ad ipsum revertamur. Quod ergo Cajetanus adunxit, si Iudaeus pater consentiat, aut etiam cogat filium suum baptizari, aut ipsemet baptizet, intendens non aliud quam ejus sanitatem corporalem, et hoc insuper manifestat, valere baptismum inauditum est absonum nimis et paradoxum, videlicet sine ulla prorsus intentione vel baptizati vel baptizantis [*emendavi*, baptizantes *cod.*], vel parentum vel Ecclesiae sacramentum conferri. Quare indigna res est super qua alterius fiat verbum.

9. Concludendum est igitur sine parentum voluntate pueros Iudaeorum aut quovismodo infidelium extra Ecclesiam existentium baptizari non posse, nec si baptizentur valere baptismum; nec aliter docuisse D. Thomam sed hoc ex ipsius doctrina neessario elici, quemadmodum Capreolus docet; licet secus visum fuit Archiepiscopo Florentino quasi D. Thomae doctrinam sectanti. Sylvester autem in sua Summa fatetur se ignorare unde ex Thomae doctrina illud elicuerit B. Antoninus. Et siquidem vero [*emendavi*, sequidem vera *cod.*] falsum videlicet et ipsum dictum, et quod ex doctrina Divi Thomae

[g] James 4.8.

ones by the Church and the elders of the Church, as we say so regarding the infants of Christians if by chance the Christian parents were to prohibit their baptism.

8. Now to analyze what Cajetan has added on his own, and first the notion that the will of the parents is not a disposition, but only an approach of the sufferer to the agent. For how does he prove this? Similarly, in fact, it will be said against him that the consent of the adult is not a disposition, and therefore he could be baptized even if he himself is unwilling, which is, far from any doubt, most false. If his will is not required, his will (so to speak) would not have had to present an obstacle, just as it also presents no obstacle for little ones who are baptized with their parents unwilling, of which parents the will, and the contrary will, is judged to be representatively the will and the contrary will of the children. Furthermore, if the consent of the parents is just an approach of the passive to the agent, certainly the agent does not act on the passive without the approach of the passive to itself. Nor is that valid which he says, that the approach can in some way happen if the agent itself should approach the passive itself, since such agent, which is God, in order to act upon the passive, requires approach of the passive to itself, as is written: approach God, and he will approach you.[24] Since we are all alienated from the God of nature, and enemies to him, and this is an obstacle against our being able to approach him, and unless this obstacle should be taken away from us, there will be no approach to him. But just as from the beginning by the will at least of the parents, which was representatively ours, we have drawn away from it, in such a way that afterwards it is necessary that by the will at least of the parents, which is ours representatively, we may return to him. And therefore Cajetan has added this: if a Jewish father should consent, or even force, his son to be baptized, or he himself should baptize him, intending nothing other than his bodily cleanliness, and moreover he should manifest this, it is unheard of that the baptism should be valid, as it is too dissonant and contradictory, that is to say, that without any direct intention either of the baptized or the the baptizer, either of the parents or of the Church, that the sacrament is conferred. Wherefore the matter is unworthy to have another word spent on it.

9. It must therefore be concluded that, without the will of the parents, the children of Jews (or those who are in any way unbelievers outside the Church) cannot be baptized, and if they should be baptized the baptism is not valid. And no differently did the Divine Thomas teach, but this is necessarily drawn from his teaching, as Capreolus teaches, although it seemed

---

24 Jas 4:8.

accipiatur. Non dubito inde tamen accipi, ubi ait periculosam esse illam assertionem de novo inducere, ut filii Iudaeorum invitis parentibus baptizentur. Si enim ante usum rationis baptismum susciperent, esset periculum fidei ne revertantur ad infidelitatem [*emendavi*, infedilitatem *cod.*] tanquam si expressus dixisset B. Thomas, quod si baptizarentur, esset in hoc periculum fidei, quod susciperent baptisma, et illud postmodo non servarent. At vero B. Thomae doctrina e diametro pugnat. Disputat (f50r) enim expresse contra illam opinionem, quae volebat tales pueros baptismum suscipere. Et ostendens hoc esse absurdum et falsum, dixit: Si enim baptismum susciperent—conditionalis est hic sermo quasi dicat: Si hoc esset verum, sicut vos dicitis, tales pueros baptismum suscipere, postmodo, quum ad perfectam rationem pervenirent, de facili possent fieri desertores.

10. Illud hic omnino advertendum [*emendavi*, advertendam *cod.*] est, quod Archiepiscopus ille sanctus admittens tales pueros vere baptismum suscipere, non tamen eo labitur, ut more Cajetani dicat sine intentione ipsius baptizati saltem interpetrative id evenire, quia alii qui offerunt tales loco parentum habentur. Sed in hoc fallitur: quia juxta doctrinam aliorum veriorem, quae certe est ipsius B. Thomae et Petri de Palude et Capreoli et evidentem prae se fert rationem, non potest Ecclesia in his supplere, qui non sunt ejus aliquo modo; quod valde erit considerandum.

11. Igitur evictum et constitutum [*emendavi*, costitutum *cod.*] est; pueros usu rationis carentes invitis parentibus non posse baptizari, nec si baptizati fuerint baptismum recipere. Superest modo ut jam eorum sententiam qui putaverunt posse, imo debere Iudaeorum infantes etiam invitis parentibus posse jussu Principum baptizari, ostendamus merito ac rationibus optimis esse explosam: quod satis fecerimus, si argumenta quibus movebantur nullius esse momenti detexerimus. Aiebat enim primum, si parentes vellent occidere filios suos, nonne liceret et pietatis esse eos de manibus parentum liberare? At prohibere ne baptizentur, quod est aliud (f50v) quam inferre mortem, et illam quidem non temporalem, sed aeternam? Adhaec nonne homo est res magis Dei, et sub ejus potestate quam parentum suorum? Haud dubium. Si igitur male sua potestate utantur parentes erga parvulos suos, cur Principes ministri Dei non possunt causam ejus suscipere et illos pueros illi reddere, et consecrare per baptismum Deo? Fingamus esse Imperatorem, Proconsulem et aliquem inferioris potestatis subordinatae tamen, et hunc qui inferioris fuerit potestatis abuti illa in detrimentum Imperatoris: nonne ad Proconsulem pertinebit emendare factum et eripere ab inferiore potestatem qua is male utitur contra dominum principalem? Ad haec: si Deus vult omnes homines salvos fieri, numquid iniquitas patris potest nocere

otherwise to the Florentine Archbishop who was supposedly following the teaching of the Divine Thomas.[25] Sylvester moreover in his Summa confesses that he does not know whence the Blessed Antoninus had drawn it from the teaching of Thomas.[26] And since it is indeed false, namely the very thing that was said, that it is taken from the teaching of the Divine Thomas. Still I do not hesitate to take from the place where he says that he induces that dangerous claim again, that children of Jews should be baptized when the parents are unwilling. For if they were to receive baptism before the use of reason, there would be a danger to the faith, that they would revert to unbelief, as if Blessed Thomas should have said expressly that if they were to be baptized, there would be in this a danger to the faith, because they would receive baptism and then not keep it afterwards. But still Blessed Thomas's teaching is diametrically opposed. For he argues expressly against that opinion that wanted such children to receive baptism. And showing that this is absurd and false, he said, "For if they were to receive baptism"—he means this word conditionally, as if to say, "If this were true, as you say, that such children receive baptism, afterwards, when they were come to the fullness of reason, they could easily become deserters."

10. Here it absolutely must be noted that that holy Archbishop, admitting that such children receive baptism, still does not err so far as to talk in the way that Cajetan does, that this comes about without the intention of the baptized, at least representatively, because such others as offer him are held to be in the place of parents. But in this he is wrong, because according to the truer teaching of others, which certainly is that of Blessed Thomas and Peter Paludanus and Capreolus, and presents plain reason, the Church is not able to supply the place for those who are not hers in any way, which will very much have to be considered.

11. Therefore we have made the proof that we set out to make, that children lacking the use of reason are not able to be baptized with the parents unwilling, and if they are baptized, they do not receive baptism. It merely remains for us to show that the opinion of those who thought that it was possible—nay, that the infants of Jews ought, that they could be baptized by the order of Princes, even with the parents unwilling—for us to show that it has already been exploded with very good merit and reasoning, which we have already done satisfactorily, if we have uncovered the fact that the arguments

---

[25] The "Florentine Archbishop" may refer to Francesco Silvestri (1323–41). Conrad Eubel, *Hierarchia Catholica medii aevi* (Regensburg, 1913), 250.

[26] The predecessor of Francesco Silvestri: Antonio Orso (1310–22). Eubel, *Hierarchia Catholica medii aevi*.

filiis suis, cum scriptum sit: Filius non portabit iniquitatem patris?[h] Ad haec: nonne certum est quod a Toletano Concilio religiosissimus Princeps vocatur Zizebutus, qui Iudaeos compulit ad baptismum. Unde comendari de eo facto videtur in Concilio. Ad haec: parvuli fidelium possunt invitis parentibus baptizari: cur non igitur et parvuli infidelium possint? Haec fere sunt quae ab opinantibus pro illa sua Sententia producta sunt: quibus sigillatim est respondendum.

12. Ad primum ergo respondentes, fatemur posse eripi filios de manu parentum Iudaeorum volentium illos occidere in eo scelere. Non enim utuntur naturali parentum officio: quoniam natura hanc illis non tribuit potestatem, sed contra potius statuit, ut quem genuerunt, (f51r) alant et servent, non ut [*emendavi*, aut *cod.*] perdant. At vero non praestare consensum filiis ad baptismum, non est ab eis auferre vitam spiritus, quam non habent, sed est tantum non adducere, aut non iuvare eos ad vitam; ad quod cogi non possunt. Si enim ipsi non possunt cogi ad consensum baptismi pro seipsis, ac propterea possunt sibi ipsis praecludere viam ad vitam, ne adipiscantur salutem, quid mirum si consequenter [*emendavi*, consequentur *cod.*] etiam suis filiis hac parte possunt non prodesse, cum filiorum consensus a patre in hujusmodi requiratur? Praeterea, si parentum factum ab ipsorum conscientia [*emendavi*, conscentia *cod.*] consideretur, longe diversi sint ejusmodi casus. Pater enim qui mortem corporalem intentat in filium manifeste contra jus naturae agit, et contra naturalem parentum affectum. Et ideo non mirum si pietas et jus naturale suadet ut e manibus eorum eripiantur, quia nulla est naturaliter in hoc patris contra filium potestas. At vero quum non vult consentire baptismo filii sui id agit non ut perdat eum, sed ut servet potius, quia putat Christi religionem esse falsam. Ius ergo naturale [*emendavi*, naturales *cod.*] parentes hoc pacto non violant, sed servant si eorum mens consideretur, cum non impendunt filiis quod putant illis noxium esse, et pro seipsis non eligunt.

---

[h] Ezech. 18.20.

by which they were moved were of no importance. For he said first, if the parents wanted to kill their children, wouldn't it be permitted, wouldn't piety even demand, that we free them from the hands of their parents? But to prohibit them from being baptized—what else is this than to bring death upon them, and that indeed not temporal but eternal? Additionally, isn't a man more a thing of God and more under his power than that of his parents? No doubt. If therefore the parents used their power toward their little ones badly, why cannot Princes, the ministers of God, be able to take up his cause and return those children to him, and consecrate them to God through baptism? Nevertheless, let us imagine an Emperor, Proconsul, and someone of lower subordinate power, and let us imagine that the one who has been of lower power is abusing it to the harm of the Emperor: is it not the Proconsul's concern to emend the deed and take away the power from the lower that he is using badly against his principal master? To this: if God wants all men to become saved, can the iniquity of the father harm his children, since it is written: the son will not bear the iniquity of the father?[27] To this: is it not certain that the prince Zizebut is called most religious by the Council of Toledo, and he compelled Jews to baptism?[28] Whence it seems that he is being commended in the Council for this deed. To this: the little ones of the faithful can be baptized with the parents unwilling; why then may also the little ones of the unbelievers not be? This is pretty nearly what has been brought forth by those who think in favor of that opinion: and we must respond to them one at a time.

12. To the first then we respond and assert that if Jewish parents want to kill their children, they can be snatched from their hands in the act of doing so. For they are not performing the natural duty of parents: since nature has not granted them this power, but has ordained rather against it, that they should nourish and keep, not destroy, one whom they have begotten. But as a matter of fact, merely not presenting consent for their children for baptism is not the same thing as taking away from them the life of the spirit, which they do not have, but is only not bringing them to it, or not helping them to the life; and they cannot be compelled to this. For if they themselves cannot be compelled to consent for baptism in regard to their own selves, and therefore they can close off the way toward life from their own selves, to stop themselves from getting salvation, is it any wonder if consequently they can also not be a boon to their children in this matter, when consent is required from the father in matters of this kind? Furthermore, if the deed should be considered from

---

[27] Ezek 18:20.
[28] Or Sisebut (see n. 35).

13. Ad illud vero quod secundo loco asserebatur, filios Iudaeorum magis esse Dei quam ipsorum parentum, quis neget? At hinc non propterea sequitur quod si parentes non curant eos ut debent, amittant ius ipsum curandi et in alio devolvatur: sed bene sequitur tales esse omnino puniendos. Quis enim dixerit hominem male usu rationis utentem, esse ipsa ratione aut usu rationis privandum? **(f51v)** Deus enim ab iis qui ratione abutuntur, rationem vel usum rationis non aufert, sed eos dignis punit suppliciis. Quapropter cum natura comparatum sit ejusmodi pueros consilio atque arbitrio parentum regi debere, si forte parentes sano consilio illis non provident, non propterea ratio naturalis dictat ut loco parentum alii substituantur, quorum cura et consilio regantur. Alioquin incinnitae [*emendavi*, Alioque insinitae *cod.*] turbae et seditiones concitarentur. Neque similitudo illa de Imperatore et Proconsule et alio inferioris gradus congruit: quoniam non erat edictum Imperatoris nostri Dei ut quisquam baptizaretur etiam invitus, sed tantum si velit. Quamobrem sicut parentes ipsi a Principabus cogi non possunt ut inviti baptizentur, ita nec eorum filii, qui tum inviti censentur cum illorum parentes renituntur. Nec valet quod tertio loco afferebatur, Deum velle omnes homines salvos fieri, et vocare omnes et invitare. Vult enim salutem nostram Deus—si tamen et nos illam velimus. Voluntatem enim nostram etiam requirit, ideo vocat et invitat ut respondeamus. Puerorum autem voluntas, cum propriam non habeant, a parentibus exigitur, quam si non praestent, inhabiles illi pueri ad consequendam salutem inveniuntur. Non ergo lex evangelica per hoc violatur, quod deficiente consensu parentum impeditur baptismus et salus filiorum: quoniam hoc in primis est evangelicae legis ut nemo sine suo consensu salvus fiat. Consensus autem, aut dissensus parentum pro filiis, ipsorum filiorum consensus aut dissensus, legis naturae interpetratione censetur. Nec filius portabit iniquitatem patris: **(f52r)** quia

the conscience of the parents themselves, cases of this kind would be quite different. For the father who intends bodily death against the son manifestly acts against natural law and against the natural feeling of parents. And so it is no wonder if piety and natural law urge that they should be snatched away from their hands, because there is in it, naturally, no power of a father against a son.[29] But as a matter of fact, when he is unwilling to consent to baptism for his son he does this not to destroy him, but to keep him rather, because he thinks that the religion of Christ is false. The parents therefore do not in this way violate the natural law, but they keep it, if their mind should be considered, when they do not apply to their children what they think is harmful to them, and do not choose it for themselves either.

13. But as for that which was being asserted in the second place, that the children of Jews are more of God than of their parents themselves, who would deny it? But it does not therefore follow from this that, if the parents do not take care of them as they ought to, they would lose the very right of taking care of them and it should devolve upon another: but it does indeed follow that such should at all events be punished. For who will have said that a man who uses the use of reason badly is to be deprived of reason itself or the use of reason? For God does not take away reason or the use of reason from those who abuse reason, but punishes them with worthy punishments. And that is why since it has been arranged by nature that children of this kind ought to be governed by the counsel and judgment of the parents, if perchance the parents do not provide for them with sound guidance, natural reason does not therefore dictate that others should be substituted in the place of the parents, by whose care and guidance they would be governed. Otherwise mobs would be stirred up and seditions aroused. Nor does the earlier example of the Emperor and the Proconsul and the other one of lower rank fit, since there was not an edict of our Emperor God that anyone should be baptized even if he were unwilling, but only if he should be willing. Wherefore just as the parents themselves are not able to be compelled by Princes to be baptized when they are unwilling, so their sons cannot either, who are considered to be unwilling when their parents are resisting it. Nor is what was brought up in the third place valid, that God wills all men to be saved, and calls and invites all. For God wills our salvation—if we should want it, too, though. For it also requires our will, and so he calls and invites us to respond. But the will of children, when they do not have their own, is claimed from the parents, and, if they do not offer it, the children are found to be unable to attain

---

29 The change to the plural pronoun *they* mid-sentence, though jarring, belongs to the author, who has perhaps chosen to refer simultaneously to the particular child of the case and to the hypothetical category of children by using both *filius* and *eripiantur*.

pater ipse solus punietur de sua duritia.[i] Filius autem ex antiquo peccato solum poenam detrimenti, seu non lucri patietur, non autem poenam sensus, ut est communis theologorum sententia.

14. Illud item quod quarto loco afferebatur, non recte concludit; Canones manifeste decernunt sub titulo de Iudaeis: et ex Concilio Toletano clare accipitur distinctione XIV. De Iudaeis. Non est verum laudari Zizibuti factum in eo Concilio, cum propria ejus Synodi constitutione reprobetur, tametsi vocetur religiosissimus princeps. Potuit enim esse pietate laudabilis, et habere zelum sed non secundum sententiam. Sed ad rem nostram.

15. Hoc est quod dicebam, si parentes ipsi non possunt cogi ad baptismum profecto nec eorum filii. At certe cogerentur, si renitentibus parentibus baptismum susciperent. Et naturae jus dicit consensum et dissensum parentum esse consensum aut disensum liberorum nondum ratione utentium. Quo pacto igitur potest concedi baptismus? Quomodo potestatis principis potest naturale vel divinum jus tollere? Sed de hoc alterius disputationis esto. Illud non praetereundum quaedam indirecte fieri, quae fieri directe non possunt. Exemplum in re proposita. Si forte exponantur pueri Iudaeorum, et in alias regiones transferantur ita ut usu potestatis ulterius parentis non habeant habentes illos pro derelictis, et sic inveniantur expositi sine patre, sine matre, quorum misereatur Deus, tunc Ecclesia suo jure quasi rem praeoccupanti expositam potest eos accipere et consecrare baptismo. Iam enim non fit injuria patri de cujus potestate ereptus est. Ac propterea nihil est miri aut novi si quaedam (ut diximus) indirecte fieri possunt, quae directe fieri (f52v) posse negantur.

16. Quod vero postremo loco adiiciebatur, posse invitis parentibus liberos eorum baptizari, nihil facit. Qui professi sunt religionem Christianam Ecclesiae placitis subduntur, de his autem qui foris sunt (ait Apostolus) quid ad nos?[j] Iudaei ergo parentes non sunt obligati Ecclesiae, nec habent nexum Spiritus cum illa. Et ideo filii eorum immundi sunt et non sanctificati, nec per Ecclesiae auxilium sanctificabiles parentibus ipsorum [*emendavi*, ipsius *cod.*] resistentibus sub quorum cura naturali lege et ordine inveniuntur, quae lex evangelica non aufert. Secus est de pueris Christianorum, quorum parentes jam obligati inveniuntur ipsi Ecclesiae ad praebendum pro filiis suis consensum. Quod si non faciunt, Ecclesia et majores supplent quod ipsi maligne subtrahunt filiis suis, qui ex ipso quod in Ecclesia procreantur mundi dicuntur apud B. Paulum, et Sanctificati, idest, habiles redditi

---

i cf. Ezech. 18.20.

j 1 Cor 5.12.

salvation. Therefore, the Gospel law is not violated in this, that the baptism and salvation of children is impeded by the lack of consent of the parents: since in the first place the Gospel law establishes this, that no one should be saved without his own consent. The consent, moreover, or dissent of the parents on behalf of the children is considered in our understanding of the natural law to be the consent or dissent of the children themselves. And the son will not bear the iniquity of the father, because the father himself alone will be punished for his stubbornness. But from the ancient sin the son will only suffer the punishment of loss, or of not profiting, but not the punishment of sense, as is the common opinion of the theologians.

14. That likewise which was brought up in the fourth place he does not conclude rightly. The Canons manifestly have decreed under the heading on the Jews, and it is clearly received in Distinction 14, "On the Jews," from the Council of Toledo. The deed of Zizibut is not really being praised in that Council, since his actions are being disapproved of in the consitution of the Synod, even though he is called "most religious prince." It was quite possible for him to be praiseworthy for his piety and to have zeal, but not according to the opinion. But to return to our affair.

15. This is what I was saying: if the parents themselves are not able to be forced to baptism, of course their sons cannot either. But certainly they would be being forced if, when the parents are resisting, they were to receive baptism. And the law of nature says that the consent and dissent of the parents is the consent and dissent of the children when they are not yet exercising reason. Therefore how can baptism be granted? How can the removal of the natural or divine law belong to the power of a prince? But as for this, let it belong to another disputation. It must not be omitted to say that some things happen indirectly which are not able to be done directly. There is an example in the proposed matter. If perchance the children of Jews should be exposed, and brought over into other regions in such a way that they no longer consider the parents to be in use of their power, considering them to be abandoned, and thus exposed they should be found to be without father, without mother, and God has mercy on them, then the Church within her right is able to receive and consecrate them to baptism, for they are as if a thing exposed to one who cares. For there is here no injury done to the father from whose power he has been snatched away. And therefore it is no wonder, nor is it strange, if some things (as we have said) can be done indirectly that we say cannot be done directly.

16. But that which is added in the last place, that their children can be baptized with the parents unwilling, does nothing. Those who profess the Christian religion are subject to the decrees of the Church, but regarding

ad Sanctificationem, ut possint de communione sanctorum participare.[k] Et quia haec a quibusdam non sunt considerata graviter aberratum est. Et haec satis ad quaestionis resolutionem.

VIII.PRAEF. (F53R) IOANNES ANTONIUS A S. GEORGIO CARD. ALEXANDRINUS IN PRIMAM DECRET. PART. COMMENT. AD CAP. III. QUI SINCERA IBI. QUAERO AN IUDAEIS SUNT AUFERENDI EORUM FILII UT BAPTIZENTUR.

1. Si filii Iudaeorum sint parvuli tunc per Christianos non possunt parvuli eis auferri, ut baptizentur. Nam Panor(mitanus) in dict(o) cap(ite) sicut de Iudaeis dicit, in hoc cap(ite) utitur verbo generali nullus Christianus et sic comprehendit tam principes quam alios quoscumque.

2. Quam sententiam tenent indistincte Cardin(alis) Florent(inus) Ioan(nes) de Anania nempe quod neque princeps neque privatus facere potest baptizari filios Iudaeorum et ita consuluit Card(inalis) cons(ultor) 3. in tit. de Iudaeis.

3. Horum autem opiniones mihi placent qui dicunt [*emendavi*, dicuntur *cod.*] quod propria mentis conversione et libero arbitrio inducendi sunt ad baptismum, quae non intervenirent in dicto baptismo dictorum parvulorum. Et hanc partem tenet Car. in Clem. prima circa finem de Iudaeis et Card. S. Xisti in Capit. de Iudaeis et S. Thomas in 2.2. q. 10 art. 17. et plus dicit do. Card. in d. cap. de Iudaeis, quod parvuli Iudaeorum vel infidelium, si de facto baptizarentur invitis parentibus, non suscipiunt sacramentum. Arg. sic, quod ad baptismum non sufficit quod in recipiente non sit objectum contrariae voluntatis, sed requiritur voluntas directa vel interpretativa. Probatur quia adultus nutritus in nemore qui numquam aliquid audivit de fide vel baptismo est in solo originali. Si talis baptizaretur dormiendo, nihil omnino

---

k cf. 1 Cor 6.11.

those who are outside it (as the Apostle says), what concern is it of ours? Therefore Jewish parents are not obligated to the Church, nor do they have the bond of the Spirit with her. And therefore their sons are unclean and not sanctified, nor are they able to be sanctified through the help of the Church, as long as their parents are resisting, under whose care they are found to be in the natural law and order, which the Gospel law does not take away. It is otherwise in regard to the children of Christians, whose parents are found to be themselves already obligated to the Church, to offer their consent for their children. And if they do not do this, the Church and the elders supply what they themselves wickedly take away from their sons, who are said to be clean, from the fact that they are procreated in the Church, in Blessed Paul, and also sanctified, that is, rendered capable of sanctification, so that they can participate in the communion of the saints. And because these things are not considered by certain persons they have erred gravely. And this is sufficient for the resolution of the question.

VIII. PREF. GIOVANNI ANTONIO SANGIORGIO (D. MARCH 14 OR 28, 1509), CARDINAL OF ALESSANDRIA.[30] I ASK WHETHER THE CHILDREN OF JEWS SHOULD BE TAKEN FROM THEM TO BE BAPTIZED.

1. If the children of Jews should be little, then when they are little they cannot be taken away from them to be baptized by Christians. For Panormitanus in the aforesaid chapter uses the general term "no Christian" and thus comprehends both princes and whomsoever else.

2. And the Florentine Cardinal Giovanni di Anania holds this opinion generally, namely, that neither prince nor private person can make the children of Jews be baptized, and the Cardinal consultor gave this opinion in the third chapter under the title On Jews.

3. But I adopt the opinions of those who are saying that with proper conversion of heart and free will they are to be brought to baptism, which would not interfere with the said baptism of the said little ones. And this is the side that the Cardinal of St. Clement holds in the first about the end regarding Jews and the Cardinal of St. Sixtus in the chapter on the Jews and St. Thomas in the *Secunda Secundae*, question 10, article 7, and the lord Cardinal says more in the distinction chapter on Jews, that the little ones of the Jews or unbelievers, if in fact they were to be baptized with the parents unwilling, do not receive the sacrament. He argues as follows, that for baptism it does not

---

30 Auditor of the Roman Rota, cardinal priest of SS Nereus and Achilleus, "considered the foremost of the jurisconsults of his time" (*habitus sui aevi Iurisconsultorum Princeps*). Augustini Oldoini Athenaeum Romanum, Apud Haeredes Sebastiani Zechini, 1676: 379–80.

esset factum. Et tamen in eo non est obiectum voluntatis contrariae, ergo praeter carentiam obiecti re(f53v)quiritur intentio sive actus voluntatis, vel propriae in adulto vel interpretative; parvulus autem nullam habet voluntatem interpretativam, nisi solum parentum, propter quod consuevit dici quod antiquitus ante datam circumcisionem salvabantur in vide parentum, non autem aliorum, nisi quatenus gerebant vicem parentis. Ergo si invitis parentibus baptizaretur parvulus, nihil videtur sibi fieri cum desit voluntas eorum directa vel interpetrativa.

4. Secundo sic: si in recipiente baptismum necessario requiritur fides Ecclesiae propria, sicut in adulto, vel aliena, sicut in parvulo. Et hoc dicit Augustinus. Sed nulla fides aliena sufficit in parvulo nisi fides parentum, tantum quia alii a parentibus nullum jus habent in eo, quantum quia ipse non pertinet ad Ecclesiam, nisi ratione suae originis: ergo ad hoc baptisma necessaria est fides parentum. Unde Aug. lib. de peccatorum remissione: Mater Ecclesia os maternum parvulis praebet [emendavi, praebat cod.], ut sacris mysteriis imbuantur, quia nondum possunt ore proprio credere ad salutem.[1] Sed isti in nullo pertinent ad fidem Ecclesiae, nisi mediantibus parentibus, cum alii super ipsos nihil juris habeant: ergo deficiente fide et voluntate parentum nihil omnino recipiuntur. Quam opinionem sequens et declarans magis Pet de Paul. in 4. dist. 10. dicit quia homo ordinatur in Deum per rationem, per quam potest Deum cognoscere. Et ideo puer antequam habeat usum rationis ordinatur in Deum per rationem parentum, quorumcurae naturaliter subiacet; secundum eorum dispositionem sunt circa eum [emendavi, cum cod.] agenda divina. (f54r) Unde si puer parentes non habeat, quicumque vult loco parentis ei sit. Et sicut in nutriendo sic in baptizando, et sufficit quia non appareat voluntas parentum contraria. Et si quidem pater et mater Iudaei mortui essent, sicut alioquin quis moritur relicta uxore pregnante quae etiam moritur in patu; vel moriuntur antequam puer habeat usum rationis, tunc propinquiores ei genere sunt tutores legitimi [emendavi, legittimi cod.] loco parentum, unde non debent nec possunt baptizari ipsis invitis, sicut nec parentibus invitis. Sed si non apparent parentes vel propinqui, loco parentum tunc succedit quicumque vult. Et ideo quicumque vellet posset eum tunc baptismo offerre, quia naturalis ratio dictat, ubi parens deficit, alius parens sit, sicut una avis alienos pullos [cod.pc puellos cod.ac] nutrit quando mater deficit.

---

[1] See Augustine, *De Peccatorum meritis et remissione*, ed. C. F. Urba and J. Zycha (Vienna: CSEL, 1913); ST III 68.9 ad. 1.

suffice that there be no objection of contrary will in the recipient, but there is required a direct or representative will. It is proved that an adult raised in the woods who has never heard anything about the faith or baptism is in only original sin. If such a one were to be baptized in his sleep, nothing at all would be done. And yet in him there is not objection of contrary will, therefore beyond the lack of an objection, there is required an intention or act of will, whether his own, in an adult, or representative; but a little one has no representative will except only that of the parents, because of which fact we usually say that of old before circumcision was given they were saved in the faith of their parents, but not of others, except insofar as they carried out the function of a parent. Therefore if a little one were to be baptized with the parents unwilling, nothing seems to be done to him, since their direct or representative will would be lacking.

4. Secondly thus: if in the one receiving baptism the faith of the church is necessarily required, his own, as in an adult, or another's, as in a little one. And Augustine says this. But no other person's faith suffices in a little one except the faith of the parents, as much because others have no right over him from the parents as because he himself does not pertain to the Church except on account of his origin: therefore the faith of the parents is necessary for this baptism. Whence Augustine says in the book *On the Remission of Sins*: "Mother Church offers her maternal mouth to her little ones so that they may be steeped in the sacred mysteries, because they are not yet able with their own mouth to believe for salvation."[31] But they pertain to the faith of the Church in no way except through the mediation of the parents, since others have no legal rights over them. Therefore if the faith and will of the parents is lacking, nothing is received at all. And following this opinion and declaring more, Peter Paludanus in distinction 10 of the *Commentary on the Four Sentences* says that man is ordered to God through reason, though which he is able to come to know God. And so the boy before he has the use of reason is ordered to God through the reason of the parents, to whose care he lies naturally subject; matters relating to God regarding him must be done according to their disposition. Therefore, if the boy should not have parents, whoever is willing would be in the place of a parent for him. And just as in upbringing, so in baptizing it also suffices that there should not appear the contrary will of the parents. And if indeed a Jewish father and the mother were dead, just as otherwise someone dies leaving a pregnant wife, and she too dies in childbirth, or they die before the boy has the use of reason,

---

[31] Note, however, that here Giovanni Antonio Sangiorgio is quoting St. Thomas, not Augustine, the latter having *praestat* where the former has the synonyom *praebet* (our manuscript in fact has praebat).

5. Ex his omnibus colligitur quod sicut parentes non possunt cogi ad ea quae sunt fidei subjecta ad legem naturae, et, si coacti non consensientes recipiant baptismum, nihil est actum, sic filii contra eorum voluntatem in his quae sunt pure juris divini, et voluntatem veram requirunt vel interpretativam: nec debet fieri nec factum valet.

(f54v)
IX. PRAEF. **(F55R)** CARDINAL. IOAN. DE TURRE CREMATA SUPER DECRETO PRIMA PARS DISTINCT. 45. CAP. DE IUDAEIS.

1. Ad idem subjungit hoc caput quod est Concilii Toletani in quo Sancta Synodus disponit quod Iudaei non sunt cogendi ad fidem. . . Pro pleniori intelligentia hujus capitis quaeruntur hic quatuor.

   1. Primum est utrum Iudaei ad fidem sint compellendi.
   2. Secundum est utrum inviti, sive coacti baptizati suscipiunt sacramentum.
   3. Tertium est, utrum parvuli Iudaeorum sint invitis parentibus baptizandi.
   4. Quartum est utrum parvuli eorum invitis parentibus baptizati suscipiant characterem baptismalem.

2. Ad primum sic proceditur. Et videtur quod Iudaei et infideles sint ad fidem compellendi. Primo sic ex illo Luc. 14. uti dicitur: Exi in vias [*emendavi*, Ex invias *cod.*] et semitas et compelle intrare ut impleatur domus mea.[m] Sed homines in domum Dei, id est Ecclesiam, intrant per fidem. Ergo videtur quod aliqui qui sunt extra (cujusmodi sunt infideles) sunt compellendi ad fidem.

3. Secundum arguitur ex illo Act. 9, ubi habetur quod Paulus coactus conversus est ad fidem Christi. Ille autem, qui poena corporis ad Evangelicum coactus introivit, plus omnibus his laboravit, qui solo verbo vocati sunt in

---

m Cf. Luke 14.23.

then his next of kin are the legitimate guardians in the place of the parents, whence they must not and are not able to be baptized if they are unwilling, just as they are not when the parents are unwilling. But if the parents or kin are not in evidence, then whoever is willing comes to the place of the parents. And therefore whoever were willing would be able to offer him then to baptism, because natural reason dictates, when the parent is lacking, there should be another parent, just as one bird raises another's chicks, when the mother is lacking.

5. From all this we gather that just as the parents are not able to be forced to the things that are of the faith and subject to the law of nature, and if, without consenting, they should be forced to receive baptism, nothing is done, so the children against their will in the things that are purely of the divine law, and they require the true or representative will: it neither ought to be done, nor, if done, is it valid.

IX. PREF. CARDINAL GIOVANNI DI TURRE CREMATA ON THE *DECRETUM*, FIRST PART, DISTINCTION 45, CHAPTER ON THE JEWS.

1. To the same he joins this chapter, which is of the Council of Toledo, in which the Holy Synod disposes that Jews are not to be forced to the faith.... For fuller understanding of this chapter the following four questions are asked.
   1. The first is whether Jews are to be compelled to the faith.
   2. The second is whether, if they are baptized while unwilling or forced, they receive the sacrament.
   3. The third is whether the little ones of the Jews are to be baptized with the parents unwilling.
   4. The fourth is whether their little ones, baptized with the parents unwilling, receive the baptismal character.

2. We thus proceed to the first. It also seems that Jews and unbelievers are to be compelled to the faith. In the first place it is thus from the passage in Luke 14, when it is said: "Go out into the roads and lanes and make them enter, so that my house will be filled."[32] But men enter into the house of God, that is the Church, through faith. Therefore, it seems that some who are outside (and unbelievers are of this sort) are to be compelled to the faith.

3. Second, it is argued from the passage of Acts 9, where it is held that Paul was forced and converted to the faith of Christ. But he, who was forced and entered into the work of the Gospel under the punishment of the body, toiled

---

32 See Luke 14:23.

Evangelio. Cur ergo cogeret Ecclesia perditos filios ut redirent, si perditi filii coegerunt alios ut perirent?

4. Tertio ad idem arguitur ex Cap. jam vero ea causa et q. ubi ait Beatus Gregorius scribens Maximo (f55v) Episcopo: "Iam vero si rusticus tantae perfidiae et obstinationis fuerit inventus, ut ad dominum minime venire consentiat tanto pensionis onere gravandus est ut ipsa exactionis suae poena compellatur ad rectitudinem festinare [*emendavi*, festinere *cod.*]."[n]

5. In oppositum est text(us) praesentis c(ausae) resp(onsionis).

6. Iuxta autem S. Thom. in II[a]-IIae q. 10 a. 8 quum infidelium quidam sunt qui numquam susceperunt fidem, sicut Gentiles et Iudaei, de istis ponitur conclusio quod tales nullo modo sunt ad fidem compellendi. Ista conclusio habetur in praesenti c(ausa) et probatur ex illo quod dicit beatus Augustinus, quod caetera potest homo nolens, credere autem non nisi volens, sed voluntas cogi non potest. Ergo conclusio vera, videlicet, quod tales infideles non sunt cogendi ad fidem. Ista conclusio est autem Raymundi in Summa Titul. de Iudaeis et Saracenis, sic dicentis, debent ad fidem auctoritatibus, rationibus, et blandimentis potius adduci quam asperitatibus; seu provocari debent; non autem compelli, quia coacta servitia Deo non placent, sed sincera. Item deducit Petrus de Palude in 4. dis. 4. Hoc etiam convenit cum divina prohibitione: a Sanctis nempe traditum habemus quod non est voluntas Dei quod Iudaei occidantur (Psal. 58): Ne occidas eos, ne unquam obliviscantur populi mei. Item quum prophetia [*emendavi*, prophetias *cod.*] praedicatione Enoch et Heliae sunt convertendi, unde usque vult Deus in sua caecitate tolerari, si autem ipsi vel eorum filii ipsis invitis baptizarentur, tunc nullo tempore Enoch et Eliae invenirentur, nec per consequen(tiam) prophetia verificaretur.

7. Ad rationes in oppositum dicendum. Ad primam de Evangelio Luc. 14. respondetur juxta Hugonem Cardinalem super (f56r) Lucam qui loquitur de compulsione per instantiam praedicationis, et non de compulsione per poenas aliquas corporales. Unde S. Thoma(s) in quaest(ione) de verit(ate) q. 22 a. 9 dicit quod compulsio illa de qua fit mentio Luc. 14. non est coactio sed efficacia persuasionis.[o]

---

n Greg. Mag. *Ep.* 4.26 (PL 77 col. 695A).

o *Quaestiones de Veritate* q. 22 a. 9 ad. 7: Ad septimum dicendum quod compulsio illa de qua ibi fit mentio, non est coactionis, sed efficacis persuasionis, vel per aspera, vel per lenia.

more than all those who were called in the Gospel by word alone. Why then would the Church force her lost children to return, if the lost children forced others to perish?

4. Third, on the same point it is argued from the chapter just now on this cause and question, when Blessed Gregory says, writing to Bishop Maximus: "But now if a country person of such faithlessness and obstinacy should have been found to consent to come to the Lord minimally, he is to be burdened with such a weight of obligation as to be compelled by the very penalty of the demand upon him to hasten to rectitude."

5. On the other side is the text of the present respondeo.

6. Now, according to Saint Thomas in the *Secunda Secundae*, question 10, article 8, whenever there are any unbelievers that have never received the faith, such as Gentiles and Jews, the conclusion is posited regarding them that such are in nowise to be compelled to the faith.[33] That conclusion is held in the present case and is proven from that which blessed Augustine says, that man is able to do everything else unwillingly, but believing he cannot do except willingly, but the will is not able to be forced: therefore the conclusion is true, when it says that such unbelievers are not to be forced to the faith. That, moreover, is the conclusion of Raymond in the *Summa* on Jews and Saracens, when he says thus: they ought to be brought to the faith by authorities, reasons, and enticements, rather than by rough treatments; or they ought to be called upon; but they ought not to be forced, because it is not forced service that is pleasing to God, but sincere. Likewise Peter Paludanus in Distinction 4.4. This also fits with the divine prohibition: we have it handed down from the saints, at least, that it is not the will of God that Jews be killed (Psalm 58): Do not kill them, lest ever my people should be forgotten. Likewise, as the prophecy states, they are to be converted at the preaching of Enoch and Elijah, whence as long as God wills them to be tolerated in their blindness, but if they themselves or their children were to be baptized while they are unwilling, then at no time would Enoch and Elijah be found, nor, consequently, would the prophecy come true.

7. We must speak in opposition to the arguments. To the first, regarding Luke's Gospel, chapter 14, the response is according to Cardinal Hugh on Luke, that he speaks about "compulsion" through the persistence of preaching, and not about compulsion though any corporal punishments. Whence Saint Thomas in the *Question Regarding Truth*, question 22, article 9, says

---

33 ST II.II 10.8: "Respondeo dicendum quod infidelium quidam sunt qui nunquam susceperunt fidem, sicut gentiles et Iudaei. Et tales nullo modo sunt ad fidem compellendi, ut ipsi credant, quia credere voluntatis est."

8. Ad Secundum respondetur, negando consequentiam. Dicit nempe Hug. in c. quis non potest 2. 3. q. 4. ubi eadem auctoritas Augustini ponitur, si quis vellet a simili argumentari, ut sicut Paulus, qui non habebat ad fidem ingressum, coactus est converti; ita etiam infideles ad fidem sunt cogendi, dico quod non est trahendum ad consequentiam, licet Augus(tinus) inde argumentatur hoc a Domino factum est de Apostolo, cui nemo dicit, "Cur ita facis?" Haec ille. Praeterea non argumentatur Augustinus quod ex exemplo Christi Ecclesia cogat infideles, qui numquam habuerunt fidem, sed quod cogat eos qui reinciperunt redire ad fidem quam susceperant, ut notanter dicit textus. Cur ergo non cogeret Ecclesia perditos filios ut redirent? Aliud est nempe redire ad fidem et aliud fidem de nova capere. Et potest dici quod licet Paulus a principio fuit renuens et contradicens Ecclesiae Dei, tamen postea factus est spontaneus cum dixit, Domine quid me vis facere; unde consentiens et non invitus [*emendavi*, invitas *cod.*] suscipit fidem.

9. Ad tertium respondetur quod c(ontra) illud loquitur de apostatis et non de paganis, aut Iudaeis, et ita non est ad propositum.

10. Ad Secundum, nempe utrum inviti sive coacti baptizati suscipiant sacramentum opponitur primo. Dicit August(ine) in Enchirid(io), "Multa bona praestantur invitis, quando eorum (f56v) compellitur utilitati non voluntati, quia ipsimet inveniuntur inimici," sed magnum praestatur beneficium, quoniam praestatur sacramentum, quo liberatur a culpa, et a poena et maxime consulitur utilitati.[p] Secundo in lege mundana est quod aliquis potest solvere pro alio et liberare eum a debito temporali ipso invito et contradicente, ergo videtur quod similiter aliquis possit praestare beneficium spirituale alicui invito et contradicenti, et liberare eum a debito spirituali. Tertio baptismus est remedium contra originale peccatum, sed peccatum originale contrahitur necessario nullo existente assensu voluntatis, ergo videtur quod baptismus similiter posset conferri alicui absque omni consensu voluntatis recipientis, sed hoc videtur conferri invito. Quarto parvulus et furiosus recipiunt sacramenta quantumcumque renuant, ergo videtur quod etiam adultus invite baptizatus suscipiet sacramentum.

---

[p] Cf. Augustine, *Enchiridion* 19.72: Multa bona praestantur invitis, quando eorum compellitur utilitati non voluntati, quia ipsi sibi inveniuntur esse inimici.

APPENDIX B

that that compulsion about which mention is made in Luke 14 is not forcing but the efficacy of persuasion.

8. To the second the response is by denying the consequence. Hugh of course says in the commentary that someone is not able (2. 3. q. 4) when the same authority of Augustine is posited. If anyone wanted to make the argument from the like—how just as Paul, who did not have a way in to the faith, was forced to convert, so also the unbelievers are to be forced to the faith—I say that it is not to be drawn to the consequence, although Augustine argues from this that that this was done by the Lord concerning the Apostle, to whom no one says, "Why do you do this?" This is what he says. Furthermore, Augustine does not argue that from the example of Christ the Church should force unbelievers who have never had the faith, but that she should force those who have begun to return again to the faith that they had received, as the text notably says. Why then will the Church not force her lost children to return? It is of course one thing to return to the faith, and another to get it in the first place. And it can be said that although Paul at first was refusing and speaking against the Church of God, nevertheless afterwards he came to it of his own free will when he said, "Lord, what do you want me to do?"; when he received the faith by consent and not unwillingly.[34]

9. The response to the third is that on the contrary that is said regarding apostates and not pagans or Jews, and so it is not relevant to the proposed.

10. To the second, namely whether they receive the sacrament if they are baptized unwillingly or forced, it is opposed to the first. Augustine says in the *Handbook*, "Many goods are presented to them who are unwilling when their utility, not their will, is being forced, because they themselves are found to be enemies," but a great benefit is being presented to them, since the sacrament is being presented to them by which freedom from fault and punishment is granted, and principally their utility is being consulted.[35] Secondly: in the law of the world is the fact that someone can pay for another and free him from a temporal debt, even if the person himself is unwilling and speaking against it, therefore it seems that similarly someone could present the spiritual benefit to someone unwilling and speaking against it, and free him from his spiritual debt. Thirdly, baptism is the remedy against original sin, but original sin is contracted necessarily with no existing assent of the will, therefore it seems that baptism similarly could be conferred on someone apart from

---

34 Acts 9:6, 22:10.

35 Cf. Augustine *Enchiridion* 19.72 (with emphasis added to show the difference), which gives a different meaning: "Many goods are presented to them who are unwilling when their utility, not their will, is being forced, because they themselves are found to be enemies *to themselves*."

11. His habitis veniendum est ad rationes in oppositum. Ad primam rationem respondetur negando consequentiam, dicimus: Iuxta magistrum Alexandrum de Hallis quod si fuerit invitus, licet posset sibi praestare beneficium temporale, non tamen beneficium baptismi, et ratio est quia sicut beneficium gratiae gratis facientis non praestatur ei qui imponit obicem voluntatis, sic nec sacramentum baptismi, quod disponit ad gratiam, non datur ei qui ponit obicem voluntatis. Ad Secundam respondetur negando consequentiam, et ratio est quia non est simile de debito spirituali et temporali. Spirituale nam debitum ita radicatur in voluntate quod manente voluntate necessaria manet debitum hujus, unde nullo (f57r) modo potest aliquis adultus ad hoc debito liberari nisi adulta radice in voluntate. Non est sic de debito temporali. Praeterea beneficio hujusmodi ingressus in Ecclesiam, ingressus nempe ad unitatem Ecclesiae, non est in adulto nisi annuente voluntate aliquo modo. Ad tertiam respondetur juxta Divum Bonaventuram negando consequentiam, et ratio est quia non est simile de peccato originali et de remedio baptismi, quum originalis contractio sit [*emendavi*, est *cod.*] quasi naturalis et ideo inevitabilis. Ad remedium baptismi non respicit naturam, sed potius voluntatem personae, et ita non est simile de parvulo et de furioso et de adulto, quia illi non habent usum voluntatis unde non statur appetitui eorum, sed voluntati offerentium.

12. Ad tertium videlicet, utrum parvuli Iudaeorum sint invitis parentibus baptizandi sic conceditur. Et videtur quod pueri Iudaeorum et vel aliorum infidelium sint baptizandi parentibus invitis. Primo sic; magis debet subveniri homini contra periculum mortis aeternae, quam contra periculum mortis temporalis existenti. Est subveniendum etiam si parentes propter maliciam contra niterentur. Ergo multo magis est subveniendum pueris infidelium contra periculum mortis aeternae etiam invitis parentibus. Secundo sic. Majus est vinculum matrimoniale quam jus patriae potestatis quia jus patriae potestatis potest per hominem solvi, cum filius familias mancipatur, vinculum autem matrimoniale non potest solvi per hominem, secundum illud Mat. 19: Quos Deus conjuxit homo non separet, sed propter infidelitatem solvitur vinculum matrimoniale. Dicit Apostolus 1. ad Cor. 7: (f57v) Quod si infidelis discedit, discedat et, ut dicit, glossa non cogitur fidelis sequi infidelem odio fidei discedentem. Ergo multo magis propter infidelitatem tollitur jus patriae potestatis in suos filios. Possunt ergo eorum filii baptizari eis invitis. Tertio sic. Quilibet homo magis est Dei a quo habet animam quam

any consent of the will of the receiver, but this seems to be conferred on one unwilling. Fourthly, a little one and a madman receive the sacraments however much they refuse, therefore it seems that even the adult baptized unwillingly will receive the sacrament.

11. With this in mind we must come to the arguments on the opposite side. To the first argument the response goes by denying the consequence. We say with the master Alexander of Hales that if he has been unwilling, even though he could present him with a temporal benefit, nevertheless he could not present him with the benefit of baptism, and the reason is that just as the benefit of grace that acts freely is not presented to him who places in the way a barrier of the will, so the sacrament of baptism, which disposes to grace, is also not given to him who places a barrier of the will.[36] To the second the response goes by denying the consequence, and the reason is that the case of a spiritual debt and a temporal debt are not alike. For the spiritual debt is so rooted in the will that as long as the necessary will remains, the debt for it remains, whence in no way can an adult be freed from this debt except from the root in the adult will. It is not so in the case of a temporal debt. Furthermore, an entrance into the Church by a benefit of this kind, that is an entrance to the unity of the Church, does not exist in an adult except one who is in some way affirming it. To the third the response goes according to the Divine Bonaventure, by denying the consequence, and the reason is that it is not like the case of original sin and the remedy of baptism, when the contraction of original sin is as if natural and therefore inevitable. For the remedy of baptism he does not look to nature, but rather to the will of the person, and so the case of a little one and a madman is not like that of an adult, because they do not have the use of the will, whence their appetite has no standing, but the will of those who are offering them does.

12. To the third, that is to say, whether the little ones of the Jews should be baptized with the parents unwilling, it is conceded thus. And it seems that the children of the Jews or even of other unbelievers should be baptized even if the parents are unwilling. In the first place thus: there is greater need to help the man against the danger of eternal death than against the danger of temporal death, when he is in it. He is even to be helped if his parents through malice strive against it. Therefore, much more are the children of unbelievers to be helped against the danger of eternal death even if the parents are unwilling. Secondly thus.[37] The matrimonial bond is greater than the right of patria potestas, because the right of patria potestas can be broken by man

---

[36] Alexander of Hales (c. 1185–1245), Franciscan.
[37] For this second argument see ST II.II 10.12 arg. 1.

patris carnalis a quo habet corpus. Non ergo est injustum si pueri Iudaeorum carnalibus parentibus auferantur.

13. Secunda opinio est huic contraria videlicet quod non sit licitum parvulos Iudaeorum invitis parentibus baptizare. Ista opinio quae est S. Thomae fulcitur et corroboratur multiplici ratione. Prima est juxta S. Thomam in 2.2. q. 10 a. 12 co. [*emendavi*, q. 10 arg. 12 *cod.*]:[q] maxime habet auctoritatem consuedudo Ecclesiae ita ut in omnibus semper est aemulanda, quia etiam ipsa doctrina Catholicorum doctorum ab Ecclesia auctoritatem habet, unde magis standum est auctoritati Ecclesiae quam auctoritati Augustini vel Hieronymi, vel cujuscumque doctoris, sed hoc usus Ecclesiae numquam habuit quod Iudaeorum filii invitis parentibus baptizarentur, quamvis fuerint retroactis temporibus multi Catholici principes potentissimi, ut Constantinus, Theodosius. Ad ergo tale nullo modo est attendendum. Secundo sic, si est forte licitum, probabile esset quod primi sancti et rectores Ecclesiae hac consuluissent principibus, quos habuerunt valde favorabiles ut Sylvester Constantinum et Ambrosius Theodosium, hoc autem numquam legitur fecisse ergo non est probabile quod hoc posset fieri licite. Tertio quia hoc videtur esse contra jus naturale. Filius enim est aliquid patris, et primo quidem non distinguitur a parentibus, nam corpus dum est in utero **(f58r)** matris postea natus ex utero carnali, antequam habeat usum liberi arbitrii, continetur sub cura parentum, quasi in quodam utero spirituali: quamdiu usum rationis non habet puer non differt ab animali irrationali, unde sicut bos et equus est alicujus ut utatur eo quum voluerit, secundum jus civile, sicut proprio instrumento, ita de jure naturali est ut filius antequam habeat usum rationis sit sub cura patris, unde contra justitiam naturalem esset si puer antequam habeat usum rationis a cura parentum subtraheretur, vel de eo aliquid ordinetur invitis parentibus. Quarto quia hoc esset valde

---

q The reference must be to ST II.II 10.12 co. The original reading of "arg. 12" would be impossible, as no article of question ten has twelve, or, for that matter, even ten, responses to arguments.

whenever a son is emancipated from his family, but the matrimonial bond cannot be broken by man, according to the passage in Matthew 19: "Whom God has joined, let man not separate," but because of unbelief the matrimonial bond is broken. The Apostle says in the first letter to the Corinthians, chapter 7: "But if an unbeliever departs, let him depart," and, as he says, the faithful tongue is not forced to follow the unbeliever who is departing through hatred of the faith. Therefore, much more because of unbelief is the right of patria potestas taken away over one's children. Therefore, their children can be baptized when they are unwilling. Thirdly thus.[38] Any man is more of God, from whom he has his life, than of his carnal father, from whom he has his body. It is not therefore unjust if the children of Jews should be taken away from their carnal parents.

13. The second opinion is contrary to this: namely, that it would not be licit to baptize the little ones of Jews with the parents unwilling. That opinion, which is St. Thomas's, is supported and corroborated with multiple reasons. The first is, according to St. Thomas, in the *Secunda Secundae*, question 10, article 12:[39] the custom of the Church especially has authority so that in all things it is to be followed, because even the teaching itself of Catholic doctors has its authority from the Church, whence one must stand more on the authority of the Church than the authority of Augustine or Jerome or any doctor whatsoever. But the usage of the Church never did hold this, that the children of Jews should be baptized with the parents unwilling, although there have been in times gone by many very powerful Catholic princes, e.g., Constantine and Theodosius. Therefore, in no way must we pay regard to such a thing. Secondly thus: if it is perhaps licit, it would be probable that the first saints and leaders of the Church would have given this counsel to the earthly princes whom they held in strong favor, as Sylvester did Constantine, and Ambrose did Theodosius. But nowhere do we read that they did this, therefore it is not probable that this could be done licitly. Thirdly, because this seems to be against natural law. For the son is something of the father, and at first at least is not distinguished from the parents, for the body, while it is in the womb of the mother, afterwards, having been born from the carnal womb, before it has the use of free will, is contained under the care of the parents, as if in a kind of spiritual womb: as long as he does not have the use of reason, the boy does not differ from an irrational animal, whence just as a cow and horse is someone's, so that he may use it whenever he wants, according to civil law, as his own instrument, so it is from natural law that the

---

[38] For this third argument see ST II.II 10.12 arg. 4.
[39] For this paragraph see ST II.II 10.12.

periculosum, si enim pueri nondum usum rationis habentes baptismum susciperent, postmodum, cum ad perfectam aetatem pervenirent, de facili possent a parentibus induci ut relinquerent quod ignorantes susceperunt, quod vergeret in fidei detrimentum. Econtra constat quod principes non possunt licite compellere Iuaeos adultos ad suscipiendum baptismum, ut habetur expresse in cap(itulo) praesenti, ergo per consequens non debet eis vim inferri auferendo filios eorum ut baptizentur, cum voluntas filii parvuli sit voluntas patris, quousque usum habeat rationis.

14. His habitis dicendum est ad rationes in oppositum, tam in principio positas quam inductas pro prima opinione. Ad primam respondetur in S. Thoma quod a morte corporali non est aliquis eripiendus contra ordinem juris civilis, puta si aliquis a suo judice condemnetur ad mortem temporalem nullus debet eum violenter eripere. Unde nec aliquis debet rumpere ordinem juris naturalis, quo filius est sub cura patris, ut eum [*emendavi*, cum *cod.*] (f58v) liberet a periculo mortis aeternae. Ad secundam respondetur negando consequentiam, et ratio est secundum S. Thomam quia non est simile, quia in vinculo matrimoniali uterque conjugum habet usum liberi arbitrii et uterque potest invito alio fidei assentire, sed hoc in puero non habet locum antequam habeat usum rationis; tunc tenet similitudo, si converti voluerit. Ad tertiam respondetur negando consequentiam, et ratio est secundum S. Thom. tam in 3. part. quam in *Secunda Secundae* et Dom. Durandum; quia cum baptizari ad jus divinum pertineat, unde quantum ad hoc quum parvulus est aliquid parentis, quantum ad ea quae Dei sunt, quantum ad usum liberi arbitrii: ergo princeps non potest parvulum violenter recipere invito parente ut baptizetur. Ad quintam [*emendavi*, quintum *cod.*] respondetur negando consequentiam et ratio est secundum jam dicta, quia in illis quae ad jus divinum pertinent non subijciuntur principibus.[r]

15. Ad quartum nempe utrum parvuli Iudaeorum invitis parentibus baptizati suscipiant sacramentum sic proceditur: et videtur quod parvuli Iudaeorum invitis parentibus baptizati suscipiant caracterem baptismalem. Respondetur [*emendavi*, Respondes *cod.*]: hic sunt duae opiniones, quarum [*emendavi*, quorum *cod.*] prima quod sic. Alia opinio est contraria dicens quod non. Pro

---

[r] It will be noticed here that the sequence of this paragraph is: *ad primam . . . ad secundam . . . ad tertiam . . . ad quintum.*

son, before he has the use of reason, is under the care of the father, whence it would be against natural justice if the boy, before he has the use of reason, should be dragged away from the care of the parents, or for anything to be ordained regarding him with the parents unwilling. Fourthly, because this would be very dangerous, for if children who do not yet have the use of reason were to receive baptism, afterwards when they were come to mature age they could easily be led by their parents to abandon what they received unknowingly, which borders on a ruination of the faith. Contrariwise it is settled that princes cannot licitly compel adult Jews to receive baptism, as is held expressly in the present chapter, therefore consequently force ought not to be brought to bear upon them in taking away their children so that they may be baptized, since the will of the little son is the will of the father until he has the use of reason.

14. With this in mind we must speak to the arguments on the opposite side, both those posited in the beginning and those introduced in favor of the first opinion. To the first the response is found in St. Thomas that no one is to be snatched away from bodily death against the order of civil law, for example, if someone should be condemned by his judge to temporal death, no one ought to snatch him away violently. Whence it is also that no one ought to break the order of natural law, by which the son is under the care of the father, to free him from the danger of eternal death. To the second the response goes by denying the consequence, and the reason is, according to St. Thomas, that it is not alike, because in the matrimonial bond each of the spouses has the use of free will and each is able, even if the other is unwilling, to assent to the faith, but this has no place in a boy before he has the use of reason; at *that* time the likeness holds, if he wants to convert. To the third the response goes by denying the consequence, and the reason is according to St. Thomas in the *Tertia* as well as in the *Secunda Secundae*, and in Dom Durand: that since being baptized pertains to divine law, whence as much as pertains to this, since the little one is something of the parent, as much as pertains to the things that are of God, as much as pertains to the use of free will: therefore a prince cannot violently take a little one for it to be baptized with the parent unwilling.

15. So we proceed to the fourth, namely whether little ones of the Jews baptized with the parents unwilling receive the sacrament: and it seems that little ones of the Jews baptized with the parents unwilling receive the baptismal character. The response goes: here there are two opinions, of which the first is yes. The other opinion is contrary, saying no. For the first the argument goes as follows. The Jew or the unbeliever has no more over his son than the faithful Christian over his, but if the son of a Christian parent is baptized

prima arguitur sic. Non plus habet Iudaeus vel infidelis super filium suum quam fidelis super suum, sed si filius parentis Christiani baptizatur invito parente recipit verum baptismum, ergo similiter si filius infidelis vel Iudaei recipiet verum Sacramentum baptismi ergo etc. Secundo idem videtur probari ex illo quod scribitur de cons. distincio 4. c. parvuli ubi videtur in(f59r) sinuare quod parvulis sufficit [*emendavi*, sufficet *cod*.] fides offerentium non facta mentione de fide parentum. Tertio sic ad susceptionem baptismi sufficit quod non inveniatur in recipiente obex contraria voluntatis, ut patet in parvulis Christianorum qui ante baptismum sunt pares parvulis. Iudaeorum sed in parvulo cujuslibet Iudaei vel infidelis non est obex contrariae voluntatis. Ergo tales suscipiunt verum Sacramentum.

16. Pro secunda opinione nempe quod [*supplevi*] parvuli Iudaeorum, si de facto baptizentur invitis parentibus, non suscipiunt caractherem, arguitur sic. Ad baptismum non sufficit quod in recipiente non sit obex contrariae voluntatis, sed requiritur voluntas directa vel interpretativa. Probatio ponatur quod adultus nutritus in nemore qui numquam aliquid audivit de fide vel de baptismo et est in solo peccato originali, si talis baptizaretur dormiendo nihil omnino esset factum, et tamen in eo non est obex voluntatis. Ergo praeter carentiam obicis requiritur intentio sive actus voluntatis, vel propriae in adulto vel interpretativae in parvulo. Parvulus autem nullam habet voluntatem interpretativam nisi per parentes; propter quod consuevit dici antiquitus, ante datam circumcisionem salvabantur in fide parentum, non autem aliorum nisi quatenus gerebant vicem parentis, ergo si invitis parentibus baptizatur parvulus, nihil fieri, cum desit voluntas vel directa vel interpretativa. Secundo sic: parvulus ita est res patris in pertinentibus ad jus humanum sicut ovis et agnus, sed qui violenter eripit ovem vel agnum non propter hoc acquirit in eo jus in foro humano, ergo similiter si quis rapit parvulum (f59v) non propter hoc acquirit in eo jus et dominium. Oportet autem quod offerens parvulum ad baptismum in ipso habeat aliquod jus et dominium. Tertio in recipiente baptismum necessario requiritur fides Ecclesiae propria sicut in adulto vel aliena, sicut in parvulo. Et hoc expresse dicit S. Aug.: sed nulla fides sufficit parvulo nisi fides parentum, tum quia alii nullum jus habent in eum, tum quia ipse non pertinet ad Ecclesiam nisi ratione stirpis suae; ergo ad hoc ut baptismum recipiat est necessaria fides parentum. Unde Augustinus in *lib. de Peccat. remissione* inquit. "Ecclesia os maternum parvulis praebet ut sacris mysteriis imbuantur, quia nondum possunt ore proprio credere ad salutem." Sed isti nullo modo pertinent ad Ecclesiam nisi mediantibus parentibus cum alii super ipsos nihil omnino recipiunt.

with the parent unwilling, he receives true baptism, therefore similarly if the son of the unbeliever or Jew, he will receive the true sacrament of baptism, therefore, etc. Secondly, the same seems to be proven from the fact that it is written in the *De Cons.*, Distinction 4, "little ones," where it seems to insinuate that the faith of those who offer them suffices for little ones, with no mention made of the faith of the parents. Thirdly, it so suffices for the reception of baptism that there be not found in the receiver a barrier of contrary will, as is plain in the little ones of Christians who before baptism are equal to the little ones of Jews, but in the little one of whatsoever Jew or unbeliever there is no barrier of contrary will. Therefore, such receive the true sacrament.

16. For the second opinion, namely, that the little ones of the Jews, if they should in fact be baptized with the parents unwilling, do not receive the character, the argument goes as follows. For baptism it does not suffice that there should be no barrier of contrary will in the receiver, but the direct or representative will is required. As proof it may be posited that an adult raised in the woods who never has heard anything about the faith or about baptism and is in only original sin, if such were baptized in the act of sleeping, nothing at all would happen and yet in him there is not a barrier of will. Therefore, beyond the lack of a barrier is required the intention or act of the will, either one's own will in the adult, or representative will in a little one. But the little one has not representative will except through the parents, because of which it is usually said that in ancient times before circumcision was given they were saved in the faith of the parents, but not of others except insofar as they carried out the role of the parent; therefore that if a little one is baptized with the parents unwilling, nothing happens, since the will, whether direct or representative, is lacking. Secondly thus: the little one is so far a thing of the father in things that pertain to human law as the sheep and the lamb is, but those who violently snatch away the little one do not for this reason acquire a right and dominion over it, but it is necessary that the one who offers the little one for baptism should have some right and dominion over it. Thirdly, in the one receiving baptism there is necessarily required the faith of the Church, his own in the case of an adult, or another's in the case of a little one. And St. Augustine says this expressly: "But no faith suffices for a little one except the faith of the parents, both because others have no right over him, and because he himself has nothing to do with the Church except in respect to his lineage; therefore, for him to receive baptism the faith of the parents is necessary." Whence Augustine in the book *On the Remission of Sins* says, "The Church offers her maternal mouth to her little ones so that they may be steeped in the sacred mysteries, because they are not yet able with their own mouth to believe for salvation." But in no way do they have to do with

17. Quam opinionem sequens et declarans magis D. Petrus de Palude dicit sic in IV Sentent(iarum) dist(inctione) IV quod homo ordinatur ad Deum per rationem per quam potest Deum cognoscere, et ideo pueri antequam habeant usum rationis ordinantur ad Deum per rationem parentum quorum curae naturaliter subjacent. Propter quam eorum dispositionem sunt circa eum [*emendavi*, cum *cod.*] agenda divina, unde si puer parentes non habet, vel non apparent [*emendavi*, comparent *cod.*], quicumque vult loco parentum ei sit, et sicut in nutriendo sic et in baptizando, et sufficit quod non appareat voluntas parentum contraria, sed si non apparent nec parentes nec propinqui loco parentum [parentium *cod.ac*] succedit tunc quicumque vult et ideo quicumque vellet posset eum tunc baptismo offerre qui naturalis ratio dictat ut **(f60r)** cui parens deficit alius parens sit. Ex his omnibus colligitur [colligetur *cod.ac*] quod, sicut parentes non possunt cogi ad ea quae sunt purae fidei, et si coacti non consentientes recipiunt baptismum nihil est actum, sic filii in eis quae sunt juris divini vel voluntatem veram requirunt vel interpretativam, nec debet fieri, nec factum valet; sed quicumque parentum consentit cujuscumque aetatis parvulus existat in favorem fidei videtur baptizandus, quia de patre expressum est extr. de convers. in Si. c. 2. De Matre vero contrar. de facto in Aug.

18. Si quis vult tenere hanc opinionem respondebitur rationibus factis pro prima opinione. Ad primam respondetur negando consequentiam, quia non est simile et ratio est quia Ecclesia prodest fidelibus non solum in actibus civilibus, sed et in his quae ad cultum Dei pertinent. Et ideo si Christianus utatur re sua contra divinum cultum, non injuriatur Ecclesia si privet eum [*emendavi*, cum *cod.*] re sua et deputet eam ad usum debitum. Et in hoc casu voluntas Ecclesiae est voluntas parvuli interpretativa [*emendavi*, inter putativa *cod.*], quia Ecclesia habet interpretrari voluntatem parentis, imo, ut verius dicatur, voluntas Ecclesiae est magis voluntas parvuli interpretativa quam voluntas parentis carnalis, eo quod de jure voluntas parentis carnalis fidelis subest voluntati Ecclesiae, non sic autem est de parvulis infidelium, quia ante baptismum non subsunt Ecclesiae, nec ratione quae filii nec ratione parentum, ut sic voluntas Ecclesiae possit esse voluntas eorum interpretativa quoque modo.

the Church except with the parents as mediators, when others get nothing at all over them.

17. And following this opinion and declaring it more, Dom Peter Paludanus says thus in the Fourth Book on the *Sentences*, Distinction Four, that man is ordered to God through reason, through which he is able to come to know God, and so children before they have the use of reason are ordered to God through the reason of the parents to whose care they naturally lie subject. And the divine things are to be done regarding him according to this disposition of theirs, whence if a boy does not have parents or they do not appear, he would have whoever is willing in the place of parents, as in upbringing so also in baptizing, and it suffices that there should not appear a contrary will of the parents, but if they do not appear, neither parents, nor kin, then whoever is willing succeeds to the place of the parents, and therefore whoever would be willing would be able to offer him then for baptism, and natural reason dictates that this person be another parent for him whose parent is lacking. From all this it is gathered that just as parents are not able to be forced to that which is purely faith-related, and if forced and not consenting they receive baptism, nothing is done, so children in the things that are of divine law require either the true or the representative will, and it ought not to be done, nor, if it is done, is it valid; but whoever of the parents consents, of whatever age the little one is, for favoring the faith, it seems that he is to be baptized, because it has been expressed regarding the father, but on the mother the opposite.[40]

18. If anyone wants to hold this opinion the response will be with the reasons made for the first opinion. To the first the response goes by denying the consequence, because it is not alike, and the reason is that the Church is good for the faithful not only in civil acts, but also in those which pertain to the worship of God. And therefore if a Christian uses his property against the divine worship, there is no injury if the Church should deprive him of his property and designate it for its proper use. And in this case the will of the Church is the representative will of the little one, because the Church is able to represent the will of the parent: indeed, to speak more truly, the will of the Church is more the representative will of the little one than the will of the carnal parent, because of the fact that legally the will of the carnal parent who is a faithful Christian is subject to the will of the Church, but it is not so regarding the little ones of unbelievers, because before baptism

---

[40] The last part of this sentence, beginning with "regarding the father," is an incomplete rendering of an extremely abbreviated Latin text, which also includes scribal corrections and is therefore very difficult to render.

19. Ad secundum de Decreto respondetur quod decretum illud non cogit, quia, qui [*supplevi*] offerentes parvulum Iudaei non offerunt eum vice sua, nihil juris habeant in offerendo fi(f60v)lium alienum nisi hoc procedat de voluntate parentum, nec offerunt eum vice parentum, cum supponamus ex titulo quaestionis quod offerant eum [*emendavi*, cum *cod.*] invitis parentibus, nec vice Ecclesiae, cum ante baptismum nihil juris habeat in parvulo infidelis et parentis. Canon ergo allegatus loquitur in casu in quo offerentes gerent vicem parentum sive Ecclesiae, quod potest esse in parvulis Christianis, non autem in parvulis Iudaeorum vel quorumcumque infidelium.

20. Ad tertiam respondetur negando majorem. Dicimus nempe quod non sufficit ad baptismum quod non inveniatur obex contrariae voluntatis in eo qui baptizatur, sed requiritur intentio directa vel indirecta sive interpretative sicut argutum est in ratione primae secundae opinionis. Cui vult Deus miseretur et per suam misericordiam ei quem vult indurat, ad Ro. 9 per suam justitiam quia illi quos induret hoc merentur ut indurentur ab ipso.

21. S Thom. super epistol. ad Rom. 9. verum ad videndum quorum obduratio et obcaecatio attribuuntur Deo, quia non solum permissive, ut tam Hug. quam Arch. exponunt.[s] Est notandum juxta S. Thomam excaecatio et induratio duo important, quorum unum motus animi humano inhaerentis malo et aversi divino lumine, et quantum ad hoc Deus non est causa excaecationis et obdurationis sicut non est causa peccati. Aliud autem est subtractio gratiae, ex qua sequitur quod mens divinitus non illuminetur ad recte videndum, et cor hominis non emolliatur ad recte [*emendavi*, recti *cod.*] vivendum, et quantum ad hoc Deus est causa excaecationis et obdurationis. Est autem considerandum quod Deus est causa illuminationis universalis animarum, secundum illud Ioannis 1.: Erat lux vera, qui illuminat omnem hominem venientem in hunc mundum, (f61r) sicut sol est universalis causa illuminationis corporum, aliter tamen et aliter. Nam sol agit illuminando per necessitatem naturae, Deus autem agit voluntaria per ordinem jure sapientiae. Sol autem, licet quantum est de se corporea illuminet, si quod tamen impedimentum inveniat in aliquo tempore, relinquit illud tenebrosum sicut patet de domo cujus fenestrae sunt clausae, sed tamen illius obscurationis causa non est sol. Non autem suo judicio agit ut lumen interius non immittit,

---

s Thomas, *Super Ep. ad Romanos*, 9.3: Quod quidem non est intelligendum hoc modo quod Deus in homine causet malitiam, sed est intelligendum permissive, quia scilicet ex iusto suo iudicio permittit aliquos ruere in peccatum propter praecedentes iniquitates.

they are not subject to the Church, neither in the reason that is the son's nor in the reason of the parents, so that thus the will of the Church can be their representative will in each way.

19. To the second, on the Decree, the response is that that decree does not have force, because those who, offering the little one of a Jew, do not offer him in their own capacity, have no right in offering someone else's son, unless this should proceed from the will of the parents, nor do those who offer him on behalf of the parents, since we suppose from the title of the question that they offer him with the parents unwilling, nor on behalf of the Church, since before baptism it has no right over the little one of a parent who is also an unbeliever. Therefore, the alleged canon speaks in the case in which those who offer will execute the function of the parents or of the Church, which can be in the little ones who are Christians, but not in the little ones of Jews or any unbelievers whatsoever.

20. To the third the response goes by denying the major. We say of course that it does not suffice for baptism that there be not found a barrier of contrary will in him who is being baptized, but the direct or indirect or representative intention is required, as has been argued in the explanation of the first part of the second opinion. If God wills to have mercy on someone, and through his mercy he hardens him whom he will (at Romans 9) through his justice, that those whom he hardens merit to be hardened by him.[41]

21. Saint Thomas, in his commentary on the Epistle to the Romans, chapter 9: "And their hardening and blinding are attributed to God for the purpose of their seeing the truth, because it is not only so permissively." It is to be noted that according to St. Thomas *blinding* and *hardening* carry two meanings, of which the one is a passion of one who inheres in a human evil and is turned away from the divine light, and as far as this is concerned God is not the cause of blinding and hardening as he is not the cause of sin. But the removal of grace is something else, from which it follows that the mind is not divinely illuminated for seeing rightly, and the heart of man is not softened for living rightly, and as far as this is concerned God is the cause of blinding and hardening. Now it must be considered that God is the cause of every illumination of souls, according to the passage in John 1: "He was the true light that illuminates every man coming into this world," just as the sun is the cause of every illumination of bodies, although in different senses. For the sun acts by illuminating through the necessity of its nature, but God acts voluntarily through order in the law of his wisdom. The sun, on the other hand, although as far as it is concerned it illuminates bodily things, but

---

[41] See Rom 9:18.

sed causa ejus est solum ille qui claudit fenestras. Deus autem proprio judicio lumen gratiae non immittit illis in quibus obstaculum invenit, unde causa subtractionis gratiae est non solum ille qui ponit obstaculum gratiae, sed etiam Deus qui suo judicio gratiam non opponit, et per hunc modum Deus est causa obdurationis cordis. Haec Sanctus Thomas.

(f61v)
X.PRAEF. **(F62R)** SYLVESTER DE PRIERIO. SUMMA SYLVESTRINA SUB VERBO BAPTISMUS DISTINCIO 4. IBI: UTRUM PUERI INFIDELIUM IUDAEORUM INFRA PUBERTATEM POSSINT INVITIS PARENTIBUS BAPTIZARI?

1. Et dico quod est una opinio quam Aurco. Sandu. et Scot(us) et Arch. et Ant(onius) de But(rio) tenent et videtur Do. de Gemi. quod sic—per principes, non autem per privatas personas. Sed ista opinio est falsa et vana cum suo fundamento. Primo quia nulla est servitus in spectantibus ad ius divinum aut naturale, unde si Iudaeus doceat filium malos mores, puta furari et adulterari, quod pertinet ad jus civile, est ei auferendum. C. de epi. aud. 1. Si lenones non autem si eum doceat malam fidem quod pertinet ad divinum, quia hoc nullo jure cavetur. Secundo nam princeps non plus sed minus habet potestatem super filios Iudaei quam super patre, et tamen patrem non potest cogere ad suscipiendum baptismum in se, licet Scotus hoc male concedat, quia hoc dicit. Iac. Hermog. et Apost. "Quid ad nos," inquit, "de his qui foris sunt judicare?" Et tex. in Cap. sicut Iudaei de Iudaeis, et XIV dis. de Iudaeis istam compulsionem prohibet. Ergo non potest inferre vim filio aut patri in filio ut baptizetur cum voluntas patris sit alia ante usum rationis in spectantibus ad praedicta jura. Tertio autem quia S. Thomas dixit quod sit illicitum in IIa IIae quaest(io) X, art(icul)o XII, et suum fundamentum est duplex naturalis aequitas quia hoc naturali iustitiae repugnat. Nam filius naturaliter est aliquid patris, et primo quidem a parentibus non distinguitur secundum corpus quamdiu in matris utero continetur. Deinde utero egressus ante usum liberi arbitrii sub **(f62v)** parentum cura, sicut sub quodam spirituali utero continetur, non differens ab irrationali animali, unde sicut bos et equus jure civili est alicujus ut eo utatur ut liber ita filius jure naturali ante usum rationis.

nevertheless if it should find an impediment at some time, it abandons that darkness, as it is plain in the case of a house whose windows are shut, but yet the sun is not the cause of that darkening. It does not, however, act by its own judgment, when it does not send its light within, but the cause of this is merely he who closes the windows. God, however, by his own judgment does not send in the light of grace into them in whom he finds an obstacle, whence the cause of the taking away of grace is not merely he who puts the obstacle in the way of grace, but also God who in his judgment does not impose grace, and in this way God is the cause of hardening of the heart. This is what St. Thomas says.

X. PREF. SYLVESTER MAZZOLINI DI PRIERIO. IN THE *SUMMA SYLVESTRINA*, UNDER THE WORD *BAPTISM*, DISTINCTION 4. THERE: WHETHER CHILDREN OF UNBELIEVER JEWS UNDER THE AGE OF MATURITY CAN BE BAPTIZED WITH THE PARENTS UNWILLING.[42]

1. And I say that there is one opinion that Scotus and Antonius of Butrio hold—and, it seems, Dom de Gemi.—that yes—but for princes, not for private persons. But that opinion is false and vain at its foundation. Firstly, because there is no servitude in those who look to the divine or natural law. Whence if a Jew should teach his son evil morals, for example to steal and commit adultery, which pertains to the civil law, he should be taken away from him. Commentary on the letter part 1. As for procurers, yes, but not if he should teach him a bad faith, which pertains to divine law, because this is provided against by no law. Secondly, for the prince has not more but less power over the children of a Jew than over the father, and nevertheless he is not able to force the father to receive baptism in himself, although Scotus hardly concedes this, because he says this. James and Hermogenes, and the Apostle, "What concern is it of ours," he says, "to judge concerning those who are outside?" And the text in the Chapter concerning Jews, and distinction 14 on Jews, prohibits that compulsion. Therefore, one cannot bring force upon a son or a father in his son for him to be baptized, since the will of the father is different before the use of reason in regard to the aforesaid laws. Thirdly, moreover, because St. Thomas has said that it is illicit in the *Secunda Secundae*, question 10, article 12, and his foundation is twofold natural equality, because this is repugnant to natural justice. For the son is naturally something of the father, and at first at least is not distinguished from the parents according to the body as long as he is contained in the mother's womb. Then when he has come out of the womb, before the use of free will, he is contained

---

[42] This chapter and subsequent chapters of the *Syllabus* have a large number of abbreviated citations of authorities; I have not been able to expand and source all of them. To make the task more difficult, in some cases there are obvious scribal errors.

2. Secundum est Ecclesiae consuetudo quae maximam habet auctoritatem, et in omnibus est aemulanda et cui magis standum est quam auctoritati Augustini et aliorum doctorum [*emendavi*, datorum *cod.*] qui ab Ecclesia habent auctoritatem, quae hoc numquam habuit, cum tamen retroactis temporibus fuerint multi Catholici principes potentissimi, ut Constantinus et Theodosius, quibus familiares fuerunt SS. Episcopi ut Sylvester et Ambrosius qui nullo modo praetermisissent ab eis impetrare nisi [*emendavi*, si *cod.*] non esset consonum rationi. Unde dicitur de pueris antiquorum quod salvati sunt in fide parentum, per quod datur intelligi quod ad eos spectet providere eis de salute. Haec ex illo. Et hanc opinionem sequitur Car. Flor. de Iudaeis in Cap. sicut Iudaei et Gaspar de Calde. in consiliis et gloss. sup. e. Iudaeorum 28. Petrus de Palude Pan(ormitanus) et Ioan(nes) de Ana(nia) in c. sicut de Iudaeis [*emendavi*, Iudaei *cod.*] et ibi de Mari. et Feli. et dicunt istud convenienter teneri et Alberti [*emendavi*, Alberi *cod.*] in Sum. vos. in v. Iudaeus quam etiam adhuc confirmat S. Thomas.

3. Nunc videndum utrum pueri infidelium invitis parentibus ante usum rationis baptizati suscipiant Sacramentum dicit Petrus de Palude quod non; quia in his quae sunt fidei, sicut parentes coacti baptizati nihil recipiunt, ita nec filii sine sua aut parentum voluntate, licet sufficiat voluntas alterius parentum. Archidiaconus autem adscribit S. Thomae quod sint vere baptizati et ad servandam fidem cogendi. Et hanc opinionem dicit sibi magis placere quia sufficiens causa baptismi est materia, forma, et voluntas propria baptizandi aut parentum, (f63r) id est offerentium, qui sunt parentes spirituales, sicut olim salvabantur in fide parentum spiritualium, idest Ecclesiae. Sed ista in S. Thoma non memini me legisse, sunt tamen vera indubitate, saltem quando juste essent subtracti a cura parentum. Et licet S. Thomas I.II. q. LXVIII. art. IX ad secund. teneat quod filii infidelium baptizati in fide Ecclesiae consequantur salutem et intelligantur offerri ab omnibus quibus placet quod offerantur, et quorum charitate ad comunionem S. Spiritus adjunguntur et non tantum ab his quorum manibus feruntur, tamen loquitur quando baptizantur invitis quidem parentibus, sed juste ab eis subtracti, ut videtur vel quando et ipsi parentes consentiunt [*emendavi*, consensiunt, *cod.*] ut pueri sint fideles, sed alio respectu puta ne sint foetentes aut energumeni, id est vexati a diabolo.

under the care of the parents as under a kind of spiritual womb, not differing from an irrational animal, whence just as a cow or horse, it lies within the civil law for someone to use him, so that the son is thus in regard to natural law free before the use of reason.

2. Next is the custom of the Church, which has the greatest authority, and in all things is to be imitated and by which we must stand more than by the authority of Augustine and the others given, who have their authority from the Church, which has never held this, even though in times gone by there have been many very powerful Catholic princes, as Constantine and Theodosius, with whom holy bishops have been familiar, as Sylvester and Ambrose, who would in no way have omitted to request it of them except that it was not harmonious with reason. Whence it is said of the children of the ancients that they are saved in the faith of the parents, through which fact it is given to be understood that we look to them to provide for their salvation. This is from that source. And this opinion the Florentine Cardinal follows in the chapter on Jews, just as Jews and Gaspar de Calde in the *consilia* and glosses on "Of Jews" 28, Peter Paludanus, Panormitanus, and Giovanni di Anania in the chapter on the Jews, etc., and they say that that is held consistently, and in the *Summa* of Albert, on the word *Jew*, which even still St. Thomas confirms.

3. Now it must be seen whether Peter Paludanus says the children of unbelievers baptized with the parents unwilling before the use of reason receive the sacrament or not, because in things which are of the faith, just as parents forced and baptized receive nothing, so neither do children without their own or their parents' will, although the will of another's parents suffices. Moreover, the archdeacon ascribes to St. Thomas that they may be truly baptized and that they must be forced to keep the faith. And this opinion he says he agrees with all the more because sufficient cause of baptism is the matter, form, and will—the proper will of the person to be baptized, or that of the parents, that is, of those offering the person, who are the spiritual parents, just as once they were saved in the faith of the spiritual parents, that is, of the Church. But I do not remember having read that in St. Thomas myself, yet it is undoubtedly true, at least when they were justly taken away from the care of the parents. And although St. Thomas in the *Prima Secundae*, question 68, article 9, in his response to the second objection holds that sons of unbelievers baptized in the faith of the Church get salvation and are understood to be offered by all those who like them to be offered, and by whose charity they are joined to the communion of the Holy Spirit, and not only by those by whose hands they are brought, nevertheless he says when they are baptized, when the parents are indeed unwilling but they are justly taken away from them,

(f63v)
XI.PRAEF. (F64R) MARCUS ANTONIUS NATTA CONSILIA SIVE RESPONSA JURIS IN CONS. 434. IBI

1. Quaedam puella octo vel novem annorum nata ex parentibus Hebraeis dicit se fieri velle Christianam et optat baptizari. Quaeritur utrum invitis parentibus et reclutantibus id fieri possit. Et quod non possit cum ad adultam nondum pervenerit aetatem vult gl. in cap. Iudaeorum 18. q. 1. Card. Io. de Lig., Abb. Io. de Ana. Maria et Fel., ubi attestatur hanc et se comunionem opinionem in c. sicut de Iudaeis Card. in Clem. 1. in fin. de Iudaeis Calder conf. 3. eod. titul. Praepos. in cap. qui sinceram 45 dist. idem tenet, S. Thomas 2. 2. q. 10 art. 12. Riccard 4. Sent. dist. 6. Art. 3 q. 6. Io Gerson in tract. regularum moralium. Idem quoque tenet Durandus et Petrus de Palude et alii plures Theologi.

2. Nec valet quod dicit Domin(us): quod principes temporales possint a Iudaeis abripere filios et baptizentur. Nam falsis utitur rationibus neque potest procedere quia Iudaei non sunt servi, quod patet quia habere bona et dominia rerum suarum possunt, nec auferuntur ab eis sine causa L. nemo exterus P. de Iudaeis C. sicut et c. multorum eodem tit. L. Christianis et ibi Bar. C. de paga: quin et rem Christiani praescribunt, gl. in c. porro 16. q. 3 et facit ad praemissa textus in L. Spadonem § jam autem de excu. tut: ubi Bal: dicit per illum textum quod Iudaei in actibus humanis nobis cum participant et Secundum Io(annem) de Ana(nia): sunt de eodem populo et corpore civitatis, licet non sint de corpore spirituali, ita dicit ipse in c. Iudaei sive Saraceni [*emendavi*, Sanaceni *cod.*] col. fin. de Iudaeis per text(um) in auth(ore) ibi "Civitas nostra (f64v) populosa et turbis diversorum hominum, ergo non sunt servi, quia servi jure civili pro nullis habentur. 1. quod attinet de reg. jur.

3. Praeterea non est major potestas principum in Iudaeorum filios quam in patres Iudaeos, sed patres non possunt compelli ad fidem nisi consentiant, et eorum patefecerint voluntatem (can. de Iudaeis 45. dist. c.) sicut de Iudaeis ergo nec filii parvuli de quorum voluntate non apparet, vi pertrahi debent ad baptismum. Non etiam est verum quod non habeant filios in potestate quia imo eos habent, ut est textus clarus in c. 2. *De Conversione Infidelium*, et vult hoc glossa in dicto capite Iudaeorum; et in cap. jus quiritum 1. dist. Bald. in 1. item in potestate, de his qui sunt sui vel alieni juris, et Alexand. et Arct. in 1. multum de verb. oblig.

as it seems even when the parents themselves consent that the children be faithful Christians, but in another respect, for example, lest they be foul or possessed, that is, tormented by the devil.

XI. MARCUS ANTONIUS NATTA. *CONSILIA* OR LEGAL RESPONSES IN CONS. 434. THERE:

1. A certain girl eight or nine years old of Hebrew parents says that she wants to become a Christian and wishes to be baptized. It is asked whether this may be done with the parents unwilling and struggling against it. And that it may not, since she has not yet arrived at the age of adulthood, is the meaning of the gloss on the chapter on Jews, 18, question 1, Cardinal Giovanni de Lig. Abb., Giovanni of Anania, Maria and Fel, where it is attested that this is the common opinion in the chapter as On Jews Cardinal in Clem. 1. at the end On the Jews Calder conf. 3. under the same title, preface on the chapter, who holds the same; St. Thomas in the *Secunda Secundae*, question 10, article 12; Riccard, commentary *On the Four Sentences*, distinction 6, article 3, question 6; Jean Gerson in the *Treatise of Moral Rules*. The same also Peter Paludanus holds, and many other theologians.

2. And that which my lord says has no validity: that temporal princes could tear children away from Jews and that they should be baptized. For he uses false reasons and it is not able to proceed, because the Jews are not slaves, because it is plain that they are able to have goods and dominion over their own things, and they are not taken away from them without cause.[43] It says through that text that Jews when they participate with us in human acts (and according to Giovanni di Anania) they are of the same people and body of the city, although they are not of the spiritual body, so he says himself in the chapter Jews or Saracens in the column at the end on Jews through the text in the author, there: "Our populous city and with crowds of diverse persons," therefore they are not slaves, because slaves are considered as nobodies in civil law. Chapter 1 that pertains to the rule of law.

3. Moreover, the power of princes over the sons of Jews is not greater than over the Jewish fathers, but the fathers cannot be compelled to the faith unless they should consent and have made their will plain (canon on Jews 45, distinction c. as on Jews); therefore, neither ought the little sons, about whose will it is not obvious, be dragged by force to baptism. It is also not true that they do not have sons in power because on the contrary they do have them, as the text is clear in chapter two on the *Conversion of Unbelievers*, and

---

[43] The remainder of this paragraph is a series of abbreviated citations of texts, as noted above, together with at least one scribal error. For indication of subsequent condensed citations an asterisk will be given.

4. In contrarium vero quod non possint principes a Iudaeis filios abducere gratia baptismi plurimae suadent rationes, quarum nonnullas adducemus. In primis movere debet Ecclesiae consuetudo (vetustae autem consuetudinis non est levis auctoritas ut inquit Imper. in 1. 2. Cod. quae sit longa consuetud.). Nam si hoc licuisset principibus Sancti olim Pontifices et Sacerdotes, qui plurima pollebant penes principes gratia, istud fieri procurassent pro animarum salute, sed istud numquam factum legitur, ergo adversus Ecclesiae consuetudinem nihil est innovandum. Nec dicatur quod exactibus negativis nec consuetudo, nec authoritas elici potest, quia istud non procedet [procedit *cod.ac*] in his quae sunt maximi ponderis, et primariae (ut sic dicatur) notae; nam talia nisi specifice **(f65r)** exprimantur, neglecta videntur 1. item apud Labeonem § hoc edictum de injur. 1. 1. § dixerit aliquis de public. Quum igitur Ecclesia antiquitus hoc praetermiserit, non modo in Iudaeorum, sed etiam in reliquorum infidelium filiis, quum id posset, censetur tacito judicio fieri noluisse, quod sane tacitum judicium consuetudinem inducit, quae observanda est praesertim, quum non careat ratione. Praeterea si licet a Iudaeis auferre filios aliquos eadem ratione licet auferre omnes non est major ratio auferendi partem quam totum, sed omnes auferre non licet, ergo nec aliquos. Nam si omnes auferantur brevi intereat Iudaeorum genus et evacuabitur illud propheticum quod praedictum est quod reliquiae Israel salvae fiant.

5. Ulterius considerandum est quod baptismus ut valeat requirit fidem et consensum baptizandi, can. de Iudaeis 45 d. C. detrahe 1. q. gloss. in can dedit in ver Hebraeus 1 q. 1. cano. verus de consecr. dist. 4 "militem namque voluntarium Christus elegit c. non est 45 q. 1. et benefacere nemo potest nisi elegerit, nisi amaverit, quo est in libera voluntate, can. ad fidem 23 q. 5.; propterea amentes et dormientes nequeunt baptizari nisi fuerint prius cathecumini, id est habuerint propositum suscipiendi baptismum, et licet ficte accedentes suscipiant baptismum, tamen illud procedit, quia illi ore consentiunt, licet corde dissentiant, et Ecclesia non judicat nec judicare potest de occultis, ut declarat Ant. de But. in d. c. majores.

6. Videndum est igitur in cujus fide fundetur baptisma istius parvuli, quia proponitur baptizandus invitis parentibus **(f65v)** Iudaeis. Certe in propria fide et voluntate pueri (seu puellae) fundari non potest, quia intelligere nec

APPENDIX B

the gloss on the said chapter of the Jews means this; and in the chapter "The Law of the Romans," first distinction, Bald. in 1st also in the power, "regarding those who are of their own or of another's right," and Alexander and Arct. in the 1st, much said on the word of obligation.

4. But on the contrary, that princes are not able to abduct Jews' sons from them for the sake of baptism, many reasons advise, and we shall adduce some. In the first place, the custom of the Church ought to influence (now the authority of ancient custom is not light, as it says in Imper. in 1. 2. Cod., what long custom is). For if this had been permitted to princes, holy Pontifices and priests, who were strongly in full favor with princes, would long ago have made sure that it be done for the salvation of souls, but it is not read that that was ever done, therefore there must not be made any innovation against the custom of the Church. And be it not said that neither custom nor authority can be elicited by ascertaining negatives, because that will not follow in things that are of the greatest weight and (so to speak) of primary note. For such things, unless they should be specifically expressed, seem to be neglected.* Whence therefore the Church in ancient times has omitted this, not only in the sons of Jews, but also in those of the other unbelievers, when it could have done it, by tacit judgment it is thought to have willed that it not be done, which tacit judgment of course induces a custom that is especially to be observed, since it does not lack reason. Moreover, if it is permitted to take away any sons from Jews, by the same account is it permitted to take away all (there is no greater reason for taking away the part than the whole)? But it is not permitted to take away all, therefore neither is it permitted to take away any. For if all should be taken away, then in a short time the race of the Jews would perish and that prophecy would be made void, when it was preached that the remnants of Israel would be saved.

5. It must further be considered that baptism requires the faith and consent of the one to be baptized to be valid, Canon On Jews 45,* "for Christ has chosen a voluntary soldier." And no one is able to do good unless he has been chosen, unless he has loved, by which he is in free will, Canon *ad fidem* 23 q. 5; wherefore the mad and the sleeping are not able to be baptized unless they should first have been catechumens, that is, have had the intention of receiving baptism, and although they should come and receive baptism in feigned fashion, nevertheless it proceeds because they consent with the mouth, even though they dissent with the heart, and the Church does not judge nor is able to judge about secrets, as Antonio di Butrio declares.*

6. It must be seen therefore in whose faith the baptism of that little one will be poured out, because he is proposed to be baptized with his Jewish parents unwilling. Certainly in the proper faith and will of the boy (or girl) it cannot

scire potest mysteria fidei, nec tenere quid sibi baptismus velit, igitur ejus voluntas nulla est; nam pupillus nec velle nec nolle intelligitur nisi tutoris accedat authoritas 1. pupillus de regulis jur. et hac ratione haereditatem adire non potest quamvis lucrosam etiam si major sit septennio § neque Inst. de auth. tut quia causam suae aditionis non intelligit. 1. pupillus de acquir. haered. ubi Bartolus dicit: quod pupillus in ea aetate nec examinare, nec descernere potest, et per consequens nec scire, quia scire est rem per causam cognoscere, et licet cognoscat multa universalia, veluti hoc quod bonum est habere aliquid, et malum non habere; tamen ista non sufficiunt, ut recte in particularibus possit judicare, ex quo fit etiam, ut in ea aetate testari nequeat quia judicium non habet. Non igitur in fide propria filii etiam majoris septennio baptismus sustineri potest, quia fidei causam non novit.

7. Quod si dicimus fundari in fide parentum, qui generaverunt, sicut in parvulis Christianorum fieri solet, c. quaeris de consecr. dist. 4. c. majores ubi gl. de baptism., respondetur hoc non procedere quia parentes infideles reluctantur. Non obstat si dicatur quod possunt parvuli suscipere impressionem in fide patrinorum qui eos offerunt Ecclesiae, et pro eis respondent, c. illud: cap. filius et c. parvuli et c. mater de consec. eist. 4. Quia respondetur quod praedicta jura intelliguntur quando patrini offerunt eos de consensu parentum a quibus ipsi parvuli traduntur et in quorum potestate sunt **(f66r)** parvulorum voluntates, quae non sunt in potestate quorumlibet extraneorum, nihil ad pueros attinentium. Et eo casu videtur baptizari in fide parentum, qui eos baptizandos tradiderunt, non eorum, qui manibus suis eos gestaverunt; quoniam actus attribuitur ordinanti non ei qui exequitur f. pater ex provincia in fi. de man. vind. 1. unum ex famil. §. fi. de falcidia et ibi Bartolus de leg. 2. 1. item eorum § si decuriores $ quod cujus univ. tradit Rom. cons. 366.

8. In baptismo (uti dicunt etiam Praeposit. et Card.) non sufficit quod in recipiente non sit obex contrariae voluntatis, sed requiritur voluntas directa vel interpretativa, unde nutritus in nemore qui numquam aliquid audisset de fide, et sic est in solo peccato originali, si dormiens baptizaretur, nihil ageret, licet in eo non sit objectus voluntatis contrariae. Requiritur ergo praeter carentiam obiectus intentio sive actus voluntatis vel prorpiae in adulto vel interpretativae in parvulo.

9. Ista autem voluntas interpretativa in parvulo consistit in fide parentum, tum quia alii a parentibus nullum jus habent in eo, tum quia ipse non alia ratione pertinet ad Ecclesiam nisi ratione suae originis; quod si parentes essent mortui, tunc genere proximiores vicem sustinent parentum, et eis invitis baptizari parvulus non debet. In his quae sunt supra legem naturae id est, quae pertinent ad jus divinum et voluntatem requirunt veram vel interpretativam, nemo cogendus, et si cogatur nihil geritur, ex quo concludunt

be founded, because he is not able to understand or know the mysteries of the faith, nor to hold what baptism means for him, therefore it is not his will; for a ward is understood neither to will nor to be unwilling unless the guardian's authority should attend, and for this reason he is not able to approach inheritance, however gainful, even if he should be older than seven years old, because he does not understand the cause of his approaching.* See "ward," *On the acquisition of inheritance*, where Bartolus says that the ward in this age is not able to examine or decide, and consequently he is also not able to know, because knowing is coming to know a thing through its cause, and although he should come to know many things in general, as for example the fact that it is good to have something and bad not to have it, nevertheless that does not suffice for his ability to judge rightly in particulars, from which it also happens that in that age he is not able to bear witness, because he does not have judgment. Baptism is not therefore able to be sustained in the proper faith of a son even older than seven years, because he does not know the cause of faith.

7. But if we say that it is founded in the faith of the parents who have begotten him, as is accustomed to be done in the little ones of Christians,* it is responded that this does not follow because the unbeliever parents are resisting. It is not an obstacle if it should be said that little ones can receive the impression in the faith of the godparents who offer them to the church and respond on their behalf.* Because it is responded that the aforesaid rights are understood when the godparents offer them from the consent of the parents by whom the littles ones are themselves handed over and in whose power are the wills of the little ones, which are not in the power of anyone outside the situation who have nothing to do with the children. And in this case it seems that they are baptized in the faith of the parents, who have given them over to be baptized, not of those who have brought them with their own hands, since the act is attributed to the one who orders it, not the one who carries it out.*

8. In baptism (as the prefect and the Cardinal also say) it does not suffice that there be no barrier of contrary will in the receiver, but there is required the direct or representative will, whence one raised in the woods who never had heard anything about the faith and thus is only in original sin, if he were to be baptized while sleeping, it would do nothing, even though in him there should be no obstacle of contrary will. It is required, therefore, beyond the lack of an obstacle, the intention or act of the will, whether one's own in an adult, or representative in a little one.

9. Now that representative will in the little one consists in the faith of the parents, both because others have no right over him from the parents, and

ipsi post Petrum de Palude, quod invitis pa(f66v)rentibus parvulus non est baptizandus, sed volentibus sic, seu eorum altero, quia sic etiam ante circumcisionem datam salvabantur parvuli in fide parentum. Ergo filii Iudaeorum ut voluit glossa in c. spiritus 1. q. 1. in versic. pueror. queunt baptizari si doli sint capaces alias non ligarentur nam tales furiosis aequiparantur.

10. Ex praedictis concluditur dictam puellam non esse baptizandam, sed parentibus Iudaeis repetentibus esse restituendam.

XII.PRAEF. (F67R) PETRUS ANCHARANUS CONSILIA SIVE JURIS RESPONSA CONSIL. 195 DE BAPTISMO.

1. In Christi nomine Amen. Secundum ea quae proposita sunt, videtur quod dictus puer Hebraeus non debet nec dici potest baptizatus; et hoc rationibus et juribus supradictis quae possunt rationibus et juribus corroborari. Deficit nempe hic primo potestas ex parte baptizantis, nam alius quam sacerdos baptizare non potest, nisi in casu necessitatis (de consec. dist. IV. cap. constat et cap. in veritate). Deficit igitur hic baptismus propter defectum personae agentis. Et sic auctoritas traditionis (de consec. dist. 4. Sanctum est baptisma).

2. Ex parte etiam suscipientis deficit hic impressio hujus Sacramenti parvulis. Nempe quia non intelligunt quid agunt non confertur nisi ab illo teneantur et offerantur, qui interrogantionibus Sacerdotis respondeat (1. quaest. Spiritus Sanctus), et est speciale hoc casu ut fides parentum obliget pueros ad fidem, et post alienum suppleat defectum. Non alias intelligitur pupillaris aetatis, quae aetas quod videt ignorat, et eorum fides nihil operatur, ut praedicta probant (de consec. dis. 4. p. tot.). In quaestione autem proposita defuit tamen satis: quia nullus respondit pro parte parvuli Hebraei et per se respondere ipse non potuit, veluti furiosus, et intellectu carens et fide (ut not. in d. cap. Spiritus Sanctus). Et si dicatur iste non est sacerdos qui infundit super caput hujus pueri Hebraei, utrumque potuit respondere pro eo, respondeo: hoc non est verum, quia sicut in ista sacramentali generatione alius debet esse, qui spiritualiter generatus, alius qui spiritualiter generat, ita (f67v) alius debet esse qui pro puero respondet, alius qui baptizat (ut d. cap. Spiritus Sanctus et c. I igitur). Sic non potest unus conferre beneficium et collationem recipere.

because he himself is related to the Church on no other account except on account of his origin; but if the parents were dead, then the next of kin uphold the role of parents, and the little one ought not to be baptized with them unwilling. In things that are above the law of nature, that is, things that pertain to the divine law, and require the true or representative will, no one must be forced, and if there should be force, nothing is accomplished, from which they who follow Peter Paludanus conclude, that the little one is not to be baptized with the parents unwilling, but if they are willing, yes, or their stand-in, because thus also before circumcision was given the little ones were saved in the faith of the parents. Therefore the sons of Jews are able to be baptized, as is the meaning of the gloss;* they can be baptized if they should be capable of deceit, otherwise they would not be bound, for such are virtually equivalent to madmen.

10. From the aforesaid it is concluded that the said girl is not to be baptized, but to be restored to the Jewish parents who are asking for her back.

XII. PREF. PETER ANCHARANUS. COUNSELS OR LEGAL RESPONSES: *CONSIL. 195 ON BAPTISM.*

1. In Christ's name, Amen. According to what has been proposed, it seems that the said Hebrew boy ought not nor is able to be said to be baptized; and this by the accounts and laws aforesaid that can be corroborated with accounts and laws. Of course here in the first place there is lacking on the part of the baptizer the power, for one other than a priest is not able to baptize except in the case of necessity (*On Consecration*, Distinction 4, and in the chapter *in veritate*). Therefore, this baptism is deficient because of the defect of the person of the agent. And thus says the authority of the tradition (*On Consecration*, Distinction 4, *Sanctum est baptisma*).

2. Even on the part of the one receiving there is lacking here the impression of this sacrament upon little ones. Of course, because they do not understand what they are doing it is not conferred unless they should be held and offered by such a one as to respond to the questions of the priest (first question *Spiritus Sanctus*), and it is special in this case that the faith of the parents obligates the children to the faith, and supplies the defect after another's. No otherwise is it understood of the age of minority, which age does not know what it sees, and their faith works nothing, as the aforesaid prove (*On Consecration*, Distinction 4). Moreover, in the proposed question sufficiency has yet been wanting: because no one responded on the part of the little Hebrew, and he himself was not able to respond by himself, just as a madman, and lacking understanding and faith (as noted in *Spiritus Sanctus*). And if it should be said that he is not a priest who has poured over the head of this

Est etiam hic defectus ex parte [*emendavi*, partae *cod.*] aquae. Unde dicit beatus Ambros. non omnis aqua sanat, sed quae habet gratiam Christi (de consec. dist. 4. per aquam et Cap. fin.). Frustra [*emendavi*, frusta *cod.*] sacrificantes ad baptismum conferentes et aqua ibi posita deputata esset si quis posset in quolibet aqua baptizari (facit c. di. in prin.), et quum ibi notatur, deficit etiam hic solemnitas catechismi [*emendavi*, cathacismi *cod.*], quae debet praecedere baptismum in pueris et in adultis, de qua solemnitate et in quibus consistat habetur de consecr. (dist. 4. baptizandi cum pluribus c. seq.) Quum ergo unus non sacerdos nulla necessitate cogente baptizando puerum Hebraeum possit subvertere tot sacrorum canonum traditiones, et parentibus subtrahere solatium filiorum discretione carentium iniquissimum videretur; et ideo concludo dictum puerum non esse baptizandum per rationem et jure praedicto [*emendavi*, praedicta *cod.*], quae possunt multis aliis rationibus confirmari gratia brevitatis omissis.

XIII.PRAEF. (F68R) TEXTUS IN LIB. 7. DECR. 5. TIT. 1. DE IUDAEIS CAP. I.

1. Quibusvis personis tam Ecclesiasticis quam secularibus expresse inhibemus ne Iudaeorum filios tam mares quam foeminas praeter formam Sacrorum Canonum quomodolibet baptizare debeant vel praesumant.

XIV.PRAEF. TEXTUS IN C. PARVULI P. 3. DE CONSECR. IV. ET IN CAP. CUM PRO PARVULIS

1. Cum pro parvulis alii respondent ut impleatur erga eos celebratio sacramenti, valet utique ad eorum consecrationem quia ipsi respondere non possunt.

XV.PRAEF. TEXTUS DECR. 3. P. DIS. IV. DE CONSEC. CAP. MULIER

1. Mulier quamvis docta et sancta aliquos baptizare non praesumat. Glossa: nisi necessitate cogente.

XVI. PRAEF. D. IOANNES CHRYSOSTOMUS IN PSAL. 44.

1. Statim sacerdos exigit ab infirma aetate pacta conventa et assertiones et minoris aetatis fide jussorem susceptorem interrogat.

Hebrew boy, whether he was able to respond for him, I respond this is not true, because just as in the sacramental generation there ought to be one who is spiritually generated, another who spiritually generates, so there ought to be one who responds for the boy, another who baptizes (as in the aforesaid chapter of *Spiritus Sanctus*). Thus, there cannot be one to confer the benefit and receive the contribution. There is also here a defect on the part of the water. Whence blessed Ambrose says, not every water heals, but that which has the grace of Christ (*On Consecration*, Distinction 4, *per aquam*, and the end of the chapter). Those who bring to baptism are sacrificing in vain, and the water placed there would have been allotted if anyone were able to be baptized in any water,* and when it is noted there, there is also lacking here the solemnity of catechism, which ought to precede baptism in children and in adults, about which solemnity and in whom it would consist is held in *On Consecration* (Distinction 4 of baptizing with many, together with what follows). Since therefore one person, not a priest, with no necessity forcing the issue, is not able to subvert so many traditions of sacred canons by baptizing the Hebrew boy; and, to take away from the parents the consolation of their children who lack discretion, would seem to be most unfair; I therefore do conclude that the said boy is not to be baptized based on the account and because of the right aforesaid, and these things can be confirmed with many other explanations that have been omitted for the sake of brevity.

XIII. PREF. TEXT IN BOOK 7, DECR. 5, TIT. 1 *ON JEWS*, CHAPTER 1.

1. We do expressly prohibit any persons, whether Ecclesiastic or secular, from being in any way under obligation or presuming to baptize the children of Jews, whether males or females, outside the form of the Sacred Canons.

XIV. PREF. TEXT IN CHAPTER "LITTLE ONES," P. 3. *ON CONSECRATION* IV AND IN THE CHAPTER *CUM PRO PARVULIS*.

1. When others respond for little ones that in relation to them the celebration of the sacrament should be fulfilled, it is valid in any case for their consecration, because they themselves are not able to respond.

XV. PREF. TEXT IN DECR. 3. P. DIST. IV. *DE CONSECRATIONE* IN THE CHAPTER *MULIER*.

1. Let no woman whatsoever, even learned and holy, presume to baptize anyone. Gloss: unless under the force of necessity.

XVII. PRAEF. GONZALEZ IN QUINQUE LIBR. DECRET. GREG. AD LIB. III. TIT. 42. DE BAPTISMO

1. Cum infantes per se respondere nequeunt susceptores eorum id debent facere eorum nomine fidem profitendo et promittendo.

XVIII. PRAEF. MARQUARDUS DE SUSANNIS CAP. IUDAEIS ET ALIIS INFIDELIBUS P. 3. C. 3. D 4.

1. Si Iudaeus non imminente necessitate baptizatus fuit sine (f68v) responsali non potest dici baptizatus cum pro seipso respondere non potuerit, nec baptizans possit aut potuerit respondere pro eo, quia sicut in ista Sacramentali generatione alius debet esse qui spiritualiter generatur, et alius qui spiritualiter generat, ita et alius debet esse qui pro baptizato respondeat, et alius qui baptizat.

XIX. PRAEF. FELINUS SUPER DECRET. LIB. V. TIT. 6. CAP. IX. IBI (IN NOTIS)

1. Adde si puer (Iudaeus) debile fuerit per saecularem baptizatus aliis non existentibus, talis puer non dicitur baptizatus. Et eodem loco num. 6. Iudaeum baptizatum sine responsali non imminente necessitate: non est baptizatus.

XX. PRAEF. PETRUS PAULUS PARISIUS S. R. E. CARDIN. CONSILIA IN CONS. 2. P. 3.

1. Cum tempore Regis Emanuelis bo: me: illi Iudaei inviti et reclamantes per vim fuerint baptizati, per talem baptismum non fuerunt effecti Christiani, nec sacramentum nec rem Sacramenti receperunt nec caracterem. Eo etiam cum in aliquibus ipsorum non appareat fuisse servatam formam in dicto sacramento requisitam et necessariam. Et eo fortius hoc praecederet et ulterius si nullus responsalis intercesserit.

XVI.PREF. DIVINE JOHN CHRYSOSTOM ON PSALM 44.

1. Immediately the priest draws from the weak age the appropriate covenant and assertions and asks the steward and guardian about the faith of the minor age.

XVII.PREF. GONZALEZ IN THE FIVE BOOKS OF DECRETALS. GREG. TO BOOK III, TIT. 42. ON BAPTISM.

1. When infants are not able to respond for themselves, their guardians ought to do this in their name by professing the faith and promising.

XVIII.PREF. MARQUARD DE SUSANNA, THE CHAPTER "JEWS AND OTHER UNBELIEVERS," P. 3. C. 3. D. 4.

1. If a Jew, not under imminent necessity, has been baptized without an answerable person, he cannot be said to have been baptized, since he has not able to respond on his own behalf, nor is or will the baptizer be able to respond for him, because just as in the sacramental generation there must be one who is spiritually generated and another who spiritually generates, so also there must be one who responds for the baptized and another who baptizes.

XIX.PREF. FELINUS ON THE *DECRETALS*, BOOK 5, TIT. 6, CAP. 9, THERE (IN THE NOTES).

1. Additionally if an infirm (Jewish) boy should be baptized by a layperson with no others present, such a boy is not said to be baptized. And in the same place, number 6, the Jew baptized without an answerable person without imminent necessity: he is not baptized.

XX.PREF. PETER PAUL PARISIUS, CARDINAL OF THE HOLY ROMAN CHURCH. COUNSELS ON CONS. 2. P. 3.

1. Since in the time of King Emanuel the Jews, unwillingly and complainingly, by force, have been baptized, through such baptism they were not made into Christians, nor did they receive the sacrament or the matter or character of the sacrament. Also because of this: since among some of them there does not appear to have been kept the requisite and necessary form in the said sacrament. And it would proceed even further more strongly than this because of this: if no answerable person shall have interceded.

XXI. PRAEF. ABBAS PANORMITANUS COMM. IN TERTIAM DECRETALIUM LIBRUM DE BAPTISMO C. DEBITUM IBI

1. In baptismo illa spiritualis generatio celebratur de qua dixit Dominus, nisi renatus fuerit ex aqua et Spiritu Sancto non intrabit in Regnum Dei; sicut in Carnali generatione alius est qui generat, alius qui generatur, sic in **(f69r)** spirituali alius debet esse qui spiritualiter generat, alius qui spiritualiter generatur. Sane cum corpus exterius, sive corpus interius baptizatur oportet et utrobique paternitas et filiatio valeat inveniri, quibus baptizatus et baptizans ad invicem referantur. Ubi aliqua requiruntur ad substantiam actus nisi illa interveniantur, non tenet actus, etiam si ex necessitate solemnitas servari non possit. In baptismo quis dicitur renasci, quia primo fuit natus carnaliter, nunc vero renascitur spiritualiter. Et ex hoc infertur et ex tex. quod ista generatio spiritualis debet imitari naturam, seu naturalem generationem in quantum potest. Unde et ex hoc nemo potest alium baptizare quia posset esse parens suus carnalis, et sic quod procedat baptizandum in plena pubertate et sit major 18. annis. Sicut et insimili dicimus in adoptione legali quia oportet, quod adoptans excedat adoptatum in plena pubertate, quod sit major 18 annis eo, quem vult adoptare ut sit certissimum quod posset esse pater carnalis ut patet Inst. de adop. §. minorem. Nam absonum videtur eum fieri patrem spiritualem qui non potest esse carnalis.

XXI. PREF. ABBOT PANORMITANUS. COMMENTARY ON THE THIRD OF THE *DECRETALS*, THE BOOK *ON BAPTISM*.

1. In baptism that spiritual generation is celebrated about which the Lord has said, unless he has been born again of water and the Holy Spirit he will not enter into the Kingdom of God; just as in carnal generation there is one who generates, another who is generated, so in the spiritual there ought to be one who spiritually generates, another who is spiritually generated. Indeed, when the body exteriorly or the body interiorly is baptized, it is necessary also that on both parts parternity and filiation should be able to be found, by which the baptized and the baptizer are related to each other. Where some things are required for the substance of the act, unless they should be interfered with, the act does not hold, even if of necessity the solemnity may not be able to be kept. In baptism someone is said to be reborn, because at first he was born carnally, but now he is being reborn spiritually. And from this it is inferred also from the text that that spiritual generation ought to imitate nature or natural generation in as much as it is able. And so it also follows from this that no one can baptize another person if that person could be his carnal parent, and thus that he should proceed to the baptism provided that he is in the fullness of age and eighteen years older. Just as also similarly we say in legal adoption that it is necessary that the adopter exceed the adopted in fullness of age, that he should be more than eighteen years older than him whom he wants to adopt, so that it should be most certain that he could be his carnal father, as is plain from *Inst. de Adopt. minorem*. For it seems absurd that he become the spiritual father who is not able to be the carnal father.

APPENDIX C

BREVI CENNI (BC)

Source: Handwritten version: AAV, Segreteria di Stato, Anno 1864, Rubrica 66, fasc. 3, ff. 173-204.
Polycopied version: AAV, Archivio particolare Pio IX, Oggetti vari, 1433.

Transcription

[p. 1]
BREVI CENNI E RIFLESSIONI SUL *PRO-MEMORIA E SILLABO*. SCRITTURE UMILIATE ALLA SANTITÀ DI NOSTRO SIGNORE PAPA PIO IX RELATIVE AL BATTESIMO CONFERITO IN BOLOGNA AL FANCIULLO EDGARDO FIGLIO DEGLI EBREI SALOMONE E MARIANNA MORTARA.

ENGLISH TRANSLATION
Translated by Saretta Marotta

[p. 1]
BRIEF NOTES AND REFLECTIONS ON THE *PRO-MEMORIA AND SYLLABUS*. WRITINGS PRESENTED TO THE HOLINESS OF OUR LORD POPE PIUS IX CONCERNING THE BAPTISM CONFERRED IN BOLOGNA ON THE CHILD EDGARDO SON OF THE JEWS SALOMONE AND MARIANNA MORTARA.

[p. 2]
I Genitori di un fanciullo prevenuto singolarmente dalla Divina Grazia, la quale togliendolo dalla cieca giudaica ostinazione, lo rendeva figlio avventurato della Chiesa, hanno fatto innalzare suppliche e querele fino all'augusto Soglio del Santo Padre ad oggetto di ottenere venga restituito il figlio già collocato in seno della Chiesa, e reso libero della libertà dei figli di Dio per il Sangue di Gesù Cristo.

Ora peraltro cotesti genitori si presentano a S. Santità non col solo sembiante di umili supplicanti, ma colla franchezza di chi credendosi oppresso da un atto arbitrario, chiede gli sia resa giustizia, e gli si restituisca l'oggetto del quale pensa esserne stato indebitamente spogliato. Cosi si pretende provare con autorità e ragioni derivate da quella medesima legge, in forza della quale i coniugi Mortara suppongono avere ricevuto oltraggio.

Portata a cotal punto l'esigenza, é ben giusto, che vengano prese ad esame le vantate autorità e ragioni, quali si espongono nel Pro-memoria,[a] e si riportano nel Sillabo[b] inserti nella Supplica al S. Padre.

Una mente venale ed una mano prezzolata ha rovistato non pochi e gravi autori per agglomerare [p. 3] testi e ragioni allo scopo di difendere una causa già decisa in senso opposto a quello, cui si mira, dai medesimi autori, ai quali si fa appello.

Vaglia il vero. Con le umiliate scritture si pretende provare:
1. *Che non si possono né si devono battezzare i figli neonati degli Ebrei contro la volontà dei parenti*
2. *Che nella ipotesi, in cui questi figli (ANTE USUM RATIONIS) venissero battezzati in onta alla contraria volontà dei parenti, cotale battesimo sarebbe del tutto invalido e di nessun effetto.*
3. *Che supposto anche valido tale battesimo, il figlio deve per diritto di natura restituirsi alla patria potestà, la quale lo reclama con ogni ragione.*
4. *Che nel caso di cui si tratta, manca la prova del Battesimo, che si pretende dato dalla fantesca Morisi al bambolo Edgardo Mortara.*
5. *Si reclama dunque per l'esposte ragioni la consegna e restituzione del figlio Edgardo ai genitori Mortara.*

---

[a] Lett. A. Pag 35.
[b] Lett B. Pag 51.

APPENDIX C

[p. 2]

The Parents of a child for whom Divine Grace has provided in a unique way, by liberating him from blind Jewish obstinacy, has made him a fortunate son of the Church, have raised petitions and complaints up to the august papal throne in order to obtain the return of their son, who has already been placed in the bosom of the Church and liberated by the Blood of Jesus Christ to the freedom of the sons of God.

Now, moreover, these parents present themselves to His Holiness not only with the appearance of humble supplicants, but with the frankness of those who, believing themselves oppressed by an arbitrary act, ask that justice be done and that the object of which they think they have been unduly deprived be restored to them. This they intend to prove by the authority and the arguments derived from the same law under which the Mortara couple claim to have been outraged.

Having brought the request to such a point, it is only right that the alleged authorities and arguments be examined, as set out in the *Pro-memoria*[1] and in the *Syllabus*[2] attached to the Supplication to the Holy Father.

[p. 3]

A venal mind and a hired hand have ransacked not a few eminent authors to collect texts and arguments in order to defend a cause that has already been decided by the same authors to whom reference is made, in the opposite direction to the one intended.

Indeed, with the submitted documents it is pretended to prove:

1. *That the newborn children of the Jews cannot and must not be baptized against the will of their parents.*
2. *That if these children (ANTE USUM RATIONIS* [of an age before the use of reason]) *were baptized in spite of the contrary will of their parents, such baptism would be completely invalid and of no effect.*
3. *That even supposing such a baptism to be valid, the child must by natural right be returned to the parental authority that claims him with every reason.*
4. *That in the present case, there is no proof of the baptism allegedly given by the nurse Morisi to the child Edgardo Mortara.*
5. *For the above reasons, the applicants therefore request the release and return of the son Edgardo to his parents Mortara.*

---

[1] Attachment A, Page 35. All footnotes are from the original document except those indicated with "translators note" in brackets.

[2] Attachment B, Page 51.

Di fronte a questi postulati si mostrerà pertanto che:
1. La verità del principale assunto nulla influisce nella [**p. 4**] fattispecie del caso avvenuto ad Edgardo Mortara.
2. Che il secondo asserto é temerario, falso, contrario alla sentenza di tutti i Canonisti e Teologi, ed opposto alla pratica costante della Chiesa universale, e già condannata dalla S. Sede in tante decisioni.
3. Che il diritto della Chiesa *acquisito* sul battezzato è di un ordine superiore, e prevale al diritto paterno; e che perciò non devesi restituire il fanciullo battezzato, ma anzi custodirlo alla Religione.
4. Che nel caso del Mortara esiste la piena prova canonica del conferito battesimo, onde non vi è più ragione e diritto per richiamare il figlio sotto la patria potestà
5. Che dunque la Chiesa madre, Maestra, e Sovrana degli uomini non lede alcun diritto, non reca onta di sorta, ma adempie alla Divina sua missione col tutelare i battezzati suoi figli togliendoli dal pericolo di apostasia.

Nel principale assunto l'innominato Teologo e Canonista unisce tutte le sue forze, onde provare che in verun modo si deve, né si può conferire il battesimo ai fanciulli Ebrei *invitis parentibus*. Ed é perciò che la miglior parte delle autorità e testi allegati nel *Pro-memoria*, ed anche nel *Sillabo*, sono dallo Scrittore diretti a provare questo asserto.

[**p. 5**]
Con tanti sforzi di erudizione non altro migliore risultato avrebbe qui ottenuto l'autore del Pro-memoria e Sillabo all'augusto cospetto di Sua Santità che quello di chi avesse recato un languido raggio di luce a far pompa di se in faccia al più brillante meriggio. Infatti la solenne proibizione di battezzare i figli degl'Infedeli ritroso dei rispettivi parenti fu mai sempre *massima* universale della Cattolica Chiesa, *massima* che da S. Tommaso si fa salire fino ai tempi Apostolici.[c] *Massima* proclamata dai SS. Padri. *Massima* decretata nei Generali Concili. *Massima* insegnata concordemente da tutti i Teologi e Canonisti. *Massima* sanzionata dalle Bolle e Decreti di tanti Sommi Pontefici.

---

c *HOC autem Ecclesiae usus NUNQUAM habuit, quod Iudaeorum filii invitis parentibus baptizarentur Quamvis fuerint retroactis temporibus multi catholici Principes potentissimi ut Constantinus, Theodosius quibus familiares fuerunt Sanctissimi Episcopi, ut Silvester Constantino, et Ambrosius Theodosio: qui nullo modo praetermisissent ab eis impetrare, si hoc esset consonum rationi. Et ideo periculosum videtur Hanc assertionem de novo inducere ut praeter consuetudinem in Ecclesia hactenus observatam, Judaeorum filii invitis parentibus baptizentur.* 2. 2. Quaest. X. Art. XII.

In the face of these assumptions, it will therefore be shown that:
1. The truth of the main assumption has no effect [p. 4] whatsoever on the case of Edgardo Mortara.
2. That the second assertion is reckless, false, contrary to the judgments of all canonists and theologians, and contrary to the constant practice of the universal Church, and has already been condemned by the Holy See in many decisions.
3. That the right of the Church *acquired over* the baptized child is of a higher order, and prevails over the paternal right; and that therefore the baptized child must not be returned, but rather kept in Religion.
4. That in Mortara's case there is full canonical proof of the conferring of baptism, so that there is no longer any reason or right to recall the child under parental authority.
5. That therefore the Church, Mother, Teacher, and Sovereign of mankind, does not infringe any right, nor bring any offence, but fulfils her divine mission by protecting her baptized children and removing them from the danger of apostasy.

In the main thesis, the anonymous theologian and canonist [the author of the *Pro-memoria*] marshals all his forces to prove that baptism of Jewish children *invitis parentibus* is in no way to be, nor can be, conferred. It is for this reason that the greater part of the authorities and texts quoted in the *Pro-memoria*, and also in the *Syllabus*, are directed by the author to prove this assertion.

[p. 5]
With so much effort of erudition, the author of the *Pro-memoria* and of the *Syllabus* would not have obtained a better result, here in the august presence of His Holiness, than that of one who has brought a languid ray of light to make a spectacle of himself in the face of the most brilliant noonday. In fact, the solemn prohibition of baptizing the children of unbelievers against the will of their respective parents has always been the universal *maxim of* the Catholic Church. A *maxim* that dates back from St. Thomas as far as the apostolic age.[3] A *maxim* proclaimed by the Holy Fathers. A *maxim* decreed by the General Councils. A *maxim* unanimously taught by all

---

3 "Now IT was NEVER the custom of the Church to baptize the children of the Jews against the will of their parents, although at time past there have been many very powerful Catholic princes, like Constantine and Theodosius, with whom most holy bishops have been on most friendly terms, as Sylvester with Constantine, and Ambrose with Theodosius, who would certainly not have failed to obtain this favor from them if it had been at all reasonable. It seems therefore hazardous to repeat this assertion, that the children of Jews should be baptized against their parents' wishes, in contradiction to the Church's custom observed hitherto." ST II.II 10.12. [Translator's note: English translations of Thomas Aquinas are based on the Benziger edition of the *Summa Theologica*: *Summa Theologica*, trans. Fathers of the English Dominican Province (New York, 1947)].

Massima definita egregiamente dal citato S. Dottore. « Consuetudine universale, che seco porta un'irrefragabile autorità ».[d]

Che se poi tutte e ciascuna delle allegate autorità si dovessero ben ponderare sarebbe facile cosa il notarne molte riportate fuori di proposito.

[p. 6]

Invero le due prime autorità riportate nel *Sillabo* dei Sommi Pontefici Clemente III e Innocenzo III sono dirette ad impedire qualsiasi violenza, che dai Cristiani trasportati da zelo indiscreto si potesse mai attentare contro gli Ebrei *adulti* forzandoli a ricevere il Battesimo, come apertamente rilevasi leggendo tutto il contesto delle citate Decretali. Giulio III poi mira soltanto ad impedire, che vengano con violenza sottratti dai genitori ebrei i figli ad oggetto di battezzarli contro il loro espresso volere.

Per verità Clemente III nella sua Decretale *sicut Iudaei* si esprime in questi termini « *Statuimus ut nullus invitos vel nolentes Iudaeos ad Baptismum venire compellat* ».

Innocenzo III mentre riprova e condanna l'abuso di chi ardisse di conferire con modi violenti e di terrore il Battesimo alli Ebrei; per isfuggire cotali minaccie ricevesse il battesimo, questo sarebbe valido:[e] eccone l'aurea Dottrina: « *Is qui terroribus, atque suppliciis vehementer attrahitur, ne detrimentum incurrat, Baptismi suscipit Sacramentum, sicut et is qui ficte ad Baptismum accedit, characterem suscipit Christianitatis impressum* ».[f] Da queste brevi citazioni ben si conosce, che i due Sommi Pontefici parlano degli Ebrei ed infedeli ADULTI e non [p. 7] già dei bambini incapaci naturalmente di violenza e minaccia.

In egual modo devono intendersi non pochi allegati di altri autori riportati nelle due scritture.

Che se la S. Chiesa ha sempre e costantemente vietato di battezzare i bambini degl'Infedeli *invitis parentibus*, vi sono però alcuni casi contemplati da tutti i Teologi e Canonisti, nei quali permette, che questi figli siano battezzati e per quanto riguarda il caso presente *è permesso* di conferire il battesimo

---

[d] *Maximam habet auctoritatem Ecclesiae consuetudo, quae "semper est in omnibus aemulanda,"* loco cit.

[e] Chi amasse conoscere la ragione, per cui si dichiara valido simile battesimo richiami alla mente la sublime dottrina del Principe dei Filosofi S. Tommaso sulli atti umani allorché insegna *quod ea quae fiunt ex metu sunt voluntaria simpliciter* etc. 1. 2. Quaest. VI. Art. 6.

[f] In capite Maiores « de Baptismo ».

theologians and canonists. A *maxim* sanctioned by the bulls and decrees of many Supreme Pontiffs. A *maxim* eloquently defined by the Holy Doctor quoted above as "a universal custom, which carries with it an irrefutable authority."[4]

Moreover, if each of the quoted authorities were carefully examined, it would be easy to see that many of them have been inappropriately cited. [p. 6] In fact, the first two quotes reported in the *Syllabus*, from the Supreme Pontiffs Clement III and Innocent III, are intended to prevent any violence that Christians, driven by indiscreet zeal, might ever use against Jewish *adults* by forcing them to receive Baptism, as can be clearly seen by reading the entire context of the quoted decrees. Moreover, Julius III's only aim was to prevent children being forcibly taken from their Jewish parents to be baptized against their express will.

Actually, Clement III in his Decree *sicut Iudaei* expressed himself in these terms: "*We decree that no one should force Jews to be baptized against their will or desire.*"

Innocent III, while denouncing and condemning the abuses of those who would dare to impose baptism on the Jews by violent and frightening means, on the other hand declares that if the Jew decides to receive baptism in order to escape such threats, this would still be valid.[5] Here is his golden Doctrine: "*Those who, attracted by terrors and tortures, in order not to be harmed by them, receive the sacrament of baptism, as well as those who approach it falsely* [i.e., with a fake conversion], *[nevertheless] receive impressed the character of Christianity.*"[6] From these brief quotations, it is easy to understand that the two Supreme Pontiffs are talking about ADULT Jews and unbelievers and not about children, who are naturally incapable of violence and threats.

[p. 7]
In the same way, not a few quotations from other authors quoted in the two attached documents must be understood.

Moreover, if the Holy Church has always and constantly forbidden to baptize the children of unbelievers *invitis parentibus*, there are, however, some cases, contemplated by all theologians and canonists, in which it allows these

---

[4] "The custom of the Church has very great authority and ought to be jealously observed in all things." ST II.II 10.12.

[5] Whoever wishes to know the reason for which such baptism is declared valid should recall the sublime teaching of the Prince of Philosophers, St. Thomas, on human acts, when he teaches "*what is done out of fear is essentially voluntary*" (ST II.I 6.6).

[6] In the chapter *Maiores* "On Baptism."

a quei bambini, i quali trovansi presso a morte, né moralmente vi é più speranza di vita. La ragione di questa indulgenza é gravissima e tutta propria di una tenera madre, quale é la Chiesa, poiché *in tali casu puer MORALITER LOQUENDO neque exponitur periculo apostasiae; neque minister, sed ipsa mors illum a parentibus eripit*. Ed invero i grandi Apostoli delle Indie e delle Americhe S. Francesco Saverio, e S. Ludovico Beltrando hanno inviato al Cielo innumerevoli comprensori col battezzare occultamente *tanti morienti bambini*.[g]

Questo appunto sarebbe il caso del bambino Edgardo battezzato in evidentissimo pericolo di morte come si vedrà a suo luogo.

La legge pertanto della Chiesa, che proibisce di battezzare i bambini prima ancora dell'uso di ragione contro la volontà dei parenti infedeli, é diretta a vietare ed impedire quest'atto che *in se* sarebbe lesivo della patria potestà fondata sul diritto di natura, ed esporrebbe il battezzato al [p. 8] manifesto pericolo di apostasia nell'età adulta in detrimento della Religione;[h] ma non riguarda in verun modo IL FATTO GIA'CONSUMATO. Onde se avvenga che anche in onta a questa legge siasi conferito il battesimo a qualche bambino di parenti infedeli, la Chiesa lo riconosce per valido, entra in potere del novello suo figlio, e adopera ogni mezzo, ogni cura per allontanarlo dalla infedeltà dei parenti, nutrirlo ed allevarlo alla grazia di Gesù Cristo. Ed é pure sempre ammirabile la Chiesa in questa economia; dappoiché se per una parte spiega il suo potere e rigore nel vietare cotali battesimi, per l'altra mostra tutta la materna sua premura e sollecitudine in soccorso di chi avesse ricevuto il battesimo riconoscendolo quale vero suo figlio. Le storie Ecclesiastiche, i Concili, e le decisioni della S. Sede ne presentano luminosissimi esempi.[i]

Il perché sembra qui appunto opportuna cosa riferire una decisione della Suprema Congregazione del S. Officio, nella quale si conferma la proibizione della Chiesa onde non vengano battezzati i figli degli Ebrei *invitis parentibus*; si cita la BULLA DI GIULIO III. che infligge ai trasgressori censure e penalità pecuniarie: si dichiara inoltre, che a fronte di questi divieti della Chiesa, il battesimo può essere valido benché conferito di contro [p. 9] al volere dei parenti Ebrei; come valido venne giudicato il battesimo del quale si trattava: tuttoché per la prova canonica non si avesse che il solo testimonio della battezzante: ed infine ordina che la battezzata bambina sia allevata dai

---

g Vedi Billuart tract. de Baptism. art. IV.

h Divus Thom. loco citato.

i Anche nei casi nei quali il battesimo é stato conferito colla debita materia, forma, ed intenzione dalli stessi ebrei, o gentili.

children to be baptized. And as far as the present case is concerned, *it is permitted* to confer baptism on those children, who are near to death, or who morally have no hope of life. The reason for this indulgence is most serious, and it is all due to a tender mother, which is the Church, since *"in such a case, MORALLY SPEAKING, neither the child is exposed to the danger of apostasy, nor is the minister, but death itself separates him from his parents."* And indeed, the great apostles of the Indies and the Americas, St. Francis Xavier and St. Louis Beltrando, sent countless blessed souls to heaven by baptizing *many dying children* in secret.[7]

This would be the case of the child Edgardo, who was baptized in clear danger of death, as will be shown below.

The Church's law, therefore, which prohibits the baptism of children before the age of reason against the will of their unbeliever parents, is intended to prohibit and prevent this act, which *in itself* would be injurious to parental authority, based on the law of nature, and would expose the baptized person to the manifest danger of apostasy in adulthood, to the detriment of religion;[8] [p. 8] but it does not in any way concern the ALREADY CONSUMMATED FACT. Therefore, if, even in spite of this law, a child of unbeliever parents were to receive baptism, the Church would recognize it as valid, take power over its new child, and use every means, every solicitude, to separate it from the unfaithfulness of its parents, and to nourish it and educate it in the grace of Jesus Christ. And the Church is always admirable in this policy; indeed, if on the one hand she deploys her power and severity to forbid such baptisms, on the other hand she shows all her motherly care and solicitude to help those who have been baptized, recognizing them as her true children. The history of the Church, the Councils, and the decisions of the Holy See provide luminous examples of this.[9]

For this reason, it seems opportune to refer here to a decision of the Supreme Congregation of the Holy Office, which confirms the prohibition of the Church not to baptize the children of the Jews *invitis parentibus*. It cites the BULL OF JULIUS III, which inflicts censures and pecuniary penalties on transgressors; it also declares that, notwithstanding these Church prohibitions, baptism can be valid even if conferred against the will of the Jewish parents; [p. 9] it judges the baptism in question to be valid, although the only canonical proof was the baptizing woman's testimony; and finally it orders

---

[7] See Billuart's treatise about Baptism, art. 4.

[8] ST II.II 10.12.

[9] Even in cases where baptism was conferred with due matter, form, and intention by the Jews or pagans themselves.

Cristiani. Tanto si rileva dalle parole e dottrina dello stesso Decreto « *Die 30 mai 1638. Circa baptismum datum parvulae puellae annorum trium circiter filiae Hebraeorum a Faustina Christiana, invitis parentibus, Eminentissimi Domini censuerunt, parvulam puellam esse vere baptizatam, concurrente materia, forma, et intentione; baptismum probari unico teste; et quamvis filii Hebraeorum non possint invitis parentibus baptizari, si tamen de facto baptizentur, valere baptismum, et characterem imprimi, et filiam baptizatam apud christianos alendam; mulierem baptizantem acriter monendam, ut in posterum caveat a similibus; notificandum vero populo, non licere invitis parentibus, filios Hebraeorum baptizare, quia licet finis sit bonus, media non sunt licita, praesertim stante Bulla Iulii Tertii imponente poenam mille ducatorum, et suspensionem baptizantibus filios Hebraeorum invitis parentibus* ». Questa dottrinale e pratica decisione basterebbe *sola* per rispondere e ribattere le citate scritture in contrario.

Devesi pertanto concludere, che la verità del principale assunto, la. quale contiene la legge e la consuetudine della Chiesa onde si vieta di battezzare *infantes infidelium invitis parentibus*; nulla influisce su di un *atto già consumato*, quale é appunto il battesimo conferito al bambino Edgardo figlio di Salomone Mortara. E poiché la [p. 10] maggior parte delle autorità allegate mirano di fatto a provare in vero una legge per se manifesta; dunque dicevasi bene in principio, che tali allegazioni sono fuori di proposito.

L'altro asserto pertanto « *che nella ipotesi, in cui i figli degli Infedeli venissero* ANTE USUM RATIONIS *battezzati contro volontà dei parenti, cotale battesimo sarebbe del tutto invalido e di nessun effetto* ». É temerario, falso, contrario alla sentenza di tutti i Canonisti e Teologi; ed opposto alla pratica costante della Chiesa universale; non che già condannato dalla Santa Sede in tante Decisioni e Decreti. Le autorità dei Canonisti e Teologi, i quali vengono riportati in favore del secondo asserto nelle due citate Scritture (se alcuno se ne eccettui col Durando) non riguardano altrimenti la validità del Battesimo in ogni caso conferito *infanti Infidelium invitis parentibus*; ma riguardano indubitatamente la lecitudine di quest'atto di fronte alle Leggi Canoniche, e consuetudine della Chiesa. Inoltre é d'avvertirsi, che gli autori riportati in favore dell'opinione contraria alla validità di tale battesimo sono quelli medesimi, i quali nelle questioni e luoghi citati sostengono colla dottrina ed assoluta sentenza di S. Tommaso la legge e consuetudine della Chiesa, che proibisce di battezzare *infantes Infidelium invitis parentibus* contro l'opinione

that the baptized child be brought up by Christians. This can be seen from the words and doctrine of the same Decree: "*30 May 1638. Concerning the baptism of a child about three years old, the daughter of Hebrews, by Faustina Cristiana, against the will of her parents, the eminent Cardinals determined that the child was truly baptized, with the participation of matter, form and intention; that a single witness proved the baptism; and that although the children of Hebrews cannot be baptized against the will of their parents, if they are in fact baptized, the baptism is valid, and that the character is imprinted and the baptized daughter should remain among Christians. That the woman who administered the baptism should be severely admonished, so that in the future she may abstain from similar things; that the people should be notified in truth that it is not lawful to baptize the children of Hebrews against the will of their parents, that although the end is good, the means are not lawful, especially since the Bull of Julius III imposes a penalty of one thousand ducats and a suspension on those who baptize the children of Hebrews against the will of their parents.*" This doctrinal and practical decision *alone* would be sufficient to answer and refute the writings cited to the contrary.

It must therefore be concluded that the truth of the [*Pro-memoria's*] main thesis, based on the law and the custom of the Church, according to which it is forbidden to baptize the children of unbelievers *invitis parentibus*, has no influence on an *act already consummated*, which is precisely the baptism given to the child Edgardo, son of Salomone Mortara. [p. 10] And since most of the attached authorities are intended to prove as true a law that is itself manifest, it is well said above that such quotations are out of order.

The other assertion, therefore, "*that in the hypothesis that the children of unbelievers were baptized, ANTE USUM RATIONIS, against the will of their parents, such baptism would be totally invalid and of no effect,*" is reckless, false, contrary to the judgment of all canonists and theologians, contrary to the constant practice of the universal Church, and already condemned by the Holy See in many decisions and decrees.

The authorities of the canonists and the theologians, quoted in favor of the second assertion in the two cited documents (with the exception of a few, among whom Durand) do not concern the validity in every case of the baptism given to the children of unbelievers *invitis parentibus*; but they undoubtedly concern the lawfulness of this act before the canonical laws and the custom of the Church. In addition, it should be noted that the authors quoted in favor of the opinion against the validity of this baptism are the same ones who, in the very questions and passages cited on the basis of the doctrine and absolute judgment of St. Thomas, support the law and custom of the Church that prohibits the baptism of the children of unbelievers *invitis*

di Scoto e di alcuni pochissimi suoi seguaci, i quali sostengono potersi battezzare anche contro la volontà dei parenti i figli degl'infedeli.

Benché da alcuni pochi autori riportati nelle due Scritture sembri richiedersi nel combattere l'opinione [p. 11] di Scoto *ad validitatem baptismi infantium Infidelum, voluntas. interpretativa parentum*, pure questa opinione è evidentemente temeraria e falsa. Infatti tutti i Teologi e Canonisti dimostrano la validità di cotale Battesimo escluso il consenso della volontà interpretativa dei parenti; e convengono nell'asserire « *validum esse baptismum sic collatum, quia omnes veri Sacramenti conditiones importat, materiam, formam intentionem, et denique subjectum idoneum* ».

Il Cardinale Cajetano fedele interprete di S. Tommaso, dichiara che questa Sentenza é cosi certa, che il S. Dottore la suppone in tutti i luoghi nei quali parla del Battesimo conferito ai figli degli infedeli « *Auctorem sentire imo supponere filios infidelium fore vere baptizatos, si invitis parentibus baptizarentur. Hoc enim supponit ratio dicens, esse periculosum, taliter filios infidelium baptizare: quia de facili ad infidelitatem redirent propter naturalem affectum ad parentes* ». In tert. part. Quaest. LXVIII Art. X

Per verità il Sacramento é sempre valido, quando vi concorrono gli estremi e le condizioni essenziali poste dal Divino Istitutore. In quanto al battesimo nulla più si richiede per la sua validità, che la materia venga applicata colla corrispondente forma ad idoneo soggetto quale può essere an- che un bambino appena nato, ed il ministro può essere qualunque uomo, purché intenda di fare *quod facit Ecclesia*. Sono questi gli estremi del Battesimo, Sacramento di necessità, come sempre ha tenuto, insegnato e deciso la Cattolica Chiesa. Né mai ha richiesto onde sia valido la volontà dei parenti in quanto ai bambini non [p. 12] ancor giunti all'uso si ragione. Cosi la discorrono i Teologi « Baptismum infantibus quorumcumque infidelium, etiam ipsis parentibus invitis collatum, esse validum, quia adsunt omnia essentialia, materia, forma, intentio ministri, et subjectum capax: neque voluntas seu intentio parentum offerentium pertinet *ad essentiam*, sed tantum *ad solemnitatem* Sacramenti ». Non enim scriptum est, inquit Augustinus epist. 23 ad Bonifac. « Nisi quis renatus fuerit ex parentum voluntate, sed nisi quis renatus fuerit ex aqua et Spiritu Sancto ». Per tutti poi conchiude l'Angelico con assoluta Sentenza affermando, che l'infedelta e l'opposizione dei parenti per nulla impedisce la validità del battesimo, e di conseguente eterna salute di cotali predestinati bambini. *Nec impeditur eorum (parvulorum) salus si parentes sint infideles.*

parentibus, against the opinion of Scotus and some very few of his followers, who maintain instead that the children of unbelievers can be baptized even against the will of their parents.

Although, in order to counter the opinion of Scotus, not all but only some of the authors mentioned in the two documents seem to require *the representative will of the parents to determine the validity of infant baptism*, this thesis too is evidently reckless and false. [p. 11] In fact, all theologians and canonists demonstrate the validity of such baptism without the consent of the representative will of the relatives; and they agree in asserting that "*baptism thus conferred is valid, because it has all the conditions of the true sacrament, namely matter, form, intention, and, finally, suitable subject.*"

Cardinal Cajetan, faithful interpreter of St. Thomas, declares that this sentence is so certain that the Holy Doctor assumes it wherever he speaks of baptism given to the children of unbelievers: "The author thinks and finally assumes that the children of unbelievers would really be baptized if they were baptized against the will of their parents. It's because he assumes this that he says it's dangerous to baptize the children of unbelievers in this way: because they would easily return to unbelief because of their natural affection for their parents." (Part III, question 68, art. 10).

In truth, the sacrament is always valid when the essential conditions and extremes established by the Divine Author are fulfilled. As far as baptism is concerned, nothing more is required for its validity than that the matter be applied with the appropriate form to a suitable subject, which can be even a newborn child, and the minister can be any man, as long as he intends to do *quod facit Ecclesia* [what the Church does]. These are the extremes of baptism, a sacrament of necessity, as the Catholic Church has always claimed, taught, and decided. Nor has it ever required the will of the parents for baptism to be valid for children who have not yet reached the use of reason. [p. 12] Theologians discuss it in this way: "The baptism of children of any unbeliever, even if it is conferred on them against the will of the parents, is valid, because all the essential elements are present: matter, form, intention of the one who administers it, and suitable subject: neither the will nor the intention of the parents of the one being baptized has anything to do *with the essence*, and still less *with the solemnity*, of the sacrament. For it is not written, Augustine says in Letter 23 to Boniface, 'Unless one has been born again of the will of his parents, but unless one has been born again of water and the Holy Spirit'? Finally, for all of them, the Angelic Doctor concludes with an absolute judgment, affirming that the unfaithfulness and opposition of the parents in no way prevent the validity of the baptism and the consequent

Il voler dunque sostenere come necessaria alla validità del battesimo la volontà dei parenti, ossia la volontà *interpretativa* sarebbe lo stesso, che il far dipendere la validità di questo Sacramento da una condizione meramente estrinseca, lo che é del tutto falso, perché si oppone alla natura della divina istituzione di si gran Sacramento.

Se si eccettui il Durando, il quale con altre azzardate proposizioni sostiene la invalidità di tali battesimi per la deficienza della volontà nel suscipiente (non propria perché il bambino non può averla, dice egli, prima dell'uso della ragione; non interpretativa, perché quella dei parenti è contraria): tutti gli altri autori citati o riferiscono semplicemente *per modum quaestionis et narrationis* l'opinione di Durando, come apertamente [p. 13] rilevasi dal *Capreolo*[j] riportato nelle due Scritture, il quale si esprime «*Quidquid sit de hoc etc.*» dimostrando cosi non esser questa la sua ferma sentenza; ovvero parlano della volontà interpretativa richiesta dai parenti infedeli per la *lecitudine* del Battesimo da conferirsi ai bambini, onde non venga lesa la loro patria potestà colla violenza.

Quanto si é finora discorso per sostenere, che le autorità riportate nelle due scritture (*una vel altera excepta*) parlano della solennità, della lecitudine della convenienza delle leggi canoniche, ed anche di potenza legale, ma non assoluta di conferire il battesimo *infantibus haebreorum invitis parentibus* è sentenza e dottrina dell'immortale Pontefice Benedetto XIV il quale nella sua lettera al Vicegerente di Roma al N. 26 cosi discorre. « Nulla de hac re inter S. Thomam (*suosque discipulos*), et Scotum dissentio est cum non in eam sententiam disputaverint, utrum baptismus Hebraeis infantibus sine parentum consensu conferri valide possit, verum an licite; ut prudenter animadvertit Cardinalis Laurea egregius Scolista[k] sermo non est de posse valido, quia si baptizarentur certum est remanere_baptizatos; sed de posse licito, idest, an licite fiat si baptizentur ».

[j] In IV Sent. Distinct. VI Quaest. 1.

eternal health of these predestined children: "*Nor is it a hindrance to their* [the children's] *salvation if their parents are unbelievers.*"[10]

To assert that the will of the parents, that is, the *representative* will, is necessary for the validity of baptism would be the same as making the validity of this sacrament dependent on a merely extrinsic condition; this would be completely false, because it contradicts the very nature of the divine institution of this great sacrament.

With the exception of Durand, who, among other bold assertions, argues for the invalidity of such baptisms because of the lack of beneficiary's will (neither his own, because the child cannot have it, he says, before the use of reason; nor the representative one, because that of the parents is contrary), all the other authors quoted either simply refer to Durand's opinion *per modum quaestionis et narrationis* [by means of questions and answers] [**p. 13**] —as is clear for Capreolus,[11] quoted in the two documents, who writes, "Whoever is of this opinion," thus showing that this is not his firm opinion—or they refer to the representative will required by the unbeliever relatives for the licit baptism of children, so that their patria potestà is not violated by force.

What has been said so far in order to sustain that the authorities mentioned in the two documents deal with the solemnity, the liceity, and the convenience of the canonical laws, and also with the legal, but not absolute power to confer baptism on the children of the Jews *invitis parentibus* is the judgement and doctrine of the immortal Pontiff Benedict XIV. This pope, in fact, in his letter to the Vicar of Rome number 26, writes: "There is no disagreement on this subject between St. Thomas (and his disciples) and Scotus, since they do not question that baptism can be validly conferred on Jewish children without the consent of their parents. As Cardinal Laurea, an excellent Scoliast,[12] wisely observes, the question is not whether it can be valid, because if they are baptized it is certain that they will remain baptized, but whether it can be licit, that is, whether they are baptized licitly."

---

10 [Translator's note: This quotation is taken from ST III 68.9.]
11 In *Sentence IV*, D. 6, question 1.
12 In *Sentence IV*, disp. 14, art. 5, num. 58.

Che se anche si voglia accordare, che alcuni autori riportati *nelle due Scritture* parlino della *validità* [p. 14] del Battesimo in ogni caso, e non già della *lecitudine*; allora risponderemo francamente con S. Tommaso, che coteste opinioni sono opposte alla consuetudine costante della Chiesa, e perciò da rigettarsi « *Maximam habet auctoritatem Ecclesiae consuetudo, quae semper est in omnibus aemulanda: quia et ipsa doctrina catholicorum Doctorum ab Ecclesia auctoritatem habet. Unde magis standum est auctoritati Ecclesiae, quam auctoritati vel Augustini, vel Hieronimi, vel cu-juscumque Doctoris»*. Nelle due Scritture non si citano già per la supposta invalidità li Agostini i Girolami, ma autori di altre avventate opinioni.[l]

Che se poi vogliasi ricercare la volontà *interpretativa* nel bambino, cui si conferisce il S. Battesimo in quanto alla *validità* del Sacramento, questa non devesi già ripetere dai parenti infedeli, ma sibbene dalla Chiesa madre e sovrana di tutti gli uomini, *quia infantes non baptizantur im fide suorum parentum, sed in fide totius Ecclesiae, ac secundum voluntatem Christi.*[m] Di cotal guisa scriveva S. Agostino a S. Bonifacio[n] « Offeruntur parvuli ad percipiendam spiritualem gratiam non tam ab eis, quorum gestantur manibus, quam ab universa Sanctorum societate atque Fidelium. Ab omnibus namque offerri intelliguntur, quibus placet, quod offeruntur, et quorum charitate ad comunionem Sancti Spiritus adjunguntur ». Perloché segue a ragionare [p. 15] sulla dottrina di Agostino l'Angelico: « Infidelitas propriorum parentum etiamsi eos (infantes) post baptismum Demoniorum sacrificiis imbuere conentur, » (qual maggior contrarietà di questa nei parenti) pueris tamen « non nocet ».[o] Inoltre con S. Agostino aggiunge S. Tommaso, che in questi casi l'intenzione della Chiesa viene rappresentata ed applicata al bambino infedele, che si battezza da quell'unica persona, che gli conferisce il Sacramento.

k In IV sentent: disp: 14 art: 5 num. 98.
l D. Th. loco citato.
m Ferraris verbo Baptismum n. 12.
n Epist. 23.
o 3. P. Q. 68. art. IX. ad. 2.

[p. 14]
Even if we admit that some of the authors mentioned in the two Documents speak of the *validity* of Baptism in every case, and not of *legitimacy*, then we will answer frankly with St. Thomas that these opinions are contrary to the constant custom of the Church, and therefore to be rejected: "*The custom of the Church has very great authority and ought to be jealously observed in all things, since the very doctrine of catholic doctors derives its authority from the Church. Hence we ought to abide by the authority of the Church rather than by that of an Augustine or a Jerome or of any doctor whatever.*" In the two Documents, it is not Augustine or Jerome who are not cited for the supposed invalidity, but authors of other reckless opinions.[13]

If, then, the *representative* will of the child on whom Holy Baptism is conferred is to be sought for the *validity* of the sacrament, it must be expressed not by the unbeliever parents, but by the Church, Mother and Sovereign of all men, "*because children are not baptized in the faith of their parents, but in the faith of the whole Church and according to the will of Christ.*"[14] The same St Augustine wrote to St Boniface:[15] "Children are offered to receive spiritual grace, not so much by those who carry them in their hands, but by the entire community of saints and faithful; in fact, they are to be offered *by all* whom it pleases to offer them, and by whose charity they are joined to the communion of the Holy Spirit." [p. 15] Therefore, the Angelic Doctor continues to reflect on the doctrine of Augustine: "The unbelief of their own parents, even if after Baptism these strive to infect them with the worship of demons, (what greater opposition than this from relatives!), hurts not the children."[16] Furthermore, Saint Thomas adds, in the same sense as St. Augustine, that in these cases the will of the Church is expressed and applied to the unbeliever child who is baptized by the one person who administers the sacrament.

---

13 ST II.II 10.12.
14 Ferraris, *verbo Baptismum*, n. 12.
15 Letter n. 23.
16 ST III. 68.9 ad. 2.

Questa dottrina é cattolica, né é lecito dubitarne menomamente, poiché é inconcussa definizione delle Decretali, dei Canoni e dei Concili Generali[p]

Passando poi a considerare i casi in particolare, e come suol dirsi *in concreto*, si ha una tradizione costante e pratica della validità del battesimo conferito *Infantibus Judaeorum insciis vel invitis parentibus*. Una piena prova di quanto affermo può ritrarsi dall'aurea lettera, che il Gran Pontefice Benedetto XIV. indirizzava al Vicegerente di Roma nel 1747 a tutti ben nota! Ma qui soltanto si accenneranno fra i molti alcuni casi e decisioni della Suprema Congregazione della S. R. Inquisizione.[q] Ed invero nel 1714 il Sommo Pontefice dichiarò valido *Baptismum collatum Augustae Taurinorim a nutrice cuidam puellae Hebraee adhuc in infantia, unde in Ecclesia* [p. 16] *Metropolitana suppleta sunt tantum sacramentalia, sive solemnitates sub die 23. Septembris eiusdem anni.*

In Fer. IV. 18. Julii 1725 *declaratum fuit validum baptisma collatum a muliere infanti Hebraeo annorum quatuor absque consensu parentum.*

Item Fer. IV. 14. Julii 1742. in generali Congregatione Supremae Inquisitionis *decretum fuit validum baptismum Avenione collatum a puella Hebraea annor. 18 infanti item ex Hebraeis parentibus nato octo mensium.*

Tandem notandum, quod in Fer. V. die 7. Septembris 1741. *propositum fuit dubium super validitate baptismi collati a quodam famulo in claustro Israelitico de Urbe infanti Hebraeo duorum annorum in hac forma* « Io ti battezzo col nome del Padre, del Figliuolo e dello Spirito Santo ».

---

[p] De Consecrat. dist. 4. Multis in locis, et in cap. Majores de Baptismo, et Concil. Trident. sess. 7. cap. 13. de baptismo.

[q] Sessa cap. LVI. De Iudaeis n. 5.

APPENDIX C

This doctrine is Catholic, and there is no right to doubt it, since it is the indisputable definition of the Decretals, the Canons, and the General Councils.[17]

Turning then to the specific cases, and, as one would say, to go to the *concrete*, there is a constant and practical tradition of the validity of the baptism given to *Infantibus Iudaeorum insciis vel invitis parentibus* [Jewish children without the knowledge or the consent of the parents]. A full proof of what I'm affirming may be found in the great letter which the Great Pontiff Benedict XIV addressed to the Vicar of Rome in 1747, and which is well known to all! But here we will only mention some of the cases and decisions of the Supreme Congregation of the Holy Roman Inquisition.[18] And indeed, in 1714, the Supreme Pontiff declared the validity of the *baptism given in Turin by a nurse to a certain Hebrew girl who was still in her infancy, so that only the sacramentals or solemnities were celebrated in the Metropolitan Church on September 25 of the same year.*

[p. 16]
On Feria IV, Wednesday, July 18, 1725, *it was declared that the baptism of a four-year-old Hebrew boy, performed by a woman without the consent of his parents, was valid.*[19]

In the same way, on Feria IV, Wednesday, July 14, 1742, in the general session of the Supreme Congregation of the Inquisition, *the baptism given in Avignon by an eighteen-year-old Hebrew girl to an eight-month-old child born of Hebrew parents was declared valid.*

Finally, it should be noted that on Feria V, Thursday, September 7, 1741, the Pope was presented with *a doubt about the validity of the baptism of a two-year-old Hebrew child, performed by a servant in the Israelite ghetto of Rome with this formula*: "I baptize you with the name of the Father, the Son, and the Holy Spirit."[20]

---

17 *De Consecrat*, dist. 4. "Multis in locis" and in chapter "Majores de Baptismo." See also the Council of Trient, session n. 7, chapter 13, "*de baptismo.*"

18 Sessa, chap. 56, *De Iudaeis* n. 5.

19 [Translator's note: Feria IV is the term used in the jargon of the Inquisition to refer to the session in which all the cardinals who were members of the Congregation met, a session that took place exactly on the fourth day of the week ("Feria IV," using the Catholic count of Sunday as the first day), that is, on Wednesday.]

20 [Translator's note: In the practice of the Inquisition and the Holy Office, on Thursday (Feria V) the assessor of the congregation would meet in audience with the pope, the supreme prefect of the congregation, to present to him the decisions made by the inquisitor cardinals in the previous day's session (Feria IV). Normally, though exceptions were not uncommon, the pope merely confirmed the decisions made by the cardinals.]

SSmus auditis Votis Eminentorum decrevit « Puerum supradictum fuisse valide baptizatum ».

Resta dunque evidente e secondo la Cattolica dottrina, che *infantes Judaeorum baptizati etiam invitis parentibus valide baptizantur recipientes in se Sacramentum, et rem Sacramenti.*

Che perciò l'asserto esposto nel Pro-memoria e sillabo *é* temerario, falso, e contrario alla sentenza di tutti i Canonisti e Teologi; opposto alla pratica costante della Chiesa universale, e già condannato dalla S. Sede in tante decisioni.

In terzo luogo si pretende dallo scrittore del Promemoria e sillabo « *Che supposto valido tale battesimo, pure devesi restituire il figlio per diritto di natura alla patria potestà, che lo reclama con ogni ragione* ».

[p. 17]
Si risponde, che il diritto della Chiesa *acquisito* sul battezzato prevale al diritto paterno degl'Infedeli, e che perciò non devesi restituire il fanciullo battezzato, che anzi si deve custodire alla Religione, cui appartiene per il carattere indelebile e Divino del S. Battesimo.

Devesi poi avvertire, che quelle poche autorità riportate nelle *due scritture* in favore della pretesa nullità del battesimo in discorso, accennano pure alla restituzione del figlio invalidamente (nel loro senso) battezzato; ma qui rispondiamo colle Scuole, *falsum antecedens, ergo et consequens.*

Di fatto i Canonisti e Teologi confermano a pieno coro questa verità: che non devesi per verun conto restituire ai parenti infedeli il figlio battezzato. Poiché non debbonsi porre di fronte Dio, e i parenti infedeli del battezzato quasi due autorità competenti sul diritto o naturale o divino di possedere il bambino: ma si deve mirare a *Dio solo* come autore del diritto naturale nei parenti infedeli, ed autore del diritto Divino nella sua Chiesa. Questo secondo, che si acquista dalla Chiesa sull'*infante* battezzato è di un ordine superiore e più nobile del primo: *ideoque iuri paterno praevalet ius, quod Ecclesia per baptismum acquisivit, cum cedat in utilitatem pueri, in honorem Dei, et Religionis, et Sacramenti, quae per apostasiam moraliter certo futuram, gravi iniuria afficerentur. Apertissime id fuit demandatum in Concilio Toletano quarto Canon. 58. hisce verbis:* « *Iudaeorum filios vel filias baptizatos, ne parentum involvantur erroribus ab eorum consortio separari decernimus:* [p. 18] *deputandos: autem Monasteriis vel Christianis viris, aut mulieribus Deum timentibus, ut in moribus et fide proficiant* ».[r]

[r] Billuart de Bapt. art. 4.

APPENDIX C

The pope, after hearing the decision of the cardinals, decreed: The said child has been validly baptized."

It remains, therefore, evident and in accordance with the Catholic doctrine that *Jewish children who are baptized, even without the consent of their parents, receive the sacrament itself and the substance of the Sacrament.*

It is also evident, therefore, that the assertion set forth in the *Pro-memoria* and the *Syllabus is* reckless, false, and contrary to the judgment of all canonists and theologians; it is contrary to the constant practice of the universal Church, and has already been condemned by the Holy See in so many decisions.

In the third place, the author of the *Pro-memoria* and *Syllabus* asserts, *"that, supposing this baptism to be valid, the child must in any case, by the right of nature, be returned to the parental authority, which claims it with every reason."*

[p. 17]

It is answered that the Church's *acquired* right over the baptized child prevails over the paternal right of the unbelievers, and that therefore the baptized child must not be returned, but must be kept in the religion to which it belongs because of the indelible and divine character of Holy Baptism.

It must then be pointed out that the few authorities quoted in the *two documents* in favor of the alleged nullity of the baptism in question also mention the restitution of the invalidly (in their sense) baptized child; but here we reply with the [propositions of the] Schools: *wrong is the premise, therefore false is the consequence.*

As a matter of fact, canonists and theologians unanimously confirm this truth: that the baptized child is not at all to be given back to the unbeliever parents. This is because God and the unbeliever parents of the baptized child must not be placed before each other as if they were two authorities with jurisdiction over the natural or divine right to possess the child; but *God alone* must be regarded as the author of the natural right in the unbeliever parents and the author of the divine right. This second right, which the Church acquires over the baptized *child*, is of a higher and nobler order than the first: *and therefore the right that the Church has acquired by baptism, prevails over the right of the father, which is relinquished for the benefit of the son, to the honor of God, religion, and the sacrament, which would suffer grave outrage from the morally certain future apostasy.* This was very clearly demanded by the Fourth Council of Toledo, Canon 58, in the following words: *"We decree that the baptized sons or daughters of the Jews should be separated from their parents, so that they may not be involved in their errors:*

L'Angelico Dottore mentre dimostra con ragioni ed autorità, che non debbonsi battezzare *infantes Judaeorum invitis parentibus*, dimostra peraltro egualmente nei luoghi citati dal Promemoria e dal Sillabo, che se avvenga di conferirsi a tali bambini il battesimo, questo é rato e valido, e che perciò non si devono lasciare cotesti figli in potere dei parenti i quali *certo certius*, in danno della Religione e della loro eterna salute li farebbero, apostatare dalla fede ricevuta nell'infanzia. Di simile guisa la discorre col S. Dottore il Cardinal Gotti « Fit iniuria baptismo et Religioni Christi ... Si quidem est moraliter impossibile, filios invitis parentibus infidelibus baptizatos, sub eorum cura in fide Christiana educari potius quam eorum erroribus imbui, ac a fide suscepta non deviare, cum ad usum rationis pervenerint. Unde S. Thomas ait: cum ad aetatem perfectam devenerint, de facili possent a parentibus induci, ut relinquerent, quod ignoranter susceperunt.... De facili ad infidelitatem redirent propter naturalem affectum ad parentes ».[s]

Lo stesso S. Tommaso nell'asserire che la Chiesa non ebbe mai in costume di battezzare i Figli degli infedeli a ritroso del loro volere fra le altre ragioni dice, che allora i parenti [p. 19] verrebbero a perdere ogni diritto sui Figli passati in potere della Chiesa in forza del Battesimo. *Fieret autem Judaeis iniuria, si eorum filii baptizarentur eis invitis; quia amitterent ius patriae potestatis in filios JAM FIDELES.*[t] Aurea Sentenza che decide e della validità del battesimo, e del pieno diritto della Chiesa di mettersi al possesso di questi novelli Figli della Grazia di Gesù Cristo. L'opinione, che sostiene potersi i figli degli Ebrei battezzati *invitis parentibus* lasciare in loro potere anche con cauzione, da pochissimi é motivata, e sostenuta dal solo Calderini, ma viene da tutti concordemente rigettata come erronea ed ingiuriosa al Divino diritto, che la Chiesa acquista sui battezzati. Anzi é stata già condannata dalla Romana Curia fino dai 22 Ottobre 1587.[u] e tante altre volte in appresso.[v] E con ogni diritto, perché opposta alle sanzioni del S.Concilio di Trento, a molti testi del Gius Canonico, ed alla costante pratica della Santa Sede.[w] Per lo che il Cardinale Albizi asserisce che la Sentenza del Calderini é stata pure condannata dalla S. Congregazione del S. Officio « *et vere scio in hac Sacra Congregatione Sententiam Calderini uti erroneam fuisse reiectam* ».[x]

s De necessitate et subjecto Baptism. Quest. V. Dub. V. § 2.
t 2.2. Quaest. X. Art. XII.
u Carena de Off. SS. Inquisitionis Part. 2 f. 14
v Sessa de Judaeis C. LV.
w Sess. 7 can. 14.
x Alibit. De Incost: in Fide Cap. 11 n. 33.

[p. 18] *instead, they should be entrusted to monasteries or to Christian men and women who fear God, so that they may grow in morals and faith."*[21]

The *Angelic Doctor*, while demonstrating with reason and authority that the children of the Jews should not be baptized *invitis parentibus*, also demonstrates in the places cited by the *Pro-memoria* and the *Syllabus* that if baptism is given to such children, it is confirmed and valid, and therefore these children should not be left in the power of parents who would *certainly*, to the detriment of religion and their eternal health, cause them to apostatize from the faith received in infancy. Cardinal Gotti argues in a similar way to Saint Thomas: "It would be an offense against baptism and the religion of Christ... since it is indeed morally impossible for children baptized against the will of unbelieving parents to be brought up under their care in the Christian faith, so that they may not be imbued with their errors and may not depart from the received faith when they come to the use of reason. Therefore St. Thomas says: 'Having reached maturity, they could easily be induced by their parents to leave what they have unconsciously received.... They would easily return to unbelief because of their natural affection for their parents.'"[22]

St. Thomas himself, in asserting that the Church has never been accustomed to baptize the sons of the unbelievers against their will, says, among other reasons, that in such a case the parents would lose all rights over their children, who have passed into the power of the Church by virtue of Baptism. [p. 19] "It would be an injustice to Jews if their children were to be baptized against their will; since they would lose the rights of paternal authority over their children AS SOON AS THESE WERE CHRISTIANS."[23] A splendid sentence that decides the validity of baptism and the full right of the Church to take possession of these new children of the grace of Jesus Christ. The opinion that the children of the Jews, baptized *invitis parentibus*, could be left in their power, even on bail, is held by very few and supported by Calderini alone, but it is unanimously rejected by all as erroneous and injurious to the Divine right that the Church acquires over the baptized.[24] On the contrary, it has already been condemned by the Roman Curia since October 22, 1587,[25] and many other times since then.[26] And rightly so, because it is contrary to

---

21 Billuart, *de Baptismo*, art. 4.

22 *De necessitate et subjecto Baptismi*, Question 5, doubt 5, § 2.

23 ST, 2.2, question 10, Art. 12.

24 [Translator's note: "Even on bail" evidently refers to the bonds (paid with gold scudi) mentioned in the various precedents of restitution of baptized Jewish children cited in the *Pro-memoria*.]

25 Carena, *de Officio SS. Inquisitionis*, Part. 2, f. 14

26 Sessa, *de Iudaeis*, chapter 55.

E per verità la S. Congregazione del Concilio rescrisse

[p. 20]

« Episeopo Fossanen, qaemdam infantem Hebraeum, qui a nutrice in domum cuiusdam Christiani delatus fuerat, et a quibusdam adolescentibus baptizatus, a parentibus segregandum, et bene custodiendum. . . . Item a S. Romana Inquisitione 1. Januari 1707. decretum fuit, infantem cuiusdam Hebraei Augustae Taurinorum a nutrice baptizatum, a parentibus segregari, et in fide Catholica educari ». Insuper sub die 16 Junii 1714 iussu SSmi per organum eiusdem supremae Congregationis separata fuit puella Hebraea a propriis parentibus, licet dubium aliquod existeret super validitate baptismi eidem a nutrice collati.

Eadem S. Congregatio ad dubium an possit cum periculo apostasiae relinqui parentibus puer baptizatus, dum annum quartum suae aetatis ageret, rescribendum censuit « Puerum Hebreum separandum. a parentum consortio, et in Religione Catholica penes Christianos esse educandum » Fer. IV, Die XVIII, Juli 1725. Item in Fer. V. coram SSmo 7 Decembris 1741 decretum fuit: « Puerum Hebraeorum a quodam famulo Romae baptizatum, removendum esse a parentibus Hebraeis, et collocandum in Domo Cathecumenorum, ibique in fide christiana instruendum, et ad R. P. D. Vicemgerentem pro executione ».[y]

---

[y] Lo stesso Sapientissimo Pontefice Benedetto XIV, nella citata lettera a Monsignor Vicegerente, conferma il diritto e la pratica della S. Romana Chiesa di mettersi al possesso dei bambini battezzati per educarli nella fede ricevuta col carattere indelebile del S. Battesimo.

the sanctions of the Holy Council of Trent, to many texts of Canon Law, and to the constant practice of the Holy See.[27] Cardinal Albizi therefore asserts that Calderini's sentence was also condemned by the Sacred Congregation of the Holy Office: "*And I truly know that in this Sacred Congregation the opinion of Calderini was rejected as erroneous.*"[28]

And indeed, the Holy Congregation of the Council wrote:

[p. 20]
"to the bishop of Fossano, that a certain Hebrew child, who had been brought by a nurse to the house of a certain Christian and baptized by some teenagers, should be separated from his parents and carefully cared for.... Likewise, on January 1, 1707, the Sacred Roman Inquisition decreed that a child of certain Hebrews in Turin, baptized by a nurse, should be separated from his parents and brought up in the Catholic faith. Furthermore, on June 16, 1714, by order of the Holy Father through the same Supreme Congregation, a Hebrew girl was separated from her parents, although there was some doubt as to the validity of the baptism conferred on her by her nurse."

The same Sacred Congregation, concerning the doubt whether a baptized child could be left to his parents, with the danger of apostasy, while he was in the fourth year of his age, gave the following answer: "The Hebrew child must be separated from his parents and brought up with Christians in the Catholic religion." (Feria IV, Wednesday, July 18, 1725.) In the same way, in Feria V, on Thursday, December 7, 1741, before the Pope it was established: "A son of the Hebrews, baptized in Rome by a servant, must be taken from his Hebrew parents, and placed in the house of catechumens, and there instructed in the Christian faith. [This was sent] to the Reverend Father Cardinal Vicar for execution."[29]

---

27 Session 7, can. 14.

28 Albizi, *De Incostantia in Fide*, Chap. 11, n. 33.

29 The Most Wise Pontiff Benedict XIV himself, in the aforementioned letter to the Vicar General, confirms the right and practice of the Holy Roman Church to take possession of baptized children in order to educate them in the faith received with the indelible character of Holy Baptism.

[p. 21]
Sub Fer. IV. Die 10. Julii 1742 dispositum fuit, ut « puer octo mensium Avenione in Gallia a puella Hebraea baptizatus omnino eripiatur e manibus parentum Hebraeorum, et omnino curandum, ut nutriatur, et educetur inter Christianos ».

Tuttavia da taluni non bene informati si fa correre voce, che la S. Sede in qualche caso ha ordinato o almeno permesso, che i bambini Ebrei battezzati *invitis parentibus* venissero restituiti ai medesimi loro parenti; e fra li altri accennano un caso di recente data accaduto a Fiumicino e Roma nel 1840.[z] Si risponde, che circa alcuni casi di data più tosto remota non vale la pena occuparsene poiché o non sussistono, o sono ben diversi dal modo, con cui si espongono: come potrebbe dimostrarsi del supposto battesimo della Ebrea Ferrarese Regina Salomoni.[aa]

[p. 22]
Il perché si darà piuttosto un'esatta e genuina relazione dell'avvenuto nel 1840 per provare ad evidenza, che fino al presente la S. Sede ha operato con prudenza, sapienza e fermezza nelle sue massime e pratiche sempre uguale, e costante.

Nel giugno 1840 prendevano terra a Fiumicino i coniugi Ebrei Daniele Montel di Nymes e Miett Cremieux. Appena discesi dal bastimento la Miett venne sorpresa dai dolori di un parto immaturo e diede alla luce una bambina. Una donna che abitava nella medesima locanda avvisando un quasi imminente pericolo di Morte fu sollecita di battezzare la neonata bambina. Però non tardarono le Autorità Ecclesiastiche a venire in cognizione dell'accaduto alla Figlia dei coniugi Montel Cremieux, i quali avevano già preso dimora in Roma. Mentre si assumevano li atti regolari per la prova del conferito battesimo si facevano sorvegliare i genitori della bambina battezzata per la personale sicurezza della medesima. Compiuti li atti venne

---

z Anche l'autore del Pro-memoria cita questo avvenimento, ma lo riporta solo per quella parte che può servire al suo scopo e tace, anzi nega la parte importante, che cioè la Figlia dei Coniugi Ebrei non fu lasciata in potere loro. Dal modo con cui cita francamente questo fatto si può argomentare sulli altri pure citati, e sulle allegate autorità ripetute quasi ad ogni pagina del Sillabo. Vedi pag. 44.

aa In Ferrara nel 1785. una donna dopo 30 e più anni asseriva, che nell'eta sua di 7 anni aveva battezzata in Padova l'ebrea Regina Salomoni allora di anni 3. Però veniva meno la prova della denunziante, la quale asseriva quanto sopra dopo avere sofferto una forte crisi e malattia mentale por la quale era stata assoggettata alli rimedi, e cura propria dei deliranti. In seguito pertanto di questa ed altre notizie la Suprema Congregazione decise in Feria III loco IV. 6. Decembris 1785 *attentis omnibus circumstantiis testem non esse fide dignam; ideoque interrogata muliere hebraea, an velit esse Christiana, quatenus renuat illico restituatur eius viro hebraeo, accepta cautione per eius maritum et universitatem hebraeorum etc.*

APPENDIX C

[p. 21]
In Feria IV, on Wednesday, July 10, 1742, it was ordered that "a boy of eight months, baptized in Avignon in France by a Hebrew girl, should be completely rescued from the hands of his Hebrew parents, and completely cared for, fed, and educated among Christians."

However, it has been rumored by some ill-informed people that in some cases the Holy See has ordered or at least allowed the return of baptized Jewish children *invitis parentibus* to their parents, mentioning among others a recent case in Fiumicino and Rome in 1840.[30] To this we reply that some cases of quite remote date are not worth dealing with, either because they do not exist, or because they are very different from the way they are presented, as could be demonstrated by the alleged baptism of the Ferrarese Jewess Regina Salomoni.[31]

[p. 22]
For this reason, we will give here an accurate and true account of what happened in 1840, in order to prove with all the evidence that the Holy See has acted with prudence, wisdom, and firmness in its principles and practices, always in the same and constant way, up to the present time.

In June 1840, the Jewish couple Daniele Montel de Nymes and Miett Cremieux landed at Fiumicino. As soon as they disembarked, Miett was surprised by the pain of premature labor and gave birth to a baby girl. A woman who lived in the same inn warned of the imminent danger of death and quickly baptized the newborn. It did not take long, however, for the ecclesiastical authorities to learn of the event that had happened to the daughter of Mr. and Mrs. Montel Cremieux, who had already settled in Rome. The parents of the baptized child were kept under surveillance for the child's personal safety while the regular acts of baptismal proof were being performed. Once

---

30 The author of the *Pro-memoria* also mentions this event, but he only mentions the part that serves his purpose, and he is silent and even denies the important part, namely that the daughter of the Jewish couple was not left in their power. From the way he cites this fact, one can argue about the others also cited and the accompanying authorities repeated on almost every page of the *Syllabus*. See p. 44.

31 In Ferrara, in 1785, a woman claimed, after thirty years and more, that she had baptized in Padua, at the age of seven, the Jewess Regina Salomoni, then three. However, there was no evidence of the complainant, who claimed this after having suffered a severe crisis and mental illness, for which she had been subjected to the remedies and treatment appropriate for delusional people. Following this and other news, the Supreme Congregation, in the Feria III loco IV [Translator's note: i.e., in a session on Tuesday instead of Wednesday] of December 6, 1785, decided, "*Taking into account all the circumstances, that the witness is not trustworthy. Therefore, after asking the Hebrew woman if she wants to be a Christian, since she refuses, she should be immediately returned to her Hebrew husband, having received a bond from her husband and from the Hebrew community, etc.*"

decretato nella Suprema Congregazione del S. Officio *in Feria IV die 1 Julii 1840. Satis constare de administratione baptismi, et de eius validitate*. Intanto si ordinava, che la figlia delli Ebrei Montel e Cremieux, venisse collocata nella Pia Casa dei Catecumeni in Roma. Però i due Ebrei avevano gia ricorso al Rappresentante di Francia presso la S. Sede quali sudditi [p. 23] di quel Regno onde non venisse loro tolta la figlia asserendo che non era battezzata.

Il Sig. Conte di Rayneval fece a tale scopo calde istanze presso la s. m. di Gregorio XVI, ma nulla poté ottenere a favore dei parenti Ebrei, non consentendolo al Sommo Pontefice il Sacro Dovere che gliene correva innanzi a Dio per la salute eterna di quell'anima rigenerata alla grazia. Ma poiché il Sig. Incaricato di Francia assicurava la S. Sede con atto officiale in nome del Suo Reale Governo, che consegnandosi la bambina Montel Cremieux al Governo medesimo, di cui era suddita, questo s'impegnava a farla educare nella Cattolica Religione, e se ne rendeva responsabile innanzi a Dio. Allora a queste espresse condizioni il Santo Padre ordinò che la battezzata bambina venisse consegnata allo stesso Sig. Incaricato; e non mai alli parenti Ebrei. A prova di quanto si asserisce si riporta *ad Verbum* la identica nota officiale della Segreteria di Stato datata 24 luglio 1840: nota comunicata officialmente alla Suprema Congregazione del S. Offizio.

« Pronunciato da cotesto Supremo Tribunale della S. Inquisizione il giudizio sulla sussistenza e validità del battesimo amministrato in Fiumicino da Flavia Simonetti ad una neonata dai coniugi Ebrei Daniele Montel e Miett Cremieux di nazione Francesi, conobbe tosto il S. Padre l'obbligo che gli correva di provvedere con sicuri mezzi alla cristiana educazione della bambina nel seno di quella Chiesa ove piacque alla Divina Provvidenza di collocarla. Né potendo per conseguenza permettere, che ne restasse [p. 24] la cura ai parenti senza rendersi responsabile innanzi a Dio della perdita di quell'anima, fra i varii mezzi, che presentaronsi al conseguimento del fine indicato piacque alla Somma Sapienza di Sua Santità nel concorso di alcune circostanze prescelier quello di far consegnare la bambina or battezzata al Sig. Incaricato di Francia sotto l'espressa condizione, che egli in nome del suo R. Governo assicurasse in antecedenza con atto officiale la S. Sede, che il Governo medesimo s'impegnava a farla educare nella cattolica Religione, rendendosene innanzi a Dio responsabile. Ed avendo il Sig. Incaricato di Francia con nota del giorno di ieri assicurato che il suo R. Governo avrebbe adempito in ogni sua parte l'espresso volere di Sua Santità, lo scrivente

these checks were completed, the Supreme Congregation of the Holy Office decreed *on July 1, 1840, in Feria IV: There is sufficient evidence of the conferral of baptism and of its validity*. In the meantime, it was ordered that the daughter of the Jews Montel and Cremieux be placed in the Pious House of Catechumens in Rome. But the two Jews had already appealed to the representative of France at the Holy See, as subjects of that kingdom, to ask that their daughter not be taken from them, on the ground that she was not baptized.

[p. 23]
The Count of Rayneval made earnest petitions to the Holy Father Gregory XVI for this purpose, but was unable to obtain anything in favor of the Jewish parents, since the Supreme Pontiff was not allowed to do so because of his sacred duty, for which he was responsible before God for the eternal health of this soul regenerated in grace. But since the French Ambassador, by an official act in the name of his royal government, assured the Holy See that, by handing over the child Montel Cremieux to the same government of which she was a subject, the latter undertook to educate her in the Catholic religion, and made himself responsible before God, the Holy Father, under these express conditions, ordered that the baptized child be handed over to the Ambassador himself, and never to her Jewish parents. As proof of what is asserted here, we report *textually* the identical official note of the Secretariat of State dated July 24, 1840, a note officially communicated to the Supreme Congregation of the Holy Office.

"After this Supreme Tribunal of the Holy Inquisition had pronounced the judgement on the existence and validity of the baptism administered in Fiumicino by Flavia Simonetti to a newborn girl of the Jewish couple Daniele Montel and Miett Cremieux of French nationality, the Holy Father soon realized the obligation he had to provide with sure means for the Christian education of the child in the bosom of that Church where it pleased Divine Providence to place her. [p. 24] Consequently, since he could not allow the care of the child to be left to her relatives without becoming responsible before God of the loss of her soul, His Holiness analyzed the various means available to achieve the desired end. In the end, a series of circumstances having also occurred in the meantime, his supreme wisdom decided to give the baptized child to the Lord Delegate of France, on the express condition that he, in the name of his Royal Government, should assure the Holy See, in advance and in the name of his Royal Government, by official document, that the government itself would undertake to educate her in the Catholic religion, making itself responsible for her before God. And as the Lord Representative of France, by a note of yesterday, has assured us that his Royal Government will fulfill in every part the express will of His Holiness,

Cardinale Segretario di Stato si é diretto all'Emo Sig. Card. Vicario pregandolo a deputare persona di sua fiducia, che prendesse li occorrenti concerti col Sig. Conte di Rayneval in concorrenza de'quali avesse luogo senz'altro indugio la consegna della bambina allo stesso Sig. Incaricato.
« Combinato in tal guisa col Divino aiuto l'affare in discorso, ed adempito dallo scrivente Cardinale il dovere di renderne istrutto cotesto supremo Tribunale della S. Romana Inquisizione Egli rinnova... etc. *firmato* L. Card. Lambruschini ».

Dall'operato adunque circa il battesimo conferito in Fiumicino alla bambina Montel Cremieux si ha una nuova prova per conchiudere, che la S. Sede non ha mai tollerato, che i bambini delli Ebrei dopo ricevuto il battesimo restino in potere dei [p. 25] loro parenti. Che se poi nell'esposto caso della Montel-Cremieux, il S. Padre ha richiesto ad una Potenza Cattolica le più assicuranti condizioni per consegnarle una bambina battezzata ma nata da parenti Ebrei fino a dichiarnela responsabile innanzi a Dio: come ora si potrebbe fare alla S. Sede la benché menoma avvertenza se nel caso presente, in cui trattasi di un proprio suddito, quale é il Mortara, ne assume la S. Sede medesima la responsabilità (anche come Governo Pontificio) e lo colloca in luogo sicuro onde il battezzato Edgardo abbia una buona educazione Religiosa, e civile? Sarebbe questo un disconoscere ogni principio e Diritto Religioso, Morale Civile. Tali pretese non possono originarsi, che da un freddo indifferentismo in fatto di Religione.

Sembra dunque evidentemente dimostrato, che non devesi più restituire alla patria potestà degl'infedeli parenti il bambino battezzato *etiamsi invitis ipsis*, perché la Chiesa ne entra in pieno diritto e potere in virtù del carattere indelebile ricevuto dal bambino nel Santo Battesimo. Che anzi la Chiesa stessa esercita il suo pieno diritto nel reclamarne effettivamente il possesso per tutelare la salute eterna del battezzato, l'onore di Dio, della Religione e del Sacramento, poiché tutto verrebbe esposto ad evidentissimo pericolo, quante volte il battezzato rimanesse in potere degl'infedeli parenti. Di cotal guisa ragionano i Teologi e Canonisti coll'Angelico Dottore S. Tommaso. Cosi decretava tanto sulla validità del Sacramento, quanto sulla necessita di sottrarre dai parenti infedeli il figlio battezzato il [p. 26] Sommo. Pontefice Innocenzo III che sul principio del Sillabo veniva citato come favorevole alla riprovata Sentenza.[ab]

[ab] Concilium Lateran. in cap. "Cum sit nimis de Judaeis" et in cap. "Maiores de Baptismo".

the undersigned Cardinal Secretary of State now writes to His Eminence the Cardinal Vicar, begging him to send a person of his confidence to make the necessary arrangements with the Count de Rayneval, in fulfilment of which the delivery of the child to the same Lord Representative should take place without further delay.

"Having thus settled the matter in question with the Divine assistance, and having fulfilled the duty of informing this Supreme Tribunal of the Holy Roman Inquisition, he undersigned Cardinal renews ... etc. signed L. Card. Lambruschini."

From the action taken regarding the baptism given at Fiumicino to the child Montel Cremieux, we have another evidence to conclude that the Holy See has never tolerated that the children of the Jews, after having been baptized, should remain in the power of their parents. [p. 25] If, then, in the reported case of Montel-Cremieux, the Holy Father demanded of a Catholic Nation the most certain conditions for the delivery of a baptized child, but born of Jewish parents, to the point of declaring that nation responsible before God, how could one ever raise the slightest objection against the Holy See if, in the present case, when dealing with one of its subjects, such as Mortara, the Holy See itself takes responsibility for him (even as the Papal Government) and places him in a safe place, so that the baptized Edgardo may receive a good religious and civil education? This would be to disregard every principle and every religious, moral, and civil right. Such demands can only come from a cold indifference to religion.

It therefore seems evidently demonstrated that the baptized child can no longer be returned to the parental authority of unbeliever parents *even against their will*, because the Church has full right and power to do so, by virtue of the indelible character received by the child in Holy Baptism. Indeed, the Church herself exercises her full right by effectively claiming possession of him in order to protect the eternal health of the baptized child and the honor of God, the religion, and the sacrament, since everything would be exposed to the most obvious danger, if the baptized child were to remain in the power of his unbeliever parents. This is the reasoning of the theologians and canonists of the same opinion as the Angelic Doctor St. Thomas. It is in this sense, with regard to the validity of the sacrament and with regard to the necessity of rescuing the baptized child from the unbeliever parents, [p. 26] that the Supreme Pontiff Innocent III, who was quoted at the beginning of the *Syllabus* as being in favor of the rejected opinion, decreed.[32]

---

[32] Lateran Council, in the chapter *"Cum sit nimis 'de Iudaeis"* and in chapter *"Maiores de Baptismo."*

In tutte e singole le riportate Decisioni e Decreti della S. Sede in favore della validità del Battesimo conferito ai bambini Ebrei *invitis parentibus*; e nei quali si decreta la perpetua separazione dai medesimi, non trovasi che un testimonio solo e per lo più una donna, che attesti del conferito battesimo, nullameno non si é mai mosso dubbio sulla realtà dei fatti, come é a vedersi nelle citate posizioni ed in tante altre conservate nell'archivio della Suprema Inquisizione. Che un solo testimonio sia pur anche una donna basti per attestare del conferito battesimo ai bambini degli Ebrei, e specialmente in caso probabile di morte, é sentenza di tutti i Teologi e Canonisti. Sentenza basata sul Diritto Canonico riportato e ripetuto in molte Decretali.[ac]

Sentenza approvata e confermata dal lodato S. P. Benedetto XIV nella citata Lettera «*Postremo mense*» la quale dovea servire d'istruzione e norma sicura a Monsignor Vicegerente per procedere in simili casi.

A ribattere per tanto l'ingiusta richiesta dell'Ebreo Salomone Mortara, il quale pretende gli venga restituito il figlio Edgardo sulla assertiva, che manchi la prova del Battesimo conferito dalla fantesca Morisi; basterà dimostrare,

[p. 27]
Che esiste la prova canonica del battesimo conferito dalla Serva Anna Morisi.

In fatti si ha in atti la denunzia formale di Marianna Bajesi nubile Bolognese di anni 40 la quale per dovere di coscienza depose di essere informata da alcune persone, che nomina, come erasi da una tale per nome Regina di anni 70 insinuato alla Serva della famiglia Ebrea Mortara, Anna Morisi, di battezzare un bambino della medesima famiglia, il quale stava in pericolo di morte (e morì di fatto); ma che la Morisi rispose di non volerlo fare altrimenti, perché in simile pericolo aveva già altra volta battezzato un altro figlio di Mortara, il quale però non venne a morte, e viveva tuttora in eta di circa anni 7.

Lettasi cotale denunzia *de relato*, non che la lettera d'officio del P. Inquisitore di Bologna, si ordinava con Decreto della Congregazione Particolare 7 Novembre 1857 l'esame formale di Anna Morisi; ed in fatti veniva questo esame rimesso alla S. Congregazione con lettera dei 15 Dicembre 1857 da quel P. Inquisitore.

Da questo fatto risulta certa la verità del conferito battesimo. Confessa la Morisi, previe le debite ammonizioni ed il giuramento *de veritate dicenda*

[ac] Vide Sessa «De Judaeis» cap. LVIII per totum.

In each and every one of the reported decisions and decrees of the Holy See in favor of the validity of the Baptism conferred on Jewish children *invitis parentibus*, and in which the perpetual separation from the parents is decreed, there is always only one witness, usually a woman, who attests to the baptism conferred, and yet there has never been any doubt about the reality of the facts, as can be seen in the above-mentioned positions and in many others preserved in the archives of the Supreme Inquisition. That a single witness, even a woman, is sufficient to testify to the baptism of the children of the Jews, especially in the case of probable death, is the judgment of all theologians and canonists. This judgment is based on the Canon Law reported and repeated in many decretals.[33]

This sentence was approved and confirmed by His Holiness Benedict XIV in the aforementioned Letter "*Postremo mense*," which was to serve as an instruction and a sure norm for his Vicar to proceed in similar cases.

In order to refute the unjust request of the Jew Salomone Mortara, who demands that his son Edgardo be returned to him, claiming that there is no proof of the baptism conferred by the servant Morisi, it will be sufficient to demonstrate:

[p. 27]
That there is canonical proof of the baptism conferred by the Servant Anna Morisi.

In fact, we have in the acts the formal denunciation of Marianna Bajesi, an unmarried Bolognese of forty years of age, who stated, out of a duty of conscience, that she had been informed by some people, whose name she gave, that a woman named Regina, aged seventy, had advised the servant of the Jewish family Mortara, Anna Morisi, to baptize a child of the same family who was in danger of death (and in fact died); But Morisi replied that she did not want to do it, because she had already baptized another son of Mortara in similar danger, but he did not die and was still alive at the age of about seven years.

Having read this denunciation on the basis of the *information reported*, as well as the official letter of the Father Inquisitor of Bologna, the Decree of the Particular Congregation of November 7, 1857, ordered the formal examination of Anna Morisi; and in fact this interrogation was referred to the Holy Congregation by letter of December 15, 1857, from this Father Inquisitor.

From this fact the truth of the baptism conferred is certain. Morisi confesses, after having taken the necessary admonitions and the oath *to tell the truth*

---

33 See Sessa, *De Iudaeis*, chapter 58.

tactis Dei Evangeliis, che nel tempo e luogo da lei indicati essendo stato colpito il figlio di Momolo Mortara di nome Edgardo dell'eta di circa due anni da un *Sinoco* così violento, che il padre e Ia madre temevano piangendo, che morisse da un momento all'altro a segno, che il padre prese dei libri Ebraici, e recitava orazioni sopra il bambino: Perloché prevedendo la morte di questa creatura, essa ne parlò con un Droghiere, [p. 28] che nomina, il quale le disse, che *Se era veramente in pericolo di morte, avrebbe fatta una buona cosa, se l'avesse battezzato*. Passa quindi a descrivere minutamente il modo, con cui il Droghiere la istruì per battezzare il bambino; e *come infatti nella susseguente notte lo battezzò versando l'acqua sul capo del Fanciullo dicendo:* « IO TI BATTEZZO NEL NOME DEL PADRE, DEL FIGLIUOLO, E DELLO SPIRITO SANTO ». Poiché vedeva, che il male sempre più si aggravava fino a sembrare, che dovesse morire da un momento all'altro. Anche in tutte le altre parti la denunzia o esame presenta tutti i caratteri di verità senza lasciare il menomo dubbio sulla realtà e validità del conferito battesimo. Inoltre ad apposite interrogazioni rispose, che *quando versò l'acqua sul capo del bambino Edgardo INTESE DI BATTEZZARLO COME COSTUMA LA CHIESA per rigenerare un'anima a Dio*, e che a ciò é stata indotta dal timore, che quell'anima andasse perduta, perché tutti quei di casa credevano, che il bambino morisse.

Con ogni ragione si può qui dichiarare a senso dell'esposto esame, che il battesimo venne conferito non pure *validamente*, ma anzi *lecitamente* poiché cosi appunto veniva deciso dalla suprema Sacra Congregazione del S. Offizio nel 1678 e 1705 come riferisce il Sommo Pontefice Benedetto XIV nella citata lettera a Monsignor Vicegerente: si riportano i termini della decisione. « Cum filius haebreorum consignatus fuisset nutrici Christianae in deficentia nutricum haebrearum, dum esset proximus morti fuit baptizatus: et sacra [p. 29] Congregatio declaravit praedictum puerum fuisse *licite* baptizatum ».[ad]

Salomone Mortara nella supplica umiliata a Sua Santità vorrebbe far credere, che il figlio Edgardo non era gravemente infermo riportando attestato del Dottor Saragoni. Si avverta peraltro che l'attestato porta la data dei 31 Luglio 1858 cioè 3 o 4 anni dopo la malattia, e quando già il battezzato era stato trasportato in Roma nella Pia Casa dei Catecumeni.

[ad] Il medesimo S. P. riferisce l'altra decisione del S. Officio del 1705 in questi termini « An Filii infantes infidelium possint baptizari invitis parentibus » Eminentissimi audito voto DD. Consultorum: dixerunt « non licere, nisi in articulo mortis ».

by touching the Gospels of God, that at the time and place indicated by her, when Momolo Mortara's son, named Edgardo, was about two years old, he was seized with a *fever* so violent that his father and mother wept and feared that he would die at any moment, so that the father took some Hebrew books and recited prayers over the child.

[p. 28]
Therefore, foreseeing the death of this creature, she spoke of it to a grocer, whose name she gives, who told her that *if he were really in danger of dying, she would have done a good thing if she had baptized him*. Then she went on to describe in detail the manner in which the grocer instructed her to baptize the child, and *how she actually baptized him the following night, pouring water on the child's head and saying: "I baptize you in the name of the Father, and of the Son, and of the Holy Spirit."* She did this because she saw that the illness was getting worse and worse and it seemed that he would die at any moment. In all the other parts, too, the report or examination presents all the characteristics of truth, without leaving the slightest doubt as to the reality and validity of the baptism conferred. Furthermore, in response to specific questions, she answered that *when she poured the water on the head of the child Edgardo, she intended to baptize him, as the Church does, in order to regenerate a soul for God*, and that she was moved to do so by the fear that this soul would be lost, since everyone in the house believed that the child was going to die.

With every reason we can declare here that the baptism was not only *valid*, but also *lawful*, since this was the decision of the Supreme Sacred Congregation of the Holy Office in 1678 and 1705, as reported by the Supreme Pontiff Benedict XIV in the aforementioned letter to Monsignor the general Vicar. We report the terms of the decision: "As the son of Jews was entrusted to a Christian nurse, because of the lack of Jewish nurses, he was baptized as he was close to death: [p. 29] and the Sacred Congregation declared that the said child was *legitimately* baptized."[34]

Salomone Mortara, in his petition presented to His Holiness, would have us believe that his son Edgardo was not seriously ill, with reference to Dr Saragoni's certificate. It should also be noted that the certificate is dated July 31, 1858, that is, three or four years after the illness, and when the baptized boy had already been taken to Rome to the Pia Casa dei Catecumeni.

---

34 The same Sovereign Pontiff refers to another decision of the Holy Office of 1705 in these terms: "Concerning the question whether the sons of the unbelievers could be baptized against the will of their parents, the Cardinals, after hearing the opinion of the Consultors of the Congregation, said: it is not licit, except in danger of death."

CONCLUSIONE

La S. Sede dunque in tutto l'operato circa la persona del battezzato Edgardo figlio di Salomone Mortara non ha menomamente violato i diritti paterni degli Ebrei suoi genitori, che anzi con modi e maniere urbane, persuasive e caritatevoli ha proceduto finora in questo delicato affare. Peraltro operando secondo la Divina missione ed autorità suprema, che ha ricevuto da Dio, e che esercita nella persona Augusta del Sommo Pontefice PIO IX Vicario dell'unigenito Divin Figlio e Salvator Nostro Gesù Cristo, si è attenuta con ogni fedeltà alle Decretali, Decisioni, e Leggi emanate costantemente per simili casi dai gloriosi predecessori del lodato Sommo Pontefice cui incombe, siccome Padre Supremo, Maestro e Pastore universale [p. 30] per ogni diritto umano e Divino di tutelare la salute spirituale di tutti gli uomini.

Si è dunque osservato.

1. Che la Chiesa ha sempre proibito il battesimo dei bambini Ebrei *invitis parentibus*. Sia per non ledere il loro diritto naturale, che per non esporre nella età adulta il battezzato all'apostasia, ed a bestemmiare il nome di Gesù Cristo, di cui porterebbe il carattere indelebile.

2. Che però se avvenga, *infantem Iudaeorum, etiam invitis parentibus baptizari*, il battesimo é valido, ed in alcuni casi anche lecito; che é valido perché vi si riscontra *nel caso* materia, forma, soggetto capace, ministro avente la intenzione di *fare ciò che fa la Chiesa*; mentre nei bambini che si battezzano non é necessaria alcuna intenzione; ma vi supplisce la Chiesa nella persona di colui che conferisce il Sacramento: *Pueri nondum habentes usum rationis non per se ipsos, sed PER ACTUM ECCLESIAE salutem suscipiunt*. Cosi S. Tommaso.

3. Che la Chiesa ha da Dio il potere, ed il diritto di mettersi al possesso dei battezzati figli degli Infedeli per tutelare in essi la Santità del ricevuto carattere, e nutrirli alla vita eterna.

4. Che nel caso esposto del battesimo di Edgardo Mortara la S. Sede ha usato del suo pieno e pacifico [p. 31] diritto nel mettersi al possesso del fanciullo adoprando modi del tutto urbani e caritatevoli, e perciò senza far onta al diritto paterno, il quale deve cedere ed essere subordinato a quello della Chiesa.

5. Che infine essendosi provata la realtà e validità del conferito battesimo, Edgardo Mortara é addivenuto figlio di redenzione e di grazia, figlio della Chiesa, figlio del Supremo Padre dei Fedeli Pio IX e, come si espresse lo stesso Edgardo: IO SONO BATTEZZATO - IL MIO PADRE È IL PAPA.

CONCLUSION

The Holy See, therefore, in all its actions concerning the person of the baptized Edgardo, son of Salomone Mortara, has not minimally violated the paternal rights of his Jewish parents, but, on the contrary, has acted in this delicate matter in a civil, persuasive, and charitable manner. Moreover, acting in accordance with the divine mission and supreme authority received from God and exercised in the august person of the Supreme Pontiff Pius IX, Vicar of the only-begotten Divine Son and our Savior, Jesus Christ, it has adhered with all fidelity to the decretals, decisions, and laws constantly issued in similar cases by the glorious predecessors of the venerable Supreme Pontiff, who, as Supreme Father, Master and Universal Pastor, [p. 30] is responsible, by reason of every human and divine right, for the protection of the spiritual health of all men.

It was therefore observed:

1. That the Church has always forbidden the baptism of Jewish children *invitis parentibus*. This was both so as not to harm their natural right, and so as not to expose the baptized child to apostasy in adulthood, and to blasphemy against the name of Jesus Christ, whose indelible mark he would bear.

2. But if it happens that *a Jewish child is baptized, even if against the will of its parents*, the baptism is valid, and in some cases even licit. It is valid because in *the case* there is matter, form, a suitable subject, a minister who had the intention of *doing what the Church does*; while, in the case of children who are baptized, no intention is necessary, but the Church makes up for it in the person of the one who administers the sacrament: "*So also children before the use of reason, receive salvation not by their own act, but BY THE ACT OF THE CHURCH.*" So said St. Thomas.[35]

3. That the Church has from God the power and the right to take possession of the baptized children of the unbelievers in order to preserve in them the holiness of their received character and to nourish them to eternal life.

[p. 31]

4. That, in the case of the baptism of Edgardo Mortara, the Holy See exercised its full and peaceful right to take possession of the child in an entirely civil and charitable manner, and therefore without violating the paternal right, which must yield and be subordinated to that of the Church.

5. Finally, having proved the reality and validity of the baptism conferred, Edgardo Mortara became a child of salvation and grace, a child of the

---

35 [Translator's note: this quotation is taken from ST III 68.9.]

Queste parole, che il Superno lume della Fede battesimale, e la divina Grazia posero sul labbro innocente e santificato del giovine Edgardo non furono vane e sterili; ma tosto produssero e seguono a germogliare in quell'animo fiori e frutti proprii delle Teologali e Cardinali Virtu, che aprono il cuore dei Superiori a belle speranze. Questo giovinetto pertanto illuminato dalla Fede infusa nella sua mente, ed acceso dalla Carità di Gesù Cristo che gli informa il cuore in oggi conosce a pieno lo spirituale beneficio ricevuto nella battesimale sua rigenerazione. Perloché essendo già in possesso del proprio libero arbitrio, e dell'uso di ragione per avere oltrepassato li anni sette, si serve della medesima sua ragione e libero arbitrio per confermare quanto la Divina Misericordia aveva già operato in lui col Sacramento di rigenerazione, e dichiara di volere essere e vivere da Cristiano, da Figlio riconoscente della Chiesa di Gesù Cristo, e del Sommo Pontefice [p. 32] Pio IX. - IO SONO BATTEZZATO - IL MIO PADRE È IL PAPA.

Ora sì, che sarebbe operare contro ogni equità e giustizia personale, contro ogni diritto naturale e Divino se si restituisse questo figlio della grazia in potere degli infedeli parenti, e perciò nella prossima occasione di pervertimento, e di morte. Ah sì! Che sentimenti cotanto ingiuusti e crudi possono trovar luogo soltanto in cuori privi di Fede, e di carità! ... Ma ogni cristiano ripeterà sempre col gran Dottore s. Tommaso « Puer autem postquam incipit habere usum liberi arbitri, iam incipit esse suus; et potest quantum ad ea, quae sunt iuris Divini, vel Naturalis, sibi ipsi provvidere: Et tunc est indicuendus ad fidem non coactione, sed persuasione; et potest etiam invitis parentibus consentire Fidei, et baptizari ».[ae]

Dunque Il Sommo Pontefice il quale come Vicario di Gesù Cristo presso tutti gli uomini, é Capo Supremo della chiesa deve sempre conservare i Diritti acquistati a prezzo della Vita, e del Sangue dello stesso Uomo Dio, Diritti che si comunicano all'uomo col battesimo per il quale addiviene membro vivo della Chiesa, Figlio di Dio, Fratello e coerede di Gesù Cristo; non può acconsentire ad una dimanda, che verrebbe a togliere dal seno della Chiesa un uomo, il quale per il battesimo é divenuto suo figlio dall'infanzia, e perciò è posto in possesso di quel diritto Divino, di cui il Pontefice stesso è il primo [p. 33] difensore, e del quale non potrebbe mai essere spogliato senza un'enorme ingiustizia. Finalmente il Sommo Pontefice costituito da Dio per tutelare quale Padre e Maestro degli Uomini, i loro diritti e ragioni non può

[ae] 2.2. Quest. X. Art. 12.

Church, a child of the Supreme Father of the faithful, Pius IX, and, as Edgardo himself said: I AM BAPTIZED — MY FATHER IS THE POPE.

These words, which the heavenly light of baptismal Faith and divine Grace placed on the innocent and sanctified lips of young Edgardo, were not vain and sterile, but soon produced and continue to produce in that soul flowers and fruits of the theological and cardinal virtues, which open the hearts of the superiors to beautiful hopes. This young man, therefore, enlightened by the faith that has been implanted in his mind, and inflamed by the charity of Jesus Christ that informs his heart, is now fully aware of the spiritual benefit that he received in his baptismal regeneration. For, already in possession of his own free will and the use of reason, having passed the age of seven, he makes use of that same reason and free will to confirm what Divine Mercy had already wrought in him through the Sacrament of Regeneration, and declares that he wishes to be and to live a Christian, a grateful son of the Church of Jesus Christ and of the Supreme Pontiff Pius IX: I AM BAPTIZED — MY FATHER IS THE POPE.

[p. 32]
Now, yes, it is true that it would be contrary to all equity and personal justice, and to all natural and divine right, if this child of grace were returned to the power of unbeliever parents, and thus to the next occasion of perversion and death. Ah yes, such unjust and cruel feelings can only find a place in hearts without faith and charity! . . . But every Christian will always repeat with the great Doctor St. Thomas: "As soon, however, as [a child] begins to have the use of its free will, it begins to belong to itself, and is able to look after itself, in matters concerning the Divine or the natural law, and then it should be induced, not by compulsion but by persuasion, to embrace the faith: it can then consent to the faith, and be baptized, even against its parents' wish."[36]

Therefore, the Supreme Pontiff, who, as Vicar of Jesus Christ before all men, is the Supreme Head of the Church, must always preserve the rights acquired at the price of the Life and Blood of the same Man God, rights communicated to man through Baptism, by which he becomes a living member of the Church, Son of God, Brother and Co-heir of Jesus Christ. Therefore, the Pope cannot consent to a petition that would remove from the bosom of the Church a man who, by baptism, has become its child from infancy, and is therefore put in possession of that divine right of which the Pontiff himself is the first defender and of which he can never be deprived without great

---

[36] ST II.II 10.12. [Translator's note: The quotation from St. Thomas ended with this caveat, which the author of *Brevi cenni* omitted: "It can then consent to the faith, and be baptized, even against its parents' will; *but not before it comes to the use of reason*" (emphasis added).]

esaudire una dimanda, la quale verrebbe a spogliare Edgardo Mortara non pure del Diritto Divino, che per il battesimo ha acquistato su di lui la Chiesa; ma del medesimo suo diritto naturale, e libero arbitrio onde protesta che é e vuol essere Cristiano, ripetendo, IO SONO BATTEZZATO - IL MIO PADRE È IL PAPA.

injustice. [p.33] Finally, the Supreme Pontiff, constituted by God to protect, as Father and Master of men, their rights and reasons, cannot grant a request that would deprive Edgardo Mortara not only of the Divine Right that the Church has acquired over him through baptism, but also of his own natural right and free will, of which he protests that he is and wants to be a Christian, repeating: I AM BAPTIZED — MY FATHER IS THE POPE.

BIBLIOGRAPHY

WORKS OF THOMAS AQUINAS

De malo. In *Sancti Thomae Aquinatis opera omnia*, vol. 23. Leonine Edition. Rome: Ex Typographia Polyglotta S.C. de Propaganda Fide, 1882–.

De potentia: Quaestiones disputatae. Vol. 2. Torino: Marietti, 1965.

De veritate. In *Sancti Thomae Aquinatis opera omnia*, vol. 22. Leonine Edition. Rome: Ex Typographia Polyglotta S.C. de Propaganda Fide, 1882–.

Sancti Thomae Aquinatis Opera omnia. Edited by Robert Busa. Stuttgart-Bad Canstatt: Frommann-Holzboog, 1980.

Summa theologiae. In *Sancti Thomae Aquinatis opera omnia*, vol. 4–12. Leonine Edition. Rome: Ex Typographia Polyglotta S.C. de Propaganda Fide, 1888–1889.

Scriptum super libros Sententiarum. Vol. 1–2 edited by P. Mandonnet; vol. 3–4 edited by M. F. Moos. Paris: Sumptibus P. Lethielleux, 1929–47.

Super Epistolas S. Pauli Lectura. Vol. 1–2. Edited by Raphael Cai. Taurini: Marietti, 1952.

Super Evangelium S. Ioannis Lectura. Edited by Raphael Cai. Turin: Marietti, 1952.

Quaestiones quodlibetales. Edited by Raymund M. Spiazzi, OP. Rome: Marietti, 1949.

MODERN TRANSLATIONS

Aquinas. *Commentary on Aristotle's Nicomachean Ethics.* Translated by C. I. Litzinger. 2 vols. Notre Dame, IN: University of Notre Dame Press, 1993.

———. *Commentary on the Gospel of John: Chapters 9–21.* Latin/English Edition of Biblical Commentaries, vol. 36. Translated by F. R. Larcher, OP. Lander, WY: Aquinas Institute for the Study of Sacred Doctrine, 2013.

———. *Commentary on the Letter of Saint Paul to the Romans.* Latin/English Edition of Biblical Commentaries, vol. 37. Translated by F. R. Larcher, OP. Edited by J. Mortensen and E. Alarcón. Lander, WY: Aquinas Institute for the Study of Sacred Doctrine, 2012.

———. *Commentary on the Letters of Saint Paul to the Corinthians.* Latin/English Edition of Biblical Commentaries, vol. 38. Translated by F. R. Larcher, OP. Edited by B. Mortensen and E. Alarcón. Lander, WY: Aquinas Institute for the Study of Sacred Doctrine, 2012.

———. *Commentary on the Sentences Book IV, 1–13.* Translated by Beth Mortensen. Latin-English Opera Omnia. Lander, WY: Aquinas Institute for the Study of Sacred Doctrine, 2017.

———. *Commentary on the Sentences Book IV, 26–42.* Translated by Beth Mortensen. Steubenville, OH: Emmaus Academic, Aquinas Institute for the Study of Sacred Doctrine, 2018.

———. *The De Malo of Thomas Aquinas.* Latin-English. Edited by Brian Davies. Translated by Richard Regan. New York: Oxford University Press, 2001.

———. *On Faith, Summa Theologiae, Part 2-2, Questions 1–16.* Translated by Mark Jordan. South Bend, IN: University of Notre Dame Press, 1990.

———. *The Power of God.* Translated by Richard J. Regan. New York: Oxford University Press, 2012.

———. *Quaestiones disputatae de Veritate.* Translated by Robert W. Schmidt, SJ. Chicago: Henry Regnery, 1954.

———. *Quodlibetal Questions 1 and 2.* Translated by Sandra Edwards. Toronto: Pontifical Institute of Medieval Studies, 1983.

———. *Summa Theologiae.* Translated by the Fathers of the English Dominican Province. New York: Benziger Brothers, 1947.

———. *Summa Theologiae: Volume 29, The Old Law: 1a2ae. 98–105.* Latin text, English translation. Translated by David Bourke and Arthur Littledale. Edited by Thomas Gilby. Cambridge, UK: Blackfriars, 1969.

———. *Summa Theologiae, Volume 32, Consequences of Faith: 2a2ae. 8–16.* Latin text, English translation. Edited by Thomas Gilby, OP. Cambridge, UK: Blackfriars, 1975.

———. *Thomas Aquinas's Quodlibetal Questions.* Translated by Brian Davies and Turner Nevitt. New York: Oxford University Press, 2020.

VATICAN APOSTOLIC ARCHIVES

"Augustine Cardinal Bea to members of the Secretariat." *Conc. Vat. II.* Box 1454. Secretariatus ad Christianorum Unitatem Fovendam Busta #8.

Brevi cenni. Segr. Stato, Rubriche, anno 1864, rubrica 66, fasc. 3, ff. 173r–204v.

Pro-memoria. Segr. Stato, Rubriche, anno 1864, rubrica 66, fasc. 1, ff. 167–74.

Syllabus. Auctoritatum comprobantium Baptisma pueris Iudaeorum invitis parentibus collatum nil prorsus valere, anno 1864, rubrica 66, fasc. 2, ff 24r–69r.

DOMINICAN THEOLOGIANS IN THE *SYLLABUS*

Capreolus, John. *Thomistarum Principis Defensiones Theologiae Divi Thomae Aquinatis.* Edited by C. Paban and T. Pègues. 7 vols. 1900–1908; repr., Turonibus: 1967.

Catharinus, Ambrosius. *De pueris iudaeorum sua sponte ad baptismum venientibus, etiam invitis parentibus, recipiendis.* In appendix to *Enarrationes in quinque priora capita libri Geneseos.* Romae: Apud Antonium Bladum, 1552.

Durandus. *In Petri Lombardi Sententias theologicas commentarium libri IIII.* In *Sent.* 4. d. 4. 2 vols. Venice: Ex Typographia Guerraea, 1571; repr., Ridgewood, NJ: Gregg Press, 1964.

Mazzolini, Silvestro di Prierio. *Summa Summarum, quæ Sylvestrina dicitur.* Vol. 1–2. Lugdunum, 1519.

Paludanus, Petrus. *Quartus Sententiarum liber.* Edited by Vincent Haerlem. Paris, 1514.

Torquemada, Juan. *Commentarium super toto Decreto* I. Venice, 1578.

———. *Summa de ecclesia.* Venice, 1561.

GENERAL BIBLIOGRAPHY

Allen, John. "Pope of Infallibility Set for Beatification: Pius IX, a Controversial Choice, Issued 'Syllabus of Errors.'" *National Catholic Reporter* 36, no. 38 (September 1, 2000): 12.

———. "Relatives of Kidnapped Boy Ask for Rule Change." *National Catholic Reporter* 36, no. 38 (September 1, 2000): 12.

Ancharanus, Petrus. *Consilia.* Pavia, 1496.

Augustine, Dom, OSB. *A Commentary on the New Code of Canon Law.* Vol. 4. London: Herder, 1920.

Augustine, Saint. *Answer to Faustus, A Manichean.* Translated by Roland Teske, SJ. Edited by Boniface Ramsey. *The Works of St. Augustine, Part I,* vol. 20. Hyde Park, NY: New City Press, 2007.

———. *The City of God, Books 11–22.* Translated by William Babcock. Edited by Boniface Ramsey. *The Works of Saint Augustine,* vol. 1. Hyde Park, NY: New City Press, 2014.

———. *The Confessions.* Translated by Maria Boulding, OSB. Edited by John E. Rotelle, OSA. *The Works of Saint Augustine,* vol. 1. Hyde Park, NY: New City Press, 1997.

———. *Homilies on the Gospel of John 1–40.* Translated by Edmund Hill, OP. Edited by Boniface Ramsey. *The Works of Saint Augustine,* vol. 3. Hyde Park, NY: New City Press, 2009.

———. *Letters Vol 1: 1–99.* Translated by Roland Teske, SJ. *The Works of Saint Augustine,* vol. 1. Hyde Park, NY: New City Press, 2001.

———. *A Treatise on the Merits and Forgiveness of Sins, and on the Baptism of Infants.* In *Nicene and Post-Nicene Fathers,* series 1, vol. 5. Edited by Philip Schaff and Henry Wace. Buffalo, NY: Christian Literature, 1887.

Augustinus, *De peccatorum meritis et remissione et de baptismo paruulorum.* Edited by C. F. Urba and J. Zycha. Vienna: Corpus scriptorum ecclesiasticorum latinorum, 1913.

Avanzolini, Maurizio, and Marilena Buscarini. "Il Caso Mortara," nella Biblioteca dell'Archiginnasio, 2022. http://bimu.comune.bologna.it/biblioweb/mostra-caso-mortara/.

Barraclough, Leo. "Marco Bellocchio Kicks Off Shoot for 'La Conversione.'" *Variety*, July 1, 2022. https://variety.com/2022/film/global/marco-bellocchio-la-conversione-1235306727/.

Barron, Robert. *The Priority of Christ: Toward a Postliberal Catholicism*. Grand Rapids, MI: Brazos Press, 2007.

Bauerschmidt, Frederick Christian. *Thomas Aquinas: Faith, Reason, and Following Christ*. New York: Oxford University Press, 2013.

———. "Reading the *Summa Theologiae*." In *The Cambridge Companion to the Summa Theologiae*, edited by Philip McCosker and Denys Turner, 9–22. New York: Cambridge University Press, 2016.

Bea, Augustin. *The Church and the Jewish People: A Commentary on the Second Vatican Council's Declaration on the Relation of the Church to Non-Christian Religions*. New York: Harper and Row, 1966.

Beal, John P., James A. Coriden, and Thomas J. Green, eds. *New Commentary on the Code of Canon Law*. New York: Paulist Press, 2000.

Benedict XVI, Pope. "Christmas Address to the Roman Curia." December 22, 2005.

———. *God and the World: A Conversation with Peter Seewald*. San Francisco: Ignatius Press, 2002.

———. "Grace and Vocation without Remorse: Comments on the Treatise De Iudaeis." *Communio: International Catholic Review* 45, no. 1 (Spring 2018): 163–84.

———. *Jesus of Nazareth*. Vol. 2: *Holy Week: From the Entrance into Jerusalem to the Resurrection*. San Francisco: Ignatius Press, 2011.

———. *Last Testament: In His Own Words*. Translated by Jacob Phillips. Edited by Peter Seewald. London: Bloomsbury, 2017.

———. *Light of the World: The Pope, the Church, and the Signs of the Times; A Conversation with Peter Seewald*. San Francisco: Ignatius Press, 2010.

———. *Many Religions–One Covenant: Israel, the Church, and the World*. Translated by Graham Harrison. San Francisco: Ignatius Press, 2013.

———. "Message for the Celebration of the World Day of Peace." January 1, 2011.

———. *What is Christianity? The Last Writings*. San Francisco: Ignatius Press, 2023.

Benedictus XIV, Pope. *Bullari Romani continuatio Summorum Pontificum* Benedictus XIV *Opera Omnia*, tt. XVIII-XXIII. Vols. 22–32. Prati: Typographia Aldina, 1843–1867.

Ben-Johanan, Karma. *Jacob's Younger Brother: Christian-Jewish Relations after Vatican II*. Cambridge, MA: Harvard Press, 2022.

Berger, David. "Mission to the Jews and Jewish-Christian Contacts in the Polemical Literature of the High Middle Ages." *American Historical Review* 91, no. 3 (1986): 575–91.

Brechenmacher, Thomas. *Das Ende der doppelten Schutzherrschaft: Der Heilige Stuhl und die Juden am Übergang zur Moderne (1775–1870)*. Päpste und Papsttum, Band 32. Stuttgart: Anton Hiersemann, 2004.

Brown, Peter. "St. Augustine's Attitude toward Religious Coercion." *Journal of Roman Studies* 54 (1964): 107–16.

Burrell, David B. *Aquinas: God and Action*. 3rd ed. Eugene, OR: Cascade, 2016.

———. *Towards a Jewish-Christian-Muslim Theology*. Oxford: Wiley-Blackwell, 2011.

Caffiero, Marina. *Forced Baptisms: Histories of Jews, Christians, and Converts in Papal Rome*. Translated by Lydia G Cochrane. Berkeley: University of California Press, 2012.

Canning, Joseph. "Torquemada, Juan de." In *The Oxford Dictionary of the Middle Ages*. New York: Oxford University Press, 2010.

Capreolus, John. *On the Virtues*. Translated by Kevin White and Romanus Cessario. Washington, DC: The Catholic University of America Press, 2001.

Catholic Church. *Catechism of the Catholic Church*. Vatican City: Libreria Editrice Vaticana; 2019.

Cessario, Romanus. "Non Possumus." *First Things* (February 2018): 55–58.

———. *A Short History of Thomism*. Washington, DC: The Catholic University of America Press, 2003.

Chadwick, Owen. *The Popes and European Revolution*. New York: Oxford University Press, 1981.

———. Review of *Das Ende der doppelten Schutzherrschaft: Der Heilige Stuhl und die Juden*, by Thomas Brechenmacher. *The Catholic Historical Review* 91, no. 1 (2005): 173–75.

Chaput, Charles J., Archbishop. "The Mortara Affair, Redux." *Jewish Review of Books*, January 29, 2018.

Chazan, Robert. *Church, State and Jew in the Middle Ages*. New York: Behrman House, 1980.

———. *Daggers of Faith: Thirteenth-Century Christian Missionizing and Jewish Response*. Berkeley: University of California Press, 1989.

———. *From Anti-Judaism to Anti-Semitism: Ancient and Medieval Christian Constructions of Jewish History*. New York: Cambridge University Press, 2016.

Chenu, Marie-Dominique, OP. *Aquinas and His Role in Theology*. Illustrated ed. Collegeville, MN: Liturgical Press, 2002.

———. *Toward Understanding Saint Thomas*. Chicago: H. Regnery, 1964.

Codex Iuris Canonici Pii X Pontificis Maximi, iussu digestus, Benedicti Papae XV, auctoritate Promulgates. Rome: Typis Polyglottis, 1917.

Codex Juris Canonici auctoritate Ioannis Pauli PP II promulgatus. Rome: Libreria Editrice Vaticana, 1983.

Cohen, Jeremy. *Christ Killers: The Jews and the Passion from the Bible to the Big Screen*. New York: Oxford University Press, 2007.

———. *The Friars and the Jews: Evolution of Medieval Anti-Judaism*. New York: Cornell University Press, 1984.

———. *Living Letters of the Law: Ideas of the Jew in Medieval Christianity*. Berkeley: University of California Press, 1999.

———. *The Salvation of Israel: Jews in Christian Eschatology from Paul to the Puritans*. New York: Cornell University Press, 2022.

———. "Supersessionism, the Epistle to the Romans, Thomas Aquinas, and the Jews of the Eschaton." *Journal of Ecumenical Studies* 52, no. 4 (Fall 2017): 527–53.

Colish, Marcia L. *Faith, Fiction, & Force in Medieval Baptismal Debates*. Washington, DC: The Catholic University of America Press, 2014.

———. *Peter Lombard*. 2 vols. Leiden: Brill, 1994.

Commission for Religious Relations with the Jews. "'The Gifts and the Calling of God Are Irrevocable' (Rom 11:29): A Reflection on Theological Questions Pertaining to Catholic-Jewish Relations, 2015." December 10, 2015.

———. "Guidelines and Suggestions for Implementing the Conciliar Declaration Nostra Aetate." December 1, 1974.

———. "Notes on the Correct Way to Present the Jews and Judaism in Preaching and Catechesis in the Roman Catholic Church." June 24, 1985.

———. "We Remember: A Reflection on the Shoah." March 16, 1998.

Condorelli, Mario. *I fondamenti giuridici della tolleranza religiosa nell'elaborazione canonistica dei secoli XII-XIX: Contributo storico-dogmatico*. Milano: Giuffrè, 1960.

Connelly, John. *From Enemy to Brother: The Revolution in Catholic Teaching on the Jews 1933–1965*. Cambridge, MA: Harvard University Press, 2012.

Coolman, Holly Taylor. "The Vatican Kidnapped a Jewish Boy in 1858. Why Are We Still Talking about It?" *America*, January 31, 2018. https://www.americamagazine.org/faith/2018/01/31/vatican-kidnapped-jewish-boy-1858-why-are-we-still-talking-about-it.

Cooney, J. R. "Ambrosius Catharinus (Lancelot Politi)." *New Catholic Encyclopedia*. 2nd ed. Vol. 1. Detroit: Gale, 2003.

Corpus iuris canonici. Edited by Aemilius Friedberg. 2 vols. Leipzig, Germany: Tauchnitz, 1879–80; repr., Union, NJ: Lawbook Exchange, 2000.

Courtney, F. "Juan de Torquemada." In *New Catholic Encyclopedia*. 2nd ed. Vol. 14. Detroit: Gale, 2003.

Cunningham, Philip A. "Gavin D'Costa: *Catholic Doctrines on the Jewish People After Vatican II*." *Studies in Christian-Jewish Relations* 15, no. 1 (2020): 1–14.

———. "Gifts and Calling: Coming to Terms with Jews as Covenantal Partners." *Studies in Christian-Jewish Relations* 12, no. 1 (2017): 1–18.

———. "The Sources behind 'The Gifts and the Calling of God Are Irrevocable' (Rom 11:29): A Reflection on Theological Questions Pertaining to Catholic-Jewish Relations on the Occasion of the 50th Anniversary of *Nostra Aetate* (no. 4)." *Studies in Christian-Jewish Relations* 12, no. 1 (2017): 1–39.

Daniélou, Jean. *The Bible and the Liturgy*. Notre Dame, IN: University of Notre Dame Press, 1966.

D'Costa, Gavin. *Catholic Doctrines on the Jewish People after Vatican II*. New York: Oxford University, 2019.

———. "Response from the Author to Reviews of *Catholic Doctrines on the Jewish People after Vatican II*." *Studies in Christian-Jewish Relations* 15, no. 1 (2020): 1–18.

Decretum magistri Gratiani. Ed. Lipsiensis secunda post Aemilii Ludovici Richteri curas ad librorum manu scriptorum et editionis Romanae fidem recognovit et adnotatione critica instruxit Aemilius. Edited by Emil Friedberg. Leipzig, Germany: 1879.

BIBLIOGRAPHY

Deferrari, Roy J. *A Latin-English Dictionary of St. Thomas Aquinas, Based on The Summa Theologica and Selected Passages of His Other Writings.* Boston: St. Paul Editions, 1986.

———. *A Lexicon of St. Thomas Aquinas Based on the Summa Theologica and Selected Passages of His Other Works.* Washington, DC: The Catholic University of America Press, 1948.

Delacouture, André Vincent. *Roma e la opinione pubblica d'Europa nel fatto Mortara: Atti, documenti, confutazioni.* Torino: Unione tipografico-editrice, 1859.

Di Nepi, Serena. *Surviving the Ghetto: Toward a Social History of the Jewish Community in 16th-Century Rome.* Translated by Paul M. Rosenberg. Leiden: Brill, 2021.

Donato, Maria Pia. "Reorder and Restore: Benedict XIV, the Index, and the Holy Office." In *Benedict XIV and the Enlightenment: Art, Science, and Spirituality,* edited by Rebecca Messbarger, Christopher Johns, and Philip Gavitt, 227–52. Toronto: University of Toronto Press, 2016.

Dreher, Rod. "The Edgardo Mortara Case." *The American Conservative,* January 9, 2018. http://www.theamericanconservative.com/dreher/the-edgardo-mortara-case/.

Dulles, Avery. "Mystery (in Theology)." In *New Catholic Encyclopedia.* 2nd ed. Vol. 10. Detroit: Gale, 2003.

Dunbabin, Jean. *A Hound of God: Pierre de La Palud and the Fourteenth-Century Church.* New York: Oxford University Press, 1991.

Dunn, Geoffrey D. *Tertullian's Aduersus Iudaeos: A Rhetorical Analysis.* Washington, DC: The Catholic University of America Press, 2008.

Dyer, G. J. "Elijah (Second Coming of)." In *New Catholic Encyclopedia.* 2nd ed. Vol. 5. Detroit: Gale, 2003.

"Ecumenism: What Catholics Think about Jews." *Time,* September 11, 1964.

Ehrlich, Ernst Ludwig. "Ehrlich to Oesterreicher." September 10, 1964, Seton Hall University Special Collections Center, John M. Oesterreicher papers, RG 26.4.1, box 2.

Elukin, Jonathan M. *Living Together, Living Apart: Rethinking Jewish-Christian Relations in the Middle Ages.* Princeton, NJ: Princeton University Press, 2013.

Faggioli, Massimo. "Obsessed with Continuity: What an Essay on the Mortara Kidnapping Confirms." *Commonweal,* January 20, 2018. https://www.commonwealmagazine.org/obsessed-continuity.

Feltoe, Charles Lett. "The Letters and Sermons of Leo the Great." In *Nicene and Post-Nicene Fathers.* Second Series. Vol. 12. Repr., Peabody, MA: Hendrickson, 1994.

Ferguson, Everett. *Baptism in the Early Church: History, Theology, and Liturgy in the First Five Centuries.* Grand Rapids, MI: Eerdmans, 2009.

Flannery, Edward H. *The Anguish of the Jews: Twenty-Three Centuries of Antisemitism.* 2nd ed. New York: Paulist Press, 2004.

Francis, Pope. *Evangelii Gaudium.* Apostolic Exhortation. November 24, 2013.

———. 'Motu Proprio' "De Concordia inter Codices." May 31, 2016.

Fredriksen, Paula. *Augustine and the Jews: A Christian Defense of Jews and Judaism.* New York: Doubleday, 2008.

———. *Paul: The Pagans' Apostle.* New Haven, CT: Yale University Press, 2017.

Friedlander, Saul. *Nazi Germany and the Jews*. Vol. 1: *The Years of Persecution, 1933–1939*. New York: HarperCollins, 1997.

Friedman, John, Jean Connell Hoff, and Robert Chazan, eds. *The Trial of the Talmud*. Toronto, Canada: Pontifical Institute of Mediaeval Studies, 2012.

Grayzel, Solomon. *The Church and the Jews in the XIIIth Century: 1254–1314*. Edited by Kenneth R. Stow. Vol. 2. New York: The Jewish Theological Seminary, 1989.

———. *The Church and the Jews in the XIIIth Century: A Study of Their Relations during the Years 1198–1254 Based on the Papal Letters and the Conciliar Decrees of the Period*. Vol. 1: *Nicaea I to Lateran V*. 1966. Repr., New York: Jewish Theological Seminary Press, 2012.

———. "The Papal Bull Sicut Judeis." In *Studies and Essays in Honor of Abraham A. Neuman*, edited by Meir Ben-Horin, Bernard D. Weinryb, and Solomon Zeitlin, 243–80. Leiden: Brill, 1962.

Harmless, William, SJ. "Baptism." In *Augustine through the Ages: An Encyclopedia*, edited by Allan D. Fitzgerald, OSA, 84–91. Grand Rapids, MI: Eerdmans, 1999.

———. "Christ the Pediatrician: Infant Baptism and Christological Imagery in the Pelagian Controversy." *Augustinian Studies* 28, no. 2 (1997): 7–34.

Healy, Nicholas. "Dignitatis Humanae." In *The Reception of Vatican II*, edited by Matthew Lamb and Matthew Levering, 367–92. New York: Oxford University Press, 2017.

Hittinger, Russell. *The First Grace: Rediscovering the Natural Law in a Post-Christian World*. Wilmington, DE: ISI Books, 2003.

Hood, John Y. B. *Aquinas and the Jews*. Philadelphia: University of Pennsylvania Press, 1995.

Hostiensis. *Lectura on the Decretals Gregorii noni*. Strassburg, 1512.

Huguccio. *Summa decretorum*, 1: *Distinctiones I–XX*. Edited by O. Přerovsky. MIC A-6. Città del Vaticano: 2006.

Hünermann, Peter, Helmut Hoping, Robert L. Fastiggi, Anne Englund Nash, and Heinrich Denzinger, eds. *Compendium of Creeds, Definitions, and Declarations on Matters of Faith and Morals*. San Francisco: Ignatius Press, 2012.

International Theological Commission. "The Hope of Salvation for Infants Who Die without Being Baptized." April 20, 2007.

———. "Memory and Reconciliation: The Church and the Faults of the Past." March 16, 1998.

Izbicki, Thomas M. *Protector of the Faith: Cardinal Johannes Turrecremata and the Defense of the Institutional Church*. Washington, DC: The Catholic University of America Press, 1981.

Jerome, Saint. *Commentary on Matthew*. Translated by Thomas P. Scheck. Washington, DC: The Catholic University of America Press, 2008.

John Paul II, Pope. "Address of the Holy Father John Paul II to an International Symposium on the Inquisition." October 31, 1998.

———. "Address to Representatives of the Jewish Community." August 8, 1991.

———. "Address to Representatives of the West German Jewish Community." November 17, 1980.

———. "Apostolic Constitution *Sacrae Disciplinae Leges* of the Supreme Pontiff Pope John Paul II for the Promulgation of the New Code of Canon Law." January 25, 1983.

———. "Apostolic Letter *Tertio millennio adveniente* for the Jubilee of the Year 2000." November 10, 1994.

———. "General Audience." September 1, 1999.

———. *Redemptor hominis*. Encyclical Letter. March 4, 1979.

———. *Redemptoris Missio*. Encyclical Letter. December 7, 1990.

———. "To the Delegates of the Episcopal Conferences for Relations with Judaism." March 6, 1982.

Katz, Solomon. "Pope Gregory the Great and the Jews." *Jewish Quarterly Review* 24, no. 2 (1933): 113–36.

Kedar, Benjamin Z. "Canon Law and the Burning of the Talmud." *Bulletin of Medieval Canon Law* 9 (1979): 79–82.

Keil, Martha. "What Happened to the 'New Christians'? The Viennese Gererah of 1410/11 and the Forced Baptism of the Jews." In *Jews and Christians in Medieval Europe: The Historiographical Legacy of Bernhard Blumenkranz*, edited by Philippe Buc, Martha Keil, and John Tolan, 97–114. Turnhout: Brepols, 2015.

Kertzer, David. "Edgardo Mortara's Doctored Memoir of a Vatican Kidnapping." *The Atlantic*, April 15, 2018.

———. "The Enduring Controversy over the Mortara Case." *Studies in Christian-Jewish Relations* 14, no. 1 (2019): 1–10.

———. *The Kidnapping of Edgardo Mortara*. New York: Vintage, 2008.

———. *The Popes against the Jews: The Vatican's Role in the Rise of Modern Anti-Semitism*. New York: Vintage, 2002.

Kleinberg, Aviad M. "Depriving Parents of the Consolation of Children: Two Legal *Consilia* on the Baptism of Jewish Children." In *De Sion exibit lex et verbum domini de Hierusalem: Essays on Medieval Law, Liturgy and Literature in Honour of Amnon Linder*, edited by Yitzhak Hen, 129–44. Turnhout: Brepols, 2001.

Knitter, Paul. "*Nostra Aetate*: A Milestone in the History of Religions? From Competition to Cooperation." In *The Future of Interreligious Dialogue: A Multireligious Conversation on Nostra Aetate*, edited by L. Charles Cohen, Paul Knitter, and Ulrich Rosenhagen, 45–60. New York: Orbis, 2017.

Korn, Bertram Wallace. *The American Reaction to the Mortara Case: 1858–1859*. Cincinnati: American Jewish Archives, 1957.

Lamb, Matthew, and Matthew Levering. *The Reception of Vatican II*. New York: Oxford University Press, 2017.

Lehner, F. C. "Mazzolini, Sylvester." In *New Catholic Encyclopedia*. 2nd ed. Vol. 9. Detroit: Gale, 2003.

Leo XIII, Pope. *Immortale Dei*. Encyclical Letter. November 1, 1885.

Lerner, Robert E. *The Feast of Saint Abraham: Medieval Millenarians and the Jews*. Philadelphia: University of Pennsylvania Press, 2001.

Levering, Matthew. *Engaging the Doctrine of Israel: A Christian Israelology in Dialogue with Ongoing Judaism*. Eugene, OR: Cascade Books, 2021.

———. *Jewish-Christian Dialogue and the Life of Wisdom: Engagements with the Theology of David Novak*. New York: Continuum, 2010.

Levine, Amy-Jill, and Marc Zvi Brettler, eds. *The Jewish Annotated New Testament*. 2nd ed. New York: Oxford University Press, 2017.

Liebeschutz, Hanz. "Judaism and Jewry in the Social Doctrine of Thomas Aquinas." *Journal of Jewish Studies* 13 (1961): 57–81.

Linder, Amnon. *The Jews in the Legal Sources of the Early Middle Ages*. Detroit: Wayne State University Press, 1997.

Livingstone, E. A., and F. L. Cross. "Ambrosius Catharinus." In *The Oxford Dictionary of the Christian Church*. 3rd ed. New York: Oxford University Press, 2005.

———. "Durandus of Saint-Pourçain." In *The Oxford Dictionary of the Christian Church*. 3rd ed. New York: Oxford University Press, 2005.

———. "Elijah and Enoch." In *The Oxford Dictionary of the Christian Church*. 3rd ed. New York: Oxford University Press, 2005.

Lombard, Peter. *The Sentences. Book 4: On the Doctrine of Signs*. Translated by Giulio Silano. Toronto: Pontifical Institute of Mediaeval Studies, 2007.

Lupano, Alberto. "Natta, Marco Antonio." In *Dizionario biografico dei giuristi Italiani*, edited by Italo Birocchi Ennio Cortese, Antonello Mattone, Marco Nicola Miletti, and Maria Luisa Carlino, 1414. Vol. 2. Bologna: Società Editrice il Mulino, 2013.

MacIntyre, Alasdair. *Dependent Rational Animals: Why Human Beings Need the Virtues*. Chicago: Open Court, 1999.

Madigan, Kevin. "We Cannot Accept This." *Commonweal*, January 25, 2018.

Marcus, Jacob R. *The Jews in the Medieval World: A Source Book, 315–1791*. New York: Hebrew Union College Press, 1990.

Marshall, Bruce. "Quasi in Figura: A Brief Reflection on Jewish Election, after Thomas Aquinas." *Nova et Vetera*, English edition 7 (2009): 477–84.

Marzoa, Ángel, Jorge Miras, Rafael Rodríguez-Ocaña, and Ernest Caparros, eds. *Exegetical Commentary on the Code of Canon Law*. Vol. 3. Montreal: Wilson & Lafleur, 2004.

Mattison, William. *Growing in Virtue: Aquinas on Habit*. Washington, DC: Georgetown University Press, 2023.

———. *Introducing Moral Theology: True Happiness and the Virtues*. Grand Rapids, MI: Brazos Press, 2008.

McCabe, Herbert. *God Still Matters*. Edited by Brian Davies. New York: Continuum, 2002.

McCosker, Philip, and Denys Turner, eds. *The Cambridge Companion to the Summa Theologiae*. New York: Cambridge University Press, 2016.

Messori, Vittorio. *Kidnapped by the Vatican? The Unpublished Memoirs of Edgardo Mortara*. San Francisco: Ignatius Press, 2017.

Miccoli, Giovanni. "Two Sensitive Issues: Religious Freedom and the Jews." In *Church as Communion: Third Period and Intersession, September 1964–September 1965*, edited by Giuseppe Alberigo and Joseph Komonchak, 95–194. Vol. 4 of *History of Vatican II*. New York: Orbis, 2003.

Michelson, Emily. *Catholic Spectacle and Rome's Jews: Early Modern Conversion and Resistance*. Princeton, NJ: Princeton University Press, 2024.

Miletto, Gianfranco. "Mortara Case." In *Religion Past and Present*. Edited by Hans Dieter Betz, Don S. Browning, Bernd Janowski, and Eberhard Jüngel. Leiden: Brill, 2011.

Miller, Robert. "The Mortara Case and the Limits of State Power: *First Things* Should Disavow Fr. Cessario's Defense of Pius IX in the Mortara Case." *Public Discourse*, January 11, 2018. http://www.thepublicdiscourse.com/2018/01/20868/.

Miranda, Salvador. "The Cardinals of the Holy Roman Church." Florida International University Libraries. 1998–2023. https://cardinals.fiu.edu/cardinals.htm.

Momigliano, Anna. "Why Some Catholics Still Defend the Kidnapping of Edgardo Mortara." *The Atlantic*, January 24, 2018.

Morselli, Marco Cassuto. *Il Memoriale di Edgardo Mortara*. Rome: Marietti, 2024.

Morrisey, Francis G. *The Canon Law Letter & Spirit: A Practical Guide to the Code of Canon Law*. Collegeville, MN: Liturgical Press, 1995.

Mortara, Elèna. "Ancora sulla breccia: battesimi forzati e codice canonico." In *150 Anni sulla breccia: Roma, una capitale in trasformazione*, edited by Marisa Patulli Trythall, 277–92. Roma: Nova Delphi Libri, 2021.

———. *Writing for Justice: Victor Séjour, the Kidnapping of Edgardo Mortara, and the Age of Transatlantic Emancipations*. Chicago: Dartmouth College Press, 2015.

Munck, Johannes. *Paul and the Salvation of Mankind*. Translated by Frank Clarke. Richmond, VA: John Knox Press, 1959.

Nanos, Mark. *Reading Romans within Judaism: The Collected Essays of Mark D. Nanos*. Vol. 2. Eugene, OR: Cascade, 2018.

"Nostra Aetate Deliberations 1–3." September 28–29, 1964. Translated by Patrick T. Brannan, SJ. Edited by Philip A. Cunningham. Council of Centers for Christian-Jewish Relations. https://ccjr.us/dialogika-resources/documents-and-statements/roman-catholic/second-vatican-council/na-debate.

Nostra Aetate Drafts. Council of Centers for Christian-Jewish Relations. https://ccjr.us/dialogika-resources/documents-and-statements/roman-catholic/second-vatican-council/na-drafts.

Nutt, Roger. *General Principles of Sacramental Theology*. Washington, DC: The Catholic University of America Press, 2017.

Ochs, Peter. *Another Reformation: Postliberal Christianity and the Jews*. Grand Rapids, MI: Baker Academic, 2011.

Oesterreicher, John M. "Declaration on the Relationship of the Church to Non-Christian Religions." In *Declaration on the Relationship of the Church to the Non-Christian Religions: Dogmatic Constitution on Divine Revelation; Decree on the Apostolate of the Laity*, edited by Herbert Vorgrimler, 1–136. Vol. 3 of *Commentary on the Documents of Vatican II*. New York: Herder and Herder, 1969.

———. *The New Encounter: Between Christians and Jews*. New York: Philosophical Library, 1986.

Pakter, Walter. *Medieval Canon Law and the Jews*. Ebelsbach, Germany: Gremler, 1988.

Paul IV, Pope. "Cum nimis absurdum." July 14, 1555. https://www.ccjr.us/dialogika-resources/primary-texts-from-the-history-of-the-relationship/paul-iv.

Paul VI, Pope. *Evangelii Nuntiandi*. Apostolic Exhortation. December 8, 1975.

Patte, Daniel. "A Post-Holocaust Biblical Critic Responds." In *Reading Israel in Romans: Legitimacy and Plausibility of Divergent Interpretations*, edited by Cristina Grenholm and Daniel Patte, 225–45. Harrisburg, PA: Trinity Press International, 2000.

Pennington, Kenneth. "Gratian and the Jews." *Bulletin of Medieval Canon Law* 31 (2014): 111–24.

———. "The Law's Violence against Medieval and Early Modern Jews." *Rivista internazionale di diritto comune* 23 (2012): 23–44.

———. *Medieval and Early Modern Jurists*. 1993. http://legalhistorysources.com/biobibl.htm.

Pennington, Kenneth, et al. "Guillelmus Redonensis." In *Bio-Bibliographical Guide to Medieval and Early Modern Jurists*. Report no. a260. Cambridge, MA: Ames Foundation, Harvard Law School, 2023. https://amesfoundation.law.harvard.edu/BioBibCanonists/Report_Biobib2.php?record_id=a260.

Peters, Edward N. *The 1917 or Pio-Benedictine Code of Canon Law: In English Translation with Extensive Scholarly Apparatus*. San Francisco: Ignatius Press, 2001.

Peters, Nathaniel. "Grace Builds Upon and Doesn't Destroy Nature: On First Things, Baptism, and the Natural Family." *Public Discourse*, January 15, 2018. http://www.thepublicdiscourse.com/2018/01/20884/.

Pinckaers, Servais. *The Sources of Christian Ethics*. Translated by Mary Thomas. Washington DC: The Catholic University of America Press, 1995.

Pius XI, Pope. "Divini Illius Magistri." December 31, 1929.

Pius XII, Pope. "Mystici Corporis." June 29, 1943.

Pontifical Biblical Commission. "The Jewish People and Their Sacred Scriptures in the Christian Bible." December, 2001.

Pontifical Council for Interreligious Dialogue. "Dialogue and Proclamation: Reflection and Orientations on Interreligious Dialogue and the Proclamation of the Gospel of Jesus Christ." May 19, 1991.

Pontificia Commissio Codici Iuris Canonici Recognoscendo, Communicationes. Vol. 3, no. 2. Rome: Typis Polyglottis Vaticanis, 1971.

Pontificia Commissio Codici Iuris Canonici Recognoscendo, Communicationes. Vol. 7, no. 1. Rome: Typis Polyglottis Vaticanis, 1975.

Pontificia Commissio Codici Iuris Canonici Recognoscendo, Communicationes, Vol. 13, no. 1. Rome: Typis Polyglottis Vaticanis, 1981.

Pontificia Commissio Codici Iuris Canonici Recognoscendo, Schema Documenti Ponuijcii quo Disciplina Canonica de Sacramentis recognoscitur. Rome: Typis Polyglottis Vaticanis, 1975.

Porter, Jean. *Natural and Divine Law: Reclaiming the Tradition for Christian Ethics.* Grand Rapids, MI: Eerdmans, 1999.

Ratzinger, Joseph. *Eschatology: Death and Eternal Life.* 2nd ed. Translated by Michael Waldstein. Washington, DC: The Catholic University of America Press, 1988.

———. *Principles of Catholic Theology: Building Stones for a Fundamental Theology.* Translated by Sister Mary Frances McCarthy, SND. San Francisco: Ignatius Press, 1982.

Ravid, Benjamin. "The Forced Baptism of Jews in Christian Europe: An Introductory Overview." In *Christianizing Peoples and Converting Individuals,* edited by Guyda Armstrong and Ian N. Wood, 157–67. Turnhout, Beglium: Brepols, 2001.

Rist, Rebecca. *Popes and Jews, 1095–1291.* New York: Oxford University Press, 2016.

Robertson, John W. "Canons 867 and 868 and Baptizing Infants Against the Will of Parents." *The Jurist* 45 (1985): 631–38.

Rosemann, Philipp W. *Peter Lombard.* New York: Oxford University Press, 2004.

———. *The Story of a Great Medieval Book.* Toronto: University of Toronto Press, 2007.

Roth, Cecil. *Gleanings: Essays in Jewish History, Letters, and Art.* New York: Bloch, 1967.

———. *Jews, Visigoths, and Muslims in Medieval Spain: Cooperation and Conflict.* Leiden: Brill, 1994.

Roth, Norman. "Church and Jews." In *Medieval Jewish Civilization: An Encyclopedia,* edited by Norman Roth, 162–72. New York: Routledge, 2003.

Rutishauser, Christian M. "Not Mission, but Dialogue." *Neue Zürcher Zeitung,* December 1, 2018. Rüdiger, Althaus. "... etiam invitis parentibus" oder: Heilsgewissheit contra Elternwille Anmerkungen zu einer problematischen Klausel im Taufrecht. *Theologie und Glaube* 113, Jahrgang 4, Heft 4, Vierteljahr (2023): 335–46.

Sacred Congregation for the Doctrine of the Faith. *Instruction on Infant Baptism: Pastoralis actio.* October 20, 1980.

Schindler, David L., and Nicholas Healy, eds. *Freedom, Truth, and Human Dignity: The Second Vatican Council's Declaration on Religious Freedom; A New Translation, Redaction History, and Interpretation of Dignitatis Humanae.* Grand Rapids, MI: Eerdmans, 2015.

Schutte, Anne Jacobson. "Palazzo del Sant'Uffizio: The Opening of the Roman Inquisition's Central Archive." *Perspectives on History: The Newsmagazine of the American Historical Association,* May 1999. https://www.historians.org/research-and-publications/perspectives-on-history/may-1999/palazzo-del-santuffizio-the-opening-of-the-roman-inquisitions-central-archive.

Schweizer, J. *Ambrosius Catharinus Politus.* Münster, Germany: 1909.

Scoti, B. Ioannis Duns. *Opera Omnia.* Civitas Vaticana: Typis Polyglottis Vaticanis, 1950–.

Scotus, Duns. *Ordinatio.* Book IV, dd. 1–7. Translated by Peter L. P. Simpson. https://aristotelophile.com/current.htm.

Sheehy, Gerard. *The Canon Law: Letter and Spirit: A Practical Guide to the Code of Canon Law.* Dublin: Veritas Publications, 1995.

Sherwin, Michael S. *By Knowledge & By Love: Charity and Knowledge in the Moral Theology of St. Thomas Aquinas*. Washington, DC: The Catholic University of America Press, 2005.

Sievers, Joseph. "'God's Gifts and Call Are Irrevocable': The Reception of Romans 11:29 through the Centuries and Christian-Jewish Relations." In *Reading Israel in Romans: Legitimacy and Plausibility of Divergent Interpretations*, edited by Cristina Grenholm and Daniel Patte, 127–73. Harrisburg, PA: Trinity Press International, 2000.

Simonsohn, Shlomo. *The Apostolic See and the Jews*. Vol. 1: *492–1404*. Toronto: Pontifical Institute of Mediaeval Studies, 1988.

———. *The Apostolic See and the Jews*. Vol. 2: *1394–1464*. Toronto: Pontifical Institute of Mediaeval Studies, 1988.

———. *The Apostolic See and the Jews*. Vol. 7: *History*. Toronto: Pontifical Institute of Mediaeval Studies, 1991.

Sokolowski, Robert. *The God of Faith and Reason: Foundations of Christian Theology*. Washington, DC: The Catholic University of America Press, 1995.

Soulen, R. Kendall. *The God of Israel and Christian Theology*. Minneapolis: Fortress Press, 1996.

———. *Irrevocable: The Name of God and the Unity of the Christian Bible*. Minneapolis: Fortress Press, 2022.

Speer, Andreas, Fiorella Retucci, Thomas Jeschke, and Guy Guldentops, eds. *Durand of Saint-Pourçain and His Sentences Commentary: Historical, Philosophical, and Theological Issues*. Leuven: Peters, 2014.

Spielberg, Steven. "The Kidnapping of Edgardo Mortara." IMDB. https://www.imdb.com/title/tt3675680/.

Spizzichino, Giancarlo. "The Ghetto and the Authorities: A Difficult Coexistence." In *Et Ecce Gaudium: The Roman Jews and the Investiture of the Popes*, edited by Daniela Di Castro, 17–21. Rome: Jewish Museum of Rome, 2010.

Stahl, Sharon. "The Mortara Affair, 1858: Reflections of the Struggle to Maintain the Temporal Power of the Papacy." PhD diss., Saint Louis University, 1987.

Stegmüller, F. *Repertorium commentariorum in Sententias Petri Lombardi*. Würzburg, Germany: 1947.

Stocking, Rachel. "Forced Converts, 'Crypto-Judaism,' and Children: Religious Identification in Visigothic Spain." In *Jews in Early Christian Law: Byzantium and the Latin West, 6th–11th Centuries*, edited by John Tolan, L. Foschia, C. Nemo-Pekelman, and N. de Lange, 243–65. Turnhout: Brepols, 2014.

Stow, Kenneth. *Anna and Tranquillo: Catholic Anxiety and Jewish Protest in the Age of Revolutions*. New Haven, CT: Yale University Press, 2016.

———. "The Cruel Jewish Father: From Miracle to Murder." In *Studies in Medieval Jewish Intellectual and Social History: Festschrift in Honor of Robert Chazan*, Supplements to the Journal of Jewish Thought and Philosophy 15, edited by David Engel, Lawrence H. Schiffman, and Eliot R. Wolfson, 245–78. Leiden: Brill, 2012.

———. *Theater of Acculturation: The Roman Ghetto in the Sixteenth Century*. Seattle: University of Washington Press, 2000.

Synan, Edward. *The Popes and the Jews in the Middle Ages.* New York: Macmillan, 1965.

———. "Review of John Hood, *Aquinas and the Jews.*" *Church History Review* 82, no. 3 (1996): 550–51.

Tanner, Norman P. *Decrees of the Ecumenical Councils.* Vol. 1. London: Georgetown University Press, 1990.

Taparelli, Luigi d'Azeglio. "Ciò Che Sa e Ciò Che Non Sa: La Revue Des Deux Mondes Intorno ad Edgardo Mortara." *Civiltà Cattolica* 12 (1858): 529–41.

———. "Il Piccolo Neofito Edgardo Mortara." *Civiltà Cattolica* 12 (1858): 385–416.

Tapie, Matthew. *Aquinas on Israel and the Church: A Study of the Question of Supersessionism in the Theology of Thomas Aquinas.* Eugene, OR: Wipf & Stock/ Pickwick, 2014.

———. "The Mortara Affair and the Question of Thomas Aquinas's Teaching against Forced Baptism." *Studies in Christian-Jewish Relations* 14, no. 1 (2019): 1–18.

———. "*Spiritualis Uterus*: The Question of Forced Baptism and Thomas Aquinas's Defense of Jewish Parental Rights." *Bulletin of Medieval Canon Law* 35 (2018): 289–329.

Tavuzzi, Michael. "Johannes Capreolus (c.1380–1444)." In *Routledge Encyclopedia of Philosophy.* Vol. 1. Oxford: Taylor and Francis, 1998.

———. *Prierias: The Life and Works of Silvestro Mazzolini Da Prierio, 1456–1527.* Durham, NC: Duke University Press, 1997.

Thatcher, Oliver Joseph, and Edgar H. McNeal, eds. *A Sourcebook for Medieval History.* New York: Scribner's Sons, 1905.

Thiessen, Matthew. *A Jewish Paul: The Messiah's Herald to the Gentiles.* Grand Rapids, MI: Baker Academic, 2023.

Tierney, Brian. *The Idea of Natural Rights: Studies on Natural Rights, Natural Law and Church Law, 1150–1625.* Grand Rapids, MI: Eerdmans, 1997.

———. *Liberty & Law: The Idea of Permissive Natural Law, 1100–1800.* Washington, DC: The Catholic University of America Press, 2014.

Tolan, John V., Nicholas de Lange, Laurence Foschia, and Capucine Nemo-Pekelman, eds. *Jews in Early Christian Law: Byzantium and the Latin West, 6th–11th Centuries.* Turnhout: Brepols, 2014.

Torrell, Jean-Pierre. *Aquinas's Summa: Background, Structure, and Reception.* Washington, DC: The Catholic University of America Press, 2005.

———. *Saint Thomas Aquinas.* Vol. 1: *The Person and His Work.* 3rd ed. Washington, DC: The Catholic University of America Press, 2023.

Turner, Nancy L. "Jewish Witness, Forced Conversion, and Island Living: John Duns Scotus on Jews and Judaism." In *Christian Attitudes toward the Jews in the Middle Ages,* edited by Michael Frassetto, 183–209. New York: Routledge, 2007.

Tutino, Stefania. "Ecclesiology/Church-State Relationship in Early Modern Catholicism." In *The Oxford Handbook of Early Modern Theology, 1600–1800,* edited by Ulrich L. Lehner, Richard A. Muller, and A. G. Roeber, 150–64. New York: Oxford University Press, 2016.

United States Conference of Catholic Bishops. "Sacraments and Sacramentals." February 22, 2024.

———. "Statement of Principles for Catholic-Jewish Dialogue." October 2, 2009.

Valkenberg, Pim, and Anthony Cirelli, eds. *Nostra Aetate: Celebrating Fifty Years of the Catholic Church's Dialogue with Jews and Muslims*. Washington, DC: The Catholic University of America Press, 2016.

Valkenberg, Pim, and Henk Schoot. "Thomas Aquinas and Judaism." In *Aquinas in Dialogue: Thomas for the Twenty-First Century*, edited by Jim Fodor and Frederick Christian Bauerschmidt, 47–66. Oxford: Wiley-Blackwell, 2004.

Van Bavel, Tarsicius J., OSA. "Augustine on Baptism: *Letter 98*." In *Augustinian Heritage: A Review of Spirituality and Tradition* 39, no. 2 (1993): 191–212.

Vatican Council II. *Ad Gentes*. December 7, 1965.

———. *Dignitatis Humanae*. December 7, 1965.

———. *Gaudium et Spes*. December 7, 1965.

———. *Lumen Gentium*. November 21, 1964.

———. *Nostra Aetate*. October 28, 1965.

Vatican News. "Pope Emeritus Benedict: Dialogue with the Jews, Not Mission." November 27, 2018. https://www.vaticannews.va/en/church/news/2018-11/pope-emeritus-benedict-dialogue-with-the-jews-not-mission.html.

Vose, Robin. *Dominicans, Muslims and Jews in the Medieval Crown of Aragon*. New York: Cambridge University Press, 2011.

Weed, Jennifer Hart. "Aquinas on the Forced Conversion of the Jews." In *Jews in Medieval Christendom: "Slay Them Not,"* Études sur le Judaïsme Médiéval 60, edited by Kristine T. Utterback and Merrall L. Price, 129–46. Leiden: Brill, 2013.

———. "Faith, Salvation, and the Sacraments in Aquinas: A Puzzle Concerning Forced Baptisms." *Philosophy, Culture, and Traditions* 10 (2014): 95–110.

Weisheipl, J. A. "Cajetan (Tommaso De Vio)." In *New Catholic Encyclopedia*. 2nd ed. Vol. 4. Detroit: Gale, 2003.

———. "Capreolus, John." In *New Catholic Encyclopedia*. 2nd ed. Vol. 3. Detroit: Gale, 2003.

———. "Durandus of Saint-Pourçain." In *New Catholic Encyclopedia*. 2nd ed. Vol. 4. Detroit: Gale, 2003.

———. *Friar Thomas D'Aquino: His Life, Thought, and Work*. 1st ed. New York: Doubleday, 1974.

White, Susan. "Baptism." In *A Dictionary of Jewish-Christian Relations*, edited by Edward Kessler and Neil Wenborn, 47. New York: Cambridge University Press, 2008.

Wilken, Robert Louis. *Liberty in the Things of God: The Christian Origins of Religious Freedom*. New Haven, CT: Yale University Press, 2019.

Winters, Michael Sean. "Fr. Cessario's Edgardo Mortara Essay Is Inexcusable." *National Catholic Reporter*, January 19, 2018. https://www.ncronline.org/news/people/distinctly-catholic/fr-cessarios-edgardo-mortara-essay-inexcusable.

Woywood, Stanislaus. *A Practical Commentary on the Code of Canon Law*, revised by Callistus Smith. 2 vols. New York: Joseph F. Wagner, 1948.

Wyschogrod, Michael. "A Jewish Reading of St. Thomas Aquinas." In *Understanding Scripture: Explorations of Jewish and Christian Traditions of Interpretation*, edited by Clemens Thoma and Michael Wyschogrod, 125–40. Mahwah, NJ: Paulist, 1987.

INDEX

A

Abraham, 126–27; and promise of Christ, 233; stock of, 204, 207n50, 213n67

Albert the Great, 387

Alexander of Hales, 61, 373

Alexander, Pope II, 89

Alexander, Pope III, 94, 96

Ambrose, Bishop, 12; in Aquinas, 117n36, 118, 119; in *Brevi cenni*, 407n3; in *Pro-memoria*, 281; in *Syllabus*, 50, 295n1, 313, 337, 343, 375, 387, 397

Anglicus, Alanus, 97

Anti-Judaism, 199

Anti-Jewish laws, 94; and crypto-Jews, 100. *See also* Fourth Council of Toledo

Antisemitism, 244n170; Christian forms of, 203, 205n39; Church's rejection of, 6, 205; Nazi racial, 203

Apostasy, 71, 73, 77, 101, 407, 411, 425, 427, 439

Apostles, 148, 185, 190, 206, 217n79, 221n91, 323, 411

Apostle Paul, 20n66, 21, 213, 221n91, 226, 233, 237, 244–45, 247, 367, 371; as interpreted by Aquinas, 159–60, 214, 227, 231; as interpreted by Benedict XVI, 236–39; as interpreted by the Second Vatican Council, 202–14, 215–16, 254; letter to the Romans, 195, 200–201, 216, 219, 222; on time of the Gentiles, 238–39. *See also* "Paul within Judaism" school of biblical scholarship

Aquinas, Thomas: on act of the will, 136, 142–44, 152, 183; on adult recipient of baptism, 137–42, 144–45, 149, 158; on analogical language concerning God and creation, 260–61; assent to the faith as God's movement of grace, 146–51, 251–52; on baptism of a child, 136; on baptism of a child of unbelievers, 136–68; on ceremonial law, 223, 227–29; on Christ's circumcision, 230; on Christ's power in baptism, 150; on the Church and spiritual judgment of outsiders, 160; on coercion, 125, 137–46; and the context of his teaching against baptism *invitis parentibus*, 110–15; and the divine law, 20, 27, 41–43, 46, 48, 50, 53–54, 59, 63, 119–21, 125–26, 131, 133, 166–67, 170, 186; defense of Jewish parental authority, 136–68; and Dominican defenders of his teaching, 31–68; on education of offspring as precept of natural law, 121, 134, 187; on emergency baptism, 12, 118; on eternal law, 122, 132–33, 251, 262–63; and interpretation of Augustine's Letter 98, 152–57; on the last end, 134; and

meaning of circumcision, 227–28, 230–31; on natural inclinations, 120–21, 132–33, 134, 187–88, 258, 262n46; on natural justice, 14, 20, 27, 35, 41n35, 117n36, 119–24, 130, 132, 146–47, 153, 163, 166–67, 252, 257, 266; on natural law, xiv, xvii, 13, 20–22, 27, 34, 35n15, 37, 51–57, 59, 62–63, 67, 99, 120–25, 128, 130, 133–35, 153, 160, 163–67, 170, 177, 180, 183, 187–88, 192, 249–51, 253, 255, 256–58, 262, 264–66; on natural right, 13–14, 20, 35, 71, 76–77, 110, 121, 122–23, 128–29, 131–32, 134, 164, 167, 251, 255, 257, 266; on "old sacraments," 126, 223n95; popes of his time, 223–24; as resource for positive interpretation of Jewish religious life, 230; on sacrament of baptism and sacramental character, 137–46; on salvation of the Jews, 231; and style of disputed question in *Summa theologiae*, 116; on toleration of Jews in Christian society, 48, 99, 112, 202; view of Jewish worship after Christ, 228–29; on virtue of faith, 149–50, 158–59; on voluntary action and fear, 72–73, 81, 136–51. See also *Expositio super Isaiam ad litteram*; *Lectura Super Evangelium S. Ioannis lectura*; *Questiones Quodlibetales*; *Scriptum super libros Sententiarum*; *Summa theologiae*; *Super I ad Corinthios*; *Super Epistolam ad Romanos*

Archivio Apostolico Vaticano, x, xvi, 2n5, 7, 11, 273n5

Aristotle, 35n18, 120–21, 134, 143, 144n151, 145

Assimilation, 200

Augustine, 11n35, 27; anti-Jewish reading of Cain and Abel, 226; in Aquinas, 118, 139n126, 148, 152–56, 164, 227; in authors of the *Syllabus*, 57, 155; on baptizing children of pagan parents, 11–12; in *Brevi cenni*, 75n25, 76, 252, 417, 419, 421; on the Church and spiritual judgment of outsiders, 160, 221n91; condemnation of the unbaptized, 256; cited in *Dignitatis Humanae*, 182; on election of Israel, 227, 247; on elements of Augustine's witness doctrine, 48, 86, 202, 229n114, 245–47; impact of his witness doctrine on papal teaching, 86, 88, 102, 236–37; cited in *Immortale Dei*, 181; cited in *Mystici Corporis*, 181; in *Pro-memoria*, 281; on relation of creation to God, 261; in *Syllabus*, 335, 345, 351, 365, 369, 371, 375, 379, 387; and teaching that Elijah would preach to Jews at end of time, 49n74; on "two witnesses" of Second Coming, Enoch and Elijah, 49, 245–47; on unbelievers must not be forced to the faith, 156, 181; witness doctrine compared with Aquinas's, 229, 245

Augustine, Dom, OSB, 174–75

B

Baptism, 8–10; and emergency cases, ix, 11–12, 99, 118, 174–75, 178, 250, 253, 256; sacrament of, 9n21; See also Aquinas, Thomas; Coercion; *favor fidei*; Forced baptism

Barron, Bishop Robert, 260–62

Bea, Augustine Cardinal, 206–8, 212–14, 216–17

Beatific vision, 14n49, 134

Beauvais, Vincent de, 115, 132, 254

Benedict XIV, Pope, 3n6, 14, 75–76, 78, 103, 105–8, 127, 166, 171–74, 176, 192, 251, 253, 419, 421, 429n29, 435, 437; view that Jewish parental rights were of human law not natural or divine law

Benedict XVI, Pope, 22; on changes to the Good Friday prayer in Tridentine Liturgy, 240n151; on difficult history of Catholic-Jewish relations, 203; on distinction of dialogue and mission, 197, 239, 245, 248; on freedom of parents to educate their children, 191; on importance of dialogue, 248; on interpretation of *Dignitatis Humanae*,

INDEX

185–86, 188, 196; interpretation of Romans 11:25–26, 197, 214, 222–23, 233, 236–37, 247; and Israel still possessor of Sacred Scripture, 246; Israel has its own mission, 239; and salvation of Jews, 237–39, 247; on the rejection of Paul's preaching by some Jews in the first century, 219; on the special status of Jewish people and Judaism, 224, 245n172; on the "time of the Gentiles," 237–38; *See also* chapter 7; Ratzinger, Cardinal Joseph

Bologna, xiii, 1–2, 23, 209, 269, 403, 437

Burrell, David, 259–62

Brechenmacher, Thomas, 102–3

Brevi cenni, x, 4n8, 7, 18, 31, 70, 192, 250, 273n5, 287n14, 289n15, 443n36; *See also chapter 3; Appendix C*; Ambrose, Bishop; Cajetan, Cardinal Thomas de Vio; Natural law; Natural right

C

Caffiero, Marina 103, 108

Cajetan, Cardinal Thomas de Vio, 144, 157; in *Brevi cenni*, 74–75, 415; in *Syllabus*, 51, 54, 56, 59, 64, 65n156, 66, 345, 347, 351, 353, 355

Callistus II, Pope, 90

Canon law, 81, 107, 132, 168; *See also chapter 4*; Code of Canon Law; Mortara, Edgardo

Capreolus, John, 18, 38–39, 51–54, 57–58, 60–61, 63–64, 65n156, 66, 110, 144, 163, 257, 265, 335, 343, 353, 355, 417

Catechism of the Catholic Church, 9, 197, 220, 225n104

Catharinus, Archbishop Ambrosius, 38, 54, 55–60, 63, 65, 142n141, 157, 164, 265, 343–63

Catholic Church, xi, xiii, 6, 9, 17, 27, 72, 75, 170, 174, 197, 225, 240, 243, 407, 415

Catholic faith, 5, 9n21, 15, 25–26, 102, 106, 179, 181, 198, 220, 242–43, 245, 281, 427

Catholic-Jewish relations, xi, xii, xiv; and the Mortara case, 2, 6, 15–17

Catholic theology, 2, 6, 196n5, 216, 226n106; and mysteries of faith, 196n5, 244, 393

Ceremonial law, 111, 226n106, 227, 228n112, 321; *See also* Aquinas, Thomas; Augustine

Cessario, Romanus, ixn1, 7, 16, 254–55; his essay, "Non Possumus," and reactions, 23–28

Chaput, Archbishop Charles, 16

Chazan, Robert, 89, 111–12

Chenu, M. D., 22n69, 51, 116n34

Christ. *See* Jesus Christ

Church Fathers, 55, 202, 230n116, 231, 246

Clement IV, Pope, 99

Code of Canon Law, or CIC (*Codex Iuris Caonici*): CIC 1917, 6, 20, 170, 174–78, 181, 183, 253; CIC 1983, 15, 20, 170–84. *See also chapter 6*

Coercion, 84, 162n219, 190, 277; and baptism: "absolute" and "conditional" forms of coerced baptism, 96–98, 107–8, 146, 151, 164; is opposed to the voluntary nature of faith, 188–89; should be excluded according to *Dignitatis Humanae*, 15, 182, 185, 188. *See also* Aquinas, Thomas

Colish, Marcia, 90, 93, 96

Congregation for the Doctrine of the Faith (CDF), 1n1, 103n101, 170. *See also* Holy Office; *Pastoralis actio*

Constantine, Emperor, 12, 50, 84–85, 117n36, 119, 295, 313, 335, 337, 375, 387, 407n3

Constitutio pro Iudaeis (Callistus II), 90

Conversion: forced, *see chapter 4*; of Jews as part of prophecy, 61, 222, 237, 245–47, 369, 391; *neofiti*, 104; question of duty, 247; view implied by *Nostra*

Aetate, 247–48, 254. *See also* Ghetto(s); Offerings

Coolman, Holly Taylor, 28

Cum nimis (Paul IV), 101–2

Cunningham, Phil, 242n162, 243n164

D

Daem, Bishop Jules Victor, 210

D'Costa, Gavin, 215–16, 221n91, 223, 243n164

Decretum (Gratian), 60, 64n148, 95–96, 127, 161n216

Dignitatis Humanae (Vatican II), 20, 184–93. *See also* Augustine; Benedict XVI, Pope; Coercion; John Paul II, Pope; Natural law

Dialogue, 28, 241; in contemporary Catholic teaching, 22, 187, 209, 220, 226n106, 241–43; as distinct from mission, 21–22, 219–20, 242n162, 243, 248; forms of Catholic-Jewish and its special status, 198–99, 219, 226n106, 240–42, 245; and question of proclamation, 241–44; as it relates to understanding Judaism, 242; as it relates to question of proclamation in USCCB's teaching, 22, 243–45. *See also* Benedict XVI; Jews and Judaism; *Nostra Aetate*; Second Vatican Council

Diaspora, 202, 217n79

Dietary laws, 228

Donin, Nicholas, 111–12

Durandus, Saint-Pourçain, 38, 39, 42–46, 49–51; Excerpt in the *Syllabus*, 293–311

E

Elchinger, Archbishop Léon-Arthur, 210

Election of the Jewish people, 198–200, 202, 204, 214–15, 217, 222, 227, 230–31, 233, 245. *See also* Augustine; Israel

Elijah, 48–49, 53, 61, 213, 245–47, 323, 369

Elukin, Jonathan, 94

Enoch, 48–49, 53, 61, 323, 369

Eschatological: elements of Paul's teaching as it relates to salvation of Jews, 196, 247; John the Baptist as symbol of Elijah, 49; salvation of Jewish people as, 246. *See also* chapter 7

Expositio super Isaiam ad litteram (Aquinas), 230n116

F

Faggioli, Massimo, 25

favor fidei (favor of the faith), 107–8, 114; not in Aquinas, 166; as basis of Benedict XIV's 1747 policies on baptism, 175

Feletti, Father Pier, 2–3

Flannery, Edward, 91, 97

Forced baptism: meritorious in certain conditions, 102, 167, 192, 253; , papal condemnations of, 12. *See also* chapter 4

Fourth Council of Toledo, 43, 47, 53, 77, 83, 92–96, 113, 151, 155, 161–62, 425; added to Gratian's *Decretum*, 95; canon 57 of, 41n34, 53, 95, 97, 151, 161n215; canon 60 of: separation of unlawfully baptized children from Jewish parents, 93; *Decretals* D.45 based on, 53; mostly ignored until after Gratian, 155

Francis, Pope, xiiin11, 222–23, 226n106

Friedländer, Saul, 199

G

Gentiles, 201; "fullness of," 208, 211, 213–14; and reconciliation with Jews, 207n50; time of, 214–15, 217–18. *See also* Apostle Paul; Benedict XVI, Pope; New Testament

Ghetto(s): "Israelite ghetto of Rome," 421; of Papal States, 4, 32, 101–2, 101, 104; relations with Christians, 104–5; Roman, 8n20, 14, 20, 84, 105–6, 108, 166, 170, 253, 264; separation of Jewish families in, 170–74

INDEX

"Gifts and the Calling of God" (Commission for Religious Relations with the Jews), 195–201, 205n38, 232n123, 236n133, 240–43, 245, 247

Grace, 249, 255, 257; against or in conflict with nature, 20, 258; of Christ, 10; as God's movement, 136, 263; as invisible reality in sacraments, 9; perfects nature, 266; supernatural gift of, 20

Gratian, 60, 95–96, 113, 127, 155, 161n216

Grayzel, Solomon, 86, 151, 224n96

Gregory the Great, Pope, 12, 86–89, 102, 224, 236, 256

Gregory, IV, Pope, 95

Gregory IX, Pope, 41n34, 53, 111, 174, 203n27, 224

Gregory XIII, Pope, 107

"Guidelines and Suggestions" 1974 (Commission for Religious Relations with the Jews), 232n122, 242nn159–60

H

Hadrian I, Pope, 95

Healy, Nicholas, 184, 190

Henry IV, Holy Roman Emperor, 95

Heresy, 1n1, 101, 111n5, 325

Heschel, Rabbi Abraham Joshua, 213n67

Hittinger, F. Russell, 258

Holocaust, 203

Holy Office, 1–2, 76n29, 78n44, 103, 105–6, 172, 411, 423n20, 427, 431, 437, 439n34. *See also* Congregation for the Doctrine of the Faith

Hostiensis, 114

House of Catechumens, 4, 264, 427, 431

Holy See, 71, 78–79, 287n14, 289n15, 407, 411, 413, 423, 427–35, 439–41

Honorius, Emperor, 256

Human freedom, 15, 150n179, 258, 262; and creation according to John Paul II, as it relates to God, 262. *See also* Coercion

Huguccio of Pisa, 97–98

I

Incarnation, 229–32, 263

Innocent III, Pope, 97, 100

Innocent IV, Pope, 224

Invincible ignorance, 197, 206, 207n47, 215–23

invitis parentibus, xi, 7–8, 13–14, 16, 18–22, 264–65; in *Brevi cenni*, 407, 411, 413, 415, 419, 421, 425, 427, 435, 439, in *Pro-memoria*, 34–37, 271, 273n6, 275, 285; in discussion of the *Syllabus*, 38–39, 41, 43, 53, 55–57, 61–67; translated as "parents unwilling" in excerpts from the *Syllabus*, 283, 299, 301, 309, 311, 315, 319, 321, 327, 329, 333, 335, 337, 343, 345, 351–57, 361–65, 367, 373–79, 383, 385–89, 391, 395. *See also* Aquinas, Thomas

Isidore of Seville, 92

Israel: connection to Christ, 202; election of, 202, 217, 230, 240, 245; of the flesh, 47, 214n74, 226, 231, 234, 247, 254; God's covenant with, 205–6, 210, 214, 220, 222; God of, 228; Messiah of, 198, 238; mission of, 238–39; mystery of, 21, 195, 201, 210, 217, 244–45, 254; people of, 207n50; problematic Christian idea of "hardening of," 233–36; salvation of, *see chapter 7*; in writings of Benedict XVI, 238–39

J

Jesus Christ, 138; and creation, 132; eschatological redemption, 196, 239; and fulfillment of God's promises or law, 198, 210, 216, 232–33; and interpretation of scripture, 49; his Passion, 147, 150, 204, 206, 215; his resurrection, 10, 147, 229–32, 307, 329. *See also* Incarnation

Jerome, 44, 117n36, 118, 297, 307, 335, 375, 419

Jerusalem, 45, 85, 204, 217n79, 238

Jews and Judaism: bearing unique witness, 200n19; community of Rome, 2n5, 4; and dangers caused by the Christian discovery of the Talmud, 19, 21, 99, 241; ethnic dimension, 215, 222, 230–31, 236, 247; and rabbinic literature, 19, 110; and references to Jews at the time of Mortara case as "Israelites," 37, 277, 281, 285, 287, 289, 291, 421; as *religio licita*, 84, 225; religious and spiritual dimension of, 222; and special status of Catholic-Jewish dialogue, 240; and Torah, 222, 230. *See also* Ghetto(s); Israel; Rabbinic Judaism

John Paul II, Pope, 9n21, 27; on Church not afraid of the truth in history, xii, xiiin11; on decision to beatify Pius IX, 17; on duty to preach the Gospel, 241n156; God's covenant with the Jewish people is irrevocable, 197, 205; interpretation of *Dignitatis Humanae*, 185, 188; jubilee teaching against violence in service to truth, 170, 184, 190–91, 253; on moral and religious memory, 200; reform of CIC 1917, 177; special status of Jewish people and olive tree metaphor, 225–26; spiritual vitality of Judaism, 223

Julius II, Pope, 64

K

Kertzer, David, ix–x, 2n5, 5n12, 102

Kleinberg, Aviad M., 107n122, 114, 255

L

Lactantius, 84, 182

Law: *See* Anti-Jewish laws; Aquinas, Thomas; canon law; ceremonial law; Code of Canon Law; Dietary laws; Jesus Christ; Jews and Judaism; Mosaic law; New Law; Old Law; rabbinic literature

Lectura Super Evangelium S. Ioannis lectura (Aquinas), 124

Leo the Great, Pope, 156n193

Leo X, Pope, 64

Leo XIII, Pope, 181

Lercaro, Cardinal Giacomo, 209

Levering, Matthew, 28, 28n19, 118n40, 221n91

Liber extra decretalium, 41n34, 53, 95n55, 96, 98, 114, 273, 421

Linder, Amnon, 91n36, 93n43

Lombard, Peter, 38–39

Lumen Gentium (Vatican II), 204, 225–26, 232

Luti, Carlo, 264–65

M

MacIntyre, Alasdair, 134n98

Madigan, Kevin, 27–28

Maiores (Innocent III), 97–98, 100, 144, 151, 409, 435

Marshall, Bruce, 229n114

Mattison, William III, xiin10, 218n84

Mazzolini, Sylvester, di Prierio, 38, 58, 64–66, 265; excerpt in the *Syllabus*, 385–87

McCabe, Herbert, 9

Messori, Vittorio, 25, 255; and the problems with English version of the Mortara memoir, 5n12

Mission. *See* Benedict XVI; Dialogue; Israel

Morisi, Anna, 1, 71, 78, 269, 271, 273, 405, 435, 437

Mortara, Edgardo: account of the removal, 1–4, 14, 16; canon law that supported removal, 24; ordained as Fr. Pio Maria, 4–5, 8; film about the case, 17; removal as a kidnapping, 166

INDEX

Mortara, Elèna, 16–17, 124n60, 266n59

Mortara family, 1, 5, 7, 14, 16, 18–19, 22, 28–29; and assistance from Jewish community, 4, 7n19; and their plea to the Vatican, *see chapter 2*. *See also* Appendix A

Mortara, Momolo, xiii, 1–4, 437

Mortara, Marianna, xiii, 1, 405

morti proximus (close to or in danger of death), 1, 8–11, 15–16, 20–21, 24, 45n53, 50, 73–74, 78n44, 79–80, 129, 130n78, 144, 155–56, 156n193, 164, 167–75, 178–84, 192, 250–53, 256–57, 263, 265, 335, 411, 429, 435, 439n34

Mosaic Law, 126, 233

Moses, 49n73, 111n7, 239, 245, 321, 323

Mystery. *See* Catholic theology; Israel; Second Vatican Council

Mystici Corporis (Pius XII), 181

N

Nanos, Mark, 234

Natural justice: in *Pro-memoria*, 277; in the authors of the excerpts of the *Syllabus*, 51–52, 60, 64, 335, 337, 345, 377, 385. *See also* Aquinas, Thomas

Natural law, 258, 262, 264–66; in *Brevi cenni*, 441; as it relates to *Dignitatis Humanae*, 177, 186–87; as it relates to parental rights in Benedict XIV, 166–67 the pope cannot dispense with, 266; in *Pro-memoria*, 34–35, 37, 275, 277, 279; as it relates to the reform of the 1917 CIC, 180, 183; in the authors of the excerpts in *Syllabus*, 41–42, 47, 51–55, 57, 59, 62–63, 67, 319, 333, 335, 337, 339, 345, 359, 361, 363, 375, 377, 385, 387. *See also* Aquinas, Thomas

Natural right, 170–71, 174–76, 188, 192; in the authors of the excerpts in *Syllabus*, 315; in *Brevi cenni*, 71, 76–77, 423, 439, 443; in *Pro-memoria*, 35, 405. *See also* Aquinas, Thomas

Nazis, 5, 203

New Israel, 199n14

New Law, 321, 323; as it relates to divine law, which includes the old law, 125n63, 147, 150; the pope cannot dispense with, 266n61

New Testament, 206, 211; and "time of the gentiles," 239, 244; unity of Old and, 225n104

Nominalism, 22, 39, 42, 45; and person and God in relation of opposition, 253–54, 258

Nostra Aetate (Vatican II), 6, 85, 193; central claims, 202–6; interreligious dialogue, 22, 187, 209, 220, 226n106, 241–43; as misinterpreted by some scholars, 198–99; Vatican II architects and fathers' interpretation of question of conversion, *see chapter 7*. *See also* Conversion

"Notes on the Correct Way to Present the Jews and Judaism" (Commission for Religious Relations with the Jews), 225, 242nn159–60

Nutt, Roger, 139

O

O'Boyle, Archbishop Patrick, 209

Ochs, Peter, 199n18

Old Law, 177, 227, 228n112

"Offerings," 34, 107, 166, 172. *See also* Ghetto(s)

Oesterreicher, John M., 203, 205–6, 208, 211, 213–14

P

Pakter, Walter, 108

Paludanus, Peter, excerpt in *Syllabus*, 311–29

Papal States, 1–2. *See also chapter 4*; *chapter 6*; Ghetto(s); *patria potestas*; Toleration of Jews in Christian society

Passover, 16, 228

Pastoralis actio, CDF Instruction on Infant Baptism, 10n29, 170–71, 176, 178, 192, 256n8

patria potestas ("the power of the father," understood to mean parental rights or authority), 20, 36, 113; arguments that sought the abrogation of, 40, 47; in conflict with *favor fidei*, 114; diminished status of Jewish in Papal States, 15, 106–7; as lower than supernatural right of Church, 175

Paul III, Pope, 101, 285

Paul IV, Pope, 32, 101, 203n27, 220

Paul VI, Pope, 185, 206, 212, 220, 241n156

"Paul within Judaism" school of biblical studies, 196–97, 233

Pennington, Kenneth, 96, 113, 115n29

Pinckaers, Servais, OP, 19, 135, 186, 258

Pius IX, Pope: critics of decision to remove, 18, 25–29, 79; defenders of decision to remove, 15, 18, 22–25, 79, 254, 256–57. *See also chapter 2; chapter 3*

Pius XII, Pope, xiiin11, 181

Porter, Jean, 13, 122

Prophets, 49n74, 148, 196, 212–13, 221n91, 222, 224, 226, 239, 244–46

Pontifical Commission for Religious Relations with the Jews, 195, 197

Postremo mense, 104n104, 107, 166, 171, 174, 192, 435

Pro-memoria, 18, 72–74, 76, 78, 80, 110, 165, 250, 252, 265. *See also chapter 2; Appendix A; Ambrose; Augustine; invitis parentibus; natural justice; natural law; natural right*

Q

Questiones Quodlibetales (Aquinas), 39, 41, 52, 55, 108, 115–16, 125, 159

R

Rabbinic Judaism, 215–16, 220–22, 223n94

Raymond de Peñafort, 96, 98

Ratzinger, Cardinal Joseph, xi, 2n3, 237n136. *See also Benedict XVI, Pope*

Ravid, Benjamin, 99–100

Replacement theory, 199

Religious freedom, 33; in early Christian arguments against coercion, 84, 168–69; according to the Second Vatican Council, 6, 16, 20–21, 181–88, 190–91, 246. *See also chapter 6;* Human freedom

Rennes, William of, 114–15, 127, 130, 132, 254

Rist, Rebecca, 88, 94

Robertson, John W., 179–80, 183

Rufinus of Bologna, 96

S

Sangiorgio, Cardinal Antonio, 57n118, 65n156, 363, 365n31

Schindler, David L., 182n45, 186–89

Scotus, John Duns, 51, 58, 74–75, 100, 104, 115, 130n82, 192, 202, 247, 254, 256

Scriptum super libros Sententiarum (Aquinas), 38, 128n73, 144–46, 159, 165

Second Council of Nicaea, 94–95

Second Temple Judaism, 232n122

Second Vatican Council, xiii, 6, 15, 243, 253, 265; condemnation of antisemitism, 205; critics of statement on the Jews, 206–7; importance of teachings on dialogue, 21n68; on mystery of Israel, *see chapter 7*; positive Catholic attitude to Jews, 202–14; rejected deicide charge, 246n177; on religious freedom, *see chapter 6*; on special status of the Jewish people, 204. *See also Dignitatis Humanae; Lumen*

INDEX

Gentium; *Nostra Aetate*; Religious freedom

Second World War, 199–200

Sicut Iudaeis (Gregory the Great), 86, 90, 96, 99, 112

Sisebut, King 92, 339, 357

Sisenand, King, 92–93

Sokolowski, Robert, 262

Soulen, Kendall, 233, 235

Stow, Kenneth, 101, 103, 107–8, 166

Summa theologiae (Aquinas), xiv, 192, 229; ST I.II (*Prima Secundae*), 72, 81, 136–37, 251, 337, 387; ST II.II (*Secunda Secundae*), xiv, 28, 35, 39–41, 53, 60–62, 72, 77–79, 104, 115–16, 126–27, 157, 159, 161–62, 165–66, 176, 229, 252, 363, 369, 375, 377, 385, 389; ST III (*Tertia Pars*), 64–66, 75, 80, 116n32, 125, 139, 141–42, 152–56, 159–60, 164–65, 293, 377; Treatise on Law, 121

Super I ad Corinthios (Aquinas), 160

Super Epistolam ad Romanos (Aquinas), 221n91, 231

Supersessionism, 199n18

Susannis, Marquardus de, 102, 273

Syllabus, 165, 250, 252, 263, 265, 273. *See also* chapter 2; Appendix B; Ambrose, Bishop; Augustine; Cajetan, Cardinal Thomas de Vio; Durandus, Saint-Pourçain; *invitis parentibus*; Mazzolini, Sylvester, di Prierio; Natural justice; Natural law; Natural right; Paludanus, Peter; Torquemada, Cardinal Juan de

Synan, Edward, 93

T

Tapie, Matthew, xn3, 18n63

Tertullian, 85, 281

Theodosius, 12, 117n36, 119, 295, 295n1, 313, 335, 337, 375, 387, 407n3

Theodosian Code, 85, 88

Tierney, Brian, 13n47, 167n229

Toleration of Jews in Christian society, 89; Augustinian tradition of, 19, 53, 61, 89–90, 110, 112; papal decrees on, 90, 102; in Papal States, 102–3

Torrell, Jean-Pierre, OP, 115n31, 116n32

Torquemada, Cardinal Juan de, 38, 60–64; Excerpt in the *Syllabus*, 367–85

Turbato corde (Clement IV), 99

V

Vatican II. *See* Second Vatican Council

W

Wilken, Robert, 85

World War II. *See* Second World War

Wyschogrod, Michael, 221n91

Z

Zion, 231, 233, 235

ALSO IN
JUDAISM AND CATHOLIC THEOLOGY

*Contemporary Catholic Approaches
to the People, Land, and State of Israel*
Edited by Gavin D'Costa and Faydra L. Shapiro
Preface by H. B. Pierbattista Pizzaballa

The Challenge of Catholic-Jewish Theological Dialogue
Edited by Alan Brill, Matthew Levering, and Matthew Tapie